Music Library Association Index and Bibliography Series
Mark Palkovic, Series Editor

1. *An Alphabetical Index to Claudio Monteverdi Tutte Le Opere,* edited by the Bibliography Committee of the New York Chapter, MLA, 1964.
2. *An Alphabetical Index to Hector Berlioz Werke,* edited by the Bibliography Committee of the New York Chapter, MLA, 1964.
3. *A Checklist of Music Bibliographies and Indexes in Progress and Unpublished,* compiled by the MLA Publications Committee, Walter Gerboth, chair; Shirley Branner; and James B. Coover; 1965; 2nd ed. by James Pruett, 1969; 3rd ed. by Linda Solow, 1974; 4th ed. by Dee Baily, 1982.
4. *A Concordance of the Thematic Indexes to the Instrumental Works of Antonio Vivaldi,* by Lenore Coral, 1965; 2nd ed., 1972.
5. *An Alphabetical Index to Tomás Luis de Victoria Opera Omnia,* edited by the Bibliography Committee of the New York Chapter, MLA, 1966.
6. *An Alphabetical Index to Robert Schumann Werke: Schumann Index, Part 1,* compiled by Michael Ochs, 1967.
7. *An Alphabetical Index to the Solo Songs of Robert Schumann: Schumann Index, Part 2,* compiled by William J. Weichlein, 1967.
8. *An Index to Maurice Frost's "English & Scottish Psalm & Hymn Tunes,"* by Kirby Rogers, 1967.
9. *Speculum: An Index of Musically Related Articles and Book Reviews,* compiled by Arthur S. Wolff, 1970; 2nd ed., 1981.
10. *An Index to "Das Chorwerk," Vols. 1–110,* compiled by Michael Ochs, 1970.
11. *Bach Aria Index,* compiled by Miriam Whaples, 1971.
12. *Annotated Bibliography of Writing about Music in Puerto Rico,* compiled by Annie Figueroa Thompson, 1975.
13. *Analyses of Twentieth-Century Music, 1940–1970,* compiled by Arthur Wenk, 1975.
14. *Analyses of Twentieth-Century Music, 1970–1975,* compiled by Arthur Wenk, 1976; 2nd ed., 1984.
15. *Analyses of Nineteenth-Century Music: 1940–1975,* compiled by Arthur Wenk, 1976; 2nd ed., *1940–1980,* 1984.
16. *Writings on Contemporary Music Notation,* compiled by Gerald Warfield, 1976.
17. *Literature for Voices in Combination with Electronic and Tape Music: An Annotated Bibliography,* compiled by J. Michele Edwards, 1977.
18. *Johannes Brahms: A Guide to His Autographs in Facsimile,* by Peter Dedel, 1978.
19. *Source: Music of the Avant Garde; Annotated List of Contents and Cumulative Indices,* by Michael D. Williams, 1978.
20. *Eighteenth-Century American Secular Music Manuscripts: An Inventory,* compiled by James J. Fuld and Mary Wallace Davidson, 1980.
21. *Popular Secular Music in America through 1800: A Checklist of Manuscripts in North American Collections,* compiled by Kate Van Winkle Keller, 1980.
22. *Palestrina: An Index to the Casimiri, Kalmus, and Haberl Editions,* by Allison Hall, 1980.
23. *E. H. Fellowes: An Index to The English Madrigalists and The English School of Lutenist Song Writers,* by Allison Hall, 1984.
24. *Music in New York during the American Revolution: An Inventory of Musical References in "Rivington's New York Gazette,"* by Gillian B. Anderson with editorial assistance by Neil Ratliff, 1987.
25. *Analyses of Nineteenth- and Twentieth-Century Music, 1940–1985,* by Arthur B. Wenk, 1987.
26. *Opera Performances in Video Format: A Checklist of Commercially Released Performances,* by Charles Croissant, 1991.
27. *A Thematic Catalog of the Works of Robert Valentine,* by J. Bradford Young, 1994.
28. *Pro-Musica: Patronage, Performance, and a Periodical—An Index to the Quarterlies,* by Paula Elliot, 1997.
29. *Musical Memorials for Musicians: A Guide to Selected Compositions,* by R. Michael Fling, 2001.
30. *Music Inspired by Art: A Guide to Recordings,* by Gary Evans, 2002.
31. *An Index to Music Published in* The Etude *Magazine, 1883–1957,* by E. Douglas Bomberger, 2004.
32. *Bibliographic Control of Music, 1897–2000,* by Richard P. Smiraglia, compiled and edited with J. Bradford Young, 2006.
33. *Grawemeyer Award for Music Composition: The First Twenty Years,* by Karen R. Little and Julia Graepel, 2007.
34. *Analyses of Nineteenth- and Twentieth-Century Music, 1940–2000,* by D. J. Hoek, 2007.

Analyses of Nineteenth- and Twentieth-Century Music, 1940–2000

D. J. Hoek

Incorporating Material By
Arthur Wenk

Music Library Association
Index and Bibliography Series, No. 34

The Scarecrow Press, Inc.
Lanham, Maryland • Toronto • Plymouth, UK
and
Music Library Association, Inc.
2007

SCARECROW PRESS, INC.

Published in the United States of America
by Scarecrow Press, Inc.
A wholly owned subsidary of The Rowman & Littlefield Publishing Group, Inc.
4501 Forbes Boulevard, Suite 200, Lanham, Maryland 20706
www.scarecrowpress.com

Estover Road
Plymouth PL6 7PY
United Kingdom

British Library Cataloguing in Publication Information Available

Library of Congress Cataloging-in-Publication Data

Hoek, D. J. (David J.), 1970–
  Analyses of nineteenth- and twentieth-century music, 1940–2000 /
D. J. Hoek ; incorporating material by Arthur Wenk.
      p. cm. — (MLA index and bibliography series, ISSN
0094-6478 ; no. 34)
  Includes bibliographical references and index.
  ISBN-13: 978-0-8108-5887-9 (pbk. : alk. paper)
  ISBN-10: 0-8108-5887-8 (pbk. : alk. paper)
1. Music—19th century—History and criticism—Bibliography.
2. Music—20th century—History and criticism—Bibliography.
3. Musical analysis—Bibliography. I. Wenk, Arthur, 1943– Analyses
of nineteenth- and twentieth-century music, 1940–1985. II. Title.

ML113.H695 2007
016.7809'034—dc22

                                                              2006032131

To Dr. C.

Contents

Abbreviations

JOURNALS

Dates in parentheses indicate publication years covered in the bibliography. Superscript daggers (†) indicate journals that have ceased publication.

ACA	*American Composers Alliance Bulletin* (1938–1965†)
ACR	*American Choral Review* (1959–2000)
ACTA	*Acta Musicologica* (1928–2000)
AM	*Archiv für Musikwissenschaft* (1918–2000)
AMF	*Archiv für Musikforschung* (1936–1945†)
AMRCJ	*American Music Research Center Journal* (1991–2000)
AMUS	*American Music* (1983–2000)
ANL	*Analisi: Rivista di teoria e pedagogia musicale* (1990–2000)
ANM	*Analyse Musicale* (1985–2000)
ASO	*Avant-scène opera* (1976–2000)
ASUC	*American Society for University Composers. Proceedings* (1966–1977†)
BBS	*Bonner Beethoven-Studien* (1999)
BF	*Beethoven Forum* (1992–2000)
BJ	*Beethoven Jahrbuch* (1953–1981†)
BM	*Beiträge zur Musikwissenschaft* (1959–1992†)
BOGM	*Beiträge: Österreichische Gesellschaft für Musik* (1967–2000)
BRJ	*Bruckner Jahrbuch* (1980–2000)
BRS	*Bruckner-Symposion* (1980–2000)
BS	*Brahms-Studien* (1974–1998)
BST	*Brahms Studies* (1994–1998)
CAD	*Cahiers Debussy* (1974–2000)
CAIR	*Cahiers de l'IRCAM. Recherche et musique* (1992–1995†)
CAUSM	*Canadian Association of University Schools of Music Journal* (1971–1979†)
CC	*Contrechamps: Musique du XXe siècle* (1983–1990†)
CCM	*Cahiers canadiens de musique* (1970–1976†)
CD	*Chord and Dischord* (1940–1969†)
CHI	*Chigiana*. Nuova ser. (1964–1993)
CI	*Critical Inquiry* (1974–2000)
CIR	*Circuit* (1991–2000)
CM	*Current Musicology* (1965–2000)
CMF	*Contemporary Music Forum* (1989–1994)
CMJ	*Canadian Music Journal* (1956–1962†)
CMR	*Contemporary Music Review* (1984–2000)

CMS	*College Music Symposium* (1961–2000)
COJ	*Cambridge Opera Journal* (1989–2000)
CPS	*Contrepoints* (1946–1953†)
CS	*Chopin Studies* (1985–2000)
CT	*Contact* (1971–1989†)
D	*Dissonance* (1969–1975†)
DAM	*Dansk Årborg for Musikforskning* (1961–2000)
DBNM	*Darmstädter Beiträge zur neuen Musik* (1958–1994†)
DI	*Dissonanz/Dissonance* (1984–2000)
DJM	*Deutsches Jahrbuch der Musikwissenschaft* (1956–1978; continued by JP)
EMM	*Essays on Modern Music* (1984–1987†)
EMR	*Electronic Musicological Review/Revista electrônica de musicologia* www.rem.ufpr.br/ (1996–2000)
ENT	*Entretemps* (1986–1992†)
EXT	*Ex tempore* (1981–2000)
FAM	*Fontes artis musicae* (1966–2000)
HJ	*Hindemith-Jahrbuch/Annales Hindemith* (1971–2000)
HJM	*Hamburger Jahrbuch für Musikwissenschaft* (1974–2000)
HS	*Haydn Studien* (1965–2000)
HY	*Haydn Yearbook* (1962–1998†)
I	*Interface* (1972–1993; continued by JNMR)
IABS	*International Alban Berg Society. Newsletter* (1968–1985†)
IAMB	*Inter-American Music Bulletin* (1957–1973†)
IAMR	*Inter-American Music Review* (1978–2000)
IKSB	*International Kodály Society. Bulletin* (1976–2000)
INH	*InHarmoniques* (1986–1991†)
INT	*Intégral* (1987–2001)
IRASM	*International Review of the Aesthetics and Sociology of Music* (1970–2000)
ISM	*Israel Studies in Musicology* (1978–1996†)
ITO	*In Theory Only* (1972–1997)
ITR	*Indiana Theory Review* (1972–2000)
JALS	*Journal of the American Liszt Society* (1977–2000)
JAMS	*Journal of the American Musicological Society* (1948–2000)
JASI	*Journal of the Arnold Schoenberg Institute* (1976–1996†)
JBR	*Journal of Band Research* (1964–2000)
JM	*Journal of Musicology* (1982–1999)
JMP	*Jahrbuch der Musikbibliothek Peters* (1894–1940†)
JMR	*Journal of Musicological Research* (1972–2000)
JMT	*Journal of Music Theory* (1957–2000)
JMTP	*Journal of Music Theory Pedagogy* (1987–2000)
JNMR	*Journal of New Music Research* (1994–2000)
JP	*Jahrbuch Peters* (1978–1987†)
JR	*Juilliard Review* (1954–1964†)
JRMA	*Journal of the Royal Musical Association* (1986–2000)
JSIM	*Jahrbuch des Staatlichen Instituts für Musicforschung, Preußischer Kulturbesitz* (1968–2000)
KJ	*Kirchenmusikalisches Jahrbuch* (1917–2000)
KN	*Key Notes* (1975–1997†)
LAMR	*Revista de Músia Latino Americana/Latin American Music Review* (1980–2000)
LMJ	*Leonardo Music Journal* (1991–2000)
M	*Musica* (1947–1996†)
MA	*Music Analysis* (1982–2000)
MAN	*Musical Analysis* (1972–1974†)
MAS	*Musik und Ästhetik* (1997–2000)
MAU	*Musicologica Austriaca* (1977–2000)
MB	*Musik und Bildung* (1970–2000)
ME	*Musikerziehung* (1947–2000)

MELOS	*Melos: Zeitschrift für Neue Musik* (1920–1974; merged with NZM to form Melos/NZM)
Melos/NZM	*Melos/Neue Zeitschrift für Musik* (1975–1979; continued by NZM)
MF	*Musikforschung* (1948–2000)
MFO	*Music Forum* (1967–1987[†])
MG	*Musik und Gesellschaft* (1951–1990[†])
MHPG	*Mitteilungen der Hans Pfitzner-Gesellschaft* (1954–2000)
MJ	*Musique en jeu* (1970–1979[†])
MK	*Musik und Kirche* (1929–2000)
ML	*Music and Letters* (1920–2000)
MM	*Modern Music* (1924–1947[†])
MMA	*Miscellanea Musicologica: Adelaide Studies in Musicology* (1966–1990[†])
MMR	*Monthly Music Record* (1871–1960[†])
MN	*Musical Newsletter* (1971–1977[†])
MO	*Musik des Ostens* (1962–1996[†])
MP	*Music Perception* (1983–2000)
MPSS	*Mitteilungen der Paul Sacher Stiftung* (1988–2000)
MQ	*Musical Quarterly* (1915–2000)
MR	*Music Review* (1940–1994[†])
MRF	*Music Research Forum* (1986–2000)
MRSQ	*Music Reference Services Quarterly* (1992–1999)
MS	*Musicology* (Sydney) (1964–1982; continued by MSA)
MSA	*Musicology Australia* (1985–2000)
MSU	*Music Survey* (1947–1952[†])
MTEA	*Music Theory Explorations and Applications* (1992–1999[†])
MTH	*Musiktheorie* (1986–2000)
MTO	*Music Theory Online* www.societymusictheory.org/mto (1993–2000)
MTS	*Music Theory Spectrum* (1979–2000)
MTX	*MusikTexte: Zeitschrift für Neue Musik* (1983–2000)
MU	*Musicology* (1945–1949[†])
MUS	*Musicae scientiae* (1997–2000)
MZ	*Musik der Zeit* (1952–1955[†])
N	*Neuland* (1980–1985[†])
NCM	*19th Century Music* (1977–2000)
NMD	*Neue Musik in der Bundesrepublik Deutschland* (1957–1958[†])
NOTES	*Notes: Quarterly Journal of the Music Library Association* (1943–2000)
NW	*Numus West* (1972–1975[†])
NZM	*Neue Zeitschrift für Musik* (1834–2000)
OM	*Orbis musicae* (1971–1998)
OMZ	*Österreichische Musikzeitschrift* (1946–2000)
OQ	*Opera Quarterly* (1983–2000)
PK	*Piano and Keyboard* (1993–2000)
PM	*Polish Music/Polnische Musik* (1967–1992[†])
PMJ	*Polish Music Journal* www.usc.edu/dept/polish_music/PMJ (1998–2000)
PNM	*Perspectives of New Music* (1962–2000)
POL	*Polyphonie* (1947–1949[†])
PQ	*Piano Quarterly* (1952–1992; continued by PK)
PRMA	*Proceedings of the Royal Musical Association* (1874–1985; continued by JRMA)
R	*Reihe* (English edition) (1957–1964[†])
RBM	*Revue belge de musicologie/Belgisch tijdschrift voor muziekwetenschap* (1946–2000)
RDM	*Revue de musicology* (1917–2000)
REP	*Repercussions* (1992–2000)
RIM	*Rivista italiana di musicologia* (1966–2000)
RM	*Revue musicale* (1920–1991[†])
RS	*Recorded Sound* (1961–1984[†])
S	*Source* (1967–1972[†])

SAG	*Saggiatore musicale* (1994–2000)
SBM	*Schweizer Beiträge zur Musikwissenschaft* (1972–1980[†])
SCORE	*Score and I. M. A. Magazine* (1949–1961[†])
SM	*Studia musicologica* (1961–2000)
SMUWO	*Studies in Music from the University of Western Ontario* (1976–1998[†])
SMZ	*Schweizerische Musikzeitung* (1861–1983[†])
SN	*Soundings* (Cardiff) (1970–1985[†])
SONUS	*Sonus* (1980–2000)
SS	*Sonorum speculum* (1958–1974; continued by KN)
STM	*Svensk Tidskrift för Musikforskning* (1919–2000)
STMO	*STM-Online* (Swedish Musicological Society) www.musik.uu.se/ssm/stmonline/index.html (1998–2000)
STU	*Studi musicali* (1972–2000)
SV	*Studi verdiani* (1982–2001)
SZM	*Studien zur Musikwissenschaft. Beihefte der Denkmäler der Tonkunst in Österreich.* New ser. (1955–1999)
T	*Tibia: Magazin für Freunde älter und neuer Bläsermusik* (1976–2000)
TCM	*20th Century Music* (1994–1999; continued by TCMU)
TCMU	*21st Century Music* (2000)
TEMPO	*Tempo: A Review of Modern Music* (1939–2000)
THE	*Theoria* (1985–1994)
TP	*Theory and Practice* (1975–2000)
TSP	*Theoretically Speaking* (1984–1992[†])
V	*Verdi: Bollettino dell' Instituto di Studi Verdiani* (1960–1987[†])
Y	*Yearbook for Inter-American Musical Research* (1965–1975[†])
ZM	*Zeitschrift für Musiktheorie* (1970–1978[†])

FESTSCHRIFTEN

F-Abert	Klaus Hortschansky, ed. *Opernstudie: Anna Amalie Abert zum 65. Geburtstag.* Tutzing: H. Schneider, 1975.
F-Abert/H	Friedrich Blume, ed. *Gedenkschrift für Hermann Abert: Von seinen Schülern.* Halle (Saale): M. Niemeyer, 1928; reprint, Tutzing: H. Schneider, 1974.
F-Abraham	Malcolm Hamrick Brown and Roland John Wiley, eds. *Slavonic and Western Music: Essays for Gerald Abraham.* Ann Arbor, Mich.: UMI Research Press; Oxford: Oxford University Press, 1985.
F-Abs	Martin Staehelin, ed. *Divertimento für Hermann J. Abs: Beethoven-Studien dargebracht zu seinem 80. Geburtstag.* Vom Verein Beethoven-Haus Beethoven-Haus und vom Beethoven-Archiv Bonn. Bonn: Beethoven-Haus, 1981.
F-Adorno/60	Max Horkheimer, ed. *Zeugnisse: Theodor W. Adorno zum 60. Geburtstag.* Im Auftrag des Instituts für Sozialforschung. Frankfurt am Main: Europaishe Verlagsanstalt, 1963.
F-Albrecht	*Hans Albrecht in Memoriam.* Kassel: Bärenreiter, 1962.
F-Albrecht/70	*Festschrift Georg von Albrecht zum 70. Geburtstag.* Stuttgart: Ichthys, 1962.
F-Albrecht/S	John Walter Hill, ed. *Studies in Musicology in Honor of Otto E. Albrecht: A Collection of Essays by His Colleagues and Former Students at the University of Pennsylvania.* Kassel: Bärenreiter, 1980.
F-Alderman	Burton L. Karson, ed. *Festival Essays for Pauline Alderman: A Musicological Tribute.* Provo, Utah: Brigham Young University Press, 1976.
F-Anglés	*Miscelánea en homenaje a Monseñor Higinio Anglés.* Barcelona: Consejo Superior de Investigaciones Científicas, 1958–1961.
F-Apel	Hans Tischler, ed. *Essays in Musicology: A Birthday Offering for Willi Apel.* Bloomington: Indiana University School of Music, 1968.
F-Bartók/S	*Studia memoriae Belae Bartók sacra.* Budapest: Aedes Academiae Scientiarum Hungaricae, 1956; 2d ed., 1957; 3d ed., 1959.
F-Bartók/T	*Béla Bartók: A Memorial Review.* New York: Boosey & Hawkes, 1950.

F-Becking	*Gustav Becking zum Gedächtnis: Eine Auswahl seiner Schriften und Beiträge seine Schüler.* Tutzing: H. Schneider, 1975.
F-Beckwith	Timothy J. McGee, ed. *Taking a Stand: Essays in Honour of John Beckwith.* Toronto: University of Toronto Press, 1995.
F-Benz	*Gegenwart in Geiste: Festschrift für Richard Benz.* Hamburg: Wegner, 1954.
F-Bernstein	Edward H. Clinkscale and Claire Brook, eds. *A Musical Offering: Essays in Honor of Martin Bernstein.* New York: Pendragon, 1977.
F-Besseler	*Festschrift Heinrich Besseler zum sechzigsten Geburtstag.* Leipzig: VEB Deutscher Verlag für Musik, 1961.
F-Bishop	*Miscellanea musicologica.* Adelaide Studies in Musicology 1. Adelaide: Libraries Board of South Australia in association with the University of Adelaide, 1966.
F-Blankenburg	Martin Geck, ed. *Bach-Interpretationen: Walter Blankenburg zum 65. Geburtstag.* Gottingen: Vandenhoeck & Ruprecht, 1969.
F-Blaukopf	Irmagard Bontinck and Otto Brusatti, eds. *Festschrift Kurt Blaukopf.* Vienna: Universal, 1975.
F-Blume	*Festschrift Friedrich Blume zum 70. Geburtstag.* Kassel: Bärenreiter, 1963.
F-Boetticher	Heinrich Hüschen and Dietz-Rudiger Moster, eds. *Convivium musicorum: Festschrift Wolfgang Boetticher zum sechzigsten Geburtstag am 19. August 1974.* Berlin: Merseburger, 1974.
F-Boulez	Josef Häusler, ed. *Pierre Boulez: Eine Festschrift zum 60. Geburtstag am 26. März 1985.* Vienna: Universal, 1985.
F-Boulez/Glock	William Glock, ed. *Pierre Boulez: A Symposium.* London: Eulenburg, 1986.
F-Brook	Allan W. Atlas, ed. *Music in the Classic Period: Essays in Honor of Barry S. Brook.* New York: Pendragon, 1985.
F-Cage	Peter Gena and Jonathan Brent, eds. *A John Cage Reader in Celebration of His 70th Birthday.* New York: Peters, 1982.
F-Cuyler	Edith Borroff, ed. *Notations and Editions: A Book in Honor of Louise Cuyler.* Dubuque, Iowa: Brown, 1974.
F-Dadelson	Volker Scherliess and Thomas Kohlhase, eds. *Festschrift Georg von Dadelson zum 60. Geburtstag.* Neuhausen-Stuttgart: Hänssler, 1978.
F-Dahlhaus	Hermann Danuser et al., eds. *Das musikalische Kunstwerk: Geschichte, Ästhetik, Theorie; Festschrift Carl Dahlhaus zum 60. Geburtstag.* Laaber: Laaber, 1988.
F-David	Gerd Sievers, ed. *Ex deo nascimur: Festschrift zum 75. Geburtstag von Johann Nepomuk David.* Wiesbaden: Breitkopf & Hartel, 1970.
F-Davison	*Essays in Honor of Archibald Thompson Davison by His Associates.* Cambridge, Mass.: Harvard University Department of Music, 1957.
F-Deutsch	Walter Gersternberg, Jan LaRue, and Wolfgang Rehm, eds. *Festschrift Otto Erich Deutsch zum 80. Geburtstag am 5. September 1963.* Kassel: Bärenreiter, 1963.
F-Dick	Anne Trenkamp and John G. Suess, eds. *Studies in the Schoenbergian Movement in Vienna and the United States: Essays in Honor of Marcel Dick.* Lewiston, N.Y.: Mellen, 1990.
F-Doflein	Lars Ulrich Abraham, ed. *Erich Doflein: Festschrift zum 70. Geburtstag.* Mainz: Schott, 1972.
F-Dürr	Wolfgang Rehm, ed. *Bachiana et alia musicologica: Festschrift Alfred Dürr zum 65. Geburtstag am 3. März 1983.* New York: Bärenreiter, 1983.
F-Emmanuel	Maurice Emmanuel. *Revue musicale* numéro special 206 (1947): 1–128.
F-Engel	*A Birthday Offering to Carl Engel.* New York: Schirmer, 1943.
F-Engel/H	*Festschrift Hans Engel zum seibzigsten Geburtstag.* Kassel: Bärenreiter, 1964.
F-Erdmann	Christof Bitter and Manfred Schloser, eds. *Begegnungen mit Eduard Erdmann.* Darmstadt: Erato, 1968.
F-Federhofer	Friedrich Wilhelm Riedel and Hubert Unverricht, eds. *Symbolae historiae musicae: Hellmut Federhofer zum 60. Geburtstag.* Mainz: Schott, 1971.
F-Federov/65	Harold Heckmann and Wolfgang Rehm, eds. *Mélanges offerts à Vladimir Féderov à l'occasion de son soixante-cinquième anniversaire 5 août 1966. Fontes artis musicae* 13 (1966): 1–152.
F-Feicht	Zofia Lissa, ed. *Studia Hieronymo Feicht seuptuagenario dedicata.* Kraków: Polskie Wydawnictwo Muzyczne, 1967.
F-Fellerer	Heinrich Hüschen, ed. *Festschrift Karl Gustav Fellerer zum sechzigsten Geburtstag.* Regensburg: Bosse, 1962.

F-Fellerer/60	Herbert Druk, ed. *Karl Gustav Fellerer zum 60. Geburtstag überreicht von den Mitgliedern der Arbeitsgemeinschafts für Rheinische Musikgeschichte.* Beiträge zur Rheinischen Musikgeschichte 52. Cologne: Volk, 1962.
F-Fellerer/70	Heinrich Hüschen, ed. *Musicae scientiae collectanea: Festschrift Karl Gustav Fellerer zum siebzigsten Geburtstag am 7. Juli 1972.* Cologne: Volk, 1973.
F-Finscher	Annegrit Laubenthal, ed. *Studien zur Musikgeschichte: Eine Festschrift für Ludwig Finscher.* Kassel: Bärenreiter, 1995.
F-Floros/60	Peter Petersen, ed. *Musikkulturgeschichte: Festschrift für Constantin Floros zum 60. Geburtstag.* Wiesbaden: Breitkoph & Härtel, 1990.
F-Floros/70	Gottfried Krieger and Matthias Spindler, eds. *Musik als Lebensprogramm: Festschrift für Constantin Floros zum 70. Geburtstag.* Frankfurt am Main: Lang, 2000.
F-Forbes	Lewis Lockwood and Phyllis Benjamin, eds. *Beethoven Essays: Studies in Honor of Elliot Forbes.* Cambridge, Mass.: Harvard University Department of Music, 1984.
F-Fox	Jerald C. Grave, ed. *Essays on Music for Charles Warren Fox.* Rochester, N.Y.: Eastman School of Music Press, 1979.
F-Ghisi	*Memorie e contributi alla musica dal medioevo all'età moderna: Offerti a F. Ghisi nel settantesimo compleanno (1901–1971).* 2 vols. Bologna: Antiquae Musicae Italicae Studiosi, 1971.
F-Göllner	Bernd Edelmann and Manfred Hermann, eds. *Altes im Neuen: Festschrift Theodor Göllner zum 65. Geburtstag.* Tutzing: Schneider, 1995.
F-Gubaidulina	*Sofia Gubaidulina: Eine Hommage zum 60. Geburtstag.* Saarbrücken: Pfau, 2000.
F-Gudewill	Uwe Haensel, ed. *Beiträge zur Musikgeschichte Nordeuropas: Kurt Gudewill zum 65. Geburtstag.* Wolfenbüttel: Möseler, 1978.
F-Haberl	Franz A. Stein, ed. *Festschrift Ferdinand Haberl zum 70. Geburtstag: Sacerdos et cantus gregoriani magister.* Regensburg: Bosse, 1977.
F-Herz	Robert L. Weaver, ed. *Essays on the Music of J. S. Bach and Other Divers Subjects: A Tribute to Gerhard Herz.* Louisville, Ky.: University of Louisville, 1981.
F-Hitchcock	Richard Crawford, R. Allen Lott, and Carol J. Oja, eds. *A Celebration of American Music: Words and Music in Honor of H. Wiley Hitchcock.* Ann Arbor: University of Michigan Press, 1990.
F-Hoboken	Joseph Schmid-Görg, ed. *Anthony van Hoboken: Festschrift zum 75. Geburtstag.* Mainz: Schott, 1962.
F-Hüschen	Detlef Altenburg, ed. *Ars musica, musica scientia: Festschrift Heinrich Hüschen zum fünfundsechzigsten Geburtstag am 2. März 1980.* Cologne: Gittare und Laute Verlagsgesellschaft, 1980.
F-Husmann	Heinz Becker and Reinhard Gerlach, eds. *Speculum musicae artis: Festgabe für Heinrich Husmann zum 60. Geburtstag am 16. Dezember 1968.* Munich: Fink, 1970.
F-Jackson	Malcolm Cole and John Koegel, eds. *Music in Performance and Society: Essays in Honor of Roland Jackson.* Warren, Mich.: Harmonie Park Press, 1997.
F-Jeppesen	Bjorn Hjelmburg and Soren Sorensen, eds. *Natalicia musicologica Knud Jeppesen suptuagenario collegis oblata.* Oslo: Hansen, 1962.
F-Kaufmann/W	Thomas Noblitt, ed. *Music East and West: Essays in Honor of Walter Kaufmann.* New York: Pendragon, 1981.
F-Kirkendale	Siegfried Gmeinwieser, David Hiley, and Jörg Riedlbauer, eds. *Musica humana: Studies in Honor of Warren and Ursula Kirkendale.* Florence: Olschki, 1994.
F-Knepler	Hanns-Werner Heister, ed. *Musik/Revolution: Festschrift für Georg Knepler zum 90. Geburtstag.* 3 vols. Hamburg: Von Bockel, 1997.
F-Kodály/80	*Zoltano Kodály octogenario sacrum.* Budapest: Akadémia Kiadó, 1962. [Also published as *Studia musicologica 3*]
F-Kretzschmar	*Festschrift Hermann Kretzschmar zum siebzigsten Geburtstage überreicht von Kollegen, Schülern und Freunden.* Leipzig: Peters, 1918. Reprint, Hildesheim: Olms, 1973.
F-LaGrange	Günther Weiß, ed. *Neue Mahleriana: Essays in Honour of Henry-Louis La Grange on His Seventieth Birthday.* Bern: Lang, 1997.
F-Lang	Edmond Strainchamps and Maria Rika Maniates, eds. *Music and Civilization: Essays in Honor of Paul Henry Lang.* New York: Norton, 1984.
F-Larsen	*Festskrift Jens Peter Larsen.* Copenhagen: Hansen, 1972.
F-LaRue	Eugene K. Wolf and Edward H. Roesner, eds. *Studies in Musical Sources and Style: Essays in Honor of Jan LaRue.* Madison, Wis.: A-R Editions, 1990.

F-Lefkowitz	John Daverio and John Ogasapian, eds. *The Varieties of Musicology: Essays in Honor of Murray Lefkowitz*. Warren, Mich.: Harmonie Park Press, 2000.
F-Lewin	Raphael Atlas and Michael Cherlin, eds. *Musical Transformation and Musical Intuition: Eleven Essays in Honor of David Lewin*. Roxbury, Mass.: Ovenbird, 1994.
F-Lichtenhahn	Antonio Baldassarre, Susanne Kübler, and Patrick Müller, eds. *Music denken: Ernst Lichtenhahn zur Emeritierung*. Bern: Lang, 2000.
F-Lissa	*Studia musicologica aesthetica, theoretics, historica*. Kraków: Polskie Wydawnictwo Muzyczne, 1979.
F-Maegaard	Mogens Andersen, Niels Bo Foltmann, and Claus Røllum-Larsen, eds. *Festskrift Jan Maegaard, 14–4–1996*. Copenhagen: Engstrøm & Sødring, 1996.
F-Marx	Erhard Karkoschka, ed. *Festschrift Karl Marx zum 70. Geburtstag*. Stuttgart: Ichthys, 1967.
F-Mauersberger	*Credo musicale: Komponistenporträts aus der Arbeit des Dresdener Kreuzchores: Festgabe zum 80. Geburtstag des Nationalpreisträgers Kreuzkantor Professor D. Dr. h. c. Rudolf Mauersberger*. Kassel: Bärenreiter, 1969.
F-Melbourne	Brenton Broadstock et al., eds. *Aflame with Music: 100 Years of Music at the University of Melbourne*. Parkville, Victoria: Centre for Studies in Australian Music, 1996.
F-Merritt	Laurence Berman, ed. *Words and Music: The Scholar's View; A Medley of Problems and Solutions Compiled in Honor of A. Tillman Merritt by Sundry Hands*. Cambridge, Mass.: Harvard University Department of Music, 1972.
F-Meyer	Eugene Narmour and Ruth A. Solie, eds. *Explorations in Music, the Arts, and Ideas: Essays in Honor of Leonard B. Meyer*. Stuyvesant, N.Y.: Pendragon, 1988.
F-Mitchell	Philip Reed, ed. *On Mahler and Britten: Essays in Honour of Donald Mitchell on His Seventieth Birthday*. Woodbridge, U.K.: Britten-Pears Library, 1995.
F-Moser	*Musik in Zeit und Raum*. Berlin: Mersburger, 1960.
F-Müller-Blattau/65	*Festgabe für Joseph Müller-Blattau zum 65. Geburtstag*. Annales Universitatis Saraviensis, Philosophie 9, fase. 1 (1960). Saarbrucken: Universität des Sarrlandes, 1960.
F-Orel	Hellmut Federhofer, ed. *Festschrift Alfred Orel zum 70. Geburtstag*. Vienna: Rohrer, 1960.
F-Osthoff/70	Ursula Aarburg and Peter Cahn, eds. *Hellmuth Osthoff zu seinen siebzigsten Geburtstag*. Tutzing: Schneider, 1969.
F-Osthoff/80	Ludwig Finscher, ed. *Renaissance-Studien: Helmut Osthoff zum 80. Geburtstag*. Tutzing: Schneider, 1979.
F-Palisca	Nancy Kovaleff Baker and Barbara Russano Hanning, eds. *Musical Humanism and Its Legacy: Essays in Honor of Claude V. Palisca*. Stuyvesant, N.Y.: Pendragon, 1992.
F-Pepping	Heinrich Poos, ed. *Festschrift Ernst Pepping zu seinem 70. Geburtstag am 12. September 1971*. Berlin: Merseberger, 1971.
F-Pfitzner	Walter Abendroth and Karl-Robert Danler, eds. *Festschrift Hans Pfitzner*. Munich: Winkler, 1969.
F-Philipp	*Franz Philipp 70 Jahre: Das Bild eines deutschen Musikers in Zeugnissen und Zeitgenossen; Gedruckt als Gabe seiner Freunde zum 70. Geburtstag, 24 August 1960*. Freiburg im Breisgau?: s.n., 1960.
F-Pisk	*Paul A. Pisk: Essays in His Honor*. Austin: University of Texas Press, 1965.
F-Plamenac	Gustav Reese and Robert J. Snow, eds. *Essays in Honor of Dragan Plamenac on His 70th Birthday*. Pittsburgh: University of Pittsburgh, 1967.
F-Ratner	Wye J. Allanbrook, Janet M. Levy, and William P. Mahrt, eds. *Convention in Eighteenth- and Nineteeth-Century Music: Essays in Honor of Leonard G. Ratner*. Stuyvesant, N.Y.: Pendragon, 1992.
F-Reger	Klaus Röhring, ed. *Max Reger 1873–1973: Ein Symposium*. In Verbindung mit dem Max-Reger-Institut (Elsa-Reger-Stiftung). Bonn-Bad Godesberg und der Internationalen Orgelwache Nürnberg. Wiesbaden: Breifkopf & Härtel, 1974.
F-Rehm	Dietrich Berke and Harald Heckmann, eds. *Festschrift Wolfgang Rehm zum 60. Geburstag am 3. September 1989*. Kassel: Bärenreiter, 1989.
F-Rohlfs	Francisco J. Oroz Anscuren, ed. *Romania cant at: Lieder in alten une neue; Chorsätzen mit sprachlichen, literarischen und musikwissenschaftlichen Interpretationen*. Tübingen: G. Narr, 1980.
F-Ronga	*Scritti in onore di Luigi Ronga*. Milan: Ricciardi, 1973.
F-Sachs/C	Gustav Reese and Rose Brandei, eds. *The Commonwealth of Music: In Honor of Curt Sachs*. Glencoe, Ill.: Free Press, 1964.
F-Savoff	Hermann Danuser and Christoph Keller, eds. *Aspekte der musikalischen Interpretation: Sava Savoff zum 70. Geburtstag*. Hamburg: Wagner, 1980.

F-Schenk	Theophil Antonicek, Rudolf Flotzinger, and Othmar Wessely, eds. *De ratione in musica: Festschrift Erich Schenk zum 5. Mai 1972*. Kassel: Bärenreiter, 1975.
F-Scheurleer	*Gedenkboek aangeboden aan Dr. D. F. Scheurleer op zijn 70sten verjaardag: Bijdragen van vrienden en vereerders op het gebied der muziek*. 's-Gravenhage: M. Nijhoff, 1925.
F-Schmidt-Görg	Dagmar Weise, ed. *Festschrift Joseph Schmidt-Görg zum 60. Geburtstag*. Bonn: Beethoven-Haus, 1957.
F-Schmidt-Görg/70	Siegfried Kross and Hans Schmidt, eds. *Colloquium amicorum: Joseph Schmidt-Görg zum 70. Geburtstag*. Bonn: Beethoven-Haus, 1967.
F-Schneider	*Festschrift für Michael Schneider zum 65. Geburtstag*. Berlin: Merseburger, 1974.
F-Schneider/80	Walter Vetter, ed. *Festschrift Max Schneider zum achtzigsten Geburtstage*. In Verbindung mit Franz von Wasenapp, Ursula Schneider und Walther Siegmund-Schultze. Leipzig: Deutscher Verlag für Musik, 1955.
F-Schnittke	*Alfred Schnittke zum 60. Geburtstag: Eine Festschrift*. Hamburg: Sikorski, 1994.
F-Schreiber	Gunther Massenkeil and Susanne Popp, eds. *Festschrift für Ottmar Schreiber zum 70. Geburtstag am 16. Februar 1976. Reger-Studien* 1. Wiesbaden: Breitkopf & Härtel, 1978.
F-Schuh	Jürg Stenzl, ed. *Art Nouveau, Jugendstil und Musik*. Zurich: Atlantis, 1980.
F-Schwarz	Malcolm Hamrick Brown, ed. *Russian and Soviet music: Essays for Boris Schwarz*. Ann Arbor, Mich.: UMI Research Press, 1984.
F-Seay	Michael D. Grace, ed. *A Festschrift for Albert Seay: Essays by His Friends and Colleagues*. Colorado Springs: Colorado College, 1982.
F-Sievers	Richard Jakoby and Gunter Katzenberger, eds. *Heinrich Sievers zum 70. Geburtstag*. Tutzing: Schneider, 1978.
F-Spohr	Hartmut Becker and Rainer Krempien, eds. *Louis Spohr: Festschrift und Ausstellungskatalog zum 200. Geburtstag*. Kassel: Wenderoth, 1984.
F-Stephan	Josef Kuckertz et al., eds. *Neue Musik und Tradition: Festschrift Rudolf Stephan zum 65. Geburtstag*. Laaber: Laaber, 1990.
F-Strecker	Carl Dahlhaus, ed. *Festschrift für einen Verlagert Ludwig Strecker zum 90. Geburtstag*. Mainz: Schott, 1973.
F-Strunk	Harold Powers, ed. *Studies in Music History: Essays for Oliver Strunk*. Princeton, N.J.: Princeton University Press, 1968.
F-Swan	Gordon Paine, ed. *Five Centuries of Choral Music: Essays in Honor of Howard Swan*. Stuyvesant, N.Y.: Pendragon, 1988.
F-Szabolcsi	Denes Bartha, ed. *Bence Szabolcsi: Septuagenario*. Kassel: Bärenreiter, 1969.
F-Tippett	Ian Kemp, ed. *Michael Tippett: A Symposium on His 60th Birthday*. London: Faber & Faber, 1965.
F-Valentin	Günther Weiss, ed. *Festschrift Erich Valentin zum 70. Geburtstag*. Regensburg: Bosse, 1976.
F-Vetter	Heinz Wegener, ed. *Musa–Mens–Musici: Im Gedenken an Walther Vetter*. Leipzig: VEB Deutscher Verlag für Musik, 1969.
F-Vogel	Heribert Schröder, ed. *Colloquium: Festschrift Martin Vogel zum 65. Geburtstag*. Bad Honnef: Schröder, 1988.
F-Vötterle	Richard Baum and Wolfgang Rehm, eds. *Musik und Verlag: Karl Vötterle zum 65. Geburtstag am 12. April 1968*. Kassel: Bärenreiter, 1968.
F-Walcha	Walter Dehnhard and Gottlob Ritter, eds. *Bachstunden: Festschrift für Helmut Walcha zum 70. Geburtstag, überreicht von seinen Schülern*. Frankfurt am Main: Evangelischer Presseverband in Hessen und Nassau, 1978.
F-Walker	Michael Saffle and James Deaville, eds. *New Lights on Liszt and His Music: Essays in Honor of Alan Walker's 65th Birthday*. Stuyvesant, N.Y.: Pendragon, 1997.
F-Wessely	Manfred Angerer et al., eds. *Festschrift Othmar Wessely zum 60. Geburtstag*. Tutzing: Schneider, 1982.
F-Wiener	*Festschrift 1817–1967 Akademie für Musik und Darstellende Kunst in Wien*. Vienna: Lafite, 1967.
F-Wiora	*Festschrift für Walter Wiora zum 30. Dezember 1966*. Kassel: Bärenreiter, 1967.
F-Yun	Hinrich Bergmeier, ed. *Isang Yun: Feschrift zum 75. Geburtstag 1992*. Berlin: Bote & Bock, 1992.

MONOGRAPHS

| M-Abbate | Carolyn Abbate and Roger Parker, eds. *Analyzing Opera: Verdi and Wagner*. Berkeley: University of California Press, 1989. |

M-Abraham	Gerald Abraham. *Essays on Russian and East European Music.* Oxford: Clarendon, 1985
M-Abraham/L	Lars Ulrich Abraham et al. *Neue Wege der musikalischen Analyse.* Berlin: Merseburger, 1967.
M-Agawu	V. Kofi Agawu. *Playing with Signs: A Semiotic Interpretation of Classic Music.* Princeton, N.J.: Princeton University Press, 1991.
M-Anhalt	István Anhalt. *Alternative Voices: Essays on Contemporary Vocal and Choral Composition.* Toronto: University of Toronto Press, 1984.
M-Arsenault	Linda Marie Arsenault. "An Introduction to Iannis Xenakis's Stochastic Music: Four Algorithmic Analyses." Ph.D. diss., University of Toronto, 2000.
M-Ayrey	Craig Ayrey and Mark Everist. *Analytical Strategies and Musical Interpretation: Essays on Nineteenth- and Twentieth-Century Music.* Cambridge: Cambridge University Press, 1996.
M-Bachfest	*Bachfest (55.) der Neuen Bachgesellschaft in Mainz, 22 bis 27 Oktober 1980: "Johann Sebastian Bach und seine Ausstrahlung auf die Nachfolgende Jahrhunderte."* Mainz: Neue Bachgesellschaft, 1980.
M-Baker	James M. Baker, David W. Beach, and Jonathan W. Bernard, eds. *Music Theory in Concept and Practice.* Rochester, N.Y.: University of Rochester Press, 1997.
M-Badura-Skoda	Eva Badura-Skoda and Peter Branscombe, eds. *Schubert Studies: Problems of Style and Chronology.* Cambridge: Cambridge University Press, 1982.
M-Battcock	Gregory Battcock. *Breaking the Sound Barrier: A Critical Anthology of the New Music.* New York: Dutton, 1981.
M-Beck	Hermann Beck, ed. *Studien zur Musikgeschichte der Stadt Regensburg.* Regensburg: Bosse, 1979.
M-Benary	Peter Benary et al. *Versuch musikalischer Analysen.* Berlin: Merseburger, 1967.
M-Bersano	James Richard Bersano. "Formalized Aspect Analysis of Sound Texture." Ph.D. diss., Indiana University, 1979.
M-Boulez	Pierre Boulez; Jean-Jacques Nattiez, ed. *Points de repère.* 2d ed. Paris: Seuil, 1985.
M-Brauneiss	Leopold Brauneiss. *Zahlen zwischen Struktur und Bedeutung: Zehn analytische Studien zu Kompositionen von Josquin bis Ligeti und Pärt.* Frankfurt am Main: Lang, 1997.
M-Breig	Werner Breig, Reinhold Brinkmann, and Elmar Budde, eds. *Analysen: Beiträge zu einer Problemgeschichte des Komponierens.* Stuttgart: Steiner, 1984.
M-Brinkmann	Reinhold Brinkmann, ed. *Die neue Musk und die Tradition: Sieben Kongress-Beiträge und eine analytische Studie.* Mainz: Schott, 1978.
M-Broekema	Andrew J. Broekema. "A Stylistic Comparison of the Solo Vocal Works of Arnold Schoenberg, Alban Berg, and Anton Webern." Ph.D. diss., University of Texas, 1962.
M-Bruhn	Siglind Bruhn, ed. *Encrypted Messages in Alban Berg's Music.* New York: Garland, 1998.
M-Brusatti	Otto Brusatti, ed. *Schubert-Kongress Wien 1978: Bericht.* Graz: Akademische Druck- und Verlagsanstalt, 1979.
M-Buccheri	John Stephen Buccheri. "An Approach to Twelve-Tone Music: Articulation of Serial Pitch Units in Piano Works of Schoenberg, Webern, Krenek, Dallapiccola, and Rochberg." Ph.D. diss., University of Rochester, 1975.
M-Budde	Elmar Budde and Rudolph Stephan, eds. *Franz-Schrecker-Symposium.* Berlin: Colloquium, 1980.
M-Campbell	Alan Douglas Campbell. "Roger Sessions' Adoption of the Twelve-Tone Method." Ph.D. diss., City University of New York, 1990.
M-Caplin	William E. Caplin. *Classical Form: A Theory of Formal Functions for the Instrumental Music of Haydn, Mozart, and Beethoven.* New York: Oxford University Press, 1998.
M-Carner	Mosco Carner. *Major and Minor.* New York: Holmes & Meier, 1980.
M-Chailley	Jacques Chailley. *Classiques et romantiques.* Vol. 2 of *Florilège d'analyses.* Paris: Leduc, 1984.
M-Chihara	Paul Seiko Chihara. "Studies in Melody in Four Twentieth-Century Composers." D.M.A. diss., Cornell University, 1965.
M-Code	David Loberg Code. "Narrative Strategies in Tonal Compositons." Ph.D. diss., University of Maryland, College Park, 1990.
M-Cohn	Richard Lawrence Cohn. "Transpositional Combination in Twentieth-Century Music." Ph.D. diss., Yale University, 1987.
M-Cope	David H. Cope. *New Directions in Music.* 4th ed. Dubuque, Iowa: Brown, 1984.
M-Cross/P	Charlotte M. Cross and Russell A. Berman, eds. *Political and Religious Ideas in the Works of Arnold Schoenberg.* New York: Garland, 2000.
M-Cross/S	Charlotte M. Cross and Russell A. Berman, eds. *Schoenberg and Words: The Modernist Years.* New York: Garland, 2000.

M-Curtis	Brandt B. Curtis. "A Comparison of Early Musical Settings of Four Poems by A. E. Housman." D.M.A. diss., Indiana University, 1979.
M-Dahlhaus	Carl Dahlhaus, ed. *Das Drama Richard Wagners als musikalisches Kunstwerk.* Regensburg: Bosse, 1970.
M-Dahlhaus/S	Carl Dahlhaus, ed. *Studien zur Musikgeschichte Berlins im fruhen 19. Jahrhundert.* Regensburg: Bosse, 1980.
M-De la Motte	Diether De la Motte. *Musikalische Analyse.* Kassel: Bärenreiter, 1968.
M-DeLio	Thomas DeLio. *Cicumscribing the Open Universe.* Lanham, Md.: University Press of America, 1984.
M-Dommel-Diény	Amy Dommel-Diény. *L'analyse harmonique en exemples de J. S. Bach à Debussy.* Neuchâtel: Delachaux & Niestlé, 1967–1970.
M-Dorroh	William James Dorroh. "A Study of Plainsong in the Organ Compositions of Six Twentieth-Century French Composers." Ph.D. diss., George Peabody College for Teachers, 1978.
M-Eitan	Zohar Eitan. *Highpoints: A Study of Melodic Peaks.* Philadelphia: University of Pennsylvania Press, 1997.
M-Enix	Margery Ann Enix. "The Dissolution of the Functional Harmonic Tonal System: 1850–1910." Ph.D. diss., Indiana University, 1977.
M-Epstein	David Epstein. *Beyond Orpheus: Studies in Musical Structure.* Cambridge, Mass.: MIT Press, 1979.
M-Forte	Allen Forte. *Contemporary Tone Structures.* New York: Teachers College Press, 1955.
M-Forte/L	Allen Forte. "Liszt's Experimental Idiom and Music of the Early Twentieth Century." NCM 10/3 (1987): 209–28. Reprinted in *Music at the Turn of the Century,* ed. Joseph Kerman, 93–112, Berkeley: University of California Press, 1990.
M-Gallatin	James Allen Gallatin. "An Overview of the Compositional Methods in Representative Works of Olivier Messiaen." Ph.D. diss., University of Cincinnati, 1986.
M-Goldschmidt	Harry Goldschmidt, Karl-Heinz Kohler, and Konrad Niemann, eds. *Bericht über den Internationalen Beethoven-Kongress 20. bis 23. März 1977 in Berlin.* Leipzig: VEB Deutscher Verlag für Musik, 1978.
M-Grasberger	Franz Grasberger and Othmar Wessely, eds. *Schubert Studien: Festgabe der Österreichischen Akademie der Wissenschaften zum Schubert-Jahr 1978, Wien 1978.* Vienna: Österreichische Akademie der Wissenschaften, 1978.
M-Greer	Taylor Aitken Greer. "Tonal Processes in the Songs of Gabriel Fauré: Two Structural Features of the Whole-Tone Scale." Ph.D. diss., Yale University, 1986.
M-Hall	Anne Carothers Hall. "Texture in Violin Concertos of Stravinsky, Berg, Schoenberg, and Bartók." Ph.D. diss., University of Michigan, 1971.
M-Hanninen	Dora A. Hanninen. "A General Theory for Context-Sensitive Music Analysis: Applications to Four Works for Piano by Contemporary American Composers." Ph.D. diss., University of Rochester, Eastman School of Music, 1996.
M-Hansler	George E. Hansler. "Stylistic Characteristics and Trends in Contemporary British Choral Music." Ph.D. diss., New York University, 1957.
M-Hart	Ralph E. Hart. "Compositional Techniques in Choral Works of Stravinsky, Hindemith, Honegger, and Britten." Ph.D. diss., Northwestern University, 1952.
M-Hines	Robert Stephan Hines, ed. *Essays on Twentieth-Century Music by Those Who Wrote It: The Orchestral Composer's Point of View.* Norman: University of Oklahoma Press, 1970.
M-Jeter	Eulalie Wilson Jeter. "The Study, Analysis, and Performance of Selected Original Two-Piano Music of Contemporary American Composers." Ed.D. diss., Columbia University, 1978.
M-Johnson	June Durkin Johnson. "Analyses of Selected Works for the Soprano Voice Written in Serial Technique by Living Composers." D.M.A. diss., University of Illinois, 1967.
M-Jones	Timothy Jones. *Beethoven: The "Moonlight" and Other Sonatas, Op. 27 and 31.* Cambridge: Cambridge University Press, 1999.
M-Kessler	Deborah Kessler. "Schubert's Late Three-Key Expositions: Influence, Design, and Structure." Ph.D. diss., City University of New York, 1996.
M-Kirchmeyer	Helmut Kirchmeyer and Hugo Wolfram Schmidt. *Aufbruch der jungen Musik: Von Webern bis Stockhausen.* Cologne: Gerig, 1970.
M-Kniesner	Virginia Elizabeth Kniesner. "Tonality and Form in Selected French Piano Sonatas: 1900–1950." Ph.D. diss., Ohio State University, 1977.
M-KNM	*Kommentare zur neuen Musik.* Cologne: Du Mont Schaubert, 1961.

M-Kolleritsch	Otto Kolleritsch, ed. *Gustav Mahler: Sinfonie und Wirklichkeit*. Graz: Universal, 1977.
M-Kolleritsch/S	Otto Kolleritsch, ed. *Alexander Skrjabin*. Graz: Universal, 1980.
M-Kramer	Lawrence Kramer. *Classical Music and Postmodern Knowledge*. Berkeley: University of California Press, 1995.
M-Kresky	Jeffrey Kresky. *Tonal Music: Twelve Analytic Studies*. Bloomington: Indiana University Press, 1977.
M-Kühn	Hellmut Kühn and Peter Nitsche, eds. *Bericht über den Internationalen Musikwissenschaftlichen Kongress, Berlin 1974*. Kassel: Bärenreiter, 1980.
M-Lambert	Philip Lambert. *The Music of Charles Ives*. New Haven, Conn.: Yale University Press, 1997.
M-Lampsatis	Raminta Lampsatis. "Dodekaphonische Werke von Balsys, Juzeliunas und der jüngeren Komponisten-generation Litauens: Dodekaphonie als integrierende Technik." Ph.D. diss., Technische Universität Berlin, 1977.
M-Lang	Paul Henry Lang. *Stravinsky: A New Appraisal of His Work*. New York: Norton, 1963. [Reprint of MQ 48 (1962): 287–384]
M-Larsen	Jens Peter Larsen, Howard Senwer, James Webster, eds. *Haydn Studies: Proceedings of the International Haydn Conference, Washington, D.C., 1975*. New York: Norton, 1981.
M-Larson	Robert Merl Larson. "Stylistic Characteristics in *a cappella* Composition in the U.S., 1940–1953, as Indicated by the Works of Jean Berger, David Diamond, Darius Milhaud, and Miklós Rozsa." Ph.D. diss., Northwestern University, 1953.
M-Leibowitz	René Leibowitz. *Schoenberg and His School*. New York: Philosophical Library, 1949.
M-Leibowitz/F	René Leibowitz. *Les Fantômes de l'opéra: Essais sur le théatre lyrique*. Paris: Gallimard, 1972.
M-Lewis	Beverly Williams Lewis. "A Study of the Musical and Literary Significance of the Lyric Portions of Goethe's Wilhelm Meisters Lehrjahre." D.M.A. diss., Memphis State University, 1979.
M-Ligeti	György Ligeti, Witold Lutosławski, and Ingvar Lidholm. *Three Aspects of New Music*. Stockholm: Nordiska Musikförlagt, 1968.
M-Little	Jean Little. "Architectonic Levels of Rhythmic Organization in Selected Twentieth-Century Music." Ph.D. diss., Indiana University, 1971.
M-Lönn	Anders Lönn and Krik Kjellberg, eds. *Analytica: Studies in the Description and Analysis of Music*. Uppsala: S. Academiae Ubsaliensis, 1985.
M-Macy	Carleton Macy. "Musical Characteristics in Selected Faust Works: A Study in Nineteenth-Century Music Rhetoric." D.M.A. diss., University of Washington, 1978.
M-Mahling	Christoph-Hellmut Mahling, ed. *Anton Bruckner: Studien zu Werk und Wirkung*. Tutzing: Schneider, 1988.
M-Marvin	Elizabeth West Marvin and Richard Hermann, eds. *Concert Music, Rock, and Jazz since 1945: Essays and Analytical Studies*. Rochester, N.Y.: University of Rochester Press, 1995.
M-Mathes	James Robert Mathes. "Texture and Musical Structure: An Analysis of First Movements of Select Twentieth-Century Piano Sonatas." Ph.D. diss., Florida State University, 1986.
M-Mertens	Wim Mertens. *American Minimal Music: An Analysis of the Music of La Monte Young, Terry Riley, Steve Reich, Philip Glass*. New York: Broude, 1983.
M-Metzger/Boulez	Hainz-Klaus Metzger, ed. *Pierre Boulez*. Munich: Text + Kritik, 1995.
M-Metzger/Brahms	Hainz-Klaus Metzger and Rainer Riehn, eds. *Aimez-vous Brahms "The Progressive."* Munich: Text + Kritik, 1989.
M-Metzger/Kfienek	Hainz-Kalus Metzger and Rainer Riehn, eds. *Ernst Kfienek*. Munich: Text + Kritik, 1984.
M-Metzger/Mahler	Hainz-Klaus Metzger and Rainer Riehn, eds. *Gustav Mahler durchgesetzt?* Munich: Text + Kritik, 1999.
M-Milstein	Silvina Milstein. *Arnold Schoenberg: Notes, Sets, Forms*. Cambridge: Cambridge University Press, 1992.
M-Mize	Lou Slem Mize. "A Study of Selected Choral Settings of Walt Whitman Poems." Ph.D. diss., Florida State University, 1976.
M-Morrison	Donald N. Morrison. "Influences of Impressionist Tonality on Selected Works of Delius, Griffes, Falla, and Respighi: Based on the Concept Developed by Robert Mueller." Ph.D. diss., Indiana University, 1960.
M-Müller	Gunther Müller and William Geissler, eds. *Schumann-Tage (1.) des Bezirkes Karl-Marx-Stadt 1976: 1. Wissenschaftliche Arbeitstagung zu Fragen der Schumann-Forschung*. Zwickau: Robert-Schumann-Gesellschaft der DDR, 1977.
M-Novak	John Kevin Novak. "The Programmatic Orchestral Works of Leoš Janáček: Their Style and Their Musical and Extramusical Content." Ph.D. diss., University of Texas at Austin, 1994.

M-Ogdon	Wilbur Lee Ogdon. "Series and Structure: An Investigation into the Purpose of the Twelve-Note Row in Selected works of Schoenberg, Webern, Krenek, and Leibowitz." Ph.D. diss., Indiana University, 1966.
M-Park	Jae-Sung Park. "A Study of Pitch-Class Structure in Anton Webern's Fourteen Early Atonal Songs (1908–1909)." Ph.D. diss., State University of New York at Buffalo, 1989.
M-Pascall	Robert Pascall, ed. *Brahms Biographical, Documentary, and Analytical Studies.* Cambridge: Cambridge University Press, 1983.
M-Pečman	Rudolf Pečman, ed. *Colloquium musica cameralis, Brno 1971.* Brno: Mezinárodní hudební festival, 1977.
M-Pečman/J	Rudolf Pečman, ed. *Colloquium Leoš Janáček et musica Europaea: Colloquia on the History and Theory of Music at the International Musical Festival in Brno.* Brno: International Musical Festival, 1970.
M-Perle	George Perle. *Serial Composition and Atonality.* 6th ed., rev. Berkeley: University of California Press, 1991.
M-Pfann	Walter Pfann. *Zur Sonatengestaltung im Spätwerk Maurice Ravels (1920–1932).* Regensburg: Bosse, 1991.
M-Potter	Keith Potter. *Four Musical Minimalists: La Monte Young, Terry Riley, Steve Reich, Philip Glass.* Cambridge: Cambridge University Press, 2000.
M-Pütz	Werner Pütz. *Studien zum Streichquartettschaffen bei Hindemith, Bartók, Schönberg und Webern.* Regensburg: Bosse, 1968.
M-Rahn	John Rahn. *Basic Atonal Theory.* New York: Longman, 1980.
M-Rathert	Wolfgang Rathert. *The Seen and Unseen: Studien zum Werk von Charles Ives.* Munich: Katzbichler, 1991.
M-Reichert	Georg Reichert and Martin Just, eds. *Bericht über den Internationalen musikwissenschaftlichen Kongress, Kassel 1962.* Kassel: Bärenreiter, 1963.
M-Rexroth	Dieter Rexroth, ed. *Erprobungen und Erfahrungen: Zu Paul Hindemiths Schaffen in den zwanziger Jahren.* Mainz: Schott, 1978.
M-Rhoades	Larry Lynn Rhoades. "Theme and Variations in Twentieth-Century Organ Literature: Analyses of Variations by Alain, Barber, Distler, Dupré, Duruflé, and Sowerby." Ph.D. diss., Ohio State University, 1973.
M-Riethmüller	Albrecht Riethmüller, ed. *Bruckner-Probleme.* Stuttgart: Steiner, 1999.
M-Roberts	Gwyneth Margaret Roberts. "Procedures for Analysis of Sound Masses." Ph.D. diss., Indiana University, 1978.
M-Rognoni	Luigi Rognoni. *Espressionismo e dodecafonia: In appendice scritti di Arnold Schoenberg, Alban Berg, Wassily Kandinsky.* Turin: Einaudi, 1954.
M-Roller	Jonathan Brian Roller. "An Analysis of Selected Movements from the Symphonies of Charles Ives Using Linear and Set Theoretical Analytical Models." Ph.D. diss., University of Kentucky, 1995.
M-Rosenbloom	Paul David Rosenbloom. "A Study of Phrase Rhythm in Late Bartók." D.M.A. diss., Cornell University, 1979.
M-Salmenhaara	Erkki Salmenhaara. *Das musikalische Material und seine Behandlung in den Werken "Apparitions," "Atmosphères," "Aventures," und "Requiem" von György Ligeti.* Trans. Heike Sander. Regensburg: Bosse, 1969.
M-Schachter	Carl Schachter. *Unfoldings: Essays in Schenkerian Theory and Analysis.* New York: Oxford University Press, 1999.
M-Schnitzler	Günter Schnitzler, ed. *Musik und Zahl: Interdisziplinäre Beiträge zum Grenzbereich zwischen Musik und Mathematik.* Bonn-Bad Godesberg: Verlag für systematische Musikwissenschaft, 1976.
M-Schnitzler/D	Günter Schnitzler, ed. *Dichtung und Musik: Kaleidoscop ihrer Beziehungen.* Stuttgart: Klett-Cotta, 1979.
M-Schreker	Franz Schreker. *Am Beginn der neuen Musik.* Graz: Universal, 1978.
M-Schultz	Wolfgang-Andreas Schultz. *Die freien Formen in der Musik des Expressionismus und Impressionismus.* Hamburg: Wagner, 1974.
M-Schultz/D	Donna Gartman Schultz. "Set Theory and Its Application to Compositions by Five Twentieth-Century Composers." Ph.D. diss., Michigan State University, 1979.
M-Schweitzer	Eugene William Schweitzer. "Generation in String Quartets of Carter, Sessions, Kirchner, and Schuller: A Concept of Forward Thrust and Its Relationship to Structure in Aurally Complex Styles." Ph.D. diss., University of Rochester, 1965.

M-Stahmer	Klaus Hinrich Stahmer, ed. *Form und Idee in Gustav Mahlers Instrumentalmusik.* Wilhelmshaven: Heinrichshofen, 1980.
M-Stephan	Rudolph Stephan, ed. *Die Musik der sechziger Jahre.* Mainz: Schott, 1972.
M-Sterling	Eugene A. Sterling. "A Study of Chromatic Elements in Selected Piano Works of Beethoven, Schubert, Schumann, Chopin, and Brahms." Ph.D. diss., Indiana University, 1966.
M-Stockhausen	Karlheinz Stockhausen. *Texte zu eigenen Werken zur Kunst anderer Aktuelles.* Vol. 2 of *Texte.* Cologne: Schauberg, 1964.
M-Stokes	Jeffrey Lewis Stokes. "Countour and Motive: A Study of 'Flight' and 'Love' in Wagner's Ring, Tristan, and Meistersinger." Ph.D. diss., State University of New York at Buffalo, 1984.
M-Straus	Joseph N. Straus. *An Introduction to Post-Tonal Music.* Englewood Cliffs, N.J.: Prentice Hall, 1990.
M-Straus/C	Joseph N. Straus. *The Music of Ruth Crawford Seeger.* Cambridge: Cambridge University Press, 1995.
M-Taruskin	Richard Taruskin. "Chernomor to Kashchei: Harmonic Sorcery, or, Stravinsky's 'Angle.'" JAMS 38 (1985): 72–142.
M-Todd	R. Larry Todd. *Mendelssohn: The Hebrides and Other Overtures.* Cambridge: Cambridge University Press, 1993.
M-Van Solkema	Sherman van Solkema, ed. *The New Worlds of Edgard Varèse: A Symposium.* New York: Institute for Studies in American Music, 1979.
M-Vogt	Hans Vogt. *Neue Musik seit 1945.* 3d ed. Stuttgart: Reclam, 1982.
M-Walts	Anthony Albert Walts. "The Significance of the Opening in Sonata Form: An Analytical Study of the First Movements from Three String Quartets by Joseph Haydn." Ph.D. diss., Yale University, 1985.
M-Webern	Österreichische Gesellschaft für Musik, ed. *Webern-Kongress, Vienna 1972: Beiträge.* Kassel: Bärenreiter, 1973.
M-Wennerstrom	Mary Hannah Wennerstrom. "Parametric Analysis of Contemporary Music Form." Ph.D. diss., Indiana University, 1967.
M-Wilson	Paul Wilson. *The Music of Béla Bartók.* New Haven, Conn.: Yale University Press, 1992.
M-Winter	Robert Winter and Bruce Carr, eds. *Beethoven, Performers, and Critics: The International Beethoven Congress, Detroit 1977.* Detroit: Wayne State University Press, 1980.
M-Wise	Ronald Eugene Wise. "Scoring in the Neoclassic Woodwind Quintets of Hindemith, Fine, Etter, and Wilder." Ph.D. diss., University of Wisconsin, 1967.
M-Wise/H	Herbert Harold Wise, Jr. "The Relationship of Pitch Sets to Formal Structure in the Last Six Piano Sonatas of Scriabin." Ph.D. diss., University of Rochester, Eastman School of Music, 1987.
M-Wolterink	Charles Paul Wolterink. "Harmonic Structure and Organization in the Early Serial Works of Igor Stravinsky, 1952–1957." Ph.D. diss., Stanford University, 1979.
M-Wozzeck	*50 Jahre Wozzeck von Alban Berg.* Studien zu Wertungsforschung 10. Graz: Universal, 1978.
M-Yeston	Maury Yeston, ed. *Readings in Schenker Analysis and Other Approaches.* New Haven, Conn.: Yale University Press, 1977.
M-Zimmerschied	Dieter Zimmerschied, ed. *Perspectiven neuer Musik: Material und didaktische Information.* Mainz: Schott, 1974.
M-Zuber	Barbara Zuber. *Gesetz + Gestalt: Studien zum Spätwerk Anton Weberns.* Munich: Musikprint, 1995.

Acknowledgments

In my days as a student and in my work as a librarian, I have consulted *Analyses of Nineteenth- and Twentieth-Century Music, 1940–1985* countless times, and I am honored for the opportunity to continue Arthur Wenk's work. I thank Dr. Wenk for welcoming me to update the bibliography and for granting me permission to incorporate the entire content of the previous edition. It is hoped that this volume will be as useful as its predecessors.

Research for this book included visits to Indiana University's Cook Music Library and the Eastman School of Music's Sibley Library. As a recipient of the Music Library Association's Walter Gerboth Award and a University Research Council Grant from Kent State University, I was fortunate to obtain monetary support that made possible these essential trips.

Claire Stewart and Tom O'Connell of Northwestern University Library's Digital Media Services provided advice and resources for scanning the previous edition of this book. Without their help, I would probably still be typing.

For assistance and encouragement, I thank Mark Palkovic, Ralph Papakhian, Debbie Campana, and Russ Clement.

The lessons taught by Lee Copenhaver have contributed fundamentally to this project, as well as to my career. Dr. C.'s musicianship, analytical curiosity, and intelligent wit continue to inspire me, and I dedicate this book to him with respect and gratitude.

Thanks also to my wife, Carol. Her unwavering patience and support through the four years spent on this book is remarkable and deeply appreciated.

And to Holly and Nina: You were disappointed to learn that Daddy's new book has no pictures, and I thank you for this and all the other funny things you say and do. You two are able to put all matters into proper perspective, and, for that, I will be forever grateful.

Introduction

This book is the latest edition of a bibliography begun by Arthur Wenk more than thirty-five years ago and published in a succession of increasingly larger volumes. While a student in Harold Samuel's music bibliography course at Cornell University in the late 1960s, Wenk compiled a list of analytical writings concerning twentieth-century music.[1] After completing the course, Wenk continued work on the bibliography, and, in 1975, the Music Library Association published *Analyses of Twentieth-Century Music, 1940–1970*, which included 1,225 references to analyses of works by 222 composers drawn from periodicals, books, theses, dissertations, and Festschriften.[2] Expanding his research beyond Cornell, Wenk visited libraries at Indiana University, Harvard University, and the University of California at Berkeley in the ensuing years. This ongoing effort resulted in a supplementary bibliography on twentieth-century music published in 1976 and, in that same year, a companion volume, *Analyses of Nineteenth-Century Music, 1940–1975*.[3] Further updates of both bibliographies were issued in 1984,[4] and Wenk's research culminated in 1987 with the publication of *Analyses of Nineteenth- and Twentieth-Century Music, 1940–1985*.[5] A compilation of all earlier bibliographies and updates with additional references through 1985, this volume offered 5,664 citations for writings on music by 779 composers and earned the Music Library Association's Vincent H. Duckles Award for the best book-length bibliography of 1987.[6]

In 2002, Mark Palkovic, editor of the Music Library Association Index and Bibliography Series, invited me to prepare a new edition of *Analyses of Nineteenth- and Twentieth-Century Music* that would bring together the content of Wenk's 1987 book with new references to analyses from 1986 through 2000. As a regular user of the bibliography, I agreed that the book's utility would be enhanced with added coverage of writings from the final fifteen years of the twentieth century, and Wenk, unable to continue his work on the bibliography, supported my interest in preparing an update.[7] Research for this new edition required a thorough review of analyses written since 1985, and, for this, I made extensive use of the music libraries at Kent State University, Indiana University, the Eastman School of Music, and Northwestern University. Many materials also were borrowed from the libraries of the Cincinnati College–Conservatory of Music and the Oberlin Conservatory.

Analyses of Nineteenth- and Twentieth-Century Music, 1940–2000 includes all entries from Wenk's 1987 edition along with additional references to writings through 2000 that address form, harmony, melody, rhythm, and other structural aspects of music by composers of the nineteenth and twentieth centuries. This updated compilation, totaling 9,306 entries for analyses of works by 1,066 composers, provides ready access to analytical writings and presents the broadest coverage and most detailed indexing of this literature available.[8] Rather than a guide to current analytical scholarship, this book serves as an extensive catalog of much of the large and diverse body of music analyses produced in the twentieth century. Adhering to the general scope of Wenk's previous editions, this bibliography includes the following features:

- References to writings in English, French, German, Italian, and other European languages
- Thorough coverage of periodical literature, including 163 print publications as well as the handful of relevant open-access electronic journals currently available
- Broad but selective coverage of analyses in theses, dissertations, Festschriften, and books, especially books published in the monographic series listed in the appendix

While this bibliography offers extensive treatment of analytical writings on nineteenth- and twentieth-century music composed in the Western art tradition, references to analyses of jazz, popular music, and world music are not included, except for the few such citations carried over from the previous edition.[9]

Throughout the bibliography, entries are arranged according to the composer whose work is analyzed, and, in cases when more than ten analyses are listed for a composer, citations are subarranged into categories for specific works or genres. Although alphabetical arrangement of composer names and subheadings is maintained in nearly all cases, the subheading "Various Works," used to collect writings that address multiple compositions by a particular composer, is consistently filed as the final element in subarranged listings. Spelling and Romanization follow the conventions of the *New Grove Dictionary of Music and Musicians*,[10] and, within citations, abbreviations are used for all journal titles and for many of the Festschriften and monographs cited. These abbreviations are delineated in the list that begins this book. An index of authors is also included.

NOTES

1. Thanks to Arthur Wenk for providing background on the bibliography's origins and development.

2. Arthur Wenk, *Analyses of Twentieth-Century Music, 1940–1970*, Music Library Association Index and Bibliography Series, no. 13 (Ann Arbor, Mich.: Music Library Association, 1975).

3. Arthur Wenk, *Analyses of Twentieth-Century Music: Supplement, 1970–1975*, Music Library Association Index and Bibliography Series, no. 14 (Ann Arbor, Mich.: Music Library Association, 1976); Arthur Wenk, *Analyses of Nineteenth-Century Music, 1940–1975*, MLA Index and Bibliography Series, no. 15 (Ann Arbor, Mich.: Music Library Association, 1976).

4. Arthur Wenk, *Analyses of Twentieth-Century Music: Supplement*, 2nd ed., Music Library Association Index and Bibliography Series, no. 14 (Boston: Music Library Association, 1984); Arthur Wenk, *Analyses of Nineteenth-Century Music*, 2nd ed. (1940–1980), MLA Index and Bibliography Series, no. 15 (Boston: Music Library Association, 1984).

5. Arthur Wenk, *Analyses of Nineteenth- and Twentieth-Century Music, 1940–1985*, Music Library Association Index and Bibliography Series, no. 25 (Boston: Music Library Association, 1987).

6. Wenk discusses the 1987 edition further in "Varieties of Analysis: Through the Analytical Sieve and Beyond," *Music Reference Services Quarterly* 2, nos. 3–4 (1993): 327–48.

7. Following the end of his musicology career in 1986, Wenk taught calculus and statistics for a number of years in Canada. Recently he completed a master's degree in psychology pursuant to a new career as a psychotherapist.

8. Harold J. Diamond's *Music Analyses: An Annotated Guide to the Literature* (New York: Schirmer, 1991) is another well-known and useful reference source, but Diamond confines his survey to publications in English and does not represent complex, scholarly analyses as extensively as the previous or present editions of this bibliography. Additionally, while online databases make information on analytical writings available quickly, they are surprisingly limited in the literature they cover and in their depth of indexing. (See Leslie Troutman, "Comprehensiveness of Indexing in Music Periodical Databases," *Music Reference Services Quarterly* 8, no. 1 [2001]: 39–51; and Alan Green, "Keeping Up with the Times: Evaluating Currency of Indexing, Language Coverage, and Subject Area Coverage in the Three Music Periodical Databases," *Music Reference Services Quarterly* 8, no. 1 [2001]: 53–68.)

9. Although no book-length bibliographies devoted to analyses of jazz, popular music, or world music are available, useful guides to this literature include D. J. Hoek, "Jazz Analyses: An Annotated Guide to Periodical Literature," *Bulletin of Bibliography* 57, no. 3 (September 2000): 147–52; Eddie S. Meadows, *Jazz Scholarship and Pedagogy: A Research and Information Guide*, 3rd ed. (New York: Routledge, 2006); Jeffrey N. Gatten, *Rock Music Scholarship: An Interdisciplinary Bibliography* (Westport, Conn.: Greenwood, 1995); Jennifer C. Post, *Ethnomusicology: A Research and Information Guide* (New York: Routledge, 2004); and the "Current Bibliography" column of *Ethnomusicology*, featured regularly in each issue of the journal since its first volume in 1953.

10. Stanley Sadie, ed., *The New Grove Dictionary of Music and Musicians*, 2nd ed., 29 vols. (New York: Grove's Dictionaries, 2000). *New Grove Online* also was consulted (www.grovemusic.com).

Bibliography

– A –

ABRAHAMSEN, HANS (b. 1952)

1. Sørensen, Søren Møller. "Ny musik, men ikke modernisme: To unge komponister i de danske 1970ere–Karl Aage Rasmussen og Hans Abrahamsen." DAM 26 (1998): 35–57.

ADAMS, JOHN (b. 1947)

2. Johnson, Timothy A. "Harmonic Vocabulary in the Music of John Adams: A Hierarchical Approach." JMT 37, no. 1 (1993): 117–56. [*The Chairman Dances, Harmonielehre, Harmonium, Phrygian Gates*]
3. ———. "Harmony in the Music of John Adams: From *Phrygian Gates* to *Nixon in China*." Ph.D. diss., State University of New York at Buffalo, 1991.
4. Kreutziger-Herr, Annette. "Politik und Postmoderne: Die Oper *Nixon in China* von John Adams." HJM 17 (2000): 323–50.
5. Ramaut-Chevassus, Béatrice. "La postmodernité musicale: Points forts d'un phénomène aux multiples facettes (Pärt, Bryars, Adams)." ANM 33 (1998): 94–103. [*The Chairman Dances*]
6. Schwarz, David. "Listening Subjects: Semiotics, Psychoanalysis, and the Music of John Adams and Steve Reich." PNM 31, no. 2 (1993): 24–56. [*Fearful Symmetries, Grand Pianola Music, Nixon in China*]
7. ———. "Postmodernism, the Subject, and the Real in John Adams's *Nixon in China*." ITR 13, no. 2 (1992): 107–35.

ADLER, SAMUEL (b. 1928)

8. Chen, Mei-chun. "The 'Sound Curtains' in Samuel Adler's Concerto for Flute and Orchestra: An Analysis of Pitch and Texture." Ph.D. diss., University of Rochester, 1998.
9. Lucas, Joan Dawson. "The Operas of Samuel Adler: An Analytical study." Ph.D. diss., Louisiana State University, 1978.

ADORNO, THEODOR W. (1903–1969)

10. Leibowitz, René. "Der Komponist Theodor W. Adorno." F-Adorno/60: 335–59. [Sechs Bagatellen für Singstimme und Klavier, op. 6]
11. Metzger, Heinz-Klaus, and Rainer Riehn, eds. *Theodor W. Adorno: Der Komponist.* Munich: Text + Kritik, 1989.
12. Spahlinger, Mathias. "Der Widersinn von Gesang: Zu Theodor W. Adornos Liedkomposition." MTX 1 (1983): 37–39.

AHRENS, JOSEPH (1904–1997)

13. Ahrens, Joseph. *Die Formprinzipien des gregorianischen Chorals und mein Orgelstil.* Heidelberg: Müller Süddeutscher Musikverlag, 1977.

ALAIN, JEHAN (1911–1940)

14. Bouchett, Richard Travis. "The Organ Music of Jehan Alain (1911–1940)." D.S.M. diss., Union Theological Seminary, 1971.
15. M-Dorroh.
16. Dunham, Ervin Jerrol. "A Stylistic Analysis of the Organ Music of Jehan Alain." D.M.A. diss., University of Arizona, 1965.
17. M-Rhoades.
18. Schauerte, Helga. *Jehan Alain (1911–1940): Das Orgelwerke.* Regensburg: Bosse, 1983.

ALBÉNIZ, ISAAC (1860–1909)
19. Mast, Paul Buck. "Style and Structure in *Iberia* by Isaac Albéniz." Ph.D. diss., University of Rochester, 1974.

ALBRECHT, GEORG VON (1891–1976)
20. Albrecht, Michael von. "Kammermusik." F-Albrecht/70: 25–34.
21. Antokoletz, Elliott. "Transformations of a Special Non-Diatonic Mode in Twentieth-Century Music: Bartók, Stravinsky, Scriabin, and Albrecht." MA 12, no. 1 (1993): 25–45. [Préludes, op. 42; Préludes, op. 61]
22. Frommel, Gerhard. "Klavier- und Orchesterwerke." F-Albrecht/70: 11–24.
23. Komma, Karl Michael. "Die Rolle der Volksmusik." F-Albrecht/70: 45–52.
24. Schwermer, Johannes. "Vokalwerke." F-Albrecht/70: 35–44.

ALIABEV, ALEXANDER ALEXANDROVICH (1787–1851)
25. Green, Carol. "The String Quartets of Alexander Alexandrovich Aliabev." MR 33 (1972): 323–29.

ALKAN, VALENTIN (1813–1888)
26. Himelfarb, Constance. "Réflexions sur la problématique de la forme dans le piano romantique français: 'Le festin d'Esope,' no. 12 des *Études dans les tons mineurs* op. 39 de C. V. Alkan (1857)." ANM 20 (1990): 24–32.

ALNAES, EYVIND (1872–1932)
27. Olson, Robert Wallace. "A Comparative Study of Selected Norwegian Romances by Halfdan Kjerulf, Edvard Grieg, and Eyvind Alnaes." Ph.D. diss., University of Illinois, 1973.

ALVAREZ, JAVIER (b. 1956)
28. Alvarez, Javier. "Rhythm as Motion Discovered." CMR 3, no. 1 (1989): 203–31. [*Caracteristicas, Temazcal, Papalotl*]

ALWYN, WILLIAM (1905–1985)
29. Conway, Paul. "William Alwyn's Symphony No. 5: Exploring *Hydriotaphia*." MR 54, nos. 3–4 (1993): 265–68.

AMBROSINI, CLAUDIO (b. 1948)
30. Quong, Meijane. "On the Recent Piano Music of Claudio Ambrosini." EXT 7, no. 2 (1995): 115–49. [*Grande ballo futurista, Rondò di forza*]

AMES, CHARLES (b. 1955)
31. Ames, Charles. "Two Pieces for Amplified Guitar." I 15, no. 1 (1986): 35–58. [*Artifacts, Excursion*]
32. Hiller, Lejaren, and Charles Ames; graphics by Robert Franki. "Automated Composition: An Installation at the 1985 International Exhibition in Tsukuba, Japan." PNM 23, no. 2 (1984–1985): 196–215. [*Mix or Match, Transitions*]

ANDERGASSEN, FERDINAND (1892–1964)
33. Gabriel, Ferdinand. "Die Instrumentalwerke von Ferdinand Andergassen." Ph.D. diss., Universität Innsbruck, 1977.

ANDERSON, T. J. (b. 1928)
34. Thompson, Bruce Alfred. "Musical Style and Compositional Technique in Selected Works of T. J. Anderson." Ph.D. diss., Indiana University, 1978.

ANDRÉ, MARK (b. 1964)
35. Conti, Luca. "(De)konstruktion und (De)fragmentation in *A B II* von Mark André." MAS 4, no. 16 (2000): 67–79.

ANDRIESSEN, HENDRIK (1892–1981)
36. Dox, Thurston J. "Hendrik Andriessen: The Path to *Il pensiero*." KN 13, no. 1 (1981): 16–24.
37. ———. "The Works of Hendrik Andriessen." Ph.D. diss., University of Rochester, 1970.
38. Klerk, Jos de. "Hendrik Andriessen: *Sonata de chiesa*, 2 studi per organo." SS 17 (1963): 14–16.
39. Paap, Wouter. "The *Symphonische Etude* by Hendrik Andriessen." SS 4 (1960): 135–36.
40. Schuyt, Nico. "*Philomela*: Opera by Hendrik Andriessen." SS 11 (1962): 10–21.

ANDRIESSEN, JURRIAAN (1925–1996)
41. Flothuis, Marius. "Jurriaan Andriessen, *Sonata de camera per flauto, viola e chitarra*." SS 15 (1963): 19–22.
42. Paap, Wouter. "Jurriaan Andriessen and Incidental Music." SS 40 (1969): 1–19.

ANDRIESSEN, LOUIS (b. 1939)
43. Andriessen, Louis, and Edward Harsh. "The Past as a Presence in Part One of Louis Andriessen's *De Materie*." CMR 6, no. 2 (1992): 59–70.
44. Coenen, Alcedo. "Louis Andriessen's *De Materie*." KN 25 (1988–1989): 2–12.

45. ———. "Musik über Music: Zu Louis Andriessens Musiktheaterstück *De Materie*." MTX 33–34 (1990): 9–14.

46. Geraedts, Jaap. "Louis Andriessen: Nocturnen for Soprano and Orchestra." SS 25 (1965): 14–16.

47. Huber, Nicolaus A. "Erlebniswanderung auf schmalem Grat: Das Hörbarmachen von Zeit und Geschwindigkeit bei Louis Andriessen." MTX 9 (1985): 24–29.

48. Potter, Keith. "The Music of Louis Andriessen: Dialectical Double-Dutch?" CT 23 (1981): 16–22.

49. Sabbe, Hermann. "Pulsierende gegen geronnene Zeit: Stenogramm einer Analyse von Andriessens *Hoketus*." MTX 9 (1985): 22–24.

50. Schönberger, Elmer. "Louis Andriessen: On the Conceiving of Time." KN 13, no. 1 (1981): 5–11.

51. Wright, David. "Louis Andriessen: Polity, Time, Speed, Substance." TEMPO 187 (1993): 7–13. [*De staat, De tijd*]

ANHALT, ISTVÁN (b. 1919)

52. Anhalt, István. "The Making of *Cento*." CCM 1 (1970): 81–89.

53. Gillmor, Alan M. "Echoes of Time and the River." F-Beckwith: 15–44. [*Simulacrum*]

ANTHEIL, GEORGE (1900–1959)

54. Albee, David Lyman. "George Antheil's *La femme 100 têtes*: A Study of the Piano Preludes." D.M.A. diss., University of Texas, 1977.

55. Whitesitt, Linda. *The Life and Music of George Antheil, 1900–1959*. Ann Arbor, Mich.: UMI Research Press, 1983.

APOSTEL, HANS ERICH (1901–1972)

56. Bischof, Rainer. "Hans Erich Apostel oder die Schönheit der Ordnung." OMZ 35 (1980): 15–27.

57. Fink, Monika. "Alfred Kubin und Hans Erich Apostel: Das bildhafte Progamm zur *Kubiniana*." MAU 9 (1989): 91–110.

ARCHER, VIOLET (1913–2000)

58. Huiner, Harvey Don. "The Choral Music of Violet Archer." Ph.D. diss., University of Iowa, 1980.

ARGENTO, DOMINICK (b. 1927)

59. Gebuhr, Ann K. "Structure and Coherence in 'The Diary' from Dominck Argento's Cycle, *From the Diary of Virginia Woolf*." ITR 1, no. 3 (1977–1978): 12–21.

60. Sabatino, Trucilla Marie. "A Performer's Commentary on *To Be Sung upon the Water* by Dominick Argento." D.M.A. diss., Ohio State University, 1980.

ARNOLD, MALCOLM (b. 1921)

61. Stasiak, Christopher. "The Symphonies of Malcolm Arnold: Eclecticism and the Symphonic Conception." TEMPO 161–62 (1987): 85–90.

ASHLEY, ROBERT (b. 1930)

62. Chen, Shu-ling. "Music and Language in Two Twentieth-Century American Operas." Ph.D. diss., University of Maryland, College Park, 1997. [*Perfect Lives (Private Parts)*]

63. DeLio, Thomas. "Structural Pluralism: Robert Ashley's *In memoriam . . . Esteban Gomez*." MQ 67, no. 4 (1981): 427–43. Reprint, M-DeLio: 69–88.

AUBER, DANIEL-FRANÇOISE-ESPRIT (1782–1871)

64. Longyear, Rey M. "D. F. E. Auber (1782–1871): A Chapter in the History of the *opéra comique*, 1800–1870." Ph.D. diss., Cornell University, 1957.

AUBIN, TONY (1907–1981)

65. M-Kniesner. [Piano Sonata, B minor]

AULIN, TOR (1866–1914)

66. Wallner, Bo. "Tor Aulin och det Svenska musiklivet." DAM 11 (1980): 31–43.

AUSTIN, LARRY (b. 1930)

67. Austin, Larry, Charles Boone, and Xavier Serra. "*Transmission Two: The Great Excursion (TT:TGE)*: The Aesthetic, Art, and Science of a Composition for Radio." LMJ 1, no. 1 (1991): 81–88.

68. Clark, Thomas. "Duality of Process and Drama in Larry Austin's *Sonata concertante*." PNM 23, no. 1 (1984–1985): 112–25.

AYERS, LYDIA

69. Ayers, Lydia. "*Merapi*: A Composition for Gamelan and Computer-Generated Tape." LMJ 6 (1996): 7–14.

– B –

BAAREN, KEES VAN (1906–1970)

70. Hill, S. Jackson. "The Music of Kees van Baaren: A Study of Transition in the Music of the Netherlands in the Second Third of the Twentieth Century." Ph.D. diss., University of North Carolina, 1970.
71. Straesser, Joep. "Kees van Baaren: *Quintetto a fiati (Sovraposizioni 2)*." SS 22 (1965): 12–19.
72. Wouters, Jos. "Kees van Baaren." SS 16 (1963): 1–14.

BABBITT, MILTON (b. 1916)

About Time

73. Mead, Andrew. "About *About Time's* Time: A Survey of Milton Babbitt's Recent Rhythmic Practice." PNM 25 (1987): 183–235.

Arie da capo

74. Mead, Andrew W. "Recent Developments in the Music of Milton Babbitt." MQ 70 (1984): 310–31.

Around the Horn

75. Mead, Andrew. "Still Being an American Composer: Milton Babbitt at Eighty." PNM 35, no. 2 (1997): 101–26.

Composition for Synthesizer

76. Morris, Robert. "Listening to Milton Babbitt's Electronic Music: The Medium and the Message." PNM 35, no. 2 (1997): 85–99.

Composition for Twelve Instruments

77. Borders, Barbara. "Formal Aspects in Selected Instrumental Works of Milton Babbitt." Ph.D. diss., University of Kansas, 1979.
78. Hush, David. "Asynordinate Twelve-Tone Structures: Milton Babbitt's *Composition for Twelve Instruments*." PNM 21 (1982–1883): 152–208; 22 (1983–1984): 103–16.
79. Westergaard, Peter. "Some Problems Raised by the Rhythmic Procedures in Milton Babbitt's *Composition for Twelve Instruments*." PNM 4, no. 1 (1965): 109–18.

Compositions for Piano

80. M-Perle: 128–34.

Cultivated Choruses

81. Schubert, Peter N. "A Multidetermined Moment in Milton Babbitt's *Three Cultivated Choruses*." TP 19 (1994): 57–82. [Madrigal no. 3]

Du

82. M-Johnson.
83. Rahn, John. "How Do You *Du* (by Milton Babbitt)." PNM 14, no. 2–15, no. 1 (1976): 61–80.

Duet

84. Escot, Pozzi. "A Duet for Betty Ann." SONUS 13, no. 1 (1992): 42–55.

Minute Waltz (3, no. 4 ± 1/8)

85. Blaustein, Susan, and Martin Brody. "Criteria for Grouping in Milton Babbitt's *Minute Waltz (or) 3, no. 4 ± 1/8*." PNM 24, no. 2 (1986): 30–79.

My Complements to Roger

86. Mead, Andrew W. "Detail and the Array in Milton Babbitt's *My Complements to Roger*." MTS 5 (1983): 89–109.
87. ———. "Recent Developments in the Music of Milton Babbitt." MQ 70 (1984): 310–31.

My Ends Are My Beginnings

88. Mead, Andrew. "'The Key to the Treasure . . . .'" TP 18 (1993): 29–56.

Paraphrases

89. Mead, Andrew W. "Recent Developments in the Music of Milton Babbitt." MQ 70 (1984): 310–31.

Reflections

90. Morris, Robert. "Listening to Milton Babbitt's Electronic Music: The Medium and the Message." PNM 35, no. 2 (1997): 85–99.
91. Peel, John, and Cheryl Cramer. "Correspondences and Associations in Milton Babbitt's *Reflections*." PNM 26, no. 1 (1988): 144–207.

Relata I
92. Babbitt, Milton. "On *Relata I.*" PNM 9, no. 1 (1970): 1–22.
93. Mead, Andrew W. "Recent Developments in the Music of Milton Babbitt." MQ 70 (1984): 310–31.

Semi-Simple Variations
94. Wintle, Christopher. "Milton Babbitt's *Semi-Simple Variations.*" PNM 14, no. 2–15, no. 1 (1976): 111–54.

Sextets
95. Borders, Barbara. "Formal Aspects in Selected Instrumental Works of Milton Babbitt." Ph.D. diss., University of Kansas, 1979.
96. Capalbo, Marc. "Charts." PNM 19, no. 2 (1980–1981): 309–31.

String Quartet No. 2
97. Cohn, Richard. "The 12 × 12 Latin Square as Found in Babbitt's String Quartet No. 2." SONUS 3, no. 1 (1982): 57–65.
98. Mead, Andrew W. "Recent Developments in the Music of Milton Babbitt." MQ 70 (1984): 310–31.
99. Zuckerman, Mark. "On Milton Babbitt's String Quartet No. 2." PNM 14, no. 2–15, no. 1 (1976): 85–110.

String Quartet No. 3
100. Arnold, Stephen, and Graham Hair. "An Introduction and a Study: String Quartet No. 3." PNM 14, no. 2–15, no. 1 (1976): 155–86.
101. Borders, Barbara. "Formal Aspects in Selected Instrumental Works of Milton Babbitt." Ph.D. diss., University of Kansas, 1979.

String Quartet No. 4
102. Mead, Andrew W. "Recent Developments in the Music of Milton Babbitt." MQ 70 (1984): 310–31.

String Quartet No. 5
103. Lake, William. "The Architecture of a Superarray Composition: Milton Babbitt's String Quartet No. 5." PNM 24, no. 2 (1986): 88–111.

Tableaux
104. Hanninen, Dora A. "A General Theory for Context-Sensitive Music Analysis: Applications to Four Works for Piano by Contemporary American Composers." Ph.D. diss., University of Rochester, 1996.

Theatrical Songs
105. Forte, Allen. "Milton Babbitt's *Three Theatrical Songs in Perspective.*" PNM 35, no. 2 (1997): 65–84.

Widow's Lament in Springtime
106. M-Johnson.

Woodwind Quartet
107. Mead, Andrew. "Twelve-Tone Organizational Strategies: An Analytical Sampler." INT 3 (1989): 93–169.

Various Works
108. Dubiel, Joseph. "Three Essays on Milton Babbitt." PNM 28, no. 2 (1990): 216–61; 29, no. 1 (1991): 90–122; 30, no. 1 (1992): 82–131.
109. M-Hines: 11–38.
110. Lake, William E. "Listening for Large-Scale Form in the Music of Milton Babbitt." CMF 2 (1990): 11–19.
111. Lewin, David. "Generalized Interval Systems for Babbitt's Lists, and for Schoenberg's String Trio." MTS 17, no. 1 (1995): 81–118.
112. Mead, Andrew. *An Introduction to the Music of Milton Babbitt.* Princeton, N.J.: Princeton University Press, 1994.
113. Sward, Rosalie La Grow. "An Examination of the Mathematical Systems Used in Selected Compositions of Milton Babbitt and Iannis Xenakis." Ph.D. diss., Northwestern University, 1981.

BACEWICZ, GRAŻYNA (1909–1969)
114. "Grażyna Bacewicz's Second Piano Sonata (1953): Octave Expansion and Sonata Form." MTO 0, no. 4 (1993).
115. Wittig, Steffen. "Höhen und Tiefen: Die Kompositionstechnik der letzten Schaffensperiode Grażyna Bacewiczs von 1960 bis 1969." MTX 71 (1997): 15–26.

BADINGS, HENK (1907–1987)
116. Ameringen, Sylvia van. "Henk Badings: Profil eines holländischen Komponisten von heute." OMZ 7 (1952): 297–300.
117. Badings, Henk. "Henk Badings: Sonata for 'Cello Solo.'" SS 7 (1961): 23–24.
118. Clardy, Mary Karen King. "Compositional Devices of Willem Pijper (1894–1947) and Henk Badings (b. 1907) in Two Selected Works." D.M.A. diss., North Texas State University 1980. [Flute Concerto No. 2]

119. Ditto, John Allen. "The Four Preludes and Fugues, the Ricercar, and the Passacaglia for Timpani and Organ by Henk Badings." D.M.A. diss., University of Rochester, 1979.
120. Geraedts, Jaap. "Badings: Symphony for String Orchestra." SS 6 (1961): 9–13.
121. Klemme, Paul T. "The Choral Music of Henk Badings." ACR 35, no. 2 (1993): 2–5.
122. Kox, Hans. "Henk Badings: Eighth Symphony." SS 16 (1963): 15–19.
123. Wouters, Jos. "Henk Badings: Largo and Allegro." SS 6 (1961): 18–20.
124. ———. "Henk Badings." SS 32 (1967): 1–23.

BAILEY, CHRISTOPHER (b. 1973)

125. Bailey, Christopher. "Realizing Musical Gestures with the Computer: Paradigms and Problems." CM 67–68 (1999): 7–30.

BAIRD, TADEUSZ (1928–1981)

126. Baird, Tadeusz. "*Sinfonia brevis* of Tadeusz Baird." PM 4, no. 1 (1969): 13–15.
127. Carper, Jeremy Lee. "The Interplay of Musical and Dramatic Structures in *Jutro,* an Opera by Tadeusz Baird." Ph.D. diss., Washington University, 1983.

BAJORAS, FELIKSAS ROMUALDAS (b. 1934)

128. M-Lampsatis.

BALAKAUSKAS, OSVALDAS (b. 1937)

129. M-Lampsatis.

BALAKIREV, MILY ALEKSEYEVICH (1837–1910)

130. Davis, Richard. "Henselt, Balakirev, and the Piano." MR 28 (1967): 173–208.
131. Garden, Edward. "Sibelius and Balakirev." F-Abraham: 215–18.
132. Gaub, Albrecht. "Balakirevs *Tamara*: Enstehung, Analyse, Programmakit." HJM 13 (1995): 165–99.

BALSYS, EDUARDAS (1919–1984)

133. Gerlach, Hannelore. "*Rührt nicht am blauen Globus*: Oratorium des litauischen Komponisten Eduardas Balsys." MG 25 (1975): 264–68.
134. M-Lampsatis.

BANK, JACQUES (b. 1943)

135. Straesser, Joep. "The Narrow Path of Jacques Bank." KN 25 (1988–1989): 25–29.

BARBER, SAMUEL (1910–1981)

Concertos

136. Maggio, Robert. "A Source of Richness in the Main Themes of Samuel Barber's Violin Concerto and Piano Concerto: Hierarchical Conflict and the Implication-Realization Model." EXT 6, no. 2 (1993): 50–78.

Piano Works (Solo)

137. Carter, Susan Blinderman. "The Piano Music of Samuel Barber." Ph.D. diss., Texas Tech University, 1980.
138. Chittum, Donald. "The Synthesis of Materials and Devices in Nonserial Counterpoint." MR 31 (1970): 123–35. [Piano Sonata]
139. Fairleigh, James P. "Serialism in Barber's Solo Piano Works." PQ 72 (1970): 13–17.
140. Haberkorn, Michael. "A Study and Performance of the Piano Sonatas of Samuel Barber, Elliott Carter, and Aaron Copland." Ed.D. diss., Columbia University, 1979.
141. Heist, Douglas R. "Harmonic Organization and Sonata Form: The First Movement of Barber's Sonata, Op. 26." JALS 27 (1990): 25–31.
142. Keyes, Christopher. "Set Classes, Twelve-Tone Rows, and Tonality in the Third Movement of Samuel Barber's Piano Sonata: The Non-Duality of Tonality and Atonality." TCM 5, no. 8 (1998): 9–15.
143. M-Mathes. [Piano Sonata]
144. Tischler, Hans. "Barber's Piano Sonata, Op. 26." ML 33 (1952): 352–54.

Songs

145. Kreiling, Jean Louise. "The Songs of Samuel Barber: A Study in Literary Taste and Text-Setting." Ph.D. diss., University of North Carolina, Chapel Hill, 1986.

Vanessa

146. Larsen, Robert L. "A Study and Comparison of Samuel Barber's *Vanessa,* Robert Ward's *The Crucible*, and Gunther Schuller's *The Visitation*." D.M.A. diss., Indiana University, 1971.

Various Works

147. Broder, Nathan. "The Music of Samuel Barber." MQ 34 (1948): 325–35.

148. ———. *Samuel Barber.* Westport, Conn.: Greenwood, 1985.

149. Friedewald, Russell Edward. "A Formal and Stylistic Analysis of the Published Music of Samuel Barber." Ph.D. diss., University of Iowa, 1957.

150. Horan, Robert. "Samuel Barber." MM 20 (1943): 161–69.

151. M-Rhoades.

152. Wathen, Lawrence Samuel. "Dissonance Treatment in the Instrumental Music of Samuel Barber." Ph.D. diss., Northwestern University, 1960.

BARKAUSKAS, VYTAUTAS (b. 1931)

153. M-Lampsatis.

BARKIN, ELAINE (b. 1932)

154. Cory, Eleanor. "Elaine Barkin: String Quartet (1969)." MQ 62 (1976): 618–20. [Record review]

BARLOW, KLARENZ (b. 1945)

155. Frisius, Rudolf. "Eine gewisse mechanische Starrheit: Zu *Çoğluotobüsişletmesi* von Klarenz Barlow." MTX 5 (1984): 45–47.

BARRAQUÉ, JEAN (1928–1973)

156. Durand, Joël. "La sonate pour piano de Jean Barraqué." ENT 5 (1987): 89–117.

157. Henrich, Heribert. "Des techniques sérielles dans le *Temps restitué*." ENT 5 (1987): 75–88.

158. Metzger, Heinz-Klaus, and Rainer Riehn, eds. *Jean Barraqué*. Munich: Text + Kritik, 1993.

159. Nicolas, François. "Le souchide developpement chez Barraqué." ENT 5 (1987): 7–24.

160. Riotte, André. "Les series proliferantes selon Barraqué: Approche formelle." ENT 5 (1987): 65–74.

BARRETT, RICHARD (b. 1959)

161. Fox, Christopher. "Music as Fiction: A Consideration of the Work of Richard Barrett." CMR 13, no. 1 (1995): 147–57.

162. Toop, Richard. "Four Facets of 'The New Complexity.'" CT 32 (1988): 4–50. [*Anatomy, Temptation*]

163. ———. "Nachdenken über den Tod: Richard Barretts *Vanity*." MAS 2, no. 5 (1998): 44–61.

BARRIÈRE, JEAN-BAPTISE (b. 1958)

164. Barrière, Jean-Baptiste. "*Chréode*: The Pathway to New Music with the Computer." CMR 1, no. 1 (1984–1985): 181–201.

BARROSO, SERGIO (b. 1946)

165. Ledroit, Christien. "Sergio Barrosso's [sic] *Íreme*: An Examination of the Music, the Ceremony, and Its Representation." EXT 9, no. 2 (1999): 34–41.

BARRY, GERALD (b. 1952)

166. Barry, Gerald. "*The Intelligence Park*." CMR 5 (1989): 229–37.

167. Volans, Kevin, and Hilary Bracefield. "A Constant State of Surprise: Gerald Barry and *The Intelligence Park*." CT 31 (1987): 9–19.

BARTEL, HANS-CHRISTIAN (b. 1932)

168. Wolf, Werner. "Neue Werke unserer Komponisten: Max Buttings X. Sinfonien; Bratschenkonzert von Hans-Christian Bartel." MG 14 (1964): 80–83.

BARTÓK, BÉLA (1881–1945)

Bagatelles Op. 6

169. Antokoletz, Elliott. "The Musical Language of Bartók's 14 Bagatelles for Piano." TEMPO 137 (1981): 8–16.

170. M-Forte: 74–90.

171. Sallis, Friedemann. "La transformation d'un heritage: Bagatelle op. 6, no. 2 de Béla Bartók et *Invenció* (1948) pour piano de György Ligeti." RDM 83, no. 2 (1997): 281–93.

172. Woodward, James. "Understanding Bartók's Bagatelle Op. 6/9." ITR 4, no. 2 (1980–1981): 11–32.

Bluebeard's Castle

173. Antokoletz, Elliott. "Bartók's *Bluebeard*: The Sources of Its 'Modernism.'" CMS 30, no. 1 (1990): 75–95.

174. ASO 149–150 (1992).

175. Frigyesi, Judit. "In Search of Meaning in Context: Bartók's *Duke Bluebeard's Castle.*" CM 70 (2000): 5–31.
176. Heath, Mary Joanne Renner. "A Comparative Analysis of Dukas's *Ariane et Barbe-bleue* and Bartók's *Duke Bluebeard's Castle.*" Ph.D. diss., University of Rochester, 1988.
177. Kroó, György. "*Duke Bluebeard's Castle.*" SM 1 (1959): 251–340.
178. Leafstedt, Carl S. "Structure in the Fifth Door Scene of Bartók's *Duke Bluebeard's Castle.*" CMS 30, no. 1 (1990): 96–102.
179. Veress, Sándor. "*Bluebeard's Castle.*" F-Bartók/T: 36–53.

Cantata profana
180. Antokoletz, Elliott. "Transformations of a Special Non-Diatonic Mode in Twentieth-Century Music: Bartók, Stravinsky, Scriabin, and Albrecht." MA 12, no. 1 (1993): 25–45.
181. Chazelle, Thierry. "La *Cantate Profane* de Bartók: Forme et perception de la forme." ANM 2 (1986): 70–76; addenda, ANM 3 (1986): 71.

Concerto for Orchestra
182. Austin, William. "Bartók's Concerto for Orchestra." MR 18 (1957): 21–47.
183. Cooper, David. Bartók: *Concerto for Orchestra.* Cambridge: Cambridge University Press, 1996.
184. French, Gilbert G. "Continuity and Discontinuity in Bartók's Concerto for Orchestra." MR 28 (1967): 122–34.
185. Kneif, Tibor. "Zur Entstehung und Kompositionstechnik von Bartóks Konzert für Orchester." MF 26 (1973): 36–51.
186. Volek, J. "Über einige interessante Beziehungen zwischen thematischer Arbeit und Instrumentation in Bartóks Werk: Concerto für Orchester." SM 5 (1963): 557–86. Reprint, *Liszt-Bartók: Bericht liber die zweite internationale musikwissenschaftliche Konferenz, Budapest 25–30 September, 1961*, ed. Z. Gárdonyi and B. Szabolcsi, 557–86. Budapest: Akadémiai Kiadó, 1963.
187. Weber, Horst. "Material und Komposition in Bartóks Concerto for Orchestra." NZM 134 (1973): 767–73.
188. M-Wilson. [Movement I.]

Contrasts
189. Folio, Cynthia J. "Analysis and Performance: A Study in *Contrasts.*" INT 7 (1993): 1–37.
190. Kárpáti, János. "Alternative Structures in Bartók's *Contrasts.*" SM 23 (1981): 201–7.
191. Oramo, Ilkka. "Marcia und Burletta: Zur Tradition der Rhapsodie in zwei Quartettsatzen Bartóks." MF 30 (1977): 14–25.

Duos (Two Violins)
192. Röbke, Peter. "Analyse im Instrumentalspiel: Ein Unterichtsentwurf: Bartóks Scherzo aus Op. 44." MB 15, no. 10 (1983): 14–17.
193. Veress, Sándor. "Béla Bartóks 44 Duos für 2 Violinen." F-Doflein: 31–57.

Improvisations on Hungarian Peasant Songs, Op. 20
194. Agawu, V. Kofi. "Analytical Issues Raised by Bartók's Improvisations for Piano, Op. 20." JMR 5 (1984–1985): 131–63.
195. Andraschke, Peter. "Folklore and Komposition: Einige Anmerkungen zu Béla Bartóks *Improvisations sur des chansons paysannes hongroises*, Op. 20." M-Breig: 393–410.
196. Antokoletz, Elliott. "Transformations of a Special Non-Diatonic Mode in Twentieth-Century Music: Bartók, Stravinsky, Scriabin, and Albrecht." MA 12, no. 1 (1993): 25–45.
197. Wilson, Paul Frederick. "Atonality and Structure in Works of Béla Bartók's Middle Period." Ph.D. diss., Yale University, 1982.
198. ———. "Concepts of Prolongation and Bartók's Opus 20." MTS 6 (1984): 79–89.

Kossuth
199. Clegg, David. "Bartók's *Kossuth* Symphony." MR 23 (1962): 215–20.

Little Piano Pieces
200. Somfai, László. "Analytical Notes on Bartók's Piano Year of 1926." SM 26 (1984): 5–58. [*Menuetto, Tambourine*]

Mikrokosmos (various; see also specific volumes)
201. Ameringen, Sylvia van. "Teaching with Bartók's *Mikrokosmos.*" TEMPO 21 (1951): 31–35.
202. Benary, Peter. "Der zweistimmige Kontrapunkt in Bartóks *Mikrokosmos.*" AM 15 (1958): 198–206.
203. Dustin, William. "Two-Voiced Texture in the *Mikrokosmos* of Béla Bartók." Ph.D. diss., Cornell University, 1959.
204. Engelmann, Hans Ulrich. *Béla Bartóks "Mikrokosmos": Versuch einer Typologie "neuer Musik."* Würzburg: Triltsch, 1953.
205. ———. "Chromatisches Ausstufung in Béla Bartóks *Mikrokosmos.*" MELOS 18 (1951): 138–41.
206. Kapst, Erich. "Bartóks Anmerkungen zum Mikrokosmos." MG 20 (1970): 585–95.
207. Loeb van Zuilenburg, Paul E. O. F. "A Study of Béla Bartók's *Mikrokosmos* with Respect to Formal Analysis, Compositional Techniques, Piano-Technical and Piano-Pedagogical Aspects." Ph.D. diss., University of Witwatersrand, Johannesburg, 1969.

208. Lowman, Edward A. "Some Striking Propositions in the Music of Béla Bartók." *Fibonacci Quarterly* 915 (1971): 527–28, 536–37.

209. Skoog, James Alfred. "Set Syntax in Bartók's *Mikrokosmos.*" Ph.D. diss., Indiana University, 1985.

210. Starr, Lawrence. "Melody-Accompaniment Textures in the Music of Bartók, As Seen in His *Mikrokosmos.*" JM 4, no. 1 (1985–1986): 91–104.

211. ———. "*Mikrokosmos*: The Tonal Universe of Béla Bartók." Ph.D. diss., University of California, Berkeley, 1973.

212. Suchoff, Benjamin. "Béla Bartók, and a Guide to the *Mikrokosmos.*" Ed.D. diss., New York University, 1956.

213. ———. *Guide to the "Mikrokosmos" of Béla Bartók.* New York: Da Capo, 1982.

214. Uhde, Jurgen. *Bartók "Mikrokosmos": Spielanweisungen und Erläuterungen; Die Einführung in das Werk und seine pädagogischen Absichten.* Regensburg: Bosse, 1954.

215. Veress, Sándor. "Le *Mikrokosmos* dans l'univers musical de Bartók." SMZ 122 (1982): 260–63.

216. Wolff, Hellmuth Christian. "Der *Mikrokosmos* von Béla Bartók." M 5 (1951): 134–40.

Mikrokosmos, Vol. III

217. Mark, Christopher. "Symmetry and Dynamism in Bartók." TEMPO 183 (1992): 2–5. [No. 70]

Mikrokosmos, Vol. IV

218. Cohn, Richard. "Bartók's Octatonic Strategies: A Motivic Approach." JAMS 44, no. 2 (1991): 262–300. [No. 109]

219. M-Schultz/D. [No. 113]

Mikrokosmos, Vol. V

220. Child, Peter. "Structural Unities in a Work of Bartók: 'Boating' from *Mikrokosmos,* Vol. 5." CMS 30, no. 1 (1990): 103–14. [No. 125]

221. Lewin, Harold F. "A Graphic Analysis of Béla Bartók's 'Major Seconds Broken and Together,' *Mikrokosmos,* Vol. V, No. 132." TP 6, no. 2 (1981): 40–46.

222. Parks, Richard S. "Harmonic Resources in Bartók's 'Fourths.'" JMT 25 (1981): 245–74. [No. 131]

Mikrokosmos, Vol. VI

223. Cohn, Richard. "Bartók's Octatonic Strategies: A Motivic Approach." JAMS 44, no. 2 (1991): 262–300. [No. 144]

224. Gollin, Edward. "Some Unusual Transformations in Bartók's 'Minor Seconds, Major Sevenths.'" INT 12 (1998): 25–51. [No. 144]

225. Simon, Albert. "Béla Bartók: 'Secondes mineures, septièmes majeures' (*Mikrokosmos* VI/144)." SMZ 123 (1983): 82–86.

226. Waldbauer, Iván F. "Intellectual Construct and Tonal Direction in Bartók's 'Divided Arpeggios.'" SM 24 (1982): 527–36. [No. 143]

227. ———. "Polymodal Chromaticism and Tonal Plan in the First of Bartók's 'Six Dances in Bulgarian Rhythm.'" SM 32 (1990): 241–62. [No. 148]

Miraculous Mandarin

228. Chailley, Jacques. "Essai d'analyse du *Mandarin merveilleux.*" SM 8 (1966): 11–39.

229. Downes, Stephen. "Eros in the Metropolis: Bartók's *The Miraculous Mandarin.*" JRMA 125, no. 1 (2000): 41–61.

230. Lendvai, Ernő. "*Der wunderbare Mandarin.*" SM 1 (1959): 363–431.

231. Lossau, Gunter. "Bartóks Pantomime *Der wunderbare Mandarin.*" MELOS 33 (1966): 173–77.

232. Persichetti, Vincent. "Current Chronicle." MQ 35 (1949): 122–26.

233. Szabolcsi, Bence. "Bartók's *Miraculous Mandarin.*" In *Bartók Studies,* ed. Todd Crow, 22–38. Detroit: Information Co-ordinators, 1976.

234. ———. "*Le Mandarin miraculeux.*" SM 1 (1959): 341–61.

235. Vinton, John. "The Case of *The Miraculous Mandarin.*" MQ 50 (1964): 1–17.

Music for Strings, Percussion, and Celesta

236. Bailey, Kathryn. "Bartók's Tonal Ellipsis in the *Music for String, Percussion and Celeste.*" SMUWO 8 (1983): 37–46.

237. Brinkmann, Reinhold. "Einige Aspekte der Bartók-Analyse." SM 24, supplement (1983): 57–66.

238. Chittum, Donald. "The Synthesis of Materials and Devices in Non-Serial Counterpoint." MR 31 (1970): 123–35.

239. Frobenius, Wolf. "Bartók und Bach." AM 41 (1984): 54–67.

240. Helm, Everett. "Bartóks *Musik für Saiteninstrumente.*" MELOS 20 (1953): 245–49.

241. Howat, Roy. "Debussy, Ravel, and Bartók: Towards Some New Concepts of Form." ML 58 (1977): 285–93.

242. Hunkemöller, Jurgen. "Bartók analysiert seine *Musik für Saiteninstrumente, Schlagzeug und Celesta.*" AM 40 (1983): 147–63.

243. ———. *Béla Bartók: Musik für Saiteninstrumente.* Munich: Fink, 1982.

244. Mark, Christopher. "Symmetry and Dynamism in Bartók." TEMPO 183 (1992): 2–5.
245. Morris, Robert D. "Conflict and Anomaly in Bartók and Webern." F-Lewin: 59–79. [Movement I]
246. ———. "Some Compositional and Analytic Applications of T-Matrices." INT 3 (1989): 37–66.
247. Mountain, Rosemary. "An Investigation of Periodicity in Music, with Reference to Three Twentieth-Century Compositons." Ph.D. diss., University of Victoria, 1993.
248. Persichetti, Vincent. "Current Chronicle." MQ 35 (1949): 297–301.
249. Pousseur, Henri. "Applications analytiques de la 'technique des réseaux.'" RBM 52 (1998): 247–98.
250. Smith, Robert. "Béla Bartók's *Music for Strings, Percussion and Celesta*." MR 20 (1959): 264–76.
251. Vauclair, Constant. "Bartók: Beyond Bi-Modality." MR 42 (1981): 243–51.
252. Weiss-Aigner, Günther. "Béla Bartók: *Musik für Saiteninstrumente, Schlagzeug und Celesta*." MB 7 (1975): 440–48.

Out of Doors
253. Chazelle, Thierry. "*En Plein Air*, suite pour piano de Béla Bartók: L'Imbrication d'une forme ternaire." ANM 7 (1987): 56–61.
254. Somfai, László. "Analytical Notes on Bartók's Piano Year of 1926." SM 26 (1984): 5–58. [*The Chase, Musettes, The Night's Music*]

Piano Concertos
255. Bartók, Béla. "The Second Piano Concerto." TEMPO 65 (1963): 5–7.
256. Guerry, Jack E. "Bartók's Concertos for Solo Piano: A Stylistic and Formal Analysis." Ph.D. diss., Michigan State University, 1964.
257. Harley, Maria Anna. "Birds in Concert: North American Birdsong in Bartók's Piano Concerto No. 3." TEMPO 189 (1994): 8–16. [Movement II]
258. Meyer, John A. "Beethoven and Bartók: A Structural Parallel." MR 31 (1970): 315–21. [Piano Concertos Nos. 2–3]
259. Michael, Frank. "Analytische Anmerkungen zu Bartóks 2. Klavierkonzert." SM 24 (1982): 425–37.
260. Nüll, Edwin von der. "Béla Bartók, Geist und Stil: Aus Anlass der 2. Klavierkonzerts." MELOS 21 (1945): 135–38.
261. Radice, Mark A. "Bartók's Parodies of Beethoven." MR 42 (1981): 252–60. [Piano Concerto No. 3]
262. Somfai, László. "Analytical Notes on Bartók's Piano Year of 1926." SM 26 (1984): 5–58. [Piano Concerto No. 1]

Piano Sonata
263. Forner, Johannes. "Zum Sonatenform-Problem bei Béla Bartók: Eine vergleichende Studie." JP (1981–1982): 62–75.
264. Somfai, László. "Analytical Notes on Bartók's Piano Year of 1926." SM 26 (1984): 5–58.
265. M-Straus: 114–17. [Movement I]
266. M-Wilson.

Piano Works (various; *see also* specific works)
267. Fenyo, Thomas. "The Piano Music of Béla Bartók." Ph.D. diss., University of California, Los Angeles, 1956.
268. Horn, Herbert A. "Idiomatic Writing in the Piano Music of Béla Bartók." D.M.A. diss., University of Southern California, 1968.
269. Hundt, Theodor. *Bartóks Satztechnik in den Klavierwerken*. Regensburg: Bosse, 1971.
270. Lammers, Joseph E. "Patterns of Change and Identity in Shorter Piano Works by Béla Bartók." Ph.D. diss., Florida State University, 1971.
271. Weissmann, John. "Bartók's Piano Music." F-Bartok/T: 60–71.
272. ———. "La musique de piano de Bartók: L'évolution d'une écriture." RM 224 (1955): 171–222.

Rhapsody No. 2 (Violin and Piano)
273. Eastman, Yasuko Tanaka. "Béla Bartók's Second Rhapsody for Violin and Its Folk Melody Sources: A study." M.M. thesis, University of Alberta, 1977.

Romanian Christmas Songs (**Piano**)
274. Arauco, Ingrid. "Bartók's Romanian Christmas Carols: Changes from the Folk Sources." JM 5, no. 2 (1987): 191–225.

Scherzo (Piano and Orchestra)
275. Mason, Colin. "Bartók: Scherzo for Piano and Orchestra." TEMPO 65 (1963): 10–13.

Sonata for Solo Violin
276. Cogan, Robert. "Spectrographic Analysis of Music Design: Fractals in Bartók's 'Melodia.'" SONUS 18, no. 1 (1997): 45–62.
277. Lenoir, Yves. "Contributions à l'étude de la Sonate pour violin solo de Béla Bartók (1944)." SM 23 (1981): 209–60.
278. M-Rosenbloom.

Sonata for Two Pianos and Percussion

279. Cohn, Richard. "Bartók's Octatonic Strategies: A Motivic Approach." JAMS 44, no. 2 (1991): 262–300. [Movement I]
280. ———. "Inversional Symmetry and Transpositional Combination in Bartók." MTS 10 (1988): 19–42.
281. M-Cohn.
282. Forner, Johannes. "Zum Sonatenform-Problem bei Béla Bartók: Eine vergleichende Studie." JP (1981–1982): 62–75.
283. Leong, Daphne. "Metric Conflict in the First Movement of Bartók's Sonata for Two Pianos and Percussion." TP 24 (1999): 57–90.
284. Nordwall, Ore. "Béla Bartók and Modern Music." SM 9 (1967): 265–80.
285. Petersen, Peter. "Rhythmik und Metrik in Bartóks Sonate für zwei Klaviere und Schlagzeug und die Kritik des jungen Stockhausen an Bartók." MTH 9, no. 1 (1994): 39–48.
286. M-Rosenbloom.
287. Russ, Michael. "Functions, Scales, Abstract Systems, and Contextual Hierarchies in the Music of Bartók." ML 75, no. 3 (1994): 401–25. [Movement I]
288. M-Stockhausen: 136–39.
289. ———. "Bartók's Sonata for Two Pianos and Percussion." *The New Hungarian Quarterly* 40 (1970): 49–53.
290. M-Wilson. [Movements I–II]

Songs

291. Arauco, Ingrid. "Methods of Translation in Bartók's *Twenty Hungarian Folksongs*." JMR 12, no. 3 (1992): 189–211. [Nos. 1, 6]
292. Gerbers, Hilda. "Béla Bartók's Öt dal (Five Songs) Op. 16." MR 30 (1969): 291–99.
293. Hough, Philip. "The Tonal Structure of Bartók's 'Autumn Tears,' Opus 16, No. l." TP 3, no. 2 (1978): 15–20.
294. Leichtentritt, Hugo. "Bartók and the Hungarian Folksong." MM 10 (1933): 130–39. [*Twenty Hungarian Folk Songs*]
295. McKinney, Bruce. "Further Reflections on 'Autumn Tears.'" TP 4, no. 1 (1979): 25–27. [Op. 16, no. 1]
296. Weissmann, John S. "Notes Concerning Bartók's Solo Vocal Music." TEMPO 36 (1955): 16–26; 38 (1956): 14–20; 40 (1956): 18–33.

String Quartets (various; *see also* specific string quartets)

297. Abraham, Gerald. "The Bartók of the Quartets." ML 26 (1945): 185–94.
298. Babbitt, Milton. "The String Quartets of Bartók." MQ 35 (1949): 377–85.
299. Boaz, Mildred Meyer. "T. S. Eliot and Music: A Study of the Development of Musical Structure in Selected Poems by T. S. Eliot and Music by Erik Satie, Igor Stravinsky, and Béla Bartók." Ph.D. diss., University of Illinois, 1977.
300. Carner, Mosco. "The String Quartets of Bartók." M-Carner: 92–121.
301. Donahue, Robert Laurence. "A Comparative Analysis of Phrase Structure in Selected Movements of the String Quartets of Béla Bartók and Walter Piston." D.M.A. diss., Cornell University, 1964.
302. Fladt, Harmut. *Zur Problematik traditionnel Formtypen in der Musik des frühen zwanzigsten Jahrhunderts: Dargestellt an Sonatensatzen in den Streichquartetten Béla Bartóks.* Munich: Katzbichler, 1974.
303. Kárpáti, János. *Bartók's String Quartets.* Budapest: Corvina, 1975.
304. Kreter, Leo Edward. "Motivic and Structural Delineation of the Formal Design in the First Three Bartók Quartets." D.M.A. diss., Cornell University, 1960.
305. Monelle, Raymond. "Bartók's Imagination in the Later Quartets." MR 31 (1970): 70–81.
306. Morrison, Charles Douglas. "Interactions of Conventional and Nonconventional Tonal Determinants in the String Quartets of Béla Bartók." Ph.D. diss., University of British Columbia, 1987.
307. Perle, George. "The String Quartets of Béla Bartók." F-Bernstein: 193–210.
308. ———. "Symmetrical Formations in the String Quartets of Béla Bartók." MR 16 (1955): 300–12.
309. M-Pütz.
310. Rands, Bernard. "The Use of Canon in Bartók's Quartets." MR 18 (1957): 183–88.
311. Schwinger, Wolfram. "Béla Bartóks Streichquartette." M 27 (1973): 13–18, 133–37, 245–50, 252, 350–55, 445–51, 569–74.
312. Seiber, Mátyás. *Béla Bartók: The String Quartets.* New York: Boosey & Hawkes, 1957.
313. ———. "Béla Bartók's Chamber Music." F-Bartók/T: 23–35.
314. Siegmund-Schultze, Walther. "Tradition und Neuerertum in Bartóks Streichquartetten." F-Kodály/80: 317–28.
315. Thomason, Leta Nelle. "Structural Significance of the Motive in the String Quartets of Béla Bartók." Ph.D. diss., Michigan State University, 1965.
316. Traimer, Roswitha. *Béla Bartóks Kompositionstechnik: Dargestellt an seinen sechs Streichquartetten.* Regensburg: Bosse, 1956.

317. Walker, Mark Fesler. "Thematic, Formal, and Tonal Structure of Bartók String Quartets." Ph.D. diss., Indiana University, 1955.

String Quartet No. 1

318. Bónis, Ferenc. "Erstes Violinkonzert–Erstes Streichquartett: Ein Wendepunkt in Béla Bartóks kompositorischer Laufbahn." M 39, no. 3 (1985): 265–73.
319. Gow, David. "Tonality and Structure in Bartók's First Two String Quartets." MR 34 (1973): 259–71.
320. Lendvai, Ernő. "Bartók und die Zahl." MELOS 27 (1960): 327–31.

String Quartet No. 2

321. Gow, David. "Tonality and Structure in Bartók's First Two String Quartets." MR 34 (1973): 259–71.
322. Whittall, Arnold. "Bartók's Second String Quartet." MR 32 (1971): 265–70.

String Quartet No. 3

323. Berry, Wallace. "Symmetrical Interval Sets and Derivative Pitch Materials in Bartók's String Quartet No. 3." PNM 18, nos. 1–2 (1979–1980): 289–379.
324. Cohn, Richard. "Inversional Symmetry and Transpositional Combination in Bartók." MTS 10 (1988): 19–42.
325. Vauclair, Constant. "Bartók: Beyond Bi-Modality." MR 42 (1981): 243–51.
326. M-Wilson.

String Quartet No. 4

327. Antokoletz, Elliott Maxim. "Principles of Pitch Organization in Bartók's Fourth String Quartet." Ph.D. diss., City University of New York, 1975.
328. ———. "Principles of Pitch Organization in Bartók's Fourth String Quartet." ITO 3, no. 6 (1977): 3–22.
329. Bayley, Amanda. "Bartók's String Quartet No. 4/III: A New Interpretive Approach." MA 19, no. 3 (2000): 353–82.
330. Buehrer, Ted. "Prolongational Structure in Bartók's Pitch-Centic Music: A Preliminary Study." ITR 18, no. 2 (1997): 1–14.
331. Cohn, Richard. "Inversional Symmetry and Transpositional Combination in Bartók." MTS 10 (1988): 19–42.
332. Forte, Allen. "Bartók's 'Serial' Composition." MQ 46 (1960): 233–45.
333. M-Forte: 139–43. [Movement I]
334. Mason, Colin. "An Essay in Analysis: Tonality, Symmetry, and Latent Serialism in Bartók's Fourth Quartet." MR 18 (1957): 189–201.
335. Monelle, Raymond. "Notes on Bartók's Fourth Quartet." MR 29 (1968): 123–29.
336. Morrison, Charles D. "Fifth Progressions in Bartók: Structural Determinants or Mimicry?" SM 34, nos. 1–2 (1992): 125–52.
337. ———. "Prolongation in the Final Movement of Bartók's String Quartet No. 4." MTS 13, no. 2 (1991): 179–96.
338. M-Perle: 52–54
339. M-Straus: 53–58. [Movement I]
340. Travis, Roy. "Tonal Coherence in the First Movement of Bartók's Fourth String Quartet." MFO 2 (1970): 298–371.
341. Treitler, Leo. "Harmonic Procedure in the Fourth Quartet of Béla Bartók." JMT 3 (1959): 292–98.
342. M-Vogt: 191–209.

String Quartet No. 5

343. Bates, Karen Anne. "The Fifth String Quartet of Béla Bartók: An Analysis Based on the Theories of Ernő Lendvai." Ph.D. diss., University of Arizona, 1986.
344. Chapman, Roger E. "The Fifth Quartet of Béla Bartók." MR 12 (1951): 296–303.
345. M-Rosenbloom.
346. Russ, Michael. "Functions, Scales, Abstract Systems, and Contextual Hierarchies in the Music of Bartók." ML 75, no. 3 (1994): 401–25. [Movement II]
347. Wilson, Paul. "Function and Pitch Hierarchy in Movement II of Bartók's Fifth Quartet." TP 14–15 (1989–1990): 179–89.
348. M-Wilson. [Movements II and IV]
349. Winrow, Barbara. "*Allegretto con indifferenza*: A Study of the 'Barrel Organ' Episode in Bartók's Fifth Quartet." MR 32 (1971): 102–6.

String Quartet No. 6

350. Kramolisch, Walter. "Das Leitthema des VI. Streichquartetts von Béla Bartók." F-Becking: 437–82.
351. Oramo, Ilkka. "Marcia und Burletta: Zur Tradition der Rhapsodie in zwei Quartettsätzen Bartóks." MF 30 (1977): 14–25.
352. Radice, Mark A. "Bartók's Parodies of Beethoven." MR 42 (1981): 252–60.
353. M-Rosenbloom.

354. Suchoff, Benjamin. "Structure and Concept in Bartók's Sixth Quartet." TEMPO 83 (1967–1968): 2–11.

355. Vauclair, Constant. "Bartók: Beyond Bi-Modality." MR 42 (1981): 243–51.

356. Vinton, John. "New Light on Bartók's Sixth Quartet." MR 25 (1964): 224–38.

Studies, Op. 18 (Piano)

357. Antokoletz, Elliott. "Organic Development and the Interval Cycles in Bartók's Three Studies, Op. 18." SM 36, nos. 3–4 (1995): 249–61.

358. Gollin, Edward. "Transformational Techniques in Bartók's Etude Op. 18, No. 2." TP 20 (1995): 13–30.

359. Hoek, D. J. "Set Structure and Large-Scale Organization in Bartók's Etude Op. 18, No. 1." M.M. thesis, Bowling Green State University, 1996.

360. Kasztelan, Helen. "Simple and Complex Games in Bartók's Studies, Op. 18." F-Melbourne: 365–79.

361. Maegaard, Jan. "Béla Bartók und 'Das Atonale.'" JP (1981–1982): 30–42. [No. 2]

362. Morrison, Charles D. "Fifth Progressions in Bartók: Structural Determinants or Mimicry?" SM 34, nos. 1–2 (1992): 125–52.

363. Rülke, Volker. "Bartòks Wende zur Atonalität: Die Études op. 18." AM 57, no. 3 (2000): 240–63.

364. Wilson, Paul Frederick. "Atonality and Structure in Works of Béla Bartók's Middle Period." Ph.D. diss., Yale University, 1982.

Suite Op. 4b (Two Pianos; Arr. of Suite No. 2 for Small Orchestra)

365. Waldbauer, Ivan. "Bartók's Four Pieces for Two Pianos." TEMPO 53–54 (1960): 17–22.

Viola Concerto

366. Kovács, Sándor. "Formprobleme beim Violakonzert von Bartók/Serly." SM 24 (1982): 381–91.

367. Serly, Tibor. "A Belated Account of the Reconstruction of a Twentieth Century Masterpiece." CMS 15 (1975): 7–25.

Violin Concerto (No. 1; Orig. Op. 5)

368. Bónis, Ferenc. "Erstes Violinkonzert—Erstes Streichquartett: Ein Wendepunkt in Béla Bartóks kompositorischer Laufbahn." M 39, no. 3 (1985): 265–73.

369. Mason, Colin. "Bartók's Early Violin Concerto." TEMPO 49 (1958): 11–16.

Violin Concerto ("No. 2")

370. Eimert, Herbert. "Das Violinkonzert von Bartók." MELOS 14 (1947): 335–37.

371. M-Hall.

372. M-Little.

373. Michael, Frank. *Béla Bartóks Variationstechnik: Dargestellt im Rahmen einer Analyse seines 2. Violinskonzert.* Regensburg: Bosse, 1976.

374. Schneider, David E. "A Context for Béla Bartók on the Eve of World War II: The Violin Concerto (1938)." REP 5, nos. 1–2 (1996): 21–68.

375. Somfai, László. "Strategies of Variation in the Second Movement of Bartók's Violin Concerto of 1937–1938." SM 19 (1977): 161–202.

376. M-Zimmerschied: 110–27.

Violin Sonata No. 1

377. Hirota, Yoko. "Past and Present Analytical Perspectives on Bartók's Sonata for Violin and Piano, No. 1 (1922): Intervallic Profiles in the Works of Experimentalism." ACTA 69, no. 2 (1997): 109–19.

Violin Sonata No. 2

378. Pleasants, Henry, and Tibor Serly. "Bartók's Historic Contribution." MM 17 (1940): 131–40.

379. Szentkirályi, András. "Bartók's Second Sonata for Violin and Piano (1922)." Ph.D. diss., Princeton University, 1976.

380. ———. "Some Aspects of Béla Bartók's Compositional Techniques." SM 20 (1978): 157–82.

381. Wilson, Paul Frederick. "Atonality and Structure in Works of Béla Bartók's Middle Period." Ph.D. diss., Yale University, 1982.

Wooden Prince

382. Wolff, Hellmuth Christian. "Béla Bartóks *Holzgeschnitzter Prinz* und seine Beziehungen zu Igor Strawinsky." MZ 2 (1952): 53–56.

Various Works

383. Antokoletz, Elliott. *The Music of Béla Bartók: A Study of Tonality and Progression in Twentieth-Century Music.* Berkeley: University of California Press, 1984.

384. ———. "Pitch-Set Derivations from the Folk Modes in Bartók's Music." SM 24 (1982): 265–74.

385. Bachmann, Tibor. *Bartók's Harmonic Language.* N.p.: Author, 1976.
386. Bachmann, Tibor, and Mario Bachmann. *Studies in Bartók's Music.* N.p.: Author, 1981.
387. Bachmann, Tibor, and Peter J. Bachmann. "An Analysis of Béla Bartók's Music Through Fibonaccian Numbers and the Golden Mean." MQ 65 (1979): 72–82.
388. Bartók, Béla. "Gypsy Music or Hungarian Music?" MQ 33 (1947): 240–57.
389. ———. "Hungarian Peasant Music." MQ 19 (1933): 267–87.
390. ———. "Das Problem der neuen Musik." MELOS 25 (1958): 232–35.
391. Berger, Gregor. *Béla Bartók.* Wolfenbüttel: Möseler, 1963.
392. Bratuz, Damiana. "Béla Bartók: A Centenary Homage." SMUWO 6 (1981): 77–111.
393. Bernard, Jonathan W. "Space and Symmetry in Bartók." JMT 30, no. 2 (1986): 185–201.
394. Brelet, Gisele. "Musique savante et musique populaire." CPS 3 (1946): 38–58.
395. Breuer, János. "Kolinda Rhythm in the Music of Bartók." SM 17 (1975): 39–58.
396. Browne, Arthur G. "Béla Bartók." ML 12 (1931): 35–45.
397. M-Chihara.
398. Citron, Pierre. *Bartók.* Paris: Seuil, 1963.
399. Cooper, David. "The Unfolding of Tonality in the Music of Béla Bartók." MA 17, no. 1 (1998): 21–38.
400. Dobszay, Lászlò. "The Absorption of Folksong in Bartók's Composition." SM 24 (1982): 303–13.
401. Downey, John W. *La musique populaire dans l'oeuvre de Béla Bartók.* Paris: Centre de Documentation Universitaire, 1966.
402. Forner, Johannes. "Die Sonatenform im Schaffen Béla Bartóks." Ph.D. diss., Wilhelm-Pieck Universität, Rostock, 1975.
403. Gergely, Jean Guillaume. "Béla Bartók, compositeur hongrois." Ph.D. diss., Strasbourg, 1975.
404. ———. "Béla Bartók, compositeur hongrois." RM 328–29 (1980): 53–88; 330–32 (1980): 137–67; 333–35 (1980): 5–114.
405. Gillies, Malcolm. "Bartók's Notation: Tonality and Modality." TEMPO 145 (1983): 4–9.
406. ———. "Bartók's Tonal Mosaics." F-Melbourne: 355–64.
407. ———. "A Theory of Tonality and Modality: Bartók's Last Works." MS 7 (1982): 120–30.
408. Griffiths, Paul. *Bartók.* London: Dent, 1984.
409. Händel, Gunter. "Bartók und die Wiener Klassik." MELOS 22 (1955): 103–6.
410. Hartzell, Lawrence W. "Contrapuntal-Harmonic Factors in Selected Works of Béla Bartók." Ph.D. diss., University of Kansas, 1970.
411. Hawthorne, Robin. "The Fugal Technique of Béla Bartók." MR 10 (1949): 277–85.
412. Hundt, Theodore. "Barocke Formelemente im Kompositionsstil Béla Bartóks." SM 24 (1982): 361–72.
413. Kapst, Erich. "Die 'polymodale Chromatik' Béla Bartóks: Ein Beitrag zur stilkritischen Analyse." Ph.D. diss., Karl-Marx Universität, 1969.
414. ———. "Stilkriterien der polymodal-chromatischen Gestaltungweise im Werk Béla Bartóks." BM 12 (1970): 1–28.
415. Kárpáti, János. "Les gammes populaires et le système chromatique dans l'oeuvre de Béla Bartók." SM 11 (1969): 227–40.
416. ———. "Tonal Divergences of Melody and Harmony: A Characteristic Device in Bartók's Musical Language." SM 24 (1982): 373–80.
417. Kramer, Jonathan. "The Fibonacci Series in Twentieth-Century Music." JMT 17 (1973): 110–48.
418. Kroó György. *A Guide to Bartók.* Trans. Ruth Pataki and Maria Steiner. N.p.: Corvina, 1974.
419. ———. "Monothematik und dramaturgie in Bartóks Bühnenwerken." SM 5 (1963): 449–67. Reprint, *Liszt-Bartók: Bericht über die zweite internationale musikwissenschaftliche Konferenz, Budapest 25–30 September, 1961,* ed. Z. Gárdonyi and B. Szabolcsi, 449–67. Budapest: Akadémiai Kiadó, 1963.
420. Kuckertz, Josef. *Gestaltvariation in den von Bartók gesammelten rümanischen Colinden.* Regensburg: Bosse, 1963.
421. Lampert, Vera. "Bartók's Choice of Theme for Folksong Arrangement: Some Lessons of the Folk-Music Sources of Bartók's Works." SM 24 (1982): 401–9.
422. Lendvai, Ernő. "Bartók und der goldene Schnitt." OMZ, Sonderheft November 1966: 23–30. Also in OMZ 21 (1966): 607–15.
423. ———. *Béla Bartók: An Analysis of His Music.* London: Kahn & Averill, 1971.
424. ———. "Duality and Synthesis in the Music of Béla Bartók." Bartók Studies, ed. Todd Crow, 39–62. Detroit: Information Coordinators, 1976.
425. ———. "Remarks on Roy Howat's 'Principles of Proportional Analysis.'" MA 3, no. 3 (1984): 255–64.
426. ———. "Über die Formkonzeption Bartóks." F-Szabolcsi: 271–80. Also in SM 11 (1969): 271–80.
427. Lesznai, Lajos. *Bartók.* Trans. Percy M. Young. London: Dent, 1973.

428. ———. "Realistische Ausdrucksmittel in der Musik Béla Bartóks." MG 11 (1961): 722–26. Reprint, SM 5 (1963): 469–79.

429. Mason, Colin. "Bartók and Folksong." MR 11 (1950): 292–302.

430. ———. "Bartók's Rhapsodies." ML 30 (1949): 26–36.

431. Maxwell, Judith Elaine Shepherd. "An Investigation of Axis-Based Structures in Two Compositions of Béla Bartók." Ph.D. diss., University of Oklahoma, 1975.

432. Michael, Frank. "Anmerkungen zu Bartóks Variationstechnik." OMZ 36 (1981): 303–10.

433. Mila, Massimo. "La natura e il mistero nell'arte di Béla Bartók." CHI 2 (1965): 147–68.

434. MZ 3 (1953). [Special issue]

435. Nelson, Mark. "Folk Music and the 'Free and Equal Treatment of the Twelve Tones': Aspects of Béla Bartòk's Synthetic Methods." CMS 27 (1978): 59–116.

436. Olsvai, I. "West-Hungarian (Trans-Danubian) Characteristic Features in Bartók's Works." SM 11 (1969): 333–47.

437. Oramo, Ilkka. "Modale Symmetrie bei Bartók." MF 33 (1980): 450–64.

438. ———. "Die notierte, die wahrgenommene, und die gedachte Strukur bei Bartók: Bermerkungen zu einem Problem der musikalischen Analyse." SM 24 (1982): 439–49.

439. Pernecky, John Martin. "A Musico-Ethnological Approach to the Instrumental Music of Béla Bartók." Ph.D. diss., Northwestern University, 1956.

440. Petersen, Peter. "Bartók-Lutosławski-Ligeti: Einige Bemerkungen zu ihrer Kompositionstechnik unter dem Aspekt der Tonhöhe." HJM 11 (1988): 289–309.

441. ———. *Die Tonalität im Instrumentalschaffen von Béla Bartók.* Hamburg: Verlag der Musikalienhandlung, 1971.

442. Petrov, Stojan. "Béla Bartók und die bulgarische musikalische Kultur." F-Lissa: 367–77.

443. Pleasants, Henry, and Tibor Serly. "Bartók's Historic Contribution." MM 17 (1940): 131–40.

444. Reaves, Florence Ann. "Bartók's Approach to Consonance and Dissonance in Selected Late Instrumental Works." Ph.D. diss., University of Kentucky, 1983.

445. Rostand, Claude. "Chemins et contrastes de la musique." CPS 3 (1946): 31–37.

446. Schlötterer-'Traimer, Roswitha. "Béla Bartók und die Tondichtungen von Richard Strauss." OMZ 36 (1981): 311–18.

447. Schoffman, Nachum. "Expanded Unisons in Bartók." JMR 4 (1982–1983): 21–38.

448. Seiber, Mátyás. "Béla Bartók's Chamber Music." TEMPO 13 (1949): 19–31.

449. Somfai, László. "*Per finire*: Some Aspects of the Finale in Bartók's Cyclic Form." F-Szabolcsi: 391–408.

450. Stenzl, Jürg. "'Wer sich der Einsamkeit ergibt . . .': Zu Béla Bartóks Bühnenwerken." AM 39 (1982): 100–12.

451. Stevens, Halsey. *The Life and Music of Béla Bartók.* Rev. ed. New York: Oxford University Press, 1964.

452. ———. "Some 'Unknown' Works of Bartók." MQ 52 (1966): 37–55.

453. Szabolcsi, Bence. *Bartók: Sa vie et son oeuvre.* Budapest: Corvina, 1956.

454. ———, ed. *Béla Bartók: Weg und Werk; Schriften und Briefe.* Kassel: Bärenreiter, 1972.

455. Szentkirályi, András. "Some Aspects of Béla Bartók's Compositional Techniques." SM 20 (1978): 157–82.

456. Taylor, Vernon H. "Contrapuntal Techniques in the Music of Béla Bartók." Ph.D. diss., Northwestern University, 1950.

457. Thayer, Fred Martin, Jr. "The Choral Music of Béla Bartók." D.M.A. diss., Cornell University, 1976.

458. Thyne, Stuart. "Bartók's 'Improvisations.'" ML 31 (1950): 30–45.

459. Tóth, Anna. "Die Dudelsack-Effekt in Bartóks Werk." SM 24 (1982): 505–17.

460. Vinton, John. "Hints to the Printers from Bartók." ML 49 (1968): 224–30.

461. Weiss, Günter. *Die frühe Schaffensentwicklung Béla Bartóks im Lichte westlicher und östlicher Traditionen.* Erlangen: n.p., 1971.

462. Weiss-Aigner, Günther. "Der Spätstil Bartóks in seiner Violinmusik: Stilistische Erscheinungsbild und spieltechnisches Perspectiven." SM 23 (1981): 261–93.

463. ———. "Tonale Perspektiven des jungen Bartók." SM 24 (1982): 537–48.

464. Weissmann, John S. "Béla Bartók: An Estimate." MR 7 (1946): 221–41.

465. Wolff, Hellmuth Christian. "Béla Bartók und die Musik der Gegenwart." MELOS 19 (1952): 209–17.

466. ———. "Zum Kompositionsstil Béla Bartóks." BM 7 (1965): 218–24.

467. Zieliński, Tadeusz A. "Die modalen Strukturen im Werk Bartóks." JP (1981–1982): 18–29.

BASSETT, LESLIE (b. 1923)

468. Campbell, Griffin Merrill. "An Analytical Approach to Leslie Bassett's *Music for Saxophone and Piano.*" Ph.D. diss., Michigan State University, 1995.

BASTIANELLI, GIANNOTTO (1883–1927)

469. Donadoni, Miriam Omodeo. "Il concerto per due pianoforti di Giannotto Bastianelli." CHI 15 (1983): 97–108.

BATISTE, EDOUARD (1820–1876)

470. Smialek, William. "Edouard Batiste's *Symphonie Militaire*: Some Thoughts on Its Conception." JBR 14, no. 2 (1978–79): 20–25.

BAUCKHOLT, CAROLA (b. 1959)

471. Bauckholt, Carola. "Anmerkungen zu *Eure Zeichen*." N 4 (1983–1984): 188–96.

472. Hilberg, Frank. "Krümel des Alltags: Carola Bauckholts Musiktheater *Es wird sich zeigen*." MTX 79 (1999): 54–56.

BAX, ARNOLD (1883–1953)

473. Foreman, R. L. E. "The Musical Development of Arnold Bax." ML 52 (1971): 59–68.

474. Mayfield, Connie E. "The Structural Function of Motives in the Piano Sonatas of Arnold Bax." Ph.D. diss., University of Kansas, 1993.

475. Scott-Sutherland, Colin. "The Symphonies of Arnold Bax." MR 23 (1962): 20–24.

BAYLE, FRANÇOIS (b. 1932)

476. Roy, Stéphane. "Functional and Implicative Analysis of *Ombres Blanches*." JNMR 27, nos. 1–2 (1998): 165–84. [*Théâtre d'ombres*, Part II]

BAYON LOUIS, MARIE EMMANUELLE (1746–1825)

477. Hayes, Deborah. "Marie-Emmanuelle Bayon, Later Madame Louis, and Music in Late Eighteenth-Century France." CMS 30, no. 1 (1990): 14–33. [Sonatas for Keyboard, op. 1]

BEACH, AMY MARCY (1867–1944)

478. Block, Adrienne Fried. "Amy Beach's Music on Native American Themes." AMUS 8, no. 2 (1990): 141–66. [*Eskimos: Four Characteristic Pieces*, op. 64; *From Blackbird Hills*, op. 83; Piano Trio, op. 150; String quartet, op. 89]

479. ———. "On Beach's *Variations on Balkan Themes*, Op. 60." AMUS 11, no. 3 (1993): 368–71. [Response to 480]

480. Bomberger, E. Douglas. "Motivic Development in Amy Beach's *Variations on Balkan Themes*, Op. 60." AMUS 10, no. 3 (1992): 326–47. [*See also* 479]

481. Chisholm Flatt, Rose Marie. "Analytical Approaches to Chromaticism in Amy Beach's Piano Quintet in F-Sharp Minor." ITR 4, no. 3 (1980–1981): 41–58.

482. Hamilton, Mary Ann. "Amy Beach, Mass in E-Flat Major: An American Classic." ACR 40, no. 2 (1998): 2–5.

483. Merrill, Lindsey E. "Mrs. H. H. A. Beach: Her Life and Music." Ph.D. diss., University of Rochester, 1963.

484. Miles, Marmaduke Sidney. "The Solo Piano Works of Mrs. H. H. A. Beach." D.M.A. diss., Peabody Conservatory, 1985.

485. Reigles, Barbara Jean. "The Choral Music of Amy Beach." Ph.D. diss., Texas Tech University, 1996.

BECK, CONRAD (1901–1989)

486. Mohr, Ernst. "Zum Kompositionsstil von Conrad Beck." SMZ 101 (1961): 150–56.

BECKWITH, JOHN (b. 1927)

487. M-Anhalt: 244–47. [*Gas!*]

488. Dixon, Gail. "Symmetry and Synthesis in Beckwith's Etudes (1983)." F-Beckwith: 70–93.

489. Mayo, John. "Coming to Terms with the Past: Beckwith's *Keyboard Practice*." F-Beckwith: 94–109.

BEDFORD, DAVID (b. 1937)

490. Barry, Malcolm, and Richard Witts. "David Bedford." CT 15 (1976–1977): 3–7.

491. Whittall, Arnold. "Post-Twelve-Tone Analysis." PRMA 94 (1967–1968): 1–17. [*Music for Albion Moonlight*]

BEETHOVEN, LUDWIG VAN (1770–1827)

Allegretto, Hess 69

492. Zanden, Jos van der. "Ein weiteres 'Ingharese' von Beethoven?" BBS 1 (1999): 112–30.

An die ferne Geliebte, Op. 98

493. Hatch, Christopher. "Ideas in Common: The *Liederkreis* and Other Works by Beethoven." F-Lang: 56–77.

494. Peake, Luise Eitel. "The Antecedents of Beethoven's *Liederkreis*." ML 63 (1982): 242–60.

495. Reynolds, Christopher. "The Representational Impulse in Late Beethoven, I: *An die ferne Geliebte*." ACTA 60, no. 1 (1988): 43–61.

Bagatelle, WoO. 60

496. Dunsby, Jonathan. "A Bagatelle on Beethoven's WoO 60." MA 3, no. 1 (1984): 57–68.

497. Gerhard, Anselm. "'Ein kühn hingeworfenes Räthselwort': Das Klavierstück WoO. 60 und die Voraussetzungen von Beethovens 'Spätstil.'" MTH 12, no. 3 (1997): 217–34.

Bagatelles, Op. 119

498. Cadwallader, Allen. "Prolegomena to a General Description of Motivic Relationships in Tonal Music." INT 2 (1988): 1–35. [No. 1]

499. Marston, Nicholas. "Trifles or a Multi-Trifle? Beethoven's Bagatelles, Op. 119, Nos. 7–11." MA 5, nos. 2–3 (1986): 193–206.

500. Poos, Heinrich. "Beethovens ars poetica: Die Bagatelle Op. 119, 7." In *Beethoven: Analecta varia*, ed. Heinz-Klaus Metzger and Rainer Riehn, 3–45. Munich: Text + Kritik, 1987.

Bagatelles, Op. 126

501. Ratz, Erwin. "Die Bagatellen Op. 126 von Beethoven." OMZ 6 (1951): 52–56.

502. Smyth, David. "Beethoven's Last Bagatelle." INT 13 (1999): 117–42. [No. 6]

Cadenzas to First and Final Movements of Mozart's Piano Concerto (K. 466), WoO. 58

503. Kramer, Richard. "Cadenza Contra Text: Mozart in Beethoven's Hands." NCM 15, no. 2 (1991): 116–31.

Cello Sonatas

504. Agmon, Eytan. "The First Movement of Beethoven's Cello Sonata, Op. 69: The Opening Solo as a Structural and Motivic Source." JM 16, no. 3 (1998): 394–406.

505. Dahlhaus, Carl. "'Von zwei Kulturen der Musik': Die Schluss-fuge aus Beethovens Cellosonate Opus 102.2." MF 31 (1978): 397–404.

506. Lockwood, Lewis. "Beethoven's Emergence from Crisis: The Cello Sonatas of Op. 102 (1815)." JM 16, no. 3 (1998): 301–22.

Choral Fantasy, **Op. 80.** *See* Fantasia, Op. 80

Diabelli Variations. See Variations on a Waltz by Diabelli, Op. 120

Eroica Variations. See Variations and a Fugue on an Original Theme, Op. 35

Fantasia, Op. 77

507. Wessel, Matthias. "Ludwig van Beethovens Fantasie für Klavier opus 77: Bekräftigung und Überwindung einer abgesunkenen Gattung." MTH 12, no. 3 (1997): 197–215.

Fantasia, Op. 80 (*Choral Fantasy*)

508. Fabre, Florence. "Beethoven: La *Fantaisie pour piano, orchestre et chœr* op. 80." ANM 34 (1999): 5–15.

509. Hess, Willy. "Zu Beethoven's *Chorfantasie*." SMZ 106 (1966): 19–23.

510. Schmidt, Hans. "Die gegenwartige Quellenlage zu Beethovens *Chorfantasie*." F-Schmidt-Görg/70: 355–71.

Fidelio, Op. 72

511. ASO 10 (1977).

512. ASO 164 (1995).

513. Brunswick, Mark. "Beethoven's Tribute to Mozart in *Fidelio*." MQ 31 (1945): 29–32.

514. M-Carner: 186–252.

515. Dahlhaus, Carl. "Idylle und Utopie: Zu Beethovens *Fidelio*." NZM 146, no. 11 (1985): 4–8.

516. Gossett, Philip. "The Arias of Marzelline: Beethoven as a Composer of Opera." BJ 10 (1978–1981): 141–83.

517. Hatch, Christopher. "The Wondrous Trumpet Call in Beethoven's *Fidelio*." OQ 15, no. 1 (1999): 5–17.

518. Hess, Willy. *Beethovens Oper "Fidelio" und ihre drei Fassungen.* Zurich: Atlantis, 1953.

519. John, Nicholas, ed. *Beethoven: Fidelio.* London: Calder, 1980.

520. Leibowitz, René. "Un rêve solitaire: *Fidelio*." M-Leibowitz/F: 61–106.

521. Nowak, Leopold. "Beethoven's *Fidelio* und die österreichischen Militarsignale." OMZ 10 (1955): 373–75.

522. Robinson, Paul. *Ludwig van Beethoven: Fidelio.* Cambridge: Cambridge University Press, 1996.

523. Tusa, Michael C. "Beethoven and Opera: The Grave-Digging Duet in *Leonore* (1805)." BF 5 (1996): 1–63.

Mass, Op. 86

524. Fillion, Michelle. "Beethoven's Mass in C and the Search for Inner Peace." BF 7 (1999): 1–15.

525. Knapp, J. Merrill. "Beethoven's Mass in C Major, Op. 86." F-Forbes: 199–216.

Mass, Op. 123 (*Missa solemnis*)

526. Dikenmann-Balmer, Lucie. *Beethovens "Missa solemnis" und ihre geisten Grundlagen.* Zurich: Atlantis, 1952.

527. Drabkin, William. *Beethoven: Missa solemnis.* Cambridge: Cambridge University Press, 1991.

528. ———. "On the *Missa solemnis*." BF 8 (2000): 173–76. [Response to 534]

529. Fiske, Roger. *Beethoven's "Missa solemnis."* London: Elek, 1979.

530. Kinderman, William. "Beethoven's Symbol for the Diety in the *Missa solemnis* and the Ninth Symphony." NCM 9, no. 2 (1985): 102–18.

531. Kirkendale, Warren. "New Roads to Old Ideas in Beethoven's *Missa solemnis*." MQ 56 (1970): 665–701.

532. Klein, Rudolf. "Die Struktur von Beethovens *Missa solemnis*." F-Valentin: 89–108.

533. Langer, Rudolf. *Missa solemnis: Über das theologische Problem in Beethovens Musik.* Stuttgart: Calwer, 1962.

534. Lodes, Birgit. "'When I Try, Now and Then, to Give Musical Form to My Turbulent Feelings': The Human and the Divine in the Gloria of Beethoven's *Missa solemnis*." BF 6 (1997): 143–79. [*See also* 528]

535. Ringwood, Alan R. "Formal Coherence in Beethoven's *Missa solemnis*." M.M. thesis, Boston University, 1994.

536. Schmidt-Görg, Joseph. "Zur melodischen Einheit im Beethovens *Missa solemnis*." F-Hoboken: 146–52.

537. Schmitz, Arnold. "Zum Verständnis des Gloria in Beethoven's *Missa solemnis*." F-Blume: 320–26.

538. Zickenheiner, Otto. "Untersuchungen zur Credo-Fuge im Beethovens *Missa solemnis*." Ph.D. diss., [Bonn?], 1981.

Missa solemnis. See Mass, Op. 123

National Airs with Variations, Op. 105 and 107

539. Misch, Ludwig. "Beethovens Variierte Themen Op. 105 und Op. 107." BJ 4 (1959–1960): 102–42.

Overtures

540. Broyles, Michael. "Stylistic Dualism in Early Beethoven and the *Leonore Challenge*." JM 5, no. 3 (1987): 419–47. [*Leonore* Overtures Nos. 2–3]

541. Göllner, Theodor. "Beethovens Ouvertüre *Die Weihe des Hauses* und Händels Trauermarsch aus Saul." F-Hüschen: 181–89.

542. Kreiner, Viktor. "Ludwig van Beethoven: Ouvertüre zu Goethes Egmont, Op. 84." NZM 148, no. 3 (1987): 30–34.

543. Mies, Paul. "Zur Coriolan-Ouvertüre Op. 62." BJ 6 (1965–1968): 260–68.

544. Oster, Ernst. "The Dramatic Character of the Egmont Overture." MU 2 (1948–1949): 269–85.

545. Wieninger, Herbert. "Beethovens Leonoren-Ouvertüren." ME 25 (1971–1972): 113–18.

Piano Concertos

546. Collier, Michael. "The Rondo Movements of Beethoven's Concerto No. 3 in C Minor, Op. 37, and Brahms's Concerto No. 1 in D Minor: A Comparative Analysis." TP 31 (1978): 5–15.

547. Cone, Edward T. "A Cadenza for Op. 15." F-Forbes: 99–107. [No. 1]

548. Goldschmidt, Harry. "Motivvariation und Gestaltmetamorphose." F-Besseler: 389–409.

549. Körner, Klaus. "Formen musikalischer Aussage im zweiten Satz des G-dur Klavierkonzertes von Beethoven." BJ 9 (1973–1977): 202–16. [No. 4]

550. Osthoff, Wolfgang. *Ludwig van Beethoven: Klavierkonzert Nr.3 C-Moll, Op.37.* Munich: Fink, 1965.

551. Rust, Ezra G. "The First Movements of Beethoven's Piano Concertos." Ph.D. diss., University of California at Berkeley, 1970.

Piano Sonatas (various; *see also* specific piano sonatas)

552. Adams, Frank John. "An Analysis of Seven Adagio and Largo Movements from the Early Piano Sonatas of Beethoven." M.A. thesis., Harvard University, 1968.

553. Bilson, Malcolm. "The Emergence of the Fantasy-Style in the Beethoven Piano Sonatas of the Early and Middle Periods." D.M.A. diss., University of Illinois, 1968.

554. Chase, Howard R. "Tonality and Tonal Factors in the Piano Sonatas of Beethoven." Ph.D. diss., University of Michigan, 1953.

555. Cittadini, Roberto. "L'espansione tonale nelle Sonate per pianoforte di Beethoven." ANL 14 (1994): 26–35.

556. Dahlhaus, Carl. "Cantabile und thematischer Prozess: Der Übergang zum Spätwerk in Beethovens Klaviersonaten." AM 37 (1980): 81–98.

557. ———. "Eine wenig beachtete Formidee: Zur Interpretation einiger Beethoven-Sonate." M-Breig: 248–56.

558. Dinslage, Patrick. Studien zum Verhältnis von Harmonik, Metrik und Form in den Klaviersonaten Ludwig van Beethovens. Munich: Katzbichler, 1987.

559. Drake, Kenneth. *The Beethoven Sonatas and the Creative Experience.* Bloomington: Indiana University Press, 1994.

560. Dreyfus, Kay. "Beethoven's Last Five Piano Sonatas: A Study in Analytical Method." BJ 9 (1973–1977): 37–45.

561. Hauschild, Peter. "Bemerkungen zu Beethovens Klaviernotation." BJ 9 (1973–1977): 147–65.

562. Huron, David. "Crescendo/Dimenuendo Asymmetries in Beethoven's Piano Sonatas." MP 7, no. 4 (1990): 395–402.

563. Kamien, Roger. "Aspects of the Recapitulation in Beethoven Piano Sonatas." MFO 4 (1976): 195–236.

564. Lorince, Frank Edell. "A Study of Musical Texture in Relation to Sonata-Form as Evidenced in Selected Keyboard Sonatas from C. P. E. Bach through Beethoven." Ph.D. diss., University of Rochester, 1966.

565. Migliaccio, Carlo. "Beethoven, Stravinskij e il problema del 'bergsonismo in musica.'" RIM 29 (1994): 157–82.

566. Pfingsten, Ingeborg. "Ökonomie der musikalischen Mittel in der formalen Gestaltung bei Mozart und Beethoven: Aufgezeigt an dreiteiligen Liedstrukturen in Klaviersonaten." MTH 1, no. 3 (1986): 217–37.

567. Reti, Rudolf. *Thematic Patterns in Sonatas of Beethoven.* London: Faber & Faber, 1967.

568. Rosenberg, Richard. Die Klaviersonaten Ludwig van Beethovens: Studien über Form und Vortrag. Olten: Urs Graf, 1957.

569. ———. "Mozart-Spuren in Beethovens Klaviersonaten." BJ 3 (1957–1958): 51–62.

570. Schick, Hartmut. "Finalität als Formprinzip: Beethovens mittlere Klaviersonaten und die Kunst, falsch zu beginnen." MTH 13, no. 3 (1998): 207–22.

571. Schmalzriedt, Siegfried. "Charakter und Drama: Zur historischen Analyse von Haydnschen und Beethovenschen Sonatensätzen." AM 42 (1985): 37–66.

572. Shamgar, Beth Friedman. "Dramatic Devices in the Retransitions of Beethoven's Piano Sonatas." ISM 2 (1979): 63–75.

573. ———. "The Retransition in the Piano Sonatas of Haydn, Mozart and Beethoven." Ph.D. diss., New York University, 1978.

574. Sheer, Miriam. "Comparison of Dynamic Practices in Selected Piano Sonatas by Clementi and Beethoven." BF 5 (1996): 85–101.

575. Stainkamph, Eileen. *Form and Analysis of the Complete Beethoven Pianoforte Sonatas.* Melbourne: Allans Music, 1968.

576. Szelényi, Istvan. "Monothematische Beziehungen in der Klaviersonaten von Beethoven." SM 12 (1970): 205–32.

577. Thompson, Harold Adams. "An Evolutionary View of Neapolitan Formations in Beethoven's Pianoforte Sonatas." CMS 20 (1980): 144–62.

578. Weber, Friedrich. *Harmonischer Aufbau und Stimmführung in den Sonatensdtzen der Klaviersonaten Beethovens.* Würzburg: Triltsch, 1940.

579. Weber, Markus. "Zu Beethovens *invenzione*: Anmerkungen insbesondere zu Reprisen in Klaviersonaten." F-Lichtenhahn: 57–79.

580. Wiora, Walter. "Tanzartige Hauptthemen von Beethovens Klaviersonaten und ihre Gestalttypen." OM 9 (1986): 192–96.

Piano Sonata, Op. 2, No. 1

581. Broyles, Michael. "The Two Instrumental Styles of Classicism." JAMS 36 (1983): 210–42.

582. Klausmeier, Friedrich. "Beethovens neuer Stil musikalisch interpretiert." M 41, no. 3 (1987): 231–40.

Piano Sonata, Op. 2, No. 2

583. Dinslage, Patrick. "Gestalt und Zusammenhang: Zum ersten Satz der Klaviersonate Opus 2, 2 von Ludwig van Beethoven." M 38, no. 5 (1984): 409–14.

Piano Sonata, Op. 2, No. 3

584. Grabócz, Márta. "A. J. Greimas's Narrative Grammar and the Analysis of Sonata Form." INT 12 (1998): 1–23. [Movement I]

Piano Sonata, Op. 7

585. Beach, David. "Phrase Expansion: Three Analytical Studies." MA 14, no. 1 (1995): 27–47. [Movement III]

586. Kamien, Roger. "Chromatic Details in Beethoven's Piano Sonata in E-Flat Major, Op. 7." MR 35 (1974): 149–56.

Piano Sonata, Op. 10, No. 1

587. Boss, Jack F. "'Schenkerian-Schoenbergian Analysis' and Hidden Repetition in the Opening Movement of Beethoven's Piano Sonata Op. 10, No. 1." MTO 5, no. 1 (1999).

588. Hager, Nancy. "The First Movement of Mozart's Sonata K. 457 and Beethoven's Opus 10, No. 1: A C Minor Connection?" MR 47, no. 2 (1986–1987): 89–100.

Piano Sonata, Op. 10, No. 3

589. De la Motte, Diether. "Ludwig van Beethoven: Klaviersonate Op.10, Nr.3, zweiter Satz in D-Moll, Largo e mesto." M-Benary: 13–20. Reprint, M-De la Motte: v. 1, 49–60.

590. Federhofer, Hellmut. "Zur Analyse des zweiten Satzes von L. van Beethovens Klaviersonate Op. 10, No. 3." F-Larsen: 339–50.

591. Finscher, Ludwig. "Beethovens Klaviersonate Opus 31, 3: Versuch einer Interpretation." F-Wiora: 385–96.

592. Huber, Ernst Friedrich. "Rhythmische Gestalten im Largo e mesto der Klaviersonate Op. 10, No. 3 von L. v. Beethoven." Ph.D. diss., Friedrich-Alexander Universität Erlangen, 1954.

593. Kamien, Roger. "Non-Tonic Settings of the Primary Tone in Beethoven Piano Sonatas." JM 16, no. 3 (1998): 379–93.

594. Rothstein, William. "Beethoven with and without 'Kunstgepräng': Metrical Ambiguity Reconsidered." BF 4 (1995): 165–93.

Piano Sonata, Op. 13 ("Pathétique")

595. Kinzler, Hartmuth. "Komplexe Abbildungen musikalischer Strukturen innerhalb eines Werkes am Beispiel von Beethovens *Pathétique* Op. 13." MTH 14, no. 2 (1999): 99–112.

596. M-Kresky: 92–107. [Movement II]

597. Sisman, Elaine R. "Pathos and the *Pathétique*: Rhetorical Stance in Beethoven's C-Minor Sonata, Op. 13." BF 3 (1994): 81–105.

Piano Sonata, Op. 14, No. 1

598. Schachter, Carl. "Beethoven's Sketches for the First Movement of Op. 14, No. 1: A Study in Design." JMT 26 (1982): 1–21

599. Swain, Joseph P. "Connections in Modulation." JMTP 1, no. 1 (1987): 13–24. [Movement II]

Piano Sonata, Op. 22

600. Lockwood, Lewis. "Reshaping the Genre: Beethoven's Piano Sonatas from Op. 22 to Op. 28 (1799–1801)." ISM 6 (1996): 1–16.

Piano Sonata, Op. 26

601. Beach, David. "The Analytic Process: A Practical Demonstration; The Opening Theme from Beethoven's Op. 26." JMTP 3, no. 1 (1989): 25–46. [Movement I]

602. Drabkin, William. "Schenker, the Consonant Passing Note, and the First-Movement Theme of Beethoven's Sonata Op. 26." MA 15, nos. 2–3 (1996): 149–89.

603. Lockwood, Lewis. "Reshaping the Genre: Beethoven's Piano Sonatas from Op. 22 to Op. 28 (1799–1801)." ISM 6 (1996): 1–16.

604. Perry, Jeffrey. "Beethoven and the Romantic Unique Subject: The Dialectic of Affect and Form in the 'Marcia funebre sulla morte d'un eroe,' Op. 26, III." ITR 18, no. 2 (1997): 47–73.

Piano Sonata, Op. 27, No. 1 ("Quasi una fantasia")

605. Benary, Peter. "Sonata quasi una fantasia: Zu Beethovens Opus 27." MTH 2, no. 2 (1987): 129–36.

606. M-Jones.

607. Lockwood, Lewis. "Reshaping the Genre: Beethoven's Piano Sonatas from Op. 22 to Op. 28 (1799–1801)." ISM 6 (1996): 1–16.

Piano Sonata, Op. 27, No. 2 ("Moonlight")

608. Benary, Peter. "Sonata quasi una fantasia: Zu Beethovens Opus 27." MTH 2, no. 2 (1987): 129–36.

609. Edelmann, Bernd. "Beethovens Phantasie Cis-Moll Op. 27 Nr. 2." F-Göllner: 269–94.

610. M-Jones.

611. Krohn, Ilmari. "Die Form des ersten Satzes der *Mondscheinsonate*." In *Beethovenzentenarfeier: Internationaler musikhistorischer Kongress, Vienna, 26–31 March 1927*, 58–65. Vienna: Universal, 1927.

612. Lockwood, Lewis. "Reshaping the Genre: Beethoven's Piano Sonatas from Op. 22 to Op. 28 (1799–1801)." ISM 6 (1996): 1–16.

Piano Sonata, Op. 28 ("Pastoral")

613. Lockwood, Lewis. "Reshaping the Genre: Beethoven's Piano Sonatas from Op. 22 to Op. 28 (1799–1801)." ISM 6 (1996): 1–16.

614. Natošević, Constanze. "Pastoraler Ideengehalt in Ludwig van Beethovens Klaviersonate D-Dur op. 28." MTH 14, no. 2 (1999): 113–20.

615. Sommer, Heinz-Dieter. "Beethovens kleine Pastorale: Zum 1. Satz der Klaviersonate Op. 28." AM 43, no. 2 (1986): 109–27.

Piano Sonata, Op. 31, No. 1

616. M-Jones.

617. Schwarting, Heino. "Komposition nach Vorbild: Vergleiche bei Schubert und Beethoven." M 38, no. 2 (1984): 130–38.

Piano Sonata, Op. 31, No. 2

618. Cooper, Barry. "The Origins of Beethoven's D-Minor Sonata Op. 31 No. 2." ML 62 (1981): 261–80.

619. Dahlhaus, Carl. "Musikalische Forme als Transformation: Bemerkungen zur Beethoven-Interpretation." BJ 9 (1973–1977): 27–36. [Movement I]

620. ———. "Zur Formidee von Beethovens D-Moll-Sonate Opus 31, 2." MF 33 (1980): 310–12.

621. M-Jones.

622. Kamien, Roger. "Non-Tonic Settings of the Primary Tone in Beethoven Piano Sonatas." JM 16, no. 3 (1998): 379–93.

623. Schmalfelt, Janet. "Form as the Process of Becoming: The Beethoven-Hegelian Tradition and the 'Tempest' Sonata." BF 4 (1995): 37–71.

Piano Sonata, Op. 31, No. 3

624. Finscher, Ludwig. "Beethovens Klaviersonate Opus 31, 3: Versuch einer Interpretation." F-Wiora: 385–96.

625. M-Jones.

626. Kamien, Roger. "Non-Tonic Settings of the Primary Tone in Beethoven Piano Sonatas." JM 16, no. 3 (1998): 379–93.

Piano Sonata, Op. 53 ("Waldstein")

627. Beach, David, Donald Mintz, and Robert Palmer. "Analysis Symposium." Jåí 13 (1969): 186–217. Also in M-Yeston: 202–26.

628. Chávez, Carlos. "Anatomic Analysis: Beethoven's *Waldstein* Op. 53." PQ 82 (1973): 17–23.

629. Guck, Marion A. "Beethoven as Dramatist." CMS 29 (1989): 8–18. [Movement I]

630. Kamien, Roger. "Subtle Enharmonic Connections, Modal Mixture, and Tonal Plan in the First Movement of Beethoven's Piano Sonata in C Major, Opus 53 ('Waldstein')." BF 1 (1992): 93–110.

631. Marion, Gregory J. "Inciting Transformational Insights." INT 9 (1995): 1–32.

632. Spitzer, Michael. "The Significance of Recapitulation in the 'Waldstein' Sonata." BF 5 (1996): 103–17.

633. Tarasti, Eero. "Beethoven's *Waldstein* and the Generative Course." ITR 12 (1991): 99–140.

Piano Sonata, Op. 57 ("Appassionata")

634. Barry, Barbara R. "Pitch Interpretation and Cyclical Procedures in Middle-Period Beethoven." MQ 76, no. 2 (1992): 184–215.

635. Dommel-Diény, Amy. *Beethoven: Appassionata Sonata.* Dommel-Diény 6. Paris: Dommel-Diény, 1972.

636. Eitan, Zohar. "Beethoven's Thematization of Musical Space: The Case of the *Appassionata* Sonata." SONUS 16, no. 1 (1995): 23–52.

637. Frohlich, Martha. *Beethoven's "Appassionata" Sonata.* Oxford: Oxford University Press, 1991.

638. ———. "Sketches for a Curious 'Imitative Motive' in Beethoven's 'Appassionata' Sonata, Op. 57." ISM 4 (1987): 27–40.

Piano Sonata, Op. 81a ("Das Lebewohl, Abwesenheit und Wiedersehn")

639. Agmon, Eytan. "Beethoven's Op. 81a and the Psychology of Loss." MTO 2, no. 4 (1996).

640. LaRue, Jan. "Proposte per un'analisi stilistica integrale con esemplificazioni dalla Sonata op. 81a di Beethoven." Trans. Manuela di Martino. ANL 1 (1990): 5–17.

641. Raab, Claus. "Von Ankunft und Aufbruch und ein 'etwas harter Gang' durch die Figurenproblematik: Ludwig van Beethovens Sonate op. 81a ('Das Lebewohl')." MF 50, no. 1 (1997): 47–73.

Piano Sonata, Op. 90

642. Danuser, Hermann. "Zum Problem musikalischer Ambiguität: Einige Aspekte von Beethovens Klaviersonate in E-Moll Opus 90." ZM 8, no. 2 (1977): 22–28.

643. Kalisch, Volker. "Beethovens Klaviersonate Op. 90: Ein analytischer Versuch." SZM 35 (1984): 89–124.

644. Krones, Hartmut. "'. . . Er habe ihm seine Liebesgeschichte in Musik setzen wollen': Ludwig van Beethovens E-moll-Sonate, op. 90." OMZ 43, no. 11 (1988): 592–601.

Piano Sonata, Op. 101

645. Schenker, Heinrich. *Beethoven: Die letzten Sonaten; Sonate A Dur Op. 101.* Vienna: Universal, 1972.

Piano Sonata, Op. 106 ("Hammerklavier")

646. Badura-Skoda, Paul. "Textprobleme in Beethovens *Hammerklaviersonate* Op. 106." Melos/NZM 3 (1977): 11–15.

647. Friedmann, Michael L. "Hexachordal Sources of Structure in Beethoven's *Hammerklavier* Sonata, Opus 106." ITO 4, no. 6 (1978): 3–17.

648. Guigue, Didier. "Beethoven et le pianoforte: L'émergence d'une pensée des timbres comme dimension autonome du discours musical." RDM 80, no. 1 (1994): 81–96.

649. Hatten, Robert S. "Interpreting Expression: The Adagio from the *Hammerklavier*." TP 19 (1994): 1–17. [Movement III]

650. Hauser, Richard. "Das AIS in der Sonate Op.106." BJ 6 (1965–1968): 243–59.

651. Klein, Rudolf. "Beethovens gebundener Stil in Opus 106." BJ 9 (1973–1977): 185–99.

652. Marston, Nicholas. "From *A* to *B*: The History of an Idea in the 'Hammerklavier' Sonata." BF 6 (1997): 97–127.

Piano Sonata, Op. 109

653. Delaigue, Olivier. "La Sonate pour piano no. 30, op. 109 de Beethoven: Rigucur et invention d'une trajectoire dialectique." ANM 15 (1989): 54–63.

654. Forte, Allen. *The Compositional Matrix.* Baldwin, N.Y.: Music Teachers National Association, 1961.

655. Marston, Nicholas. *Beethoven's Piano Sonata in E, Op. 109.* Oxford: Oxford University Press, 1995.

656. ———. "Schenker and Forte Reconsidered: Beethoven's Sketches for the Piano Sonata in E, Op. 109." NCM 10, no. 1 (1986): 24–42.

657. Mulder, Michael. "An Unpublished Letter Treating the Piano Sonata, Op.109, by Ludwig van Beethoven." ITO 5, no. 4 (1979–1981): 16–20. [Analysis presented as a fictional letter by Beethoven]

658. Schenker, Heinrich. *Beethoven: Die letzten Sonaten; Sonata E Dur Op. 109.* Vienna: Universal, 1971.

Piano Sonata, Op. 110

659. Ashforth, Alden. "The Relationship of the Sixth in Beethoven's Piano Sonata, Opus 110." MR 32 (1971): 93–101.

660. Beach, David. "Motivic Repetition in Beethoven's Piano Sonata Op. 110, Part I: The First Movement." INT 1 (1987): 1–29.

661. ———. "Motivic Repetition in Beethoven's Piano Sonata Op. 110, Part II: The Trio of the Second Movement and the Adagio-Arioso." INT 2 (1988): 75–97.

662. Hoyt, Reed J. "Rhythmic Process in the Scherzo of Beethoven's Sonata Op. 110: Analysis as a Basis for Interpretation and Criticism." ITR 9, no. 2 (1988): 99–133.

663. Kinderman, William. "Integration and Narrative Design in Beethoven's Piano Sonata in A-Flat Major, Opus 110." BF 1 (1992): 111–45.

664. Uhde, Jurgen, and Renate Wieland. "Von der Analyse zur Darstellung: Zur Artikulation der Zeitgestalt in Beethovens Sonate As-Dur Op.110." M 36 (1982): 13–18.

665. Van Beek, Johan. "Der zweite Takt des Rezitativs in Beethovens Klaviersonate As-Dur Opus 110." MTH 12, no. 3 (1997): 235–54.

666. Voss, Egon. "Zu Beethovens Klaviersonate As-Dur Op.110." MF 23 (1970): 256–268.

Piano Sonata, Op. 111

667. Drabkin, William. "The Sketches for Beethoven's Piano Sonata in C Minor, Opus 111." Ph.D. diss., Princeton University, 1977.

668. ———. "Some Relationships between the Autographs of Beethoven's Sonata in C Minor, Opus 111." CM 13 (1972): 38–47.

669. Hackman, Willis H. "Rhythmic Analysis as a Clue to Articulation in the Arietta of Beethoven's Op. 111." PQ 93 (1976): 26–37.

670. Schenker, Heinrich. *Beethoven: Die letzten Sonaten; Sonate C Moll Op. 111.* Vienna: Universal, 1971.

Piano Trios

671. M-Code. [Op. 70, no. 1]

672. Hiebert, Elfrieda F. "Beethoven's Trios for Pianoforte, Violin, and Violoncello: Problems in History and Style." Ph.D. diss., University of Wisconsin, 1970.

673. McCreless, Patrick. "Roland Barthes's *S/Z* from a Musical Point of View." ITO 10, no. 7 (1988): 1–29. [Op. 70, no. 1 (Movement I)]

Piano Works (various; *see also* specific piano works)

674. Batta, András, and Sándor Kovács. "Typbildung und Grossform in Beethovens frühen Klaviervariationen." SM 20 (1978): 125–56.

675. Cockshoot, John V. *The Fugue in Beethoven's Piano Music.* London: Routledge, 1959.

676. Goldschmidt, Harry. "Chopiniana bei Beethoven." F-Lissa: 209–22.

677. Laufer, Edward. "Voice-Leading Procedures in Development Sections." SMUWO 13 (1991): 69–120.

678. M-Sterling.

Quintet for Piano and Winds, Op. 16

679. Dittrich, Raymond. "Anmerkungen zu den Kompositionstechniken der Sonatenhauptsätze von Mozarts und Beethovens Quintetten für Bläser und Klavier." T 17, no. 3 (1992): 169–78.

***Rondo a capriccio*, Op. 129**

680. Hertzmann, Erich. "The Newly Discovered Autograph of Beethoven's Rondo à capriccio, Op. 129." MQ 32 (1946): 171–95.

***Sehnsucht*, WoO. 134**

681. Forbes, Elliot. "*Nur wer die Sehnsucht kennt*: An Example of a Goethe Lyric Set to Music." F-Merritt: 59–82.

Songs (various; *see also* specific songs)

682. Richter, Lukas. "Zur Kompositionstechnik von Beethovens Britischen Liedern." BM 17 (1975): 257–79.

683. Stuber, Robert. *Die Klavierbegleitung im Liede von Haydn, Mozart, und Beethoven: Eine Stilstudie.* Biel: Graphische Anstalt Schüler, 1958.

Songs, Op. 48

684. Schollum, Robert. "Zur Wiedergabe der *Gellert-Lieder* Op. 48 von Beethoven." M 33 (1979–1980): 99–104, 153–57.

Songs, Op. 75

685. Broeckx, Jan L., and Walter Landrieu. "Comparative Computer Study of Style, Based on Five Liedermelodies." I 1 (1972): 29–92. [No. 1]

686. Cooper, Barry. *Beethoven's Folksong Settings: Chronology, Sources, Style.* Oxford: Oxford University Press, 1994.

687. M-Lewis.

String Quartets (various; *see also* specific string quartets)

688. Brusatti, Otto. "Klangexperimente in Beethovens Streichquartetten." SZM 29 (1978): 69–88.

689. Carr-Richardson, Amy. "Phrase Rhythm and Form: The Scherzi of Beethoven's Late String Quartets." Ph.D. diss., Florida State University, 1995.

690. Cooke, Deryck. "The Unity of Beethoven's Late Quartets." MR 24 (1963): 30–49.

691. Drabkin, William. "Beethoven and the Open String." MA 4, nos. 1–2 (1985): 15–28.

692. ———. "The Cello Part in Beethoven's Late Quartets." BF 7 (1999): 45–66.

693. Dullo, W. A. "The Mysterious Four-Note Motive in Beethoven's Late String Quartets." MS 1 (1964): 10–15.

694. Forchert, Arno. "Zur Satztechnik von Beethovens Streichquartetten." F-Hüschen: 151–58.

695. Galo, Ellen Gillespie. "Analysis of the Rasumovsky Quartets Op. 59, Nos. 1, 2, and 3 of Beethoven." M.A. diss., State University College, Potsdam, New York, 1977.

696. Hübsch, Lini. *Ludwig van Beethoven: Die Rasumowsky Quartette Op. 59, Nr.1, F-Dur, Nr.2 E-Moll, Nr.3, C-Dur.* Munich: Fink, 1983.

697. Kerman, Joseph. *The Beethoven Quartets.* New York: Knopf, 1967.

698. Kreft, Ekkehard. *Die späten Quartette Beethovens: Substanz und Substanzverarbeitung.* Bonn: Bouvier, 1959.

699. Krummacher, Friedhelm. "Synthesis des Disparaten: Zu Beethovens späten Quartetten und ihrer frühen Rezeption." AM 37 (1980): 99–134.

700. Levy, Janet M. "Texture as a Sign in Classic and Early Romantic Music." JAMS 35 (1982): 482–531.

701. Radliffe, Philip. *Beethoven's String Quartets.* London: Hutchinson, 1965.

702. Ratner, Leonard G. "Texture: A Rhetorical Element in Beethoven's Quartets." ISM 2 (1979): 51–62.

703. Siegele, Ulrich. *Beethoven: Formale Strategien der späten Quartette.* Munich: Text + Kritik, 1990.

704. Stephan, Rudolf. "Zu Beethovens letzten Quartetten." MF 23 (1970): 245–56.

705. Tepping, Susan E. "Fugue Process and Tonal Structure in the String Quartets of Haydn, Mozart, and Beethoven." Ph.D. diss., Indiana University, 1987.

706. Wildberger, Jacques. "Versuch über Beethovens späte Streichquartette." SMZ 110 (1970): 1–8.

String Quartet, Op. 18, No. 1

707. Green, Michael D. "Beethoven's Path toward Large-Scale Rhythmic Development: The Exposition of the First Movement of Opus 18, No. 1." ITR 7, no. 1 (1986): 3–22.

708. Klausmeier, Friedrich. "Beethovens neuer Stil musikalisch interpretiert." M 41, no. 3 (1987): 231–40.

709. Levy, Janet M. *Beethoven's Compositional Choices: The Two Versions of Op. 18, No. 1, First Movement.* Philadelphia: University of Pennsylvania Press, 1982.

710. Renger, Jens. "Zum Klassizismus in Beethovens Streichquartett Op. 18, 1." M 50, no. 6 (1996): 407–13.

String Quartet, Op. 18, No. 3

711. Burstein, L. Poundie. "Surprising Returns: The VII# in Beethoven's Op. 18, No. 3, and Its Antecedents in Haydn." MA 17, no. 3 (1998): 295–312.

String Quartet, Op. 18, No. 6

712. Mitchell, William J. "Beethoven's *La Malinconia* from the String Quartet, Op. 16, No. 6: Techniques and Structure." MFO 3 (1973): 269–80.

String Quartet, Op. 59, No. 1 ("Rasumovsky")

713. Chailley, Jacques. "Sur la signification du quatuor de Mozart K.465, dit 'Les Dissonances,' et du 7ème quatuor de Beethoven." F-Jeppesen: 283–92.

714. M-Chailley.

715. Del Mar, Jonathan. "A Problem Resolved? The Form of the Scherzo of Beethoven's String Quartet in F, Op. 59, No. 1." BF 8 (2000): 165–72. [Response to 718]

716. Eiseman, David. "Half-Notes Demystified in the First Movement of Beethoven's String Quartet, Op. 59, No. 1." CMS 24 (1984): 21–27.

717. Headlam, Dave. "A Rhythmic Study of the Exposition in the Second Movement of Beethoven's Quartet Op. 59, No. 1." MTS 7 (1985): 114–38.

718. Lockwood, Lewis. "A Problem of Form: The 'Scherzo' of Beethoven's String Quartet in F Major, Op. 59, No. 1." BF 2 (1993): 85–95. [*See also* 715]

String Quartet, Op. 59, No. 2 ("Rasumovsky")

719. Barry, Barbara R. "Pitch Interpretation and Cyclical Procedures in Middle-Period Beethoven." MQ 76, no. 2 (1992): 184–215.

String Quartet, Op. 59, No. 3 ("Rasumovsky")

720. Hatten, Robert S. "An Approach to Ambiguity in the Opening of Beethoven's String Quartet, Op. 59, No. 3, I." ITR 3, no. 3 (1979–1980): 28–35.

String Quartet, Op. 74

721. Marston, Nicholas. "Analysing Variations: The Finale of Beethoven's String Quartet Op. 74." MA 8, no. 3 (1989): 303–24.

String Quartet, Op. 95 ("Serioso")

722. Carpenter, Patricia. "Musical Form and Musical Idea: Reflections on a Theme of Schoenberg, Hanslick, and Kant." F-Lang: 394–427.

723. Fischer, Kurt von. "*Never to Be Performed in Public*: Zu Beethovens Streichquartett, Op. 95." BJ 9 (1973–1977): 87–96.

724. Livingstone, Ernest F. "Die Coda in Beethovens Streichquartett F-Moll Op. 95." M-Kühn: 358–69.

725. ———. "The Final Coda in Beethoven's String Quartet in F Minor, Op. 95." F-Fox: 132–44.

String Quartet, Op. 127

726. McKee, Eric. "Alternative Meanings in the First Movement of Beethoven's String Quartet in E-Flat Major, Op. 127: Emergence and Growth from Stagnation and Decline." TP 24 (1999): 1–27.

727. Smyth, David H. "Patterning Beyond Hypermeter." CMS 32 (1992): 79–98. [Movement I]

String Quartet, Op. 130

728. Barry, Barbara R. "Recycling the End of the 'Liebquartett': Models, Meaning, and Propriety in Beethoven's Quartet in B-Flat Major, Opus 130." JM 13, no. 3 (1995): 355–76.

729. Brügge, Joachim. "Zu Ferdinand Zehentreiter, 'Bruch und Kontinuitat in Beethovens spaten Quartetten.'" MTH 12, no. 2 (1997): 165–68. [Response to 733]

730. Churgin, Bathia. "The *Andante con moto* in Beethoven's String Quartet Op. 130: The Final Version and Changes on the Autograph." JM 16, no. 2 (1998): 227–53. [Movement III]

731. Fischer, Kurt von. "Zur Cavatina aus Beethovens Streichquartett Op. 130." F-Dahlhaus: 493–501.

732. MacArdle, Donald. "Beethoven's Quartet in B Flat, Op. 130." MR 8 (1947): 11–24.

733. Zehentreiter, Ferdinand. "Bruch und Kontinuität in Beethovens späten Quartetten: Einige Überlegungen zur Werk-und Bedeutungsanalyse." MTH 11, no. 3 (1996): 211–40. [*See also* 729]

String Quartet, Op. 131

734. Barry, Barbara R. "Teleology and Structural Determinants in Beethoven's C-Sharp Minor Quartet, Op. 131." CMS 30, no. 2 (1990): 57–73.

735. Carr-Richardson, Amy. "Rotational Symmetry as a Metaphor for the Scherzo of Beethoven's Opus 131." ITR 20, no. 1 (1999): 1–23.

736. Crotty, John Edward. "Design and Harmonic Organization in Beethoven's String Quartet, Opus 131." Ph.D. diss., University of Rochester, 1986.

737. Dougherty, William Patrick. "An Examination of Semiotics in Musical Analysis: The Neapolitan Complex in Beethoven's Op. 131." Ph.D. diss., Ohio State University, 1985.

738. Firca, Gheorghe. "Werkanalyse und Möglichkeiten einer neuen Lesert von Beethovens Schaffen." M-Goldschmidt: 323–27.

739. Glauert, Amanda. "The Double Perspective in Beethoven's Opus 131." NCM 4 (1980–1981): 113–20.

740. Platen, Emil. "Eine Frühfassung zum ersten Satz des Streichquartetts Op. 131 von Beethoven." BJ 10 (1978–1981): 277–304.

741. Winter, Robert S., III. "Compositional Origins of Beethoven's String Quartet in C-Sharp Minor, Op.131." Ph.D. diss., University of Chicago, 1978.

String Quartet, Op. 132

742. Agawu, V. Kofi. "A Semiotic Interpretation of the First Movement of Beethoven's String Quartet in A Minor, Op. 132." M-Agawu: Chap. 6.

743. ———. "The First Movement of Beethoven's Opus 132 and the Classical Style." CMS 27 (1987): 30–45.

744. Firca, Gheorghe. "Werkanalyse und Möglichkeiten einer neuen Lesert von Beethovens Schaffen." M-Goldschmidt: 323–27.

745. Kirk, Ken. "Discontinuity and Closure: The First Movement of Beethoven's Quartet in A Minor, Op. 132." MRF 2, no. 1 (1987): 1–6.

746. Kirkendale, Warren. "Gregorianischer Stil in Beethovens Streichquartett Op.132." M-Kühn: 373–76.

747. Schwindt-Gross, Nicole. "Zwischen Kontrapunkt und Divertimento: Zum zweiten Satz aus Beethovens Streichquartett Op. 132." F-Finscher: 446–56. [Movement II]

748. Vitercik, Greg. "Structure and Expression in Beethoven's Op. 132." JMR 13, nos. 3–4 (1993): 233–53.

749. Wallace, Robin. "Background and Expression in the First Movement of Beethoven's Op. 132." JM 7, no. 1 (1989): 3–20.

String Quartet, Op. 133

750. Firca, Gheorghe. "Werkanalyse und Möglichkeiten einer neuen Lesert von Beethovens Schaffen." M-Goldschmidt: 323–27.

751. Kirkendale, Warren. "The *Great Fugue* Op. 133: Beethoven's *Art of Fugue.*" ACTA 35 (1963): 14–24.

752. Mahnkopf, Claus-Steffen. "Beethovens *Große Fuge*: Multiperspekivität im Spätwerk." MAS 2, no. 8 (1998): 12–38.

753. Mila, Massimo. "Lettura della *Grande fuga* Op. 133." F-Ronga: 345–66.

String Quartet, Op. 135

754. Cacioppo, Curt. "Color and Dissonance in Late Beethoven: Quartet Op. 135." JMR 6, no. 3 (1986): 207–48.

755. Fischer, Kurt von. "*Der schwer gefasste Entschluss*: Eine Interpretationsstudie zu Beethovens Streichquartett Op. 135." BM 18 (1976): 117–21.

756. Kluge, Reiner. "*Der schwer gefasste Entschluss*: Über eine Verbindung biogener, logogener und musikogener Elemente in Beethovens Op. 135." BM 26 (1984): 225–36.

757. Kramer, Jonathan D. "Multiple and Non-Linear Time in Beethoven's Opus 135." PNM 11, no. 2 (1973): 122–45.

758. ———. "Postmodern Concepts of Musical Time." ITR 17, no. 2 (1996): 21–61. [Movement I]

759. Reynolds, Christopher. "The Representational Impulse in Late Beethoven, II: String Quartet in F Major, Op. 135." ACTA 60, no. 1 (1988): 180–94.

String Quintet, Op. 29

760. Hatch, Christopher. "Thematic Interdependence in Two Finales by Beethoven." MR 45 (1984): 194–207.

761. Levy, Janet M. "Texture as a Sign in Classic and Early Romantic Music." JAMS 35 (1982): 482–531.

String Trios

762. Kerman, Joseph. "*Tändelne Lazzi*: On Beethoven's Trio in D Major, Opus 70, No. 1." F-Abraham: 109–22.

763. Platen, Emil. "Beethovens Streichtrio D-Dur, Opus 9, Nr. 2: Zum Prob em der thematischen Einheit mehrsätziger Formen." F-Schmidt-Görg/70: 260–82.

Symphonies (various; *see also* specific symphonies)

764. Cooper, Barry. "Newly Identified Sketches for Beethoven's Tenth Symphony." ML 66 (1985): 9–18.

765. Gülke, Peter. "Zur Bestimmung des Sinfonsichen bei Beethoven." DJM 15 (1970): 67–95.

766. LaRue, Jan. "Harmonic Rhythm in the Beethoven Symphonies." MR 18 (1957): 8–20.

767. Schulze, Werner. *Temporelationen in symphonischen Werk von Beethoven, Schubert und Brahms.* Bern: Kreis & Freude um Hans Kayser, 1981.

768. Steunenberg, Thomas B. "Rhythmic Continuity in Slow Movements from Beethoven's Symphonies." Ph.D. diss., University of Rochester, 1954.

Symphony No. 1, Op. 21

769. Hantz, Edwin. "A Pitch for Rhythm: Rhythmic Patterns in Beethoven's First Symphony: III (Minuetto)." ITO 1, no. 4 (1975–1976): 17–21.

770. Misch, Ludwig. "Der persönliche Stil in Beethovens erster Symphonie: Organismus und Idee des ersten Satzes." BJ 2 (1955–1956): 55–101.

771. Seidel, Wilhelm. *Ludwig van Beethoven: I. Symphonie C-Dur.* Munich: Fink, 1979.

Symphony No. 2, Op. 36

772. Hill, Cecil. "Early Versions of Beethoven's Second Symphony." MS 6 (1980): 90–110.

773. Marston, Nicholas. "Stylistic Advance, Strategic Retreat: Beethoven's Sketches for the Finale of the Second Symphony." BF 3 (1994): 127–50.

774. Pazur, Robert. "The Development of the Fourth Movement of Beethoven's Second Symphony Considered as a Variation of the Development of the First Movement." ITO 2, nos. 1–2 (1976): 3–4.

775. Westphal, Kurt. *Vom Einfall zur Symphonie: Einblick in Beethovens Schaffenweise.* Berlin: Gruyter, 1965.

Symphony No. 3, Op. 55 ("Eroica")

776. Antonicek, Theophil. "Humanitätssymbolik im *Eroica*-Finale." F-Schenk: 144–55.

777. Barry, Barbara R. "Pitch Interpretation and Cyclical Procedures in Middle-Period Beethoven." MQ 76, no. 2 (1992): 184–215.

778. Berry, Wallace. "Formal Process and Performance in the *Eroica* Introductions." MTS 10 (1988): 3–18. [Movements I, IV]

779. Cavett-Dunsby, Esther. "Schenker's Analysis of the *Eroica* Finale." TP 11 (1986): 43–51.

780. Degen, Helmut. "Der erste Satz der *Eroica.*" NZM 118 (1957): 156–59.

781. Downs, Philip G. "Beethoven's 'New Way' and the *Eroica.*" MQ 56 (1970): 585–604.

782. Engelsmann, Walther. "Beethovens Werkthematik: Dargestelle an der *Eroica.*" AM 5 (1940): 104–13.

783. Epstein, David. "Unity in Beethoven's *Eroica* Symphony (First Movement)." In *Beyond Orpheus: Studies in Musical Structure.* Cambridge: MIT Press, 1979.

784. Floros, Constantin. *Beethovens "Eroica" und "Prometheus" Musik: Subjekt-Studien.* Wilhelmshaven: Heinrichshofen, 1978.

785. Hauschild, Peter. "Melodische Tendenzen in Beethovens *Eroica.*" DJM 14 (1969): 41–75.

786. Hollander, Hans. "Zur Psychologie des Helden in Beethovens Eroica." NZM 128 (1967): 205–7.

787. Huber, Anna Gertrud. *Der Held der "Eroica": Beethovens Es Dur Symphonie in ihrem Aufbau.* Strassbourg: Heitz, 1947.

788. Lochhead, Judy. "Musical Reference: A Source of Meaning in the First Movement of the *Eroica.*" TP 5, no. 2 (1980): 32–39.

789. Lockwood, Lewis. "Beethoven's Earliest Sketches for the *Eroica* Symphony." MQ 67 (1981): 457–78.

790. Maruyama, Keisuke. "Die Sinfonie des Prometheus: Zur Dritten Sinfonie." In *Beethoven: Analecta varia*, ed. Heinz-Klaus Metzger and Rainer Riehn, 46–82. Munich: Text + Kritik, 1987.

791. Meikle, Robert B. "Thematic Transformation in the First Movement of Beethoven's *Eroica* Symphony." MR 32 (1971): 205–18.

792. Poirier, Alain. "Pour en revenir à Beethoven: La question fondamentale de l'intelligibilité de la forme." ANM 1 (1985): 40–43.

793. Ringer, Alexander L. "Clementi and the *Eroica.*" MQ 47 (1961): 454–68.

794. Schleuning, Peter. "Beethoven in alter Deutung: Der 'neue Weg' mit der 'Sinfonia eroica.'" AM 44, no. 3 (1987): 165–94.

795. Sheer, Miriam. "Patterns of Dynamic Organization in Beethoven's *Eroica* Symphony." JM 10, no. 4 (1992): 483–504.

796. Sipe, Thomas. *Beethoven: Eroica Symphony.* Cambridge: Cambridge University Press, 1998.

Symphony No. 4, Op. 60

797. Dahlhaus, Carl. *Ludwig van Beethoven: IV. Symphonie B-Dur.* Munich: Fink, 1979.

798. Feil, Arnold. "Zur Satztechnik in Beethovens vierter Sinfonie." AM 16 (1959): 391–99.

799. Hatch, Christopher. "Internal and External References in Beethoven's Fourth Symphony." CMS 24 (1984): 107–17.

800. Mayeda, Akio. "Zur Kernmotivik in den mittleren Symphonien Ludwig van Beethovens." F-Finscher: 432–45.

Symphony No. 5, Op. 67

801. Atlas, Raphael. "Enharmonic *Trompe-l'oreille*: Reprise and the Disguised Seam in Nineteenth-Century Music." ITO 10, no. 6 (1988): 15–36. [Movement I]

802. Bielitz, Matthias. "Zur Geschichte des Anfangsmotivs der 5. Symphonie von L. v. Beethoven als Geschichte der kompositorischen Verwendung eines Archetyps elementarer musikalischer Gestaltbildung." SZM 39 (1988): 275–312.

803. Canisius, Claus Heinrich. "Quellenstudien und satztechnische Untersuchungen zum dritten Satz aus Beethovens C-Moll-Sinfonie." Ph.D. diss., Ruprecht-Karl-Universität, Heidelberg, 1966.

804. Forbes, Elliot, ed. *Beethoven: Symphony No. 5 in C Minor.* Norton Critical Scores. New York: Norton, 1971.

805. Gülke, Peter. "Motive aus französischer Revolutionsmusik in Beethovens fünfter Sinfonie." MG 21 (1971): 636–41.

806. Jung-Kaiser, Ute. "Ein Bänkelsang als Vorlage? Zum idellen Programm der 'Fünften' von Ludwig van Beethoven." M 45, no. 1 (1991): 4–10. [Movement II]

807. Kerman, Joseph. "Taking the Fifth." F-Dahlhaus: 483–91.

808. Knapp, Raymond. "A Tale of Two Symphonies: Converging Narratives of Divine Reconciliation in Beethoven's Fifth and Sixth." JAMS 53, no. 2 (2000): 291–343.

809. Lockwood, Lewis. "On the Coda of the Finale of Beethoven's Fifth Symphony." F-Abs: 41–48.

810. Mayeda, Akio. "Zur Kernmotivik in den mittleren Symphonien Ludwig van Beethovens." F-Finscher: 432–45.

811. Messiaen, Olivier. "Entwicklung durch Verkürzung: Eine Rede über Beethoven." MTX 16 (1989): 24–25.

Symphony No. 6, Op. 68

812. Bockholdt, Rudolf. *Ludwig van Beethoven: VI. Symphonie F-Dur, Op.68, "Pastorale."* Munich: Fink, 1981.

813. Gossett, Philip. "Beethoven's Sixth Symphony: Sketches for the First Movement." JAMS 27 (1974): 248–84.

814. Kirby, F. E. "Beethoven's *Pastoral Symphony* as a *Sinfonia caracteristica.*" MQ 56 (1970): 605–23.

815. Knapp, Raymond. "A Tale of Two Symphonies: Converging Narratives of Divine Reconciliation in Beethoven's Fifth and Sixth." JAMS 53, no. 2 (2000): 291–343.

816. Mayeda, Akio. "Zur Kernmotivik in den mittleren Symphonien Ludwig van Beethovens." F-Finscher: 432–45.
817. M-Taruskin.
818. Ujfalussy, Joszef. "Dramatischer Bau und Philosophie in Beethovens VI. Symphonie." SM 11 (1969): 439–47. Reprint, F-Szabolcsi: 439–47.
819. Will, Richard. "Time, Morality, and Humanity in Beethoven's *Pastoral Symphony*." JAMS 50, nos. 2–3 (1997): 271–329.
820. Wyn Jones, David. *Beethoven: The Pastoral Symphony*. Cambridge: Cambridge University Press, 1995.

Symphony No. 7, Op. 92

821. Bässler, Hans, and Andreas Jung. "Beethoven: Scherzo aus der VII. Sinfonie; Theorie und Praxis." MB 14, no. 1 (1982): 27–30.
822. Below, Robert. "Some Aspects of Tonal Relationships in Beethoven's Seventh Symphony." MR 37 (1976): 1–4.
823. Carner, Mosco. "A Beethoven Movement and Its Successors." M-Carner: 9–20.
824. Gauldin, Robert. "Beethoven's Interrupted Tetrachord and the Seventh Symphony." INT 5 (1991): 77–100.
825. Gerstenberg, Walter. "Das Allegretto in Beethovens VII. Symphonie." F-Hüschen: 171–74.
826. Lespinard, Bernadette. "Ludwig van Beethoven: VIIe symphonie, op. 42." ANM 25 (1991): 5–17.
827. Levarie, Siegmund. "A Pitch Cell in Beethoven's Seventh Symphony." F-Brook: 181–93.
828. Osthoff, Wolfgang. "Zum Vorstellungsgehalt des Allegretto in Beethovens 7. Symphonie." AM 34 (1977): 159–79.
829. Richter, Christoph. "Beethovens Scherzo aus der VII. Sinfonie: Ein musikalisches Puzzle." MB 12 (1980): 595–602.
830. Silliman, A. Cutler. "Familiar Music and the a priori: Beethoven's Seventh Symphony." JMT 20 (1976): 215–26.
831. Temperley, Nicholas. "Schubert and Beethoven's Eight-Six Chord." NCM 5 (1981–1982): 142–54.
832. Winking, Hans. "Ludwig van Beethoven: Sinfonie Nr. 7 A-Dur Op. 92." NZM 144, nos. 7–8 (1983): 39–43.

Symphony No. 8, Op. 93

833. Dahlhaus, Carl. "Bermerkungen zu Beethovens 8. Symphonie." SZM 110 (1970): 205–9.
834. De la Motte, Diether. "Scherzando–für wen? Analyse des zweiten Satzes der 8. Sinfonie von Beethoven." M-Goldschmidt: 130–37.
835. Gauldin, Robert. "A Labyrinth of Fifths: The Last Movement of Beethoven's Eighth Symphony." ITR 1, no. 3 (1977–1978): 4–11.
836. Gülke, Peter. "Zum Allegretto der 8. Sinfonie." M-Goldschmidt: 106–12.
837. Holopov, Jurij. "Modulation und Formbildung: Zur Analyse des Allegretto scherzando aus der Sinfonie Nr. 8 F-Dur von Beethoven." M-Goldschmidt: 97–106.
838. Kaden, Christian. "Ludwig van Beethoven, Sinfonie Nr. 8 Op. 93, zweiter Satz Allegretto scherzando: Ansätze zu einer statistischen Strukturanalyse." M-Goldschmidt: 113–30.
839. Laaff, Ernst. "Der musikalische Humor in Beethovens achter Symphonie." AM 19–20 (1962–1963): 213–29.
840. Schneider, Frank. "Das Allegretto scherzando aus der 8. Sinfonie von Beethoven." M-Goldschmidt: 137–46.
841. ———. "Überlegungen zur VIII. Sinfonie." MG 27 (1977): 158–64.

Symphony No. 9, Op. 125

842. Cohn, Richard L. "The Dramatization of Hypermetric Conflicts in the Scherzo of Beethoven's Ninth Symphony." NCM 15, no. 3 (1992): 188–206.
843. Cook, Nicholas. *Beethoven: Symphony No. 9*. Cambridge: Cambridge University Press, 1993.
844. Eichhorn, Andreas. "Das 'Hauptthema' im ersten Satz von Beethovens Neunter Symphonie: Überlegungen zur Form und historischen Substanz." MF 49, no. 1 (1996): 2–19.
845. Friedheim, Philip. "On the Structural Integrity of Beethoven's Ninth Symphony." MR 46, no. 2 (1985): 93–117.
846. Kinderman, William. "Beethoven's Symbol for the Diety in the *Missa solemnis* and the Ninth Symphony." NCM 9, no. 2 (1985): 102–18.
847. Sanders, Ernest. "Form and Content in the Finale of Beethoven's Ninth Symphony." MQ 50 (1964): 59–76.
848. ———. "The Sonata-Form Finale of Beethoven's Ninth Symphony." NCM 22, no. 1 (1998): 54–60.
849. Schenker, Heinrich. *Beethoven's Ninth Symphony: A Portrayal of Its Musical Content with Running Commentary on Performance and Literature as Well*. Trans. and ed. John Rothgeb. New Haven, Conn.: Yale University Press, 1992. [Orig. German ed. published in 1912]
850. Soloman, Maynard. "Beethoven's Ninth Symphony: A Search for Order." NCM 10, no. 1 (1986): 3–23.
851. Steglich, Rudolf. "Motivischer Dualismus und thematische Einheit in Beethovens neunter Sinfonie." F-Besseler: 411–24.
852. Tusa, Michael C. "*Noch einmal*: Form and Content in the Finale of Beethoven's Ninth Symphony." BF 7 (1999): 113–37.
853. Webster, James. "The Form of the Finale of Beethoven's Ninth Symphony." BF 1 (1992): 25–62.
854. Winter, Robert. "The Sketches for the 'Ode to Joy.'" M-Winter: 176–214.

Variations and a Fugue on an Original Theme, Op. 35 ("Eroica Variations")

855. Derr, Ellwood. "Beethoven's Long-Term Memory of C. P. E. Bach's Rondo in E Flat, W.61/1 (1787), Manifest in the Variations in E-Flat for Piano, Opus 35 (1802)." MQ 70 (1984): 45–76.
856. Fischer, Kurt von. "*Eroica-Variationen* Op. 5 und Eroica-Finale." SMZ 89 (1949): 282–86.
857. Heinemann, Michael. "'Altes' und 'Neues' in Beethovens '*Eroica*'-*Variationen* Op. 35." AM 49, no. 1 (1992): 38–45.
858. Hering, Hans. "Beethovens Klaviervariationen Opus 35 und das Eroica-Finale." M 29 (1975): 304–6.
859. Huber, Anna Gertrud. *Beethoven-Studien*. Zurich: Hug, 1961.
860. Kunze, Stefan. "Die 'wirklich gantz neue Manier' in Beethovens *Eroica-Variationen* Op. 35." AM 29 (1972): 124–29.

Variations on a Waltz by Diabelli, Op. 120

861. Abraham, Lars Ulrich. "Trivialität und Persiflage in Beethovens *Diabellivariationen*." M-Abraham/L: 7–17.
862. Chazelle, Thierry. "Musique et littérature: Deux exemples d'alternative." ANM 4 (1986): 42–46.
863. Dahlhaus, Carl. "Zur Rhythmik in Beethovens *Diabelli Variationen*." *Veröffentlichungen des Institut für neue Musik und Musikerziehung, Darmstadt* 6 (1967): 18–22.
864. Geiringer, Karl. "The Structure of Beethoven's *Diabelli Variations*." MQ 50 (1964): 496–503.
865. Huber, Anna Gertrud. *Beethoven-Studien*. Zurich: Hug, 1961.
866. Kinderman, William. *Beethoven's Diabelli Variations*. Oxford: Oxford University Press, 1987.
867. ——. "Beethoven's *Variations on a Waltz by Diabelli*: Genesis and Structure." Ph.D. diss., University of California, Berkeley, 1980.
868. ——. "The Evolution and Structure of Beethoven's *Diabelli Variations*." JAMS 35 (1982): 306–28.
869. Munster, Arnold. *Studien zu Beethovens "Diabelli-Variationen."* Munich: Henle, 1982.
870. Porter, David H. "The Structure of Beethoven's *Diabelli Variations*, Op. 120." MR 31 (1970): 295–301.
871. ——. "The Structure of Beethoven's *Diabelli Variations*, Op. 120–Again." MR 52, no. 4 (1991): 294–98.
872. Schaeffer, Erwin. "Die *Diabelli-Variationen* von Beethoven." SMZ 107 (1967): 202–10.
873. Uhde, Jurgen. "Reflexionen zu Beethovens Op.120 (*33 Veränderungen über einen Walzer von A. Diabelli*)." ZM 7, no. 1 (1976): 30–53.
874. Weißgerber, Lydia. "Intervallsatz beim späten Beethoven: Zur 20. *Diabelli-Variation*." MTH 14, no. 2 (1999): 171–78.
875. Zenck, Martin. "Rezeption von Geschichte im Beethovens *Diabelli-Variation*: Zur Vermittlung analytischer, ästhetischer und historischer Kategorien." AM 37 (1980): 61–75.

Violin Concerto, Op. 61

876. Jander, Owen. "Romantic Form and Content in the Slow Movement of Beethoven's Violin Concerto." MQ 69 (1983): 159–79.
877. Kojima, Shin Augustinus. "Die Solovioline-Fassungen und -Varianten von Beethovens Violinkonzert Op. 61." BJ 8 (1971–1972): 97–145.
878. Mohr, Wilhelm. "Die Klavierfassung von Beethovens Violonkonzert." OMZ 27 (1972): 71–75.
879. Moser, Hans Joachim. "Die Form von Beethovens Violonkonzert." F-Moser: 198–205.
880. Scholz, Werner. "Zur Interpretation des Violinkonzertes von Beethoven." MG 12 (1962): 732–36.
881. Stowell, Robin. *Beethoven: Violin Concerto*. Cambridge: Cambridge University Press, 1998.

Violin Sonatas

882. Ahn, Suhnne. "Genre, Style, and Compositional Procedure in Beethoven's 'Kreutzer' Sonata, Opus 47." Ph.D. diss., Harvard University, 1997.
883. Eppstein, Hans. "Duo und Dialog: Zu einem Struktur- und Stilproblem der Kammermusik." MF 49, no. 3 (1996): 252–75.
884. Hatch, Christopher. "Thematic Interdependence in Two Finales by Beethoven." MR 45 (1984): 194–207. [Op. 23]
885. Hollander, Hans. "Tektonische Probleme in Beethovens *Kreutzer*-sonate." SMZ 115 (1975): 237–43. [Op. 47]
886. Kramer, Richard A. "The Sketches for Beethoven's Violin Sonatas, Opus 30: History, Transcription, Analysis." Ph.D. diss., Princeton University, 1974.
887. Schachter, Carl. "The Sketches for the Sonata for Piano and Violin, Op. 24." BF 3 (1994): 107–25.
888. Zeeuw, Anne Marie de. "Overall Structure and Design in a Variation Form." JMTP 1, no. 1 (1987): 39–56. [Op. 30, no. 1 (Movement III)]

Various Works

889. Arnold, Denis, and Nigel Fortune, eds. *The Beethoven Companion*. London: Faber & Faber, 1971.
890. Badura-Skoda, Paul. "Fehlende und Überzählige Takte bei Schubert und Beethoven." OMZ 33 (1978): 284–94.
891. Bartha, Dénes. "Drei Finale-Themen von Beethoven." F-Federhofer: 210–16.
892. Becker, Heinz. "Das modulierende Zwischenglied in der engeren Sonatenform: Beobachtungen an Beethovens Frühwerk." F-Dadelson: 20–32.

893. Becking, Gustav. "Studien zu Beethovens Personalstil: Das Scherzothema." F-Becking: 1–68.

894. Beling, Renate. "Der Marsch bei Beethoven." Ph.D. diss., Rhenische Friedrich Wilhelms-Universität, 1960.

895. Berry, Wallace. "Rhythmic Accelerations in Beethoven." JMT 22, no. 2 (1978): 177–240.

896. Blumröder, Christoph von. "Von Wandel musikalischer Aktualität: Anmerkungen zum Spätstil Beethovens." AM 40 (1983): 24–37.

897. BM 12 (1970). [Special issue]

898. Broyles, Michael E. "Rhythm, Metre, and Beethoven." MR 33 (1972): 300–22.

899. Bruce, I. M. "Calculated Unpredictability in Beethoven's Sonata-Designs." SN 1 (1970): 36–53.

900. Brusatti, Otto. "Die thematisch-melodische Einheit im Spätwerk Beethovens." MAU 2 (1979): 117–40.

901. Cahn, Peter. "Aspekte der Schlussgestaltung in Beethovens Instrumentalwerken." AM 39 (1982): 19–31.

902. M-Caplin.

903. M-Chailley.

904. Cole, Malcolm S. "Techniques of Surprise in the Sonata-Rondos of Beethoven." SM 12 (1970): 232–62.

905. Cooper, Martin. *Beethoven: The Last Decade.* Oxford: Oxford University Press, 1985.

906. Dürr, Walther. "Wer vermag nach Beethoven noch etwas zu machen? Gedanken über die Beziehungen Schuberts zu Beethoven." BJ 9 (1973–1977): 47–67.

907. Eibner, Franz. "Einige Kriterien für die Apperzeption und Interpretation von Beethovens Werk." BOGM (1976–1978): 20–36.

908. M-Epstein.

909. Eversole, James Atlee. "A Study of Orchestrational Style through the Analysis of Representative Works of Mozart and Beethoven." Ed.D. diss., Columbia University, 1966.

910. Fischer, Kurt von. *Die Beziehungen von Form und Motiv in Beethovens Instrumentalwerke.* 2d augmented ed. Baden-Baden: Korner, 1972.

911. Garner, Chet H. "Principles of Periodic Structure in the Instrumental Works of Haydn, Mozart, and Beethoven." Ph.D. diss., University of Iowa, 1977.

912. Goldschmidt, Harry. *Beethoven-Studien.* Leipzig: Deutscher Verlag für Musik, 1974.

913. ———. "Zitat oder Parodie?" BM 12 (1970): 171–98.

914. Greene, David B. *Temporal Processes in Beethoven's Music.* New York: Gordon & Breach, 1981.

915. Gülke, Peter. "Kantabilität und thematische Abhandlung." BM 12 (1970): 252–73.

916. Hess, Willy. *Beethoven-Studien.* Bonn: Beethoven-Haus, 1972.

917. Kolisch, Rudolf. "Tempo and Character in Beethoven's Music." MQ 29 (1943): 169–87, 291–312.

918. Kopferman, Michael. *Beiträge zur musikalischen Analyse später Werke Ludwig van Beethovens.* Munich: Katzbichler, 1975.

919. Kropfinger, Klaus. "Zur thematischen Funktion der langsamen Einleitung bei Beethoven." F-Schmidt-Görg/70: 197–216.

920. Lang, Paul Henry, ed. *The Creative World of Beethoven.* New York: Norton, 1971. [Reprinted from MQ 56 (1970)]

921. Liebermann, Ira. "Some Representative Works from Beethoven's Early Period Analyzed in Light of the Theories of Ernst Kurt and Kurt von Fischer." Ph.D. diss., Columbia University, 1968.

922. Linde, Bernard S. van der. "Die Versunkenheitsepisode bei Beethoven." BJ 9 (1973–1977): 319–37.

923. Lippman, Edward A. "The Formation of Beethoven's Early Style." F-Lang: 102–16.

924. Lubin, Steven. "Techniques for the Analysis of Development in Middle Period Beethoven." Ph.D. diss., New York University, 1974.

925. Luxner, Michael David. "The Evolution of the Minuet/Scherzo in the Music of Beethoven." Ph.D. diss., University of Rochester, 1978.

926. Mahaim, Ivan. *Beethoven.* Paris: Desclée de Brouwer, 1964.

927. Mainka, Jürgen. "Das Weltbild des jungen Beethoven." BM 12 (1970): 199–251.

928. Mies, Paul. "Die Bedeutung der Pauke in den Werken Ludwig van Beethovens." BJ 8 (1971–1972): 49–71.

929. ———. "Friedrich Silchers Liederarbeitungen Beethovenscher Melodien." BJ 3 (1957–1958): 111–26.

930. ———. "Ludwig van Beethovens Werke über seinen Kontretanz in Es-Dur." BJ 1 (1953–1954): 80–102.

931. ———. "Sehnsucht von Goethe und Beethoven." BJ 2 (1955–1956): 112–19.

932. Miller, Hugh. "Beethoven's Rhythm: Some Observations and Problems." F-Apel: 165–74.

933. Misch, Ludwig. *Beethoven Studies.* Trans. G. I. C. De Courey. Norman: University of Oklahoma Press, 1953.

934. ———. *Neue Beethoven-Studien und andere Themen.* Munich: Henle, 1967.

935. ———. "Wiedergeburt aus dem Geist der Sonate: Fuge und Fugato in Beethovens Variationsform." NZM 119 (1958): 75–81.

936. Newman, William S. "Tempo in Beethoven's Instrumental Music: Its Choice and Its Flexibility." PQ 116 (1981–1982): 22–29; 117 (1981–1982): 22–31.
937. Preston, Sandra Elaine. "An Investigation of Beethoven's Use of Tonality." Ph.D. diss., Sheffield University, 1975.
938. Ratner, Leonard G. "Key Definition: A Structural Idea in Beethoven's Music." JAMS 23 (1970): 472–83.
939. Ratz, Erwin. "Analyse und Hermeneutik in ihrer Bedeutung für die Interpretation Beethovens." OMZ 25 (1970): 756–66. English trans. Mary Whittall in MA 3, no. 3 (1984): 243–54.
940. ———. *Einführung in der musikalische Formenlehre: Über Formprinzipien in den Inventionen J. S. Bachs und ihre Bedeutung für die Kompositionstechnik Beethovens.* Vienna: Österreichischer Bundesverlag für Unterricht, Wissenschaft & Kunst, 1951.
941. Rienäcker, Gerd. "Zum Problem des attacca in Instrumentalwerken Ludwig van Beethovens." BM 18 (1976): 39–68.
942. Rosen, Charles. *The Classical Style: Haydn, Mozart, Beethoven.* Expanded ed. New York: Norton, 1997.
943. Rummenhöller, Peter. "Beethovens 'Nebengedanken': Zur Hierarchie thematischer Gestalten in Beethovens Sonatenformen." M 50, no. 6 (1996): 397–405.
944. Samarotto, Frank Paul. "A Theory of Temporal Plasticity in Tonal Music: An Extension of the Schenkerian Approach to Rhythm with Special Reference to Beethoven's Late Music." Ph.D. diss., City University of New York, 1999.
945. Schenkman, Walter. "The Tyranny of the Formula in Beethoven." CMS 18 (1978): 158–74.
946. Schneider, Norbert J. "Mediantische Harmonik bei Ludwig van Beethoven." AM 35 (1978): 210–30.
947. Schwager, Myron. "A Fresh Look at Beethoven's Arrangements." ML 54 (1973): 142–60.
948. ———. "Some Observations on Beethoven as an Arranger." MQ 60 (1974): 89–93.
949. Sheer, Miriam. "Dynamics in Beethoven's Late Instrumental Works: A New Profile." JM 16, no. 3 (1998): 358–78.
950. Sisman, Elaine R. "Tradition and Transformation in the Alternating Variations of Haydn and Beethoven." ACTA 62, nos. 2–3 (1990): 152–82.
951. Souchay, Marc-André. "Zur Sonate Beethovens." F-Abert/H: 133–53.
952. Stanley, Glenn, ed. *The Cambridge Companion to Beethoven.* Cambridge: Cambridge University Press, 2000.
953. Steglich, Rudolf. "Über Beethovens Märsche." F-Orel: 187–95.
954. Steinbeck, Wolfram. "Ein wahres Spiel mit musikalischen Forme Zum Scherzo Ludwig Beethovens." AM 38 (1981): 194–226.
955. Thym, Jürgen. "The Instrumental Recitative in Beethoven's Compositions." F-Fox: 230–40.
956. Tyson, Alan. *Beethoven Studies.* New York: Norton, 1973.
957. Wagner, Günther. "Motivgruppierung in der Expositionsgestaltung bei C. Ph. E. Bach und Beethoven: Zur Kompositionsgeschichtlichen Kontinuität im 18. Jahrhundert." JSIM (1978): 43–71.
958. Warch, Willard F. "A Study of the Modulation Technique of Beethoven." Ph.D. diss., University of Rochester, 1955.
959. Wiesel, Henry Meir. "Thematic Unity in Beethoven's Sonata Works of the Period 1796–1802." Ph.D. diss., City University of New York, 1976.
960. Zickenheiner, Otto. "Zur kontrapunktischen Satztechnik in späten Werken Beethovens." BJ 9 (1973–1977): 553–69.

BELCHER, SUPPLY (1751–1836)
961. Owen, Earl M., Jr. "The Life and Music of Supply Belcher (1751–1836), 'Handel of Maine.'" D.M.A. diss., Southern Baptist Theological Seminary, 1969.

BELLINI, VINCENZO (1801–1835)
962. ASO 29 (1980). [*Norma*]
963. ASO 96 (1987). [*I puritani*]
964. ASO 122 (1989). [*I Capuleti e i Montecchi*]
965. ASO 178 (1997). [*La sonnambula*]
966. Kimbell, David. *Vincenzo Bellini: Norma.* Cambridge: Cambridge University Press, 1998.
967. Lippmann, Friedrich. "Donizetti und Bellini: Ein Beitrag zur Interpretation von Donizettis Stil." STU 4 (1975): 193–243.
968. ———. *Vincenzo Bellini und die italienische Opera seria seiner Zeit: Studien über Libretto, Arienform, und Melodik.* Cologne: Böhlau, 1969.
969. Weinstock, Herbert. *Vincenzo Bellini: His Life and Operas.* New York: Knopf, 1971.

BENDER, JAN (1909–1994)
970. Herman, H. David. "Jan Bender and His Organ Music." D.M.A. diss., University of Kansas, 1974.

BENJAMIN, ARTHUR (1893–1960)
971. Keller, Hans. "Arthur Benjamin and the Problem of Popularity." TEMPO 15 (1950): 4–15.
972. Seiber, Mátyás. "Arthur Benjamin: Symphony, An analysis." TEMPO 32 (1954): 9–12.

BENJAMIN, GEORGE (b. 1960)

973. Nieminen, Risto, ed. *George Benjamin.* Paris: IRCAM, 1996. English edition, London: Faber and Faber, 1997.

BENNETT, RICHARD RODNEY (b. 1936)

974. Marston, Marlene G. "The Serial Keyboard Music of Richard Rodney Bennett." Ph.D. diss., University of Wisconsin, 1968.

BENOLIEL, BERNARD (b. 1943)

975. MacDonald, Calum. "An American in Albion: The Music of Bernard Benoliel." TEMPO 142 (1982): 20–30.

BENSON, WARREN (b. 1924)

976. Ferguson, Thomas. "A Theoretical Analysis of Symphony for Drums and Wind Orchestra by Warren Benson." JBR 10, no. 1 (1974): 9–22.

977. Harbinson, William G. "*The Passing Bell* of Warren Benson." JBR 21, no. 2 (1986): 1–8.

BENTZON, NIELS VIGGO (1919–2000)

978. Krarup, Bertel. "En klaverstil folder sig ud: Niels Viggo Bentzons klaviermusik i 1940'erne og 1950'erne." DAM 27 (1999): 45–64.

BERG, ALBAN (1885–1935)

Altenberg Lieder. See Orchesterlieder nach Ansichtkartentexten von Peter Altenberg

Frühe Lieder

979. Eberle, Gottfried. "Alban Berg: *Sieben frühe Lieder.*" NZM 146, no. 2 (1985): 23–26.

Kammerkonzert

980. Brauneiss, Leopold. "Überlegungen zur Rhythmic im Kammerkonzert Alban Bergs." OMZ 41, no. 11 (1986): 553–59.

981. Congdon, David. "Composition in Berg's Kammerkonzert." PNM 24, no. 1 (1985): 234–69.

982. Floros, Constantin. "Das verschwiegene Programm des Kammerkonzerts von Alban Berg: Eine semantische Analyse." NZM 148, no. 11 (1987): 11–22.

983. Hilmar, Rosemary. "Metrische Proportionen und serielle Rhythmik im Kammerkonzert von Alban Berg." SMZ 120 (1980): 355–60.

984. Lambert, J. Philip. "Berg's Path to Twelve-Note Composition: Aggregate Construction and Association in the Chamber Concerto." MA 12, no. 3 (1993): 321–42.

985. Pinkas, Sally. "A Rhythmic and Metric Analysis of the Rondo Ritmico, the Third Movement of the Chamber Concerto by Alban Berg." Ph.D. diss., Brandeis University, 1991.

986. Votta, Michael, Jr. "Pitch Structures and Extra-Musical References in Alban Berg's Kammerkonzert." JBR 26, no. 2 (1991): 1–32.

Lieder (various; *see also* specific Lieder and song cycles)

987. Adorno, Theodor W. "Die Instrumentation von Bergs frühen Lieder." In *Klangfiguren-Musikalischen Schriften,*vol. 1, 138–56. Berlin: Suhrkamp, 1959.

988. M-Broekema.

989. Chadwick, Nicholas. "Berg's Unpublished Songs in the Österreichische Nationalbibliothek." ML 52 (1971): 123–30.

990. Dopheide, Bernhard. "Zum frühen Liedschaffen Alban Bergs." MF 43, no. 3 (1990): 222–44.

991. Pittman, Elmer Everett. "Harmony in the Songs of Alban Berg." Ph.D. diss., Florida State University, 1966.

992. Venus, Dankmar. *Vergleichende Untersuchung zur melodischen Struktur der Singstimmen in den Liedern von Arnold Schönberg, Alban Berg, Anton Webern, und Paul Hindemith.* Göttingen, 1965.

993. Wilkey, Jay W. "Certain Aspects of Form in the Vocal Music of Alban Berg." Ph.D. diss., Indiana University, 1965.

Lieder, Op. 2

994. Ayrey, Craig. "Berg's *Scheideweg*: Analytical Issues in Op. 2/ii." MA 1 (1982): 189–202.

995. ———. "Berg's 'Warm die Lüfte' and PC Set Genera: A Preliminary Reading." MA 17, no. 2 (1998): 163–76.

996. Breivik, Magnar. "The Representation of Sleep and Death in Berg's 'Piano Songs,' op. 2." M-Bruhn: 109–35.

997. Doerksen, John F. "Set-Class Salience and Forte's Theory of Genera." MA 17, no. 2 (1998): 195–205. [No. 4]

998. Gauldin, Robert. "Reference and Association in the Vier Lieder Op. 2 of Alban Berg." MTS 21, no. 1 (1999): 32–42.

999. Jarman, Douglas. "Alban Berg: The Origins of a Method." MA 6, no. 3 (1987): 273–88. [No. 2]

1000. Kennett, Chris. "Take Me Out to the Analysis Conference: Sets, Stats, Sport, and Competence." MA 17, no. 2 (1988): 182–94. [No. 4]

1001. Metz, Paul W. "Set Theory, Clock Diagrams, and Berg's Op. 2, No. 2." ITO 12, nos. 1–2 (1991): 1–17.

1002. Parks, Richard S. "Pitch-Class Set Genera: My Theory, Forte's Theory." MA 17, no. 2 (1998): 206–26. [No. 4]

1003. Simms, Bryan R. "Alban Berg's Four Songs, Op. 2: A Tribute to Schoenberg." F-Palisca: 487–501.

1004. M-Straus: 84–88. [No. 2]

1005. Tucker, Gary Richard. "Tonality and Atonality in Alban Berg's Four Songs, Op. 2." Ph.D. diss., University of Western Ontario, 1995.

1006. Wennerstrom, Mary H. "Pitch Relationships in Berg's Songs, Op. 2." ITR 1, no. 1 (1977–1978): 12–22.

1007. Witzenmann, Wolfgang. "'Text von Theodor Storm': Zu den Klavierliedern Alban Bergs." MF 41, no. 2 (1988): 127–41.

Lulu

1008. ASO 181–182 (1998).

1009. Baragwanath, Nicholas. "Alban Berg, Richard Wagner, and Leitmotivs of Symmetry." NCM 23, no. 1 (1999): 62–83.

1010. Bitter, Christof. "Notizen zu Mozarts *Don Giovanni* und Bergs *Lulu.*" F-Strecker: 123–24.

1011. Boulez, Pierre. "*Lulu*: Le second opéra." M-Boulez: 307–25.

1012. DeVoto, Mark. "The Death Leitmotif in *Wozzeck* and *Lulu.*" M-Bruhn: 243–48.

1013. Eitan, Zohar. "Peaks in Berg: Romantic Gesture in a New Context." M-Eitan: Chap. 5. [Acts I–II]

1014. Ertelt, Thomas F. "'Hereinspaziert . . .': Ein früher Entwurf des Prologs zu Alban Bergs *Lulu.*" OMZ 41 (1986): 15–25.

1015. Foldi, Andrew. "The Enigma of Schigolch: A Character Analysis." IABS 9 (1980): 4–7.

1016. Fuß, Hans-Ulrich. *Musikalisch-dramatische Prozesse in den Opern Alban Bergs.* Hamburg: Verlag der Musikalienhandlung K. D. Wagner, 1991.

1017. Headlam, Dave. "The Derivation of Rows in *Lulu.*" PNM 24, no. 1 (1985): 198–233.

1018. Hirsbrunner, Theo. "Vom Tristan-Akkord zu den Zwölftonakkorden Alban Bergs." DI 43 (1995): 16–21.

1019. Jarman, Douglas. *Alban Berg: Lulu.* Cambridge: Cambridge University Press, 1991.

1020. ———. "Alban Berg: The Origins of a Method." MA 6, no. 3 (1987): 273–88.

1021. ———. "Berg's Surrealist Opera." MR 31 (1970): 232–40.

1022. ———. "Dr. Schön's Five-Strophe Aria: Some Notes on Tonality and Pitch Association in Berg's *Lulu.*" PNM 8, no. 2 (1970): 23–48.

1023. ———. "*Lulu*: The Sketches." IABS 6 (1978): 4–8.

1024. ———. "Some Rhythmic and Metric Techniques in Alban Berg's *Lulu.*" MQ 56 (1970): 349–66.

1025. M-Leibowitz: 177–85.

1026. Massow, Albrecht von. *Halbwelt, Kultur, und Natur in Alban Bergs "Lulu."* Stuttgart: Steiner, 1992.

1027. Neumann, Karl. "Wedekind's and Berg's *Lulu.*" MR 35 (1974): 47–57.

1028. Perle, George. "The Film Interlude of *Lulu.*" IABS 11 (1982): 3–8.

1029. ———. "Das Film-Zwischenspiel in Bergs Opera *Lulu.*" OMZ 36 (1981): 631–38.

1030. ———. "Inhaltliche und formale Strukturen in Alban Bergs Oper *Lulu.*" OMZ 32 (1977): 427–41.

1031. ———. "An Introduction to *Lulu.*" OQ 3 (1985): 87–111.

1032. ———. "*Lulu*: The Formal Design." JAMS 17 (1964): 179–92.

1033. ———. "*Lulu*: Thematic Materials and Pitch Organization." MR 26 (1965): 269–302.

1034. ———. "The Music of *Lulu*: A New Analysis." JAMS 12 (1959): 185–200. [Corrections in JAMS 14 (1961): 96]

1035. ———. *The Operas of Alban Berg.* Vol. 2: *Lulu.* Berkeley: University of California Press, 1985.

1036. ———. "Die Personen in Berg's *Lulu.*" AM 24 (1967): 283–90.

1037. ———. "Some Thoughts on an Ideal Production of *Lulu.*" JM 7, no. 2 (1989): 244–53.

1038. ———. "Der Tod der Beschwitz." OMZ 36 (1982): 19–28.

1039. ———. "The Tone-Row as Symbol in Berg's *Lulu.*" F-Herz: 309–18.

1040. Pople, Anthony. "Serial and Tonal Aspects of Pitch Structure in Act III of Berg's *Lulu.*" SN 10 (1983): 36–57.

1041. Reich, Willi. "Alban Berg's *Lulu.*" MQ 22 (1936): 383–401.

1042. ———. "*Lulu*: The Text and Music." MM 12 (1935): 103–11.

1043. Reiter, Manfred. *Die Zwölftontechnik in Alban Bergs Oper "Lulu."* Regensburg: Bosse, 1973.

1044. M-Rognoni: 165–87.

1045. Scherliess, Volker. "Alban Bergs analytische Tafeln zur *Lulu*-Reihe." MF 30 (1977): 452–64.

1046. Stephan, Rudolf. "Zur Sprachmelodie in Alban Bergs *Lulu*-Musik." M-Schnitzler/D: 246–64.

Lulu Suite. See Symphonische Stücke aus der Oper "Lulu"

Lyrische Suite

1047. Ashby, Arved. "The Development of Berg's Twelve-Tone Aesthetic as Seen in the *Lyric Suite* and Its Sources." Ph.D. diss., Yale University, 1995.

1048. Berg, Alban. "Berg's Notes for the *Lyric Suite*." IABS 2 (1971): 5–7.

1049. Blankenship, Shirley Meyer. "Berg: Lines, Opus 3, *Lyrische Suite*." D.M.A. diss., University of Illinois, 1977.

1050. Bouquet, Fritz. "Alban Berg's *Lyrische Suite*: Eine Studie über Gestalt, Klang, und Ausdruck." MELOS 15 (1948): 227–31.

1051. Brindle, Reginald Smith. "The Symbolism in Berg's *Lyric Suite*." SCORE 21 (1957): 60–63.

1052. Budday, Wolfgang. *Alban Bergs "Lyrische Suite."* Neuhausen-Stuttgart: Hänssler, 1979.

1053. Eitan, Zohar. "Peaks in Berg: Romantic Gesture in a New Context." M-Eitan: Chap. 5.

1054. Floros, Constantin. "Das esoterische Programm der *Lyrischen Suite* von Alban Berg: Eine semantische Analyse." HJM 1 (1974): 101–45.

1055. Green, Douglass. "The Allegro Misterioso of Berg's *Lyric Suite*: Iso- and Retrorhythms." JAMS 30 (1977): 507–16.

1056. ———. "Berg's 'De Profundis': The Finale of the *Lyric Suite*." JABS 5 (1977): 13–23.

1057. ———. "Das Largo Desolato der *Lyrischen Suite* von Alban Berg." OMZ 33 (1978): 79–85.

1058. Parish, George D. "Motive and Cellular Structure in Alban Berg's *Lyric Suite*." Ph.D. diss., University of Michigan, 1970.

1059. Perle, George. "Das geheime Programm der *Lyrischen Suite*." OMZ 33 (1978): 64–79, 113–19.

1060. ———. "The Secret Program of the *Lyric Suite*." IABS 5 (1977): 4–12.

1061. M-Perle: 72–77.

1062. Straus, Joseph N. "Tristan and Berg's *Lyric Suite*." ITO 8, no. 3 (1983–1984): 33–41.

Orchesterlieder nach Ansichtkartentexten von Peter Altenberg, Op. 4

1063. Ashby, Arved. "Singing the Aphoristic Text: Berg's *Altenberg-Lieder*." M-Bruhn: 191–226.

1064. Bruhn, Siglind. "Symbolism and Self-Quotation in Berg's *Picture Postcard Songs*." M-Bruhn: 157–90.

1065. Chadwick, Nicholas. "Thematic Integration in Berg's *Altenberg Songs*." MR 29 (1968): 300–4.

1066. Danuser, Hermann. "Zu den *Altenberg-Liedern* von Alban Berg." MB 17, no. 12 (1985): 837–45.

1067. DeVoto, Mark. "Alban Berg's Picture Postcard Songs." Ph.D. diss., Princeton University, 1966.

1068. ———. "Alban Berg's Picture Postcard Songs." EMM 1, no. 2 (1984): 11–19.

1069. Jarman, Douglas. "Alban Berg: The Origins of a Method." MA 6, no. 3 (1987): 273–88.

1070. Leibowitz, René. "Alban Berg's Five Orchestral Songs." MQ 34 (1948): 487–511.

1071. Mayer-Rosa, Eugen. "Alban Bergs *Altenberg-Lieder* im Unterricht." MB 4 (1972): 123–28.

1072. Redlich, Hans. "Alban Berg's *Altenberg Songs*, Op 4." MR 31 (1970): 43–53.

1073. Ringger, Rolf Urs. "Zur formbildener Kraft des vertonten Wortes: Analytische Untersuchungen an Liedern von Hugo Wolf und Alban Berg." SMZ 99 (1959): 225–29.

1074. Stenzl, Jürg. "Franz Schreker und Alban Berg: Bemerkungen zu den Altenberg-Liedern Op. 4." M-Schreker: 44–58.

1075. Stroh, Wolfgang Martin. "Alban Bergs Orchesterlieder." NZM 130 (1969): 89–94.

Piano Sonata, Op. 1

1076. Estero, Andrea. "Nuove gerarchie strutturali nella 'fase di transizione': La Sonata per pianoforte di Alban Berg." ANL 29 (1999): 6–17.

Schliesse mir die Augen beide (1925)

1077. Dopheide, Bernhard. "Zu Alban Bergs Zweitvertonung von Theodor Storms Gedicht 'Schließe mir die Augen beide.'" MTH 7, no. 1 (1992): 33–46.

1078. Smith, Joan Allen. "Some Sources for Berg's *Schliesse mir bei die Augen beide* II." IABS 6 (1978): 9–13.

1079. Witzenmann, Wolfgang. "'Text von Theodor Storm': Zu den Klavierliedern Alban Bergs." MF 41, no. 2 (1988): 127–41.

String Quartet, Op. 3

1080. Krämer, Ulrich. "Quotation and Self-Borrowing in the Music of Alban Berg." JMR 12, nos. 1–2 (1992): 53–82.

1081. Porter, Charles. "Interval Cycles in Alban Berg's String Quartet Opus 3." TP 14–15 (1989–1990): 139–77.

1082. Rockmaker, Jody Darien. "Articulating Form in Alban Berg's String Quartet, Opus 3: An Analysis of the First Movement and the Sketches." Ph.D. diss., Princeton University, 1989.

Stücke, Op. 5 (Clarinet and Piano)

1083. Borris, Siegfried. "Vergleichende Stilanalyse: Alban Berg–Paul Hindemith." M-Benary: 35–47. [No. 1]

1084. ———. "Vergleichende Werkanalyse: Alban Berg, Op. 5 Nr. 1; Paul Hindemith, Aus der Violinsonate 1939." MB 5 (1973): 138–41.

1085. Fisher, George, and Judy Lochhead. "Analysis, Hearing, and Performance." ITR 14, no. 1 (1993): 1–36. [Nos. 1–2]

1086. De Fotis, William. "Berg's Op. 5: Rehearsal Instructions." PNM 17, no. 1 (1978–1979): 131–37.

1087. M-De la Motte: 131–45. [No. 1]

1088. Eitan, Zohar. "Peaks in Berg: Romantic Gesture in a New Context." M-Eitan: Chap. 5.

1089. Jarman, Douglas. "Alban Berg: The Origins of a Method." MA 6, no. 3 (1987): 273–88. [No. 1]

1090. M-Leibowitz: 150–52.

1091. Lewis, Christopher. "Tonal Focus in Atonal Music: Berg's Op.5/3." MTS 3 (1981): 84–97.

1092. Perone, James. "Tonal Implications and the Role of the Symmetrical Hexachord in Alban Berg's Four Pieces for Clarinet and Piano, Opus 5, No. 2." I 16, nos. 1–2 (1987): 49–54.

1093. Schatt, Peter W. "Zahl, Symbolik und Kryptogrammatik in Alban Bergs Vier Stücken für Klarinette und Klavier." AM 43, no. 2 (1986): 128–35.

Stücke, Op. 6 (Orchestra)

1094. Archibald, Bruce. "The Harmony of Berg's 'Reigen.'" PNM 6, no. 2 (1968): 73–91.

1095. DeVoto, Mark. "Alban Berg's 'Marche Macabre.'" PNM 22 (1983–1984): 386–447.

1096. Falck, Robert. "Two 'Reigen': Berg, Schnitzler, and Cyclic Form." M-Bruhn: 91–105.

1097. Jameux, Dominque. "Interminable analyse: Études atonales III; La première pièce de l'opus 6 de Berg: Präludium." MJ 19 (1975): 49–70; 20 (1975): 33–41.

1098. Micznik, Vera. "Gesture as Sign: A Semiotic Interpretation of Berg's Op. 6, No. 1." ITO 9, no. 4 (1986): 19–35.

1099. Rost, Cornelia. "Alban Berg: Drei Orchesterstücke Op. 6." NZM 143, no. 12 (1982): 37–40.

Symphonische Stücke aus der Oper "Lulu" (Lulu-Suite)

1100. Headlam, David. "The Musical Language of the 'Symphonic Pieces' from *Lulu*." Ph.D. diss., University of Michigan, 1985.

Violin Concerto

1101. Barcaba, Peter. "Zur Tonalität in Alban Bergs Violinkonzert." M 32 (1978–1979): 158–64.

1102. Delaigue, Olivier. "Le requiem d'Alban Berg: Quelques éléments pour l'analyse du 'Concerto à la mémoire d'un ange.'" ANM 18 (1990): 54–60.

1103. Floros, Constantin. "Alban Berg 'Requiem': Das verschwiegene Programm des Violinkonzerts." NZM 146, no. 4 (1985): 4–8.

1104. Forneberg, Erich. "Der Bach-Choral in Alban Bergs Violinkonzert." MELOS 23 (1956): 247–49.

1105. Fuhrmann, Roderich. "Alban Berg (1885–1935): Violinkonzert (1935)." M-Zimmerschied: 73–109.

1106. M-Hall.

1107. Headlam, Dave. "Sketch Study and Analysis: Berg's Twelve-Tone Music." CMS 3334 (1993–1994): 155–71.

1108. Jarman, Douglas. "Alban Berg, Wilhelm Fliess, and the Secret Programme of the Violin Concerto." IABS 12 (1982): 5–11.

1109. ———. "Alban Berg, Wilhelm Fliess und das geheime Programm des Violinkonzerts." OMZ 40 (1985): 12–21.

1110. Knaus, Herwig. "Die Kärntner Volksweise aus Alban Bergs Violinkonzert." ME 23 (1970): 117–18.

1111. ———. "Die Reihenskizzen zu Alban Bergs Violinkonzert." OMZ 37 (1982): 105–8.

1112. ———. "Studien zu Alban Bergs Violinkonzert." F-Schenk: 255–74.

1113. Krämer, Ulrich. "Quotation and Self-Borrowing in the Music of Alban Berg." JMR 12, nos. 1–2 (1992): 53–82.

1114. M-Leibowitz: 162–67.

1115. M-Little.

1116. Pople, Anthony. *Berg: Violin Concerto.* Cambridge: Cambridge University Press, 1991.

1117. Redlich, Hans. "Alban Bergs Violinkonzert." MELOS 24 (1957): 316–21, 352–57.

1118. Schneider, Frank. "Alban Bergs Violinkonzert: Metaphern zu einer transzendierenden Musik." BM 18 (1976): 219–33.

1119. Schreffler, Theodore Wilson, III. "An Analysis of the Violin Concerto (1935) by Alban Berg." Ph.D. diss., University of California, Los Angeles, 1979.

1120. Stephan, Rudolf. *Alban Berg: Violinkonzert (1935).* Munich: Fink, 1988.

Wein

1121. Eitan, Zohar. "Peaks in Berg: Romantic Gesture in a New Context." M-Eitan: Chap. 5.

1122. Headlam, David. "Row Derivation and Contour Association in Berg's *Der Wein*." PNM 28, no. 1 (1990): 256–92.

1123. Jarman, Douglas. "Some Row Techniques in Alban Berg's *Der Wein*." SN 2 (1971–1972): 46–56.

1124. Knaus, Herwig. "Alban Bergs Skizzen und Vorarbeiten zur Konzartarie *Der Wein*." F-Wessely: 355–80. Reprint, M 38 (1984–1985): 194–204.

Wozzeck, Op. 7

1125. ASO 35 (1981).

1126. Berg, Alban. "Conférence sur *Wozzeck* (1929)." MJ 14 (1974): 77–94.

1127. Bruhn, Siglind. *Die musikalische Darstellung psychologischer Wirklichkeit in Alban Bergs "Wozzeck."* Frankfurt am Main: Lang, 1986.
1128. Chittum, Donald. "The Triple Fugue in Berg's *Wozzeck.*" MR 28 (1967): 52–62.
1129. DeVoto, Mark. "The Death Leitmotif in *Wozzeck* and *Lulu.*" M-Bruhn: 243–48.
1130. Forneberg, Erich. *"Wozzeck" von Alban Berg.* Berlin: Lienau, 1963.
1131. Fritz, Rebecca. *Text and Music in German Operas of the 1920s.* Frankfurt am Main: Lang, 1998.
1132. Fuß, Hans Ulrich. "'Die Brücken zur Vergangenheit sind schmale und zerbrechliche Stege': Spätromantische Elemente in der Harmonik von Alban Bergs *Wozzeck.*" HJM 17 (2000): 57–74.
1133. ———. *Musikalisch-dramatische Prozesse in den Opern Alban Bergs.* Hamburg: Verlag der Musikalienhandlung K. D. Wagner, 1991.
1134. Gervasoni, Pierre. "*Wozzeck*: Une gestion symboliste de drame." ANM 27 (1992): 54–58.
1135. Hirsbrunner, Theo. "Tonale Fixpunkte in Alban Bergs *Wozzeck.*" MTH 13, no. 1 (1998): 43–53.
1136. ———. "Vom Tristan-Akkord zu den Zwölftonakkorden Alban Bergs." DI 43 (1995): 16–21.
1137. Hyde, Martha MacLean. "George Perle: *The Operas of Alban Berg*, Vol. I: '*Wozzeck.*'" JAMS 34 (1981): 573–87. [Review of 1153]
1138. Jarman, Douglas. *Alban Berg: Wozzeck.* Cambridge: Cambridge University Press, 1989.
1139. Jouve, Pierre, and Michel Fano. *"Wozzeck" d'Alban Berg.* Paris: Union Générale, 1964.
1140. ———. "*Woozeck* d'Alban Berg (acte III, scène IV)." RM 212 (1952): 87–98.
1141. Klein, Rudolf. "Zur Frage der Tonalität in Alban Bergs Oper *Wozzeck.*" M-Wozzeck: 32–45.
1142. König, Werner. *Tonalitätstructkturen in Alban Bergs Oper "Wozzeck."* Tutzing: Schneider, 1974.
1143. Krämer, Ulrich. "Die Suite als Charakterstudie des Hauptmanns in Alban Bergs *Wozzeck.*" HJM 10 (1988): 47–75.
1144. ———. "Quotation and Self-Borrowing in the Music of Alban Berg." JMR 12, nos. 1–2 (1992): 53–82.
1145. Lederer, Josef Horst. "Zu Alban Berg's Invention über den Ton H." M-Wozzeck: 57–67.
1146. M-Leibowitz: 171–77.
1147. Mahler, Fritz. *Zu Alban Bergs Oper "Wozzeck": Szenische und musikalische Übersicht.* Vienna: Universal, 1957. Translated under the title *Concerning Alban Berg's Opera "Wozzeck": Scenic and Musical Analysis* (Vienna: Universal, 1965).
1148. Mauser, Siegfried. *Das expressionistische Musiktheater der Wiener Schule: Stilistische und entwicklungsgeschichtliche Untersuchungenen zu Arnold Schönbergs "Erwartung" und "Die glückliche Hand," und Alban Bergs "Wozzeck."* Regensburg: Bosse, 1982.
1149. McCredie, Andrew D. "A Half Centennial New Look at Alban Berg's *Wozzeck*: Its Antecedents and Influence on German Expressionist Music Theatre." MMA 9 (1977): 156–205.
1150. Metzger, Heinz-Klaus, and Rainer Riehn, eds. *Alban Berg: Wozzeck.* Munich: Text + Kritik, 1985.
1151. Noske, Frits. "The Captain and the Doctor in *Wozzeck.*" M-Lönn: 269–75. [Act I, Scene I]
1152. Perle, George. "The Musical Language of *Wozzeck.*" MFO 1 (1967): 204–59.
1153. ———. *The Operas of Alban Berg.* Vol. I: *Wozzeck.* Berkeley: University of California Press, 1980. [*See also* 1137]
1154. ———. "Representation and Symbol in the Music of *Wozzeck.*" MR 32 (1971): 281–308.
1155. ———. "*Woyzeck* and *Wozzeck.*" MQ 53 (1967): 206–19.
1156. Petersen, Peter. "Berg und Büchner—*Wozzeck* und *Woyzeck*: Von der 'offenen Form' des Dramas zur 'geschlossenen Form' der Oper." HJM 14 (1997): 169–88.
1157. ———. "Leitmotive und andere Semanteme in Bergs *Wozzeck.*" MB 17, no. 12 (1985): 853–61.
1158. ———. "Wozzecks persönliche Leitmotive: Ein Beitrag zur Deutung des Sinngehalts der Musik in Alban Bergs *Wozzeck.*" HJM 4 (1980): 33–84.
1159. Ploebsch, Gerd. *Alban Berg's "Wozzeck."* Strasbourg: Heitz, 1968. [Includes extensive bibliography]
1160. Radice, Mark A. "The Anatomy of a Libretto: The Music Inherent in Büchner's *Woyzeck.*" MR 41 (1980): 223–33.
1161. Redlich, Hans. "*Wozzeck*: Dramaturgie und musikalische Form." M 10 (1956): 120–25.
1162. Reich, Willi. "Alban Berg: *Wozzeck.*" MZ 6 (1954): 27–34.
1163. ———. "A Guide to *Wozzeck.*" MQ 38 (1952): 1–21. Also published as *Alban Berg's "Wozzeck": A Guide to the Text and Music of the Opera* (New York: Schirmer, 1952).
1164. Reiman, Erika. "Tonality and Unreality in Berg's *Wozzeck.*" M-Bruhn: 229–42.
1165. Richter, Christoph. "Die Wirthausszene aus Alban Bergs *Wozzeck*: Unterrichtsmodell; Verhältnis von Musik und Sprache in der Oper." MB 14, no. 9 (1982): 553–63.
1166. Sabin, Robert. "Alban Berg's *Wozzeck.*" *Musical America* (April 1951): 6. [Includes chart of the form by Fritz Mahler]
1167. Schmalfeldt, Janet. *Berg's "Wozzeck": Harmonic Language and Dramatic Design.* New Haven, Conn.: Yale University Press, 1983.

1168. ———. "Berg's *Wozzeck*: Pitch-Class Set Structures and the Dramatic Design." Ph.D. diss., Yale University, 1979.
1169. Stephan, Rudolf. "Aspekte der *Wozzeck*-Musik." M-Wozzeck: 9–21.
1170. Treitler, Leo. "*Wozzeck* and the Apocalypse: An Essay in Historical Criticism." CI 3, no. 2 (1976–1977): 251–70. French translation, SMZ 116 (1976): 249–62.
1171. Tsang, Lee. "Musical Timbre in Context: The Second Viennese School, 1909–1925." Ph.D. diss., University of Southampton, 2000.

Various Works

1172. Archibald, Robert Bruce. "Harmony in the Early Works of Alban Berg." Ph.D. diss., Harvard University, 1965.
1173. Buchanan, Herbert Herman. "An Investigation of Mutual Influences among Schoenberg, Webern, and Berg (with an Emphasis on Schoenberg and Webern, ca. 1904–1908)." Ph.D. diss., Rutgers University, 1974.
1174. Cahn, Peter. "Klassizismen bei Alban Berg?" In *Colloquium Klassizität, Klassizismus, Klassik in der Musik 1920–1950*, ed. Wolfgang Osthoff and Reinhard Wiesend, 95–129. Tutzing: Schneider, 1988.
1175. Carner, Mosco. *Alban Berg: The Man and the Work.* London: Duckworth, 1975.
1176. Chadwick, Nicholas. "Franz Schreker's Orchestral Style and Its Influence on Alban Berg." MR 35 (1974): 29–46.
1177. DeVoto, Mark, and Joan Allen Smith. "Berg's Seventeen Four-Part Canons: The Mystery Solved." IABS 3 (1975): 4–7.
1178. Gervink, Manuel. "Alban Bergs kompositorische Annäherung an die Zwölftontechnik." MTH 13, no. 1 (1998): 55–74.
1179. Godwin, Paul Milton. "A Study of Concepts of Melody, with Particular Reference to Some Music of the Twentieth Century and Examples from the Compositions of Schoenberg, Webern, and Berg." Ph.D. diss., Ohio State University, 1972.
1180. Headlam, Dave. *The Music of Alban Berg.* New Haven, Conn.: Yale University Press, 1996.
1181. Hier, Ethel Glenn. "To Alban Berg: A Tribute." MU 1 (1946–1947): 275–87.
1182. Hollander, Hans. "Alban Berg." MQ 22 (1936): 375–82.
1183. Jarman, Douglas. *The Music of Alban Berg.* Berkeley: University of California Press, 1979.
1184. König, Werner. "Alban Bergs Zwölftonreihen und ihre harmonische Grundbedeutung." OMZ 55, no. 6 (2000): 25–33.
1185. Maegard, Jan. "Ein Beispiel atonalen Kontrapunkts im Frühstadium." ZM 3, no. 1 (29–34).
1186. Murray, Robert P. "The String Quartets of Alban Berg." Ph.D. diss., Indiana University, 1975.
1187. Nelson, Robert U. "Form and Fancy in the Variations of Berg." MR 31 (1970): 54–69.
1188. Perle, George. "Berg's Master Array of Interval Cycles." MQ 63 (1977): 1–30.
1189. Pernye, Andras. "Alban Berg und die Zahlen." SM 9 (1967): 141–61.
1190. Pople, Anthony, ed. *The Cambridge Companion to Berg.* Cambridge: Cambridge University Press, 1997.
1191. Redlich, Hans Ferdinand. *Alban Berg: The Man and His Music.* New York: Abelard Schumann, 1957.
1192. Reich, Willi. *The Life and Work of Alban Berg.* London: Thames & Hudson, 1965.
1193. M-Rognoni.
1194. Schollum, Robert. *Die Wiener Schule: Schonberg-Berg-Webern: Entwicklung und Ergebnis.* Vienna: Lafite, 1969.
1195. Schweitzer, Klaus. *Die Sonatensatzform im Schaffen Alban Bergs.* Stuttgart: Musikwissenschaftliche Verlagsgesellschaft, 1970.
1196. Spring, Glenn Ernest, Jr. "Determinants of Phrase Structure in Selected Works of Schoenberg, Berg, and Webern." D.M.A. diss., University of Washington, 1972.
1197. Stroh, Wolfgang Martin. "Alban Berg's 'Constructive Rhythm.'" PNM 7, no. 1 (1968): 18–31.

BERGER, ARTHUR (1912–2003)

1198. Barkin, Elaine. "Post Impressions: Arthur Berger's Trio for Violin, Guitar and Piano (1972)." PNM 17, no. 1 (1978–1979): 23–37. Reprint, M-Battcock: 215–20.
1199. Silver, Sheila. "Pitch and Registral Distribution in Arthur Berger's Music for Piano." PNM 17, no. 1 (1978–1979): 68–76.

BERGER, JEAN (1909–2002)

1200. Johnson, Axie Allen. "Choral Settings of the Magnificat by Selected Twentieth-Century Composers." D.M.A. diss., University of Southern California, 1968.
1201. M-Larson.
1202. Pritchard, W. Douglas. "The Choral Style of Jean Berger." ACR 8, no. 1 (1965): 4–5, 15.
1203. Roller, Dale Alvin. "The Secular Choral Music of Jean Berger." Ed.D. diss., University of Illinois, 1974.
1204. Smith, Kenyard Earl. "The Choral Music of Jean Berger." Ph.D. diss., University of Iowa, 1972.

BERGSMA, WILLIAM (1921–1994)

1205. Skulsky, Abraham. "The Music of William Bergsma." JR 3, no. 2 (1956): 12–26.

BERIO, LUCIANO (1925–2003)

Allelujah I–II
1206. Berio, Luciano. "Aspects d'un artisanat formel." CC 1 (1983): 10–23.

Chemins I–III
1207. Osmond-Smith, David. "Joyce, Berio et l'art de l'exposition." CC 1 (1983): 83–89.

Circles
1208. Demierre, Jacques. "*Circles*: e. e. Cummings lu par Luciano Berio." CC 1 (1983): 123–80.
1209. Hermann, Richard. "Luciano Berio's *Circles*, First Movement." SONUS 4, no. 2 (1984): 26–45.
1210. Jones, David Evan. "Text and Music in Luciano Berio's *Circles*." EXT 4, no. 2 (1987–1988): 108–14.
1211. Schnaus, Peter. "Anmerkungen zu Luciano Berios *Circles*." MB 10 (1978): 489–97.

Coro
1212. M-Anhalt: 252–66.

Formazioni
1213. Hander-Power, Janet. "Strategies of Meaning: A Study of the Aesthetic and the Musical Language of Luciano Berio." Ph.D. diss., University of Southern California, 1988.

Laborintus II
1214. Flynn, George W. "Listening to Berio's Music." MQ 61 (1975): 388–421.

Nones
1215. Hicks, Michael. "Exorcism and Epiphany: Luciano Berio's *Nones*." PNM 27, no. 2 (1989): 252–68.

O King
1216. Prost, Christine. "De l'écoute à l'analyse: Une expérience pédagogique autour d'*O King* de Luciano Berio." ANM 30 (1993): 25–28.
1217. Stoianowa, Iwanka. "Verbe et son: 'Centre et absence'; Sur *cummings ist der Dichter* de Boulez, *O King* de Berio, et *Für Stimmen (. . . Missa est)* de Schnebel." MJ 16 (1974): 79–102.

Opera
1218. Ramaut, Béatrice. "Deux mises en scène d'une conscience de la tradition: *Opera* de Berio (1969) et *Accanto* de Lachenmann (1976)." RDM 79, no. 1 (1993): 109–41.

Passaggio
1219. Noller, Joachim. "Musiktheater als Brennpunkt künstlerischer Avantgarde: Zur Dramaturgie von Berios *Passaggio*." F-Knepler, vol. 3: 95–115.

Sequenzas I–IX (*see also* specific Sequenzas)
1220. Albèra, Philippe. "Introduction aux neuf séquences." CC 1 (1983): 90–122.

Sequenza I
1221. Betz, Marianne. "Versuch über Berio: Eine Analyse der *Sequenza* per flauto solo." T 17, no. 1 (1992): 26–32.
1222. Gartmann, Thomas. "Das offene Kunstwerk, Neu erschlossen: Zu Luciano Berios Uberarbeitung der *Sequenza*." F-Lichtenhahn: 219–33.
1223. Magnani, Francesca. "La *Sequenza 1* de Berio dans les poétiques musicales des années 50." ANM 14 (1989): 74–81.

Sequenza III
1224. Anhalt, István. "Luciano Berio's *Sequenza III*." CCM 7 (1973): 23–60. Reprint, M-Anhalt: 25–40.
1225. Gruhn, Wilfried. "Luciano Berio (1925): *Sequenza III* (1965)." M-Zimmerschied: 234–49.
1226. Lyotard, Jean-François, and Dominique Avron. "A Few Words to Sing (sur *Sequenza III* de Berio)." MJ 2 (1971): 30–44.

Sequenza IV
1227. Hermann, Richard. "Theories of Chordal Shape, Aspects of Linguistics, and Their Roles in an Analysis of Pitch Structure in Berio's *Sequenza IV* for Piano." M-Marvin: 364–98.
1228. MacKay, John. "Aspects of Post-Serial Structuralism in Berio's *Sequenza IV* and *VI*." I 17, no. 4 (1988): 223–39.

Sequenza V
1229. Pellman, Samuel Frank. "An Examination of the Role of Timbre in a Musical Composition as Exemplified by an Analysis of *Sequenza V* by Luciano Berio." D.M.A. diss., Cornell University, 1979.

Sequenza VI
1230. Deliège, Irène, and Abdessadek El Ahmadi. "Mécanisme d'extraction d'indices dans le groupement: Etude de perception sur la *Sequenze VI* pour alto solo de Luciano Berio." CC 10 (1989): 85–104.

1231. MacKay, John. "Aspects of Post-Serial Structuralism in Berio's *Sequenza IV* and *VI*." I 17, no. 4 (1988): 223–39.

1232. Uscher, Nancy. "Luciano Berio, *Sequenza VI* for Solo Viola: Performance Practices." PNM 21 (1982–1983): 286–93.

Sequenza VII

1233. Förtig, Peter. "Zu Luciano Berios *Sequenza per Oboe solo*." T 1, no. 2 (1976–1977): 72–76.

Sequenza XI

1234. Delume, Caroline. "Luciano Berio: *Sequenza 11* pour guitare." ENT 10 (1992): 41–56.

Serenata I

1235. M-Wennerstrom.

Sinfonia

1236. Altmann, Peter. *"Sinfonia" von Luciano Berio: Eine analytische Studie.* Vienna: Universal, 1977.

1237. Bayer, Francis. "Thèmes et citations dans le 3eme mouvement de la *Sinfonia* de Luciano Berio." ANM 13 (1988): 69–73.

1238. Budde, Elmar. "Zum dritten Satz der *Sinfonia* von Luciano Berio." M-Stephan: 128–44.

1239. M-Cope: 345–51.

1240. Flynn, George W. "Listening to Berio's Music." MQ 61 (1975): 388–421.

1241. Hicks, Michael. "Text, Music, and Meaning in Berio's *Sinfonia*, 3rd Movement." PNM 20 (1981–1982): 199–224.

1242. Jahnke, Sabine. "Materialien zu einer Unterrichtssequenz: Des Antonius von Padua Fischpredigt bei Orff-Mahler-Berio." MB 5 (1973): 615–22.

1243. Krieger, Georg, and Wolfgang Martin Stroh. "Probleme der Collage in der Musik: Aufgezeigt am 3. Satz der *Sinfonia* von Luciano Berio." MB 3 (1971): 229–35.

1244. Osmond-Smith, David. "From Myth to Music: Lévi-Strauss's *Mythologiques* and Berio's *Sinfonia*." MQ 67 (1981): 230–60.

1245. ———. *Playing on Words: A Guide to Luciano Berio's "Sinfonia."* London: Royal Musical Association, 1985.

1246. ———. "*Sinfonia* de Luciano Berio (*O King*)." INH 5 (1989): 181–200.

1247. Ravizza, Victor. "*Sinfonia* für acht Singstimmen und Orchester von Luciano Berio." MELOS 41 (1974): 291–97.

1248. Zeichner, Sam. "Sound in Luciano Berio's *Sinfonia*: A La Rue Style Analysis." D 5, no. 2 (1973): 2–12.

Tempi concertati

1249. Jarvlepp, Jan. "Compositional Aspects of *Tempi concertati* by Luciano Berio." I 11 (1982): 179–93.

Thema (Omaggio a Joyce)

1250. Berio, Luciano. "Poésie et musique: Une expérience." CC 1 (1983): 24–35.

1251. Delalande, François. "*L'Omaggio a Joyce* de Luciano Berio." MJ 15 (1974): 45–54.

1252. Di Scipio, Agostino. "Da un'esperienza in ascolto di phonè e logos: Testo, suono e struttura in *Thema (Omaggio a Joyce)* di Berio." SAG 7, no. 2 (2000): 325–59.

Visage

1253. Flynn, George W. "Listening to Berio's Music." MQ 61 (1975): 388–421.

Various Works

1254. Dressen, Norbert. "Luciano Berios Vokalkompositionen: Sprachliche Vorlagen und kompositorische Beispiele." *Sprache im technischen Zeitalter* 74 (1980): 109–22.

1255. ———. *Sprache und Musik bei Luciano Berio.* Regensburg: Bosse, 1982.

1256. Holmes, Reed Kelley. "Relational Systems and Process in Recent Works of Luciano Berio." Ph.D. diss., University of Texas, 1981.

1257. Miller, Robert W. "A Style Analysis of the Published Solo Piano Works of Luciano Berio, 1950–1975." D.M.A. diss., Peabody Conservatory, 1979.

1258. Sams, Carol Lee. "Solo Vocal Writing in Selected Works of Berio, Crumb, and Rochberg." D.M.A. diss., University of Washington, 1975.

1259. Stoianova, Ivanka. "Luciano Berio: Chemins en musique." RM 375–377 (1985): 5–512.

BERKELEY, LENNOX (1903–1989)

1260. Hull, Robin. "Two Symphonies: Eugene Goossens and Lennox Berkeley." MR 4 (1943): 229–42.

BERLIOZ, HECTOR (1803–1869)

Benvenuto Cellini

1261. ASO 142 (1991).

Damnation de Faust

1262. Albright, Daniel. "Berlioz's Faust: The Funeral March of a Marionette." JMR 13, nos. 1–2 (1993): 79–97.

1263. ASO 22 (1979).

1264. Ferchault, Guy. *Faust: Une légende et ses musiciens.* Paris: Larousse, 1948.

1265. M-Macy.

1266. Rushton, Julian. "The Genesis of Berlioz's *La Damnation de Faust*." ML 56 (1975): 129–46.

Grande messe des morts (**Requiem**)

1267. Cone, Edward T. "Berlioz's Divine Comedy: The *Grande Messe des Morts*." NCM 4 (1980–1981): 3–16.

1268. George, Graham. "The Ambiguities of Berlioz." CAUSM 6 (1976): 1–10.

Harold en Italie

1269. Dahlhaus, Carl. "Allegro frenetico: Zum Problem des Rhythmus bei Berlioz." Melos/NZM 3 (1977): 212–14.

1270. Danuser, Hermann. "Symphonisches Subjekt und Form in Berlioz' *Harold en Italie*." Meloz/NZM 3 (1977): 203–12.

1271. Schenkman, Walter. "Fixed Ideas and Recurring Patterns in Berlioz's Melody." MR 40 (1979): 24–48.

Lélio, ou Le retour à la vie

1272. Bloom, Peter. "Orpheus' Lyre Resurrected: A *Tableau musical* by Berlioz." MQ 61 (1975): 189–211.

Nuits d'été

1273. Kiem, Eckehard. "Grenzbereich und Ausdruckskonstruktion: Hector Berlioz und Théophile Gautier; *Nuits d'été*." MAS 2, no. 6 (1998): 21–41. ["Au cimetière, clair de lune"]

1274. Lütteken, Laurenz. "'. . . Erfordert eine ziemlich große Sensibilität bei der Ausführung': Anmerkungen zum Liedzyklus *Les nuits d'éte* von Hector Berlioz." MAU 8 (1988): 41–64.

Operas (various; *see also* specific operas)

1275. Langford, Jeffrey. "The Operas of Hector Berlioz: Their Relationship to the French Operatic Tradition of the Early Nineteenth Century." Ph.D. diss., University of Pennsylvania, 1978.

Overtures

1276. Adelson, Deborah M. "Interpreting Berlioz's *Overture to King Lear*, Opus 4: Problems and solutions." CM 35 (1983): 46–56.

1277. Sandford, Gordon T. "The Overtures of Hector Berlioz: A Study in Musical Style." Ph.D. diss., University of Southern California, 1964.

Requiem. *See Grande messe des morts*

Roméo et Juliette

1278. Albright, Daniel. "Berlioz's *Roméo et Juliette:* Symphonic Metamorphoses on a Theme by Shakespeare." JMR 19, no. 2 (2000): 135–76.

1279. M-Chailley. [*Scène d'amour*]

1280. Friedheim, Philip. "Berlioz' *Roméo* Symphony and the Romantic Temperament." CM 36 (1983): 101–11.

1281. Micznik, Vera. "Of Ways of Telling, Intertextuality, and Historical Evidence in Berlioz's *Roméo et Juliette*." NCM 24, no. 1 (2000): 21–61.

1282. Rushton, Julian. *Berlioz: Roméo et Juliette.* Cambridge: Cambridge University Press, 1994.

1283. Schacher, Thomas. *Hector Berlioz: "Roméo et Juliette."* Munich: Fink, 1998.

1284. Shamgar, Beth. "Program and Sonority: An Essay in Analysis of the 'Queen Mab' Scherzo from Berlioz's *Romeo and Juliet*." CMS 28 (1988): 40–52.

Songs (various; *see also Nuits d'été*)

1285. Bullard, Truman Campbell. "Hector Berlioz and the Solo Song in France." M.A. thesis, Harvard University, 1963.

1286. Dickinson, A. E. F. "Berlioz's Songs." MQ 55 (1969): 329–43.

Symphonie fantastique

1287. Banks, Paul. "Coherence and Diversity in the *Symphonie fantastique*." NCM 8 (1984–1985): 37–43.

1288. Berger, Christian. *Phantastik als Konstruktion: Hector Berlioz' "Symphonie fantastique."* Kassel: Bärenreiter, 1983.

1289. Bockholdt, Rudolf. "Die idée fixe der *Phantastischen Symphonie*." AM 30 (1973): 190–207.

1290. Cone, Edward T., ed. *Berlioz: Fantastic Symphony.* Norton Critical Scores. New York: Norton, 1971.

1291. Dömling, Wolfgang. *Hector Berlioz: Symphonie fantastique.* Munich: Fink, 1986.

1292. Schenkman, Walter. "Fixed Ideas and Recurring Patterns in Berlioz's Melody." MR 40 (1979): 24–48.

1293. Temperley, Nicholas. "The *Symphonie fantastique* and Its Program." MQ 57 (1971): 593–608.

Symphonies (various; *see also* specific symphonies)

1294. Bass, Edward. "Thematic Procedures in the Symphonies of Berlioz." Ph.D. diss., University of North Carolina, 1964.

1295. Langford, Jeffrey. "The 'Dramatic Symphonies' of Berlioz as an Outgrowth of the French Operatic Tradition." MQ 69 (1983): 85–103.

1296. Nowalis, Sister Susan Marie. "Timbre as a Structural Device in Berlioz's Symphonies." Ph.D. diss., Case Western Reserve University, 1975.

Troyens

1297. ASO 128–29 (1990).

1298. Goldberg, Louise. "Aspects of Dramatic and Musical Unity in Berlioz's *Les Troyens*." JMR 13, nos. 1–2 (1993): 99–112.

1299. Kemp, Ian. *Hector Berlioz: Les Troyens.* Cambridge: Cambridge University Press, 1988.

1300. Kühn, Hellmut. "Antike Massen: Zu einigen Motiven in *Les Troyens* von Hector Berlioz." F-Abert: 141–52.

1301. Rushton, Julian. "The Overture to *Les Troyens*." MA 4, nos. 1–2 (1985): 119–44.

Various Works

1302. Alexander, Metche Franke. "The Choral-Orchestral Works of Hector Berlioz." Ph.D. diss., North Texas State University, 1978.

1303. Bass, Edward. "Musical Time and Space in Berlioz." MR 30 (1969): 211–24.

1304. ———. "Thematic Unification of Scenes in Multi-Movement Works of Berlioz." MR 28 (1967): 45–51.

1305. Bloom, Peter, ed. *The Cambridge Companion to Berlioz.* Cambridge: Cambridge University Press, 2000.

1306. Bockholdt, Rudolf. *Berlioz-Studien.* Tutzing: Schneider, 1979.

1307. ———. "Musikalischer Satz und Orchesterklang im Werk von Hector Berlioz." MF 32 (1979): 122–35.

1308. Chailley, Jacques. "Berlioz harmoniste." RM 223 (1956): 15–30.

1309. Dickinson, A. E. F. "Berlioz's Rome Prize Works." MR 25 (1964): 163–85.

1310. ———. "Berlioz' Stage Works." MR 31 (1970): 136–57.

1311. ———. *The Music of Berlioz.* London: Faber & Faber, 1972.

1312. Dömling, Wolfgang. "'En songeant au temps . . . à l'espace . . .': Über einzige Aspekte der Musik Hector Berlioz." AM 33 (1976): 241–60.

1313. ———. *Hector Berlioz: Die symphonisch-dramatischen Werke.* Stuttgart: Reclam, 1979.

1314. Friedheim, Philip. "Berlioz and Rhythm." MR 37 (1976): 5–44.

1315. ———. "Radical Harmonic Procedures in Berlioz." MR 21 (1960): 282–95.

1316. Guiomar, Michel. *Le masque et le fantasme: L'imagination de la matière sonore dans la pensée musicale de Berlioz.* Paris: Corti, 1970.

1317. Hirshberg, Jehoash. "Berlioz and the Fugue." JMT 18 (1974): 152–88.

1318. Primmer, Brian. *The Berlioz Style.* New York: Oxford University Press, 1973. Reprint, New York: Da Capo, 1984.

1319. Rushton, Julian. *The Musical Language of Berlioz.* New York: Cambridge University Press, 1983.

1320. Silverman, Richard S. "Synthesis in the Music of Hector Berlioz." MR 34 (1973): 346–52.

1321. Tanner, Peter H. "Timpani and Percussion Writing in the Works of Hector Berlioz." Ph.D. diss., Catholic University, 1967.

BERNSTEIN, LEONARD (1918–1990)

1322. Boelzner, David E. "The Symphonies of Leonard Bernstein: An Analysis of Motivic Character and Form." M.A. thesis, University of North Carolina, 1976.

1323. Gottlieb, Jack. "The Choral Music of Leonard Bernstein." ACR 10 (1958): 156–74.

1324. ———. "The Music of Leonard Bernstein: A Study of Melodic Manipulations." D.M.A. diss., University of Illinois, 1964.

1325. ———. "Symbols of Faith in the Music of Leonard Bernstein." MQ 66 (1980): 287–95.

1326. Gradenwitz, Peter. "Leonard Bernstein." MR 10 (1949): 191–202.

1327. Lehrman, Leonard Jordan. "Leonard Bernstein's *Serenade* after Plato's *Symposium*: An Analysis." D.M.A. diss., Cornell University, 1977.

1328. Pearlmutter, Alan Jay. "Leonard Bernstein's *Dybbuk*: An Analysis Including Historical, Religious, and Literary Perspectives of Hasidic Life and Lore." D.M.A. diss., Peabody Conservatory, 1985.

BERWALD, FRANZ (1796–1868)

1329. Brüll, Erich. "*Sinfonie singulière*: Information über Berwald." MG 18 (1968): 246–52.

1330. Stahmer, Klaus. "Ein Beitrag Barwalds zur romantischen Sonaten-form: Das Duo für Violoncello und Klavier (1858)." STM 59, no. 2 (1977): 23–33.

1331. ———. "Zur zyklischen Sonatenform: Franz Berwalds Duo für Violoncello und Klavier (1858)." F-Gudewill: 79–90.

BEVERSDORF, THOMAS (1924–1981)
1332. Ferguson, Thomas. "An Analysis of Symphony for Winds and Percussion by Thomas Beversdorf." JBR 9, no. 1 (1972–1973): 17–31.

BEYERS, FRANK MICHAEL (b. 1928)
1333. Dorfmüller, Joachim. "Musik der Sensibilität und Transparenz: Zum Orgelschaffen Frank Michael Meyers." MK 48 (1948) 273–77.

BIALAS, GÜNTER (1907–1995)
1334. Huber, Nicolaus. "Der Komponist Günter Bialas." M 26 (1972): 333–37.

BIERMANN, WOLF (b. 1936)
1335. Reinhardt, Klaus. "Eine Ballade von Wolf Biermann." MB 4 (1972): 200–201.

BIJSTER, JACOB (1902–1958)
1336. Beechey, Gwilym. "The Organ Music of Jacob Bijster (1902–1958)." SS 36 (1968): 1–7.

BINKERD, GORDON (1916–2003)
1337. Griffith, Patricia Barnes. "The Solo Piano Music of Gordon Binkerd." D.M.A. diss., Peabody Conservatory, 1985.
1338. Hawthorne, Loyd Furman. "The Choral Music of Gordon Binkerd." D.M.A. diss., University of Texas, 1973.

BIRTWISTLE, HARRISON (b. 1934)
1339. Adlington, Robert. *The Music of Harrison Birtwistle.* Cambridge: Cambridge University Press, 2000.
1340. Cross, Jonathan. "Birtwistle's Secret Theatres." M-Ayrey: 207–25. [*Tragoedia, Verses for Ensembles, Secret Theatre*]
1341. ———. "Lines and Circles: On Birtwistle's *Punch and Judy* and *Secret Theatre*." MA 13, nos. 2–3 (1994): 203–26.
1342. Smalley, Roger. "Birtwistle's *Nomos*." TEMPO 86 (1968): 7–10.
1343. Whittall, Arnold. "Comparatively Complex: Birtwistle, Maxwell Davies, and Modernist Analysis." MA 13, nos. 2–3 (1994): 139–59. [*Earth Dances*]
1344. ———. "The Mechanisms of Lament: Harrison Birtwistle's *Pulse Shadows*." ML 80, no. 1 (1999): 86–102.

BITTNER, JULIUS (1874–1939)
1345. Zauner, Waltraud. "Studien zu den musikalischen Bühnenwerken von Julius Bittner: Mit Beiträgen zur Lebensgeschichte des Komponisten." Ph.D. diss., Universität Wien, 1983.
1346. ———. "Studien zu den musikalischen Bühnenwerken von Julius Bittner, I." SZM 38 (1987): 135–214. [Early operas]
1347. ———. "Studien zu den musikalischen Bühnenwerken von Julius Bittner, II." SZM 39 (1988): 313–85. [*Die Kohlhaymerin, Mondnacht, Das Rosengärtlein, Das Veilchen*]

BIZET, GEORGES (1838–1875)
Carmen
1348. ASO 26 (1980).
1349. Beardsley, Thomas S. "The Spanish Musical Sources of Bizet's *Carmen*." IAMR 10, no. 2 (1989): 143–46.
1350. Bleiler, Ellen H., ed. *Georges Bizet: Carmen.* New York: Dover, 1970.
1351. Cooper, Martin. *Bizet: Carmen.* London: Boosey & Hawkes, 1947.
1352. Dean, Winton. "*Carmen:* An Attempt at a True Evaluation." MR 7 (1946): 209–20.
1353. Huebner, Steve. "Carmen as *corrida de toros*." JMR 13, nos. 1–2 (1993): 3–29.
1354. John, Nicholas, ed. *Bizet: Carmen.* London: Calder, 1982.
1355. Malherbe, Henry. *Carmen.* Paris: Michel, 1951.
1356. McClary, Susan. *Georges Bizet: Carmen.* Cambridge: Cambridge University Press, 1992.

Pêcheurs de perles
1357. ASO 124 (1989).

Variations chromatiques
1358. Luck, Ray. "An Analysis of Three Variation Sets for Piano by Bizet, d'Indy and Pierné." D.M.A. diss., Indiana University, 1978.

Various Works
1359. Dean, Winton. *Georges Bizet: His Life and Work.* London: Dent, 1965.
1360. Muller, Monique. "L'oeuvre pianistique originale de Georges Bizet." Ph.D. diss., Université de Neuchâtel, 1976.

1361. Shanet, Howard. "Bizet's Suppressed Symphony." MQ 44 (1958): 461–76.
1362. Stefan, Paul. *Georges Bizet.* Zurich: Atlantis, 1952.

BLACHER, BORIS (1903–1975)

1363. Gray, John H. "Variable Meter and Parametric Progression in the Music of Boris Blacher." D.M.A. diss., Cornell University, 1979.
1364. Jahnke, Sabine. "Boris Blacher: Ornamente für Klavier, Op. 37." MB 1 (1969): 508–10.
1365. M-Vogt: 253–60. [*Abstrakte Oper No. 1*]

BLAUSTEIN, SUSAN (b. 1953)

1366. Kramer, Lawrence. "Text and Music: Some New Directions." CMR 5 (1989): 143–53. [*Songs of "The World" (A Naive Poem): Warsaw, 1943*]

BLITZSTEIN, MARC (1905–1964)

1367. Dietz, Robert James. "The Operatic Style of Marc Blitzstein in the American 'Agit-Prop' Era." Ph.D. diss., University of Iowa, 1970.

BLOCH, AUGUSTYN (b. 1929)

1368. Erhardt, Ludwig. "*Wordsworth Songs* by Augustyn Bloch." PM 12, no. 1 (1977): 30–35.
1369. Kominek, Mieczyslaw. "Augustyn Bloch *Anenaiki, Carmen biblicum.*" PM 15, no. 4 (1980): 11–14.

BLOCH, ERNEST (1880–1959)

Chamber Works

1370. Guibbory, Yenoin Ephraim. "Thematic Treatment in the String Quartets of Ernest Bloch." Ph.D. diss., University of West Virginia, 1970.
1371. Jones, William M. "Ernest Bloch's Five String Quartets." MR 28 (1967): 112–21.
1372. Raditz, Edward. "An Analytical Study of the Violin and Piano Works of Ernest Bloch." Ph.D. diss., New York University, 1975.
1373. Rimmer, Frederick. "Ernest Bloch's Second String Quartet." TEMPO 52 (1959): 11–16.

Choral Works

1374. Móricz, Klára. "The Confines of Judaism and the Illusiveness of Universality in Ernest Bloch's *Avodath Hakodesh (Sacred Service).*" REP 5, nos. 1–2 (1996): 184–241.

Orchestral Works

1375. Kushner, David. "Ernest Bloch and His Symphonic Works." Ph.D. diss., University of Michigan, 1966.
1376. Sharp, Geoffrey. "Ernest Bloch's Violin Concerto." MR 1 (1940): 72–78.

Piano Works

1377. Wheeler, Charles Lynn. "The Solo Piano Music of Ernest Bloch." D.M.A. diss., University of Oregon, 1976.

Various Works

1378. Knapp, Alexander. "The Jewishness of Bloch: Subconscious or Conscious." PRMA 97 (1970–1971): 99–112.
1379. Jones, William M. "The Music of Ernest Bloch." Ph.D. diss., Indiana University, 1963.
1380. Minsky, Henri S. "Ernest Bloch and His Music." Ph.D. diss., George Peabody College for Teachers, 1945.
1381. Newlin, Dika. "The Later Works of Ernest Bloch." MQ 33 (1947): 443–59.

BLOMDAHL, KARL-BIRGER (1916–1968)

1382. Ostrander, Arthur Eugene. "Style in the Orchestral Works of Karl-Birger Blomdahl." Ph.D. diss., Indiana University, 1973.

BOCCHERINI, LUIGI (1743–1805)

1383. Cattoretti, Anna. "1771–1773: Gli ultimi quintetti per archi di Giovanni Battista Sammartini i primi di Luigi Boccherini." CHI 43/nuova serie n. 23 (1993): 193–229. [Early string quartets]
1384. Churgin, Bathia. "Sammartini and Boccherini: Continuity and Change." CHI 43/nuova serie n. 23 (1993): 171–91.
1385. Tchernowitz-Neustadtl, Miriam. "Aspects of the Cycle and Tonal Relationships in Luigi Boccherini's String Trios." CHI 43/nuova serie n. 23 (1993): 157–69.

BOESMANS, PHILIPPE (b. 1936)

1386. ASO 160 (1994). [*Reigen*]
1387. ASO 198 (2000). [*Wintermärchen*]

BOIELDIEU, ADRIEN (1775–1834)
1388. ASO 176 (1997). [*La dame blanche*]

BON, WILLEM FREDERIK (1940–1983)
1389. Vermeulen, Ernst. "Willem Frederik Bon: *Usher-Symphony.*" SS 48 (1971): 1–8.

BORNEFELD, HELMUT (1906–1990)
1390. Braun, Gerhard. "Dan andere Arkadien: Gedanken zur Flötenmusik von Helmut Bornefeld." T 12, no. 2 (1987): 401–5.

BORODIN, ALEKSANDR PORFIR'YEVICH (1833–1887)
1391. Abraham, Gerald. "Borodin as a Symphonist." ML 11 (1930): 352–59.
1392. ———. *Borodin: The Composer and His Music; A Descriptive and Critical Analysis of His Works and a Study of His Value as an Art-Force.* London: Reeves, 1927. Reprint, New York: AMS, 1976.
1393. ASO 168 (1995). [*Prince Igor*]
1394. Bobeth, M. *Borodin und seine oper "Furst Igor": Geschichte, Analyse, Konsequenzen.* Munich: Katzbichler, 1982.
1395. Dianin, Serge Aleksandrovich. *Borodin.* London: Oxford University Press, 1963.
1396. Josephson, Nors S. "Westeuropäische Stilmerkmale in der Musik Borodins (1833–1887)." JSIM (1994): 278–303.

BORTNYANSKY, DMITRY STEPANOVICH (1751–1825)
1397. Seaman, Gerald. "D. S. Bortnyansky (1751–1825)." MR 21 (1960): 106–13.

BOSSEUR, JEAN-YVES (b. 1947)
1398. Witts, Richard. "Jean-Yves Bosseur." CT 15 (1976–1977): 8–11.

BOUCOURECHLIEV, ANDRÉ (1925–1997)
1399. Boucourechliev, André. "*Le Nom d'Oedipe*: Protocole musical." ASO 18 (1978): 90–101.
1400. Rigoni, Michel. "*Archipel III* d'André Boncourechliev [*sic*]: Naviguer dans l'œuvre ouverte." ANM 30 (1993): 57–64.

BOUDREAU, WALTER (b. 1947)
1401. Boudreau, Walter. "Circuits-multiples circa 1970–1980: Les années 'hard core' (faire 'respirer' la musique)." CIR 8, no. 1 (1997): 31–42. [*Variations*]

BOULANGER, LILI (1893–1918)
1402. Chailley, Jacques. "L'oeuvre de Lili Boulanger." RM 353–54 (1982): 15–44.
1403. Dopp, Bonnie Jo. "Numerology and Cryptography in the Music of Lili Boulanger: The Hidden Program in *Clairières dan le ciel.*" MQ 78, no. 3 (1994): 557–83.
1404. Giesbrecht-Schutte, Sabine. "Lili Boulanger: *Clairières dans le Ciel*–ästhetischer Ausdruck und musikalische Form." MF 47, no. 4 (1994): 384–402.
1405. Rosenstiel, Leonie. *The Life and Works of Lili Boulanger.* Rutherford, N.J.: Fairleigh Dickinson University Press, 1978.

BOULEZ, PIERRE (b. 1925)
Cummings ist der Dichter
1406. Gottwald, Clytus. "Anmerkungen zur Harmonik von *cummings ist der Dichter.*" MTH 12, no. 1 (1997): 53–59.
1407. Morton, Lawrence. "*cummings ist der Dichter.*" F-Boulez: 128–53. [In English and German]
1408. Stoianowa, Iwanka. "Verbe et son: 'Centre et absence'; Sur *cummings ist der Dichter* de Boulez, *O King* de Berio, et *Für Stimmen (. . . Missa est)* de Schnebel." MJ 16 (1974): 79–102.

Dérive I
1409. Bösche, Thomas. "Zwischen Opazität und Klarheit: Einige abschweifende Bemerkungen zu *Dérive* 1." In *Pierre Boulez II*, ed. Heinz-Klaus Metzger and Rainer Riehn, 62–92. Munich: Text + Kritik, 1997.

Dialogue de l'ombre double
1410. Ramaut, Béatrice. "*Dialogue de l'ombre double* de Pierre Boulez: Analyse d'un processus citationnel." ANM 28 (1992): 69–75.
1411. Rogers, Joe. "*Dialogue de l'ombre double*: Construction by Assemblage." PNM 38, no. 2 (2000): 30–51.

Doubles
1412. Edwards, Allen. "Boulez's *Doubles* and *Figures Doubles Prismes*: A Preliminary Study." TEMPO 185 (1993): 6–17.

Eclat
1413. Schœller, Phillippe. "Mutation de l'écriture: *Éclat, Stria, Désintégrations.*" INH 1 (1986): 197–208.

Etudes for Tape

1414. Decroupet, Pascal. "Timbre Diversification in Serial Tape Music and Its Consequence on Form." CMR 10, no. 2 (1994): 13–23. [No. 2]

1415. Decroupet, Pascal, and Elena Ungeheuer. "Karel Goeyvaerts und die serielle Tonbandmusik." RBM 48 (1994): 95–118. [No. 1]

Figures-Doubles-Prismes. *See Doubles*

Livre pour quatuor

1416. Bösche, Thomas. "A propos du *Livre pour quatuor*." M-Metzger/Boulez: 91–111.

Marteau sans maître

1417. Bard, Maja, and Hans Vogt. "Pierre Boulez: *Le marteau sans maître* (1954)." M-Vogt: 274–87.

1418. Bösche, Thomas. "Einige Beobachtungen zu Technik und Ästhetik des Komponierens in Pierre Boulez' *Marteau sans maître*." MTH 5, no. 3 (1990): 253–69. [Response to 1425]

1419. Fink, Wolfgang. "'Schönes Gebäude und die Vorahnungen': Zur Morphologie des 5. Satzes von Pierre Boulez' *Le marteau sans maître*." In *Pierre Boulez II*, ed. Heinz-Klaus Metzger and Rainer Riehn, 3–61. Munich: Text + Kritik, 1997.

1420. Heinemann, Stephen. "Pitch-Class Set Multiplication in Theory and Practice." MTS 20, no. 1 (1998): 72–96.

1421. Hoffman, Michael. "Pierre Boulez's *Le marteau sans maître*: An Overview Analysis." TCM 4, no. 10 (1997): 4–11.

1422. Koblyakov, Lev. "P. Boulez *Le marteau sans maître*: Analysis of Pitch Structure." ZM 8, no. 1 (1977): 24–39.

1423. Lerdahl, Fred. "Cognitive Constraints on Compositional Systems." CMR 6, no. 2 (1992): 97–121.

1424. Levin, Gregory. "An Analysis of Movements III and IX from *Le marteau sans maître* by Pierre Boulez." Ph.D. diss., Brandeis University, 1975.

1425. Mosch, Ulrich. "Disziplin und Indisziplin: Zum seriellen Komponieren im 2. Satz des *Marteau sans maître* von Pierre Boulez." MTH 5, no. 1 (1990): 39–66. [*See also* 1418]

1426. Piencikowski, Robert T. "René Char et Pierre Boulez: Esquisse analytique du *Marteau sans maître*." SBM 4 (1980): 193–264.

1427. Stockhausen, Karlheinz. "Music and Speech." R 6 (1964): 40–64.

1428. Wentzel, Wayne. "Dynamic and Attack Associations in Boulez's *Le marteau sans maître*." PNM 29, no. 1 (1991): 142–70.

1429. Winick, Steven. "Symmetry and Pitch-Duration Associations in Boulez' *Le marteau sans maître*." PNM 24, no. 2 (1986): 280–321.

Messagesquisse

1430. Bonnet, Antoine. "*Ecriture* and Perception: On *Messagesquisse* by Pierre Boulez." CMR 2, no. 1 (1987): 173–209. French translation in INH 3 (1988): 211–43.

Notations

1431. Ofenbauer, Christian. "Vom Faltenlegen: Versuch einer Lektüre von Pierre Boulez' *Notation(s) I(1)*." M-Metzger/Boulez: 55–75. [Piano and orchestral versions]

Piano Sonata No. 1

1432. Jedrzejewski, Franck. "La mise en œuvre du principe dodécaphonique dans la 1re Sonate de Pierre Boulez." ANM 7 (1987): 69–76.

1433. Rosen, Charles. "The Piano Music." F-Boulez/Glock: 85–97.

Piano Sonata No. 2

1434. Dechario, Joseph L. "A Phrase Structure Analysis of the Third Movement of Boulez's Second Piano Sonata: An Essay Together with a Comprehensive Project in Piano Performance." D.M.A. diss., University of Iowa, 1977.

1435. M-Mathes.

1436. Rosen, Charles. "The Piano Music." F-Boulez/Glock: 85–97.

Piano Sonata No. 3

1437. Black, Robert. "Boulez's Third Piano Sonata: Surface and Sensibility." PNM 20 (1981–1982): 182–98.

1438. Boulez, Pierre. "Sonate, que me veux-tu?" PNM 1, no. 2 (1962): 32–44. Reprinted in M-Boulez: 163–75.

1439. ———. "Zu meiner III. Sonate." DBNM 3 (1960): 27–40.

1440. Harbinson, William G. "Performer Indeterminacy and Boulez's Third Sonata." TEMPO 169 (1989): 16–20.

1441. Ligeti, György. "À propos de la troisième Sonate de Boulez (1959)." MJ 16 (1974): 6–8.

1442. Pereira, Rosângela. "La troisième sonate de Pierre Boulez." DI 36 (1993): 4–7.

1443. Piret, Anne. "Pierre Boulez: Troisième sonate pour piano." ANM 29 (1992): 61–74.

1444. Rosen, Charles. "The Piano Music." F-Boulez/Glock: 85–97.

1445. Stahnke, Manfred. "Beelzebuboulez: Über eine romantische Kategorie der Dritten Klaviersonate." F-Boulez: 118–27.

1446. ———. *Struktur und Aesthetik bei Boulez: Untersuchung zum Formanten "Trope" der dritten Klaviersonate.* Hamburg: Wagner, 1979.

1447. Stoianowa, Iwanka. "La Troisième Sonate de Boulez et le projet mallarméen du Livre." MJ 16 (1974): 9–28.

1448. Trenkamp, Wilma Anne. "The Concept of Aléa in Boulez's *Constellation-Miroir*." ML 57 (1976): 1–10.

1449. Wait, Mark. "Aspects of Literary and Musical Structure as Reflected by the Third Piano Sonata of Pierre Boulez." D.M.A. diss., Peabody Conservatory, 1976.

1450. ———. "Liszt, Scriabin, and Boulez: Considerations of Form." JALS 1 (1977): 9–16.

Piano Works (various; *see also* specific piano works)

1451. Nemecek, Robert. "Tendenz und Kontinuität im frühen Klavierschaffen von Pierre Boulez." MPSS 6 (1993): 18–22. [Piano works 1942–1945]

Pli selon pli

1452. Boulez, Pierre. "Construire une improvisation (*Deuxième improvisation sur Mallarmé*)." M-Boulez: 143–62.

1453. ———. "Wie arbeitet die Avantgarde." MELOS 28 (1961): 301–8. [*Improvisations sur Mallarmé I–II*]

1454. Brunner, Raphaël. "*L'Improvisation III sur Mallarmé* de Pierre Boulez: Eléments pour une mise en perspective." DI 50 (1996): 4–14.

1455. Cross, Anthony. "Form and Expression in Boulez' *Don*." MR 36 (1975): 215–30.

1456. Deliège, Cèlestin. "The Convergence of Two Poetic Systems." Trans. L. M. Peugniez. F-Boulez/Glock: 99–125. [*Improvisation sur Mallarmé I*]

1457. Krastewa, Iwanka. "*Pli selon pli*: Portrait de Mallarmé." SMZ 113 (1973): 16–24, 76–82, 143–50.

1458. McCalla, James. "Sea-Changes: Boulez's *Improvisations sur Mallarmé*." JM 6, no. 1 (1988): 83–106.

1459. Miller, Roger L. "*Pli selon pli*: Pierre Boulez and the 'New Lyricism.'" Ph.D. diss., Case Western Reserve University, 1978.

Polyphonie X

1460. Boulez, Pierre. "Le système mis à nu: *Polyphonie X* et *Structures* pour deux pianos." M-Boulez: 129–42.

1461. Strinz, Werner. "'Que d'interférences à provoquer...': Bemerkungen zur Kompositionstechnik in Pierre Boulez' *Polyphonie X* pour 18 instruments." MPSS 12 (1999): 39–45.

Répons

1462. Deliège, Cèlestin. "Moment de Pierre Boulez sur l'introduction orchestrale de *Répons*." INH 4 (1988): 181–202.

1463. Gerzso, Andrew. "Reflections on *Répons*." CMR 1, no. 1 (1984–1985): 23–34.

1464. Nattiez, Jean-Jacques. "*Répons* et la crise de la 'communication' musicale contemporaine." INH 2 (1987): 193–210.

1465. Oehlschlägel, Reinhard. "Koordination von Akustik und Musik: Répons 3 von Pierre Boulez." MTX 9 (1985): 51–54.

Rituel: In Memoriam Bruno Maderna

1466. Beiche, Michael. "Serielles Denken in *Rituel* von Pierre Boulez." AM 38 (1981): 24–56.

1467. Stoianova, Ivanka. "Narrativisme, téléologie et invariance dans l'oeuvre musicale: À propos de *Rituel* de Pierre Boulez." MJ 25 (1976): 15–31.

Sonatina (Flute and Piano)

1468. Baron, Carol K. "An Analysis of the Pitch Organization in Boulez's Sonatine for Flute and Piano." CM 20 (1975): 87–95.

Structures

1469. Boulez, Pierre. "Le système mis à nu (*Polyphonie X* et *Structures* pour deux pianos)." M-Boulez: 129–42.

1470. De Young, Lynden. "Pitch Order and Duration Order in Boulez' *Structure* Ia." PNM 16, no. 2 (1977–1978): 26–34.

1471. Febel, Reinhard. *Musik für zwei Klaviere seit 1950 als Spiegel der Kompositionstechnik.* Herrenberg: Döring, 1978.

1472. Fuhrmann, Roderich. "Boulez, Pierre (1925): *Structures* I (1952)." M-Zimmerschied: 170–87.

1473. Ivanova, Irina. "Transformations and Invariant Structure in *Structures* 1B." TCMU 7, no. 4 (2000): 6–10.

1474. M-Kirchmeyer: 179–86.

1475. Ligeti, György. "Pierre Boulez." R 4 (1960): 36–62.

1476. M-Wennerstrom.

Various Works

1477. Bennett, Gerald. "The Early Works." F-Boulez/Glock: 41–84.

1478. Bradshaw, Susan. "The Instrumental and Vocal Music." F-Boulez/Glock: 127–229.

1479. Decroupet, Pascal. "Renverser la vapeur...: Zu Musikdenken und Kompositionen von Boulez in den fünfziger Jahren." M-Metzger/Boulez: 112–31.

1480. Griffiths, Paul. *Boulez.* London: Oxford University Press, 1978.
1481. Häusler, Josef, and Pierre Stoll. "Musikalische Technik." DBNM 5 (1963): 29–123.
1482. McCalla, James Wesley. "'Between Its Human Accessories': The Art of Stéphane Mallarmé and Pierre Boulez." Ph.D. diss., University of California, Berkeley, 1976.
1483. Piencikowski, Robert. "Fonction relative du timbre dans la musique contemporaine: Messiaen, Carter, Boulez, Stockhausen." ANM 3 (1986): 51–53.
1484. ———. "Nature morte avec guitare; Stilleben mit Gitarre." F-Boulez: 66–98. [In French and German]
1485. Trenkamp, Wilma Anne. "A Throw of the Dice: An Analysis of Selected Works by Pierre Boulez." Ph.D. diss., Case Western Reserve University, 1973.

BOWLES, PAUL (1910–1999)

1486. Holden, Jon W. "Form and Harmonic Technique in the Two-Piano Works by Paul Bowles." Ph.D. diss., New York University, 1995.

BOYKAN, MARTIN (b. 1931)

1487. Harbison, John, and Eleanor Cory. "Martin Boykan: String Quartet (1967); Two views." PNM 11, no. 2 (1973): 204–48. [Includes entire score]

BOZZA, EUGÈNE (1905–1991)

1488. Rowan, Denise Cecile Rogers. "The Contributions for Bassoon with Piano Accompaniment and Orchestral Accompaniment of Eugene Bozza with Analyses of Representative Solo Compositions." D.M.A. diss., University of Southern Mississippi, 1978.

BRAHMS, JOHANNES (1833–1897)

Alto Rhapsody. *See* Rhapsody, Op. 53

Cello Sonata No. 1, Op. 38

1489. Graybill, Roger. "Brahms' Integration of Traditional and Progressive Tendencies: A Look at Three Sonata Expositions." JMR 8, nos. 1–2 (1988): 141–68. [Movement I]

Cello Sonata No. 2, Op. 99

1490. Graybill, Roger. "Harmonic Circularity in Brahms's F major Cello Sonata: An Alternative to Schenker's Reading in *Free Composition*." MTS 10 (1988): 43–55. [Movement I]
1491. Notley, Magaret. "Brahms's Cello Sonata in F Major and Its Genesis: A Study in Half-Step Relations." BST 1 (1994): 139–60.
1492. Smith, Peter H. "Liquidation, Augmentation, and Brahms's Recapitulatory Overlaps." NCM 17, no. 3 (1994): 237–61. [Movement I]

Choral Works (various; *see also* specific choral works)

1493. Bellamy, Sister Katherine Elizabeth. "Motivic Development in the Larger Choral Works of Johannes Brahms." Ph.D. diss., University of Wisconsin, 1973.
1494. Kross, Siegfried. *Die Chorwerke von Johannes Brahms.* Berlin: Hesse, 1958.
1495. ———. "The Choral Music of Johannes Brahms." ACR 25, no. 4 (1983): 5–30.
1496. Roeder, Michael T. "The Choral Music of Brahms: Historical Models." CAUSM 5, no. 2 (1975): 26–46.
1497. Rose, Michael Paul. "Structural Integration in Selected Mixed a Capella Choral Works of Brahms." Ph.D. diss., University of Michigan, 1971.

Clarinet Sonata, Op. 120, No. 1

1498. Graybill, Roger. "Brahms' Integration of Traditional and Progressive Tendencies: A Look at Three Sonata Expositions." JMR 8, nos. 1–2 (1988): 141–68. [Movement I]
1499. Pfisterer, Manfred. "Eingriffe in die Syntax: Zum Verfahren der metrisch-rhythmischen Variation bei Johannes Brahms." M-Metzger/Brahms: 76–85. [Movement I]
1500. Schmidt, Christian Martin. *Verjähren der motivischthematischen Vermittlung in der Musik von Johannes Brahms, dargestellt an der Klarinettensonate F-Moll, Op. 120, 1.* Munich: Katzbichler, 1971.
1501. Smith, Peter H. "Brahms and the Neapolitan Complex: bII, bVI and Their Multiple Functions in the First Movement of the F-Minor Clarinet Sonata." BST 2 (1998): 169–208.

Clavierstücke, Op. 118

1502. Baud, Jean-Marc. "Con molta espressione." SMZ 123 (1983): 141–47.
1503. Cadwallader, Allen. "Foreground Motivic Ambiguity: Its Clarification at Middleground Levels in Selected Late Piano Pieces of Johannes Brahms." MA 7, no. 1 (1988): 59–92. [No. 2]

1504. Cai, Camilla. "Forms Made Miniature: The Intermezzi of Brahms." F-Lefkowitz: 135–50. [No. 1]

1505. Cone, Edward T. "Three Ways of Reading a Detective Story: Or, a Brahms Intermezzo." *Georgia Review* 31 (1977): 554–74. [No. 1]

1506. Lamb, James Boyd. "A Graphic Analysis of Brahms' Opus 118 with an Introduction to Shenkerian Theory and the Reduction Process." Ph.D. diss., Texas Tech University, 1979.

1507. Miller, Lynus Patrick. "From Analysis to Performance: The Musical Landscape of Johannes Brahms's Opus 118, No. 6." Ph.D. diss., University of Michigan, 1979.

1508. Scott, Ann Besser. "Thematic Transmutation in the Music of Brahms: A Matter of Musical Alchemy." JMR 15, no. 3 (1995): 177–206. [No. 6]

1509. Snarrenberg, Robert. "The Play of *Différance*: Brahms's Intermezzo Op. 118, No. 2." ITO 10, no. 3 (1987): 1–25.

Clavierstücke, Op. 119

1510. Baud, Jean-Marc. "Con molta espressione." SMZ 123 (1983): 141–47.

1511. Braus, Ira. "An Unwritten Metrical Modulation in Brahms's Intermezzo in E Minor, Op. 119, No. 2." BST 1 (1994): 161–69.

1512. Cadwallader, Allen. "Foreground Motivic Ambiguity: Its Clarification at Middleground Levels in Selected Late Piano Pieces of Johannes Brahms." MA 7, no. 1 (1988): 59–92. [No. 2]

1513. ———. "Motivic Unity and Integration of Structural Levels in Brahms's B Minor Intermezzo, Op. 119, No. 1." TP 8, no. 2 (1983): 5–24.

1514. Clements, Peter J. "Johannes Brahms: Intermezzo, Opus 119, No. 1." CAUSM 7 (1977): 31–51.

1515. Dunsby, Jonathan Mark. "Analytical Studies of Brahms." Ph.D. diss., University of Leeds, 1976. [No. 1]

1516. ———. "Structural Ambiguity in Brahms: Analytical Approaches to Four Works." Ann Arbor, Mich.: UMI Research Press, 1981. [No. 1]

1517. Goebels, Franzpeter. "Adagio h-moll: Bemerkungen zum Intermezzo h-moll op. 119 Nr. 1 von Johannes Brahms." M 37, no. 3 (1983): 230–31.

1518. Jordan, Roland, and Emma Kafalenos. "The Double Trajectory: Ambiguity in Brahms and Henry James." NCM 13, no. 2 (1989): 129–44. [No. 1]

1519. Newbould, Brian. "A New Analysis of Brahms's Intermezzo in B Minor, Op. 119, No. 1." MR 38 (1977): 33–43.

Des Abends kann ich nicht schlafen gehn

1520. Klenz, William. "Brahms, O. 38: Piracy, Pillage, Plagiarism, Parod." MR 34 (1973): 39–50.

Deutsches Requiem, Op. 45

1521. Hollander, Hans. "Gedanken zum strukturellen Aufbau des Brahmsschen Requiem." SMZ 105 (1965): 326–33.

1522. Musgrave, Michael. *Brahms: A German Requiem*. Cambridge: Cambridge University Press, 1996.

1523. ———. "Historical Influences in the Growth of Brahms's Requiem." ML 53 (1972): 3–17.

1524. Newman, William S. "A 'basic motive' in Brahms' *German Requiem*." MR 24 (1963): 190–94.

1525. Reinhardt, Klaus. "Motivisch-thematisches im *Deutschen Requiem* von Brahms: Zum 100. Jahrestag der ersten voellstandigen Aufführung im Leipzig am 28. Februar 1869." MK 39 (1969): 13–17.

1526. Westafer, Walter. "Overall Unity and Contrast in Brahms's *German Requiem*." Ph.D. diss., University of North Carolina, 1973.

Duets (Vocal)

1527. Atlas, Raphael. "Text and Musical Gesture in Brahms's Vocal Duets and Quartets with Piano." JM 10, no. 2 (1992): 231–60.

1528. Bozart, George Severs, Jr. "Brahms's Duets for Soprano and Alto, Op. 61: A Study in Chronology and Compositional Process." SM 25 (1983): 191–210.

Ernste Gesänge, Op. 121

1529. Whittall, Arnold. "The *Vier ernste Gesänge* Op. 121: Enrichment and Uniformity." M-Pascall: 191–207.

Fantasien, Op. 116

1530. Baud, Jean-Marc. "Con molta espressione." SMZ 123 (1983): 141–47.

1531. Cai, Camilla. "Forms Made Miniature: The Intermezzi of Brahms." F-Lefkowitz: 135–50. [No. 4]

1532. Dunsby, Jonathan. "The Multi-Piece in Brahms: Fantasien Op. 116." M-Pascall: 167–90.

1533. Horne, William. "Brahms's Düsseldorf Suite Study and His Intermezzo, Opus 116, No. 2." MQ 73, no. 2 (1989): 249–83.

1534. Kraus, Detlef. "Brahms' op. 116: Das Unikum der sieben Fantasien." BS 8 (1990): 49–60.

1535. Mastroianni, Thomas Owen. "Elements of Unity in Fantasies, Opus 116, by Brahms." D.M.A. diss., Indiana University, 1970.

1536. Scott, Ann Besser. "Thematic Transmutation in the Music of Brahms: A Matter of Musical Alchemy." JMR 15, no. 3 (1995): 177–206. [No. 4]

1537. Smith, Charles Justice, III. "Patterns and Strategies: Four Perspectives of Musical Characterization." Ph.D. diss., University of Michigan, 1980. [No. 4]

1538. Torkewitz, Dieter. "Die entwickelte Zeit: Zum Intermezzo Op. 116, IV von Johannes Brahms." MF 32 (1979): 135–40.

1539. Wick, Norman L. "Shifted Downbeats in Classic and Romantic Music." ITR 15, no. 2 (1994): 73–87. [Nos. 3, 6]

Fugue, WoO. 8 (Organ)

1540. Hartmann, Günter. "Zur Orgelfuge in As-Moll von Johannes Brahms." BS 7 (1987): 9–19.

Gesänge, Op. 3

1541. Braus, Ira. "Brahms's 'Liebe und Frühling' II, Op. 3, No. 3: A New Path to the Artwork of the Future?" NCM 10, no. 2 (1986): 135–56.

Gesänge, Op. 43

1542. Platt, Heather. "Dramatic Turning Points in Brahms Lieder." ITR 15, no. 1 (1994): 69–104. [No. 1]

Gesänge, Op. 104

1543. Larson, Brook C. "A Study of Brahms' Fünf Gesänge, Op. 104." M.M. thesis, Bowling Green State University, 1999.

Hungarian Dances, WoO. 1

1544. Sheveloff, Joel. "Dance, Gypsy, Dance!" F-Lefkowitz: 151–65.

Intermezzos, Op. 117

1545. Baud, Jean-Marc. "Con molta espressione." SMZ 123 (1983): 141–47.

1546. Budde, Elmar. "Johannes Brahms' Intermezzo op. 117, Nr. 2." M-Breig: 324–37.

1547. Cadwallader, Allen. "Foreground Motivic Ambiguity: Its Clarification at Middleground Levels in Selected Late Piano Pieces of Johannes Brahms." MA 7, no. 1 (1988): 59–92. [No. 2]

1548. ———. "Schenker's Unpublished Graphic Analysis of Brahms's Intermezzo Op. 117, No. 2: Tonal Structure and Concealed Motivic Repetition." MTS 6 (1984): 1–13.

1549. Cai, Camilla. "Forms Made Miniature: The Intermezzi of Brahms." F-Lefkowitz: 135–50. [No. 2]

1550. Gamer, Carlton. "Busnois, Brahms, and the Syntax of Temporal Proportions." F-Seay: 201–15. [No. 3]

1551. Grippe, Kerry. "An Analysis of the Three Intermezzi, Op. 117, by Johannes Brahms." D.M.A. diss., Indiana University, 1980.

1552. Scott, Ann Besser. "Thematic Transmutation in the Music of Brahms: A Matter of Musical Alchemy." JMR 15, no. 3 (1995): 177–206. [No. 2]

1553. Velten, Klaus. "Entwicklungsdenken und Zeiterfahrung in der Musik von Johannes Brahms: Das Intermezzo Op. 117, Nr. 2." MF 34 (1981): 56–59.

1554. Zabrack, Harold. "Musical Timing: A View of Implicit Musical Reality." JALS 16 (1984): 89–97. [No. 1]

Klavierstücke, Op. 76

1555. Atlas, Raphael. "Enharmonic *Trompe-l'oreille*: Reprise and the Disguised Seam in Nineteenth-Century Music." ITO 10, no. 6 (1988): 15–36. [No. 4]

1556. Cadwallader, Allen. "Echoes and Recollections: Brahms's Op. 76, No. 6." TP 13 (1988): 65–78.

1557. Cahn, Peter. "Johannes Brahms: Intermezzo B-dur Op. 76, Nr. 4." M 42, no. 1 (1988): 47–51.

1558. Carpenter, Patricia. "A Problem in Organic Form: Schoenberg's Tonal Body." TP 13 (1988): 31–63. [No. 6]

1559. M-Code. [No. 4]

1560. M-Kresky: 120–34. [No. 7]

1561. Lewin, David. "On Harmony and Meter in Brahms's Op. 76, No. 8." NCM 4 (1980–1981): 261–65.

1562. Trucks, Amanda Louise. "The Metric Complex in Johannes Brahms's Klavierstücke, Op. 76." Ph.D. diss., University of Rochester, 1992.

Liebeslieder (Waltzes), Op. 52a

1563. Brodbeck, David. "Compatibility, Coherence, and Closure in Brahms's *Liebeslieder Waltzes*." F-Meyer: 411–37.

Lieder (various; *see also* specific *Lieder, Gesänge*, and collections)

1564. Bozart, George Severs, Jr. "The Lieder of Johannes Brahms, 1868–1871: Studies in Chronology and Compositional Process." Ph.D. diss., Princeton University, 1978.

1565. Gerber, Rudolf. "Formprobleme im Brahmsschen Lied." JMP 39 (1932): 23–42.

1566. Giebeler, Konrad. *Die Lieder von Johannes Brahms*. Münster/Westfalen: Kramer, 1959.

1567. Harrison, Max. *The Lieder of Brahms*. London: Cassell, 1972.

1568. Helms, Siegmund. "Die Melodiebildung in den Liedern von Johannes Brahms und ihr Verhältnis zu Volksliedern und volkstümlichen Weisen." Ph.D. diss., Freie Universität, Berlin, 1968.

1569. Jacobsen, Christiane. *Das Verhältnis von Sprache und Musik in ausgewählten Liedern von Johannes Brahms, dargestellt an Parallelvertonungen.* Hamburg: Wagner, 1975.

1570. Kinsey, Barbara. "Mörike Poems Set by Brahms, Schumann, and Wolf." MR 29 (1968): 257–67.

1571. Misch, Ludwig. "Kontrapunkt und Imitation im Brahmsschen Lied." MF 11 (1958): 155–60.

1572. Rieger, Erwin. "Die Tonartencharacteristik im einstimmigen Klavierlied von Johannes Brahms." SZM 22 (1955): 142–216.

1573. Stohrer, Sister M. Baptist. "The Selection and Setting of Poetry in the Solo Songs of Johannes Brahms." Ph.D. diss., University of Wisconsin, 1974.

Lieder, Op. 47

1574. Thym, Jürgen, and Ann Clark Fehn. "Sonnet Structure and the German Lied: Shackles or Spurs?" JALS 32 (1993): 3–15. [No. 5]

Lieder, Op. 85

1575. Platt, Heather. "Unrequited Love and Unrealized Dominants." INT 7 (1993): 119–48. [No. 6]

Lieder, Op. 94

1576. Platt, Heather. "Unrequited Love and Unrealized Dominants." INT 7 (1993): 119–48. [No. 5]

Lieder, Op. 95

1577. Platt, Heather. "Dramatic Turning Points in Brahms Lieder." ITR 15, no. 1 (1994): 69–104. [No. 5]

Lieder, Op. 96

1578. Kielian, Marianne, Marion A. Guck, and Charles J. Smith. "Analysis Symposium: Brahms's 'Der Tod, das ist die kühle Nacht.'" ITO 2, no. 6 (1976): 16–43.

1579. Pisk, Paul A. "Dreams of Death and life: A Study of Two Songs by Johannes Brahms." F-Alderman: 227–34. [No. 1]

1580. Platt, Heather. "Unrequited Love and Unrealized Dominants." INT 7 (1993): 119–48. [No. 3]

Lieder, Op. 105

1581. Braus, Ira. "Poetic-Musical Rhetoric in Brahms's 'Auf dem Kirchhofe,' Op. 105, No. 4." TP 13 (1988): 15–30.

1582. Clarkson, Austin, and Edward Laufer. "Analysis Symposium: Brahms Op. 105/1." JMT 15, nos. 1–2 (1971): 2–57. Reprint, M-Yeston: 227–74.

1583. Pisk, Paul A. "Dreams of Death and life: A Study of Two Songs by Johannes Brahms." F-Alderman: 227–34. [No. 2]

1584. Schenker, Heinrich. "Graphic Analysis of Brahms's 'Auf dem Kirchhofe,' Op. 105, No. 4." Introduction by Hedi Siegel; commentary by Arthur Maisel. TP 13 (1988): 1–14.

Lieder und Gesänge, Op. 58

1585. Bozart, George Severs, Jr. "Synthesizing Word and Tone: Brahms' Setting of Hebbel's 'Vorüber.'" M-Pascall: 77–98. [No. 7]

Lieder und Gesänge, Op. 59

1586. McKinney, Timothy R. "Beyond the 'Rain-Drop' Motif: Motivic and Thematic Relationships in Brahms's Opera 59 and 78." MR 52, no. 2 (1991): 108–22.

Lieder und Gesänge, Op. 63

1587. Bruckmann, Annett. "'O wüßt ich doch den Weg zurück . . .': Ein Beitrag zum Brahmsschen Liedschaffen." BS 9 (1992): 49–73. [Nos. 7–9]

Motets, Op. 29

1588. Beller-McKenna, Daniel. "Brahms's Motet 'Es ist das Heil uns kommen her' and the 'Innermost Essence of Music.'" BST 2 (1998): 31–61.

1589. Blume, Jürgen. "Johannes Brahms: *Schaffe in mir, Gott, ein reine Herz* (Op. 29, Nr. 2)." NZM 146, no. 5 (1985): 34–36.

Motets, Op. 74

1590. Beller-McKenna, Daniel. "The Great *Warum?* Job, Christ, and Bach in a Brahms Motet." NCM 19, no. 3 (1996): 231–51. [No. 1]

1591. Hohlfeld, Christoph. "Johannes Brahms: Zwei Motetten für gemischten Chor a capella, Op. 74." BS 12 (1999): 119–33.

Piano Concertos (various; *see also* specific piano concertos)

1592. Vallis, Richard. "A Study of Late Baroque Instrumental Style in the Piano Concertos of Brahms." Ph.D. diss., New York University, 1978.

Piano Concerto No. 1, Op. 15

1593. Böttinger, Peter. "Jahre der Krise, Krise der Form: Beobachtungen am 1. Satz des Klavierkonzertes op. 15 von Johannes Brahms." M-Metzger/Brahms: 41–68. [Movement I]
1594. Collier, Michael. "The Rondo Movements of Beethoven's Concerto No. 3 in C Minor, Op. 37, and Brahms's Concerto No. 1 in D Minor: A Comparative Analysis." TP 31 (1978): 5–15.
1595. Dahlhaus, Carl. *Johannes Brahms: Klavierkonzert Nr. 1 D-Moll, Op. 15.* Munich: Fink, 1965.
1596. Dubiel, Joseph. "Contradictory Criteria in a Work of Brahms." BST 1 (1994): 81–110. [Movement I]
1597. Rosen, Charles. "Influence: Plagiarism and Inspiration." NCM 4 (1980–1981): 87–100. [No. 1]

Piano Concerto No. 2, Op. 83

1598. Mahlert, Ulrich. *Johannes Brahms: Klavierkonzert B-Dur op. 83.* Munich: Fink, 1994.

Piano Quartet No. 1, Op. 25

1599. Breslauer, Peter Seth. "Motivic and Rhythmic Contrapuntal Structure in the Chamber Music of Johannes Brahms." Ph.D. diss., Yale University, 1984.

Piano Quartet No. 3, Op. 60

1600. Dunsby, Jonathan Mark. "Analytical Studies of Brahms." Ph.D. diss., University of Leeds, 1976.
1601. ———. "Structural Ambiguity in Brahms: Analytical Approaches to Four Works." Ann Arbor, Mich.: UMI Research Press, 1981.
1602. Pfisterer, Manfred. "Eingriffe in die Syntax: Zum Verfahren der metrisch-rhythmischen Variation bei Johannes Brahms." M-Metzger/Brahms: 76–85. [Movement I]

Piano Sonata No. 3, Op. 9

1603. Schläder, Jürgen. "Zur Funktion der Variantentechnik in den Klaviersonaten F-Moll von Johannes Brahms und G-Moll von Franz Liszt." HJM 7 (1984): 171–99.

Piano Trio No. 1, Op. 8

1604. Baldassarre, Antonio. "Johannes Brahms and Johannes Kreisler: Creativity and Aesthetics of the Young Brahms Illustrated by the Piano Trio in B major, Opus 8." ACTA 72, no. 2 (2000): 145–67.

Piano Trio No. 3, Op. 101

1605. Daverio, John. "From 'Concertante Rondo' to 'Lyric Sonata': A Commentary on Brahms's Reception of Mozart." BST 1 (1994): 111–36. [Movement I]
1606. Scott, Ann Besser. "Thematic Transmutation in the Music of Brahms: A Matter of Musical Alchemy." JMR 15, no. 3 (1995): 177–206. [Movement II]
1607. Thompson, Christopher K. "Forming Brahms: Sonata Form and the Piano Trio in C Minor, Op. 101." MTEA 6 (1997): 49–68.

Piano Works (various; *see also* specific piano works)

1608. Floros, Constantin. "Studien zu Brahms' Klaviermusik." BS 5 (1983): 25–64.
1609. Hübler, Klaus K. "Die Kunst, ohne Einfälle zu komponieren: Dargestellt an Johannes Brahms' späten Intermezzi." M-Metzger/Brahms: 24–40.
1610. Mason, Colin. "Brahms's Piano Sonatas." MR 5 (1944): 112–18.
1611. M-Sterling.

Quartets (Vocal)

1612. Atlas, Raphael. "Text and Musical Gesture in Brahms's Vocal Duets and Quartets with Piano." JM 10, no. 2 (1992): 231–60.
1613. Kolb, G. Roberts. "The Vocal Quartets of Brahms (Ops. 31, 64, and 92): A Textual Encounter." F-Swan: 323–55.

Quintet, Op. 115

1614. Breslauer, Peter Seth. "Motivic and Rhythmic Contrapuntal Structure in the Chamber Music of Johannes Brahms." Ph.D. diss., Yale University, 1984.
1615. Häfner, Roland. *Johannes Brahms: Klarinettenquintett.* Munich: Fink, 1978.
1616. Lawson, Colin. *Brahms: Clarinet Quintet.* Cambridge: Cambridge University Press, 1998.
1617. Salvetti, Guido. "Johannes Brahms: Quintette avec clarinette, op. 115." Trans. Nicolas Meeùs. ANM 21 (1990): 45–53.

Requiem. *See Deutsches Requiem, Op. 45*

Rhapsodies, Op. 79

1618. Greenberg, Beth. "Brahms' Rhapsody in G Minor, Op. 79, No. 2." ITO 1, no. 9 (1975): 21–32.

Rhapsody, Op. 53

1619. Berry, Wallace. "Text and Music in the *Alto Rhapsody*." JMT 27 (1983): 239–53.

1620. Forte, Allen. "Motive and Rhythmic Contour in the *Alto Rhapsody*." JMT 27 (1973): 255–71.

Rinaldo, **Op. 50**

1621. Ingraham, Mary Isabel. "Brahms's *Rinaldo*, Op. 50: A Structural and Contextual Study." Ph.D. diss., University of Nottingham, 1994.

Romanzen (*Magelone-Lieder*), Op. 33

1622. Boyer, Margaret Gene. "A Study of Brahms' Setting of the Poems from Tieck's *Liebesgeschichte der schönen Magelone und des Grafen Peter von Provence*." Ph.D. diss., Washington University, 1980.

1623. Jost, Peter. "Brahms und die romantische Ironie: Zu den 'Romanzen aus L. Tieck's Magelone' Op. 33." AM 47, no. 1 (1990): 27–61.

Scherzo, Op. 4

1624. Joseph, Charles M. "Origins of Brahms's Structural Control." CMS 21 (1981): 8–24.

Schicksalslied, **Op. 54**

1625. Cooper, John Michael. "Dialectic Thought and Musical Form in Johannes Brahms's *Schicksalslied*, Opus 54." TSP 4 (1987): 41–47.

String Quartet No. 3, Op. 67

1626. Fenske, David. "Contrapuntal Textures in the String Quartets, Op. 51, No. 2, and Op. 67 of Johannes Brahms." F-Kaufmann/W: 351–69.

1627. Wilke, Rainer. *Brahms, Reger, Schönberg, Streichquartette: Motivisch-thematische Prozesse und formale Gestalt.* Hamburg: Wagner, 1980.

String Quartets, Op. 51

1628. Breslauer, Peter Seth. "Motivic and Rhythmic Contrapuntal Structure in the Chamber Music of Johannes Brahms." Ph.D. diss., Yale University, 1984.

1629. Daverio, John. "From 'Concertante Rondo' to 'Lyric Sonata': A Commentary on Brahms's Reception of Mozart." BST 1 (1994): 111–36. [No. 1 (Movement IV)]

1630. Fenske, David. "Contrapuntal Textures in the String Quartets, Op. 51, No. 2, and Op. 67 of Johannes Brahms." F-Kaufmann/W: 351–69.

1631. Forte, Allen. "Motivic Design and Structural Levels in the First Movement of Brahms's String Quartet in C Minor." MQ 69 (1983): 471–502. [No. 1]

1632. Graybill, Roger. "Brahms' Integration of Traditional and Progressive Tendencies: A Look at Three Sonata Expositions." JMR 8, nos. 1–2 (1988): 141–68. [No. 1 (Movement I)]

1633. Hill, William G. "Brahms' Opus 51: A Diptych." MR 13 (1952): 110–24.

1634. Krummacher, Friedhelm. "Reception and Analysis: On the Brahms Quartets, Op. 51, Nos. 1 and 2." NCM 18, no. 1 (1994): 24–45.

1635. Smith, Peter H. "Liquidation, Augmentation, and Brahms's Recapitulatory Overlaps." NCM 17, no. 3 (1994): 237–61. [No. 1 (Movement I)]

1636. Wilke, Rainer. *Brahms, Reger, Schönberg, Streichquartette: Motivisch-thematische Prozesse und formale Gestalt.* Hamburg: Wagner, 1980.

String Quintet No. 1, Op. 88

1637. Ravizza, Victor. "Möglichkeiten des Komischen in der Musik: Der letzte Satz des Streichquintetts in F Dur, Op. 88 von Johannes Brahms." AM 31 (1974): 137–50.

1638. Redlich, Hans F. "Bruckner and Brahms Quintets in F." ML 36 (1955): 253–58.

1639. Seidel, Wilhelm. "Das Streichquintett in F-Dur im Œuvre von Anton Bruckner und Johannes Brahms." BRS (1983): 183–89.

Symphonies (various; *see also* specific symphonies)

1640. Andrieux, Françoise. "Le thème dan les formes sonate des symphonies de Brahms." ANM 13 (1988): 58–68.

1641. ASO 53 (1983).

1642. Cuyler, Louise E. "Progressive Concepts of Pitch Relationships as Observed in the Symphonies of Brahms." F-Fox: 164–80.

1643. Floros, Constantin. "Zur Gegensätzlichkeit der Symphonik Brahms' und Bruckners." BRS (1983): 145–53.

1644. Fuchs, Ingrid. "Aspekte der Instrumentation der Symphonien Brahms' und Bruckners." BRS (1983): 133–44.

1645. Hendrickson, Hugh. "Rhythmic Activity in the Symphonies of Brahms." ITO 2, no. 6 (1976): 5–15.

1646. Klein, Rudolf. "Die konstructiven Grundlagen der Brahms-Symphonien." OMZ 23 (1968): 258–63.

1647. Rittenhouse, Robert J. "Rhythmic Elements in the Symphonies of Johannes Brahms." Ph.D. diss., University of Iowa, 1967.

1648. Schubert, Giselher. "Themes and Double Themes: The Problem of the Symphonic in Brahms." NCM 18, no. 1 (1994): 10–23.

1649. Schulze, Werner. *Temporelationen in symphonischen Werk von Beethoven, Schubert und Brahms.* Bern: Kreis & Freude um Hans Kayser, 1981.

1650. Steilfeld, Bent. "Kontrapunktik og den funktion i Brahms's orkestervoeker." DAM 14 (1983): 115–32.

Symphony No. 1, Op. 68

1651. Brodbeck, David Lee. *Brahms: Symphony No. 1.* Cambridge: Cambridge University Press, 1997.

1652. Carrozzo, Mario. "Le due versioni del secondo movimento della Sinfonia n. 1 op. 68 di Johannes Brahms: Un problema storiografico o analitico?" ANL 13 (1994): 16–28. [Movement II]

1653. Fink, Robert. "Desire, Repression, and Brahms's First Symphony." REP 2, no. 1 (1993): 75–103.

1654. Floros, Constantin. "Tradition und Innovation in der Ersten Symphonie von Johannes Brahms." BRS (1997): 233–42.

1655. Kross, Siegfried. "Brahms und Bruckner: Über Zusammenhänge von Themenstruktur und Form." BRS (1983): 173–81.

1656. Moser, Hans Joachim. "Zur Sinndeutung der Brahms'schen C-Moll Symphonie." OMZ 8 (1953): 21–24.

1657. Musgrave, Michael. "Brahms's First symphony: Thematic Coherence and Its Secret Origin." MA 2 (1983): 117–34.

1658. Ravizza, Victor. "Konflikte in Brahms'scher Musik: Zum ersten Satz der C-Moll-Sinfonie Op. 68." SBM 2 (1974): 75–90.

1659. Seedorf, Thomas. "Brahms' 1. Symphonie: Komponieren als Auseinandersetzung mit der Geschichte." MB 15, no. 5 (1983): 10–14.

1660. Winkler, Gerhard J. "Anton Bruckner—ein Neudeutscher? Gedanken zum Verhältnis zwischen Symphonie und symphonischer Dichtung." BRS (1984): 149–62.

Symphony No. 2, Op. 73

1661. Brinkmann, Reinhold. *Johannes Brahms: Die Zweite Symphonie, späte Idylle.* Munich: Text + Kritik, 1990.

1662. M-Epstein.

1663. Komma, Karl Michael. "Das Scherzo der 2. Symphonie von Johannes Brahms." F-Wiora: 448–57.

1664. Schachter, Carl. "The First Movement of Brahms's Second Symphony: The First Theme and Its Consequences." MA 2 (1983): 55–68.

Symphony No. 3, Op. 90

1665. Beveridge, David. "Echoes of Dvořák in the Third Symphony of Brahms." MO 11 (1989): 221–30.

1666. Brown, A. Peter. "Brahms' Third Symphony and the New German School." JM 2 (1983): 434–52.

1667. Moore, Hilarie Clark. "The Structural Role of Orchestration in Brahms's Music: A Study of the Third Symphony." Ph.D. diss., Yale University, 1991.

1668. Musgrave, Michael. "*Frei aber Froh*: A Reconsideration." NCM 3 (1979–1980): 251–58.

Symphony No. 4, Op. 98

1669. Doebel, Wolfgang. "Zum Prozeß der Formentstehung im Finalsatz der Vierten Sinfonie von Johannes Brahms." BS 11 (1997): 19–40. [Movement IV]

1670. Dunsby, Jonathan Mark. "Analytical Studies of Brahms." Ph.D. diss., University of Leeds, 1976.

1671. ———. "Structural Ambiguity in Brahms: Analytical Approaches to Four Works." Ann Arbor, Mich.: UMI Research Press, 1981.

1672. Hekkers, William. "Johannes Brahms: Symphonie no. 4 en mi mineur, op. 98, 1er et 4e mouvements: Structure thématique et économie des moyens." ANM 23 (1991): 51–63.

1673. Hull, Kenneth. "Allusive Irony in Brahms's Fourth Symphony." BST 2 (1998): 135–68.

1674. Klein, Rudolf. "Die Doppelgerüsttechnik in der Passacaglia der IV. Symphonie von Brahms." OMZ 27 (1972): 641–48.

1675. Knapp, Raymond. "The Finale of Brahms's Fourth Symphony: The Tale of the Subject." NCM 13, no. 1 (1989): 3–17.

1676. Mäckelmann, Michael. *Johannes Brahms: IV. Symphonie e-Moll op. 98.* Munich: Fink, 1991.

1677. Osmond-Smith, David. "The Retreat from Dynamism: A Study of Brahms's Fourth Symphony." M-Pascall: 147–66.

1678. Pascall, Robert. "Genre and the Finale of Brahms's Fourth Symphony." MA 8, no. 3 (1989): 233–45.

1679. Siegmund-Schultze, Walter. "Brahms' vierte Sinfonie." F-Schneider/80: 241–54.

1680. Smith, Peter H. "Liquidation, Augmentation, and Brahms's Recapitulatory Overlaps." NCM 17, no. 3 (1994): 237–61. [Movement I]

1681. Weber, Horst. "Melancholia: Versuch über Brahms' Vierte." F-Stephan: 281–95.

Tragic Overture, Op. 81

1682. Webster, James. "Brahms's *Tragic Overture*: The Form of Tragedy." M-Pascall: 99–124.

Trio, Op. 40

1683. Thompson, Christopher K. "Re-forming Brahms: Sonata Form and the Horn Trio, Op. 40." ITR 18, no. 1 (1997): 65–96. [Movement I]

Variations and Fugue on a Theme by G. F. Handel, Op. 24

1684. Agmon, Eytan. "Rhythmic Displacement in the Fugue of Brahms's *Handel Variations*: The Refashioning of a Traditional Device." SMUWO 13 (1991): 1–20.

1685. Dunsby, Jonathan Mark. "Analytical Studies of Brahms." Ph.D. diss., University of Leeds, 1976.

1686. ———. "Structural Ambiguity in Brahms: Analytical Approaches to Four Works." Ann Arbor, Mich.: UMI Research Press, 1981.

Variations on a Theme by J. Haydn, Op. 56a–b

1687. Forte, Allen. "The Structural Origin of Exact Tempi in the *Brahms-Haydn Variations*." MR 18 (1957): 138–49.

1688. McCorkle, Donald M., ed. *Johannes Brahms: Variations on a Theme by Haydn for Orchestra, Op. 56a and for Two Pianos, Op. 56b.* Norton Critical Scores. New York: Norton, 1976.

Variations on a Theme by Paganini, Op. 35

1689. Auh, Mijai Youn. "Piano Variations by Brahms, Liszt, and Friedman on a Theme by Paganini." D.M. diss., Indiana University, 1980.

1690. Mies, Paul. "Zu Werdegang und Strukturen der *Paganini-Variationen* Op. 35 für Klavier von Johannes Brahms." SM 11 (1969): 323–32. Also in F-Szabolcsi: 323–32.

1691. Schädler, Stefan. "Technik und Verfahren in den Studien für Pianoforte: *Variationen über ein Thema von Paganini* op. 35 von Johannes Brahms." M-Metzger/Brahms: 3–23.

Variations on a Theme by R. Schumann, Op. 9

1692. Neighbour, Oliver. "Brahms and Schumann: Two Opus Nines and Beyond." NCM 7 (1983–1984): 266–70.

Variations, Op. 21

1693. Struck, Michael. "Dialog über die Variation, präzisiert: Joseph Joachims *Variationen über ein irisches Elfenlied* und Johannes Brahms' Variationenpaar Op. 21 im Licht der gemeinsamen gattungstheoretischen Diskussion." F-Floros/60: 105–54.

Viola Sonata, Op. 120, No. 1. *See* Clarinet Sonata, Op. 120, No. 1

Violin Concerto, Op. 77

1694. Weiss-Aigner, Günter. *Johannes Brahms: Violinkonzert D-Dur.* Munich: Fink, 1979.

1695. ———. "Komponist und Geiger: Joseph Joachims Mitarbeit am Violinkonzert von Johannes Brahms." NZM 135 (1974): 232–36.

Violin Sonata, No. 1, Op. 78

1696. Hollander, Hans. "Der melodische Aufbau in Brahms' *Regenlied* Sonate." NZM 125 (1964): 5–7.

1697. McKinney, Timothy R. "Beyond the 'Rain-Drop' Motif: Motivic and Thematic Relationships in Brahms's Opera 59 and 78." MR 52, no. 2 (1991): 108–22.

Violin Sonata No. 2, Op. 100

1698. Eppstein, Hans. "Duo und Dialog: Zu einem Struktur- und Stilproblem der Kammermusik." MF 49, no. 3 (1996): 252–75. [Movement I]

Violin Sonata No. 3, Op. 108

1699. Daverio, John. "From 'Concertante Rondo' to 'Lyric Sonata': A Commentary on Brahms's Reception of Mozart." BST 1 (1994): 111–36. [Movement IV]

1700. Fischer, Richard S. "Brahms' Technique of Motive Development in His Sonata in D Minor, Opus 108, for Piano and Violin." D.M.A. diss., University of Arizona, 1964.

Waltzes, Op. 39

1701. Brodbeck, David. "*Primo* Schubert, *Secondo* Schumann: Brahms's Four-Hand Waltzes, Op. 39." JM 7, no. 1 (1989): 58–80.

1702. Kirsch, Winfried. "Die Klavier-Walzer Op. 39 von Johannes Brahms und ihre Tradition." JSIM 1969: 38–67.

Various Works

1703. Azzaroni, Loris. "Elusività dei processi cadenzali in Brahms: Il ruolo della sottodominante." RIM 24, no. 1 (1989): 74–94.

1704. Beveridge, David. "Non-Traditional Functions of the Development Section in Sonata Forms by Brahms." MR 51, no. 1 (1990): 25–35.

1705. Borchardt, Georg. "Ein Viertonmotiv als melodische Komponente in Werken von Brahms." HJM 7 (1984): 101–12.

1706. Braun, Hartmut. "Ein Zitat: Beziehungen zwischen Chopin und Brahms." MF 25 (1972): 317–21.

1707. Brusatti, Otto. "Zur thematischen Arbeit bei Johannes Brahms." SZM 31 (1980): 191–206.

1708. Cone, Edward T. "Brahms: Songs with Words and Songs without Words." INT 1 (1987): 31–56.

1709. Czesla, Werner. "Motivische Mutationen in Schaffen von Johannes Brahms." F-Schmidt-Görg/70: 64–72.

1710. ———. "Studien zum Finale in der Kammermusik von Johannes Brahms." Ph.D. diss., Rheinische Friedrich-Wilhelms-Universität, Bonn, 1968.

1711. Epstein, David. "Brahms and the Mechanisms of Motion: The Composition of Performance," *American Brahms Society Newsletter* 8, no. 2 (1990): 1–6. German translation under the title "Brahms und die Mechanismen der Bewegung: Die Komposition der Aufführung" (BS 10 [1994]: 9–21).

1712. Federhofer, Hellmut. "Johannes Brahms–Arnold Schönberg und der Fortschritt." SZM 34 (1983): 111–30.

1713. Fenske, David. "Texture in the Chamber Music of Johannes Brahms." Ph.D. diss., University of Wisconsin, 1973.

1714. Frisch, Walter Miller. *Brahms and the Principle of Developing Variation.* Berkeley: University of California Press, 1984.

1715. ———. "Brahms's Sonata Structures and the Principle of Developing Variation." Ph.D. diss., University of California, Berkeley, 1981.

1716. Hiebert, Elfrieda. "The Janus Figure of Brahms: A Future Built upon the Past." JALS 16 (1984): 72–88.

1717. Hirsch, Hans. *Rhythmisch-metrische Untersuchungen zur Variationstechnik bei Johannes Brahms.* Hamburg: n.p., 1963.

1718. Hollander, Hans. "Die Terzformel als musikalisches Bauelement bei Brahms." NZM 133 (1972): 439–41.

1719. Jordahl, Robert. "A Study of the Use of the Chorale in the Works of Mendelssohn, Brahms, and Reger." Ph.D. diss., University of Rochester, 1965.

1720. Kirsch, Winfried. "Das Scherzo bei Brahms und Bruckner." BRS (1983): 155–72.

1721. Kohlhase, Hans. "Brahms und Mendelssohn: Strukturelle Parallelen in der Kammermusik für Streicher." HJM 7 (1984): 59–86.

1722. Kraus, Detlef. "Konstanten im Schaffen von Johannes Brahms." BS 11 (1997): 41–48.

1723. Kross, Siegfried. "Brahms und der Kanon." F-Schmidt-Görg: 175–87.

1724. Lesznai, Lajos. "Auf den Spuren einer ungarischen Intonation in den Werken von Johannes Brahms." MG 21 (1971): 455–58.

1725. Mitschka, Arno. "Der Sonatensatz in den Werken von Johannes Brahms." Ph.D. diss., Johannes-Gutenberg-Universität, Mainz, 1961.

1726. Morik, Werner. *Johannes Brahms und sein Verhältnis zum deutschen Volkslied.* Tutzing: Schneider, 1965.

1727. Musgrave, Michael. *The Cambridge Companion to Brahms.* Cambridge: Cambridge University Press, 1999.

1728. Nivans, David Brian. "Brahms and the Binary Sonata: A Structuralist Interpretation." Ph.D. diss., University of California, Los Angeles, 1992.

1729. Pacun, David Edward. "Large-Scale Form in Selected Variation Sets of Johannes Brahms." Ph.D. diss., University of Chicago, 1998.

1730. Sisman, Elaine R. "Brahms and the Variation Canon." NCM 14, no. 2 (1990): 132–53.

1731. Smith, Peter H. "Brahms and Motivic 6, no. 3 Chords." MA 16, no. 2 (1997): 175–217.

1732. Truscott, Harold. "Brahms and Sonata Style." MR 25 (1964): 186–201.

1733. Velten, Klaus. "Das Princip der entwickelnden Variation bei Johannes Brahms und Arnold Schönberg." MB 6 (1974): 547–55.

1734. Webster, James. "Schubert's Sonata Form and Brahms's First Maturity." NCM 2, no. 1 (1978): 18–35; 3, no. 1 (1979–1980): 52–71.

1735. Wetschky, Jürgen. *Der Kanontechnik in der Instrumentalmusik von Johannes Brahms.* Regensburg: Bosse, 1967.

1736. Zingerle, Hans. "Chromatische Harmonik bei Brahms und Reger: Ein Vergleich." SZM 27 (1966): 151–85.

BRANT, HENRY (b. 1913)

1737. Drennen, Dorothy Carter. "Henry Brant's Use of Ensemble Dispersion." MR 38 (1977): 65–68.

1738. ———. "Relationship of Ensemble Dispersion to Structure in the Music of Henry Brant." Ph.D. diss., University of Miami, 1975.

1739. Harley, Maria Anna. "An American in Space: Henry Brant's 'Spatial Music.'" AMUS 15, no. 1 (1997): 70–92.

1740. Sankey, Stuart. "Henry Brant's *Grand Universal Circus*." JR 3, no. 3 (1956): 21–37.

BRAUN, GERHARD (b. 1932)
1741. Devroop, Chatradari. "Monologe eine Blockflötenspielers: Anmerkungen zu den Kompositionen für Blockflöte solo von Gerhard Braun." T 17, no. 2 (1992): 85–90.

BREDEMEYER, REINER (1929–1995)
1742. Kneipel, Eberhard. "Die Analyse: Konzert für Oboe und Orchester von Reiner Bredemeyer." MG 29 (1979): 286–89.
1743. Thiel, Wolfgang. "Reiner Bredermeyers Film- und Fernsehmusiken." MG 23 (1973): 648–53.

BRÉGENT, MICHEL-GEORGES (1948–1993)
1744. Petrowska-Brégent, Christina. "The Concept of *Geste*." CCM 9 (1974): 65–79.

BRESGEN, CESAR (1913–1988)
1745. Zaunschirm, Franz. "Cesar Bresgen: *Requiem für Anton Webern*." M 37, no. 6 (1983): 525–28.

BRETTINGHAM SMITH, JOLYON (b. 1949)
1746. Schmidt, Christian Martin. "Jolyon Brettingham Smith." NZM 144, no. 6 (1983): 22–26.

BRÉVILLE, PIERRE DE (1861–1949)
1747. Daitz, Mimi Segal. "The Songs of Pierre de Bréville (1861–1949)." Ph.D. diss., New York University, 1974.
1748. M-Kniesner. [Piano Sonata]

BRIAN, HAVERGAL (1876–1972)
1749. Pike, Lionel. "The Tonal Structure of Brian's *Gothic Symphony*." TEMPO 138 (1981) 33–40.
1750. Truscott, Harold, and Paul Rapoport. *Havergal Brian's "Gothic Symphony": Two Studies*. Potters Bar: Havergal Brian Society, 1978.

BRICHT, WALTER (1904–1970)
1751. Martin, Paul David. "The Seven Solo Piano Sonatas of Walter Bricht." D.M.A. diss., Indiana University, 1977.
1752. Wylie, Ted David. "A Survey of the Solo Vocal Compositions of Walter Bricht with Analyses of Selected Songs." D.M.A. diss., Indiana University, 1979.

BRIDGE, FRANK (1879–1941)
1753. Howells, Herbert. "Frank Bridge." ML 22 (1941): 208–15.
1754. Keating, Roderic Maurice. "The Songs of Frank Bridge." D.M.A. diss., University of Texas, 1970.
1755. Kennett, Chris. "Segmentation and Focus in Set-Generic Analysis." MA 17, no. 2 (1998): 127–59. [*Gargoyle*, Piano Sonata]
1756. Payne, Anthony. "The Music of Frank Bridge." TEMPO 106 (1973): 18–25; 107 (1973): 11–18.
1757. Wade, Bryan Lee. "The Four String Quartets of Frank Bridge." Ph.D. diss., Catholic University of America, 1995.

BRISTOW, GEORGE FREDERICK (1825–1898)
1758. Kauffman, Byron F. "The Choral Works of George F. Bristow (1825–1898) and William H. Fry (1815–1864)." D.M.A. diss., University of Illinois, 1975.

BRITTEN, BENJAMIN (1913–1976)

Albert Herring
1759. Hindley, Clifford. "Not the Marrying Kind: Britten's *Albert Herring*." COJ 6, no. 2 (1994): 159–74.
1760. Keller, Hans. *Benjamin Britten, Albert Herring: Analytical Notes*. New York: Boosey & Hawkes, 1949.

Beggar's Opera
1761. Keller, Hans. "Britten's *Beggar's Opera*." TEMPO 10 (1948–1949): 7–13.
1762. Wolff, Hellmuth Christian. "Britten und die *Beggar's Opera*." MZ 11 (1955): 62–65.

Billy Budd
1763. ASO 158 (1994).
1764. Cescotti, Diego. "Britten e la favola del 'Bel marinaio.'" RIM 21, no. 1 (1986): 170–93.
1765. Cooke, Mervyn. *Benjamin Britten: Billy Budd*. Cambridge: Cambridge University Press, 1993.
1766. Hindley, Clifford. "Britten's *Billy Budd*: The 'Interview Chords' Again." MQ 78, no. 1 (1994): 99–126.
1767. McKellar, Shannon. "Re-Visioning the 'Missing' Scene: Critical and Tonal Trajectories in Britten's *Billy Budd*." JRMA 122, no. 2 (1997): 258–80.
1768. Porter, Andrew. "Britten's *Billy Budd*." ML 33 (1952): 111–18.

1769. Rupprecht, Philip. "Tonal Stratification and Uncertainty in Britten's Music." JMT 40, no. 2 (1996): 311–46.

1770. Schuh, Willi. "*Billy Budd*: Zur musikalischen Struktur." MZ 11 (1955): 14–17.

1771. Whittall, Arnold. "'Twisted Relations': Method and Meaning in Britten's *Billy Budd*." COJ 2, no. 2 (1990): 145–71.

Cantata academica, carmen basiliense
1772. Bradshaw, Susan. "Britten's *Cantata academica*." TEMPO 53–54 (1960): 22–34.

Canticles
1773. Brown, David. "Britten's Three Canticles." MR 21 (1960): 55–65.

1774. Gordon, Samuel S. "Benjamin Britten's Canticles I, II, and III: A Structural and Stylistic Analysis." D.M. diss., Indiana University, 1974.

1775. Roseberry, Eric. "'Abraham and Isaac' Revisited: Reflections on a Theme and Its Inversion." F-Mitchell: 253–66. [Canticle II]

Cello Sonata
1776. Evans, Peter. "Britten's Cello Sonata." TEMPO 58 (1961): 8–19.

Chansons françaises
1777. Mark, Christopher. "Britten's *Quatre chansons françaises*." SN 10 (1983): 22–35.

Curlew River
1778. Flynn, William T. "Britten the Progressive." MR 44 (1983): 44–52.

1779. Laade, Wolfgang. "Benjamin Brittens Mysterienspiel *Curlew River* und die japanischen Vorbilder." MB 1 (1969): 562–65.

1780. Rhoads, Mary Ruth Schneyer. "Influences of Japanese *hogaku* Manifest in Selected Compositions by Peter Mennin and Benjamin Britten." Ph.D. diss., Michigan State University, 1969.

Death in Venice
1781. Corse, Sandra, and Larry Corse. "Britten's *Death in Venice*: Literary and Musical Structures." MQ 73, no. 3 (1989): 344–63.

1782. Dickinson, A. E. F. "Current Chronicle: Britten's New Opera." MQ 60 (1974): 470–78.

1783. Evans, John. "Britten's Venice Workshop: 1. The Sketch Book." SN 12 (1984–1985): 7–24.

1784. ———. "*Death in Venice*: The Apollonian/Dionysian Conflict." OQ 4, no. 3 (1986): 102–15.

1785. Milliman, Joan Ann. "Benjamin Britten's Symbolic Treatment of Sleep, Dream, and Death as Manifest in His Opera *Death in Venice*." Ph.D. diss., University of Southern California, 1977.

1786. Mitchell, Donald. *Benjamin Britten: Death in Venice*. Cambridge: Cambridge University Press, 1987.

1787. Travis, Roy. "The Recurrent Figure in the Britten/Piper Opera *Death in Venice*." MFO 6, no. 1 (1987): 129–246.

Gloriana
1788. Mitchell, Donald. "Some Observations on *Gloriana*." MMR 83 (1953): 255–60.

Holy Sonnets of John Donne
1789. Docherty, Barbara. "Sentence into Cadence: The Word-Setting of Tippett and Britten." TEMPO 166 (1988): 2–11.

1790. ———. "Syllogism and Symbol: Britten, Tippett, and English Text." CMR 5 (1989): 37–63.

Hymn to St. Cecilia
1791. Jennings, John Wells. "The Influence of W. H. Auden on Benjamin Britten." D.M.A. diss., University of Illinois, 1979.

Illuminations
1792. Mark, Christopher. "Contextually Transformed Tonality in Britten." MA 4, no. 3 (1985): 265–87. ["Villes"]

Metamorphoses after Ovid
1793. Slogteren, Koen van. "Benjamin Britten: *Six Metamorphoses after Ovid* für Oboe solo." T 15, no. 4 (1990): 268–73.

1794. ———. "Brittens *Metamorphosen* für Oboe: *Phaeton*." T 17, no. 2 (1992): gelbe Seite: ix–xii.

Midsummer Night's Dream
1795. ASO 146 (1992).

1796. Bach, Jan Morris. "An Analysis of Britten's *A Midsummer Night's Dream*." D.M.A. diss., University of Illinois, 1971.

1797. Cooke, Mervyn. "Britten and Shakespeare: Dramatic and Musical Cohesion in *A Midsummer Night's Dream*." ML 74, no. 2 (1993): 246–68.

1798. Evans, Peter. "Britten's New Opera: A Preview." TEMPO 53–54 (1960): 34–48.

Missa brevis
1799. Roseberry, Eric. "A Note on Britten's *Missa Brevis*." TEMPO 53–54 (1960): 11–16.

Nocturnal after John Dowland: Reflections on "Come Heavy Sleep"
1800. Rupprecht, Philip. "Tonal Stratification and Uncertainty in Britten's Music." JMT 40, no. 2 (1996): 311–46.

Nocturne
1801. Whitesell, Lloyd. "Translated Identities in Britten's Nocturne." REP 6, no. 1 (1997): 109–34.

Noye's Fludde
1802. Roseberry, Eric. "The Music of *Noye's Fludde.*" TEMPO 49 (1958): 2–11.

On This Island
1803. Jennings, John Wells. "The Influence of W. H. Auden on Benjamin Britten." D.M.A. diss., University of Illinois, 1979.

Operas (various; *see also* specific operas)
1804. Brauneiss, Leopold. "Zur Aktualität Benjamin Brittens." MTH 11, no. 2 (1996): 125–37.
1805. MZ 22 (1955). [Special issue]
1806. Simons, Harriett Rose. "The Use of the Chorus in the Operas of Benjamin Britten." D.M.A. diss., Indiana University, 1970.

Our Hunting Fathers
1807. Jennings, John Wells. "The Influence of W. H. Auden on Benjamin Britten." D.M.A. diss., University of Illinois, 1979.
1808. Mark, Christopher. "Contextually Transformed Tonality in Britten." MA 4, no. 3 (1985): 265–87. ["Rats Away!"]

Owen Wingrave
1809. ASO 173 (1996).
1810. McKellar, Shannon. "Music, Image, and Ideology in Britten's *Owen Wingrave*: Conflict in a Fissured Text." ML 80, no. 3 (1999): 390–410.
1811. Whittall, Arnold. "Britten's Lament: The World of Owen Wingrave." MA 19, no. 2 (2000): 145–66.

Paul Bunyan
1812. Ketukaenchan, Somsak. "A (Far Eastern) Note on *Paul Bunyan.*" F-Mitchell: 275–79.

Peter Grimes
1813. ASO 31 (1981).
1814. Brett, Philip. *Benjamin Britten: Peter Grimes.* Cambridge: Cambridge University Press, 1983.
1815. Deavel, R. Gary. "A Study of Two Operas by Benjamin Britten: *Peter Grimes* and *The Turn of the Screw.*" Ph.D. diss., University of Rochester, 1970.
1816. Foerster, Lilian. "*Peter Grimes* in Score and Performance." MU 1 (1946–1947): 221–41.
1817. Garbutt, J. W. "Music and Motive in *Peter Grimes.*" ML 44 (1963): 334–42.
1818. Kovnatskaya, Ludmila. "Notes on a Theme from *Peter Grimes.*" F-Mitchell: 172–85. [Act 1, scene 1]
1819. McGiffert, Genevieve. "The Musico-Dramatic Techniques of Benjamin Britten: A Detailed study of *Peter Grimes.*" Ph.D. diss., University of Denver, 1970.
1820. Nelson, John C. "Tonal and Dramatic Design in *Peter Grimes*: A Preliminary Study." TSP 3 (1986): 13–31.
1821. ———. "Tonal and Dramatic Design in *Peter Grimes*: Continuation and Conclusions." TSP 5 (1988): 34–64.
1822. Payne, Anthony. "Dramatic Use of Tonality in *Peter Grimes.*" TEMPO 66/67 (1963): 22–26.
1823. Stein, Erwin. "Benjamin Britten: *Peter Grimes.*" MZ 6 (1954): 51–55.
1824. ———. "*Peter Grimes*: Form und Geist." MZ 11 (1955): 10–14.

Praise We Great Men
1825. Stimpson, Mansel. "Britten's Last Work." TEMPO 155 (1985): 34–36.

Prince of the Pagodas
1826. Mitchell, Donald. "An Afterword on Britten's *Pagodas*: The Balinese Sources." TEMPO 152 (1985): 7–11.
1827. ———. "Catching on to the Technique in Pagoda-Land." TEMPO 146 (1983): 13–24.

Rape of Lucretia
1828. Squire, W. H. Haddon. "The Aesthetic Hypothesis and *The Rape of Lucretia.*" TEMPO 1 (1946): 1–9.

Rejoice in the Lamb
1829. LePage, Peter V. "Benjamin Britten's *Rejoice in the Lamb.*" MR 33 (1972): 122–37.

Saint Nicolas
1830. Holst, Imogen. "*Saint Nicholas.*" MZ 7 (1954): 33–34.

Songs from the Chinese
1831. Noble, Jeremy. "Britten's *Songs from the Chinese.*" TEMPO 52 (1959): 25–29.

Songs (various; *see also* specific songs and song cycles)
1832. Whittall, Arnold. "Tonality in Britten's Song Cycles with Piano." TEMPO 96 (1971): 2–11.

Sonnets of Michelangelo
1833. Mark, Christopher. "Simplicity in Early Britten." TEMPO 147 (1983): 8–14.

Spring Symphony
1834. Stein, Erwin. "Britten's *Spring Symphony.*" TEMPO 15 (1950): 19–24.

String Quartet No. 1
1835. Mark, Christopher. "Contextually Transformed Tonality in Britten." MA 4, no. 3 (1985): 265–87.

String Quartet No. 2
1836. Keller, Hans. "Benjamin Britten's Second Quartet." TEMPO 3 (1947): 6–8.

String Quartet No. 3
1837. Seedorf, Thomas. "Tonalität und Form in Benjamin Brittens 3. Streichquartett." MTH 6, no. 3 (1991): 245–56.

Symphony for Cello and Orchestra
1838. Evans, Peter. "Britten's Cello Symphony." TEMPO 66–67 (1963): 2–15.

Turn of the Screw
1839. ASO 173 (1996).
1840. Brett, Philip. "Britten's Bad Boys: Male Relations in *The Turn of the Screw.*" REP 1, no. 2 (1992): 5–25.
1841. Deavel, R. Gary. "A Study of Two Operas by Britten: *Peter Grimes* and *The Turn of the Screw.*" Ph.D. diss., University of Rochester, 1970.
1842. Howard, Patricia. *Benjamin Britten: The Turn of the Screw.* Cambridge: Cambridge University Press, 1985.
1843. Mitchell, Donald. "*Turn of the Screw*: A Note on Its Thematic Organization." MMR 85 (1955): 95–100.
1844. Stein, Erwin. "*Turn of the Screw* and Its Musical Idiom." TEMPO 34 (1955): 6–14. German translation in MZ 11 (1955): 53–61.
1845. Whitesell, Lloyd. "Doubt and Failure in Britten's *The Turn of the Screw.*" ITR 13, no. 2 (1992): 41–87.

War Requiem
1846. Bagley, Peter B. E. "Benjamin Britten's *War Requiem*: A Structural Analysis." D.M. diss., Indiana University, 1972.
1847. Boyd, Malcolm. "Britten, Verdi, and the Requiem." TEMPO 86 (1968): 2–6.
1848. Cooke, Mervyn. *Britten: War Requiem.* Cambridge: Cambridge University Press, 1996.
1849. Evans, Peter. "Britten's *War Requiem.*" TEMPO 61–62 (1961–1962): 20–39.
1850. Roseberry, Eric. "'Abraham and Isaac' Revisited: Reflections on a Theme and Its Inversion." F-Mitchell: 253–66. [Offertorium]
1851. Rowold, Helge. "'To Achieve Perfect Clarity of Expression, That Is My Aim': Zum Verhältnis von Tradition und Neuerung in Benjamin Brittens *War Requiem.*" MF 52, no. 2 (1999): 212–19.
1852. Shaw, Robert. "The Texts of Britten's *War Requiem.*" F-Swan: 357–83.
1853. Whittall, Arnold M. "Tonal Instability in Britten's *War Requiem.*" MR 24 (1963): 201–4.

Wedding Anthem (Amo ergo sum)
1854. Mitchell, Donald. "*Wedding Anthem.*" MZ 7 (1954): 31–32.

Winter Words: Lyrics and Ballads of Thomas Hardy
1855. Docherty, Barbara. "Syllogism and Symbol: Britten, Tippett, and English Text." CMR 5 (1989): 37–63.
1856. Paetsch, Annabelle. "Aspects of Narrativity and Temporality in Britten's *Winter Words.*" ML 79, no. 4 (1998): 538–54.

Various Works
1857. Brewster, Robert G. "The Relationship between Poetry and Music in the Original Solo-Vocal Music of Benjamin Britten through 1965." Ph.D. diss., Washington University, 1967.
1858. Cooke, Mervyn, ed. *The Cambridge Companion to Benjamin Britten.* Cambridge: Cambridge University Press, 1999.
1859. Damp, Alice Bancroft. "The Fusion of Sacred and Secular Elements in Benjamin Britten's Vocal and Choral Literature." D.M.A. diss., University of Rochester, 1973.
1860. Dundore, Mary Margaret. "The Choral Music of Benjamin Britten." D.M.A. diss., University of Washington, 1964.
1861. Evans, Peter. "Britten's Fourth Creative Decade." TEMPO 106 (1973): 8–17.
1862. ———. *The Music of Benjamin Britten.* London: Dent; Minneapolis: University of Minnesota Press, 1979.
1863. Garvie, Peter. "'Darkly Bright': Britten's Moral Imagination." CCM 1 (1970): 59–66.
1864. Handel, Darrell. "Britten's Use of the Passacaglia." TEMPO 94 (1970): 2–6.
1865. M-Hansler.

1866. M-Hart.

1867. Holst, Imogen. "Let's Make an Opera!" MZ 11 (1955): 46–50.

1868. Howard, Patricia. *The Operas of Benjamin Britten: An Introduction.* London: Barrie & Rockcliff, 1969.

1869. Mark, Christopher. "Britten's Revisionary Practice: Practical and Creative." TEMPO 66/67 (1963): 15–22.

1870. Mitchell, Donald, and Hans Keller, eds. *Benjamin Britten: A Commentary on His Works from a Group of Specialists.* London: Tinling, 1952.

1871. MZ 7 (1954). [Special issue]

1872. Rupprecht, Philip Ernst. "Tonal Stratification and Conflict in the Music of Benjamin Britten." Ph.D. diss., Yale University, 1993.

1873. Stein, Erwin. "Benjamin Britten und die englische Tradition." MZ 7 (1954): 11–20.

1874. ———. "Brittens Sinfonien." MZ 7 (1954): 46–53.

1875. Whittall, Arnold. *The Music of Britten and Tippett: Studies in Themes and Techniques.* Cambridge: Cambridge University Press, 1982.

1876. ———. "The Study of Britten: Triadic Harmony and Tonal Structure." PRMA 106 (1979–1980): 27–41.

BROD, MAX (1884–1968)

1877. Jost, Peter. "Max Brods Kafka-Vertonungen *Tod und Paradies*, Op. 35." AM 44, no. 4 (1987): 282–305.

BRONS, CAREL (1931–1983)

1878. Visser, Piet. "The Schnitger Organ and the Schnitger Prize of the City of Zwolle Awarded to Carel Brons for His Composition *Prisms.*" SS 36 (1968): 9–20.

BROWN, EARLE (1926–2002)

1879. Quist, Pamela Layman. "Indeterminate Form in the Work of Earle Brown." D.M.A. diss., Peabody Conservatory, 1984.

1880. M-Vogt: 314–21. [*Available Forms II*]

1881. Welsh, John P. "Open Form and Earle Brown's *Modules I* and *II* (1967)." PNM 32, no. 1 (1994): 254–90.

BRUCH, MAX (1838–1920)

1882. Vick, Bingham Lafayette, Jr. "The Five Oratorios of Max Bruch (1838–1920)." Ph.D. diss., Northwestern University, 1977.

BRUCKNER, ANTON (1824–1896)

Christus factus est

1883. Fellinger, Imogen. "Die drei Fassungen des 'Christus factus est' in Bruckners kirchenmusikalischem Schaffen." BRS (1985): 145–53. [1873 and 1884 settings]

1884. Hoffmann, Wolfgang. "Die Motette *Christus factus est* (1884) von Anton Bruckner: Zur Adaption und Integration älterer Kompositionsverfahren im Kirchenmusikschaffen Anton Bruckners." KJ 77 (1993): 135–46.

1885. Jackson, Timothy. "The Enharmonics of Faith: Enharmonic Symbolism in Bruckner's *Christus factus est* (1884)." BRJ (1987–1988): 7–20.

Helgoland

1886. Grandjean, Wolfgang. "Anton Bruckners *Helgoland* und das Symphonische." MF 48, no. 4 (1995): 349–68.

Locus iste

1887. Bister, Heribert. "Harmonische Grundlagen der Intonation aufgezeigt am *Locus iste* von Anton Bruckner." M 48, no. 5 (1994): 269–74.

Masses (various; *see also* specific masses)

1888. Gruber, Gerold Wolfgang. "Die Credo-Kompositionen Anton Bruckners." BRS (1985): 129–43.

1889. Mathews, Theodore Kenneth. "The Masses of Anton Bruckner: A Comparative Analysis." Ph.D. diss., University of Michigan, 1974.

1890. Newlin, Dika. "Bruckner's Three Great Masses." CD 2, no. 8 (1958): 3–16.

1891. Scholz, Horst-Günther. *Die Form der reifen Messen Anton Bruckners.* Berlin: Merseburger, 1961.

1892. Wellesz, Egon. "Anton Bruckner and the Process of Musical Creation." MQ 24 (1938): 265–90.

Mass, F Major

1893. Fellinger, Imogen. "Die drei Fassungen des 'Christus factus est' in Bruckners kirchenmusikalischem Schaffen." BRS (1985): 145–53.

Mass No. 1, D Minor

1894. Wessely, Othmar. "Vergangenheit und Zukunft in Bruckners Messe in D-Moll." OMZ 29 (1974): 412–18.

Mass No. 2, E Minor

1895. Diether, Jack. "An Introduction to Bruckner's Mass in E Minor." CD 2, no. 6 (1950): 60–65.

1896. Nowak, Leopold. "Studien zu den Formverhältnissen in der E-Moll-Mess von Anton Bruckner." In *Bruckner Studien*, ed. Othmar Wessely, 249–70. Vienna: Öesterreichischen Akademie der Wissenschaften, 1975.

1897. Simpson, Robert. "Thoughts on Bruckner's E Minor Mass." CD 2, no. 4 (1946): 30–35.

Mass No. 3, F Minor

1898. Brauneiss, Leopold. "Skizzen und Zahlen: Überlegungen zur F-Moll-Messe von Anton Bruckner." BRJ (1997–2000): 47–61.

1899. Jackson, Timothy. "Bruckner's 'Oktaven.'" ML 78, no. 3 (1997): 391–409.

Organ Works

1900. Vogel, Martin. "Bruckner in reiner Stimmung: Eine Analyse des Orgelpräludiums in C-Dur." BRJ (1981): 159–66.

1901. Swinden, Kevin J. "Bruckner's *Perger Prelude*: A Dramatic Revue of Wagner?" MA 18, no. 1 (1999): 101–24. [Prelude, C Major]

Os justi

1902. David, Johann Nepomuk. *Die "Jupiter Symphonie": Eine Studie über die thematische-melodischen Zusammenhänge*, 35–39. Göttingen: Vandenhoeck und Reuprecht, 1960.

Psalm 150

1903. Hoffmann, Wolfgang. "'Sextaccord'-Folgen im geistlichen Vokalschaffen Anton Bruckners." BRJ (1994–1996): 157–73.

Songs

1904. Dürr, Walther. "Das romantische Lied." BRS (1987): 153–66. [*Mein Herz und deine Stimme*]

String Quartet

1905. Grandjean, Wolfgang. "Anton Bruckners frühe Scherzi." BRJ (1994–1996): 47–66.

1906. Nowak, Leopold. "Form und Rhythmus in ersten Satz des Streichquartetts von Anton Bruckner." F-Engle/H: 260–73.

String Quintet

1907. Gruber, Gerold W. "Anton Bruckner, Streichquintett in F-Dur (WAB 112)." BRJ (1994–1996): 99–133.

1908. Seidel, Wilhelm. "Das Streichquintett in F-Dur im Œuvre von Anton Bruckner und Johannes Brahms." BRS (1983): 183–89.

Symphonies (various; *see also* specific symphonies)

1909. Bauer, Moritz. "Zur Form in den sinfonischen Werken Anton Bruckners." F-Kretzschmar: 12–14.

1910. Benary, Peter. "Zu Anton Bruckners Personalstil." MTH 8, no. 2 (1993): 119–30.

1911. Buschler, David Martin. "Development in the First Movements of Bruckner's Symphonies." Ph.D. diss., City University of New York, 1975.

1912. Dahlhaus, Carl. "Ist Bruckners Symphonik formbildend?" BRJ (1982–1983): 19–26.

1913. Doernberg, Erwin. *The Life and Symphonies of Anton Bruckner*. London: Barrie & Rockcliff, 1960.

1914. Dokalik, Alfred. "Anton Bruckners Symphonien: Auswahl und Darbietung an der A.HS." ME 28 (1974–1975): 8–14, 109–13, 206–12.

1915. Engel, Gabriel. *The Symphonies of Anton Bruckner*. New York: Bruckner Society of America, 1955.

1916. Floros, Constantin. "Bruckners Symphonik und die Musik Wagners." BRS (1984): 177–83.

1917. ———. "Die Zitate in Bruckners Symphonik." BRJ (1982–1983): 7–18.

1918. ———. "Zur Gegensätzlichkeit der Symphonik Brahms' und Bruckners." BRS (1983): 145–53.

1919. Fuchs, Ingrid. "Aspekte der Instrumentation der Symphonien Brahms' und Bruckners." BRS (1983): 133–44.

1920. Grunsky, Karl. *Bruckners Symphonien*. Berlin: Schlesinger, 1907.

1921. Halm, August. *Die Symphonie Anton Bruckners*. Munich: Müller, 1923.

1922. Hinrichsen, Hans-Joachim. "Bruckners Wagner–Zitate." M-Riethmüller: 115–33.

1923. Kirsch, Winfried. "Das Scherzo bei Brahms und Bruckner." BRS (1983): 155–72.

1924. Krohn, Ilmari Henrik Reinhold. *Anton Bruckners Symphonien: Untersuchung über Formenbau und Stimmungsgehalt*. 3 vols., ser. 13, 86, 99, 109. Helsinki: Suomalainen Tiedeakat; Wiesbaden: Harrassowitz, 1955–1957.

1925. Lechleitner, Gerda. "Bruckner–Wagner: Ein meßbarer Unterschied: Betrachtungen zur Instrumentation in Melodie und Begleitung." BRS (1984): 123–48.

1926. ———. "Die Rolle der Holzblasinstrumente in Scherzosätzen bei Bruckner und Mahler." BRS (1986): 119–27.

1927. Moravesik, Michael J. "The Coda in the Symphonies of Anton Bruckner." MR 34 (1973): 241–58.

1928. Murphy, Edward. "Bruckner's Use of Numbers to Indicate Phrase Lengths." BRJ (1987–1988): 39–52.

1929. Notter, Werner. *Schematismus und Evolution in der Sinfonik Anton Bruckners.* Munich: Katzbichler, 1983.

1930. Oeser, Fritz. *Die Klangstruktur der Bruckner-Symphonie: Eine Studie zur Frage der Originalfassungen.* Leipzig: Musikwissenschaftlicher Verlag, 1939.

1931. Röder, Thomas. "Zu Bruckners Scherzo: der 'responsoriale' Thementyp, die Kadenz, die Coda und der Zyklus." BRJ (1994–1996): 67–77.

1932. Schön, Werner. "Studien zur Symphonik Bruckners: Motivisch-thematische Substanz und musikalischer Prozess." Ph.D. diss., Marburg, n.d.

1933. Steinbeck, Wolfram. "'Dona nobis pacem': Religiöse Symbolik in Bruckners Symphonien." M-Riethmüller: 87–96.

1934. Werner, Eric. "Nature and Function of the Sequence in Bruckner's Symphonies." F Plamenac: 365–84.

1935. Wilcox, James H. "Bruckner and Symphonic Form." CD 2, no. 9 (1960): 89–99.

1936. ———. "The Symphonies of Anton Bruckner." Ph.D. diss., Florida State University, 1956.

1937. Wohlfahrt, Frank. *Anton Bruckners sinfonisches Werk: Stil- und Formerläuterung.* Leipzig: Musikwissenschaftlicher Verlag, 1943.

1938. Wünschmann, Theodor. *Anton Bruckners Weg als Symphoniker.* Beiträge zur Musikreflexion 4. Steinfeld: Salvator, 1976.

Symphony, D Minor ("Nullte")

1939. Grandjean, Wolfgang. "Anton Bruckners frühe Scherzi." BRJ (1994–1996): 47–66.

Symphony, F Minor ("Study Symphony")

1940. Grandjean, Wolfgang. "Anton Bruckners frühe Scherzi." BRJ (1994–1996): 47–66.

Symphony No. 1

1941. Grandjean, Wolfgang. "Anton Bruckners frühe Scherzi." BRJ (1994–1996): 47–66.

1942. Schipperges, Thomas. "Zur Wiener Fassung von Anton Bruckners Erster Sinfonie." AM 47, no. 4 (1990): 272–85.

Symphony No. 2

1943. Grasberger, Franz. "Anton Bruckners II. Symphonie." In *Bruckner Studien,* ed. Othmar Wessely, 303–31. Vienna: Verlag der Öesterreichischen Akademie der Wissenschaften, 1975.

1944. Hinrichsen, Hans-Joachim. "'Himmlische Länge' und 'symphonischer Strom': Bruckner, Schubert und das Problem der 'Form.'" BRS (1997): 99–116.

1945. Jackson, Timothy L. "Bruckner's Metrical Numbers." NCM 14, no. 2 (1990): 101–31.

1946. ———. "Bruckner's Rhythm: Syncopated Hyperrhythm and Diachronic Transformation in the Second Symphony." BRS (1992): 93–106.

Symphony No. 3

1947. Kühnen, Wolfgang. "Die Botschaft als Chiffre: Zur Syntax musikalischer Zitate in der ersten Fassung von Bruckners Dritter Symphonie." BRJ (1991–1993): 31–43.

1948. Röder, Thomas. *Auf dem Weg zur Bruckner Symphonie: Untersuchungen zu den ersten beiden Fassungen zu Anton Bruckners Dritter Symphonie.* Stuttgart: Steiner, 1987.

1949. Schnebel, Dieter. "Der erhörte Klang: Höranalyse am Beispiel von Bruckners Dritter." MB 11 (1979): 159–64.

1950. Stephan, Rudolf. "Zu Anton Bruckners dritter Symphonie." BRS (1980): 65–73.

1951. Tröller, Josef. *Anton Bruckner: III. Symphonie D-moll.* Munich: Fink, 1976.

1952. Voss, Egon. "Wagner-Zitate in Bruckners Dritter Sinfonie? Ein Beitrag zum Begriff des Zitats in der Musik." MF 49, no. 4 (1996): 403–6.

1953. Winkler, Gerhard J. "Anton Bruckner–ein Neudeutscher? Gedanken zum Verhältnis zwischen Symphonie und symphonischer Dichtung." BRS (1984): 149–62.

Symphony No. 4

1954. Nowak, Leopold. "Die Drei Final-Sätze zur IV. Symphonie von Anton Bruckner." OMZ 36 (1981): 2–11.

1955. Röder, Thomas. "Motto und symphonischer Zyklus: Zu den Fassungen von Anton Bruckners vierter Symphonie." AM 42 (1985): 166–77.

1956. Stephan, Rudolf. "Bruckners Romantische Sinfonie." M-Mahling: 171–87.

Symphony No. 5

1957. Cohrs, Gunnar. "Zahlenphänomene in Bruckners Symphonik: Neues zu den Strukturen der Fünften und Neunten Symphonie." BRJ (1989–1990): 35–75.

1958. Horn, Erwin. "Analyse der Scherzo-Themen der Symphonien V, VI, VII, und VIII." BRJ (1991–1993): 45–60.

1959. Kross, Siegfried. "Brahms und Bruckner: Über Zusammenhänge von Themenstruktur und Form." BRS (1983): 173–81.

1960. Nowak, Leopold. "Anton Bruckners Formwille, dargestellt am Finale seiner V. Symphonie." F-Anglés: 609–13.

1961. Wieninger, Herbert. "Das Finale von Bruckners V. Sinfonie." ME 24 (1970–1971): 9–13.

Symphony No. 6

1962. Brauneiss, Leopold. "Die Architektuer der sechsten Symphonie Anton Bruckners." M-Brauneiss: 72–84.

1963. Halbreich, Harry. "Bruckners Sechste: Kein Stiefkind mehr." BRS (1982): 85–92.

1964. Hinrichsen, Hans-Joachim. "'Himmlische Länge' und 'symphonischer Strom': Bruckner, Schubert und das Problem der 'Form.'" BRS (1997): 99–116.

1965. Horn, Erwin. "Analyse der Scherzo-Themen der Symphonien V, VI, VII, und VIII." BRJ (1991–1993): 45–60.

1966. Jackson, Timothy L. "Die Wagnersche Umarmungs-Metapher bei Bruckner und Mahler." M-Riethmüller: 134–52.

Symphony No. 7

1967. Brauneiss, Leopold. "Zahlen und Proportionen in Bruckners Siebenter Symphonies." BRJ (1994–1996): 33–46.

1968. Horn, Erwin. "Analyse der Scherzo-Themen der Symphonien V, VI, VII, und VIII." BRJ (1991–1993): 45–60.

1969. Murphy, Edward W. "The Dominant Complex/Climax in Selected Works of the Late Nineteenth Century." MR 55, no. 2 (1994): 104–18. [Movement I]

1970. Nowak, Adolf. "Die Wiederkehr in Bruckners Adagio." M-Mahling: 159–70. [Movement II]

1971. Parkany, Stephen. "Kurth's *Bruckner* and the Adagio of the Seventh Symphony." NCM 11, no. 3 (1988): 262–81.

1972. Simpson, Robert. "The Seventh Symphony of Bruckner." MR 8 (1947): 178–87.

1973. ———. "The Seventh Symphony of Bruckner: An Analysis." CD 2/10 (1961): 57–67.

1974. Steinbeck, Wolfram. "Schema als Form bei Anton Bruckner: Zum Adagio der VII. Symphonie." M-Breig: 304–23.

Symphony No. 8

1975. Dahlhaus, Carl. "Bruckner und die Programmmusik: Zum Finale der Achten Symphonie." M-Mahling: 7–32.

1976. Dowson-Bowling, Paul. "Thematic and Tonal Unity in Bruckner's Eighth Symphony." MR 30 (1969): 225–36.

1977. Floros, Constantin. "Die Fassungen der Achten Symphonie von Anton Bruckner." BRS 1980: 53–63.

1978. Gilliam, Bryan. "The Two Versions of Bruckner's Eighth Symphony." NCM 16, no. 1 (1992): 59–69.

1979. Gloede, Wilhelm. "Eine Hommage Anton Bruckners an Mozart?" BRJ (1984–1986): 7–14. (Movement IV)

1980. Hansen, Mathias. "Persönlichkeit im Werk: Zum Bild Anton Bruckners in der Analyse seiner Musik." BRS (1992): 187–93.

1981. Horn, Erwin. "Analyse der Scherzo-Themen der Symphonien V, VI, VII, und VIII." BRJ (1991–1993): 45–60.

1982. ———. "Evolution und Metamorphose in der Achten Symphonie von Anton Bruckner: Darstellung der thematischen Zusammenhänge." BRJ (1989–1990): 7–33.

1983. Korstvedt, Benjamin M. *Bruckner: Symphony No. 8.* Cambridge: Cambridge University Press, 2000.

1984. Marschner, Bo. "Den cykliske formproces i Anton Bruckners Symfoni Nr. 8 og dens arketypiske grundlag." DAM 12 (1981): 19–68.

Symphony No. 9

1985. Adensamer, Michael. "Bruckners Einfluss auf die Modern (mit Beispielen aus dem Adagio der 9. Symphonie)." BRJ 1 (1980): 27–31.

1986. Cohrs, Gunnar. "Zahlenphänomene in Bruckners Symphonik: Neues zu den Strukturen der Fünften und Neunten Symphonie." BRJ (1989–1990): 35–75.

1987. Floros, Constantin. "Zur Deutung der Symphonik Bruckners: Das Adagio der neunten Symphonie." BRJ (1981): 89–96.

1988. Murphy, Edward W. "The Dominant Complex/Climax in Selected Works of the Late Nineteenth Century." MR 55, no. 2 (1994): 104–18. [Movement III]

1989. Puffett, Derrick. "Bruckner's Way: The Adagio of the Ninth Symphony." MA 18, no. 1 (1999): 5–99.

1990. Steinbeck, Wolfram. *Anton Bruckner: Neunte Symphonie D-Moll.* Munich: Fink, 1993.

Te Deum

1991. Griesbacher, Peter. *Bruckners "Te Deum": Studie.* Regensburg: Pustet, 1919.

1992. Hoffmann, Wolfgang. "'Sextaccord'-Folgen im geistlichen Vokalschaffen Anton Bruckners." BRJ (1994–1996): 157–73.

1993. Müller-Blattau, Wendelin. "Chor- und Orchestersatz im *Te Deum* von Anton Bruckner." M-Mahling: 149–58.

Vexilla regis

1994. Jackson, Timothy L. "Bruckner's Metrical Numbers." NCM 14, no. 2 (1990): 101–31.

Various Works

1995. Fellinger, Imogen. "Anton Bruckner und Hugo Wolf: Ein kompositorischer Vergleich." BRS (1984): 91–101.

1996. Floros, Constantin. "Parallelen zwischen Schubert und Bruckner." F-Wessely: 133–46.

1997. Grant, Parks. "Bruckner and Mahler: The Fundamental Dissimilarity of Their Styles." MR 32 (1971): 36–55.

1998. Grunsky, Hans. "Rang und Wesen der Musik Anton Bruckners." M 18 (1964): 190–97.
1999. Hoffmann, Wolfgang. "Über Anton Bruckners Klang-Kontrapunkt." MF 54, no. 4 (1999): 466–72.
2000. Howie, A. C. "Traditional and Novel Elements in Bruckner's Sacred Music." MQ 67 (1981): 544–67.
2001. Kirsch, Winfried. *Studien zum Vokalstil der mittleren und späten Schaffensperiode Anton Bruckners.* Frankfurt am Main: n.p., 1958.
2002. Kurth, Ernst. *Bruckner.* Berlin: Hesse, 1925.
2003. Maier, Elisabeth. "Der Choral in den Kirchenwerken Bruckners." BRS (1985): 111–22.
2004. Neumann, Friedrich. "Zum Verhaltnis von Akkordik und Melodik bei Anton Bruckner." BRJ (1981): 167–70.
2005. Newlin, Dika. *Bruckner, Mahler, Schoenberg.* New York: King's Crown Press, 1947.
2006. OMZ 29, no. 9 (1974). [Special issue]
2007. Redlich, Hans F. *Bruckner and Mahler.* Rev. ed. London: Dent, 1963.
2008. Schurtz, H. Paul. "The Small Sacred Choral Works of Anton Bruckner." M.A. thesis, Brigham Young University, 1976.
2009. Smith, Warren Storey. "The Cyclic Principle in Musical Design and the Use of It by Bruckner and Mahler." CD 2, no. 9 (1960): 3–32.
2010. Unger, Klaus. "Studien zur Harmonik Bruckners: Einwirkung und Umwandlung älterer Klangstruckturen." Ph.D. diss., University of Heidelberg, 1969.
2011. Wagner, Karl. "Bruckners Themenbildung als Kriterium seiner Stilentwicklung." OMZ 25 (1970): 159–65.
2012. Wagner, Manfred. "Der Quint-Octayschrift als 'Maiestas'-Symbol bei Anton Bruckner." KJ 56 (1972): 97–103.
2013. Wellesz, Egon. "Anton Bruckner and the Process of Musical Creation." MQ 24 (1938): 265–290.

BRUNEAU, ALFRED (1857–1934)
2014. Bishop, Raymond James, Jr. "The Operas of Alfred Bruneau (1857–1934)." Ph.D. diss., University of North Carolina at Chapel Hill, 1987.

BRUNELLI, LOUIS JEAN (b. 1925)
2015. Neilson, James. "*Essay for Cyrano*: Concert Overture for Band by Louis Jean Brunelli; Analysis by Dr. James Neilson from Notes Provided by the Composer." JBR 15, no. 1 (1979–1980): 58–65.

BRUNSWICK, MARK (1902–1971)
2016. Gideon, Miriam. "The Music of Mark Brunswick." ACA 13, no. 1 (1965): 1–10.

BRUYNÈL, TON (1934–1998)
2017. Paagiviströmm, John. "Ton Bruynèl: Trying to Set the Ear Free." KN 15 (1982): 24–29. [*Phases, Serene, Soft Song, Toccare, Translucent II*]
2018. Vermeulen, Ernst. "*Signs* by Ton Bruynèl." SS 42 (1970): 17–30.

BRYARS, GAVIN (b. 1943)
2019. Potter, Keith. "Just the Tip of the Iceberg: Some Aspects of Gavin Bryars's Music." CT 22 (1981): 4–15.
2020. Ramaut-Chevassus, Béatrice. "La postmodernité musicale: Points forts d'un phénomène aux multiples facettes (Pärt, Bryars, Adams)." ANM 33 (1998): 94–103. [*Incipit vita nova*]

BUCK, DUDLEY (1839–1909)
2021. Gallo, William K. "The Life and Church Music of Dudley Buck (1839–1909)." Ph.D. diss., Catholic University of America, 1968.

BURGMÜLLER, NORBERT (1810–1836)
2022. Vogt, Hans. "Romantische Sinfonik, frühvollendet: Zu den Sinfonien Norbert Burgmüllers." M 43, no. 2 (1989): 126–33.

BURKHARD, WILLY (1900–1955)
2023. Burkhard, Simon. "Die Klavierlieder von Willy Burkhard." SMZ 100 (1960): 154–58.
2024. Burkhard, Willy. "Mein Oratorium *Das Gesicht Jesajas* und die Musik unserer Zeit." SMZ 100 (1960): 136–46.
2025. Eckhardt, Paul. "Musikalische Einführung in Burkhards Oratorium *Das Gesicht Jesajas.*" MK 22 (1952): 148–54.
2026. Indermühle, Fritz. "Die erzählende Musik im Schaff Willy Burkhards." SMZ 100 (1960): 147–54.
2027. ———. "*Die Musikalische Übung*, Op. 39, von Willy Burkhard." MK 41 (1971): 79–88.
2028. Mohr, Ernst. "Betrachtungen zum Stil Willy Burkhards." SMZ 87 (1947): 1–8.
2029. ———. "Die Messe von Willy Burkhard." M 12 (1950): 67–72.
2030. Schmidt, Erich. "'Ahnung einer neuen Weltordnung': Willy Burkhard (1900–1955)." F-Mauersberger: 111–25.
2031. Sievers, Gerd. "Das Ezzolied in der Vertonung von Willy Burkhard und Johann Nepomuk David: Ein Vergleich." F-Engel/H: 335–63.

BUSH, ALAN (1900–1995)

2032. Stevenson, Ronald. "Alan Bush: Committed Composer." MR 25 (1964): 232–42.

BUSONI, FERRUCCIO (1866–1924)

2033. ASO 193 (1999). [*Doktor Faust*]

2034. Leshowitz, Myron Howard. "A Study of the Life and Work of Ferruccio Busoni and Analyses of His *Waffentanz, All'Italia!*, and Toccata for Use in Performance and Interpretation." Ph.D. diss., New York University, 1979.

2035. Meloncelli, Raoul. "La *Turandot* di Busoni." CHI 31 (1974): 167–86.

2036. Meyer, Heinz. *Die Klaviermusik Ferruccio Bussonis: Eine stilkritische Untersuchung.* Wolfenbüttel: Möseler, 1969.

2037. Previtali, Fernando. "La *Turandot* di Busoni." CHI 31 (1974): 249–58.

2038. Raessler, Daniel M. "The '113' Scales of Ferruccio Busoni." MR 43 (1982): 51–56.

2039. Sitsky, Larry. "The Six Sonatinas for Piano of Ferruccio Busoni." STU 2 (1973): 155–73.

2040. Winfield, George. "Ferruccio Busoni's Compositional Art: A Study of Selected Works for Piano Solo Composed between 1907 and 1923." Ph.D. diss., Indiana University, 1981.

BUSSOTTI, SYLVANO (b. 1931)

2041. Attinello, Paul. "Signifying Chaos: A Semiotic Analysis of Sylvano Bussotti's *Siciliano*." REP 1, no. 2 (1992): 84–110. [*Memoria*]

BUTTERWORTH, GEORGE (1885–1916)

2042. M-Curtis.

BUTTING, MAX (1888–1976)

2043. Vetter, Walther. "Max Butting als schaffender Musiker der Gegenwart: Eine Improvisation zur seinem 75. Geburtstag." MG 13 (1963): 604–11.

2044. Wolf, Werner. "Neue Werke unserer Komponisten: Max Buttings X. Sinfonien; Bratschenkonzert von Hans-Christian Bartel." MG 14 (1964): 80–83.

– C –

CAGE, JOHN (1912–1992)

Amores

2045. Welsh, John. "John Cage's 'Trio' from *Amores* (1943): A Study of Rhythmic Structure and Density." EXT 4, no. 2 (1987–1988): 80–92.

2046. Williams, Barry Michael. "The Early Percussion Music of John Cage, 1935–1943." Ph.D. diss., Michigan State University, 1990.

Atlas eclipticalis

2047. Beeler, Charles Alan. "*Winter Music, Cartridge Music, Atlas eclipticalis*: A Study of Three Seminal Works by John Cage." Ph.D. diss., Washington University, 1973.

Cartridge Music

2048. Beeler, Charles Alan. "*Winter Music, Cartridge Music, Atlas eclipticalis*: A Study of Three Seminal Works by John Cage." Ph.D. diss., Washington University, 1973.

2049. M-Cope: 289–96.

Cheap Imitation

2050. Huber, Nicolaus A. "John Cage: *Cheap Imitation*." N 1 (1980): 135–41.

Concerto for Prepared Piano

2051. Kessler, Howard. "Rhythmic Cycles and Self-Similarity in John Cage's Concerto for Prepared Piano and Orchestra, First Movement." SONUS 15, no. 2 (1995): 113–29.

2052. Pritchett, James. "From Choice to Chance: John Cage's Concerto for Prepared Piano." PNM 26, no. 1 (1988): 50–81.

First Construction (in Metal)

2053. Williams, Barry Michael. "The Early Percussion Music of John Cage, 1935–1943." Ph.D. diss., Michigan State University, 1990.

HPSCHD

2054. Cage, John, and Lejaren Hiller. "*HPSCHD*." S 2, no. 2 (1968): 10–19.

2055. Husarik, Stephen. "John Cage and Lejaren Hiller: *HPSCD*, 1969." AMUS 1, no. 2 (1983): 1–21.

Hymns and Variations
2056. Brooks, William. "John Cage and History: *Hymns and Variations*." PNM 31, no. 2 (1993): 74–103.

James Joyce, Marcel Duchamp, Erik Satie: An Alphabet
2057. Hinz, Klaus-Michael. "Ein Museum ohne Taschen: Zum Hörspiel *James Joyce, Marcel Duchamp, Erik Satie: Ein Alphabet* von John Cage." MTX 10 (1985): 35–38.

Metamorphosis
2058. Davidian, Teresa. "From Crawford to Cage: Parallels and Transformations." MQ 84, no. 4 (2000): 664–95.

Mushrooms et variationes
2059. Gronemeyer, Gisela. "'Paul Zukovsky Does Not Agree': *Mushrooms et Variationes*; Eine neue Textkomposition von John Cage." MTX 10 (1985): 26–31.

Music of Changes
2060. Klüppelholz, Werner. "Schlüsselwerk der experimentellen Musik: *Music of Changes* von John Cage." MTX 15 (1989): 34–39.

103
2061. Frobenius, Wolf. "John Cage und sein Orchesterstück *103* (1991)." AM 56, no. 2 (1999): 146–57.

Piano Works (various; *see also* specific piano works)
2062. Francis, John Richard. "Structure in the Solo Piano Music of John Cage." Ph.D. diss., Florida State University, 1976.
2063. Fürst-Heidtmann, Monika. *Das präparierte Klavier des John Cage*. Regensburg: Bosse, 1978.

Roaratorio, An Irish Circus on Finnegans Wake
2064. Reichert, Klaus. "*Finnegans Wake* auf der Spur bei John Cage: James Joyce und *Roaratorio*." åfi 10 (1985): 23–26.

Sonatas and Interludes
2065. Goebels, Franzpeter. "Bemerkungen und Materialien zum Studium neuer Klaviermusik (II)." SMZ 113 (1973): 331–36.

Themes and Variations
2066. Radano, Ronald M. "*Themes and Variations* by John Cage." PNM 21 (1982–1983): 417–24.

Three
2067. Geddert, Geesche. "*Three*: Das Blockflötentrio von John Cage." T 19, no. 1 (1994): 40–43.

Variations I
2068. M-Zimmerschied: 188–200.

Variations II
2069. DeLio, Thomas. "John Cage's *Variations II*: The Morphology of a Global Structure." PNM 19, no. 2 (1980–1981): 351–71. Reprint, M-DeLio: 9–27.
2070. ———. "Sound, Gesture, and Symbol: The Relation between Notation and Structure in American Experimental Music." I 10 (1981): 199–219.

Variations IV
2071. Dasilva, Fabio B., and Allan M. Hunchuk. "Musical Spaces: A Phenomenological Analysis of John Cage's *Variations IV*." MR 50, nos. 3–4 (1989): 281–96.

Winter Music
2072. Beeler, Charles Alan. "*Winter Music, Cartridge Music, Atlas Eclipticalis*: A Study of Three Seminal Works by John Cage." Ph.D. diss., Washington University, 1973.

Various Works
2073. Blum, Eberhard. "John Cage und seine Kompositionen für und mit Flöten." T 5, no. 6 (1980–1981): 407–11.
2074. Brooks, William. "Choice and Change in Cage's Recent Music." F-Cage: 82–100.
2075. Campana, Deborah Ann. "Form and Structure in the Music of John Cage." Ph.D. diss., Northwestern University, 1985.
2076. ———. "Sound, Rhythm, and Structure: John Cage's Compositional Process Before Chance." I 18, no. 4 (1989): 223–41.
2077. Duckworth, William Ervin. "Expanding Notational Parameters in the Music of John Cage." Ed.D. diss., University of Illinois, 1972.
2078. Gillmor, Alan. "Satie, Cage, and the New Asceticism." CT 25 (1982): 15–20.
2079. Gresser, Clemens. "'. . . A music made by everyone . . .': Eine analytische Annäherung an John Cages Number Pieces." MTX 76–77 (1998): 41–47.
2080. Griffiths, Paul. *Cage*. London: Oxford University Press, 1981.

2081. Gronemeyer, Gisela. "'I'm Finally Writing Beautiful Music': Das numerierte Spätwerk von John Cage." MTX 48 (1993): 19–24.

2082. Mahrt, Jürgen. "Die Temperatur der Sprache: Zu Texten von John Cage." åfï 10 (1985): 38–40.

2083. Metzger, Heinz-Klaus, and Rainer Riehn, eds. *John Cage*. Munich: Text + Kritik, 1978.

2084. ———. *John Cage II*. Munich: Text + Kritik, 1990.

2085. Pritchett, James. *The Music of John Cage*. Cambridge: Cambridge University Press, 1993.

2086. Shimoda, Kimiko. "Cage and Zen." CT 25 (1982): 28–29.

2087. Zukovsky, Paul. "John Cage's Recent Violin Music." F-Cage: 101–6.

CAMBINI, GIUSEPPE MARIA (1746–1825)

2088. Fertonani, Cesare. "Gli ultimi quartetti di Giuseppe Maria Cambini." CHI 43/nuova serie n. 23 (1993): 247–79.

CAMPHOUSE, MARK (b. 1954)

2089. Simmons, Gregory C. "*Elegy* by Mark Camphouse." JBR 27, no. 2 (1992): 45–53.

CAPDEVILLE, CONSTANÇA (1937–1992)

2090. Miranda, Gil. "*Libera me* by Constança Capedeville [*sic*]." EXT 8, no. 2 (1997): 16–32.

CARDEW, CORNELIUS (1936–1981)

2091. Tilbury, John. "Cornelius Cardew." CT 26 (1983): 4–12.

CARPENTER, JOHN ALDEN (1876–1951)

2092. Pierson, Thomas C. "The Life and Music of John Alden Carpenter." Ph.D. diss., University of Rochester, 1952.

CARRILLO, JULIÁN (1875–1965)

2093. Benjamin, Gerald R. "Julián Carrillo and *Sonido Trece*." Y 3 (1967): 33–68. [*Fantasía "Sonido 13"*]

CARTER, ELLIOTT (b. 1908)

Brass Quintet

2094. Lochhead, Judy. "Temporal Structure in Recent Music." JMR 6, nos. 1–2 (1986): 49–93.

Canon for 3: In Memoriam Igor Stravinsky

2095. DeLio, Thomas. "Spatial Design in Elliott Carter's Canon for 3." ITR 4, no. 1 (1980–1981): 1–12.

Cello Sonata

2096. Bernard, Jonathan W. "The Evolution of Elliott Carter's Rhythmic Practice." PNM 26, no. 2 (1988): 164–203.

Concerto for Orchestra

2097. Bernard, Jonathan W. "Poem as Non-Verbal Text: Elliott Carter's *Concerto for Orchestra* and Saint-John Perse's *Winds*." M-Ayrey: 169–204.

2098. Hicken, Steve. "Structural Cross-Rhythms." TSP 7 (1992): 28–48.

2099. Santana, Rosário. "Musical Discourse and Rhythm in Elliott Carter." EXT 9, no. 1 (1998): 37–83.

Double Concerto

2100. Bernard, Jonathan W. "The Evolution of Elliott Carter's Rhythmic Practice." PNM 26, no. 2 (1988): 164–203.

2101. Santana, Rosário. "Musical Discourse and Rhythm in Elliott Carter." EXT 9, no. 1 (1998): 37–83.

2102. Simmons, Greg. "The Rhythmic Structure of the 'Introduction' to Elliott Carter's *Double Concerto*." TSP 6 (1989): 66–90. Reprinted in TSP 7 (1992): 72–98.

2103. Strizich, Robert. "Notation in Elliott Carter's *Double Concerto*." EXT 2, no. 1 (1982): 46–80.

2104. Whittall, Arnold. "Post-Twelve-Note Analysis." PRMA 94 (1967–1968): 1–17.

Duo for Violin and Piano

2105. Derby, Richard. "Carter's Duo for Violin and Piano." PNM 20 (1981–1982): 149–68.

Esprit rude/esprit doux

2106. Truniger, Matthias. "Elliott Carter: *Esprit rude/esprit doux*." SONUS 19, no. 1 (1998): 26–52.

Figment

2107. Cox, Frank. "Elliott Carter zum 90. Geburtstag: *Figment* for Solo Cello." MAS 3, no. 9 (1999): 5–25.

Four Lauds

2108. Mead, Andrew. "The Role of Octave Equivalence in Elliott Carter's Recent Music: A Birthday Celebration." SONUS 14, no. 1 (1993): 13–37. ["Riconoscenza per Goffredo Petrassi"]

In Sleep, in Thunder

2109. Schiff, David. "*In Sleep, in Thunder*: Elliott Carter's Portrait of Robert Lowell." TEMPO 142 (1982): 2–9.

Mirror on which to Dwell

2110. Durieux, Frédéric. "*A Mirror on which to Dwell*: Domaines d'une écriture." ENT 4 (1987): 55–67.

2111. Ravenscroft, Brenda. "The Anatomy of a Song: Text and Texture in Elliott Carter's 'O Breath.'" EXT 9, no. 1 (1998): 84–102.

2112. ———. "Texture in Elliott Carter's *A Mirror on which to Dwell*." Ph.D. diss., University of British Columbia, 1992.

2113. Zimmermann, Robert. "The Poetics of Polyrhythm in Elliott Carter's 'Anaphora.'" SONUS 19, no. 1 (1998): 67–85.

Night Fantasies

2114. Darbellay, Étienne. "Continuité, cohérence, et formes de temps: A propos des *Night Fantasies* d'Elliott Carter." SAG 2, no. 2 (1995): 297–327.

2115. Hicken, Steve. "Structural Cross-Rhythms." TSP 7 (1992): 28–48.

2116. Link, John F. "The Composition of Elliott Carter's *Night Fantasies*." SONUS 14, no. 1 (1993): 67–89.

2117. Mead, Andrew. "Twelve-Tone Composition and the Music of Elliott Carter." M-Marvin: 67–102.

2118. Warburton, Thomas. "A Literary Approach to Carter's *Night Fantasies*." MR 51, no. 3 (1990): 208–20.

Piano Concerto

2119. Grau, Irene Rosenberg. "Compositional Techniques Employed in the First Movement of Elliott Carter's Piano Concerto." Ph.D. diss., Michigan State University, 1973.

2120. Mead, Andrew. "Twelve-Tone Composition and the Music of Elliott Carter." M-Marvin: 67–102.

2121. Stone, Kurt. "Current Chronicle." MQ 55 (1969): 559–72.

Piano Sonata

2122. Below, Robert. "Elliott Carter's Piano Sonata." MR 34 (1973): 283–93.

2123. Haberkorn, Michael. "A Study and Performance of the Piano Sonatas of Samuel Barber, Elliott Carter, and Aaron Copland." Ed.D. diss., Columbia University, 1979.

Sonata for Flute, Oboe, Cello, and Harpsichord

2124. Shinn, Randall. "An Analysis of Elliott Carter's Sonata for Flute, Oboe, Cello, and Harpsichord (1952)." D.M.A. diss., University of Illinois, 1975.

Pieces for Four Timpani

2125. Uno, Yayoi. "The Tempo-Span GIS as a Measure of Continuity in Elliott Carter's Eight Pieces for Four Timpani." INT 10 (1996): 53–91.

String Quartets (various; *see also* specific string quartets)

2126. Morgan, Robert P. "Elliott Carter's String Quartets." MN 4, no. 3 (1974): 3–11.

String Quartet No. 1

2127. Bernard, Jonathan W. "The Evolution of Elliott Carter's Rhythmic Practice." PNM 26, no. 2 (1988): 164–203.

2128. ———. "Problems of Pitch Structure in Elliott Carter's First and Second String Quartets." JMT 37, no. 2 (1993): 231–66.

2129. Lochhead, Judy. "On the 'Framing' Music of Elliott Carter's First String Quartet." F-Lewin: 179–98.

2130. McElroy, William Wiley. "Elliott Carter's String Quartet No. 1: A Study of Heterogeneous Rhythmic Elements." M.M. thesis, Florida State University, 1973.

2131. Schreiner, Martin. "Expansion as Design in the *Fantasia* of Elliott Carter's String Quartet No. 1." SONUS 12, no. 2 (1992): 11–26.

2132. Tingley, George Peter. "Metric Modulation and Elliott Carter's First String Quartet." ITR 4, no. 3 (1980–1981): 3–11.

String Quartet No. 2

2133. Bernard, Jonathan W. "The Evolution of Elliott Carter's Rhythmic Practice." PNM 26, no. 2 (1988): 164–203.

2134. ———. "Problems of Pitch Structure in Elliott Carter's First and Second String Quartets." JMT 37, no. 2 (1993): 231–66.

2135. Gass, Glenn. "Elliott Carter's Second String Quartet: Aspects of Time and Rhythm." ITR 4, no. 3 (1980–1981): 12–23.

2136. Hoffman, Michael. "Carter's String Quartet No. 2: An Overview Analysis." TCM 6, no. 1 (1999): 11–18.

2137. Koivisto, Tiina. "Aspects of Motion in Elliott Carter's Second String Quartet." INT 10 (1996): 19–52.

2138. Mead, Andrew. "The Role of Octave Equivalence in Elliott Carter's Recent Music: A Birthday Celebration." SONUS 14, no. 1 (1993): 13–37.

2139. Schmidt, Dörte. "Formbildende Tendenzen der musikalischen Zeit: Elliott Carters Konzept der Tempo-Modulation im zweiten Streichquartett als Folgerung aus dem Denken Schönbergs." JSIM (1999): 118–36.

2140. M-Schweitzer.

2141. Steinberg, Michael. "Elliott Carter's Second String Quartet." SCORE 27 (1960): 22–26.

2142. ———. "Elliott Carters 2. Streichquartett." MELOS 28 (1961): 35–37.

2143. M-Wennerstrom.

String Quartet No. 3

2144. Godfrey, Daniel. "A Unique Vision of Musical Time: Carter's String Quartet No. 3." SONUS 8, no. 1 (1987): 40–59.

2145. Mead, Andrew W. "Pitch Structure in Elliott Carter's String Quartet No. 3." PNM 22 (1983–1984): 31–60. French translation by Hubert Guery under the title "Le troisieme quatuor a cordes: Structure des hauteurs," ENT 4 (1987): 77–94.

2146. ———. "The Role of Octave Equivalence in Elliott Carter's Recent Music: A Birthday Celebration." SONUS 14, no. 1 (1993): 13–37.

2147. ———. "Twelve-Tone Composition and the Music of Elliott Carter." M-Marvin: 67–102.

Syringa

2148. Vermaelen, Denis. "Aspects de la pensée musicale d'Elliott Carter dans *Syringa*: Invention formelle et réflexion sur le temps." RDM 85, no. 1 (1999): 97–118.

Variations for Orchestra

2149. Bernard, Jonathan W. "The Evolution of Elliott Carter's Rhythmic Practice." PNM 26, no. 2 (1988): 164–203.

2150. Stewart, Robert. "Serial Aspects of Elliott Carter's Variations for Orchestra." MR 34 (1973): 62–65.

Various Works

2151. Bernard, Jonathan W. "Spatial Sets in Recent Music of Elliott Carter." MA 2 (1983): 5–34.

2152. Breedon, Daniel Franklin. "An Investigation of the Influence of the Metaphysics of Alfred North Whitehead upon the Formal-Dramatic Compositional Procedures of Elliott Carter." D.M.A. diss., University of Washington, 1975.

2153. Carter, Elliott. *Collected Essays and Lectures, 1937–1995.* Ed. Jonathan W. Bernard. Rochester: University of Rochester Press, 1997.

2154. Geissler, Fredrick Dietzmann. "Considerations of Tempo as a Structural Basis in Selected Orchestral Works of Elliott Carter." D.M.A. diss., Cornell University, 1974.

2155. Glock, William. "A Note on Elliott Carter." SCORE 12 (1955): 47–52.

2156. Goldman, Richard Franko. "The Music of Elliott Carter." MQ 43 (1957): 151–70.

2157. M-Hines: 36–91.

2158. Nicolas, François. "Le feuillete du tempo: Essai sur les 'modulations métriques.'" ENT 9 (1990): 51–77.

2159. Northcott, Bayan. "Carter the Progressive." In *Elliott Carter: A Seventieth-Birthday Tribute*, 4–7, 10–11. London: Schirmer, 1978.

2160. Noubel, Max. "Ausdruck und Struktur bei Carter: Die musikalischen Charaktere und die Formen der Komposition." DI 58 (1990): 10–17.

2161. Piencikowski, Robert. "Fonction relative du timbre dans la musique contemporaine: Messiaen, Carter, Boulez, Stockhausen." ANM 3 (1986): 51–53.

2162. Rosen, Charles. "Les langages musicaux d'Elliot Carter." Trans. Thierry Baud. CC 6 (1986): 123–39.

2163. ———. *The Music Languages of Elliott Carter.* Washington, D.C.: Music Division, Research Services, Library of Congress, 1984.

2164. Schiff, David. "Elliott Carter's Harvest Home." TEMPO 167 (1988): 2–13.

2165. ———. *The Music of Elliott Carter.* London: Eulenberg Books; New York: Da Capo, 1983.

2166. Skulsky, Abraham. "Elliott Carter." ACA 3, no. 2 (1953): 2–16.

CASTALDO, JOSEPH (b. 1927)

2167. Chittum, Donald. "Current Chronicle." MQ 53 (1967): 254–56. [*Dichotomy* for Woodwind Quartet]

2168. ———. "Current Chronicle." MQ 55 (1969): 95–99. [*Flight*]

2169. ———. "Current Chronicle." MQ 57 (1971): 138–41. [*Cycle*]

CASTELNUOVO-TEDESCO, MARIO (1895–1968)

2170. Higham, Peter Anthony. "Castelnuovo-Tedesco's Works for Guitar." M.M. thesis, University of Alberta, 1977. [Opp. 143, 152]

2171. Holmberg, Mark Leonard. "Thematic Contours and Harmonic Idioms of Mario Castelnuovo-Tedesco as Exemplified in the Solo Concertos." Ph.D. diss., Northwestern University, 1974.

2172. Scalin, Burton Howard. "Operas by Mario Castelnuovo-Tedesco." Ph.D. diss., Northwestern University, 1980.

CASTÉRÈDE, JACQUES (b. 1926)
2173. Delente, Gail Buchanan. "Selected Piano Music in France since 1945." Ph.D. diss., Washington University, 1966. [*Diagrammes,* 4 Études, Passacaglia and Fugue]

CASTRO, JUAN JOSÉ (1895–1968)
2174. Arias, Enrique Alberto. "Juan José Castro's *Corales criollos.*" LAMR 7, no. 1 (1986): 25–50.

CAZDEN, NORMAN (1914–1980)
2175. Haufrecht, Herbert. "The Writings of Norman Cazden: Composer and Musicologist." ACA 8, no. 2 (1958): 2–9.

CERHA, FRIEDRICH (b. 1926)
2176. McShane, Catherine Albertson. "The Music of Friedrich Cerha and an Analysis of His Opera *Der Rattenfänger.*" Ph.D. diss., University of Texas at Austin, 1995.

CHABRIER, EMMANUEL (1841–1894)
2177. Schwartz, Manuela. "'Leitmotiver tout un orchestre sous la déclamation': Emmanuel Chabriers *Briséïs* im Spannungsfeld zwischen Wagner und Frankreich." JSIM (1997): 211–34.

CHADWICK, GEORGE WHITEFIELD (1854–1931)
2178. Campbell, Douglas G. "George W. Chadwick: His Life and Works." Ph.D. diss., University of Rochester, 1957.
2179. Yellin, Victor. "The Life and Operatic Works of George Whitefield Chadwick." Ph.D. diss., Harvard University, 1957.

CHAMPAGNE, CLAUDE (1891–1965)
2180. Walsh, Anne. "The Life and Works of Claude Adonai Champagne." Ph.D. diss., Catholic University of America, 1972.

CHANCE, JOHN BARNES (1932–1972)
2181. Chance, John Barnes. "*Variations on a Korean Folk Song.*" JBR 3, no. 1 (1966–1967): 13–16.
2182. Rohrer, Thomas P. "An Analysis of *Blue Lake: Overture for Concert Band* by John Barnes Chance." JBR 31, no. 2 (1996): 52–85.

CHANLER, THEODORE (1902–1961)
2183. Cox, Donald Ray. "Theodore Ward Chanler: A Biographical and Analytical Study of the Man and Three Song Cycles." D.M.A. diss., University of Southern Mississippi, 1976.
2184. Kolb, Bruce Lanier. "The published songs of Theodore Chanler." DMA dissertation (Performance): Louisiana State University, 1976.
2185. Nordgren, Elliott Alfred. "An Analytical Study of the Songs of Theodore Chanler (1902–1961)." Ph.D. diss., New York University, 1980.

CHARPENTIER, GUSTAVE (1860–1956)
2186. ASO 197 (2000). [*Louise*]

CHATHAM, RHYS (b. 1952)
2187. Gann, Kyle. "Downtown Beats for the 1990s: Rhys Chatham, Mikel Rouse, Michael Gordon, Larry Polansky, Ben Neill." CMR 10, no. 1 (1994): 33–49.

CHAUSSON, ERNEST (1855–1899)
2188. Barricelli, Jean-Pierre, and Leo Weinstein. *Ernest Chausson: The Composer's Life and Works.* Norman: Oklahoma University Press, 1955.
2189. M-Chailley. [*Poème,* op. 25]
2190. Grover, Ralph S. "The Influence of Franck, Wagner, and Debussy on Representative Works of Ernest Chausson." Ph.D. diss., University of North Carolina, 1966.
2191. Hirsbrunner, Theo. "Debussy-Maeterlinck-Chausson: Musikalische und literarische Querverbindungen." Fs. Schuh: 47–66. English translation, MMA 13 (1984): 57–85. [*Serres chaudes*]

CHÁVEZ, CARLOS (1899–1978)
2192. Nordyke, Diane. "The Piano Works of Carlos Chávez." Ph.D. diss., Texas Tech University, 1982.
2193. Parker, Robert L. *Carlos Chávez: Mexico's Modern-Day Orpheus.* Boston: Hall, 1983.
2194. ———. "Carlos Chávez's Orchestral Tribute to the Discovery of San Francisco Bay." LAMR 15, no. 2 (1994): 177–88. [*Discovery*]

2195. ———. "Clare Boothe Luce, Carlos Chávez, and Sinfonía No. 3." LAMR 5, no. 1 (1984): 48–65.

2196. ———. "A Recurring Melodic Cell in the Music of Carlos Chávez." LAMR 12, no. 2 (1991): 160–72.

CHEN YI (b. 1953)

2197. Chen Yi. "Tradition and Creation." CM 67–68 (1999): 59–72. [*Duo Ye, The Points, Qi, Sparkle*]

CHERNEY, BRIAN (b. 1942)

2198. Spiteri, Vivienne. "*Déploration–In Memoriam Morton Feldman* by Brian Cherney, and in Conversation." CMR 19, no. 4 (2000): 73–103.

CHERUBINI, LUIGI (1760–1842)

2199. Cadenbach, Rainer. "Cherubinis 'symphonistisches' Quartett zwischen 'neuem Pariser Ton' und 'roccoco, perruque u.s.w.'" F-Stephan: 209–31. [String Quartet No. 2 (arr. of Symphony, D major)]

2200. Fend, Michael. "Literary Motifs, Musical Form, and the Quest for the 'Sublime': Cherubini's *Eliza ou Le voyage aux glaciers du Mont St. Bernard.*" COJ 5, no. 1 (1993): 17–38.

2201. Hohenegger, Maximilian. "L'acquisizione della forma-sonata in L. Cherubini: Dall cantata *Amphion* all'opera *Anacréon.*" ANL 33 (2000): 9–15.

2202. ———. "Formstrukturen in den Ouverturen von Cherubinis frühen Opern." SZM 46 (1998): 95–142.

2203. Saak, Siegfried. *Studien zur Instrumentalmusik Luigi Cherubinis.* Kassel: Bärenreiter-Antiquariat, 1979. [Overtures, String Quartets, String Quintets, Symphony in D major]

2204. Selden, Margery J. S. "The French Operas of Luigi Cherubini." Ph.D. diss., Yale University, 1951.

2205. White, Maurice L. "The Motets of Luigi Cherubini." Ph.D. diss., University of Michigan, 1968.

CHESLOCK, LOUIS (1898–1981)

2206. Sprenkle, Elam Ray. "The Life and Works of Louis Cheslock." D.M.A. diss., Peabody Conservatory, 1979.

CHESNOKOV, PAVEL GREGORYEVICH (1877–1944)

2207. Elzinga, Harry. "The Sacred Choral Compositions of Paval Gregoryevich Chesnokov (1877–1944)." Ph.D. diss., Indiana University, 1970.

CHOPIN, FRYDERYK FRANCISZEK (1810–1849)

Ballades (various; *see also* specific ballades)

2208. Griffel, L. Michael. "The Sonata Design in Chopin's Ballades." CM 36 (1983): 125–36.

2209. Samson, Jim. *Chopin: The Four Ballades.* Cambridge: Cambridge University Press, 1992.

2210. Witten, Neil David. "The Chopin Ballades: An Analytical Study." D.M.A. diss., Boston University, 1979.

Ballade, Op. 23

2211. Berger, Karol. "The Form of Chopin's Ballade, Op. 23." NCM 20, no. 1 (1996): 46–71.

2212. Gut, Serge. "Interferences entre le langage et la structure dans la Ballade en sol mineur opus 23 de Chopin." CS 5 (1995): 64–72.

2213. Rothstein, William. "Ambiguity in the Themes of Chopin's First, Second, and Fourth Ballades." INT 8 (1994): 1–50.

2214. Tarasti, Eero. "A Narrative Grammar of Chopin's G Minor Ballade." CS 5 (1995): 38–63.

2215. Ünlü, Altug. "Fréderic Chopins Ballade G-Moll op. 23 und ihr Stellenwert im zyklischen Zusammenhang: Ein Strukturanalyse." F-Floros/70: 47–62.

Ballade, Op. 38

2216. Rothstein, William. "Ambiguity in the Themes of Chopin's First, Second, and Fourth Ballades." INT 8 (1994): 1–50.

2217. Samson, Jim. "The Second Ballade: Historical and Analytical Perspectives." CS 5 (1995): 73–81.

2218. Zakrzewska, Dorota. "Alienation and Powerlessness: Adam Mickiewicz's *Ballady* and Chopin's Ballades." PMJ 2, nos. 1–2 (1999). Shortened version, MRF 15 (2000): 31–87.

Ballade, Op. 52

2219. Nettheim, Nigel. "The Derivation of Chopin's Fourth Ballade from Bach and Beethoven." MR 54, no. 2 (1993): 95–111.

2220. Noden-Skinner, Cheryl. "Tonal Ambiguity in the Opening Measures of Selected Works by Chopin." CMS 24 (1984): 28–34.

2221. Rothstein, William. "Ambiguity in the Themes of Chopin's First, Second, and Fourth Ballades." INT 8 (1994): 1–50.

2222. Suurpää, Lauri. "The Path from Tonic to Dominant in the Second Movement of Schubert's String Quintet and in Chopin's Fourth Ballade." JMT 44, no. 2 (2000): 451–85.

Barcarolle, Op. 60

2223. Gajewski, Ferdinand. "A Hidden Aspect of Chopin's Invention." STU 24, no. 1 (1995): 125–30.

Berceuse, Op. 57
2224. Lissa, Zofia. "Max Regers Metamorphosen der Berceuse Op.57 von Frederic Chopin." F-Wiener: 35–40.

Cello Sonata, Op. 65
2225. Gajewski, Ferdinand. "A Hidden Aspect of Chopin's Invention." STU 24, no. 1 (1995): 125–30.
2226. Sutcliffe, W. Dean. "Chopin's Counterpoint: The Largo from the Cello Sonata, Opus 65." MQ 83, no. 1 (1999): 114–33.

Concertos
2227. Rink, John. *Chopin: The Piano Concertos.* Cambridge: Cambridge University Press, 1997.

Etudes (various; *see also* specific études)
2228. Ganz, Peter. "The Development of the Etude for Pianoforte." Ph.D. diss., Northwestern University, 1960.

Etudes, Op. 10
2229. Cinnamon, Howard. "E Major Tonality as Dominant or Mediant in Chopin's Op. 10/1: Schenker's Graphs from *Free Composition.*" ITR 15, no. 1 (1994): 1–20.
2230. Eitan, Zohar. "Associative Convergence and the Structure of Chopin's 'Revolutionary Etude.'" ISM 6 (1996): 153–78. [No. 12]
2231. Phipps, Graham H. "A Response to Schenker's Analysis of Chopin's Étude, Opus 10, No. 12, Using Schoenberg's *Grundgestalt* Concept." MQ 69 (1983): 543–69.
2232. Prost, Christine. "Modernité de Chopin: La dynamique et le timbre comme éléments constitutifs de la forme." ANM 8 (1987): 27–30. [No. 9]
2233. Smith, Charles Justice, III. "Patterns and Strategies: Four Perspectives of Musical Characterization." Ph.D. diss., University of Michigan, 1980. [NÓ. 1]
2234. ———. "(Supra-) Durational Patterns in Chopin's 'Revolutionary' Etude." ITO 2, no. 5 (1976): 3–12. [No. 12]
2235. ———. "Toward the Construction of Intersecting Divergent Models for Chopin's 'Three Against Two' Etude." ITO 1, no. 3 (1975–1976): 19–25.
2236. Spicer, Mark J. "Root Versus Linear Analysis of Chromaticism: A Comparative Study of Selected Excerpts from the Oeuvres of Chopin." CMS 36 (1996): 138–47. [No. 3]

Etudes, Op. 25
2237. Salzer, Felix. "Chopin's Étude in F Major, Opus 25, No. 3: The Scope of Tonality." MFO 3 (1973): 281–90.
2238. Smith, Charles Justice, III. "Registering Distinctions: Octave Non-Equivalence in Chopin's 'Butterfly' Etude." ITO 3, no. 5 (1977–1978): 32–40.

***Fantaisie-Impromptu,* Op. 66.** *See* Impromptu, Op. 66

Fantasy, Op. 49
2239. Gojowy, Detlej. "Frédéric Chopin: Fantaisie F-Moll, Op. 49." NZM 146, no. 6 (1985): 29–31.
2240. Samson, Jim. "Chopin and Genre." MA 8, no. 3 (1989): 213–31.
2241. Schachter, Carl. "Chopin's Fantasy, Op. 49: The Two-Key Scheme." M-Schachter: Chap. 11.
2242. Tomaszewski, Mieczysław. "Fantasie F-moll op. 49: Genese, Struktur, Rezeption." Trans. Antoni Buchner. CS 5 (1995): 210–23.

Impromptus (various; *see also* specific impromptus)
2243. Samson, Jim. "Chopin and Genre." MA 8, no. 3 (1989): 213–31.

Impromptu, Op. 36
2244. Samson, Jim. "Chopin's F-Sharp Impromptu: Notes on Genre, Style, and Structure." CS 3 (1990): 297–304.

Impromptu, Op. 66
2245. Ekier, Jan. "Das Impromptu Cis-Moll von Frédéric Chopin." Melos/NZM 4 (1978): 201–4.
2246. Oster, Ernst. "The Fantaisie-Impromptu: A Tribute to Beethoven." MU 1 (1946–1947): 407–29.

Mazurkas (various; *see also* specific mazurkas)
2247. Eitan, Zohar. "Chopin: Melodic Peaks, Salience, and Intensity." M-Eitan: Chap. 4.
2248. Swartz, Anne. "Folk Dance Elements in Chopin's Mazurkas." JMR 4 (1982–1983): 417–26.
2249. ———. "The Mazurkas of Chopin: Certain Aspects of Phrasing." Ph.D. diss., University of Pittsburgh, 1973.
2250. Witkowska-Zaremba, Elżbieta. "Versification, Syntax, and Form in Chopin's Mazurkas." Trans. Maria Pilatowicz. PMJ 3, no. 1 (2000).

Mazurkas, Op. 6
2251. Hyer, Brian. "Chopin and the In-F-able." F-Lewin: 147–66. [No. 1]
2252. Viljoen, Nicol. "The Drone Bass and Its Implications for the Tonal Voice-Leading Structure in Two Selected Mazurkas by Chopin." ITR 6, nos. 1–2 (1982–1983): 17–35. [No. 2]

Mazurkas, Op. 7

2253. Meeùs, Nicolas. "Questions de méthode: La Mazurka op. 7 no. 5 de Chopin." ANM 32 (1993): 58–63.

Mazurkas, Op. 17

2254. Beach, David. "Chopin's Mazurka, Op. 17, No. 4: Analysis." TP 2, no. 3 (1977): 12–16.

2255. Noden-Skinner, Cheryl. "Tonal Ambiguity in the Opening Measures of Selected Works by Chopin." CMS 24 (1984): 28–34.

Mazurkas, Op. 56

2256. Viljoen, Nicol. "The Drone Bass and Its Implications for the Tonal Voice-Leading Structure in Two Selected Mazurkas by Chopin." ITR 6, nos. 1–2 (1982–1983): 17–35. [No. 2]

Mazurkas, Op. 59

2257. Belotti, Gastone. "Una nuova mazurca di Chopin." STU 6 (1977): 161–206. [No. 3]

Mazurkas, Op. 68

2258. Bronarski, Louis. "La dernière Mazurka de Chopin." SMZ 95 (1955): 380–87. [No. 4]

2259. Kallberg, Jeffrey. "Chopin's Last Style." JAMS 38 (1985): 264–315. [No. 4]

2260. M-Kresky: 80–91. [No. 3]

2261. Nowik, Wojciech. "Chopins Mazurka F Moll, Op. 68, Nr. 4: Die letzte Inspiration des Meisters." AM 30 (1973): 109–27.

Nocturnes, Op. 9

2262. Rink, John. "'Structural Momentum' and Closure in Chopin's Op. 9, No. 2." CS 5 (1995): 82–104.

Nocturnes, Op. 15

2263. Kallberg, Jeffrey. "The Rhetoric of Genre: Chopin's Nocturne in G Minor." NCM 11, no. 3 (1988): 238–61. [No. 3]

2264. Kirsch, Winfried. "*Languido, Religioso*: Zu Chopins Nocturnes in G-moll Op. 15 Nr. 3 und Op. 37 Nr. 1." CS 5 (1995): 105–19.

2265. Meeùs, Nicolas. "Techniques modales dans l'harmonie des Mazurkas de Chopin." ANM 21 (1990): 102–12.

Nocturnes, Op. 27

2266. Levy, Janet M. "Texture as a Sign in Classic and Early Romantic Music." JAMS 35 (1982): 482–531. [No. 1]

2267. Salzer, Felix. "Chopin's Nocturne in C-Sharp Minor, Op. 27, No. 1." MFé 2 (1970): 283–97.

2268. Tuchowski, Andrzej. "Chopin's Integrative Technique and Its Repercussions for Twentieth-Century Polish Music." PMJ 2, nos. 1–2 (1999). [Nos. 1–2]

Nocturnes, Op. 32

2269. Carapezza, Paolo Emilio. "Chopin's Nocturne Op. 32, No. 1: The Source of Mahler's Sixth Symphony?" CS 5 (1995): 126–44.

2270. Mainka, Jürgen. "Zu Chopins G-Dur-Nocturno Opus 32 Nr. 1: Ein Aspekt der Tonsprache Chopins in ihrem Verstältnis zur deutschen Romantik." BM 22 (1980): 309–16.

Nocturnes, Op. 37

2271. Kirsch, Winfried. "*Languido, Religioso*: Zu Chopins Nocturnes in G-moll op. 15 Nr. 3 und op. 37 Nr. 1." CS 5 (1995): 105–19.

Nocturnes, Op. 48

2272. Rothgeb, John. "Chopin's C-Minor Nocturne, Op. 48, No. 1, First Part: Voice Leading and Motivic Content." TP 5, no. 2 (1980): 26–31.

Nocturnes, Op. 62

2273. Wick, Norman L. "Shifted Downbeats in Classic and Romantic Music." ITR 15, no. 2 (1994): 73–87. [No. 1]

***Polonaise-Fantasy*, Op. 61**

2274. Kallberg, Jeffrey. "Chopin's Last Style." JAMS 38 (1985): 264–315.

2275. Rink, John. "Chopin and Schenker: Improvisation and Musical Structure." CS 3 (1990): 219–31.

2276. Rothstein, William. "The Form of Chopin's *Polonaise-Fantasy*." M-Baker: 337–59.

2277. Spicer, Mark J. "Root versus Linear Analysis of Chromaticism: A Comparative Study of Selected Excerpts from the Oeuvres of Chopin." CMS 36 (1996): 138–47.

2278. Tarasti, Eero. "Pour une narratologie de Chopin." IRASM 15, no. 1 (1984): 53–75.

Preludes, Op. 28 (various; *see also* specific preludes)

2279. Agawu, V. Kofi. "Concepts of Closure and Chopin's Opus 28." MTS 9 (1987): 1–17.

2280. Cole, Ronald Eugene. "Analysis of the Chopin Preludes, Opus 28." M.M. diss., Florida State University, 1968.

2281. Eigeldinger, Jean-Jacques. "Le Vingt-quatre Préludes op. 28 de Chopin: Genre, structure, signification." RDM 75, no. 2 (1989): 201–28. English translation published under the title "Twenty-Four Preludes, Op. 28: Genre, Structure, Significance," in *Chopin Studies,* 167–94 (Cambridge: Cambridge University Press, 1988).
2282. Higgins, Thomas. *Chopin: Preludes, Op. 28.* Norton Critical Scores. New York: Norton, 1975.
2283. Kirk, Kenneth Patrick. "The Golden Ratio in Chopin's Preludes, Opus 28." Ph.D. diss., University of Cincinnati, 1987.
2284. Schwarz, David Bunker. "Structuralism, Post-Structuralism, and a Classical Musical Text: A New Look at Chopin's Preludes, Opus 28." Ph.D. diss., University of Texas at Austin, 1987.
2285. Smith, Charles J. "On Hearing the Chopin Preludes as a Coherent Set: A Survey of some Possible Structural Models for Op. 28." ITO 1, no. 4 (1975–1976): 5–16.

Prelude, Op. 28, No. 1
2286. Pestelli, Giorgio. "Sul preludio di Chopin op. 28 n. 1." ACTA 63, no. 1 (1991): 98–114.

Prelude, Op. 28, No. 2
2287. Hoyt, Reed J. "Chopin's Prelude in A Minor Revisited: The Issue of Tonality." ITS 8, no. 6 (1984–1985): 7–16.
2288. Kielian-Gilbert, Marianne. "Motive Transfer in Chopin's A Minor Prelude." ITO 9, no. 1 (1986): 21–32.
2289. Kramer, Lawrence. "Romantic Meaning in Chopin's Prelude in A Minor." NCM 9, no. 2 (1985): 145–55.
2290. Noden-Skinner, Cheryl. "Tonal Ambiguity in the Opening Measures of Selected Works by Chopin." CMS 24 (1984): 28–34.
2291. Rogers, Michael R. "Chopin, Prelude in A Minor, Op. 28, No. 2." NCM 4 (1980–1981): 245–50.
2292. Spicer, Mark J. "Root Versus Linear Analysis of Chromaticism: A Comparative Study of Selected Excerpts from the Oeuvres of Chopin." CMS 36 (1996): 138–47.

Prelude, Op. 28, No. 4
2293. Kirsch, Winfried. "Chopins Préludes E-Moll und G-Moll (op. 28): Ein Analyse- und Interpretationsversuch." F-Finscher: 572–81.
2294. M-Kresky: 41–55.
2295. Pierce, Alexandra. "Climax in Music: Structure and Phrase (Part III)." ITO 7, no. 1 (1983–1984): 3–30.

Prelude, Op. 28, No. 5
2296. Schachter, Carl. "Chopin's Prelude in D Major, Opus 28, No. 5: Analysis and Performance." JMTP 8 (1994): 27–45.

Prelude, Op. 28, No. 6
2297. Cinnamon, Howard. "New Observations on Voice Leading, Hemiola, and Their Roles in Tonal and Rhythmic Structures in Chopin's Prelude in B Minor, Op. 28, No. 6." INT 6 (1992): 66–106.
2298. Kirsch, Winfried. "Chopins Préludes E-Moll und G-Moll (op. 28): Ein Analyse- und Interpretationsversuch." F-Finscher: 572–81.
2299. Warburton, Thomas. "Possible Models for Chopin's Preludes, Opus 28." TSP 4 (1987): 1–24.

Prelude, Op. 28, No. 16
2300. Prost, Christine. "Modernité de Chopin: La dynamique et le timbre comme éléments constitutifs de la forme." ANM 8 (1987): 27–30.

Prelude, Op. 28, No. 22
2301. Hoyt, Reed J. "Harmonic Process, Melodic Process, and Interpretive Aspects of Chopin's Prelude in G Minor." ITR 5, no. 3 (1981–1982): 22–42.

Prelude, Op. 45
2302. Eigeldinger, Jean-Jacques. "Chopin and 'La note bleue': An Interpretation of the Prelude Op. 45." ML 78, no. 2 (1997): 233–53.

Scherzos
2303. Fang, Julia Lam. "Chopin's Approach to Form in His Four Piano Scherzos." Ph.D. diss., Michigan State University, 1979.
2304. Krebs, Harald. "Tonal and Formal Dualism in Chopin's Scherzo, Op. 31." MTS 13, no. 1 (1991): 48–60.
2305. Noden-Skinner, Cheryl. "Tonal Ambiguity in the Opening Measures of Selected Works by Chopin." CMS 24 (1984): 28–34. [Op. 39]
2306. Nowik, Wojciech. "Fryderyk Chopin's Scherzo in B Minor Op. 20: Form and Thematic Process." Trans. Katharine Tylko-Hill. CS 5 (1995): 174–89.
2307. Tuchowski, Andrzej. "Scherzo C Sharp Minor: The Problem of Structural Consistency and Motivic Transformations." CS 5 (1995): 190–97. [Op. 39]

Sonata, Op. 35, B-Flat Minor

2308. Arnold, Janice Margaret. "The Role of Chromaticism in Chopin's Sonata Forms: A Schenkerian View." Ph.D. diss., Northwestern University, 1992. [Movement I]

2309. Bisgaard, Lars. "Musikalsk hermeneutik på hierarkisk grundlag: Bidrag til en musikalsk fænomenologi." DAM 16 (1985): 75–125. [Movement I]

2310. Bollinger, John Simon. "An Integrative and Schenkerian Analysis of the B-Flat Minor Sonata by Frederic Chopin." Ph.D. diss., Washington University, 1981.

2311. Chołopow, Jurij. "Über die Kompositionsgrundsätze bei Frédéric Chopin: Das Rätsel des Finales der Sonate b-moll." Trans. Maria Weronika Janssen. CS 3 (1990): 269–95.

2312. Petty, Wayne C. "Chopin and the Ghost of Beethoven." NCM 22, no. 3 (1999): 281–99.

2313. Rosen, Charles. "Chopin, poésie et métier: À propos de la Sonate op. 35 en si bémol mineur." Trans. Nasreen Hussein. ANM 21 (1990): 96–101.

2314. ———. "The First Movement of Chopin's Sonata in B-Flat Minor, Op. 35." NCM 14, no. 1 (1990): 60–66.

2315. Tuchowski, Andrzej. "Chopin's Integrative Technique and Its Repercussions for Twentieth-Century Polish Music." PMJ 2, nos. 1–2 (1999).

2316. Wessely, Othmar. "Chopins B-Moll Sonate." OMZ 4 (1949): 283–86.

Sonata, Op. 58, B Minor

2317. Arnold, Janice Margaret. "The Role of Chromaticism in Chopin's Sonata Forms: A Schenkerian View." Ph.D. diss., Northwestern University, 1992. [Movement I]

Songs

2318. Gajewski, Ferdinand. "Unriddling Chopin's 'Sphinx.'" STU 15, no. 2 (1986): 299–310. [Śpiew grobowy (Hymn from the Tomb), op. 74, no. 17]

2319. Matracka-Kościelny, Alicja. "The Relationship between Words and Music in Chopin's Songs." Trans. Rosemary Hunt. CS 2 (1987): 63–70.

Waltzes

2320. Eitan, Zohar. "Chopin: Melodic Peaks, Salience, and Intensity." M-Eitan: Chap. 4.

2321. Sittner, Hans. "Der Walzer bei Chopin und Johann Strauss." OMZ 4 (1949): 287–93.

Various Works

2322. Barbag-Drexler, Irena. "Zur Harmonik Chopins." ME 27 (1973–1974): 202–6.

2323. Belotti, Gastone. Les origini italiane del "rubato" chopiniano. Wroclaw: Zakld Narodowy Im. Ossolińskich, 1968.

2324. ———. "Le Polacche dell'Op. 26 nel testo autentico di Chopin." STU 2 (1973): 267–313.

2325. ———. "Le prime composizione di Chopin: Problemi e osservazioni." RIM 7 (1972): 230–91.

2326. Braun, Hartmut. "Ein Zitat: Beziehungen zwischen Chopin und Brahms." MF 25 (1972): 317–21.

2327. Bronarski, Louis. "Le plus 'chopinesque' des accords de Chopin." SMZ 85 (1945): 382–85.

2328. Burdick, Michael Francis. "A Structural Analysis of Melodic Scale-Degree Tendencies in Selected Themes of Haydn, Mozart, Schubert, and Chopin." Ph.D. diss., Indiana University, 1977.

2329. Chomifiski, Józef Michat. "Das Entwicklungsprobleme des chopinschen Stils." F-Besseler: 437–46.

2330. Dammeier-Kirpal, Ursula. Der Sonatensatz bei Frédéric Chopin. Wiesbaden: Breitkopf & Härtel, 1973.

2331. Dommel-Diény, Amy. Chopin. Dommel-Diény 7. Paris: Éditions Transatlantiques, 1970.

2332. Eigeldinger, Jean-Jacques. "Un autographe musical inédit de Chopin." SMZ 115 (1975): 18–23.

2333. ———. "Chopin et l'heritage baroque." SBM 2 (1974): 51–74.

2334. Goepfert, Robert Harold. "Ambiguity in Chopin's Rhythmic Notation." D.M.A. diss., Boston University, 1981.

2335. Gołąb, Maciej. "Das Problem der Haupttonart in den Werken von Chopin." Trans. Beatrysa Hirszenberg. CS 5 (1995): 235–44.

2336. ———. "Über den Tristan-Akkord bei Chopin." Trans. Beatrysa Hirszenberg. CS 3 (1990): 246–56.

2337. Goldschmidt, Harry. "Chopiniana bei Beethoven." F-Lissa: 209–22.

2338. Hutchinson, William R. "Implication, Closure, and Interpolated Change as Exemplified in the Works of Frédéric Chopin." Ph.D. diss., University of Chicago, 1960.

2339. Kallberg, Jeffrey. "Compatibility in Chopin's Multipartite Publications." JM 2 (1983): 391–417.

2340. Kholopov, Yuri. "Aufzeichnungen uber Chopins Metrik." CS 5 (1995): 245–61.

2341. Kinzler, Hartmuth. Frédéric Chopin: Über den Zusammenhang von Satztechnik und Klavierspiel. Munich: Katzbichler, 1977.

2342. Klein, Rudolf. "Chopins Sonatentechnik." OMZ 22 (1967): 389–99.

2343. Koszewskik, Andrzej. "Das Walzerelement im Schaffen Chopins." DJM 5 (1960): 48–66.

2344. Lissa, Zofia, ed. *The Book of the First International Musicological Congress Devoted to the Works of Frédérick Chopin.* Warsaw: Panstwowe Wydawnictwo Naukowe, 1963.

2345. Lissa, Zofia. "Chopin und die polnische Volksmusik." MG 10 (1960): 65–74.

2346. ———. "Die chopinische Harmonik aus dÂr Perspective der Klangtechnik des 20. Jahrhunderts." DJM 2 (1957): 68–84; 3 (1958): 74–91.

2347. ———. "Über den Einfluss Chopins aus Ljadow." DJM 13 (1968): 5–42.

2348. Matter, Jean. "De l'harmonie complémentaire et de l'expression du dépaysement dans la musique de Chopin." SMZ 101 (1961): 93–97.

2349. McGinnis, Francis. "Chopin: Aspects of Melodic Style." Ph.D. diss., Indiana University, 1969.

2350. Meloncelli, Raoul. "Coerenza et continuità dÂl linguaggio chopiniano." F-Haberl: 187–95.

2351. Metzger, Heinz-Klaus, and Rainer Riehn, eds. *Fryderyk Chopin.* Munich: Text + Kritik, 1985.

2352. Moore, Kevin Morris. "Linearity of Voice Structure in Selected Works of Frédéric Chopin and Its Implications in Performance." Ph.D. diss., New York University, 1979.

2353. Parks, Richard S. "Voice Leading and Chromatic Harmony in the Music of Chopin." JMT 20 (1976): 189–214.

2354. Société Frédéric Chopin. *Annales Chopin.* Kraków: Polskie Wydawn. Muzyczne, 1956–1969.

2355. M-Sterling.

2356. Thomas, Betty J. "Harmonic Materials and Treatment of Dissonance in the Pianoforte Music of Frédéric Chopin." Ph.D. diss., University of Rochester, 1963.

2357. Wagner, Günther. "Die Melodik Chopins unter dem Einfluss italienischer Opernmusik." JSIM (1975): 80–95.

2358. Walker, Alan, ed. *Frédéric Chopin: Profiles of the Man and the Musician.* London: Barrie & Rockcliff, 1966.

2359. Węcowski, Jan. "Religious Folklore in Chopin's Music." PMJ 2, nos. 1–2 (1999).

2360. YaDeau, William Ronald. "Tonal and Formal Structure in Selected Larger Works of Chopin." Ph.D. diss., University of Illinois, 1980.

CHOU WEN-CHUNG (b. 1923)

2361. Lai, Eric Chiu Kong. "A Theory of Pitch Organization in the Early Music of Chou Wen-chung." Ph.D. diss., Indiana University, 1995.

2362. ———. "Modal Formations and Transformations in the First Movement of Chou Wen-chung's *Metaphors.*" PNM 35, no. 1 (1997): 153–85.

CHOWNING, JOHN M. (b. 1934)

2363. Schœller, Phillippe. "Mutation de l'écriture: *Éclat, Stria, Désintégrations.*" INH 1 (1986): 197–208. [*Stria*]

CILEA, FRANCESCO (1866–1950)

2364. ASO 155 (1993). [*Adriana Lecouvreur*]

CILENŠEK, JOHANN (1913–1998)

2365. Felix, Werner. "Die V. Sinfonie von Johann Cilenšek." MG 10 (1960): 541–48.

2366. Junghanns, Bernd. "Johannes Cilenšek: Sein sinfonisches Werk." Ph.D. diss., Martin-Luther-Universiät, 1977.

2367. Markowski, Liesel. "Johann Cilenšek: II. Sinfonie." MG 12 (1962): 489–90.

2368. Schmidt, Gerhard. "Johann Cilenšek: Konzertstück für Klavier und Orchester." MG 2 (1952): 86–89.

CLAPP, PHILIP GREELEY (1888–1954)

2369. Kleinknecht, Daniel. "*A Chant of Darkness.*" ACR 35, no. 1 (1993): 3–4.

CLARKE, HENRY LELAND (1907–1992)

2370. Verrall, John. "Henry Leland Clarke." ACA 9, no. 3 (1959): 2–8.

CLARKE, REBECCA (1886–1979)

2371. Curtis, Lianc. "Rebecca Clarke and Sonata Form: Questions of Gender and Genre." MQ 81, no. 3 (1997): 393–429. [Viola Sonata, various other works]

2372. MacDonald, Calum. "Rebecca Clarke's Chamber Music (I)." TEMPO 160 (1986): 15–26.

2373. Richards, Deborah. "'And You Should Have Seen Their Faces When They Saw It Was by a Woman!': Gedanken zu Rebecca Clarkes Klaviertrio." N 4 (1983–1984): 201–8.

CLEMENTI, ALDO (b. 1925)

2374. Bortolotto, Mario. "Aldo Clementi." MELOS 30 (1963): 364–69.

2375. Osmond-Smith, David. "Au creux néant musicien: Recent Work by Aldo Clementi." CT 23 (1981): 5–9.

CLEMENTI, MUZIO (1752–1832)

2376. Allorto, Riccardo. *Le Sonate per pianoforte di Muzio Clementi: Studio critico e catalogo tematico.* Florence: Olschki, 1959.

2377. Grave, Jerald C. "Clementi's Self-Borrowings: The Refinement of a Manner." F-Fox: 57–71.

2378. Hill, John Walter. "The Symphonies of Muzio Clementi." M.A. thesis, Harvard University, 1965.

2379. Sheer, Miriam. "Comparison of Dynamic Practices in Selected Piano Sonatas by Clementi and Beethoven." BF 5 (1996): 85–101.

2380. Tighe, Alice Eugene. "Muzio Clementi and His Sonatas Surviving as Solo Piano Works." Ph.D. diss., University of Michigan, 1964.

COE, TONY (b. 1934)

2381. Barry, Malcolm. "Tony Coe's *Zeitgeist.*" CT 19 (1978): 12–14.

COGAN, ROBERT (b. 1930)

2382. Shreffler, Anne. "Cogan's *Utterances* and the Polyphony of Oppositions." SONUS 16, no. 1 (1995): 53–68.

COHEN, DENIS (b. 1952)

2383. Nieminen, Risto, ed. *Denis Cohen.* Paris: IRCAM, 1993.

COLE, BRUCE (b. 1947)

2384. Potter, Keith. "Bruce Cole and *Fenestrae sanctae.*" TEMPO 107 (1973): 19–22.

COLERIDGE-TAYLOR, SAMUEL (1875–1912)

2385. Batchman, John Clifford. "Samuel Coleridge-Taylor: An Analysis of Selected Piano Works and an Examination of His Influence on Black American Musicians." Ph.D. diss., Washington University, 1977.

COLGRASS, MICHAEL (b. 1932)

2386. Mathes, James. "*Winds of Nagual* by Michael Colgrass." JBR 23, no. 1 (1987): 3–16.

COLTRANE, JOHN (1926–1967)

2387. Cole, William Shadrack. "The Style of John Coltrane, 1955–1967." Ph.D. diss., Wesleyan University, 1975.

CONVERSE, FREDERICK SHEPHERD (1871–1940)

2388. Garofalo, Robert J. "The Life and Works of Frederick Shepherd Converse (1871–1940)." Ph.D. diss., Catholic University of America, 1969.

COOKE, ARNOLD (b. 1906)

2389. Clapham, John. "Arnold Cooke's Symphony." MR 11 (1950): 118–21. [Symphony No. 1]

2390. Gaulke, Stanley Jack. "The Published Solo and Chamber Works for Clarinet of Arnold Cooke." D.M.A. diss., University of Rochester, 1978.

COPLAND, AARON (1900–1990)

Connotations

2391. Evans, Peter. "Copland on the Serial Road." PNM 2, no. 2 (1964): 141–49.

Dance Symphony

2392. Hilliard, Quincy Charles. "A Theoretical Analysis of the Symphonies of Aaron Copland." Ph.D. diss., University of Florida, 1984.

Danzón cubano

2393. M-Jeter.

Duo for Flute and Piano

2394. Perlove, Nina. "Inherited Sound Images: Native American Exoticism in Aaron Copland's Duo for Flute and Piano." AMUS 18, no. 1 (2000): 50–77.

Nonet

2395. Plaistow, Stephen. "Some Notes on Copland's Nonet." TEMPO 64 (1962): 6–11.

2396. Salzman, Eric, and Paul Des Marais. "Aaron Copland's Nonet: Two views." PNM 1, no. 1 (1962): 172–79.

Passacaglia

2397. Coolidge, Richard. "Aaron Copland's Passacaglia: An Analysis." MAN 2 (1974): 33–36.

Piano Blues No. 3

2398. M-Forte: 63–73.

Piano Fantasy

2399. Berger, Arthur. "Aaron Copland's *Piano Fantasy.*" JR 5, no. 1 (1957–1958): 13–27.

2400. Lively, David. "La recherche du style à travers les œuvres pianistiques d'Aaron Copland: De la forme consciente à la forme symbolique." ANM 17 (1989): 23–30.

Piano Sonata

2401. Haberkorn, Michael. "A Study and Performance of the Piano Sonatas of Samuel Barber, Elliott Carter, and Aaron Copland." Ed.D. diss., Columbia University, 1979.

2402. Kirkpatrick, John. "Aaron Copland's Piano Sonata." MM 19 (1942): 246–50.

2403. Lively, David. "La recherche du style à travers les œuvres pianistiques d'Aaron Copland: De la forme consciente à la forme symbolique." ANM 17 (1989): 23–30.

Piano Variations

2404. Lively, David. "La recherche du style à travers les œuvres pianistiques d'Aaron Copland: De la forme consciente à la forme symbolique." ANM 17 (1989): 23–30.

2405. Remson, Michael. "Copland's *Piano Variations*: A Forgotten Masterpiece?" PK 178 (1996): 31–35.

Piano Works (various; *see also* specific piano works)

2406. Case, Nelly Maude. "Stylistic Coherency in the Piano Works of Aaron Copland." Ph.D. diss., Boston University, 1984.

Poems of Emily Dickinson

2407. Cherlin, Michael. "Thoughts on Poetry and Music, on Rhythms in Emily Dickinson's 'The World Feels Dusty' and Aaron Copland's Setting of It." INT 5 (1991): 55–75.

2408. Daugherty, Robert Michael. "An Analysis of Aaron Copland's *Twelve Poems of Emily Dickinson.*" D.M.A. diss., Ohio State University, 1980.

2409. Mabry, Sharon Cody. "*Twelve Poems of Emily Dickinson* by Aaron Copland: A Stylistic Analysis." D.M.A. diss., George Peabody College for Teachers, 1977.

2410. Soll, Beverly, and Ann Dorr. "Cyclical Implications in Aaron Copland's *Twelve Poems of Emily Dickinson.*" CMS 32 (1992): 99–128.

2411. Young, Douglas. "Copland's *Dickinson Songs.*" TEMPO 103 (1972): 25–37.

Symphonies

2412. Berger, Arthur. "The Third Symphony of Aaron Copland." TEMPO 9 (1948): 20–27.

2413. Crist, Elizabeth Bergman. "Aaron Copland's Third Symphony (1946): Context, Composition, and Consequence." Ph.D. diss., Yale University, 2000.

2414. Hilliard, Quincy Charles. "A Theoretical Analysis of the Symphonies of Aaron Copland." Ph.D. diss., University of Florida, 1984.

Various Works

2415. Berger, Arthur. "The Music of Aaron Copland." MQ 31 (1945): 420–47.

2416. Brookhart, Charles E. "The Choral Works of Aaron Copland, Roy Harris, and Randall Thompson." Ph.D. diss., George Peabody College for Teachers, 1960.

2417. Cole, Hugo. "Aaron Copland." TEMPO 76 (1966): 2–6; 77 (1966): 9–15.

2418. Evans, Peter. "The Thematic Technique of Copland's Recent Works." TEMPO 51 (1959): 2–13.

2419. Metzer, David. "'Spurned Love': Eroticism and Abstraction in the Early Works of Aaron Copland." JM 15, no. 4 (1997): 417–43.

2420. Sayers, Richard. "Tonal Organization in Selected Early Works of Aaron Copland." Ph.D. diss., Catholic University of America, 2000.

2421. Smith, Julia Frances. "Aaron Copland: His Work and Contribution to American music." Ph.D. diss., New York University, 1952.

2422. Starr, Lawrence. "Copland's Style." PNM 19, no. 1 (1980–1981): 68–89.

CORDERO, ROQUE (b. 1917)

2423. Ennett, Dorothy Maxine. "An Analysis and Comparison of Selected Piano Sonatas by Three Contemporary Black Composers: George Walker, Howard Swanson, and Roque Cordero." Ph.D. diss., New York University, 1973.

2424. Sider, Ronald R. "Roque Cordero: The Composer and His Style Seen through Three Representative Works." IAMB 61 (1967): 1–17.

CORIGLIANO, JOHN (b. 1938)

2425. Dickson, John Howard, Jr. "The Union of Poetry and Music in John Corigliano's *A Dylan Thomas Trilogy.*" D.M.A. diss., University of Texas, 1985.

2426. M-Jeter. [*Kaleidoscope*]

2427. Olfert, Warren D. "An Analysis of John Corigliano's *Gazebo Dances for Band.*" JBR 29, no. 1 (1993): 25–42.

CORNELIUS, PETER (1824–1874)

2428. Federhofer, Hellmut, and Kurt Oehl, eds. *Peter Cornelius als Komponist, Dichter, Kritiker und Essayist.* Regensburg: Bosse, 1977.

2429. Porter, Ernest Graham. "The Songs of Peter Cornelius." MR 27 (1966): 202–6.

COSME, LUIZ (1908–1965)

2430. Béhague, Gerard. "Luiz Cosme (1908–1965): Impulso creador versus conciencia formal." Y 5 (1969): 67–89.

COULTHARD, JEAN (1908–2000)

2431. Rowley, Vivienne Wilda. "The Solo Piano Music of the Canadian Composer Jean Coulthard." Ph.D. diss., Boston University, 1973.

COWELL, HENRY (1897–1965)

2432. Cowell, Henry. "Mein Weg zu den Clusters." MELOS 40 (1973): 288–96.

2433. Gerschefski, Edwin. "Henry Cowell." MM 23 (1946): 255–60.

2434. Godwin, Joscelyn R. J. C. "The Music of Henry Cowell." Ph.D. diss., Cornell University, 1969.

2435. Hitchcock, H. Wiley. "Henry Cowell's *Ostinato pianissimo.*" MQ 70 (1984): 23–44.

2436. Nicholls, David. "Henry Cowell's *United Quartet.*" AMUS 13, no. 2 (1995): 195–217. [String Quartet No. 4]

2437. O'Neel, Roger Lee. "Pitch Organization and Text Setting in Songs of Charles Seeger, Ruth Crawford Seeger, and Henry Cowell." Ph.D. diss., University of Texas at Austin, 1996.

2438. Saylor, Bruce. "The Tempering of Henry Cowell's 'Dissonant Counterpoint.'" EMM 2 (1985): 3–11. [String Quartets Nos. 1–4]

2439. Smith, Leland. "Henry Cowell's *Rhythmicana.*" Y 9 (1973): 134–47.

2440. Weisgall, Hugo. "The Music of Henry Cowell." MQ 45 (1959): 484–507.

COX, FRANK (b. 1961)

2441. Ulman, Erik, and Steven Kazuo Tagasugi. "Frank Cox' *Spuren.*" MAS 2, no. 7 (1988): 53–68.

CRAWFORD, RUTH (1901–1953)

2442. Gaume, Mary Matilda. "Ruth Crawford Seeger: Her Life and Works." Ph.D. diss., Indiana University, 1974.

2443. Hisama, Ellie M. "The Question of Climax in Ruth Crawford's String Quartet, Mvt. 3." M-Marvin: 285–312.

2444. Karpf, Juanita. "'Pleasure from the Very Smallest Things': Trichordal Transformation in Ruth Crawford's *Diaphonic Suites.*" MR 53, no. 1 (1992): 32–45. [*Diaphonic Suite No. 4*]

2445. O'Neel, Roger Lee. "Pitch Organization and Text Setting in Songs of Charles Seeger, Ruth Crawford Seeger, and Henry Cowell." Ph.D. diss., University of Texas at Austin, 1996.

2446. Pace, Cynthia. "Accent on Form-against-Form: Ruth Crawford's *Piano Study in Mixed Accents.*" TP 20 (1995): 125–47.

2447. Seragg, Deborah. "Time and Intervallic Language in Crawford's *Diaphonic Suite No. 3.*" SONUS 3, no. 1 (1982): 39–56.

2448. M-Straus/C. [Songs ("Prayers of Steel," "Rat Riddles"), String Quartet (Movements III, IV), Suite for Wind Quintet (Movements I, III)]

2449. Tick, Judith. "Dissonant Counterpoint Revisited: The First Movement of Ruth Crawford's *String Quartet 1931.*" F-Hitchcock: 405–22.

2450. ———. "Ruth Crawford's *Proletarian Ricercari.*" SONUS 15, no. 2 (1995): 54–79. [Two Ricercari]

CROSSE, GORDON (b. 1937)

2451. Blacker, Terry. "Gordon Crosse: Towards a Style." TEMPO 155 (1985): 22–27.

CROTCH, WILLIAM (1775–1847)

2452. Renwick, William J. "'A Subject of Four Notes': William Crotch's Experiment in Motivic Saturation." MTO 0/10 (1994). [*Introduction and Fugue on a Subject of Four Notes*]

CRUMB, GEORGE (b. 1929)

Ancient Voices of Children

2453. Spitz, Ellen Handler. "*Ancient Voices of Children*: A Psychoanalytic Interpretation." CM 40 (1985): 7–21.

Echoes of Time and the River (Echoes II)

2454. M-Bersano. [Processional IV]

Eleven Echoes of Autumn (Echoes I)

2455. Thomas, Jennifer. "The Use of Color in Three Chamber Works of the Twentieth Century." ITR 4, no. 3 (1980–1981): 24–40.

Gnomic Variations

2456. Kessner, Dolly Eugenio. "Structural Coherence in Late Twentieth-Century Music: The Linear-Extrapolation Paradigm." MTEA 2 (1993): 5–16.

Madrigals

2457. Chatman, Stephen. "George Crumb's *Madrigals Book III*: A Linear Analysis." ITO 1, no. 9 (1975): 55–79.

Makrokosmos I–II

2458. Bass, Richard. "Models of Octatonic and Whole-Tone Interaction: Geogre Crumb and His Predecessors." JMT 38, no. 2 (1994): 155–86.

2459. ———. "Sets, Scales, and Symmetries: The Pitch-Structural Basis of George Crumb's *Makrokosmos I* and *II*." MTS 13, no. 1 (1991): 1–20.

2460. Carbon, John. "Astrological, Numerological, and Mythological Symbolism in George Crumb's *Makrokosmos, Vol. I*." TCM 2, no. 6 (1995): 1–5; 2, no. 9 (1995): 10–11; 2, no. 12 (1995): 5–7.

2461. ———. "Astrological, Numerological, and Mythological Symbolism in George Crumb's *Makrokosmos, Vol. II*." TCM 3, no. 4 (1996): 7–10.

2462. ———. "Astrological Symbolic Order in George Crumb's *Makrokosmos*." SONUS 10, no. 2 (1990): 65–80.

2463. Kaiser, Andrew. "George Crumb's *Makrokosmos, Vol. 1*: Music, Mysticism, and Analysis." MTEA 3 (1994): 4–9.

2464. Lajoinie, Vincent. "*Makrokosmos* de George Crumb: 24 pièces en quête d'auteur." CC 6 (1986): 88–101.

2465. M-Schultz/D. [*Makrokosmos II*, Movement III]

Music for a Summer Evening (Makrokosmos III)

2466. Moevs, Robert. "George Crumb: *Music for a Summer Evening (Makrokosmos III)*." MQ 62 (1976): 293–302. [Record review]

Night Music I

2467. Lewis, Robert Hall. "George Crumb: *Night Music I*." PNM 3, no. 2 (1965): 143–51.

Night of the Four Moons

2468. Chatman, Stephen. "George Crumb: *Night of the Four Moons*." JMR 1 (1973–1975): 215–24.

2469. White, John D. "Systematic Analysis for Musical Sound." JMR 5 (1984–1985): 165–90.

Vocal Works (various; *see also* specific vocal works)

2470. De Dobay, Thomas R. "The Evolution of Harmonic Style in the Lorca Works of Crumb." JMT 28, no. 1 (1984): 89–112.

2471. Rouse, Christopher Chapman, III. "The Music of George Crumb: A Stylistic Metamorphosis as Reflected in the Lorca Cycle." D.M.A. diss., Cornell University, 1977.

2472. Sams, Carol Lee. "Solo Vocal Writing in Selected Works of Berio, Crumb, and Rochberg." D.M.A. diss., University of Washington, 1975.

Vox balaenae (Voice of the Whale)

2473. Timm, Kenneth N. "A Stylistic Analysis of George Crumb's *Vox balaenae*." D.M.A. diss., Indiana University, 1977.

Various Works

2474. Bruns, Steven M. "'In stilo Mahleriano': Quotation and Allusion in the Music of George Crumb." AMRCJ 3 (1993): 9–39.

2475. Schuffett, Robert V. "The Music, 1971–1975, of George Crumb: A Style Analysis." D.M.A. diss., Peabody Conservatory, 1979.

2476. Steinitz, Richard. "George Crumb." CT 15 (1976–1977): 11–13.

2477. ———. "The Music of George Crumb." CT 11 (1975): 14–22.

CUI, CÉSAR (1835–1918)

2478. Abraham, Gerald. "Heine, Cui, and William Ratcliff." M-Abraham: 56–67.

CURRAN, ALVIN (b. 1938)

2479. Lowy, Stephen. "Vom Nebelhorn zum Schofar: Gedanken zu den neueren Jagdgründen von Alvin Curran." MTX 53 (1994): 48–53.

CZERNOWIN, CHAYA (b. 1957)

2480. Takasugi, Steven Kazuo. "Chaya Czernowins *Afatism*: Melodische Resynthetisierung und Zeitentstellung." MAS 1, no. 3 (1997): 66–81.

CZERNY, CARL (1791–1857)

2481. Neumeyer, David. "The Three-Part *Ursatz*." ITO 10, nos. 1–2 (1987): 3–29. [*Der kleine Klavierschüler*, op. 823]

2482. Sweets, Randall. "Carl Czerny Reconsidered: Romantic Elements in His Sonata Op. 7." JALS 16 (1984): 54–71.

– D –

DAHL, INGOLF (1912–1970)

2483. Kloecker, John H. "An Analysis of Ingolf Dahl's Sinfonietta for Concert Band." JBR 28, no. 2 (1993): 37–90.

DALAYRAC, NICOLAS-MARIE (1753–1809)

2484. Charlton, David. "Motif and Recollection in Four Operas of Dalayrac." SN 7 (1978): 38–61.

2485. Moss, Llewellyn. "The One-Act *Opéra comiques* by Nicolas Dalayrac (1753–1809)." Ph.D. diss., New York University, 1969.

DALBAVIE, MARC-ANDRÉ (b. 1961)

2486. Nieminen, Risto, ed. *Marc-Andre Dalbavie*. Paris: IRCAM, 1993.

DALLAPICCOLA, LUIGI (1904–1975)

Canti

2487. Michel, Pierre. "Quelques aspects du timbre chez Luigi Dallapiccola." RDM 78, no. 2 (1992): 307–30.

2488. Wildberger, Jacques. "Dallapiccolas Cinque canti." MELOS 26 (1959): 7–10.

Canti di liberazione

2489. Dallapiccola, Luigi. "Notes for an Analysis of the *Canti di liberazione*." Trans. F. Chloë Stodt. PNM 38, no. 1 (2000): 5–24.

2490. Engelmann, Hans Ulrich. "Dallapiccolas *Canti di liberazione*." MELOS 23 (1956): 73–76.

Canti di prigionia

2491. Arasimowicz, George. "Luigi Dallapiccola *Canti di prigionia*." EXT 2, no. 1 (1982): 33–45.

Commiato

2492. Kämper, Dietrich. "*Commiato*: Bemerkungen zu Dallapiccolas letztem Werk." SMZ 111 (1975): 194–200.

Goethe Lieder

2493. DeLio, Thomas. "A Proliferation of Canons: Luigi Dallapiccolas's *Goethe Lieder* No. 2." PNM 23, no. 2 (1984–1985): 186–95.

2494. ———. "A Proliferation of Canons II: Luigi Dallapiccola's *Goethe Lieder* No. 6." I 16, nos. 1–2 (1987): 39–47.

2495. Eckert, Michael. "Text and Form in Dallapiccola's *Goethe-Lieder*." PNM 17, no. 2 (1978–1979): 98–111.

2496. M-Johnson.

2497. Neumann, Peter Horst, and Jürg Stenzl. "Luigi Dallapiccolas *Goethe-Lieder*." SBM 4 (1980): 171–92.

Liriche di Antonio Machado

2498. M-Johnson.

Liriche greche

2499. Michel, Pierre. "Quelques aspects du timbre chez Luigi Dallapiccola." RDM 78, no. 2 (1992): 307–30. [*Sex carmina Alcaei*]

Piano Works (various; *see also* specific piano works)

2500. M-Buccheri.

Prigioniero

2501. Rufer, Josef. "Luigi Dallapiccola: *Il prigioniero*." MZ 6 (1954): 46–64.

Quaderno musicale di Annalibera

2502. Marvin, Elizabeth West. "A Generalization of Contour Theory to Diverse Musical Spaces: Analytical Applications to the Music of Dallapiccola and Stockhausen." M-Marvin: 135–71.

2503. Shackelford, Rudy. "Dallapiccola and the Organ." TEMPO 111 (1974): 15–22.

Requiescant

2504. Michel, Pierre. "Quelques aspects du timbre chez Luigi Dallapiccola." RDM 78, no. 2 (1992): 307–30.

Three Questions with Two Answers

2505. Petrobelli, Pierluigi. "Dallapiccola's Last Orchestral Piece." TEMPO 123 (1977): 2–6.

Various Works

2506. Brown, Rosemary. "Continuity and Recurrence in the Creative Development of Luigi Dallapiccola." Ph.D. diss., University College of North Wales, 1977.

2507. ———. "Dallapiccola's Use of Symbolic Self-Quotation." STU 4 (1975): 277–304.

2508. ———. "La sperimentazione ritmica in Dallapiccola tra libertà e determinazione." RIM 13 (1978): 142–73.

2509. Eckert, Michael. "Octatonic Elements in the Music of Luigi Dallapiccola." MR 46, no. 1 (1985): 35–48.

2510. Gould, Glen Hibbard. "A Stylistic Analysis of Selected Twelve-Tone Works of Luigi Dallapiccola." Ph.D. diss., Indiana University, 1964.

2511. Kämper, Dietrich. "'Ricerca ritmica e metrica': Beobachtungen am Spätwerk Dallapiccolas." NZM 135 (1974): 94–99.

2512. Mancini, David L. "Twelve-Tone Polarity in Later Works of Luigi Dallapiccola." JMT 30, no. 2 (1986): 203–24.

2513. Mereni, Anthony Ekemezie. "Die Chorwerke Luigi Dallapiccolas." Ph.D. diss., Salzburg Universität, 1979.

2514. Nathan, Hans. "On Dallapiccola's Working Methods." PNM 15, no. 2 (1977): 34–57.

2515. ———. "The Twelve-Tone Compositions of Luigi Dallapiccola." MQ 44 (1958): 289–310.

2516. Perkins, John MacIvor. "Dallapiccola's Art of Canon." PNM 1, no. 2 (1963): 95–106.

2517. Vlad, Roman. "Dallapiccola 1948–1966." SCORE 15 (1956): 39–62.

DAMASE, JEAN-MICHEL (b. 1928)

2518. M-Kniesner. [Piano Sonata, Op.24]

DANZI, FRANZ (1763–1826)

2519. Abert, Anna Amalie. "*Oberon* in Nord und Süd." F-Gudewill: 51–68. [*Der Triumph der Treue*]

DASHOW, JAMES (b. 1944)

2520. Dashow, James. "Looking into *Sequence Symbols*." PNM 25 (1987): 108–37.

DAVID, JOHANN NEPOMUK (1895–1977)

Choralwerk

2521. Johns, Donald Charles. "Johann Nepomuk David's *Choralwerk*: A Study in the Evolution of a Contemporary Liturgical Organ Style." Ph.D. diss., Northwestern University, 1960.

2522. ———. "Technik und Problematik der Cantus firmus-Bearbeitung in Johann Nepomuk Davids *Choralwerk*." MK 35 (1965): 242–52.

Partita über B–A–C–H

2523. Bertram, Hans George. "Johann Nepomuk David: *Partita über B–A–C–H* für Orgel." MK 40 (1970): 411–24.

2524. Klein, Rudolf. "Die jüngsten Werke von Johann Nepomuk David." OMZ 20 (1965): 566–71.

Spiegelkabinett

2525. Sievers, Gerd. "Johann Nepomuk Davids *Spiegelkabinett*: Analytische Studie." F-David: 160–87.

Symphony No. 8

2526. Klein, Rudolf. "Die jüngsten Werke von Johann Nepomuk David." OMZ 20 (1965): 566–71.

Variationen über ein Thema von Josquin Desprez

2527. Sievers, Gerd. "Johann Nepomuk Davids *Josquin-Variationen* (1966): Entstehung–Analyse–Deutung." HJM 4 (1980): 115–44.

Violin Concerto No. 1

2528. Kaufmann, Harold. "J. N. David und das Ganzheitsstreben seiner Musik." ME 9 (1955): 158–60. [Movement I]

Violin Concerto No. 2

2529. Sievers, Gerd. "Polyphonie mit zwölf Tönen: Johann Nepomuk Davids 2. Violinkonzert." MF 41, no. 3 (1988): 213–30.

Various Works

2530. Bertram, Hans Georg. "Flöte und Horn: Instrument und Instrumentation bei Johann Nepomuk David." F-David: 126–49.

2531. ———. *Material, Struktur, Form: Studien zur musikalischen Ordnung bei Johann Nepomuk David*. Wiesbaden: Breitkopf & Härtel, 1965.

2532. ———. "Von der Einheit in der Vielfalt der Stilepochen bei J.N. David." NZM 127 (1966): 424–28.

2533. Dallmann, Wolfgang. "Johann Nepomuk Davids späte Orgelwerke." MK 52 (1982): 15–23.

2534. ———. "Poetik der Polyphonie: Zum 100. Geburtstag von Johann Nepomuk David." MK 65, no. 6 (1995): 328–33.

2535. Klein, Rudolf. *Johann Nepomuk David: Eine Studie.* Vienna: Österreichischer Bundesverlag, 1964.

2536. ———. "Neue Orgelmusik von Johann Nepomuk David." OMZ 26 (1971): 691–97.

2537. Kolneder, Walter. "Unbekannte Werke von Johann Nepomuk David." OMZ 20 (1965): 572–77.

2538. Marsh, Lawrence Bernhard. "The Choral Music of Johann Nepomuk David (1895–)." D.M.A. diss., University of Washington, 1974.

2539. Sievers, Gerd. "Das Ezzolied in der Vertonung von Willy Burkhard und Johann Nepomuk David: Ein Vergleich." F-Engel/H: 335–63.

DAVIDOVSKY, MARIO (b. 1934)

2540. Serrouya, Meir. "An Analysis of Mario Davidovsky's *Scenes from Shir-ha-shirim.*" Ph.D. diss., Brandeis University, 2000.

2541. Soule, Richard Lawrence. "*Synchronisms* Nos. 1, 2, 3, 5, and 6 of Mario Davidovsky: A Style Analysis." D.M.A. diss., Peabody Conservatory, 1978.

2542. Susser, Peter M. "Attack, Sustain, and Decay as Metaphor in *Synchronisms* No. 3 by Mario Davidovsky." CMF 3 (1991): 27–36.

2543. True, Wesley. "Men, Music, and Machines: Some Thoughts Generated by the Practice and Performance of Mario Davidovsky's *Synchronisms* No. 6 for Piano and Electronic Sounds." JALS 9 (1981): 50–54.

2544. Wuorinen, Charles. "Mario Davidovsky: *Contrastes* No. l." PNM 4, no. 2 (1966): 144–49.

DAVIES, PETER MAXWELL (b. 1934)

Ave maris stella

2545. Pruslin, Stephen. "The Triangular Space: Peter Maxwell Davies's *Ave maris stella.*" TEMPO 120 (1977): 16–22.

Dark Angels

2546. McNamee, Ann K. "Elision and Structural Levels in Peter Maxwell Davies's *Dark Angels.*" M-Baker: 481–520.

Klee Pictures

2547. Knussen, Oliver. "Peter Maxwell Davies's *Five Klee Pictures.*" TEMPO 124 (1978): 17–21.

Motets

2548. Payne, Anthony. "Peter Maxwell Davies's Five Motets." TEMPO 72 (1965): 7–11.

Piano Sonata (1981)

2549. Griffiths, Paul. "Maxwell Davies's Piano Sonata." TEMPO 140 (1982): 5–9.

Second Fantasia on John Taverner's In Nomine

2550. Pruslin, Stephen. "Maxwell Davies's *Second Taverner Fantasia.*" TEMPO 73 (1965): 2–11.

2551. Whittall, Arnold. "Post-Twelve-Note Analysis." PRMA 94 (1967–1968): 1–17.

Shepherd's Calendar

2552. Andrewes, John. "Maxwell Davies's *The Shepherd's Calendar.*" TEMPO 87 (1968): 6–9.

2553. Peat, Donald. "Peter Maxwell Davies: *The Shepherd's Calendar.*" MMA 1 (1966): 249–55. Reprint, F-Bishop: 249–55.

Songs for a Mad King

2554. M-Cope: 128–33.

2555. Harvey, Jonathan. "Maxwell Davies's *Songs for a Mad King.*" TEMPO 89 (1969): 2–6.

2556. Skoog, James. "Pitch Material in Peter Maxwell Davies's *Eight Songs for a Mad King.*" M.A. thesis, University of Rochester, 1976.

Stone Litany: Runes from a House of the Dead

2557. Pruslin, Stephen. "Returns and Departures: Recent Maxwell Davies." TEMPO 113 (1975): 22–28.

2558. Silsbee, Ann Loomis. "Peter Maxwell Davies's *Stone Litany*: Integration and Dynamic Process." D.M.A. diss., Cornell University, 1979.

Symphony No. 3

2559. Jones, Nicholas. "Peter Maxwell Davies's 'Submerged Cathedral': Architectural Principles in the Third Symphony." ML 81, no. 3 (2000): 402–32.

2560. ———. "'Preliminary Workings': The Precompositional Process in Maxwell Davies's Third Symphony." TEMPO 204 (1998): 14–22.

2561. Whittall, Arnold. "Comparatively Complex: Birtwistle, Maxwell Davies, and Modernist Analysis." MA 13/ 2–3 (1994): 139–59.

Taverner
2562. Harbison, John. "Peter Maxwell Davies's *Taverner.*" PNM 11, no. 1 (1972): 233–40.
2563. TEMPO 101 (1972). [Special issue]

Vesalii icones
2564. Jacob, Jeffrey Lynn. "Peter Maxwell Davies' *Vesalii icones*: Origins and Analysis." D.M.A. diss., Peabody Conservatory, 1980.
2565. Potter, Keith. "The Music of Peter Maxwell Davies." CT 4 (1972): 3–9.
2566. Pruslin, Stephen. "'One if by land, two if by sea': Maxwell Davies the Symphonist." TEMPO 153 (1985): 2–6.
2567. ——, ed. *Peter Maxwell Davies: Studies from Two Decades*. London: Boosey & Hawkes, 1979. [Collection of articles originally published in TEMPO]
2568. Taylor, Michael. "Maxwell Davies's *Vesalii icones.*" TEMPO 92 (1970): 22–27.

Westerlings
2569. Warnaby, John. "*Westerlings*: A Study in Symphonic Form." TEMPO 147 (1983): 15–22.

Worldes Blis
2570. Pruslin, Stephen. "Returns and Departures: Recent Maxwell Davies." TEMPO 113 (1975): 22–28.

Various Works
2571. Griffiths, Paul. *Peter Maxwell Davies*. London: Robson, 1982.
2572. McGregor, Richard E. "Peter Maxwell Davies: The Early Works." TEMPO 160 (1986): 2–7.
2573. Owens, Peter. "Revelation and Fallacy: Observations on Compositional Technique in the Music of Peter Maxwell Davies." MA 13/ 2–3 (1994): 161–202.

DAVIS, LESLIE N.
2574. Davis, Leslie N. "Chemical Composition: Chiral Rows (*Lactic No. 1*)." PNM 23, no. 1 (1984–1985): 108–11.

DEBUSSY, CLAUDE (1862–1918)

Ariettes, paysages belges et aquarelles (**Revised as *Ariettes oubliées***)
2575. Fischer, Kurt von. "Bemerkungen zu der zwei Ausgaben von Debussys *Ariettes oubliées.*" F-Federhofer: 283–89.

Ballades de Villon
2576. Youens, Susan Lee. "From the Fifteenth Century to the Twentieth: Considerations of Musical Prosody in Debussy's *Trois ballades de François Villon.*" JM 2 (1983): 418–33.

Cello Sonata
2577. Davidian, Teresa. "Intervallic Process and Autonomy in the First Movement of Debussy's Sonata for Cello and Piano." TP 14–15 (1989–1990): 1–12.
2578. Moevs, Robert. "Intervallic Procedures in Debussy: Serenade from the Sonata for Cello and Piano, 1915." PNM 8, no. 1 (1969): 82–101.

Chansons de Bilitis
2579. Rumph, Stephen. "Debussy's *Trios Chansons de Bilitis*: Song, Opera, and the Death of the Subject." JM 12, no. 4 (1994): 464–90.
2580. Youens, Susan. "Music, Verse, and 'Prose Poetry': Debussy's *Trios Chansons de Bilitis.*" JMR 7, no. 1 (1986): 69–94.

Chansons de Charles d'Orléans
2581. Alfred, Everett Maurice. "A Study of Selected Choral Works of Claude Debussy." Ph.D. diss., Texas Tech University, 1980.
2582. Báhmer, Helga. "Claude Debussy (1862–1918): 'Yver, vous n'estes qu'un vilain' für vierstimmigen Chor a cappella aus den *Trois chansons de Charles d'Orléans.*" F-Rohlfs: 453–54.

Children's Corner
2583. Koptschewski, Nikolai. "*Children's Corner* von Claude Debussy: Stilistische Parallelen und Probleme der Interpretation." JP 1 (1978): 173–209.

Damoiselle élue
2584. Alfred, Everett Maurice. "A Study of Selected Choral Works of Claude Debussy." Ph.D. diss., Texas Tech University, 1980.

Diane au bois

2585. Briscoe, James R. "'To Invent New Forms': Debussy's *Diane au bois*." MQ 74, no. 1 (1990): 131–69.

D'un cahier d'esquisses

2586. Howat, Roy. "En Route for *L'isle joyeuse*: The Restoration of a Triptych." CAD 19 (1995): 37–52.

En blanc et noir

2587. Dunsby, Jonathan. "The Poetry of Debussy's *En blanc et noir*." M-Ayrey: 149–68.

2588. Vis, Jurjen. "Debussy and the War–Debussy, Luther, and Janequin: Remarks on Part II ('Lent. Sombre.') of *En blanc et noir*." CAD 15 (1991): 31–50.

2589. Watson, Linda Lee. "Debussy: A Programmatic Approach to Form." Ph.D. diss., University of Texas, Austin, 1978.

Épigraphes antiques

2590. Hirsbrunner, Theo. "Claude Debussy und Pierre Louÿs: Zu den *Six épigraphes antiques* von Debussy." MF 31 (1978): 426–42.

2591. Watson, Linda Lee. "Debussy: A Programmatic Approach to Form." Ph.D. diss., University of Texas, Austin, 1978.

Estampes

2592. Kopp, David. "Pentatonic Organization in Two Piano Pieces of Debussy." JMT 41, no. 2 (1997): 261–87. [*Pagodes*]

Etudes

2593. Brauner, Jürgen. "Pianistisches oder kompositorisches Exerzitium? Anmerkungen zu zwei späten Klavieretüden von Claude Debussy und Aleksandr Skrjabin." MF 53, no. 3 (2000): 254–71. [No. 3]

2594. Gauldin, Robert, William E. Benjamin, and Elaine Barkin. "Analysis Symposium: Debussy, Etude *Pour les sixtes*." JMT 22 (1978): 241–312.

2595. Kaufmann, Harold. "Zur Wertung des Epigonentums in der Musik." NZM 129 (1968): 397–404. [No. 10]

2596. Parks, Richard Samuel. "Organizational Procedures in Debussy's *Douze études*." Ph.D. diss., Catholic University of America, 1973.

2597. Peterson, William John. "Debussy's *Douze études*: A Critical Analysis." Ph.D. diss., University of California, Berkeley, 1981.

2598. Schneider, John. "The Debussy Etudes: A Challenge to Mind and Fingers." JALS 14 (1983): 59–63.

Fantaisie (Piano and Orchestra)

2599. Mueller, Richard. "Javanese Influence on Debussy's *Fantaisie* and Beyond." NCM 10, no. 2 (1986): 157–86.

Fêtes galantes **(Sets 1 and 2)**

2600. Nichols, Roger. "Debussy's Two Settings of *Clair de lune*." ML 48 (1967): 229–35.

2601. Youens, Susan Lee. "Debussy's setting of Verlaine's *Colloque sentimental*: From the Past to the Present." SMU 15 (1981): 93–105.

Gladiateur

2602. Clevenger, John R. "Debussy's First 'Masterpiece,' *Le gladiateur*." CAD 23 (1999): 3–34.

Hommage à Haydn

2603. Mahlert, Ulrich. "Gebannte Improvisation und Maskentanz: Die 'Haydn'-Stücke von Claude Debussy und Maurice Ravel." MB 19, no. 12 (1987): 912–19.

2604. Mies, Paul. "Widmungsstück mit Buchstaben: Motto bei Debussy und Ravel." SZM 25 (1962): 363–68.

Images **(Orchestra)**

2605. Bein, Joseph H. "Debussy's Orchestral *Images*: Other Features of the Style." Ph.D. diss., University of Rochester, 1970.

2606. M-Schultz: 49–52. [*Rondes de printemps*]

Images **(Piano)**

2607. Howat, Roy. "Debussy, Ravel and Bartók: Towards Some New Concepts of Form." ML 58 (1977): 285–93. [Series 1, *Reflets dans l'eau*]

2608. Meredith, David. "Computer-Aided Comparison of Syntax Systems in Three Piano Pieces by Debussy." CMR 9 (1993): 285–304. [Series 1, *Reflets dans l'eau*; Series 2, *Cloches à travers les feuilles*]

2609. Reiche, Jens Peter. "Die theoretischen Grundlagen javanischer Gamelan-Musik und ihre Bedeutung für Claude Debussy." ZM 3, no. 1 (1972): 5–15. [Series 2, *Cloches à travers le feuilles*]

Isle joyeuse

2610. Howat, Roy. "Debussy, *Masques*, *L'isle joyeuse* and a Lost Sarabande." MSA 10 (1987): 16–30.

2611. ———. "En Route for *L'isle joyeuse*: The Restoration of a Triptych." CAD 19 (1995): 37–52.

Jeux

2612. Berman, Laurence D. "*Prelude to the Afternoon of a Faun* and *Jeux*: Debussy's Summer Rites." NCM 3 (1979–1980): 225–38.
2613. Eimert, Herbert. "Debussy's *Jeux*." R 5 (1961): 3–20.
2614. Gut, Serge. "Konstante und bewegliche Elemente in *Jeux* von Claude Debussy." M-Kühn: 395–98.
2615. Leibowitz, René. "L'interpretation de Debussy." In *Le compositeur et son double: Essais sur l'interpretation musicale*, 201–9 (Paris: Gallimard, 1971).
2616. McGinness, John. "From Movement to Moment: Issues of Expression, Form, and Reception in Debussy's *Jeux*." CAD 22 (1998): 51–74.
2617. M-Schultz: 53–57.
2618. Zenck-Maurer, Claudia. "Form- und Farbenspiele: Debussys *Jeux*." AM 33 (1976): 28–47.

Khamma

2619. Chimènes, Myriam. "La chimie musicale de *Khamma*." CAD 12–13 (1988–1989): 123–40.
2620. McFarland, Mark. "Debussy and Stravinsky: Another Look into Their Musical Relationship." CAD 24 (2000): 79–112.

Martyre de St Sébastien

2621. Watson, Linda Lee. "Debussy: A Programmatic Approach to Form." Ph.D. diss., University of Texas, Austin, 1978.

Masques

2622. Howat, Roy. "Debussy, *Masques, L'isle joyeuse* and a Lost Sarabande." MSA 10 (1987): 16–30.
2623. ———. "En Route for *L'isle joyeuse*: The Restoration of a Triptych." CAD 19 (1995): 37–52.

Mer

2624. Barraqué, Jean. "*La Mer* de Debussy, ou la naissance des formes ouvertes: Essai de méthodologie comparative; La forme musicale considérée non plus comme un archétype mais comme un devenir." ANM 12 (1988): 15–62.
2625. Dömling, Wolfgang. *Claude Debussy: La mer.* Munich: Fink, 1976.
2626. Gousset, Bruno. "Prééminence du timbre dans le langage musical de *La mer* de Debussy." ANM 3 (1986): 37–45.
2627. Howat, Roy. "Dramatic Shape and Form in *Jeux de vagues*, and Its Relationship to *Pelléas, Jeux*, and Other Scores." CAD 7 (1983): 7–23.
2628. Monnard, Jean-François. "Claude Debussy: *La mer*." SMZ 121 (1981): 11–16.
2629. Rolf, Marie. "Debussy's *La mer*: A Critical Analysis in the Light of Early Sketches and Editions." Ph.D. diss., University of Rochester, 1976.
2630. Trezise, Simon. *Debussy: La mer.* Cambridge: Cambridge University Press, 1994.

Nocturnes (Orchestra)

2631. Fischer, Kurt von. "Debussy and the Climate of Art Nouveau: Some Remarks on Debussy's Aesthetics." MMA 13 (1984): 49–56.
2632. Gelleny, Sharon. "Cyclic Form and Debussy's Nocturnes." CAD 20 (1996): 25–40.
2633. Lang-Becker, Elke. *Debussy: Nocturnes.* Munich: Fink, 1982.
2634. Prey, Stefan. "Zur Harmonik in Debussy's Nocturnes für Orchester." M 41, no. 1 (1987): 7–12.

No-ja-li (Le palais du silence)

2635. Orledge, Robert. "Debussy's Second English Ballet: *Le palais du silence* or *No-ja-li*." CM 22 (1976): 73–87.

Ode à la France

2636. Alfred, Everett Maurice. "A Study of Selected Choral Works of Claude Debussy." Ph.D. diss., Texas Tech University, 1980.

Pelléas et Melisande

2637. Abbate, Carolyn. "*Tristan* in the Composition of *Pelléas*." NCM 5 (1981–1982): 117–41.
2638. Andreani, Éveline. "Texte et musique ou las aventures du sens: À propos de *Pelléas et Melisande;* Maeterlinck et Debussy." ANM 9 (1987): 21–28.
2639. Appledorn, Mary Jeanne van. "A Stylistic Study of Claude Debussy's Opera *Pelléas et Mélisande*." Ph.D. diss., University of Rochester, 1966.
2640. Bugeanu, Constantin. "La forme musicale dans le Pelléas de Debussy." *Revue roumaine d'histoire de l'art* 6 (1969): 243–60.
2641. Emmanuel, Maurice. *"Pelléas et Mélisande" de Claude Debussy: Étude historique et critique, analyse musicale.* Paris: Mellottée, 1925.
2642. M-Enix.

2643. Gilman, Lawrence. *Debussy's "Pelléas et Mélisande": A Guide to the Opera with Musical Examples from the Score.* New York: Schirmer, 1907.

2644. Grayson, David A. "The Interludes of Pelléas et Mélisande." CAD 12–13 (1988–1989): 100–122.

2645. ———. "The Libretto of Debussy's *Pelléas et Mélisande.*" ML 66 (1985): 34–50.

2646. Gut, Serge. "Le prélude de *Pelléas*: Les ambiguïtés du contraste et de la cohésion." ANM 31 (1993): 6–14.

2647. John, Nicholas, ed. *Debussy: Pelléas et Mélisande.* London: Calder, 1982.

2648. Kunze, Stefan. "Le chant parlé et l'indicible: Remarques sur le *Pelléas et Mélisande* de Debussy." Trans. Nicolas Meeùs. Part I, ANM 30 (1993): 46–51; Part II, ANM 31 (1993): 15–21.

2649. Leibowitz, René. *"Pelléas et Mélisande*, ou les fantômes de lä réalité." M-Leibowitz/F: 291–326.

2650. Neuwirth, Gösta. "Musik um 1900." F-Schuh: 89–134.

2651. Nichols, Roger. *Claude Debussy: Pelléas et Mélisande.* Cambridge: Cambridge University Press, 1989.

2652. Philips, Mary Kathryn. "Recitativo-Arioso: A Survey with Emphasis on Contemporary Opera." Ph.D. diss., University of California, Los Angeles, 1965.

2653. Schumann, Margit. "Une esquisse pour *Pelléas et Mélisande*: La 'Scène des moutons.'" CAD 17–18 (1993–1994): 35–56.

2654. Setaccioli, Giacomo. *Debussy: Eine kritische-aesthetische Studie.* Leipzig: Breitkopf & Härtel, 1911.

2655. Spieth-Weissenbacher, Christine Elisabeth. "Le Recitatif mélodique dans *Pelléas et Mélisande* de Claude Debussy." Ph.D. diss., Strasbourg, 1979.

2656. Staempfli, Edward. *"Pelléas und Mélisande*: Eine Gegenüberstellung der Werke von Claude Debussy und Arnold Schönberg." SMZ 112 (1972): 65–72.

2657. Stirnemann, Knut. "Zur Frage des Leitmotivs in Debussys *Pelléas et Mélisande.*" SBM 4 (1980): 151–70.

2658. Terrasson, René. *"Pelléas et Mélisande,"* ou l'initiation. Paris: EDIMAF, 1982.

2659. Unseld, Melanie. "Augenblicke des Sterbens: Salome und Melisande als Entwürfe von Weiblichkeit um die Jahrhundertwende." HJM 15 (1998): 301–18.

2660. Van Ackère, Jules. *Pelléas et Mélisande.* Bruxelles: Librairie Encyclopédique, 1952.

2661. Velly, Jean-Jacques. "Quelques aspects de l'orchestration dans *Pelléas et Melisande*: Économie de moyens et richesse sémantique." ANM 31 (1993): 22–26.

2662. Wenk, Arthur. "Claude Debussy and the Art Nouveau Image of Woman." MMA 13 (1984): 67–74.

Piano Trio

2663. Derr, Ellwood. "Sein erstes überliefertes Instrumentalwerk: Zur Erstveröffentlichung von Claude Debussys frühem Klaviertrio." NZM 146, no. 12 (1985): 10–16.

Piano Works (various; *see also* specific piano works)

2664. Adams, John Kenneth. "Debussy: The Early Piano Works." PQ 137 (1987): 36–40.

2665. ———. "Debussy: The Later Piano Works." PQ 138 (1987): 48–53.

2666. Barras, Marie-Cécile. "La présence de Chopin dans la musique de piano de Debussy." CAD 20 (1996): 41–60.

2667. Chun, Edna Breinig. "Debussy's Piano Music, 1903–1907." D.M. diss., Indiana University, 1980.

2668. Dommel-Diény, Amy. *Debussy.* Dommel-Diény 16. Neuchâtel: Delachaux & Niestlé, 1967.

2669. Holden, Calvin. "The Organization of Texture in Selected Piano Compositions of Claude Debussy." Ph.D. diss., University of Pittsburgh, 1973.

2670. Jakobik, Albert. *Die assoziative Harmonik in den Klavierwerkern Claude Debussys.* Würzburg: Triltsch, 1940.

2671. Martins, José Eduardo. "Quelques aspects comparatifs dans les langages pianistiques de Debussy et Scriabin." CAD 7 (1983): 24–37.

2672. Porten, Maria. *Zum Problem der "Form" bei Debussy: Untersuchungen am Beispiel der Klavierwerke.* Munich: Katzbichler, 1974.

2673. Schmitz, Elie Robert. *The Piano Works of Claude Debussy.* New York: Duell, Sloan, & Pearce, 1950.

2674. Storb, Ilse. "Untersuchungen zur Auflösung der funktionalen Harmonik in den Klavierwerken von Claude Debussy." Ph.D. diss., University of Cologne, 1967.

2675. Zulueta, Jorge, and Jacobo Romano. *Claude Debussy: La Obra completo para piano; Analisis y manuscritos.* Buenos Aires: Universidac Nacional de Tucumona, 1964.

Poèmes de Baudelaire

2676. Bergeron, Katherine. "The Echo, the Cry, and the Death of Lovers." NCM 18, no. 2 (1994): 136–51. ["La mort des amants"]

2677. Goldman, David Paul. "Esotericism as a Determinant of Debussy's Harmonic Language." MQ 75, no. 2 (1991): 130–47. ["Le balcon"]

2678. Routley, Nicholas. "Debussy and Baudelaire's *Harmonie du soir.*" MSA 15 (1992): 77–82. ["Harmonie du soir"]

Poèmes de Mallarmé
2679. Wheeldon, Marianne. "Debussy's 'Soupir': An Experiment in Permutational Analysis." PNM 38, no. 2 (2000): 134–60.

Prélude à l'après-midi d'un faune
2680. Austin, William W., ed. *Claude Debussy: Prelude to the Afternoon of a Faun.* Norton Critical Scores. New York: Norton, 1970.
2681. Berman, Laurence D. "*Prelude to the Afternoon of a Faun* and *Jeux*: Debussy's Summer Rites." NCM 3 (1979–1980): 225–38.
2682. Brauneiss, Leopold. "Debussys geheimnisvolle Mathematik: Zum *Prélude à L'après-midi d'un faune.*" M-Brauneiss: 55–71.
2683. Brown, Matthew. "Tonality and Form in Debussy's *Prélude à L'Après-midi d'un faune.*" MTS 15, no. 2 (1993): 127–43.
2684. Crotty, John E. "Symbolist Influence in Debussy's *Prelude to the Afternoon of a Faun.*" ITO 6, no. 2 (1981–1983): 17–30.
2685. Gülke, Peter. "Musik aus dem Bannkreis einer literarischen Aesthetik: Debussy's *Prélude à l'après-midi d'un faune.*" JP 1 (1978): 103–46.
2686. Haug, Wiltrud. *Claude Debussy, Historische Einordnung: Analyse "L'après-midi d'un faune."* Ravensburg: Holzschuh, 1977.
2687. Leibowitz, René. "L'interpretation de Debussy." In *Le compositeur et son double: Essais sur l'interpretation musicale,* 201–9 (Paris: Gallimard, 1971).
2688. Mataigne, Viviane. "Une analyse du *Prélude à l'après-midi d'un faune* de Claude Debussy." ANM 12 (1988): 89–102.
2689. Meeùs, Nicolas. "Le *Prélude à l'après-midi d'un faune*: Une analyse harmonique." ANM 13 (1988): 81–87.
2690. Parks, Richard S. "A Viennese Arrangement of Debussy's *Prélude á l'après-midi d'un faune*: Orchestration and Musical Structure." ML 80, no. 1 (1999): 50–73. [Analysis of arrangement attributed to Benno Sachs]

Préludes (various; *see also* specific books of preludes)
2691. Buck, Charles Henry, III. "Structural Coherence in the Preludes for Piano by Claude Debussy." Ph.D. diss., University of California, Berkeley, 1975.
2692. Charru, Philippe. "Une analyse des 24 Préludes pour piano de Debussy: Le mouvement musical au rythme de la forme." ANM 12 (1988): 63–86.
2693. Freundlich, Irwin. "Random Thoughts on the Preludes of Claude Debussy." CM 13 (1972): 48–57. Reprint, PQ 87 (1974): 17–24.
2694. Hepokoski, James A. "Formulaic Openings in Debussy." NCM 8 (1984–1985): 44–59.
2695. Hirbour-Paquette, Louise. "Analyse sémiologique des Préludes pour piano de Claude Debussy: Vers une characterisation stylistique de la 'mélodie.'" Ph.D. diss., Université de Montréal, 1975.
2696. Imberty, Michel. *Signification and Meaning in Music: On Debussy's Préludes pour le piano.* Montréal: Groupe de recherches en sémiologie musicale, Université de Montréal, 1976.
2697. Keil, Werner. *Untersuchungen zur Entwicklung des frühen Klavierstils von Debussy und Ravel.* Wiesbaden: Breitkopf & Härtel, 1982.
2698. Kinariwala, Neela Delia. "Debussy and Musical Coherence: A Study of Succession and Continuity in the Preludes." Ph.D. diss., University of Texas at Austin, 1987.
2699. Morrill, Dexter. "Rhythmic Innovations and Conventions in Debussy's Piano Preludes." F-Ratner: 257–81.
2700. Réfols, Alberto. "Debussy and the Symbolist Movement: The Preludes." D.M.A. diss., University of Washington, 1975.
2701. Schoffman, Nachum. "Pedal Points, Old and New." JMR 4 (1982–1983): 369–98.
2702. Seldin, H. D. "An Analytical Study of the Debussy Preludes for Piano." M.A. thesis, Columbia University, 1965.
2703. Watson, Lorne. "Cadences in Debussy's Preludes, Books I and II." D.M.A. diss., Indiana University, 1976.
2704. Wenk, Arthur B. "An Analysis of Debussy's Piano Preludes, Book I." M.A. thesis, Cornell University, 1967.

Préludes, Book 1
2705. Bass, Eddie C. "Tonality and Pitch-Class Set Relations in Debussy's Prelude No. 4, Book I." TSP 5 (1988): 14–33. [*Les sons et les parfums tournent dans l'air du soir*]
2706. Benedetto, Renato di. "Congetture su *Voiles.*" RIM 13 (1978): 312–44.
2707. Böckl, Rudolf. "Claude Debussys Prélude II (*Voiles*): Über Material und Form; Ein Versuch." MF 25 (1972): 321–23.
2708. Charru, Philippe. "*La cathédrale engloutie* prélude de Claude Debussy: Le mouvement musical au rythme de la forme." ANM 4 (1986): 72–77.
2709. Forte, Allen. "Generative Processes in a Debussy Prelude." F-Palisca: 471–86. [*La fille aux cheveux de lin*]
2710. Guck, Marion A. "One Path through Debussy's *Des par sur la neige.*" ITO 1, no. 5 (1975–1976): 4–8.

2711. ———. "Tracing Debussy's *Des pas sur la neige*." ITO 1, no. 8 (1975–1976): 4–12.

2712. Guertin, Marcelle. "Lecture-audition du texte musical: Une Étude de la mélodie dans le Livre I des Préludes pour piano de Debussy." Ph.D. diss., Université Laval, 1985.

2713. ———. "A Stylistic Approach to Debussy's Preludes for Piano." In *Three Musical Analyses*, 36–58. Toronto: Victoria University, 1981.

2714. Guigue, Didier. "Uma demonstração da reflexão Debussysta sobre o pós-tonalismo." EMR 4 (1999). [*Ce qu'a vu le vent d'ouest*]

2715. Gut, Serge. "*La cathédrale engloutie* prélude de Claude Debussy: Interférences entre le matériau, la structure et la forme." ANM 4 (1986): 78–81.

2716. Imberty, Michel. "De la perception du temps musical à sa signification psychologique: À propos de la *Cathédrale engloutie* de Debussy." ANM 6 (1987): 28–37.

2717. Kopp, David. "Pentatonic Organization in Two Piano Pieces of Debussy." JMT 41, no. 2 (1997): 261–87. [*Les collines d'Anacapri*]

2718. M-Kresky: 151–63. [*La fille aux cheveux de lin*]

2719. Lewin, David. "Some Instances of Parallel Voice-Leading in Debussy." NCM 11, no. 1 (1987): 59–72. Reprinted in *Music at the Turn of the Century*, ed. Joseph Kerman, 57–70. Berkeley: University of California Press, 1990. [*Le vent dans la plaine*]

2720. Miller, Cynthia Fayne. "Parallelism and Symmetry in Three Debussy Preludes." Ph.D. diss., City University of New York, 2000. [*Des pas sur la neige, Les sons et les parfums tournent dans l'air du soir, Le vent dans la plaine*]

2721. Pousseur, Henri. "Applications analytiques de la 'technique des réseaux.'" RBM 52 (1998): 247–98. [*Des pas sur la neige*]

2722. Routley, Nicholas. "Debussy and Baudelaire's *Harmonie du soir*." MSA 15 (1992): 77–82. [*Les sons et les parfums tournent dans l'air du soir*]

2723. ———. "*Des pas sur la neige*: Debussy in Bilitis's Footsteps." MSA 16 (1993): 19–27.

Préludes, Book 2

2724. Amiot, Emmanuel. "Pour en finir avec le Désir: La notion de symétrie en analyse musicale." ANM 22 (1991): 87–92. [*La terrasse des audiences du clair de lune*]

2725. Biget, Michelle. "*La terrasse des audiences du clair de lune* ou le primat du geste instrumental." ANM 16 (1989): 85–91.

2726. Delalande, François. "*La terrasse des audiences du clair de lune*: Un essai d'analyse esthésique." ANM 16 (1989): 75–84.

2727. Forte, Allen. "*La terrasse des audiences du clair de lune*: Approche motivique et linéaire." Trans. Nasreen Hussein. ANM 16 (1989): 23–29.

2728. Friedmann, Michael L. "Approaching Debussy's *Ondine*." CAD 6 (1982): 22–35.

2729. Lewin, David. "Some Instances of Parallel Voice-Leading in Debussy." NCM 11, no. 1 (1987): 59–72. Reprinted in *Music at the Turn of the Century*, ed. Joseph Kerman, 57–70. Berkeley: University of California Press, 1990. [*Canope*]

2730. Marion, Gregory J. "A Foreground Mist? Debussy's *Brouillards*." CM 66 (1999): 21–65.

2731. Mesnage, Marcel. "*La terrasse des audiences du clair de lune*: Esquisse d'analyse modélisée." ANM 16 (1989): 31–43.

2732. Nadeau, Roland. "*Brouillards*: A Tonal Music." CAD 4–5 (1980–1981): 38–50.

2733. Narmour, Eugene. "Implication et réalisation mélodique dans *La terrasse des audiences du clair de lune* de Debussy." Trans. Nasreen Hussein. ANM 16 (1989): 44–53.

2734. Parks, Richard Samuel. "Pitch Organization in Debussy: Unordered Sets in *Brouillards*." MTS 2 (1980): 119–34.

2735. Riotte, André. "Les matériaux du clair de lune: Préalables à une étude formalisée du style chez Debussy." ANM 17 (1989): 55–58. [*La terrasse des audiences du clair de lune*]

2736. Schnebel, Dieter. "*Brouillards*: Tendenzen bei Debussy." R 6 (1964): 33–39.

2737. Tarasti, Eero. "L'analyse sémiotique d'un prélude de Debussy: *La terrasse des audiences du clair de lune*." ANM 16 (1989): 67–74.

2738. Wheeldon, Marianne. "Interpreting 'Strong Moments' in Debussy's *La terrasse des audiences du clair de lune*." INT 14–15 (2000–2001): 181–208.

Proses lyriques

2739. Hirsbrunner, Theo. "Debussy–Maeterlinck–Chausson: Musikalische und literarische Querverbindungen." F-Schuh: 47–66. Translated under the title "Debussy–Maeterlinck–Chausson: Literary and Musical Connections," MMA 13 (1984): 57–65.

2740. ———. "Musik und Dichtung im französischen *Fin de siècle* am Beispiel der *Proses lyriques* von Claude Debussy." M-Schnitzler/D: 152–74.

Sonata for Flute, Viola, and Harp
2741. Allen, Judith Shatin. "Tonal Allusion and Illusion: Debussy's Sonata for Flute, Viola, and Harp." CAD 7 (1983): 38–48.
2742. Martins, José Eduardo. "Le langage pianistique des deux dernieres sonates." CAD 14 (1990): 55–71.
2743. Whitman, Ernestine. "Analysis and Performance Critique of Debussy's Flute Works." D.M.A. diss., University of Wisconsin, 1977.

Songs (various; *see also* specific song cycles)
2744. Briscoe, James R. "Debussy *d'après* Debussy: The Further Resonance of Two Early Mélodies." NCM 5 (1981–1982): 110–16. [*Fête galante, La fille aux cheveux de lin (Leconte de Lisle)*]
2745. ———. "Debussy's Earliest Songs." CMS 24, no. 2 (1984): 81–94.
2746. Hirsbrunner, Theo. "Zu Debussys und Ravels Mallarmé-Vertonungen." AM 35 (1978): 81–103.
2747. Hsu, Samuel. "Imagery and Diction in the Songs of Claude Debussy." Ph.D. diss., University of California, Santa Barbara, 1972.
2748. Koechlin, Charles. "Quelques anciennes mélodies inédites de Claude Debussy." RM Special Number (1926): 115 (211)–140 (236).
2749. Monelle, Raymond. "A Semantic Approach to Debussy's Songs." MR 51, no. 3 (1990): 193–207.
2750. Nichols, Roger. "Debussy's Two Settings of *Clair de lune*." ML 48 (1967): 229–35.
2751. Ruschenburg, Peter. "Stilkritische Untersuchungen zu den Liedern Claude Debussys." Ph.D. diss., University of Hamburg, 1966.
2752. Somer, Avo. "Chromatic Third-Relations and Tonal Structure in the Songs of Debussy." MTS 17, no. 2 (1995): 215–41.
2753. Velten, Klaus. "Über die Heilung der Musik vom 'Blutandrang': Ein analytischer Beitrag zum Verständnis der Kunstanschauung Claude Debussys." M 45, no. 1 (1991): 18–22. [*Clair de lune* (1882)]
2754. Wenk, Arthur B. "Claude Debussy and the Poets." Ph.D. diss., Cornell University, 1970. [Includes several appendices not contained in 2755]
2755. ———. *Claude Debussy and the Poets.* Berkeley: University of California Press, 1976. [Includes several chapters not contained in 2754]

String Quartet
2756. Dietschy, Marcel. "Wagner et le Quatuor de Debussy." SMZ 121 (1981): 243–47.
2757. Gouttenoire, Philippe. "Un jeu de métamorphoses." ANM 37 (2000): 36–46.
2758. Guye, Jean-Philippe. "Notes sur les procédures harmoniques et la modalité." ANM 37 (2000): 47–53.
2759. Yih, Annie K. "Analysing Debussy: Tonality, Motivic Sets, and the Referential Pitch-Class Specific Colleciton." MA 19, no. 2 (2000): 203–29.
2760. ———. "Continuity and Formal Organization in Debussy's String Quartet." Ph.D. diss., Yale University, 1992.

Suite bergamasque
2761. Meredith, David. "Computer-Aided Comparison of Syntax Systems in Three Piano Pieces by Debussy." CMR 9 (1993): 285–304. [*Clair de lune*]
2762. Velten, Klaus. "Über die Heilung der Musik vom 'Blutandrang': Ein analytischer Beitrag zum Verständnis der Kunstanschauung Claude Debussys." M 45, no. 1 (1991): 18–22. [*Clair de lune*]

Syrinx
2763. Bopp, Joseph. "*Syrinx* von Claude Debussy." T 7, no. 8 (1982–1983): 265–67.
2764. Borris, Siegfried. "Claude Debussy: *Syrinx* für Soloflöte." MB 4 (1969): 173–75.
2765. Deliège, Irène. "Le parallélisme, support d'une analyse auditive de la musique: Vers un modèle des parcours cognitifs de l'information musicale." ANM 6 (1987): 73–79.
2766. Mahlert, Ulrich. "Die 'göttliche Arabeske': Zu Debussys *Syrinx*." AM 43, no. 3 (1986): 181–200.
2767. Whitman, Ernestine. "Analysis and Performance Critique of Debussy's Flute Works." D.M.A. diss., University of Wisconsin, 1977.

Violin Sonata
2768. Lewin, David. "Some Instances of Parallel Voice-Leading in Debussy." NCM 11, no. 1 (1987): 59–72. Reprinted in *Music at the Turn of the Century*, ed. Joseph Kerman, 57–70. Berkeley: University of California Press, 1990.
2769. Martins, José Eduardo. "Le langage pianistique des deux dernieres sonates." CAD 14 (1990): 55–71.

Various Works
2770. Berman, Laurence D. "The Evolution of Tonal Thinking in the Works of Claude Debussy." Ph.D. diss., Harvard University, 1965.
2771. Brăiloiu, Constantin. "Pentatony in Debussy's Music." F-Bartók/S: 377–417.

2772. Briscoe, James Robert. "The Compositions of Claude Debussy's Formative Years (1879–1887)." Ph.D. diss., University of North Carolina, 1979.

2773. Brynside, Ronald Lee. "Debussy's Second Style." Ph.D. diss., University of Illinois, 1971.

2774. Carner, Mosco. "Debussy and Puccini." M-Carner: 139–47.

2775. Cnattingius, Claes M. "Notes sur les oeuvres de jeunesse de Claude Debussy." STM 44 (1962): 31–53.

2776. Crapes, Lyra Nabors. "Compensatory Change as a Formal Element in Selected Compositions of Debussy." M.M. thesis, Florida State University, 1970.

2777. Davidian, Teresa Maria. "Debussy's Sonata Forms." Ph.D. diss., University of Chicago, 1988.

2778. DeLone, Peter. "Claude Debussy, *contrapuntiste malgré lui.*" CMS 17, no. 2 (1977): 48–63.

2779. Denissow, Edison. "Über einige Besonderheiten der Kompositionstechnik Claude Debussys." JP 1 (1978): 147–72.

2780. Dionisi, Renato. "Aspetti tecnici e sviluppo storica del sistema 'esacordale' da Debussy in poi." RIM 1 (1966): 49–67.

2781. Faltin, Peter. "Debussy, der Impressionismus und die strukturbildende Kraft des immanenten Klanges." HJM 9 (1986): 121–51.

2782. Flothuis, Marius. "Claude Debussys Neuerungen und ihre historischen Hintergründe." MTH 9, no. 3 (1994): 211–25.

2783. Forte, Allen. "Debussy and the Octatonic." MA 10, nos. 1–2 (1991): 125–69.

2784. Gervais, Françoise. "Étude comparée des langages harmoniques de Fauré et de Debussy." Ph.D. diss., 1954. Published as book, Paris: Richard-Masse, 1971.

2785. ———. "Structures Debussystes." RM 258 (1962): 77–88.

2786. Gitter, Felix. "Die Programmatik in klavieristischen und orchestralen Schaffen von Claude Debussy." Ph.D. diss., Halle-Salle, 1973.

2787. Gruber, Gernot. "Zur Funktion der 'primären Klangformen' in der Musik Debussys." F-Federhofer: 272–82.

2788. Hilse, Walter Bruno. "Hindemith and Debussy." HJ 2 (1972): 48–90.

2789. Holloway, Robin. *Debussy and Wagner.* London: Eulenberg Books, 1979.

2790. Howat, Roy. *Debussy in Proportion: A Musical Analysis.* Cambridge: Cambridge University Press, 1983.

2791. ———. "Proportional Structure in the Music of Claude Debussy." Ph.D. diss., King's College, Cambridge, 1979.

2792. Jakobik, Albert. *Claude Debussy oder die lautlose Revolution in der Musik.* Würzburg: K. Triltsch, 1977.

2793. Koechlin, Charles. "Sur l'evolution de la musique française avant et après Debussy." RM 16 (1935): 264–80.

2794. Liess, Andreas. "Claude Debussy und der Art nouveau: Ein Entwurf." Part I, STU 4 (1975): 245–76; Part II, STU 5 (1976): 143–234.

2795. Lockspeiser, Edward. "Musorgsky and Debussy." MQ 23 (1937): 421–27.

2796. Mueller, Robert Earl. "The Concept of Tonality in Impressionist Music: Based on the Works of Debussy and Ravel." Ph.D. diss., Indiana University, 1954.

2797. Orledge, Robert. *Debussy and the Theatre.* Cambridge: Cambridge University Press, 1982.

2798. Park, Raymond. "The Later Style of Claude Debussy." Ph.D. diss., University of Michigan, 1966.

2799. Parks, Richard S. *The Music of Claude Debussy.* New Haven, Conn.: Yale University Press, 1989.

2800. Ringgold, John Robert. "The Linearity of Debussy's Music and Its Correspondences with the Symbolist Esthetic: Developments before 1908." Ph.D. diss., University of Southern California, 1972.

2801. Schmidt-Garre, Helmut. "Die Klangstruktur Debussy: In ihrem Beziehung zur Mehrstimmigkeit des Mittelalters." MELOS 17 (1950): 104–6.

2802. Seraphin, Hellmut. *Debussys Kammermusik der mittleren Schaffenzeit.* Kassel: Bärenreiter, 1964.

2803. Sowa-Winter, Sylvia. *Die Harfe im Art Nouveau.* Munich: Katzbichler, 1988.

2804. Starr, Lawrence. "The Modern Composer, the Conservative Audience . . . and Debussy." CAD 8 (1984): 13–17.

2805. Stuckenschmidt, H. H. "Debussy or Berg? The Mystery of a Chord Progression." MQ 51 (1965): 453–59.

2806. Warburton, Thomas. "Bitonal Miniatures by Debussy from 1913." CAD 6 (1982): 5–15.

2807. Weber, Edith, ed. *Debussy et l'évolution de la musique au XXe siècle.* Paris: Editions du Centre National de la Recherche Scientifique, 1965.

2808. Wenk, Arthur B. *Claude Debussy and Twentieth-Century Music.* Boston: G. K. Hall, 1983.

2809. ———. "Varieties of Analysis: Through the Analytical Sieve and Beyond." MRSQ 2, nos. 3–4 (1993): 327–48.

2810. Wheeldon, Marianne. "Interpreting Discontinuity in the Late Works of Claude Debussy." Ph.D. diss., University of Rochester, 1997.

2811. Whittall, Arnold. "Tonality and the Whole-Tone Scale in the Music of Debussy." MR 36 (1975): 261–71.

2812. Wilson, Eugene N. "Form and Texture in the Chamber music of Debussy and Ravel." Ph.D. diss., University of Washington, 1968.

2813. Winzer, Dieter. *Claude Debussy und die französische musikalische Tradition.* Wiesbaden: Breitkopf & Härtel, 1981.

2814. Woollen, Russell. "Episodic Compositional Techniques in Late Debussy." JAMS 11 (1958): 79–80.

2815. Zenck-Maurer, Claudia. *Versuch über die wahre Art, Debussy zu analysieren.* Munich: Katzbichler, 1974.

DECAUX, ABEL (1869–1943)
2816. Schenewerk, Joyce L. "Abel Decaux's *Clairs de lune.*" M.A. thesis, University of Rochester, 1977.

DELÁS, JOSÉ LUIS (b. 1928)
2817. Metzger, Heinz-Klaus, and Rainer Riehn, eds. *José Luis de Delás.* Munich: Text + Kritik, 1992.

DEL BORGO, ELLIOT (b. 1938)
2818. Toering, Ronald J. "An Analysis of Elliot Del Borgo's *Do Not Go Gentle into That Good Night.*" JBR 21, no. 1 (1985): 1–21.

DELDEN, LEX VAN (1919–1988)
2819. Delden, Lex van. "Lex van Delden: Impromptu for Solo Harp, Op. 48." SS 7 (1961): 25–27.

DELIBES, LÉO (1836–1891)
2820. ASO 183 (1998). [*Lakmé*]

DELIO, THOMAS (b. 1951)
2821. Hamman, Michael. "Toward a Morphology of Presence: The Sound Installations of Thomas DeLio." I 16, nos. 1–2 (1987): 55–73.

DELIUS, FREDERICK (1862–1934)

Koanga
2822. Randel, William. "*Koanga* and Its Libretto." ML 52 (1971): 141–56.

Magic Fountain
2823. Threlfall, Robert. "Delius's Unknown Opera: *The Magic Fountain.*" SMU 11 (1977): 60–73.

Mass of Life
2824. Boyle, Andrew J. "*A Mass of Life* and Its 'Bell-Motif.'" MR 42 (1982): 44–50.
2825. Puffett, Derrick. "A Nietzschean Libretto: Delius and the Text for *A Mass of Life.*" ML 79, no. 2 (1998): 244–67.

Requiem
2826. Payne, Anthony. "Delius's Requiem." TEMPO 76 (1966): 12–17.

Songs (various)
2827. Holland, Arthur Keith. *The Songs of Delius.* London: Oxford University Press, 1951.
2828. Hutchings, Edward Gillmore, III. "The Published Solo Songs of Frederick Delius." D.M.A. diss., University of Miami, 1980.

Various Works
2829. Bacon-Shone, Frederic. "Form in the Chamber Music of Frederick Delius." Ph.D. diss., University of Southern California, 1976.
2830. Cooke, Deryck. "Delius the Unknown." PRMA 89 (1962–1963): 17–29.
2831. Grimes, Doreen. "Form in the Orchestral Music of Frederick Delius." Ph.D. diss., North Texas State University, 1966.
2832. Jones, Philip B. R. "The American Sources of Delius's Style." Ph.D. diss., 1982.
2833. M-Morrison.
2834. Palmer, Christopher. "Delius and Percy Grainger." ML 52 (1971): 418–25.
2835. Payne, Anthony. "Delius's Stylistic Development." TEMPO 60 (1961): 6–16.
2836. TEMPO 26 (1952–1953). [Special issue]

DELLO JOIO, NORMAN (b. 1913)
2837. Boston, Nancy J. "The Piano Sonatas and Suites of Norman Dello Joio (1940–1948)." D.M.A. diss., Peabody Conservatory, 1984.
2838. Bumgardner, Thomas Arthur. "The Solo Vocal Works of Norman Dello Joio." D.M.A. diss., University of Texas, 1973.
2839. Downes, Edward. "The Music of Norman Dello Joio." MQ 48 (1962): 149–72.
2840. M-Jeter. [Aria and Toccata]
2841. M-Mize.
2842. Whalen, J. Robert. "A Comparative Study of the Sonata Number Three for Piano and the *Variations, Chaconne, and Finale* for Orchestra by Norman Dello Joio." D.M. diss., Indiana University, 1968.

DEL TREDICI, DAVID (b. 1937)
2843. Earls, Paul. "David Del Tredici: *Syzygy.*" PNM 9, no. 2–10, no. 1 (1970): 304–13.
2844. Knussen, Oliver. "David Del Tredici and *Syzygy.*" TEMPO 118 (1976): 8–15.

DELZ, CHRISTOPH (1950–1993)

2845. Brotbeck, Roman. "Zwischen Transkomposition und Zitat: Zum Komponieren von Christoph Delz." DI 48 (1996): 4–9.

DEMESSIEUX, JEANNE (1921–1968)

2846. M-Dorroh.

DENCH, CHRIS (b. 1953)

2847. Toop, Richard. "Beyond the 'Crisis of Material': Chris Dench's *Funk.*" CMR 13, no. 1 (1995): 85–115.

2848. ———. "Four Facets of 'The New Complexity.'" CT 32 (1988): 4–50. [*Énoncé, Tilt*, Symphony No. 3 (*Afterimages*)]

2849. ———. "*Sulle Scale della Fenice.*" PNM 29, no. 2 (1991): 72–92.

DENNIS, BRIAN (1941–1998)

2850. Hill, Peter. "The Chinese Song-Cycles of Brian Dennis." TEMPO 137 (1981): 23–29.

DESSAU, PAUL (1894–1979)

2851. Hennenberg, Fritz. "Kosmosforschung als sinfonisches Subjekt: Kommentar zur Orchestermusik Nr. 2 *Meer der Stürme* von Paul Dessau." MG 18 (1968): 177–83.

2852. ———. "Mozart-Modern: Bermerkungen zu Paul Dessaus 'Sinfonischer Adaptation' des Streichquintetts in Es Dur von W. A. Mozart (KV 614)." MG 16 (1966): 375–79.

2853. ———. "Paul Dessaus Theatermusik: Kommentar, Deutung, Werkübersicht: Zum 65. Geburtstag des Komponisten." MG 9, no. 12 (1959): 3–10.

2854. Müller, Gerhard. "Paul Dessaus Konzeption einer politischen Musik." JP 3 (1980): 9–26.

2855. Rienäcker, Gerd. "Analytische Bemerkungen zu Dessaus Oper *Einstein.*" MG 24 (1974): 711–17.

2856. ———. "Zur Dialektik musikdramaturgischer Gestaltung: Analytische Notate zum zwölften Bild der Oper *Lanzelot* von Paul Dessau." DJM 64 (1972): 79–97.

2857. Spieler, Heinrich. "Tradition und Zeitgenössisches Denken: Paul Dessaus Bach-Variationen." MG 14 (1964): 714–24.

DETT, R. NATHANIEL (1882–1943)

2858. McBrier, Vivian F. "The Life and Works of Robert Nathaniel Dett." Ph.D. diss., Catholic University of America, 1967.

DHOMONT, FRANCIS (b. 1926)

2859. Lewis, Andrew. "Francis Dhomont's *Novars.*" JNMR 27, nos. 1–2 (1998): 67–83. [*Cycle du son*]

DIAMOND, DAVID (1915–2005)

2860. Friday, Raymond. "Analyses and Interpretations of Selected Songs of David Diamond." Ph.D. diss., New York University, 1984.

DICK, MARCEL (1898–1991)

2861. Ogasapian, John K. "Marcel Dick's *Choral, Passacaglia, and Fugue*: Some Considerations of Form and Color in Row-Based Organ Music." F-Dick: 135–52.

2862. Rockmaker, Jody D. "Marcel Dick's Suite for Piano." F-Dick: 181–94.

DIDKOVSKY, NICHOLAS (b. 1958)

2863. Didkovsky, Nick. "*Lottery*: Toward a Unified Rational Strategy for Cooperative Music-Making." LMJ 2, no. 1 (1992): 3–12.

DIEPENBROCK, ALPHONS (1862–1921)

2864. Braas, Ton. "The Verlaine Songs of Alphons Diepenbrock." KN 30, no. 4 (1996): 16–20.

2865. Reeser, Eduard. "Alphons Diepenbrock: Music for *Elektra.*" SS 12 (1962): 12–14.

2866. ———. "Alphons Diepenbrock: The Commemoration of the Centenary of His Birth." SS 12 (1962): 1–11.

2867. ———. "Some Melodic Patterns in the Music of Alphons Diepenbrock." KN 3 (1976): 16–25.

DIEREN, BERNARD VAN (1887–1936)

2868. Grouse, Gordon. "Bernard van Dieren: Three Early Songs in Relation to His Subsequent Development." MR 29 (1968): 116–22.

2869. Riley, Patrick Robert. "The String Quartets of Bernard van Dieren." Ph.D. diss., University of Iowa, 1985.

2870. Williams, Robert. "The Life and Work of Bernard van Dieren." Ph.D. diss., University of Wales, Aberystwyth, 1980.

DIESENDRUCK, TAMAR

2871. Moe, Eric. "Beyond Right and Wrong Ways to Write Music: Tsontakis, Rosenblum, and Diesendruck." CMR 10, no. 1 (1994): 149–95. [*Coming to Terms with the Tower of Babel*]

DIETRICH, KARL (b. 1927)

2872. Kneipel, Eberhard. "Die Analyse: Dramatische Szenen für drei Flöteninstrumente und grosses Orchester (1974) von Karl Dietrich." MG 25 (1975): 525–29.

2873. Kober, Kleinhardt. "Karl Dietrichs sinfonisches Schaffen als Ausdruck sozialistischen Lebensgefühls." Ph.D. diss., Martin-Luther-Universität, Halle-Wittenberg, 1981.

DILLON, JAMES (b. 1950)

2874. Alexander, Michael J. "The Changing States of James Dillon." CMR 13, no. 1 (1995): 65–84.

2875. Toop, Richard. "Four Facets of 'The New Complexity.'" CT 32 (1988): 4–50. [String Quartet, *Überschreiten*, *Zone (. . . de azul)*]

DIMOV, BOJIDOR (b. 1931)

2876. Zelinsky, Beate, and David Smeyers. "Neue Musik, die aufhorchen läßt: *Rituals for Clarinet Duo* von Bojidor Dimov." T 14, no. 1 (1989): 327–30.

DINESCU, VIOLETA (b. 1953)

2877. Dinescu, Violeta. "Allgemeine Gedanken zum Komponieren." N 4 (1983–1984): 46–52.

DISTLER, HUGO (1908–1942)

2878. Bergaas, Mark Jerome. "Compositional Style in the Keyboard Works of Hugo Distler (1908–1942)." Ph.D. diss., Yale University, 1978.

2879. Neumann, Friedrich. "Anmerkungen zum Kompositionsstil Hugo Distlers." M 33 (1979–1980): 16–21.

2880. M-Rhoades.

2881. Schmolzi, Herbert. "Das Wort-Ton-Verhältnis in Distlers Choralpassion." M 7 (1953): 556–61.

DITTRICH, PAUL-HEINZ (b. 1930)

2882. Hansen, Mathias. "Die Analyse: Violoncellokonzerte von Paul-Heinz Dittrich, Siegfried Matthus und Christfried Schmidt." MG 29 (1979): 591–99.

DOBROWOLSKI, ANDRZEJ (1921–1990)

2883. Zieliński, Tadeusz. "New Works by Andrej Dobrowolski." PM 20, nos. 3–4 (1985): 35–42. [*Music for Orchestra No. 5 (Passacaglia)*, *Music for Orchestra No. 6*]

DOHNÁNYI, ERNŐ (1877–1960)

2884. DeFoor, Keith Alex. "The Symphonies of Ernst von Dohnányi." Ph.D. diss., Florida State University, 1991.

2885. Hallman, Milton. "Ernő Dohnanyi's Solo Piano Works." JALS 17 (1985): 48–54.

2886. Kiszely, Deborah. "Editions and Recordings: An Analysis of Ernő Dohnányi's *Ruralia hungarica*, Op. 32/a, No. 4." SM 36, nos. 1–2 (1995): 73–90.

2887. Mabry, George Louis. "The Vocal and Choral Works of Ernst von Dohnanyi." Ph.D. diss., George Peabody College, 1973.

2888. Mintz, George Jacob. "Textural Patterns in the Solo Piano Music of Ernst von Dohnanyi." Ph.D. diss., Florida State University, 1976.

DONATONI, FRANCO (1927–2000)

2889. Piencikowski, Robert. "Sauf-conduit: Analyse d'*Etwas ruhiger im Ausdruck*." ENT 2 (1986): 75–86.

2890. Stoianova, Ivanka. "Franco Donatoni: *Souvenir*." MR 20 (1975): 4–14. [*Souvenir* (Kammersymphonie op. 18)]

DONIZETTI, GAETANO (1797–1848)

Ange de Nisida

2891. Ashbrook, William. "*L'ange de Nisida* di Donizetti." RIM 16 (1981): 96–14.

Anna Bolena

2892. Gossett, Philip. *Anna Bolena and the Artistic Maturity of Gaetano Donizetti*. Oxford: Clarendon Press, 1985.

2893. Levy, Janet M. "Texture as a Sign in Classic and Early Romantic Music." JAMS 35 (1982): 482–31.

Don Pasquale

2894. ASO 108 (1988).

Elisir d'amore

2895. ASO 95 (1987).

Fille du régiment

2896. ASO 179 (1997).

Lucia di Lammermoor

2897. ASO 55 (1983).

Lucrezia Borgia

2898. Zoppelli, Luca. "Narrative Elements in Donizetti's Operas." Trans. William Ashbrook. OQ 10, no. 1 (1993): 23–32.

Item numbers 2899 through 2998 were intentionally not used.

Maria di Rohan

2999. Lamacchia, Saverio. "Un tempo, due affetti: Una risorsa dell'aria romantica." SV 14 (1999): 51–68. [Act III]

Various Works

3000. Ashbrook, William. *Donizetti.* London: Cassell, 1965.

3001. ———. *Donizetti and His Operas.* Cambridge: Cambridge University Press, 1982.

3002. Dean, Winton. "Donizetti's Serious Operas." PRMA 100 (1973–1974): 123–41.

3003. Lippmann, Friedrich. "Donizetti und Bellini: Ein Beitrag zur Interpretation von Donizettis Stil." STU 4 (1975): 193–243.

DORATI, ANTAL (1906–1988)

3004. MacDonald, Calum. "Antal Dorati, Composer: A Catalog of His Works." TEMPO 143 (1982): 16–24.

DRAESEKE, FELIX (1835–1913)

3005. Follert, Udo-R. "'Christus'–Mysterium in einem Vorspiel und drei Oratorien für Soli, Chor, und Orchester von Felix Draeseke (1835–1913)." Part I, MK 60, no. 2 (1990): 81–92; Part II, MK 60, no. 4 (1990): 202–9; Part III, MK 60, no. 5 (1990): 245–52. [*Mysterium: Christus*]

3006. ———. "Felix Draeseke (1835–1913): Eine Bekanntmachung am Beispiel seines Requiem G-moll, Op. 22." MK 52 (1982): 226–35.

DRESHER, PAUL (b. 1951)

3007. Carl, Robert. "Three Points on the Spectrum: The Music of Louis Karchin, Lois V. Vierk, and Paul Dresher." CMR 10, no. 1 (1994): 11–31.

DREYFUS, GEORGE (b. 1928)

3008. Lucas, Kay. "George Dreyfuss *Garni Sands*: A Forward Step for Australian Opera." SMU 7 (1973): 78–87.

DRIESSLER, JOHANNES (b. 1921)

3009. Platen, Emil. "Johannes Driesslers Oratorium *Dein Reich komme.*" MK 21 (1951): 113–22.

DRUCKMAN, JACOB (1928–1996)

3010. Uscher, Nancy. "Two Contemporary Viola Concerti: A Comparative Study." TEMPO 147 (1983): 23–29.

DRUMMOND, JOHN (b. 1944)

3011. Drummond, John. "*Narcissus* and Tonality." CT 2 (1971): 18–19.

DUFOUR, DENIS (b. 1953)

3012. Fischer, Michel. "Acuité d'écoute 'acousmatique' et itinéraire timbrique." ANM 30 (1993): 29–37. [*Collection de timbres*]

DUFOURT, HUGUES (b. 1943)

3013. Fervers, Andreas. "Priorität der Farbgebung: Hugues Dufourts *The Watery Star.*" MTX 79 (1999): 31–36.

DUKAS, PAUL (1865–1935)

3014. Abbate, Carolyn. "What the Sorcerer Said." NCM 12, no. 3 (1989): 221–30. [*L'apprenti sorcier*]

3015. ASO 149–50 (1992). [*Ariane et Barbe-bleue*]

3016. Boyd, Everett Vernon, Jr. "Paul Dukas and the Impressionist Milieu: Stylistic Assimilation in Three Orchestral works." Ph.D. diss., University of Rochester, 1980. [*L'apprenti sorcier, Ariane et Barbe-bleue, La Péri*]

3017. Favre, Georges. *L'oeuvre de Paul Dukas.* Paris: Durand, 1969.

3018. Heath, Mary Joanne Renner. "A Comparative Analysis of Dukas's *Ariane et Barbe-bleue* and Bartók's *Duke Bluebeard's Castle.*" Ph.D. diss., University of Rochester, 1988.

3019. M-Kniesner. [Piano Sonata]

3020. Minger, Frederick. "The Piano Works of Paul Dukas." D.M.A. diss., Peabody Conservatory, 1982.

3021. Reinfandt, Karl-Heintz. "Unterrichtsplanung im Fachmusik am Beispiel *Der Zauberlehrling* von Paul Dukas." MB 6 (1973): 389–96. [*L'apprenti sorcier*]

3022. Schubert, Giselher. "'Vibrierende Gedanken' und das 'Katasterverfahren' der Analyse: Zu den Klaviersonaten von Dukas und d'Indy." F-Dahlhaus: 619–34.

DUNCAN, JOHN (1913–1975)

3023. Spence, Martha Ellen Blanding. "Selected Song Cycles of Three Contemporary Black American Composers: William Grant Still, *Songs of Separation*; Hale Smith, *Beyond the Rim of Day*; John Duncan, *Blue Set*." D.M.A. diss., University of Southern Mississippi, 1977.

DUNHAM, HENRY MORTON (1853–1929)

3024. Gamble, Jane Council. "The Organ Sonatas of Henry Morton Dunham." D.M.A. diss., Memphis State University, 1980.

DUPARC, HENRI (1848–1933)

3025. Elst, Nancy van der. *Henri Duparc: L'homme et son oeuvre.* Lille Service de Reproduction des Thèses, Université de Lille, 1972.

DUPRÉ, MARCEL (1886–1971)

3026. Delestre, R. *L'oeuvre de Marcel Dupré.* Paris: Éditions Musique Sacrée, 1952.

3027. M-Dorroh.

3028. Pagett, John Mason. "The Music of Marcel Dupré." S.M.D. diss., Union Theological Seminary, 1975.

3029. M-Rhoades.

3030. Van Wye, Benjamin. "Marcel Dupré's Marian Vespers and the French *alternatim* tradition." MR 43 (1982): 192–224.

DURIEUX, FRÉDÉRIC (b. 1959)

3031. Nieminen, Risto, ed. *Frédéric Durieux.* Paris: IRCAM, 1995.

DURUFLÉ, MAURICE (1902–1986)

3032. Beechey, Gwilym. "The Music of Maurice Duruflé." MR 32 (1971): 146–55.

3033. M-Dorroh.

3034. Forst, Inge. "Maurice Duruflé und sein Requiem." KJ 75 (1991): 107–17.

3035. McIntosh, John Stuart. "The Organ Music of Maurice Duruflé." D.M.A. diss., University of Rochester, 1973.

3036. M-Rhoades.

DUSSEK, JAN LADISLAV (1760–1812)

3037. Grossman, Orin Louis. "The Solo Piano Sonatas of Jan Ladislav Dussek." Ph.D. diss., Yale University, 1975.

3038. Schwarting, Heino. "The Piano Sonatas of Johann Ladislaus Dussek." PQ 91 (1975): 41–45.

DUTILLEUX, HENRI (b. 1916)

3039. Delente, Gail Buchanan. "Selected Piano Music in France since 1945." Ph.D. diss., Washington University, 1966. [Piano Sonata]

3040. M-Kniesner.

3041. Kühnl, Claus. "Poet der Nacht: Henri Dutilleux, Altmeister der Neuen Musik in Frankreich." NZM 150, no. 1 (1989): 4–9. [*Tout un monde lointain*]

3042. Lessing, Wolfgang. "Hommage à Sacher: Henri Dutilleux' und Heinz Holligers Kompositionen für Violoncello solo über den Namen Sacher." MTH 6, no. 2 (1991): 151–80. [*3 strophes sur le nom de Sacher*]

DVOŘÁK, ANTONÍN (1841–1904)

Alfred

3043. Smaczny, Jan. "*Alfred*: Dvořák's First Operatic Endeavour Surveyed." JRMA 115, no. 1 (1990): 80–106.

Biblical Songs, Op. 99

3044. Vojtěch, Ivan. "Vertonte Sprache in der geistigen Tradition der tschechischen Musik: A. Dvořák, *Biblische Lieder* op. 99, Nr. 4, 'Hospodin jest můj pastýř.'" F-Dahlhaus: 579–88.

Cello Concerto, A Major (1865)

3045. Clapham, John. "Dvořák's First Cello Concerto." ML 37 (1956): 350–55.

Cello Concerto, Op. 104, B Minor

3046. Clapham, John. "Dvořák's Cello Concerto in B Minor: A Masterpiece in the Making." MR 40 (1979): 123–40.

3047. Smaczny, Jan. *Dvořák: Cello Concerto.* Cambridge University Press, 1999.

Cypresses

3048. Smaczny, Jan. "Dvořák's *Cypresses*: A Song Cycle and Its Metamorphoses." ML 72, no. 4 (1991): 552–68.

Legends, Op. 59

3049. Fischer, Kurt von. "Bemerkungen zu Antonin Dvořáks *Legenden* Op. 59 für Klavier zu vier Händen." OM 9 (1986): 197–204.

Operas (various; *see also* specific operas)
3050. Clapham, John. "The Operas of Antonin Dvořák." PRMA 84 (1957–1958): 55–69.

***Othello*, Op. 93**
3051. Cooper, John Michael. "Program and Form in Dvořák's *Othello,* Op. 93." TSP 3 (1986): 66–81.

Piano Quintet, Op. 81
3052. Beveridge, David. "Dvořák's 'Dumka' and the Concept of Nationalism in Music Historiography." JMR 12, no. 4 (1993): 303–25. [Movement II]
3053. Hollander, Hans. "Schubertsches bei Dvořák." M 28 (1974): 40–43.

Piano Trios
3054. Case, Barbara Betty Bacik. "The Relation between Structure and the Treatment of Instruments in the First Movements of Dvořák's Piano Trios Opus 21, 26, and 65." D.M.A. diss., University of Texas, 1977.

Requiem, Op. 89
3055. Longyear, Rey M., and Kate R. Covington. "Motivic Unity and Harmonic Variety in Dvořák's Requiem." ITO 12, nos. 5–6 (1992): 51–64.

***Rusalka*, Op. 114**
3056. Schläder, Jürgen. "Märchenoper oder symbolistisches Musik-drama? Zum Interpretationsrahmen der Titelrolle in Dvořáks *Rusalka.*" MF 34 (1981): 25–39.

Serenade, Op. 44
3057. Woodford, Paul G. "An Analysis on Antonin Dvořák's Serenade in D Minor, Opus 44." JBR 34, no. 1 (1998): 38–58.

String Quartet No. 12, Op. 96 ("The American")
3058. Beveridge, David. "Sophisticated Primitivism: The Significance of Pentatonicism in Dvořák's 'American Quartet.'" CM 24 (1977): 25–36.

Symphony No. 5, Op. 76
3059. Beveridge, David. "Echoes of Dvořák in the Third Symphony of Brahms." MO 11 (1989): 221–30.

Symphony No. 6, Op. 60
3060. Josephson, Nors S. "On Some Apparent Beethoven Reminiscences and Quotations in Dvořák's Sixth Symphony." MR 54, no. 2 (1993): 112–22.

Symphony No. 7, Op. 70
3061. Clapham, John. "Dvořák's Symphony in D Minor: The creative process." ML 42 (1961): 103–16.

Symphony No. 9, Op. 95 ("From the New World")
3062. Beckerman, Michael. "Dvořák's 'New World' Largo and *The Song of Hiawatha.*" NCM 16, no. 1 (1992): 35–48.
3063. Clapham, John. "The Evolution of Dvořák's Symphony *From the New World.*" MQ 44 (1958): 167–83.

Various Works
3064. Abraham, Gerald. "Verbal Inspiration in Dvořák's Instrumental Music." SM 11 (1969): 27–34.
3065. Beveridge, David. "Romantic Ideas in a Classical Frame: The Sonata Forms of Dvořák." Ph.D. diss., University of California, Berkeley, 1980.
3066. Boese, Helmut. *Zwei Urmusikanten: Smetana, Dvořák.* Zurich: Almathea, 1955.
3067. Clapham, John. *Antonin Dvořák: Musician and Craftsman.* London: Faber & Faber, 1966.
3068. ———. "Dvořák's Relations with Brahms and Hanslick." MQ 57 (1971): 241–54.
3069. ———. "The National Origins of Dvořák's Art." PRMA 89 (1962–1963): 75–88.
3070. Hollander, Hans. "Die tschechisch-amerikanische Synthese in Dvořáks Musik aus der Neuen Welt." M 29 (1975): 122–24.
3071. Komma, Karl Michael. "Die Pentatonik in Antonín Dvořáks Werk." MO 1 (1962): 63–75.
3072. Kull, Hans. *Dvořáks Kammermusik.* Bern: Haupt, 1948.
3073. Šourek, Otakar. *Antonín Dvořák: Werkanalysen.* Prague: Artia, 1956.
3074. ———. *The Chamber Music of Antonín Dvořák.* Prague: Artia, 1956.
3075. ———. *The Orchestral Works of Antonín Dvořák.* Prague: Artia, 1957.

– E –

EBEN, PETR (b. 1929)
3076. Koch, Timothy. "The A Capella Music of Petr Eben." ACR 40, no. 1 (1998): 3–5.
3077. Landale, Susan. "Die Orgelmusik von Petr Eben." MK 50 (1980): 248–59.

EBERL, ANTON (1765–1807)

3078. White, A. Duane. "The Piano Works of Anton Ebert (1765–1807)." Ph.D. diss., University of Wisconsin, 1971.

ECKARDT, JASON (b. 1971)

3079. Eckardt, Jason. "Listening and Composing." CM 67–68 (1999): 73–91. [*Polarities*]

EGK, WERNER (1901–1983)

3080. Häusler, Josef. "'Choucoun': Reflexion und Verwandlung (*Variations über ein karibisches Thema).*" MELOS 26 (1959): 373–76.

EIMERT, HERBERT (1897–1972)

3081. Oesch, Hans. "Herbert Eimert: Pionier der Zwölftontechnik." MELOS 41 (1974): 211–14.

EINEM, GOTTFRIED VON (1918–1996)

3082. Kaatz, Klemens. "Eine Hinrichtung Büchners: *Dantons Tod* von Gottfried von Einem." HJM 14 (1997): 131–67.

3083. Klein, Rudolf. "Gottfried von Einems Oper *Jesu Hochzeit.*" OMZ 35 (1980): 189–99.

3084. ———. "Gottfried von Einems Oper *Kabale und Liebe.*" OMZ 31 (1976): 633–39.

3085. Revers, Peter. "Aspekte einer Kinderoper: Zu Lotte Ingrisches/Gottfried von Einems *Tulifant.*" M 47, no. 2 (1993): 86–90.

3086. Saathen, Friedrich. "Committed Opera: Gottfried von Einem's *The Visit of the Old Lady.*" TEMPO 104 (1973): 22–29. [*Der Besuch der alten Dame*]

3087. Schollum, Robert. "Die Klavierlieder Gottfried von Einems." OMZ 28 (1973): 80–86.

EISLER, HANNS (1898–1962)

Balladen, Op. 22

3088. Phleps, Thomas. "'Das wird ein Winter, mein Junge!': Anmerkungen zu Hanns Eislers 'Ballade von den Säckeschmeißern.'" BM 31, no. 2 (1989): 118–30.

Cantatas

3089. Grabs, Manfred. "Über Hanns Eislers Kammerkantaten." MG 18 (1968): 445–54.

Deutsche Sinfonie

3090. Phleps, Thomas. *Hann Eislers "Deutsche Sinfonie": Ein Beiträg zur Ästhetik des Widerstands.* Kassel: Bärenreiter, 1988.

3091. Szeskus, Richard. "Bemerkungen zur Eislers *Deutscher Sinfonie.*" MG 23 (1973): 390–96.

Ernste Gesänge

3092. Dümling, Albrecht. "Für ein Leben ohne Angst: 'XX. Parteitag' aus den *Ernste Gesänge* von Hanns Eisler." BOGM 10 (2000): 9–25.

Klavierstücke, Op. 3

3093. Münch, Stephan. "Hanns Eislers Klaviersonate op. 1 und die Vier Klavierstücke op. 3: Ein Beitrag zur Entwicklung dodekaphoner Kompositionstechnik." MF 39, no. 1 (1986): 37–44.

Nonet No. 1

3094. Helbing, Volker. "Pastorale, zwölftönig: Anmerkungen zu einer Filmpartitur Hanns Eislers." MAS 4, no. 14 (2000): 25–39.

Piano Sonata No. 1

3095. Münch, Stephan. "Hanns Eislers Klaviersonate op. 1 und die Vier Klavierstücke op. 3: Ein Beitrag zur Entwicklung dodekaphoner Kompositionstechnik." MF 39, no. 1 (1986): 37–44.

Septet No. 1

3096. Mainka, Jürgen. "Zum Finale von Eislers Septett Nr. 1." MG 28 (1978): 412–13.

Songs (various; *see also* specific songs and song cycles)

3097. Elsner, Jürgen. "Zum 70. Geburtstag Hanns Eislers: Die Majakowski-Vertonungen." MG 18 (1968): 435–44.

3098. Grabs, Manfred. "*Wir, so gut es gelang, haben das Unsre getan*: Zur Aussage der Hölderlin-Vertonungen Hanns Eislers." BM 15 (1973): 49–60.

3099. Keller, Christoph. "Parallele und Parodie: Über Beziehungen zwischen der Vokal- und Klaviermusik Hanns Eislers." DI 19 (1989): 4–9.

3100. ———. "Der verschwundene Text: Zu Eislers *Rotem* [i.e., *Roter*] *Wedding* und der *DDR-Hymne* aus heutiger Sicht." F-Knepler, vol. 3: 183–99.

3101. Krones, Hartmut. "Musikalische Semantik im Dienste politischer, humanitärer und persönlicher Aussage: Zu Hanns Eislers Liedschaffen." BOGM 10 (2000): 40–55.

3102. Rösler, Walter. "Zu einigen Tucholsky-Liedern Hanns Eislers." BM 15 (1973): 81–92.

Wiegenlieder für Arbeitermütter

3103. Phleps, Thomas. "Die Kunst zu erben, oder: Was haben Hanns Eislers *Wiegenlieder* mit Franz Schubert zu tun?" NZM 149, no. 11 (1988): 9–13.

Winterschlacht-Suite

3104. Hauska, Hans. "Hanns Eisler: *Winterschlact-Suite*." MG 12 (1962): 416–17.

Zeitungsausschnitte

3105. Stephan, Rudolf. "*Zeitungsausschnitte* und *Kinderreime*: Zu einigen Liedern von Hanns Eisler und Theodor W. Adorno." OMZ 39 (1984): 18–22.

Various Works

3106. Allihn, Ingeborg. "Die Musik Hanns Eislers zu Stücken von Bertolt Brecht." Ph.D. diss., Humboldt-Universität, Berlin, 1979.
3107. BM 15 (1973). [Special issue]
3108. Csipák, Karoly. *Probleme der Volkstümlichkeit bei Hanns Eisler.* Munich: Katzbichler, 1975.
3109. Hauska, Hans. "Hanns Eisler: Ouvertüre zu einem Lustpiel." MG 13 (1963): 148–49.
3110. Knepler, Georg. "Was des Eislers ist . . . ." BM 15 (1973): 29–48.
3111. Schweinhardt, Peter. "Eislers Walzer: Anwendungen des Dreivierteltaktes." BOGM 10 (2000): 26–39.
3112. Stern, Dietrich. "Hanns Eislers Balladen für Gesang und kleines Orchester." SM 18 (1976): 169–82.

ELGAR, EDWARD (1857–1934)

3113. Dann, Mary G. "Elgar's Use of the Sequence." ML 19 (1938): 255–64.
3114. Gimbel, Allen. "Elgar's Prize Song: Quotation and Allusion in the Second Symphony." NCM 12, no. 3 (1989): 231–40.
3115. Newbould, Brian. "'Never Done Before': Elgar's Other Enigma." ML 77, no. 2 (1996): 228–41. [String Quartet]
3116. Porte, John F. *Sir Edward Elgar.* London: K. Paul, Trench, Truber, 1921.
3117. Ridout, Godfrey. "Elgar, the Angular Saxon." CMJ 1, no. 4 (1957): 33–40.
3118. Rushton, Julian. *Elgar: Enigma Variations.* Cambridge: Cambridge University Press, 1999.
3119. Westrup, Jack A. "Elgar's Enigma." PRMA 86 (1959–1960): 79–97.

ELOY, JEAN-CLAUDE (b. 1938)

3120. Felder, John. "The Structural Function of Wind Role Transformations in *Equivalences* by J. C. Eloy." EXT 1, no. 1 (1981): 18–35.

EMMANUEL, MAURICE (1862–1938)

3121. Carlson, Eleanor Anne. "Maurice Emmanuel and the Six Sonatinas for Piano." D.M.A. diss., Boston University, 1974.
3122. F-Emmanuel.

ENESCU, GEORGE (1881–1955)

3123. Lejtes, Ruf. "*Oedipe* by Georges Enesco." Ph.D. diss., Inst. Istorii iskusstv, Leningrad, 1970.
3124. Newman, Elaine W. "Enesco's *Oedipe*: A Little-Known Masterpiece." CM 26 (1978): 99–105.

ERB, DONALD (b. 1927)

3125. Cope: 232–35. [*Souvenir*]
3126. Suess, John G. "The Solo Concerti of Donald Erb." F-Dick: 111–34.

ERBER, JAMES (b. 1951)

3127. Erber, James. "Music for 25 Solo Strings." CMR 13, no. 1 (1995): 117–32.

ERDMANN, EDUARD (1896–1958)

3128. Baumgartner, Paul. "Das Konzertstück Op. 18." F-Erdmann: 152–55.
3129. Scherliess, Volker. "Zum Streichquartett Op. 17." F-Erdmann: 156–62.

ERICKSON, ROBERT (1917–1997)

3130. Erickson, Robert. "*Loops*: An Informal Timbre Experiment." EXT 6, no. 2 (1993): 99–107.
3131. MacKay, John. "On the Music of Robert Erickson: A Survey and Some Selected Analyses." PNM 26, no. 2 (1988): 56–85. [Concerto for Piano and Seven Instruments, *The Idea of Order at Key West*, *Kryl*, *Ricercar à 5*, *Solstice*, String Quartet no. 2]
3132. ———. "On the Recent Music of Robert Erickson." EXT 6, no. 2 (1993): 108–36.

ESCHER, RUDOLF (1912–1980)

3133. Escher, Rudolf. "Rudolf Escher: Musique pour l'esprit en deuil." SS 20 (1964): 15–33.

3134. ———. "Rudolf Escher: Quintette a fiati." SS 34 (1968): 24–34.

3135. Paap, Wouter. "*Le tombeau de Ravel* by Rudolf Escher." SS 4 (1960): 136–37.

ESCOT, POZZI (b. 1933)

3136. Hearon, Jim. "Escot's *Mirabilis I*: 'Pulses with the Beauty of Mathematics.'" SONUS 16, no. 2 (1996): 66–79.

ESSER, HEINRICH (1818–1872)

3137. Müller, Karl-Josef. *Heinrich Esser als Komponist.* Kassel: Bärenreiter-Antiquariat, 1969.

ETLER, ALVIN (1913–1973)

3138. Nichols, William Roy. "The Wind Music of Alvin Etler." D.M.A. diss., University of Iowa, 1976.

3139. Painter, Noel Thomas. "Exploring Contour Associations through Transformation Networks: Identification and Classification of Contour Relations in Modern Multiple Percussion Music." Ph.D. diss., University of Rochester, 2000. [*XL Plus 1*]

3140. Shelden, Paul Melvin. "Alvin Etler (1913–1973): His Career and the Two Sonatas for Clarinet." D.M.A. diss., University of Maryland, 1978.

3141. M-Wise.

EVANGELISTA, JOSÉ (b. 1943)

3142. Evangelista, José. "Pourquoi composer de la musique monodique." CIR 1, no. 2 (1990): 55–70.

EVANGELISTI, FRANCO (1926–1980)

3143. Giomi, Francesco, and Marco Ligabue. "Evangelisti's Composition *Incontri di fasce sonore* at W. D. R.: Aesthetic-Cognitive Analysis in Theory and Practice." JNMR 27, nos. 1–2 (1998): 120–45.

3144. Metzger, Heinz-Klaus, and Rainer Riehn, eds. *Franco Evangelisti.* Munich: Text + Kritik, 1985.

EYBLER, JOSEPH LEOPOLD (1765–1846)

3145. Ricks, Robert W. "The Published Masses of Joseph Eybler, 1765–1846." Ph.D. diss., Catholic University of America, 1967.

– F –

FALLA, MANUEL DE (1876–1946)

3146. ASO 177 (1997). [*El amor brujo, El retablo de maese Pedro, La vida breve*]

3147. Brownscombe, Peter. "Spanish Nationalism and Impressionism as Represented in Manuel de Falla's *Homenaje: Pour le tombeau de Debussy.*" D 5, no. 1 (1973): 1–10.

3148. Budwig, Andrew. "Manuel de Falla's *Atlantida*: An Historical and Analytical Study." Ph.D. diss., University of Chicago, 1984.

3149. Concepción, Elman Augusto. "An Analysis of Twelve Published Works of Manuel de Falla y Matheu for Voice and Piano." D.M.A. diss., University of Miami, 1981.

3150. Mayer-Serra, Otto. "Falla's Musical Nationalism." MQ 29 (1943): 1–17.

3151. M-Morrison.

3152. Rigoni, Michel. "De Falla: Le concerto pour clavecin." ANM 21 (1990): 55–64.

3153. ———. "*Nuits dans les jardins d'Espagne* de Manuel de Falla: De la couleur locale au classicisme." ANM 18 (1990): 49–53.

3154. Walters, D. Gareth. "Thematic Metamorphosis in Falla's *El amor brujo.*" MR 53, no. 2 (1992): 137–44.

FANO, MICHEL (b. 1929)

3155. Toop, Richard. "Messiaen/Goeyvaerts, Fano/Stockhausen, Boulez." PNM 13, no. 1 (1974–1975): 141–69. [Sonata for Two Pianos]

FARWELL, ARTHUR (1872–1952)

3156. Kirk, Edgar L. "Toward American Music: A Study of the Life and Music of Arthur Farwell." Ph.D. diss., University of Rochester, 1959.

FAUCHET, PAUL ROBERT MARCEL (1881–1937)

3157. Mitchell, Jon C. "Paul Robert Marcel Fauchet: *Symphonie pour musique d'harmonie* (Symphony in B Flat)." JBR 20, no. 2 (1983–1984): 8–26.

FAURÉ, GABRIEL (1845–1924)

Barcarolle, Op. 41

3158. De Martino, Pier Paolo. "'L'entêtement à écrire pour le piano': Per una rilettura dei morceaux de salon del primo Fauré." RIM 29 (1994): 459–89.

Cello Sonata No. 2, Op. 117

3159. Labussière, Annie. "Gabriel Fauré: 2e sonate pour violoncelle et piano, op. 117." ANM 25 (1991): 19–35.

Nocturnes

3160. Crouch, Richard Henry. "The Nocturnes and Barcarolles for Solo Piano of Gabriel Fauré." Ph.D. diss., Catholic University of America, 1980.

3161. De Martino, Pier Paolo. "'L'entêtement à écrire pour le piano': Per una rilettura dei morceaux de salon del primo Fauré." RIM 29 (1994): 459–89. [No. 1, op. 33; No. 5, op. 37]

3162. Dommel-Diény, Amy. *Gabriel Fauré*. Dommel-Diény 12. Paris: Dommel-Diény, 1974. [Nos. 1–3, op. 33]

3163. Johansen, Ken. "Gabriel Fauré and the Art of Ambiguity." JALS 43 (1998): 8–44. [No. 10, op. 99; No. 11, op. 104, no. 1]

3164. Valicenti, Joseph Anthony. "The Thirteen Nocturnes of Gabriel Fauré." D.M.A. diss., University of Miami, 1980.

Pelléas et Mélisande

3165. Nectoux, Jean-Michel. "Le *Pelléas* de Fauré." RDM 67 (1981): 169–90.

Piano Works (various; *see also* specific piano works)

3166. Crouch, Richard Henry. "The Nocturnes and Barcarolles for Solo Piano of Gabriel Fauré." Ph.D. diss., Catholic University of America, 1980.

3167. Johansen, Ken. "Gabriel Fauré, un art de l'équivoque." RDM 85, no. 1 (1999): 63–96.

3168. Sanger, G. Norman. "Chromaticism in the Keyboard Works of Franck and Fauré." Ph.D. diss., University of Pittsburgh, 1976.

Preludes, Op. 103

3169. Austin, William W. "Tonalität und Form in den Preludes Op. 103 von Gabriel Fauré." M-Kühn: 399–401.

3170. Johansen, Ken. "Gabriel Fauré and the Art of Ambiguity." JALS 43 (1998): 8–44.

Songs

3171. Bland, Stephen F. "The Songs of Gabriel Fauré." Ph.D. diss., Florida State University, 1976.

3172. Dommel-Diény, Amy. *Fauré*. Dommel-Diény 13. Neuchâtel: Delachaux et Niestlé, 1967. [*Au cimetière*, op. 51, no. 2; *L'horizon chimérique*, op. 118; *Prison*, op. 83, no. 1; *Les roses d'Isapahan*, op. 39, no. 4; *Le secret*, op. 23, no. 3]

3173. Fortassier, Pierre. "Le rythme dans les mélodies de Gabriel Fauré." RDM 62 (1976): 257–74.

3174. Greer, Taylor. "Modal Sensibility in Gabriel Fauré's Harmonic Language." TP 16 (1991): 127–42. [*Les présents*, op. 46, no. 1; *La rose*, op. 51, no. 4; "Une sainte en son auréole," op. 61, no. 1 (from *La bonne chanson*)]

3175. M-Greer. [*La lune blanche luit dans les bois*, op. 61, no. 3; *Le parfum impérissable*, op. 76, no. 1; *Puisque l'aube grandit*, op. 61, no. 2; *La rose*, op. 51, no. 4]

3176. Jackson, Timothy L. "Gabriel Fauré's Expansions of Nonduple Hypermeter in *La fleur qui va sur l'eau*, Op. 85, No. 2." ITO 12, nos. 3–4 (1992): 1–27.

3177. Jankélévitch, Vladimir. *Gabriel Fauré et ses mélodies*. Paris: Librarie Plon, 1938.

3178. Johansen, Ken. "Gabriel Fauré and the Art of Ambiguity." JALS 43 (1998): 8–44. [*Lydia*, op. 4, no. 2]

3179. Kurtz, James Lawrence. "Problems of Tonal Structure in Songs of Gabriel Fauré." Ph.D. diss., Brandeis University, 1970.

3180. Orledge, Robert. "The Two Endings of Fauré's *Soir*." ML 60 (1979): 316–22.

3181. Phillips, Edward R. "Smoke, Mirrors, and Prisms: Tonal Contradiction in Fauré." MA 12, no. 1 (1993): 3–24.

3182. Sommers, Paul Bartholin. "Fauré and His Songs: The Relationship of Text, Melody, and Accompaniment." D.M.A. diss., University of Illinois, 1969.

String Quartet, Op. 121

3183. Knox, Roger Martin. "Counterpoint in Gabriel Fauré's String Quartet, Op. 121." MA diss., Indiana University, 1978.

Thème et variations, Op. 73

3184. Dommel-Diény, Amy. *Gabriel Fauré*. Dommel-Diény 12. Paris: Dommel-Diény, 1974.

Violin Sonata No. 1, Op. 13
3185. Rorick, William C. "The A Major Violin Sonatas of Fauré and Franck: A Stylistic Comparison." MR 42 (1981): 46–55.
3186. Tubergen, David Gene. "A Stylistic Analysis of Selected Violin and Piano Sonatas of Fauré, Saint-Saëns, and Franck." Ph.D. diss., New York University, 1985.

Various Works
3187. Favre, Max. *Gabriel Faurés Kammermusik.* Zurich: Niehans, 1947.
3188. Gervais, Françoise. *Étude comparée des langages harmoniques de Fauré et de Debussy.* Paris: Revue musicale, 1971.
3189. Nectoux, Jean-Michel. "Works Renounced, Themes Rediscovered: *Elements pour une thématique fauréenne.*" NCM 2 (1978–1979): 231–44.

FEBEL, REINHARD (b. 1952)
3190. Febel, Reinhard. "Anmerkungen zu *Komitas* und Variationen für Orchester." N 2 (1981–1982): 35–40.
3191. Heiland, Tilman. "Reinhard Febel: Variationen für Orchester." N 2 (1981–1982): 41–44.
3192. Hinz, Klaus-Michael. "The Tradition of Mannerism: Reinhard Febel." CMR 12, no. 1 (1995): 103–23.

FEDELE, IVAN (b. 1953)
3193. Nieminen, Risto, ed. *Ivan Fedele.* Paris: IRCAM, 1996.

FELCIANO, RICHARD (b. 1930)
3194. Christiansen, Sigurd Olaf. "The Sacred Music of Richard Felciano: An Analytical Study." D.M.A. diss., University of Illinois, 1977.

FELDMAN, MORTON (1926–1987)

Coptic Light
3195. Karallus, Manfred. "Résistance gegen die Welt: Morton Feldmans *Coptic Light.*" MTX 52 (1994): 47–50.

Crippled Symmetry
3196. Gronemeyer, Gisela. "Momente von grosser Schönheit: Zu Morton Feldmans neuem Stück *Crippled Symmetry.*" MTX 4 (1984): 5–9.

Durations III
3197. DeLio, Thomas. "Toward an Art of Imminence: Morton Feldman's *Durations III, #3.*" I 12, no. 3 (1983): 465–80. Reprint, M-DeLio: 29–47.

For Bunita Marcus
3198. Franke, Daniël. "Analytische Contemplation des Feldmanschen Klavierstückes *For Bunita Marcus.*" In *Morton Feldman,* ed. Heinz-Klaus Metzger and Rainer Riehn, 135–47. Munich: Text + Kritik, 1986.

Instruments I
3199. Böttinger, Peter. "Das exakt Ungefähre: Ein analytischer Versuch über *Instruments 1* (1974) von Morton Feldman." In *Morton Feldman,* ed. Heinz-Klaus Metzger and Rainer Riehn, 105–14. Munich: Text + Kritik, 1986.

Last Pieces
3200. Hirata, Catherine Costello. "The Sounds of the Sounds Themselves: Analyzing the Early Music of Morton Feldman." PNM 34, no. 1 (1996): 6–27.

Palais de Mari
3201. Mörchen, Raoul. "Music as a Musical Process: Morton Feldmans *Palais de Mari.*" MTX 66 (1996): 53–62.

Patterns in a Chromatic Field (Untitled Composition)
3202. Hummel, Thomas. "Qualitativer Sprung: Morton Feldmans Untitled Composition." MTX 52 (1994): 51–56.

Piano and Orchestra
3203. Guillot, Matthieu. "Poétique sonore de Morton Feldman: Lenteur, douceur et fragilité (sur *Piano & Orchestra*)." ANM 37 (2000): 80–90.

Rothko Chapel
3204. Johnson, Steven. "*Rothko Chapel* and Rothko's Chapel." PNM 32, no. 2 (1994): 6–53.

Three Voices
3205. McGuire, John. "Wiederholung und Veränderung: Morton Feldmans *Three Voices.*" MTX 20 (1987): 26–29.

Various Works
3206. Gruhn, Wilfried. "Klang und Stille: Gedanken zur kompositorischen Arbeit Morton Feldmans." MB 14, no. 3 (1982): 147–52.

FERGUSON, HOWARD (1908–1999)

3207. McBurney, Gerard. "Howard Ferguson in 1983." TEMPO 147 (1983): 2–6.
3208. Russell, John. "Howard Ferguson's Concerto for Piano and String Orchestra." TEMPO 24 (1952): 24–25.

FERNEYHOUGH, BRIAN (b. 1943)

Bone Alphabet

3209. Schick, Steven. "Developing an Interpretive Context: Learning Brian Ferneyhough's *Bone Alphabet*." PNM 32, no. 1 (1994): 132–53.

Carceri d'invenzione I–III

3210. Cavallotti, Pietro. "Einige Bermerkungen über die Tonhöhenorganisation in Brian Ferneyhoughs Zyklus Carceri d'invenzione." MPSS 13 (2000): 48–53.
3211. Toop, Richard. "'Prima le parole . . .' (On the Sketches for Ferneyhough's *Carceri d'invenzione I–III*)." PNM 32, no. 1 (1994): 154–75.

Cassandra's Dream Song

3212. Waterman, Ellen. "*Cassandra's Dream Song*: A Literary Feminist Perspective." PNM 32, no. 2 (1994): 154–72.

Kurze Schatten II

3213. Andersson, Magnus. "Brian Ferneyhough: *Kurze Schatten II*, considérations d'un interprète." CC 8 (1988): 128–38.

Lemma-Icon-Epigram

3214. Melchiorre, Alessandro. "Les labyrinthes de Ferneyhough: À propos du Deuxième Quatour et de *Lemma-Icon-Epigram*." ENT 3 (1987): 69–88.
3215. Toop, Richard. "Brian Ferneyhough's *Lemma-Icon-Epigram*." PNM 28, no. 2 (1990): 52–100. French translation, CC 8 (1988): 86–127.

String Quartet No. 2

3216. Ferneyhough, Brian. "Deuxième quatour à cordes." Trans. Terence Waterhouse. CC 8 (1988): 149–62.
3217. Melchiorre, Alessandro. "Les labyrinthes de Ferneyhough: À propos du Deuxième Quatour et de *Lemma-Icon-Epigram*." ENT 3 (1987): 69–88.

String Quartet No. 4

3218. Lippe, Klaus. "'Pitch Systems' im Vierten Streichquartett von Brian Ferneyhough." MPSS 13 (2000): 54–60.

String Trio

3219. Mahnkopf, Claus-Steffen. "Ferneyhoughs Streichtrio." MAS 1, nos. 1–2 (1997): 93–104.

Superscriptio

3220. Toop, Richard. "On *Superscriptio*: An Interview with Brian Ferneyhough, and an Analysis." CMR 13, no. 1 (1995): 3–17.
3221. ———. "*Superscriptio* pour flute piccolo solo." ENT 3 (1987): 95–106.

Terrain

3222. Feller, Ross. "Slippage and Strata in Brian Ferneyhough's *Terrain*." EXT 9, no. 2 (1999): 77–122.

Trittico per Gertrude Stein

3223. Feller, Ross. "Random Funnels in Brian Ferneyhough's *Trittico per Gertrude Stein*." MPSS 10 (1997): 32–38.

Unity Capsule

3224. Ferneyhough, Brian. "*Unity Capsule*: Un journal de bord." Trans. Terence Waterhouse. CC 8 (1988): 139–48.

Various Works

3225. Ferneyhough, Brian, interviewed by Paul Driver. "Speaking with Tongues: Composing for the Voice–A Correspondence-Conversation." CMR 5 (1989): 155–83.
3226. Potter, Keith, Kathryn Lukas, Kevin Corner, and Malcolm Barry. "Brian Ferneyhough." CT 20 (1979): 4–15.
3227. Szendy, Peter, ed. *Brian Ferneyhough*. Paris: IRCAM, 1999.

FERRERO, LORENZO (b. 1951)

3228. Ferrero, Lorenzo. "*Marilyn*: Anmerkungen zur Oper." N 3 (1982–1983): 142–46.

FIELD, JOHN (1782–1837)

3229. Branson, David. *John Field and Chopin*. London: Barrie & Jenkins, 1972.
3230. Hibbard, Trevor Davies. "John Field's *Rondeaux* on 'Speed the Plough.'" MR 24 (1963): 139–46.
3231. Piggott, Patrick. *The Life and Music of John Field, 1782–1837, Creator of the Nocturne*. Berkeley: University of California Press, 1973.

3232. Southall, Geneva Handy. "John Field's Piano Concertos: An Analytical and Historical Study." Ph.D. diss., University of Iowa, 1966.

FINE, IRVING (1914–1962)
3233. Epstein, David. "Symphony (1962)." PNM 3, no. 2 (1965): 160–64.
3234. M-Wise.

FINNEY, ROSS LEE (1906–1997)
3235. Amman, Douglas D. "The Choral Music of Ross Lee Finney." Ph.D. diss., University of Cincinnati, 1972.
3236. Cooper, Paul. "The Music of Ross Lee Finney." MQ 53 (1967): 1–21
3237. Finney, Ross Lee. "Concerning My *Fantasy in Two Movements* (1958)." F-Cuyler: 182–90.
3238. Haines, Don Robert. "The Eight String Quartets of Ross Lee Finney." D.M.A. diss., University of Rochester, 1973.
3239. M-Hines: 62–75.
3240. Onderdonk, Henry. "Aspects of Tonality in the Music of Ross Lee Finney." PNM 6, no. 2 (1968): 125–45.

FINNISSY, MICHAEL (b. 1946)
3241. Barrett, Richard. "Michael Finnissy: An Overview." CMR 13, no. 1 (1995): 23–43.
3242. Toop, Richard. "Four Facets of 'The New Complexity.'" CT 32 (1988): 4–50. [String Trio; *Verdi Transcriptions*, Book I]

FIRST, C. P. (b. 1960)
3243. First, C. P. "Metapraxis and Compositional Process in *Tantrum*." TCM 4, no. 6 (1997): 1–4.

FISCHER, IRWIN (1903–1977)
3244. Borroff, Edith. "Spelling and Intention: A Setting of William Alexander Percy's Lyric *A Sea-Bird* (1933) by Irwin Fischer." F-Cuyler: 172–81.

FIŠER, LUBOŠ (1935–1999)
3245. Locke, John R. "An Analysis of *Report* by Luboš Fišer." JBR 20, no. 1 (1984–1985): 9–19.

FLEURY, ANDRÉ (1903–1995)
3246. M-Dorroh.

FLORENTZ, JEAN-LOUIS (b. 1947)
3247. Florentz, Jean-Louis. "The Question of Timbre and Harmonic Vibratos in *Les Laudes* (op. 5) for Organ." CMR 8, no. 1 (1993): 95–111.

FLOTHUIS, MARIUS (1914–2001)
3248. Geraedts, Jaap. "Marius Flothuis: *Canti e Giuochi*." SS 25 (1965): 16–19.

FLOYD, CARLISLE (b. 1926)
3249. Pollack, Howard. "The Reconstruction of *Jonathan Wade*." OQ 8, no. 1 (1991): 62–83.

FOOTE, ARTHUR (1853–1937)
3250. Alviani, Doric. "The Choral Church Music of Arthur William Foote." S.M.D. diss., Union Theological Seminary, 1962.

FÖRSTER, EMANUEL ALOYS (1748–1823)
3251. Longyear, Rey M. "Klassik und Romantik in Emanuel Aloys Försters Nachlass." MAU 2 (1979): 108–16.

FORTNER, WOLFGANG (1907–1987)
3252. Dangel, Arthur. "Wolfgang Fortner: Impromptus." MELOS 27 (1960): 79–84, 107–12.
3253. Döhl, Friedhelm. "Fortners Lorca-Vertonung: *In seinem Garten liebt Don Perlimplin Belisa*." NZM 125 (1964): 183–87.
3254. Engelmann, Hans Ulrich. "Fortners *Phantasie über B-A-C-H*." MELOS 21 (1954): 131–35.
3255. Günther, Siegfried. "Wolfgang Fortner: *The Creation*." MELOS 29 (1961): 109–12.
3256. Kroeker, Dieter. "Fortners Fantasia aus der Pfingstgeschichte." F-Schneider: 50–61.
3257. Lindlar, Heinrich, ed. *Wolfgang Fortner: Eine Monographie, Werkanalysen, Aufsätze, Reden, Offene Briefe 1950–1959*. Rodenkirches/Rhein: P. J. Tonger, 1960.
3258. Lohrmann, Uwe. "Zum geistlichen Werk Wolfgang Fortners: Dem Komponisten zum 75. Geburtstag." MK 52 (1982): 215–25.
3259. Schuhmacher, Gerhard. "Aktualität und Geschichtsbewusstsein als Vernügen: Zu Wolfgang Fortners kompositorischen Prinzipien." NZM 143, no. 11 (1982): 20–28.

FOSS, LUKAS (b. 1922)

3260. Bailey, Donald Lee. "A Study of Stylistic and Compositional Elements of *Anthem* (Stravinsky), *Fragments of Archilochos* (Foss), and *Creation Prologue* (Ussachevsky)." D.M.A. diss., University of Northern Colorado, 1976.

3261. Browne, Bruce Sparrow. "The Choral Music of Lukas Foss." D.M.A. diss., University of Washington, 1976.

3262. Foss, Lukas. "Work-notes for *Echoi*." PNM 3, no. 1 (1964): 54–61.

3263. Gruhn, Wilfried. "Bearbeitung als kompositorische Reflexion in neuer Musik." M 28 (1974): 522–28. [*Baroque Variations*]

3264. ———. "Lukas Foss *Phorion*: Die Obsession einer Melodie von Johann Sebastian Bach in den *Baroque Variations*." MB 13 (1981): 140–53.

3265. M-Wennerstrom. [*Echoi*]

FOSTER, STEPHEN C. (1826–1864)

3266. Gombosi, Otto. "Stephen Foster and 'Gregory Walker.'" MQ 30 (1944): 133–46.

FOULDS, JOHN (1880–1939)

3267. MacDonald, Calum. "John Foulds and the String Quartet." TEMPO 132 (1980): 16–25.

FRANCHETTI, ARNOLD (1905–1993)

3268. Morrison, Watson Wilbur. "The Piano Sonatas of Arnold Franchetti." D.M.A. diss., Boston University, 1972.

FRANCK, CÉSAR (1822–1890)

Mélodies de François Schubert

3269. Scheres, Bernd. "Cesar Francks Bearbeitung der vier Schubert-Lieder." RBM 45 (1991): 61–76.

Organ Works

3270. Dommel-Diény, Amy. *Franck.* Dommel-Diény 11. Paris: Dommel-Diény, 1973. [*Trois chorals*]

3271. Dufourcq, Norbert. *César Franck et la genèse des premières oeuvres d'orgue.* Paris: Schola Cantorum, 1973.

3272. Haag, Herbert. *César Franck als Orgelkomponist.* Kassel: Bärenreiter, 1936.

Prélude, choral et fugue

3273. Dommel-Diény, Amy. *Franck.* Dommel-Diény 11. Paris: Dommel-Diény, 1973.

Quintette

3274. Mompellio, Federico. "Valori cromatici nell Quintetto di César Franck." F-Ghisi (vol.2): 311–30.

String Quartet

3275. Rathert, Wolfgang. "Form und Zeit im Streichquartett César Francks." F-Stephan: 311–32.

3276. Wegener, Bernd. "Cesar Francks Harmonik dargestellt am Streichquartett D-dur." RBM 45 (1991): 109–26.

Symphony, D Minor

3277. Gülke, Peter. "Wider die Übermacht des Thematischen: Zum Verständnis César Franks anhand seinen D-Moll-Sinfonie." BM 13 (1971): 261–72.

3278. Hollander, Hans. "Die tonpoetische Idee in der Sinfonie César Francks." SMZ 99 (1959): 425–27.

Violin Sonata

3279. Rorick, William C. "The A Major Violin Sonatas of Fauré and Franck: A Stylistic Comparison." MR 42 (1981): 46–55.

3280. Schneider, Herbert. "Analyse der Violinsonate A-dur von C. Franck." RBM 45 (1991): 127–44.

3281. Tubergen, David Gene. "A Stylistic Analysis of Selected Violin and Piano Sonatas of Fauré, Saint-Saëns, and Franck." Ph.D. diss., New York University, 1985.

Various Works

3282. Cranford, Dennis Ray. "Harmonic and Contrapuntal Techniques in the Late Keyboard Works of César Franck." Ph.D. diss., University of North Texas, 1992.

3283. Kreutzer, Peter. *Die sinfonische Form César Francks.* Düsseldorf: Dissertations-Verlag Nolte, 1938.

3284. Matter, Jean. "De quelques sources beethoveniennes de César Franck." SMZ 99 (1959): 231–34.

3285. Monnikendam, Marius. *César Franck.* Regensburg: Bosse, 1976.

3286. Sanger, G. Norman. "Chromaticism in the Keyboard Works of Franck and Fauré." Ph.D. diss., University of Pittsburgh, 1976.

3287. Seipt, Angelus. *César Francks symphonische Dichtungen.* Regensburg: Bosse, 1981.

3288. Wegener, Bernd. *César Francks Harmonik.* Regensburg: Bosse, 1976.

FRANCK, EDUARD (1817–1893)

3289. Bittner, Johannes. "Die Klaviersonaten Eduard Francks (1817–1893) und anderer Kleinmeister seiner Zeit." Ph.D. diss., Universität Hamburg, 1968.

FRAZZI, VITO (1888–1975)

3290. Prosperi, Carlo. "Vito Frazzi e il *Re Lear.*" CHI 14 (1981): 333–60.

FREEDMAN, HARRY (b. 1922)

3291. Dixon, Gail. "Cellular Metamorphosis and Structural Compartmentalization in Harry Freedman's *Chalumeau.*" SMUWO 6 (1981): 48–76.

3292. ———. "Harry Freedman: A Survey." SMUWO 5 (1980): 122–44.

FRENCH, JACOB (1754–1817)

3293. Genuchi, Marvin C. "The Life and Music of Jacob French (1754–1817), Colonial American Composer." Ph.D. diss., University of Iowa, 1963.

FRICKER, PETER RACINE (1920–1990)

3294. M-Hines: 76–88.

3295. Kimbell, Michael Alexander. "Peter Racine Fricker's Second String Quartet: An Analysis." D.M.A. diss., Cornell University, 1973.

FRID, GÉZA (1904–1989)

3296. Wijdeveld, Wolfgang. "Géza Frid." SS 18 (1964): 1–9.

FRIEDMAN, IGNACY (1882–1948)

3297. Auh, Mijai Youn. "Piano Variations by Brahms, Liszt, and Friedman on a Theme by Paganini." D.M. diss., Indiana University, 1980.

FRITZE, GREGORY (b. 1954)

3298. Camejo, Francisco Carlos Bueno, and Oscar Creus Ortola. "Gregory P. Fritze's String Quartet (1994)." TCM 6, no. 8 (1999): 17–20.

FROMMEL, GERHARD (1906–1984)

3299. Osthoff, Wolfgang. "'In Ketten tanzen': Symphonische Scherzi im totalitären Staat." JSIM (1994): 158–98. [Symphony No. 1]

3300. ———. "Symphonien beim Ende des Zweiten Weltkriegs: Strawinsky–Frommel–Schostakowitsch." ACTA 60, no. 1 (1988): 62–104. [Symphony No. 2]

FRY, WILLIAM HENRY (1813–1864)

3301. Kauffman, Byron F. "The Choral Works of George F. Bristow (1825–1898) and William Henry Fry (1813–1864)." D.M.A. diss., University of Illinois, 1975.

FURRER, BEAT (b. 1954)

3302. Becher, Christoph. "Der freie Fall des Architekten: Beat Furrers Oper *Die Blinden.*" NZM 151, nos. 7–8 (1990): 34–40.

FURRER-MÜNCH, FRANZ (b. 1924)

3303. Meyer, Thomas. "Aus dem Notenbuch eines Träumers: Der Komponist Franz Furrer-Münch." DI 37 (1993): 6–9.

– G –

GABURO, KENNETH (1926–1993)

3304. Logan, Jackie Dale. "*Mouthpiece* by Kenneth Gaburo: A Performer's Analysis of the Composition." Ph.D. diss., University of California, San Diego, 1977.

GADE, NIELS W. (1817–1890)

3305. Hong, Barbara Blanchard. "Gade Models for Grieg's Symphony and Piano Sonata." DAM 15 (1984): 27–28. [Piano Sonata, op. 28; Symphony no. 1, op. 5 ("Paa Sjølunds fagre sletter")]

GÁL, HANS (1890–1987)

3306. Oliver, Roger. "Hans Gál at 95." TEMPO 155 (1985): 2–7.

GALINDO DIMAS, BLAS (1910–1993)

3307. Conant, Richard Paul. "The Vocal Music of Blas Galindo: A Study of the Choral and Solo Vocal Works of a Twentieth-Century Mexican Composer." D.M.A. diss., University of Texas, 1977.

GAMER, CARLTON (b. 1929)

3308. Gamer, Carlton. "Notes on the Structure of *Piano Raga Music*." PNM 12, nos. 1–2 (1973–1974): 217–30. [Includes complete score: 191–216]

GÄNSBACHER, JOHANN (1778–1844)

3309. Schneider, Manfred. "Studien zu den Messenkompositionen Johann Baptist Gänsbachers (1778–1884)." Ph.D. diss., University of Innsbruck, 1976.

GASSER, ULRICH (b. 1950)

3310. Gasser, Ulrich. "Bilderbuch für zwei Klaviere: Vier Paprikafrüchte." N 2 (1981–1982): 110–19.

3311. ———. "*Passion II/Stationen* (75)1976(77)." SMZ 119 (1979): 274–79.

GAUDIBERT, ERIC (b. 1936)

3312. Barras, Vincent, Jacques Demierre, and Alfred Zimmerlin. "Les œuvres récentes d'Eric Gaudibert." DI 12 (1987): 4–9.

3313. Gaudibert, Eric. "*Variations lyriques* pour violoncello solo (1966–1976)." SZM 117 (1977): 150–53.

GEERS, DOUGLAS (b. 1968)

3314. Geers, Douglas. "Oblique Strategies." CM 67–68 (1999): 109–28. [*Reality House, Ripples*]

GEHLHAAR, ROLF (b. 1943)

3315. Gehlhaar, Rolf. "*Fünf deutsche Tänze*." DBNM 16 (1977): 56–64.

GEIJER, ERIK GUSTAF (1783–1847)

3316. Geijerstam, Claes af. "Kring Erik Gustaf Geijers cellosonat." STM 67 (1985): 59–76.

GEISSLER, FRITZ (1921–1984)

Handzettel an einige Nachbarn

3317. Kapst, Erich. "Fritz Geisslers *Handzettel an einige Nachbarn*." MG 9, no. 1 (1959): 10–14.

Schöpfer Mensch

3318. Schönfelder, Gerd. "Fritz Geisslers Oratorium *Schöpfer Mensch*." MG 23 (1973): 408–12.

Symphonies

3319. Heinecke-Oertel, Walther. "*Sinfonische Suite* von Fritz Geissler." MG 16 (1966): 242–43. [No. 1, rev. as *Sinfonische Suite*]

3320. Hennenberg, Fritz. "Das Sinfonische und das Dramatische: Kommentar zu Fritz Geisslers III. Sinfonie." MG 18 (1968): 610–15.

3321. Kapst, Erich. "Fritz Geisslers Sinfonische Sätze." MG 10 (1960): 146–49.

3322. Klement, Udo. "Analysen: Sinfonie Nr. 9 von Fritz Geissler." MG 30 (1980): 325–29.

3323. Schneider, Frank. "Gedenken zur V. Sinfonie von Fritz Geissler." MG 20 (1970): 595–99.

3324. ———. "Gedenken zur VIII. Sinfonie von Fritz Geissler." MG 25 (1975): 204–7.

3325. Schönfelder, Gerd. "VII. Sinfonie von Fritz Geissler." MG 24 (1974): 199–202.

3326. Wolf, Werner. "Fritz Geisslers II. Sinfonie." MG 16 (1966): 91–98.

Zerbrochene Krug

3327. Schneider, Frank. "*Der zerbrochene Krug*: Oper von Fritz Geissler." MG 24 (1974): 11–18.

GENZMER, HARALD (b. 1909)

3328. Müllisch, Hermann. *Die A-Capella-Chorwerke Harald Genzmers: Stilkritische Untersuchungen zur Textausdeutung.* Berlin: Ries & Erler, 1982.

GEORGESCU, CORNELIU DAN (b. 1938)

3329. Redepenning, Dorothea. "Die Idee einer 'Musiqe atemporelle': Zum *Model Mioritic* von Corneliu Dan Georgescu." HJM 16 (1999): 291–307.

GERHARD, ROBERTO (1896–1970)

Alta naixença del rei en Jaume

3330. Walker, Geoffrey J., and David Drew. "Gerhard's Cantata." TEMPO 139 (1981): 12–18.

Concerto for Orchestra

3331. Sproston, Darren. "Thematicism in Gerhard's Concerto for Orchestra." TEMPO 184 (1993): 18–22.

Soirées de Barcelone

3332. MacDonald, Calum. "*Soirées de Barcelone*: A Preliminary Report." TEMPO 139 (1981): 19–26.

Symphonies

3333. Ballantine, Christopher. "The Symphony in the Twentieth Century: Some Aspects of Its Tradition and Innovation." MR 32 (1971): 219–32. [No. 1]

3334. Bradshaw, Susan. "Symphony No. 2/*Metamorphoses*: The Compositional Background." TEMPO 39 (1981): 28–32.

3335. Cunningham, Michael Gerald. "An Analysis of the First Symphony of Roberto Gerhard." Ph.D. diss., Indiana University, 1973.

3336. MacDonald, Calum. "Sense and Sound: Gerhard's Fourth Symphony." TEMPO 100 (1972): 25–29.

Wind Quintet

3337. Nash, Peter Paul. "The Wind Quintet." TEMPO 139 (1981): 5–11.

Various Works

3338. Davies, Hugh. "The Electronic Music." TEMPO 139 (1981): 36–38.

3339. Donat, Misha. "Thoughts on the Late Works." TEMPO 139 (1981): 39–43.

3340. Glock, William, ed. "A Tribute to Roberto Gerhard on His Sixtieth Birthday." SCORE 17 (1956): 5–72. [Special issue]

GERSCHEFSKI, EDWIN (1909–1992)

3341. Vaglio, Anthony Joseph, Jr. "The Compositional Significance of Joseph Schillinger's System of Musical Composition as Reflected in the Works of Edwin Gerschefski." Ph.D. diss., University of Rochester, 1977.

3342. Yerlow, Stanley Clinton. "Edwin Gerschefski's Preludes, Op. 6, Nos. 1–6, and Three Dances, Op. 11, Nos. 1–3." D.M.A. diss., University of Rochester, 1980.

GERSHWIN, GEORGE (1898–1937)

Concerto in F

3343. Shirley, Wayne D. "Scoring the Concerto in F: George Gershwin's First Orchestration." AMUS 3, no. 3 (1985): 277–98.

3344. Vinay, Gianfranco. "Gershwin e l'analisi impertinente." RIM 26 (1991): 59–78.

"I Got Rhythm" Variations

3345. Beyer, Richard. "George Gershwins *Variations on 'I Got Rhythm.'*" M 49, no. 4 (1995): 233–38.

Porgy and Bess

3346. ASO 103 (1987).

3347. Nauert, Paul. "Theory and Practice in *Porgy and Bess*: The Gershwin-Schillinger Connection." MQ 78, no. 1 (1994): 9–33.

3348. Puzan, Matthew Davis. "Dynamic Symmetry in the Music of George Gershwin and Arnold Schoenberg." TCM 2, no. 12 (1995): 1–4. ["Summertime"]

3349. Starr, Lawrence. "Gershwin's 'Bess, You Is My Woman Now': The Sophistication and Subtlety of a Great Tune." MQ 72, no. 4 (1986): 429–48.

3350. ———. "Toward a Reevaluation of Gershwin's *Porgy and Bess*." AMUS 2, no. 2 (1984): 25–37.

3351. Vinay, Gianfranco. "Gershwin e l'analisi impertinente." RIM 26 (1991): 59–78. ["Bess, You Is My Woman Now"]

Rhapsody in Blue

3352. Schiff, David. *Gershwin: Rhapsody in Blue.* Cambridge: Cambridge University Press, 1997.

3353. Vinay, Gianfranco. "Gershwin e l'analisi impertinente." RIM 26 (1991): 59–78.

Various Works

3354. Gilbert, Steven E. "Gershwin's Art of Counterpoint." MQ 70 (1984): 423–56.

3355. ———. *The Music of Gershwin.* New Haven, Conn.: Yale University Press, 1995.

3356. Schwartz, Charles M. "The Life and Orchestral Works of George Gershwin." Ph.D. diss., New York University, 1969.

GERTILUCCI, ARMANDO (1939–1989)

3357. Heister, Hanns-Werner. "Kantabilität und Klangkonstruktion: Ein Werkporträt des italienischen Komponisten Armando Gentilucci." MTX 12 (1985): 6–10.

GIANNINI, VITTORIO (1903–1966)

3358. Mullins, Joe Barry. "A Comparative Analysis of Three Symphonies for Band." JBR 6, no. 1 (1969–1970): 17–28. [Symphony No. 3]

3359. Parris, Robert. "Vittorio Giannini and the Romantic Tradition." JR 4, no. 2 (1957): 32–46.

3360. Wynn, James Leroy. "An Analysis of the First Movement of the Symphony No. 3 for Band by Vittorio Giannini." JBR 1, no. 2 (1964–1965): 19–26.

GIBBS, CECIL ARMSTRONG (1889–1960)
3361. M-Curtis.

GIDEON, MIRIAM (1906–1996)
3362. Fertig, Judith Pinnolis. "An Analysis of Selected Works of the American Composer Miriam Gideon (1906–) in Light of Contemporary Jewish Musical Trends." M.A. thesis, University of Cincinnati, 1978.
3363. Perle, George. "The Music of Miriam Gideon." ACA 7, no. 4 (1957): 2–8.

GILBERT, HENRY F. (1868–1928)
3364. Longyear, Katherine E. "Henry F. Gilbert: His Life and Works." Ph.D. diss., University of Rochester, 1968.
3365. Longyear, Katherine E., and Rey M. Longyear. "Henry F. Gilbert's Unfinished *Uncle Remus* Opera." Y 10 (1974): 50–67.

GILLINGHAM, DAVID (b. 1947)
3366. Schnoor, Neal H. "An Analysis of David Gillingham's *Prophecy of the Earth* (1993)." JBR 34, no. 2 (1999): 63–82.

GINASTERA, ALBERTO (1916–1983)
3367. Bottazzi, Bruno G. "A Performance Guide to Selected Piano Music of Alberto Ginastera." Ph.D. diss., New York University, 1984.
3368. Chase, Gilbert. "Alberto Ginastera: Argentine Composer." MQ 43 (1957): 439–60.
3369. Hanley, Mary Ann. "The Solo Piano Compositions of Alberto Ginastera (1916–)." D.M.A. diss., University of Cincinnati, 1969.
3370. Kuss, Malena. "Type, Derivation, and Use of Folk Idioms in Ginastera's *Don Rodrigo* (1964)." LAMR 1 (1980): 176–95.
3371. Paik, Eui. "An Analysis of the First Piano Concerto (1961) by Alberto Ginastera." D.M.A. diss., Indiana University, 1979.
3372. Richards, James Edward, Jr. "Pitch Structure in the Opera *Don Rodrigo* of Alberto Ginastera." Ph.D. diss., University of Rochester, 1986.
3373. Suarez Urtubey, Pola. "Alberto Ginastera's *Don Rodrigo*." TEMPO 74 (1965): 11–18.
3374. ———. "Ginastera's *Bomarzo*." TEMPO 84 (1968): 14–21.
3375. Tabor, Michelle. "Alberto Ginastera's Late Instrumental Style." LAMR 15, no. 1 (1994): 1–31. [Guitar Sonata, Piano Quintet, *Puneña* No. 2]
3376. Wallace, David Edward. "Alberto Ginastera: An Analysis of His Style and Technique of Composition." Ph.D. diss., Northwestern University, 1964.

GIORDANO, UMBERTO (1867–1947)
3377. ASO 121 (1989). [*Andrea Chénier*]

GIULIANI, MAURO (1781–1829)
3378. Heck, Thomas F. "The Birth of the Classic Guitar and Its Cultivation in Vienna, Reflected in the Career and Compositions of Mauro Giuliani (d. 1829)." Ph.D. diss., Yale University, 1970.

GLASS, PHILIP (b. 1937)
3379. Cebulla, Gregor. "*Koyaanisquatsi*: Eine bebilderte musikalische Rede." MB 18, no. 9 (1986): 789–95.
3380. Lassetter, Leslie. "The Position of *Satyagraha* in the Operatic Triology of Philip Glass." MRF 1 (1986): 15–40.
3381. Lemieux, Glenn Claude. "Construction, Reconstruction, and Deconstruction: *Music in Twelve Parts* by Philip Glass." Ph.D. diss., University of Iowa, 2000.
3382. M-Mertens: 67–86.
3383. M-Potter.
3384. Raickovich, Milos. "*Einstein on the Beach* by Philip Glass: A Musical Analysis." Ph.D. diss., City University of New York, 1994.
3385. Smith, Dave. "The Music of Phil Glass." CT 11 (1975): 27–33.
3386. Welch, Allison. "Meetings Along the Edge: *Svara* and *Tāla* in American Minimal Music." AMUS 17, no. 2 (1999): 179–99. [*Satyagraha*]
3387. York, Wesley. "Form and Process in *Two Pages* by Philip Glass." SONUS 1, no. 2 (1980): 28–50.

GLAUS, DANIEL (b. 1957)
3388. Nyffeler, Max. "Zur Kammeroper *Zerstreute Wege* von Daniel Glaus." DI 11 (1987): 12–13.

GLAZUNOV, ALEKSANDR KONSTANTINOVICH (1865–1936)

3389. Abraham, Gerald. "Glazunov and the String Quartet." TEMPO 73 (1964): 16–21.

3390. Cherbuliez, Antoine-Elisée. "Alexander Glasunows Kammermusik." MO 4 (1967): 45–64.

3391. M-Taruskin. [*The Seasons*, Symphony No. 3]

GLINKA, MIKHAIL IVANOVICH (1804–1857)

3392. DeVoto, Mark. "The Russian Submediant in the Nineteenth Century." CM 59 (1995): 48–76. [*Ruslan and Lyudmila*]

3393. Rennicke, Klaus. "Sonatenform–einmal auf russisch: Die Ouverture zu Glinkas Oper *Ruslan und Ludmilla*." MB 18, no. 12 (1986): 1079–81.

3394. Rowen, Ruth Halle. "Glinka's Tour of Folk Modes on the Wheel of Harmony." F-Schwarz: 35–54. [*Ruslan and Lyudmila*]

3395. Woodside, Mary S. "Leitmotiv in Russia: Glinka's Use of the Whole-Tone Scale." NCM 14, no. 1 (1990): 67–74. [*Ruslan and Lyudmila*]

GLOBOKAR, VINKO (b. 1934)

3396. Bachmann, Claus-Henning. "Der Weg nach draussen." NZM 144, no. 1 (1983): 15–18. [*Miserere*]

3397. Klüppelholz, Werner. "Von Nächtlichen Schrecken: Zu Vinko Globokars *Discours VI* für Streichquartett." N 5 (1984–1985): 252–55.

3398. König, Wolfgang. *Vinko Globokar: Komposition und Improvisation.* Wiesbaden: Breitkopf & Härtel, 1977.

3399. Wilson, Peter Niklas. "'Das Malheur ist schon gemacht': Vinko Globokars *Elégie balkanique*." MTX 53 (1994): 11–16.

GOEHR, ALEXANDER (b. 1932)

3400. Ballantine, Christopher. "The Symphony in the Twentieth Century: Some Aspects of Its Tradition and Innovation." MR 32 (1971): 219–32. [*Little Symphony*]

3401. Northcott, Bayan. "Alexander Goehr: The Recent Music." TEMPO 124 (1978): 10–15; 125 (1978): 12–18.

3402. Rowlands, Jeffrey. "Twelve-Note Methodology in the Music of Alexander Goehr." Ph.D. diss., University of Surrey, 1989.

3403. Wood, Hugh. "The Choral Work of Alexander Goehr." ACR 8, no. 2 (1965): 6–8.

GOETHALS, LUCIEN (b. 1931)

3404. Geysen, Frans. "Lucien Goethals' muziek voor orgel-solo." RBM 54 (2000): 179–88.

3405. Moelants, Dirk. "Rhythm in Lucien Goethals' Electroacoustic Works." RBM 54 (2000): 143–56. [*Contrapuntos, Otros Momentos, Study II*]

3406. Rathé, Filip. "De vocaal-instrumentale muziek van Lucien Goethals, musicus poeticus in de twintigste eeuw." RBM 54 (2000): 157–78.

3407. Sabbe, Hermann. "Lucien Goethals: Le Constructivisme bifonctionnel." *Jaarboek IPEM* (1967): 33–59.

GOEYVAERTS, KAREL (1923–1993)

3408. Decroupet, Pascal, and Elena Ungeheuer. "Karel Goeyvaerts und die serielle Tonbandmusik." RBM 48 (1994): 95–118. [*Compositie no. 4 met dode tonen*]

3409. Delaere, Mark, and Jeroen D'Hoe. "Structural Aspects of the New Tonality in Goeyvaerts' String Quartet *The Seven Seals*." RBM 48 (1994): 133–50. [*De Zeven Zegels*]

3410. Sabbe, Hermann. "Vom Serialismus zum Minimalismus: Der Werdegang eines Manierismus; Der Fall Goeyvaerts, 'Minimalist avant la letter.'" N 3 (1982–1983): 203–8.

3411. Toop, Richard. "Messiaen/Goeyvaerts, Fano/Stockhausen, Boulez." PNM 13, no. 1 (1974–1975): 141–69. [Sonata for Two Pianos]

3412. Vervloft, Willy. "Transformatietechnieken in een repetitief werk: Een analyse van Karel Goeyvaerts' *Pas à Pas*." RBM 48 (1994): 119–32.

3413. Wauters, Christine, Mark Delaere, and Jef Lysens. "Karel Goeyvaerts' *Litanie V* for Harpsichord and Tape or Several Harpsichords." CMR 19, no. 4 (2000): 115–27.

GOLDMAN, RICHARD FRANKO (1910–1980)

3414. Lester, Noel K. "Richard Franko Goldman: His Life and Works." D.M.A. diss., Peabody Conservatory, 1984.

GOLDMANN, FRIEDRICH (b. 1941)

3415. Schneider, Frank. "Die Analyse: Friedrich Goldmann: *Sing Lessing*, Komposition für Bariton und 6 Spieler." MG 29 (1979): 137–43.

3416. ———. "Die Analyse: Sinfonie 2 von Friedrich Goldmann." MG 28 (1978): 30–35.

3417. ———. "Analysen: Fünf Gesichtspunkte zum Konzert für Oboe und Orchester von Friedrich Goldman." MG 30 (1980): 329–33.

3418. ———. "Angemessene Reaktionen: Friedrich Goldmanns *Ensemblekonzert 2.*" MTX 23 (1988): 10–13.

3419. ———. "Dialog ohne Kompromiß: Das Klavierkonzert von Friedrich Goldmann." BM 31, no. 4 (1989): 244–53.

3420. ———. "Rebellion gegen mauerfeste Gefangennahme? *Sonata a quattro* von Friedrich Goldmann." MTX 39 (1991): 16–18.

3421. ———. "Sinfonie für Orchester von Friedrich Goldmann." MG 24 (1974): 143–49.

GOLDMARK, KARL (1830–1915)

3422. Kecskeméti, István. "Liturgical Elements in the Opera *The Queen of Sheba* (1875) by Karl Goldmark." OM 10 (1990–1991): 229–40.

GOLDSCHMIDT, BERTHOLD (1903–1996)

3423. Matthews, David. "Berthold Goldschmidt: The Chamber and Instrumental Music." TEMPO 145 (1983): 20–25.

GOOSSENS, EUGENE (1893–1962)

3424. Hull, Robin. "Two Symphonies: Eugene Goossens and Lennox Berkeley." MR 4 (1943): 229–42.

3425. Smith, Judith Carla. "The Instrumental Chamber Music of Sir Eugene Goossens." Ph.D. diss., University of Cincinnati, 1985.

GORDON, MICHAEL (b. 1956)

3426. Gann, Kyle. "Downtown Beats for the 1990s: Rhys Chatham, Mikel Rouse, Michael Gordon, Larry Polansky, Ben Neill." CMR 10, no. 1 (1994): 33–49.

GÓRECKI, HENRYK MIKOŁAJ (b. 1933)

3427. Thomas, Adrian. "The Music of Henryk Mikotaj Górecki: The First Decade." CT 27 (1983): 10–20.

3428. ———. "A Pole Apart: The Music of Górecki since 1965." CT 28 (1984): 20–31.

GÖRNER, HANS-GEORG (1908–1984)

3429. Vetter, Walther. "Görners Cello-Konzert Opus 41: Uraufführung in Gotha." MG 14 (1964): 533–34.

GOTTSCHALK, ARTHUR (b. 1952)

3430. DeFoor, Keith. "Arthur Gottschalk's Concerto for Wind and Percussion Orchestra." JBR 22, no. 1 (1986): 9–19.

GOTTSCHALK, LOUIS MOREAU (1829–1869)

3431. Doyle, John G. "The Piano Music of Louis Moreau Gottschalk (1829–1869)." Ph.D. diss., New York University, 1960.

3432. Korf, William E. "Gottschalk's One-Act Opera Scene, *Esceñas campestres.*" CM 26 (1978): 62–73.

3433. ———. *The Orchestral Music of Louis Moreau Gottschalk.* Henryville, Pa.: Institute of Mediaeval Music, 1983.

3434. Marrocco, W. Thomas. "America's First Nationalist Composer: Louis Moreau Gottschalk (1829–1869)." F-Ronga: 293–313.

3435. Smith, Paul Ely. "Gottschalk's 'The Banjo,' Op. 15, and the Banjo in the Nineteenth Cenury." CM 50 (1991): 47–61.

GOULD, MORTON (1913–1996)

3436. Mullins, Joe Barry. "A Comparative Analysis of Three Symphonies for Band." JBR 6, no. 1 (1969–1970): 17–28. [Symphony for Band]

3437. ———. "Morton Gould: Symphony for Band." JBR 4, no. 2 (1967–1968): 24–35; 5, no. 1 (1968–1969): 29–47.

GOUNOD, CHARLES-FRANÇOIS (1818–1893)

3438. ASO 2 (1976). [*Faust*]

3439. ASO 41 (1982). [*Roméo et Juliette*]

3440. Ferchault, Guy. *Faust: Une Legende et ses musiciens.* Paris: Larousse, 1948.

3441. Langevin, Kenneth W. "'Au silence des belles nuits': The Earlier Songs of Charles Gounod." Ph.D. diss., Cornell University, 1978.

3442. M-Macy. [*Faust*]

GRAÇA, FERNANDO LOPES (1906–1994)

3443. Peixinho, Jorge. "*Canto de Amore e de Morte*: Introduction and Essay in Morphological Interpretation." EXT 8, no. 2 (1997): 1–8.

GRAETTINGER, BOB (1923–1957)

3444. Morgan, Robert Badgett. "The Music and Life of Robert Graettinger." D.M.A. diss., University of Illinois, 1974.

GRAINGER, PERCY (1882–1961)

3445. Anderson, Peter James. "The Innovative Music of Percy Grainger: An Examination of the Origins and Development of Free Music." M.M. thesis, University of Melbourne, 1979.

3446. Fred, Herbert W. "Percy Grainger's Music for Wind Band." JBR 1, no. 1 (1964–1965): 10–16.

3447. Slattery, Thomas C. "The Hill Songs of Percy Aldridge Grainger." JBR 8, no. 1 (1971–1972): 6–10.

3448. ———. "The Wind Music of Percy Aldridge Grainger." Ph.D. diss., University of Iowa, 1967.

GRANGE, PHILIP (b. 1956)

3449. Williamson, Clive. "Philip Grange." TEMPO 146 (1983): 25–30.

GRECHANINOV, ALEXANDER TIKHONOVICH (1864–1956)

3450. Yasser, Joseph. "Gretchaninoff's 'Heterdox' Compositions." MQ 28 (1942): 309–17.

GRIEG, EDVARD (1843–1907)

Lyric Suite, Op. 54

3451. Sutcliffe, W. Dean. "Grieg's Fifth: The Linguistic Battleground of 'Klokkeklang.'" MQ 80, no. 1 (1996): 161–81.

Peer Gynt Suite No. 1

3452. Saby, Pierre. "Edvard Grieg: *Peer Gynt,* suit d'orchestra no. 1." ANM 29 (1992): 19–29.

Piano Sonata, Op. 7

3453. Hong, Barbara Blanchard. "Gade Models for Grieg's Symphony and Piano Sonata." DAM 15 (1984): 27–28.

Slåtter, Op. 72

3454. Kleiberg, Ståle. "Grieg's *Slåtter,* Op. 72: Change of Musical Style or New Concept of Nationality?" JRMA 121, no. 1 (1996): 46–57.

Symphony, C Minor

3455. Benestad, Finn. "A Note on Edvard Grieg's 'Forbidden' Symphony." M-Lönn: 203–10.

3456. Hong, Barbara Blanchard. "Gade Models for Grieg's Symphony and Piano Sonata." DAM 15 (1984): 27–28.

Various Works

3457. Abraham, Gerald. *Grieg: A Symposium.* London: Drummond, 1948.

3458. Bauer, Werner. "Edvard Grieg." SMZ 97 (1957): 349–52.

3459. Fischer, Kurt von. *Griegs Harmonik und die nordländische Folklore.* Bern: Haupt, 1938.

3460. Kortsen, Bjarne. *Zur Genesis von Edvard Griegs G-Moll Streichquartett, Op. 27.* Haugesund, 1967.

3461. Olson, Robert Wallace. "A Comparative Study of Selected Norwegian Romances by Halfdam-Kjerulf, Edvard Grieg, and Eyvind Alnaes." Ph.D. diss., University of Illinois, 1973.

3462. Sandvik, O. M. "Edward Grief und die norwegische Volksmusik." F-Scheurleer: 271–75.

3463. Schjelderup-Ebbe, Dag. *A Study of Grieg's Harmony, with Special References to His Contributions to Musical Impressionism.* Oslo: Tanum, 1953.

GRIESBACH, KARL-RUDI (1916–2000)

3464. Felix, Werner. "*Afrikanische Sinfonie* von Karl-Rudi Griesbach." MG 17 (1967): 460–66.

3465. Marfordt, Torsten. "Noch einmal *Kolumbus.*" MG 10 (1960): 203–8, 278–83.

3466. Pollack, Hans. "Das *Planetarische Manifest* von Karl-Rudi Griesbach." MG 14 (1964): 530–32.

3467. Winter, Ilse. "*Marike Weiden*: Karl-Rudi Griesbachs neue Oper." MG 10 (1960): 707–12.

GRIFFES, CHARLES T. (1884–1920)

3468. Boda, Daniel. "The Music of Charles T. Griffes." Ph.D. diss., Florida State University, 1962.

3469. Johnson, Richard Oscar. "The Songs of Charles Tomlinson Griffes." D.M.A. diss., University of Iowa, 1977.

3470. M-Morrison.

3471. Nash, Nancy Lee. "Syllogistic Form as a Heuristic Principle in Musical Analysis: Based on the Music of Charles Griffes." M.M. thesis, Florida State University, 1972.

3472. Pratt, Hoon Mo Kim. "The Complete Piano Works of Charles Griffes." D.M.A. diss., Boston University, 1975.

GRISEY, GÉRARD (1946–1998)

3473. Anderson, Juliana. "Dans le contexte." Trans. Jean-Philippe Guye. ENT 8 (1989): 13–23.

3474. Castanet, P. A. "Gérard Grisey and the Foliation of Time." CMR 19, no. 3 (2000): 29–40.

3475. Grisey, Gérard. "*Tempus ex Machina*: A Composer's Reflections on Musical Time." CMR 2, no. 1 (1987): 239–75. French version, ENT 8 (1989): 83–119.

3476. Hervé, Jean-Luc. "*Vortex temporum* von Gérard Grisey: Die Auflösung des Materials in die Zeit." MAS 1, no. 4 (1997): 51–66.

3477. Luminet, Jean-Pierre. "Musique avec pulsar obligé: A propos du *Noir d'étoile* de Gérard Grisey." CAIR 4 (1993): 133–43.

3478. Rose, François. "Introduction to the Pitch Organization of French Spectral Music." PNM 34, no. 2 (1996): 6–39.

3479. Stahnke, Manfred. "Die Schwelle des Hörens: 'Liminales' Denken in *Vortex temporum* von Gérard Grisey." OMZ 54, no. 6 (1999): 21–30.

3480. ———. "Zwei Blumen der reinen Stimmung im 20. Jahrhundert: Harry Partch und Gérard Grisey." HJM 17 (2000): 369–89.

3481. Wilson, Peter Niklas. "Vers une 'écologie des sons': *Partiels* de Gérard Grisey et l'esthétique du groupe de l'Itinéraire." ENT 8 (1989): 55–81. Reprint, ANM 36 (2000): 36–52.

GROLL, EVERMOD (1755–1810)

3482. Lederer, Franz. *Evermod Groll (1755–1810): Leben und Werke eines süddeutschen Klosterkomponisten.* Regensburger Beiträge zur Musikwissenschaft 5. Regensburg: Bosse, 1978.

GRUENBERG, LOUIS (1884–1964)

3483. Nisbett, Robert F. "Louis Gruenberg's American Idiom." AMUS 3, no. 1 (1985): 25–41.

GRÜNEWALD, JEAN-JACQUES (1911–1982)

3484. M-Dorroh.

GUBAYDULINA, SOFIYA ASGATOVNA (b. 1931)

3485. Hamer, Janice Ellen. "Sofia Gubaidulina's Compositional Strategies in the String Trio (1988) and Other Works." Ph.D. diss., City University of New York, 1994.

3486. Meyer-Grotjahn, Hans-Olaf. "Anmerkungen zur Symbolik der *Sieben Worte.*" F-Gubaidulina: 47–51.

3487. Redepenning, Dorothea. "Klingende Symbole des Glaubens: Zur Musik von Sofia Gubaidulina." KJ 84 (2000): 33–49.

GUILMANT, ALEXANDRE (1837–1911)

3488. Johnson, Calvert. "The Organ Sonatas of Félix-Alexandre Guilmant." D.M.A. diss., Northwestern University, 1973.

GÜMBEL, MARTIN (b. 1923)

3489. Gümbel, Martin. "Zu meinem Divertimento für Streicher (1960)." F-Marx: 98–101.

– H –

HAAS, PAVEL (1899–1944)

3490. Karbusicky, Vladimir. "Der Exotismus der Absurdität." HJM 15 (1998): 25–63.

HÁBA, ALOIS (1893–1973)

3491. Vyslouzil, Jirí. "Alois Hába und die Dodekaphonie." SMZ 118 (1978): 95–102.

HADLEY, HENRY (1871–1937)

3492. Canfield, John Clair, Jr. "Henry Kimball Hadley: His Life and Work (1871–1937)." Ed.D. diss., Florida State University, 1960.

HAHN, REYNALDO (1874–1947)

3493. Barber, Carolyn A. "An Introduction to Reynaldo Hahn's *Le Bal de Béatrice d'Este (Suite pour instruments à vent, deux harpes et un piano).*" JBR 36, no. 1 (2000): 47–64.

3494. Gorrell, Lorraine. "Reynaldo Hahn: Composer of Song, Mirror of an Era." MR 46, no. 4 (1985): 284–301.

3495. Schuh, Willi. "Zum Liedwerk Reynaldo Hahns." SBM 2 (1974): 103–26.

HALÉVY, FROMENTAL (1799–1862)

3496. ASO 100 (1987). [*La Juive*]

HALFFTER, CHRISTÓBAL (b. 1930)

3497. Andraschke, Peter. "Traditionsmomente in Kompositionen von Christóbal Halffter, Klaus Huber, und Wolfgang Rihm." M-Brinkmann: 130–52.

HALFFTER, RUDOLFO (1900–1987)

3498. Harper, Nancy Lee. "Rodolfo Halffter and the Superposiciones of Manuel de Falla: Twelve-Tone Applications of 'Apparent Poly-Tonality.'" EXT 8, no. 1 (1996): 57–91. [*Escolio*]

HALLER, HERMANN (b. 1914)

3499. Haller, Hermann. "Komponisten präsentieren neue Arbeiten: 2. Streichquartett." SMZ 113 (1973): 348–52.

HAMBRAEUS, BENGT (1928–2000)

3500. Howard, Chris. "Completing the Circle: Bengt Hambræus's Concerto for Piano and Orchestra." EXT 8, no. 2 (1997): 56–76.

3501. Jacob, Andreas. "Bengt Hambraeus: *Extempore.*" MK 66, no. 4 (1996): 229–33.

3502. MacKay, John. "'Les jeux sont faits!' Ensemble Strategies and Historical 'Borrowing' in the Music of Bengt Hambræus." EXT 10, no. 1 (2000): 12–67.

3503. MacKay-Simmons, Margo. "Aspects of Orchestration in Bengt Hambraeus' *Transfiguration* for Orchestra: Composed Resonance as a Gererator of Musical Texture." EXT 3, no. 2 (1985–1986): 38–55.

3504. Schmiedeke, Ulrich. *Der Beginn der neuen Orgelmusik: Die Orgelkompositionen von Hambraeus, Kagel, und Ligeti.* Munich: Katzbichler, 1981.

3505. Waters, Laraine Olson. "Bengt Hambræus's *Livre d'orgue*: An Exploration of the French Classic Tradition and Beyond." EXT 8, no. 2 (1997): 77–119.

HAMEL, PETER MICHAEL (b. 1947)

3506. Vill, Suzanne. "Gral-Bilder: Zu Peter Michael Hamels *Merlin-Musik.*" NZM 143, no. 11 (1982): 8–13.

HAMILTON, IAIN (1922–2000)

3507. Ballantine, Christopher. "The Symphony in the Twentieth Century: Some Aspects of Its Tradition and Innovation." MR 32 (1971): 219–32. [Sinfonia for Two Orchestras]

3508. Thompson, Randall Scott. "The Solo Clarinet Works of Iain Hamilton." D.M.A. diss., University of Maryland, 1976.

HANISCH, JOSEPH (1812–1892)

3509. Kraus, Eberhard. "Der gregorianische Choral im Orgelschaffen der Regensburger Domorganisten Joseph Hanisch (1812–1892) und Joseph Renner (1868–1934)." F-Haberl: 151–67.

HANKE, KARL (1750–1803)

3510. Abert, Anna Amalie. "*Oberon* in Nord und Süd." F-Gudewill: 51–68. [*Hüon und Amande*]

HANSON, HOWARD (1896–1981)

3511. Carnine, Albert, Jr. "The Choral Music of Howard Hanson." D.M.A. diss., University of Texas, 1977.

3512. M-Mize.

3513. Tuthill, Burnet C. "Howard Hanson." MQ 22 (1936): 140–53.

HARBISON, JOHN (b. 1938)

3514. Harbison, John. "Symmetries and the 'New Tonality.'" CMR 6, no. 2 (1992): 71–79. [String Quartet No. 1, *Words from Paterson*]

3515. Markoch, Jerome R. "*Music for Eighteen Winds* by John Harbison." JBR 30, no. 2 (1995): 1–26.

HARRIS, ROY (1898–1979)

3516. Brookhart, Charles E. "The Choral Works of Aaron Copland, Roy Harris, and Randall Thompson." Ph.D. diss., George Peabody College for Teachers, 1960.

3517. Cox, Sidney Thurber. "The Autogenic Principle in the Melodic Writing of Roy Harris." D.M.A. diss., Cornell University, 1948.

3518. Evett, Robert. "The Harmonic Idiom of Roy Harris." MM 23 (1946): 100–107.

3519. Farwell, Arthur. "Roy Harris." MQ 18 (1932): 18–32.

3520. Mendel, Arthur. "The Quintet of Roy Harris." MM 17 (1939): 25–28.

3521. M-Mize.

3522. Piston, Walter. "Roy Harris." MM 11 (1934): 73–83.

3523. Pye, Richard. "'Asking About the Inside': Schoenberg's 'Idea' in the Music of Roy Harris and William Schuman." MA 19, no. 1 (2000): 69–98. [Symphonies Nos. 1–2]

3524. Slonimsky, Nicolas. "Roy Harris." MQ 33 (1947): 17–37.

3525. Stehman, Dan. "The Symphonies of Roy Harris: An Analytical Study of Linear Materials." Ph.D. diss., University of Southern California, 1973.

HARRISON, LOU (1917–2003)

3526. Harrison, Lou. "About My Fourth Symphony." CM 67–68 (1999): 129–32.

3527. Miller, Leta E., and Fredric Lieberman. "Lou Harrison and the American Gamelan." AMUS 17, no. 2 (1999): 146–78.

3528. Ravenscroft, Brenda. "Working Out the 'Is-tos' and the 'As-tos': Lou Harrison's Fugue for Percussion." PNM 38, no. 1 (2000): 25–43.
3529. Rutman, Neil Clark. "The Solo Piano Works of Lou Harrison." D.M.A. diss., Peabody Conservatory, 1983.

HART, FRITZ (1874–1949)
3530. Forbes, Ann-Marie H. "The Songs of Fritz Bennicke Hart: A Contribution to Literature on Twentieth Century English Solo Song." MMA 15 (1986): 172–86.

HARTING, JULIE (b. 1957)
3531. Harting, Julie. "*Hoc est corpus meum.*" CM 67–68 (1999): 133–37.

HARTMANN, KARL AMADEUS (1905–1963)
Concerto for Piano, Winds, and Percussion
3532. M-Vogt: 260–63.

Piano Sonata (1945, rev. 1947; "den 27. April 1945")
3533. Heister, Hanns-Werner. "Karl Amadeus Hartmann: 2. Klaviersonate '27. April 1945.'" NZM 146, no. 10 (1985): 29–31.
3534. ———. "Voller Angst vor dem Nazi-Terror: Wort und Sinn in Karl Amadeus Hartmanns Instrumentalmusik: Die Klaviersonate '27. April 1945.'" MTX 11 (1985): 9–15.

Symphonie divertissement
3535. McCredie, Andrew D. "Karl Amadeus Hartmann's Envisaged *Symphonie-Divertissement*: Some Reflections around a Fragment in the Bayerische Staatsbibliothek." F-Göller: 387–403.

Symphonies
3536. Distefano, Joseph P. "The Symphonies of Karl Amadeus Hartmann." Ph.D. diss., Florida State University, 1972.
3537. Günther, Siegfried. "Hartmanns achte Sinfonie." MELOS 30 (1963): 190–93.
3538. ———. "6. Sinfonie von Karl Amadeus Hartmann." MELOS 29 (1962): 74–77.
3539. Heister, Hanns-Werner. "Zur Semantik musikalischer Strukturen: Der Schluss-Satz aus K. A. Hartmanns 1. Symphonie." BM 18 (1976): 137–47.

Symphonische Hymnen
3540. McCredie, Andrew D., ed. *Karl Amadeus Hartmann: Symphonische Hymnen für grosser Orchester.* Mainz: Schott, 1976.

Various Works
3541. McCredie, Andrew D. "Karl Amadeus Hartmann (1905–1963): New Documents and Sources in a Decennial Perspective." MMA 7 (1975): 142–87.
3542. ———. "The Role of Sources and Antecedents in the Compositional Process of Karl Amadeus Hartmann." MMA 10 (1979): 166–212.

HARVEY, JONATHAN (b. 1939)
3543. Griffiths, Paul. "Three Works by Jonathan Harvey: The Electronic Mirror." CMR 1, no. 1 (1984–1985): 87–109. [*Bhakti, Inner Light 1–3, Mortuos piango, vivos vovo*]
3544. Harvey, Jonathan, Denis Lorrain, Jean-Baptiste Barrière, and Stanley Haynes. "Notes on the Realization of *Bhakti.*" CMR 1, no. 1 (1984–1985): 111–29.
3545. Palmer, John. "An Introduction to Jonathan Harvey's *Bhakti.*" TCM 5, no. 11 (1998): 6–15. [*Bhakti, Inner Light 1–3*]
3546. ———. "Structural Strategies and Pitch Gestalt in Jonathan Harvey's *Bhakti.*" TCM 5, no. 12 (1990): 4–24.
3547. Smith, Pamela. "Towards the Spiritual: The Electroacoustic Music of Jonathan Harvey." CT 34 (1989): 11–16. [*Bhakti, Inner Light 1–3, Mortuos plango, vivos voco*]
3548. Whittall, Arnold. *Jonathan Harvey.* London: Faber & Faber, 1999. French edition, Paris: IRCAM, 2000.

HASELBACH, JOSEF (b. 1936)
3549. Haselbach, Josef. "Komponisten präsentieren neue Arbeiten: *Moving-Theatre I.*" SMZ 114 (1974): 149–54.

HAUER, JOSEF MATTHAIS (1883–1959)
3550. Covach, John R. "The *Zwölftonspiel* of Josef Matthias Hauer." JMT 36, no. 1 (1992): 149–84.
3551. Lagaly, Klaus. "Zelluläre Verbandsstrukturen: Die Tropen von J. M. Hauer als individuelles Erkennungsmerkmal von Zwölftonreihen und ihrem Potential." AM 47, no. 3 (1990): 163–91; 47, no. 4 (1990): 286–316.
3552. Leuchtmann, Horst. "'Möglichkeiten logischer Formgebung bei der Benützung von 12 Tönen': J. M. Hauers Op. 22,1." F-Sievers: 103–14.
3553. OMZ 21 (1966): 98–144. [Special issue]

3554. Sengstschmid, Johann. "Anatomie eines Zwolftonspiels: Ein Block in der Werkstatt Josef Matthais Hauers." ZM 2, no. 1 (1971): 14–34.

3555. ———. *Zwischen Trope und Zwölftonspiel: J. M. Hauers Zwölftontechnik in ausgewählten Beispielen.* Regensburg: Bosse, 1980.

3556. Szmolyan, Walter. "Hauer als Opernkomponist." OMZ 21 (1966): 226–32.

HAUFRECHT, HERBERT (1909–1998)

3557. Cazden, Norman. "Herbert Haufrecht: The Composer and the Man." ACA 8, no. 4 (1958): 2–11.

HAWKINS, JOHN (b. 1944)

3558. Mather, Bruce. "Le collage musical: *Remembrances* de John Hawkins." CCM 3 (1971): 99–102.

3559. McLean, Don. "Of Things Past: John Hawkins's *Remembrances* (1969)." F-Beckwith: 45–69.

3560. Plawutsky, Eugene. "The Music of John Hawkins." CAUSM 8, no. 1 (1978): 112–34.

HAYDN, JOSEPH (1732–1809)

Ah tu non senti . . . Qual destra omicida, H. XXIVb:10

3561. Brown, A. Peter. "Tommaso Traetta and the Genesis of a Haydn Aria (Hob. XXIVb:10)." CHI 16 (1984): 101–42.

Armida

3562. Rice, John A. "Sarti's *Giulio Sabino,* Haydn's *Armida,* and the Arrival of opera seria at Eszterháaza." HY 15 (1984): 181–98.

Baryton Trios

3563. Wollenberg, Susan. "Haydn's Baryton Trios and the *Gradus.*" ML 54 (1973): 107–78.

Creation. See *Schöpfung*

Fedeltà premiata

3564. Clark, Caryl. "Intertextual Play and Haydn's *La fedeltà premiata.*" CM 51 (1991): 59–81.

3565. Lippmann, Friedrich. "Haydns *La fedelta premiata* and Cimarosas *L'infedeltà fedele.*" HS 5 (1982–1983): 1–15.

Jahreszeiten (The Seasons)

3566. Brown, A. Peter. *"The Creation* and *The Seasons*: Some Allusions, Quotations, and Models from Handel to Mendelssohn." CM 51 (1991): 26–58.

3567. Moe, Orin, Jr. "Structure in Hadyn's *The Seasons.*" HY 9 (1975): 340–48.

3568. Schmidt, Karl. "Die Sprache der Tonarten in Hadyns *Jahreszeiten.*" M 36 (1982–1983): 211–14.

Keyboard Trios

3569. Chapman, Roger E. "Modulation in Haydn's Piano Trios in the Light of Schoenberg's Theories." M-Larsen: 471–75.

3570. Komlós, Katalin. "Haydn's Keyboard Trios Hob. XV:5–17: Interaction between Texture and Form." SM 28 (1986): 351–400.

3571. Steinberg, Lester. "A Numerical Approach to Activity and Movement in the Sonata-Form Movements of Haydn's Piano Trios." M-Larsen: 515–22.

3572. ———. "The Piano Trios of Joseph Haydn: Analysis of Style in Sonata-Form Movements." Ph.D. diss., New York University, 1976.

3573. Sutcliffe, W. Dean. "Haydn's Piano Trio Textures." MA 6, no. 3 (1987): 319–32.

Lieder für das Clavier, H. XXVIa:1–12

3574. Trembath, Shirley. "Joseph Haydn's *XII Lieder für das Clavier* (Erster Teil) of 1781: Song Cycle or Collection?" SZM 43 (1994): 145–57.

Masses (various; *see also* specific masses)

3575. Brand, Carl Maria. *Die Messen von Joseph Haydn.* Würzburg: Triltsch, 1941. Reprint, Walluf bei Wiesbaden: Sandig, 1973.

3576. Gibbs, Thomas Jordan, Jr. "A Study of Form in the Late Masses of Joseph Haydn." Ph.D. diss., University of Texas, 1972.

3577. Krummacher, Friedhelm. "Symphonische Verfahren in Haydns späten Messen." F-Dahlhaus: 455–81.

3578. MacIntyre, Bruce C. "Die Entwicklung der konzertierenden Messen Joseph Haydns und seiner Wiener Zeitgenossen." HS 6, no. 2 (1988): 80–87.

3579. Nafziger, Kenneth J. "The Masses of Haydn and Schubert: A Study in the Rise of Romanticism." D.M.A. diss., University of Oregon, 1970.

3580. Otto, Craig A. "The Use of the Sonata-Allegro Form in the Kyrie Movements of Joseph Hadyn's Late Masses." D 4, no. 2 (1972): 3–12.

3581. Runestad, Cornell J. "The Masses of Joseph Haydn: A Stylistic Study." D.M.A. diss., University of Illinois, 1970.
3582. Schützeichel, Harald. "Der Aufblau der späten Messen Haydns im Verglich zu den frühen." SZM 38 (1987): 65–88.
3583. Town, Stephen. "Toward an Understanding of Fugue and Fugato in the Masses of Joseph Haydn." JMR 6, no. 4 (1986): 311–51.

Mass, H. XXII:8 (*Missa Cellensis; Mariazellermesse*)
3584. Town, Stephen. "A Contrafactum by Joseph Haydn." ACR 33, no. 2 (1991): 4–6. [Benedictus]

Mass, H. XXII:11 (*Nelsonmesse; Imperial Mass; Coronation Mass*)
3585. Guye, Jean-Philippe. "Joseph Haydn: *Messe in Angustiis (Nelsonmesse).*" ANM 33 (1998): 5–35.

Mass, H. XXII:13 (*Schöpfungsmesse*)
3586. Kalisch, Volker. "Haydn und die Kirchenmusik: Ein analytischer Versuch am Beispiel des Benedictus aus der *Schöpfungsmesse.*" MK 54 (1984): 159–70.

Operas (various; *see also* specific operas)
3587. Hunter, Mary. "Haydn's Sonata-Form Arias." CM 37–38 (1984): 19–32.
3588. ———. "Text, Music, and Drama in Haydn's Italian Opera Arias: Four Case Studies." JM 7, no. 1 (1989): 29–57.
3589. Lawner, George. "Form and Drama in the Operas of Joseph Haydn." Ph.D. diss., University of Chicago, 1959.
3590. Lippmann, Friedrich. "Haydns opere serie: Tendenzen and Affinitäten." STU 12 (1983): 301–32.

Oratorios (various; *see also* specific oratorios)
3591. Riedel-Martiny, Anke. "Das Verhältnis von Text und Musik in Haydns Oratorien." HS 1 (1965–1967): 205–40.

Piano Sonatas (various; *see also* specific piano sonatas)
3592. Andrews, Harold L. "Tonality and Structure in the First Movements of Haydn's Solo Keyboard Sonatas." Ph.D. diss., University of North Carolina, 1967.
3593. Brown, Alfred P. "The Solo and Ensemble Keyboard Sonatas of Joseph Haydn: A Study of Structure and Style." Ph.D. diss., Northwestern University, 1970.
3594. Eitan, Zohar. "Peaks in Haydn: The Attenuation of Climax." M-Eitan: Chap. 3.
3595. Fillion, Michelle. "Sonata-Exposition Procedures in Haydn's Keyboard Sonatas." M-Larsen: 475–81.
3596. Reed, Carl H. "Motivic Unity in Selected Keyboard Sonatas and String Quartets of Joseph Haydn." Ph.D. diss., University of Washington, 1966.
3597. Shamgar, Beth Friedman. "The Retransition in the Piano Sonatas of Haydn, Mozart, and Beethoven." Ph.D. diss., New York University, 1978.
3598. Vignal, Marc. "L'oeuvre pour piano seul de Joseph Haydn." RM 249 (1961): 7–19.
3599. Wackernagel, Bettina. *Joseph Haydns frühe Klaviersonaten: Ihre Beziehungen zur Klaviermusik um d. Mitte d. 18. Jahrhunderts.* Tutzing: Schneider, 1975.
3600. Zeller, Hans Rudolf. "Abweichungen vom Thema." In *Joseph Haydn*, ed. Heinz-Klaus Metzger and Rainer Riehn, 47–66. Munich: Text + Kritik, 1985.

Piano Sonata, H. XVI:20, C Minor
3601. Broyles, Michael. "The Two Instrumental Styles of Classicism." JAMS 36 (1983): 210–42.

Piano Sonata, H. XVI:38, E-Flat Major
3602. Petty, Wayne. "Cyclic Integration in Haydn's E-Flat Piano Sonata Hob. XVI:38." TP 19 (1994): 31–55.

Piano Sonata, H. XVI:49, E-Flat Major
3603. Spitzer, Michael. "The Retransition as Sign: Listener-Oriented Approaches to Tonal Closure in Haydn's Sonata-Form Movements." JRMA 121, no. 1 (1996): 11–45.

Piano Sonata, H. XVI:50, C Major
3604. Broyles, Michael. "The Two Instrumental Styles of Classicism." JAMS 36 (1983): 210–42.
3605. Willner, Channan. "Chromaticism and the Mediant in Four Late Haydn Works." TP 13 (1988): 79–114.

Piano Sonata, H. XVI:52, E-Flat Major
3606. Agawu, Kofi. "Haydn's Tonal Models: The First Movement of the Piano Sonata in E-Flat Major, Hob. XVI:52." F-Ratner: 3–22.
3607. Broyles, Michael. "The Two Instrumental Styles of Classicism." JAMS 36 (1983): 210–42.
3608. Moss, Lawrence K. "Haydn's Sonata Hob. XVI:52 (ChL.62) in E-Flat Major: An Analysis of the First Movement." M-Larsen: 496–501.
3609. Schenker, Heinrich. "Haydn: Sonata in E-Flat Major." Trans. Wayne Petty. THE 3 (1998): 105–60.

Piano Sonata, H. XVII:6, F Minor (*Un piccolo divertimento*; variations)

3610. Goebels, Franzpeter. "'Meine Sprache versteht man durch die ganze Welt': Bemerkungen zu den Variationen F-Moll (Hob.XVII.6) von Joseph Haydn." MB 14 (1982): 338–40, 349–50.

Piano Trios. *See* Keyboard Trios

***Salve regina*, H. XXIIIb:2, G Minor**

3611. Webster, James. "Haydns *Salve regina* in G-Moll (1771) und die Entwicklung zum durchkomponierten Zyklus." HS 6, no. 4 (1994): 245–60.

Schöpfung (The Creation)

3612. Brown, A. Peter. "*The Creation* and *The Seasons*: Some Allusions, Quotations, and Models from Handel to Mendelssohn." CM 51 (1991): 26–58.

3613. Kramer, Lawrence. "Haydn's Chaos, Schenker's Order; or, Hermeneutics and Musical Analysis: Can They Mix?" NCM 16, no. 1 (1992): 3–17.

3614. M-Kramer: 67–97.

3615. Ravizza, Victor. *Joseph Haydn: Die Schöpfung.* Munich: Fink, 1981.

3616. Sohet, Dominique. "La *Création* de Joseph Haydn: Une œuvre pour l'histoire." ANM 1 (1985): 84–91.

3617. Temperley, Nicholas. *Haydn: The Creation.* Cambridge: Cambridge University Press, 1991.

Seasons. *See Jahreszeiten*

Seven Last Words. *See Sieben letzten Worte unseres Erlösers am Kreuze*

Sieben letzten Worte unseres Erlösers am Kreuze (The Seven Last Words)

3618. Hailparn, Lydia. "Haydn: *The Seven Last Words*: A New Look at an Old Masterpiece." MR 34 (1973): 1–21.

3619. Suurpää, Lauri. "Programmatic Aspects of the Second Sonata of Haydn's *Seven Last Words.*" TP 24 (1999): 29–55.

String Quartets (various; *see also* specific string quartets)

3620. Barrett-Ayres, Reginald. *Joseph Haydn and the String Quartet.* London: Barrie & Jenkins, 1974.

3621. Bartha, Dénes. "Thematic Profile and Character in the Quartet-Finales of Joseph Haydn." SM 11 (1969): 35–62.

3622. Demaree, Robert W., Jr. "The Structural Proportions of the Haydn Quartets." Ph.D. diss., Indiana University, 1973.

3623. Edwards, George. "The Nonsense of an Ending: Closure in Haydn's String Quartets." MQ 75, no. 3 (1991): 227–54.

3624. Germann, Jörg. *Die Entwicklung der Exposition in Joseph Haydn Streichquartetten.* Teufen AR: Kunz-Druck, 1964.

3625. Kohlhase, Hans. "Der Fauxbourdonsatz in den Streichquartetten von Joseph Haydn." F-Floros/60: 155–65.

3626. Moe, Orin, Jr. "Texture in Haydn's Early Quartets." MR 35 (1974): 4–22.

3627. ———. "Texture in the String Quartets of Haydn to 1787." Ph.D. diss., University of California, Santa Barbara, 1970.

3628. Pankaskie, Lewis V. "Tonal Organization in the Sonata-Form Movements of Haydn's String Quartets." Ph.D. diss., University of Michigan, 1957.

3629. Reed, Carl H. "Motivic Unity in Selected Keyboard Sonatas and String Quartets of Joseph Haydn." Ph.D. diss., University of Washington, 1966.

3630. Silbert, Doris. "Ambiguity in the String Quartets of Joseph Haydn." MQ 36 (1950): 562–73.

3631. Tepping, Susan E. "Fugue Process and Tonal Structure in the String Quartets of Haydn, Mozart, and Beethoven." Ph.D. diss., Indiana University, 1987.

3632. Webster, James. "Freedom of Form in Haydn's Early String Quartets." M-Larsen: 522–30.

3633. Wiesel, Siegfried. "Klangfarbendramaturgie in den Streichquartetten von Joseph Haydn." HS 5 (1982–1983): 16–22.

String Quartets, Op. 9

3634. M-Walts. [No. 1 (Movement I)]

String Quartets, Op. 20

3635. M-Walts. [No. 2 (Movement I)]

String Quartets, Op. 33

3636. Ballstaedt, Andreas. "'Humor' und 'Witz' in Joseph Haydn's Musik." AM 55, no. 3 (1998): 195–219. [No. 2]

3637. Kaschmitter, Walter. "Streichquartett Op. 33 Nr. 2 oder Humor bei Joseph Haydn." M 36 (1982–1983): 168–71.

3638. Moe, Orin, Jr. "The Significance of Haydn's Op. 33." M-Larsen: 445–50.

3639. Steinbeck, Wolfram. "Mozarts 'Scherzi': Zur Beziehung zwischen Haydns Streichquartetten Op. 33 und Mozarts Haydn-Quartetten." AM 41 (1984): 208–31.

3640. M-Walts. [No. 3 (Movement I)]

String Quartets, Op. 50

3641. Sutcliffe, W. Dean. *Haydn: String Quartets, Op. 50.* Cambridge: Cambridge University Press, 1992.

String Quartets, Op. 64

3642. Anson-Cartwright, Mark. "Haydn's Hidden Homage to Mozart: Echoes of 'Voi che sapete' in Opus 64, No. 3." INT 14–15 (2000–2001): 121–36.

3643. Spitzer, Michael. "The Retransition as Sign: Listener-Oriented Approaches to Tonal Closure in Haydn's Sonata-Form Movements." JRMA 121, no. 1 (1996): 11–45. [No. 6]

String Quartets, Op. 71

3644. Anson-Cartwright, Mark. "Chromatic Features of E-Flat Major Works of the Classical Period." MTS 22, no. 2 (2000): 177–204. [No. 3]

String Quartets, Op. 74

3645. Levy, Janet M. "Texture as a Sign in Classic and Early Romantic Music." JAMS 35 (1982): 482–531. [Nos. 1, 3]

3646. Suurpää, Lauri. "Continuous Exposition and Tonal Structure in Three Late Haydn Works." MTS 21, no. 2 (1999): 174–99. [No. 3 (Movement I)]

String Quartets, Op. 76

3647. Agawu, V. Kofi. "A Semiotic Interpretation of the First Movement of Haydn's String Quartet in D Minor, Op. 76, No. 2." M-Agawu: Chap. 5.

3648. Levy, Janet M. "Texture as a Sign in Classic and Early Romantic Music." JAMS 35 (1982): 482–531. [No. 1]

3649. Löber, Burckhard. *Strukturwissenschaftliche Darstellung der ersten und letzten Satze der sechs Streichquartette Op. 76 von Joseph Haydn.* Münster: Forschungsstelle für theoretische Musikwissenschaft, 1983.

3650. Randall, J. K. "Haydn: String Quartet in D, Op. 76, No. 5." MR 21 (1960): 94–105.

3651. Salzer, Felix. "Haydn's Fantasia from the String Quartet, Opus 76, No. 6." MFO 4 (1976): 161–94.

3652. Somfai, László. "Le *style savant* de Haydn: Les stratégies thématiques dans le quatuor 'Les quintes.'" Trans. Agnès Ausseus. ANM 13 (1988): 51–57. [No. 2]

3653. ———. "'Learned Style' in Two Late String Quartet Movements of Haydn." SM 28 (1986): 325–49. [Nos. 2–3]

3654. Suurpää, Lauri. "Continuous Exposition and Tonal Structure in Three Late Haydn Works." MTS 21, no. 2 (1999): 174–99. [No. 2 (Movement I)]

String Trios

3655. Brook, Barry. "Haydn's String Trios: A Misunderstood Genre." CM 36 (1983): 61–77.

Symphonies (various; *see also* specific symphonies)

3656. Alston, Charlotte LeNora. "Recapitulation Procedures in the Mature Symphonies of Haydn and Mozart." Ph.D. diss., University of Iowa, 1972.

3657. Bard, Raimund. *Untersuchungen zur motivischen Arbeit in Haydns sinfonischem Spätwerken.* Kassel: Bärenreiter, 1982.

3658. Bawel, Frederick Henry. "A Study of Developmental Techniques in Selected Hadyn Symphonies." Ph.D. diss., Ohio State University, 1972.

3659. Cole, Malcolm S. "Haydn's Symphonic Rondo Finales: Their Structural and Stylistic Evolution." HY 13 (1982): 113–42.

3660. Fisher, Stephen C. "Further Thoughts on Haydn's Symphonic Rondo Finales." HY 17 (1992): 85–107.

3661. ———. "Sonata Procedures in Hadyn's Symphonic Rondo Finales of the 1770s." M-Larsen: 481–87.

3662. Gresham, Carolyn D. "Stylistic Features of Hadyn's Symphonies from 1768 to 1772." M-Larsen: 431–34.

3663. Haimo, Ethan. "Haydn's Altered Reprise." JMT 32, no. 2 (1988): 335–51.

3664. ———. *Haydn's Symphonic Forms: Essays in Compositional Logic.* Oxford: Oxford University Press, 1995.

3665. Klein, Rudolf. "Wo kann die Analyse von Haydns Symphonik ansetzen?" OMZ 37 (1982): 234–41.

3666. LaRue, Jan. "Bifocal Tonality in Haydn Symphonies." F-Ratner: 59–73.

3667. Marillier, C. G. "Computer Assisted Analysis of Tonal Structure in the Classical Symphony." HY 14 (1983): 187–99.

3668. Menk, Gail E. "The Symphonic Introductions of Joseph Haydn." Ph.D. diss., University of Iowa, 1960.

3669. Riehm, Diethard. "Zur Anlage der Exposition in Joseph Haydns letzten Sinfonien." OMZ 21 (1966): 255–60.

3670. Scheideler, Ullrich. "Das Ohr hört mit: Quint- und Oktavparallelen in frühen Sinfonien Joseph Haydns." HS 8, no. 1 (2000): 1–38.

3671. Schroeder, David Peter. "Joseph Haydn's Symphonic Language: A Critical Approach." Ph.D. diss., King's College, Cambridge, 1982.

3672. Schwartz, Judith L. "Thematic Asymmetry in First Movements of Haydn's Early Symphonies." M-Larsen: 501–9.

3673. Worbs, Hans Christoph. *Die Sinfonik Haydns.* Heidenau/Sa.: Mitteldeutsche Kunstanstalt, 1956.

Symphony, H. I:38, C Major

3674. Ballstaedt, Andreas. "'Humor' und 'Witz' in Joseph Haydn's Musik." AM 55, no. 3 (1998): 195–219.

Symphony, H. I:45, F-Sharp Minor ("Farewell")

3675. Schwartz, Judith L. "Periodicity and Passion in the First Movement of Haydn's 'Farewell' Symphony." F-LaRue: 293–338.

3676. Webster, James. "The D-Major Interlude in the First Movement of Haydn's 'Farewell' Symphony." F-LaRue: 339–80.

3677. ———. *Haydn's "Farewell" Symphony and the Idea of Classical Style: Through-Composition and Cyclic Integration in His Instrumental Music.* Cambridge: Cambridge University Press, 1991.

Symphony, H. I:58, F Major

3678. Ballstaedt, Andreas. "'Humor' und 'Witz' in Joseph Haydn's Musik." AM 55, no. 3 (1998): 195–219.

Symphony, H. I:76, E-Flat Major

3679. Broyles, Michael. "The Two Instrumental Styles of Classicism." JAMS 36 (1983): 210–42.

Symphonies, H. I:82–87 ("Paris Symphonies")

3680. Harrison, Bernard. *Haydn: The "Paris" Symphonies.* Cambridge: Cambridge University Press, 1998.

Symphony, H. I:92, G Major

3681. Levy, Janet M. "Texture as a Sign in Classic and Early Romantic Music." JAMS 35 (1982): 482–531.

Symphonies, H. I:93–104 ("London Symphonies")

3682. Ballstaedt, Andreas. "'Humor' und 'Witz' in Joseph Haydn's Musik." AM 55, no. 3 (1998): 195–219. [No. 94]

3683. Butcher, Norma Perkins. "A Comparative-Analytical Study of Sonata-Allegro Form in the First Movements of the London Symphonies of Franz Joseph Haydn." Ph.D. diss., University of Southern California, 1971.

3684. Cole, Malcolm S. "Momigny's Analysis of Hadyn's Symphony No. 103." MR 30 (1969): 261–84.

3685. Eberle, Gottfried. "Joseph Haydn: Sinfonia G-Dur Hob.1:100 ('Militär-Sinfonie')." NZM 143, no. 2 (1982): 31–33.

3686. Geiringer, Karl, ed. *Franz Joseph Haydn: Symphony No. 103 in E-Flat Major ("Drum-Roll").* Norton Critical Scores. New York: Norton, 1974.

3687. Gwilt, Richard. "Sonata-Allegro Revisited." ITO 7, nos. 5–6 (1983–1984): 3–33. [Nos. 93–97, 100, 103]

3688. Keefe, Simon P. "Dialogue and Drama: Haydn's Symphony No. 102." MRF 11, no. 1 (1996): 1–21.

3689. M-Kresky: 12–26. [No. 104 (Movement I)]

3690. Lazar, Joel. "Thematic Unity in the First Movements of Haydn's London Symphonies." M.A. thesis, Harvard University, 1963.

3691. Livingstone, Ernest F. "Unifying Elements in Hadyn's Symphony No. 104." M-Larsen: 493–96.

3692. Martinez-Gollner, Marie Louise. *Joseph Haydn: Symphonie Nr. 94 (Paukenschlag).* Munich: Fink, 1979.

3693. Marx, Karl. "Über thematische Beziehungen in Haydns Londoner Symphonien." HS 4 (1976–1980): 1–20.

3694. Riehm, Diethard. *Die ersten Sätze von Joseph Haydns Londoner Sinfonien.* N.p.: 1971.

3695. Schlager, Karl-Heinz. *Joseph Haydn: Sinfonie Nr. 104 D-Dur.* Munich: Fink, 1983.

3696. Schroeder, David Peter. "Audience Reception and Haydn's London Symphonies." IRASM 16, no. 1 (1985): 57–72.

3697. Suurpää, Lauri. "Continuous Exposition and Tonal Structure in Three Late Haydn Works." MTS 21, no. 2 (1999): 174–99. [No. 96 (Movement I)]

3698. Willner, Channan. "Chromaticism and the Mediant in Four Late Haydn Works." TP 13 (1988): 79–114. [No. 98 (Movement IV), No. 101 (Movement I), No. 104 (Movement IV)]

3699. Wolf, Eugene K. "The Recapitulations in Hadyn's London Symphonies." MQ 52 (1966): 71–89.

Various Works

3700. Andrews, Harold L. "The Submediant in Hadyn's Development Sections." M-Larsen: 465–71.

3701. Arnold, Denis. "Haydn's Counterpoint and Fux's *Gradus*." MMR 87 (1957): 52–58.

3702. Bartha, Dénes. "Volkstanz-Stilisierung in Joseph Haydns Finale-Themen." F-Wiora: 375–84.

3703. Brown, A. Peter. "Critical Years for Haydn's Instrumental Music: 1787–1790." MQ 62 (1976): 374–94.

3704. Burdick, Michael Francis. "A Structural Analysis of Melodic Scale-Degree Tendencies in Selected Themes of Haydn, Mozart, Schubert, and Chopin." Ph.D. diss., Indiana University, 1977.

3705. M-Caplin.

3706. Cushman, David Stephen. "Joseph Haydn's Melodic Materials: An Exploratory Introduction to the Primary and Secondary Sources Together with an Analytical Catalogue and Tables of Proposed Melodic Correspondence and/or Variance." Ph.D. diss., Boston University, 1973.

3707. Danckwardt, Marianne. *Die langsame Einleitung: Ihre Herkunft und ihr Bau bei Haydn und Mozart.* 2 vols. Tutzing: Schneider, 1977.

3708. Edwall, Harry R. "Ferdinand IV and Haydn's Concertos for the *Lira organizzata.*" MQ 48 (1962): 190–203.

3709. Feder, Georg. "Haydn und Bach: Versuch eines musikhistorischen Vergleichs." Dürr: 75–87.

3710. ———. "Typisches bei Haydn: Eine Methode der Stiluntersuchung." OMZ 24 (1969): 11–17.

3711. Finscher, Ludwig. "Joseph Haydn: Ein unbekannten Komponist?" NZM 143, no. 10 (1982): 12–18.

3712. Garner, Chet H. "Principles of Periodic Structure in the Instrumental Works of Haydn, Mozart, and Beethoven." Ph.D. diss., University of Iowa, 1977.

3713. Grave, Floyd. "Metrical Dissonance in Haydn." JM 13, no. 2 (1995): 168–202.

3714. Haimo, Ethan. "Remote Keys and Multi-Movement Unity: Haydn in the 1790s." MQ 74, no. 2 (1990): 242–68.

3715. Harutunian, John Martin. "Haydn and Mozart: A Study of Their Mature Sonata-Style Procedures." Ph.D. diss., University of California, Los Angeles, 1981.

3716. ———. "Haydn and Mozart: Tonic-Dominant Polarity in Mature Sonata-Style Works." SM 31 (1989): 217–40; reprint, JMR 9, no. 4 (1990): 273–98.

3717. Josephson, Nors S. "Modulatory Patterns in Haydn's Late Development Sections." HY 17 (1992): 181–91.

3718. Lang, Paul Henry, ed. *Haydn Commemorative Issue of "The Musical Quarterly."* Introduction by Karl Geiringer. New York: Da Capo, 1982.

3719. Müllers, Christian. "De Einfluss des Konzertsatzes auf die Formentwicklung im 18. Jahrhundert." ZM 9, no. 2 (1978): 34–46.

3720. Neubacher, Jürgen. "'Idee' und 'Ausführung': Zum Kompositionsprozess bei Joseph Haydn." AM 41 (1984): 187–207.

3721. Prey, Stefan. "Originalität in Haydns Harmonik." M 36 (1982): 136–39.

3722. Reindl, Johannes. "Zur Entstehung des Refrains der Kaiserhymne Joseph Haydns." SZM 25 (1966): 417–33.

3723. Rosen, Charles. *The Classical Style: Haydn, Mozart, Beethoven.* London: Faber & Faber, 1971.

3724. Scholz, Gottfried. "Der dialektische Prozess in Hadyns Doppelvariationen." MAU 2 (1979): 97–107.

3725. Schroeder, David. "Melodic Source Material and Haydn's Creative Process." MQ 68 (1982): 496–515.

3726. Schwarting, Heino. "Ungewöhnliche Repriseneintritte in Haydns späterer Instrumentalmusik." AM 17 (1960): 168–82.

3727. Sisman, Elaine Rochelle. "Haydn's Variations." Ph.D. diss., Princeton University, 1978.

3728. ———. "Tradition and Transformation in the Alternating Variations of Haydn and Beethoven." ACTA 62, nos. 2–3 (1990): 152–82.

3729. Sponheuer, Bernd. "Haydns Arbeit am Finalproblem" ZM 34 (1977): 199–224.

3730. Steinbeck, Wolfram. *Das Menuett in der Instrumentalmusik Joseph Haydns.* Munich: Katzblichler, 1973.

3731. Stuber, Robert. *Die Klavierbegleitung im Liede von Haydn, Mozart, und Beethoven: Eine Stilstudie.* Biel: Graphische Anstalt Schuler, 1958.

HAYDN, MICHAEL (1737–1806)

3732. Pauly, Reinhard G. "Michael Haydn's Latin *Proprium Missae* Compositions." Ph.D. diss., Yale University, 1956.

3733. Poland, Jeffrey T. "Michael Haydn and Mozart: Two Requiem Settings." ACR 29, no. 1 (1987): 3–14. [*Pro defuncto Archiepiscopo Sigismundo*]

HAYER, RALF

3734. Hansen, Mathies. "Die Analyse: Streichquartett Nr. 1 von Ralf Hayer." MG 30 (1980): 528–32.

HEIDEN, BERNHARD (1910–2000)

3735. Langosch, Marlene Joan. "The Instrumental Chamber Music of Bernhard Heiden." Ph.D. diss., Indiana University, 1974.

HEIDER, WERNER (b. 1930)

3736. Jacob, Andreas. "Im Geflecht musikalischer Nervenbahnen: *Inneres* von Werner Heider." MK 68, no. 6 (1998): 392–96.

3737. Kelber, Sebastian. "Werner Heiders *Katalog für einen Blockflötenspieler*: Eine Analyse." T 1, no. 2 (1976–1977): 145–48.

HEILLER, ANTON (1923–1979)

3738. Gant, Robert Edward. "The Organ Works of Anton Heiller." D.M.A. diss., University of Rochester, 1975.

3739. Wieninger, Herbert. "Anton Heiller: Choralmotette *Ach, wie nichtig, ach, wie flüchtig.*" ME 21 (1968): 122–27.

HEINRICH, ANTHONY PHILIP (1781–1861)

3740. Maust, Wilbur. "The Symphonies of Anthony Philip Heinrich Based on American Themes." Ph.D. diss., Indiana University, 1973.

HEISS, HERMANN (1897–1966)

3741. DBNM 15 (1975). [Special issue]

HELLER, STEPHEN (1813–1888)
3742. Booth, Ronald E., Jr. "The Life and Music of Stephen Heller." Ph.D. diss., University of Iowa, 1969.

HEMEL, OSCAR VAN (1892–1981)
3743. Paap, Wouter. "The Second Violin Concerto by Oscar van Hemel." SS 45 (1970): 1–5.

3744. Wouters, Jos. "Oscar van Hemel." SS 13 (1962): 1–7.

HENKEMANS, HANS (1913–1995)
3745. Flothuis, Marius. "Hans Henkemans." SS 14 (1963): 1–9.

3746. ———. "Hans Henkemans: Quintet No. 2 for Flute, Oboe, Clarinet, Bassoon, and Horn." SS 22 (1965): 19–24.

3747. Geraedts, Jaap. "Henkemans: Partita per orchestra." SS 6 (1961): 13–15.

3748. ———. "*Winter Cruise*: An Opera by Hans Henkemans." KN 9 (1979): 13–16.

3749. Henkemans, Hans. "Hans Henkemans: Piano Sonata." SS 7 (1961): 20–22.

HENRY, PIERRE (b. 1927)
3750. Delalande, François. "Music Analysis and Reception Behaviors: *Sommeil* by Pierre Henry." JNMR 27, nos. 1–2 (1998): 13–66.

HENSELT, ADOLPH (1814–1889)
3751. Graham, Daniel M. "An Analytical Study of Twenty-Four Etudes by Adolph von Henselt." D.M.A. diss., Peabody Conservatory, 1979.

3752. Ho, Allan. "A Stylistic Analysis of the Piano Music of Adolph von Henselt (1814–1889)." M.A. thesis, University of Hawaii, Manoa, 1980.

HENZE, HANS WERNER (b. 1926)

Absences
3753. Flammer, Ernst Helmuth. "Hans Werner Henze: *Six Absences;* Strukturanalyse und Gegenüberstellung zur Jazzfassung von George Gruntz." MB 10 (1978): 88–95.

Barcarola
3754. Rothkamm, Jörg. "'In Memoriam Paul Dessau': Hans Werner Henzes *Barcarola per grande orchestra.*" HJM 17 (2000): 279–311.

Being Beauteous
3755. Vogt, Hans. "*Being Beauteous* von Hans Werner Henze." MELOS 40 (1973): 359–65. Reprint, M-Vogt: 322–33.

Cimarrón
3756. Klüppelholz, Werner. "Henzes *El Cimarrón*: Eine didaktische Analyse für die Sekundarstufe II." MB 10 (1978): 95–104.

König Hirsch
3757. Oehl, Klaus. "RICERCAR: Auf der Suche nach sozialer, politischer und künstlerischer Identitt; Die Oper *König Hirsch* als autobiographische Allegorie." In *Hans Werner Henze: Politisch-humanitäres Engagement als künstlerische Perspektive,* 55–71. Osnabrück: Universitätsverlag Rasch, 1998.

Langwierige Weg in die Wohnung der Natascha Ungeheuer
3758. Flammer, Ernst Helmuth. "Form und Gehalt III: Eine Analyse von Hans Werner Henzes *Der langwierige Weg in die Wohnung der Natascha Ungeheuer.*" Melos/NZM 4 (1978): 486–95.

Nachtstücke und Arien
3759. Fürst, Marion. "'Gegenbild der heillosen Zeit': Ingeborg Bachmanns und Hans Werner Henzes Gemeinschaftswerk *Nachtstücke und Arien* (1957)." F-Knepler, vol. 3: 47–71.

Piano Concerto No. 2
3760. Berger, Gregor. "Henzes zweites Klavierkonzert." MELOS 40 (1973): 33–40.

3761. Fuhrmann, Roderich. "Hans Werner Henze (1926): 2. Konzert für Klavier und Orchester (1967)." M-Zimmerschied: 267–85.

3762. Fürst, Marion. "'Bruderschaft mit der Dichtkunst': Beobachtungen am Skizzenmaterial zu Hans Werner Henzes zweitem Klavierkonzert." MPSS 9 (1996): 24–29.

Piano Sonata
3763. M-Wennerstrom.

Prinz von Homburg

3764. De la Motte, Diether. *Hans Werner Henze: Der Prinz von Homburg; Ein Versuch über die Komposition und den Komponisten.* Mainz: Schott, 1960.

String Quartets

3765. Bruderreck, Markus. "Harmonik und Reihenstrukturen im Triptychon der Streichquartette Nr. 3–5 von Hans Werner Henze." MTH 15, no. 1 (2000): 41–56.

Symphonies

3766. Hamilton, Phillips Howard. "Serialism in the Third, Fourth, and Fifth Symphonies of Hans Werner Henze." Ph.D. diss., University of Rochester, 1981.

3767. Ketas, Sheila. "Current Chronicle." MQ 57 (1971): 141–48. [No. 6]

3768. Schmidt, Christian Martin. "Über die Unwichtigkeit der Konstruktion: Anmerkungen zu Hans Werner Henzes 6. Symphonie." Melos/NZM 2 (1976): 275–80.

Tristan

3769. Fürst, Marion. *Hans Werner Henzes "Tristan": Ein Werkmonographie.* Neckargemünd: Männeles, 2000.

Voices

3770. Petersen, Peter, Hanns-Werner Heister, and Hartmut Lück, eds. *"Stimmen" für Hans Werner Henze: Die 22 Lieder aus "Voices."* Mainz: Schott, 1996.

We Come to the River

3771. Hatten, Robert S. "Pluralism of Theatrical Genre and Musical Style in Henze's *We Come to the River.*" PNM 28, no. 2 (1990): 292–311.

Various Works

3772. M-Hines: 89–104.

3773. Pauli, Hansjürg. "Hans Werner Henze's Italian Music." SCORE 25 (1959): 26–37.

3774. Symons, David. "Hans Werner Henze: The Emergence of a Style." SMU 3 (1969): 35–52.

HEPPENER, ROBERT (b. 1925)

3775. Paap, Wouter. "The Composer Robert Heppener." SS 39 (1969): 1–11.

HERSCHEL, WILLIAM (1738–1822)

3776. Duckles, Vincent. "William F. Herschel's Concertos for Oboe, Viola, and Violin." F-Deutsch: 66–74.

HESPOS, HANS-JOACHIM (b. 1938)

3777. Brauen, Gerhard. "Schattenhaft ruhig, grob gekaut': Anmerkungen zu den Flötenkompositionen von H.-J. Hespos." T 7, no. 8 (1982–1983): 418–21.

3778. Fleck, Theresia. "'Von flirrender dichte': Zu *überRASCH* und *duma* von Hans-Joachim Hespos." MTX 83 (2000): 8–12.

3779. Oehlschlägel, Reinhard. "Zwischen Handlungsoper und absurdem Theater: Zu *Itzo-hux* von Hans-Joachim Hespos und Peter Wagenbreth." MTX 8 (1985): 46–48.

HESSENBERG, KURT (1908–1994)

3780. Albrecht, Christoph. "'. . . Weil ich die Möglichkeiten der Tonalität noch nicht für erschöpt halte': Kurt Hessenberg (geboren 17-8-1908)." F-Mauersberger: 165–75.

3781. Osthoff, Wolfgang. "'In Ketten tanzen': Symphonische Scherzi im totalitären Staat." JSIM (1994): 158–98. [Symphony No. 2 (Movement III)]

3782. Riemer, Otto. "Unausgeschöpfte Tonalität: Gedanke zum Schaffen von Kurt Hessenberg." M 7 (1953): 56–60.

3783. Zimmermann, Heinz Werner. "Kurt Hessenbergs Motette *O Herr, mache mich zum Werkzeug deines Friedens,* Opus 37, Nr. 1." MK 48 (1978): 211–17.

HILL, WILLIAM H.

3784. Harbinson, William G. "Analysis: William Hill's *Dances Sacred and Profane.*" JBR 19, no. 1 (1983–1984): 5–10.

HILLER, LEJAREN (1924–1994)

3785. Cage, John, and Lejaren Hiller. "*HPSCHD.*" S 2, no. 2 (1968): 10–19.

3786. Hiller, Lejaren, and Charles Ames; graphics by Robert Franki. "Automated Composition: An Installation at the 1985 International Exhibition in Tsukusa, Japan." PNM 23, no. 2 (1984–1985): 196–215. [*Circus Piece, Mix or Match*]

HINDEMITH, PAUL (1895–1963)

Cardillac

3787. Rexroth, Dieter. "Zum Stellenwert der Oper *Cardillac* im Schaffen Hindemiths." M-Rexroth: 56–59.

3788. Schilling, Hans Ludwig. *Paul Hindemith's "Cardillac": Beitrage zu einem Vergleich der beiden Opernfassungen; Stilkriterien im Schaffen Hindemiths.* Würzburg: Triltsch, 1964.

3789. Willms, Franz. *Führer zur Oper "Cardillac" von Paul Hindemith.* Mainz: Schott, 1926.

Cello Sonata (1948)

3790. Traub, Andreas. "Zur Sonate für Violoncello und Klavier (1948)." HJ 19 (1990): 39–54.

3791. M-Zimmerschied: 153–69.

Chansons

3792. Gros, Raymond. "Hindemith et les poèmes français de Rilke." HJ 8 (1979): 79–101.

3793. Neumann, Friedrich. "Kadenzen, Melodieführung, und Stimmführung in den *Six chansons* und *Five Songs on Old Texts* von Hindemith." HJ 8 (1979): 49–78.

Choral Works (various; *see also* specific choral works)

3794. M-Hart.

3795. Rubeli, Alfred Ulrich. *Paul Hindemiths a cappella Werke.* Mainz: Schott, 1975.

3796. Walker, Alvah John. "The a cappella Choral Music of Paul Hindemith." Ph.D. diss., University of Rochester, 1971.

Clarinet Sonata

3797. Kidd, James C. "Aspects of Mensuration in Hindemith's Clarinet Sonata." MR 38 (1977): 211–22.

Concerto for Orchestra

3798. Booth, Paul J. H. "Hindemith's Analytical Method and an Alternative: Two Views of His Concerto for Orchestra." SN 7 (1978): 117–36.

3799. Haack, Helmut. "Der Finalsatz aus Hindemiths Konzert für Orchester Op. 38." HJ 1 (1971): 63–79.

Concerto for Trumpet, Bassoon, and Strings

3800. Schubert, Giselher. "Zu einigen Spätwerken Hindemiths." Melos/NZM 3 (1977): 108–14.

English Horn Sonata

3801. Heimer, Ann-Katrin."Eine unbekannte Quelle für Hindemiths Englischhorm-Sonate." HJ 24 (1995): 42–65.

Gesänge, Op. 9

3802. Schmierer, Elisabeth. "Monumentalität und Pathos: Zu den Orchestergesängen Op. 9 von Hindemith." HJ 21 (1992): 97–131.

Harmonie der Welt

3803. Briner, Andres. "Eine Bekenntnisoper Paul Hindemiths: Zu seiner Oper *Die Harmonie der Welt.*" SMZ 99 (1959): 1–5, 50–56.

3804. D'Angelo, James. "Tonality Symbolism in Hindemith's Opera *Die Harmonie der Welt.*" HJ 14 (1985): 99–128.

Horn Concerto

3805. Neumeyer, David. "Tonal, Formal, and Proportional Design in Hindemith's Music." MTS 9 (1987): 93–116.

Kammermusik Nos. 1–4

3806. Kohlhase, Hans. "Aussermusikalische Tendenzen im Frühschaffen Paul Hindemiths: Versuch über die *Kammermusik* No. 1 mit Finale 1921." HJM 6 (1983): 183–224.

3807. Metz, Günther. "Paul Hindemith: *Kammermusik* Nr. 4, Op. 36, Nr. 3, für Solo-Violine und größeres Kammerorchester." HJ 16 (1987): 175–211.

3808. Ross, Walter Beghtol. "Principles of Melodic Construction in Paul Hindemith's Chamber Concerti, Op. 36." D.M.A. diss., Cornell University, 1966. [Nos. 2–4]

Kleine Kammermusik

3809. M-Wise.

Kleine Lieder für amerikanische Schulliederbuch

3810. Richter, Eckhart. "'Spider, spider what art thou spinning?' Paul Hindemith's *Songs for American School Children.*" HJ 15 (1986): 106–57.

Konzertmusik, Op. 50

3811. Schubert, Giselher. "Kontext und Bedeutung der Konzertmusiken Hindemiths." HJM 4 (1980): 85–114.

Ludus tonalis

3812. Delaere, Mark. "Analysing Contrapuntal Music: Some Remarks on the Fugues in C and F from Hindemith's *Ludus Tonalis.*" HJ 24 (1995): 66–86.

3813. M-Forte: 91–190. [Fugue No. 11]

3814. Neumann, Friedrich. "Hindemith: *Ludus tonalis,* Fuga nona in B." ZM 8, no. 1 (1977): 19–33.

3815. Neumeyer, David. "The Genesis and Structure of Hindemith's *Ludus tonalis.*" HJ 7 (1978): 72–103.
3816. Saguer, Louis. "*Ludus tonalis* de Paul Hindemith." CPS 4 (1946): 20–40.
3817. Tischler, Hans. "Hindemith's *Ludus tonalis* and Bach's *Well-Tempered Clavier:* A Comparison." MR 20 (1959): 217–27.

Madrigals
3818. Klyce, Stephen W. "Hindemith's Madrigals: Some Analytical Comments." ACR 14 (1972): 3–13.

Marienleben
3819. Davis, Donna Loomis. "Hindemith's Theory of Composition and *Das Marienleben.*" D 5, no. 2 (1973): 13–15.
3820. Metz, Gunther. "Hindemiths Lied 'Stillung Mariä mit dem Auferstandenen.'" HJ 12 (1983): 53–78.
3821. Schilling, Hans Ludwig. "Hindemith's Passacagliathemen in den beiden *Marienleben.*" AM 11 (1954): 65–70. Reprint, MELOS 23 (1956): 106–9.
3822. Schubert, Giselher. "Werkfassung und Werkidee: Kompositorische Probleme im Oeuvre Hindemiths." MF 45, no.1 (1992): 21–36.
3823. Starobinski, Georges. "Rythme, mètre et ton poétique dans *Das Marienleben* de Paul Hindemith." HJ 29 (2000): 8–38.
3824. Stephan, Rudolf. "Hindemith's *Marienleben* (1922–1948)." MR 15 (1954): 275–87.

Mass
3825. French, Richard F. "Hindemith's Mass 1963: An Introduction." F-Merritt: 83–91.
3826. Gottwald, Clytus. "Hindemiths Messe." MELOS 32 (1965): 386–91.
3827. ———. "Hindemiths Messe." MB 6 (1974): 370–73.
3828. Hirsbrunner, Theo. "Paul Hindemiths Traditionsverständnis dargestellt am Gloria der Messe." HJ 13 (1984): 111–21.
3829. Rössler, Franz-Georg. *Paul Hindemith: Messe (1963).* Munich: Fink, 1985.
3830. M-Vogt: 333–48.

Mathis der Maler
3831. Hitchcock, H. Wiley. "Trinitarian Symbollism in the 'Engelkonzert' of Hindemith's *Mathis der Maler.*" F-Seay: 217–29.
3832. Kilian, Gerald. "Paul Hindemiths Symphonie *Mathis der Maler:* Eine Deutung musikalischer Ausdruckscharaktere und formaler Strukturen als semiotische Gestaltqualitäten symbolischer Musik." HJ 28 (1999): 254–72.
3833. Schneider, Norbert J. "Prinzipien der rhythmischen Gestaltung in Hindemiths Oper *Mathis der Maler.*" HJ 8 (1979): 7–48.

Motets
3834. Thilman, Johannes Paul. "Zu Hindemiths Motetten." M 28 (1974): 15–17.

Octet
3835. Metz, Günther. "Hindemiths Oktett." HJ 14 (1985): 154–75.
3836. Wörner, Karl H. "Hindemiths neues Oktett." MELOS 25 (1958): 356–59.

Organ Works
3837. Bolitho, Albert G. "The Organ Sonatas of Paul Hindemith." Ph.D. diss., Michigan State University, 1969.
3838. Bruckner, Otto. "Betrachtungen zu Paul Hindemiths Orgelsonaten." HJ 24 (1995): 87–128.
3839. Gibson, Emily. "A Study of the Major Organ Works of Hindemith: The Three Sonatas and the Two Concerti." D.M.A. diss., University of Rochester, 1968.
3840. Rehm, Gottfried. "Ein Beitrag zur tonal-atonikalen Harmonik: Harmonische Analyse von Hindemiths 1. Orgelsonate (letzter Satz) und Strawinskys *Agnus Dei.*" MK 55 (1985): 172–80.
3841. Schilling, Hans Ludwig. "Hindemiths Orgelsonaten." MK 33 (1963): 202–9.

Philharmonisches Konzert
3842. Sannemüller, Gerd. "Das *Philharmonische Konzert* von Paul Hindemith." HJ 6 (1977): 76–103.

Piano Sonatas
3843. Billeter, Bernhard. "Die kompositorische Entwicklung Hindemiths am Beispiel seiner Klavierwerke." HJ 6 (1977): 104–21. [No. 1]
3844. ———. "Zur Wiedergewinnung von Hindemiths Klaviersonate op. 17." HJ 16 (1987): 111–23.
3845. Kraemer, Uwe. "Hindemiths 2. Klaviersonate (1936), 1. Satz." MB 1 (1969): 74–77.

Pittsburgh Symphony
3846. Briner, Andres. "Hindemith's *Pittsburgh Symphony.*" MELOS 26 (1959): 252–55.
3847. Metz, Günther. "Das Webern-Zitat in Hindemiths *Pittsburgh Symphony.*" AM 42 (1985): 200–12.
3848. Neumeyer, David. "Hindemiths Auseinandersetzung mit der Reihentechnik." MTH 2, no. 1 (1987): 55–72.

Plöner Musiktag
3849. Sannemüller, Gerd. *Der "Plöner Musiktag" von Paul Hindemith.* Neumünster: K. Wachholtz, 1976.

Sancta Susanna

3850. Kube, Michael. "Die Faktur der Ekstase: Zu Kontext, Form und Harmonik von Hindemiths *Sancta Susanna.*" HJ 22 (1993): 46–67.

3851. Laubenthal, Annegrit. "Skizzen, Entstehung und Formkonzept der *Sancta Susanna.*" HJ 16 (1987): 124–37.

Septet (Winds)

3852. Neumeyer, David. "Tonal, Formal, and Proportional Design in Hindemith's Music." MTS 9 (1987): 93–116.

Serenaden

3853. Konold, Wulf. "Paul Hindemiths Serenaden." HJ 4 (1974): 88–96.

3854. Neumeyer, David Paul. "Letter-Name Mottoes in Hindemith's 'Gute Nacht.'" ITO 2, no. 8 (1976): 5–19. Reprint, HJ 6 (1977): 22–46.

Sinfonietta

3855. Kemp, Ian. "Sinfonietta 1950: Colour as Design." HJ 27 (1998): 180–96.

Sing und Spielmusik für Liebhaber und Musikfreunde

3856. Austin, William W. "Hindemith's 'Frau musica': The Versions of 1928 and 1943 Compared." F-Davison: 265–71.

Songs (various; *see also* specific songs and song cycles)

3857. Danuser, Hermann. "Paul Hindemiths amerikanische Lieder." HJ 27 (1998): 155–79.

3858. Fischer, Kurt von. "Hindemith's Early Songs for Voice and Piano." PRMA 109 (1982–1983): 147–59.

3859. Venus, Dankmar. *Vergleichende Untersuchungen zur melodischen Struktur der Singstimmen in den Liedern von Arnold Schönberg, Alban Berg, Anton Webern, und Paul Hindemith.* Göttingen: n.p., 1965.

Songs on Old Texts

3860. Neumann, Friedrich. "Kadenzen, Melodieführung, und Stimmführung in den *Six chansons* und *Five Songs on Old Texts* von Hindemith." HJ 8 (1979): 49–78.

String Quartets

3861. Doflein, Erich. "Die sechs Streichquartette von Paul Hindemith." SMZ 95 (1955): 413–21.

3862. Dorfman, Joseph. "Hindemith's Fourth Quartet." HJ 7 (1978): 54–71.

3863. ——. "Thematic Organization in the String Quartets of Paul Hindemith." OM 6 (1978): 45–58.

3864. Espey, Sister Jule Adele. "Formal, Tonal, and Thematic Structure of the Hindemith String Quartets." Ph.D. diss., Indiana University, 1974.

3865. Krummacher, Friedhelm. "Concordantia dissonans: Zum Quartettsatz Paul Hindemiths." JSIM (1998): 163–94.

3866. Kube, Michael. "Zum Stilwandel in Paul Hindermiths frühen Streichquartetten (1915–23)." HJ 25 (1996): 56–83. [Nos. 1–5]

3867. M-Pütz.

3868. Rexroth, Dieter. "Tradition und Reflexion beim frühen Hindemith: Analytische und interpretatorische Anmerkungen zu Op. 16." HJ 2 (1972): 91–113. [No. 3]

3869. Stephan, Rudolf. "Paul Hindemiths Streichquartett Op. 32." HJ 24 (1995): 25–41. [No. 5]

Stücke (Flute)

3870. Metz, Günther. "Paul Hindemiths Acht Stücke für Flöte allein." T 10, no. 2 (1985): 335–46.

Symphonic Metamorphosis after Themes by Carl Maria von Weber

3871. Anderson, Gene. "Musical Metamorphoses in Hindemith's March from *Symphonic Metamorphoses of Themes by Carl Maria von Weber.*" JBR 30, no. 1 (1994): 1–10.

3872. ——. "The Triumph of Timelessness over Time in Hindemith's 'Turandot Scherzo' from *Symphonic Metamorphosis of Themes by Carl Maria von Weber.*" CMS 36 (1996): 1–15.

3873. Brennecke, Wilfried. "Die Metamorphosen: Werke von Richard Strauss und Paul Hindemith." F-Albrecht: 268–84. Reprint, SMZ 103 (1963): 129–36, 199–208.

Symphony, E-Flat Major

3874. Konold, Wulf. "Hindemiths Symphonie in Es." HJ 15 (1986): 70–105.

Symphony for Concert Band

3875. Gallagher, Charles. "Hindemith's Symphony for Band." JBR 2, no. 1 (1966): 19–27.

Symphony serena

3876. Laaff, Ernst. "Hindemiths *Symphony serena.*" MELOS 15 (1948): 328–33.

3877. Neumeyer, David. "Tonal, Formal, and Proportional Design in Hindemith's Music." MTS 9 (1987): 93–116.

Tuba Sonata

3878. Neumeyer, David. "Hindemiths Auseinandersetzung mit der Reihentechnik." MTH 2, no. 1 (1987): 55–72.

Unaufhörliche

3879. Fehn, Ann Clark. "*Das Unaufhörliche*: Gottfried Benns Text in der Vertonung von Paul Hindemith." HJ 5 (1976): 43–101.

Viola Sonatas

3880. Hilse, Walter Bruno. "Hindemith and Debussy." HJ 2 (1972): 48–90. [Op. 11, no. 4]

3881. Neumeyer, David. "Hindermith's *hommages à Bach* in Two Early Viola Sonatas." HJ 16 (1987): 153–74. [Op. 11, no. 5; Op. 31, no. 4]

Violin Sonatas

3882. Borris, Siegfried. "Vergleichende Werkanalyse: Alban Berg, Op. 5, Nr.1; Paul Hindemith, aus der Violinsonate 1939." M-Benary: 35–47. Reprint, MB 5 (1973): 138–41.

3883. M-Chihara.

3884. Hambourg, Klement Main. "Three Sonatas for Violin and Piano by Paul Hindemith: A Stylistic and Interpretive Study." D.M.A. diss., University of Oregon, 1977.

3885. Hilse, Walter Bruno. "Hindemith and Debussy." HJ 2 (1972): 48–90. [Op. 11, no. 1]

Various Works

3886. Bobbitt, Richard. "Hindemith's Twelve-Tone Scale." MR 26 (1965): 104–17.

3887. Borris, Siegfried. "Hindemiths posthum fertiggestelltes Lehrsystem." MB 2, no. 11 (1970): 484–89.

3888. Brennecke, Dietrich. "'Ein Ideal edler und möglichst vollkommenen Musik': Paul Hindemiths Verhältnis zur Tradition." JP 3 (1980): 86–115.

3889. Briner, Andres. *Paul Hindemith*. Zurich: Atlantis; Mainz: Schott, 1971.

3890. Browne, Arthur G. "Paul Hindemith and Neo-Classic Music." ML 13 (1932): 42–58.

3891. Cahn, Peter. "Hindemiths Cadenzen." HJ 1 (1971): 80–134.

3892. Decker, Jay C. "A Comparative Textural Analysis of Selected Orchestral Works of William Walton and Paul Hindemith." D.M.A. diss., University of Missouri, 1971.

3893. Dorfman, Joseph. "Tonal Concepts in the Instrumental Chamber Works of Paul Hindemith." ISM 2 (1979): 141–56.

3894. ———. "Counterpoint-Sonata Form." HJ 19 (1990): 55–67.

3895. Hilse, Walter B. "Factors Making for Coherence in the Works of Paul Hindemith, 1919–1926." Ph.D. diss., Columbia University, 1972.

3896. Hindemith, Paul. "Methods of Music Theory." MQ 30 (1944): 20–28.

3897. Hymanson, William. "Hindemith's Variations: A Comparison of Early and Recent Works." MR 13 (1952): 20–33.

3898. Kleemann, Paul. "Die Kompositionsprinzip Paul Hindemiths und sein Verhältnis zur Atonalität." F-Albert/H: 80–92.

3899. Koper, Robert Peter. "A Stylistic and Performance Analysis of the Bassoon Music of Paul Hindemith." Ed.D. diss., University of Illinois, 1972.

3900. Landau, Victor. "The Harmonic Theories of Paul Hindemith in Relation to His Practice as a Composer of Chamber Music." Ph.D. diss., New York University, 1957.

3901. ———. "Hindemith the System Builder: A Critique of His Theory of Harmony." MR 22 (1961): 137–51.

3902. ———. "Paul Hindemith: A Case Study in Theory and Practice." MR 21 (1960): 36–54.

3903. Lanza, Andrea. "Libertà e determinazione formale nel giovane Hindemith." RIM 5 (1970): 234–91.

3904. Mason, Colin. "Hindemiths Kammermusik." MELOS 24 (1957): 171–77, 255–58.

3905. ———. "Some Aspects of Hindemith's Chamber Music." ML 41 (1960): 150–55.

3906. Metz, Günther. *Melodische Polyphonie in der Zwölftonordnung: Studien zum Kontapunkt Paul Hindemiths*. Baden-Baden: Koener, 1976.

3907. Neumeyer, David Paul. "Counterpoint and Pitch Structure in the Early Music of Hindemith." Ph.D. diss., Yale University, 1976.

3908. ———. *The Music of Paul Hindemith*. New Haven, Conn.: Yale University Press, 1986.

3909. Ohlsson, Jean Mary. "Paul Hindemith's Music for Flute: Analysis of Solo Works and Stylistic and Formal Considerations of Chamber Works." D.M.A. diss., Ohio State University, 1975.

3910. Payne, Dorothy Katherine. "Contrapuntal Techniques in the Accompanied Brass and Woodwind Sonatas of Hindemith." Ph.D. diss., University of Rochester, 1974.

3911. Redlich, Hans. "Paul Hindemith: A Re-Assessment." MR 25 (1964): 241–53.

3912. Reich, Willi. "Paul Hindemith." MQ 17 (1931): 486–96.

3913. Rosteck, Jens. "Das 'nette Spiel' der Polytonalität: Zur Wahlverwandtschaft zwischen Darius Milhaud und Paul Hindemith." MF 46, no. 3 (1993): 268–84.

3914. Salmen, Walter. "Alte Töne und Volksmusik in Kompositionen Paul Hindemiths." MB 6 (1974): 362–69.

3915. Schilling, Hans Ludwig. "Melodischer Sequenzbau im Werke Paul Hindemiths." SMZ 96 (1956): 429–33.

3916. Schollum, Robert. "Metamorphosen über Thema Hindemith." M 9 (1955): 533–38.

3917. Strobel, Heinrich. *Paul Hindemith.* Mainz: Schott, 1948.

3918. Thomson, William. "Hindemith's Contribution to Music Theory." JMT 9 (1965): 52–71.

3919. Tischler, Hans. "Remarks on Hindemith's Contrapuntal Technique." F-Apel: 175–84.

3920. Zwinck, Eberhard. *Paul Hindemiths "Unterweisung im Tonsatz" als Konsequenz der Entwicklung seiner Kompositonstechnik: Graphische und statistische Musikanalyse.* Goppingen: Kummerle, 1974.

HOCH, FRANCESCO (b. 1943)

3921. Hoch, Francesco. "Francesco Hoch: *Memorie da requiem.*" DI 35 (1993): 4–8.

3922. ———. "*Idra* per 11 archi (1973)." SMZ 115 (1975): 77–85.

HODDINOTT, ALUN (b. 1929)

3923. Clark, Stewart Jay. "The Choral Music of Alun Hoddinott: An Analysis and Related Conclusions Concerning Performance." D.M.A. diss., University of Texas, 1977.

HOFFMANN, E. T. A. (1776–1822)

3924. Dechant, Hermann. *E. T. A. Hoffmanns Oper "Aurora."* Regensburg: Bosse, 1975.

3925. Garlington, Aubrey S., Jr. "Notes on Dramatic Motives in Opera: Hoffmann's *Undine.*" MR 32 (1971): 136–45.

HOHENSEE, WOLFGANG (b. 1927)

3926. Rebling, Eberhard. "Ein gelungenes Experiment: Das *Poem* für zwei Klaviere und Orchester von Wolfgang Hohensee." MG 16 (1966): 659–62.

HOLBROOKE, JOSEPH (1878–1958)

3927. Forbes, Anne-Marie H. "Josef Holbrooke's *Cauldron of Annwn* and Metempsychosis in Music." MSA 17 (1994): 43–59.

HÖLLER, YORK (b. 1944)

3928. Battier, Marc, and Thierry Lancino. "Simulation and Extrapolation of Instrumental Sounds Using Direct Synthesis at IRCAM (a propos of *Resonance*)." CMR 1, no. 1 (1984–1985): 77–81.

3929. Haynes, Stanley. "Report on the Realization of York Holler's *Arcus.*" CMR 1, no. 1 (1984–1985): 41–66.

3930. Höller, York. "*Resonance*: Composition Today." CMR 1, no. 1 (1984–1985): 67–76.

3931. Karallus, Manfred. "Schlangenbeschwörung und Pythagoras verbindend . . . der Komponist York Höller." NZM 144, no. 11 (1983): 14–18.

HOLLIGER, HEINZ (b. 1939)

3932. Häusler, Josef. "Heinz Holliger: Versuch eines Porträts." SMZ 107 (1967): 64–73.

3933. Lessing, Wolfgang. "Hommage à Sacher: Henri Dutilleux' und Heinz Holligers Kompositionen für Violoncello solo über den Namen Sacher." MTH 6, no. 2 (1991): 151–80. [Chaconne for Solo Cello]

3934. Rigoni, Michel. "Le Cycle-Scardanelli de Heinz Holliger." INH 8–9 (1991): 348–68. [*Scardanelli-Zyklus*]

3935. Roth, Markus. "Der Gang ins Verstummen: Heinz Holligers *Beiseit-Zyklus* nach Robert Walser." MAS 4, no. 14 (2000): 40–51.

HOLLOWAY, ROBIN (b. 1943)

3936. Burn, Andrew. "Holloway's Viola Concerto and Ballad." TEMPO 155 (1985): 33–34.

3937. Nash, Peter Paul. "*Cantata on the Death of God* and *Clarissa.*" TEMPO 129 (1979): 27–34.

HOLST, GUSTAV (1874–1934)

Egdon Heath (Homage to Hardy)

3938. Greene, Richard. "A Musico-Rhetorical Outline of Holst's *Egdon Heath.*" ML 73, no. 2 (1992): 244–67.

Hammersmith

3939. Cantrick, Robert. "*Hammersmith* and the Two Worlds of Gustav Holst." JBR 12, no. 1 (1975–1977): 3–11.

Hymn of Jesus

3940. Boyer, D. Royce. "Holst's *The Hymn of Jesus*: An Investigation into Mysticism in Music." MR 36 (1975): 272–83.

Planets

3941. Greene, Richard. *Holst: The Planets.* Cambridge: Cambridge University Press, 1995.

3942. Macan, Edward. "Holst's 'Mars': A Model of Goal-Oriented Bitonality." F-Jackson: 411–22.

Songs without Words
3943. Greene, Richard. "*Country Song*: An Example of Gustav Holst's Rhetorical Method." MR 50, nos. 3–4 (1989): 240–69.

Suites for Military Band
3944. Gallagher, Charles. "Thematic Derivations in the Holst First Suite in E Flat." JBR 1, no. 2 (1964–1965): 6–10.
3945. Mitchell, Jon Ceander. "Gustav Holst's Three Folk Tunes: A Source for the Second Suite in F." JBR 19, no. 1 (1983–1984): 1–4.

Various Works
3946. Holst, Imogen. *The Music of Gustav Holst.* London: Oxford University Press, 1951.
3947. Krone, Max T. "The Choral Works of Gustav Holst." Ph.D. diss., Northwestern University, 1940.
3948. Mitchell, Jon Ceander. "Gustav Holst: The Works for Military Band." Ed.D. diss., University of Illinois, 1980.

HÖLSZKY, ADRIANA (b. 1953)
3949. Büchter-Römer, Ute. "Chaos der Gefühle: Adriana Hölszky: *Bremer Freiheit*–Singwerk auf ein Frauenleben." MTX 65 (1996): 60–62.
3950. Hiekel, Jörn-Peter. "Der Boden unter den Füßen schwankt: Momente des 'Anästhetischen' im Werk von Adriana Hölszky." MTX 65 (1996): 63–67.
3951. Houben, Eva-Maria. "Durchsichtige Wände in Bewegung: Die neueren Werke von Adriana Hölszky." MTX 65 (1996): 39–45.
3952. Stegen, Gudrun. "Komponistenporträt Adriana Hölszky." N 4 (1983–1984): 54–67.

HOLT, SIMEON TEN (b. 1923)
3953. Holt, Simeon ten. "*Tripticon* by Simeon ten Holt." SS 39 (1969): 33–40.

HONEGGER, ARTHUR (1892–1955)

Amphion
3954. Calmel, Huguette. "La collaboration Valéry-Honegger à travers *Amphion* (1929)." SMZ 120 (1980): 5–11.

Choral Works (various; *see also* specific choral works)
3955. Headley, Harrold Eugene. "The Choral Works of Arthur Honegger." Ph.D. diss., North Texas State University, 1959.
3956. Voss, Hans-Dieter. "Die Oratorien von Arthur Honegger." Ph.D. diss., Heidelberg, 1982.

Piano Works
3957. Ehrler, Hanno. *Untersuchungen zur Klaviermusik von Francis Poulenc, Arthur Honegger, und Darius Milhaud.* Tutzing: Schneider, 1990.

Roi David
3958. Spratt, Geoffrey Kenneth. "Honegger's *Le roi David*: A Reassessment." MR 39 (1978): 54–60.

Rugby (*Mouvement symphonique* No. 2)
3959. Waters, Keith John. "Rhythmic and Contrapuntal Structures in the Music of Arthur Honegger." Ph.D. diss., University of Rochester, 1997.

Symphonies
3960. Maillard, Jean, and Jacques Nahoum. *Les Symphonies d'Arthur Honegger.* Paris: Leduc, 1974.
3961. Parker, Daniel Quienton, II. "The Symphonies of Arthur Honegger: An Examination of Stylistic Factors and Form." Ph.D. diss., University of Kentucky, 1990.
3962. Silver, Hector. "Honegger: Lithurgische Sinfonie." MELOS 14 (1947): 383–86. [*Symphonie liturgique* (Symphony No. 3)]
3963. Waters, Keith John. "Rhythmic and Contrapuntal Structures in the Music of Arthur Honegger." Ph.D. diss., University of Rochester, 1997. [Symphony No. 2 ("Symphonie pour cordes")]

Violin Sonata, D Minor (1912)
3964. Waters, Keith J. "Rhythm and Meter in an Early Composition of Arthur Honegger." MPSS 8 (1995): 22–24.

Various Works
3965. Castanet, Pierre-Albert. "L'appareil cinétique dans l'œuvre instrumentale d'Arthur Honegger." ANM 8 (1987): 31–35.
3966. M-Hart.
3967. Spratt, Geoffrey Kenneth. "A Critical Study of the Complete Works of Arthur Honegger with Particular Reference to His Dramatic Works." Ph.D. diss., Bristol, 1980.
3968. Tappolet, Willy. *Arthur Honegger.* Zurich: Atlantis, 1954.
3969. Trickey, Samuel Miller. "Les Six." Ph.D. diss., North Texas State University, 1955.

HÖNIGSBERG, DAVID (b. 1959)

3970. Hönigsberg, David. "Chamber Symphony 1998." CM 67–68 (1999): 139–56.

HORN, CHARLES EDWARD (1786–1849)

3971. Montague, Richard A. "Charles Edward Horn: His Life and Works (1786–1849)." Ed.D. diss., Florida State University, 1959.

HORST, ANTHON VAN DER (1899–1965)

3972. Geraedts, Jaap. "Anthon van der Horst: *Réflexions* pour orchester." SS 21 (1964): 35–41.

3973. Wouters, Jos. "Dr. Anthon van der Horst (1899–1965)." SS 23 (1965): 1–17.

HOVHANESS, ALAN (1911–2000)

3974. Cox, Dennis Keith. "Aspects of the Compositional Styles of Three Selected Twentieth-Century American Composers of Choral Music: Alan Hovhaness, Ron Nelson, and Daniel Pinkham." D.M.A. diss., University of Missouri, 1978.

3975. Gerbrandt, Carl James. "The Solo Vocal Music of Alan Hovhaness." D.M.A. diss., Peabody Conservatory, 1974.

3976. M-Jeter. [*Vijag*, op. 37]

3977. Johnson, Axie Allen. "Choral Settings of the Magnificat by Selected Twentieth Century Composers." D.M.A. diss., University of Southern California, 1968.

3978. Rosner, Arnold. "An Analytical Survey of the Music of Alan Hovhaness." Ph.D. diss., State University of New York, Buffalo, 1979.

3979. Tircuit, Heuwell. "Alan Hovhaness: An American Choral Composer." ACR 9, no. 1 (1966): 8, 10–11, 17.

HOWELLS, HERBERT (1892–1983)

3980. Hodgson, Peter John. "The Music of Herbert Howells." Ph.D. diss., University of Colorado, 1970.

HUBER, KLAUS (b. 1924)

Erinnere dich an G . . .

3981. Piencikowski, Robert. "Hors-Texte: *Erinnere dich an G* . . . ." ENT 7 (1988): 127–33.

Erniedrigt-Geknechtet-Verlassen-Verachtet

3982. Nyffeler, Max. "Klaus Huber: *Erniedrigt-Geknechtet-Verlassen-Verachtet.*" Trans. Martin Kaltenecker. ENT 7 (1988): 97–125.

Litania instrumentalis

3983. Pauli, Hansjurg. "Klaus Huber." M 17 (1963): 10–17.

Senfkorn

3984. Gasser, Ulrich. "Klaus Hubers *Senfkorn*: Informatives, Analytisches, und Spekulatives." SMZ 118 (1978): 142–49.

Tempora

3985. Keller, Kjell. "*Tempora*: Konzert für Violine und Orchester von Klaus Huber." MELOS 40 (1973): 165–172.

Tenebrae

3986. Flammer, Ernst Helmuth. "Form und Gehalt (II): Eine Analyse von Klaus Hubers *Tenebrae.*" Melos/NZM 4 (1978): 294–304.

Turnus

3987. Keller, Kjell. "Öffnen der Fenster: Klaus Hubers Orchestermusik *Turnus.*" MTX 51 (1993): 47–48.

Umgepflügte Zeit

3988. Fervers, Andreas. "*Die umgepflügte Zeit*: Klaus Hubers Stuck nach Texten von Ossip Mandelstam in memoriam Luigi Nono." NZM 153, no. 9 (1992): 23–27.

Von Zeit zu Zeit

3989. Oehlschlägel, Reinhard. "'. . . immer mit stärkstem Ausdruck!' Zu Klaus Hubers Zweitem Streichquartett . . . *von Zeit zu Zeit* . . . ." MTX 51 (1993): 43–46.

Various Works

3990. Andraschke, Peter. "Traditionsmomente in Kompositionen von Christobal Halffter, Klaus Huber und Wolfgang Rihm." M-Brinkmann: 130–52.

3991. Muggler, Fritz. "Das Porträt Klaus Hubers." MELOS 41 (1974): 339–44.

3992. Schweizer, Klaus. "Geschichte, eingespannt in Gegenwart: Choräle in Partituren von Klaus Huber." NZM 146, nos. 7–8 (1985): 32–38.

HUBER, NICOLAUS A. (b. 1939)

3993. Huber, Nicolaus. "*Gespenster*: Vorspruch-Tutti-Lied." N 2 (1981–1982): 51–67.

HUGGLER, JOHN (1928–1993)

3994. M-Chihara.

HUMMEL, FRANZ (b. 1939)

3995. Schneider, Norbert Jürgen. "'Ich flüchte, wenn ich kann': Musik und Psychoanalyse in Franz Hummels Oper *Blaubart*." MTX 19 (1987): 17–23.

HUMMEL, JOHANN NEPOMUK (1778–1837)

3996. Davis, Richard. "The Music of J. N. Hummel: Its Derivations and Development." MR 26 (1965): 169–91.

3997. Mitchell, Francis H. "The Piano Concertos of Johann Nepomuk Hummel." Ph.D. diss., Northwestern University, 1957.

3998. Zimmerschied, Dieter. "Die Kammermusik Johann Nepomuk Hummels." Ph.D. diss., Mainz, 1966.

HUMPERDINCK, ENGELBERT (1854–1921)

3999. ASO 104 (1987). [*Hänsel und Gretel*]

4000. Gerstner, Annette. *Drei Klavierlieder Engelbert Humperdincks.* Berlin: Merseburger, 1984.

HURÉ, JEAN (1877–1930)

4001. M-Kniesner. [Piano Sonata No. 1]

HUREL, PHILIPPE (b. 1955)

4002. Nieminen, Risto, ed. *Philippe Hurel.* Paris: IRCAM, 1994.

HUSA, KAREL (b. 1921)

4003. Hartzell, Lawrence W. "Karel Husa: The Man and the Music." MQ 62 (1976): 87–104.

4004. Molineux, Allen. "The Elements of Unity and Their Applications on Various Levels of the First Movement of Karel Husa's Concerto for Wind Ensemble." JBR 21, no. 1 (1985): 43–49.

4005. Rollin, Robert. "Pitch Structure, Form, and Notation in Husa's Concerto for Orchestra." SONUS 13, no. 2 (1993): 45–63.

HYLA, LEE (b. 1952)

4006. Wheeler, Scott. "Beyond the Flat Surface: Form and Rhetoric in Machover, Hyla, and Lindroth." CMR 10, no. 1 (1994): 75–100. [*Pre-Pulse Suspended*]

– I –

IANNACCONE, ANTHONY (b. 1943)

4007. Kalib, Sylvan. "Anthony Iannaccone's *Apparitions*." JBR 25, no. 1 (1989): 2–67.

4008. Renshaw, Jeffrey. "Analysis: Anthony Iannaccone's *Sea Drift*." 35, no. 1 (1999): 36–62.

IBERT, JACQUES (1890–1962)

4009. Failoni, Judith Weaver. "Tradition and Innovation in Jacques Ibert's Opera *Persée et Andromède*." Ph.D. diss., Washington University, 1994.

4010. Timlin, Francis Eugene. "An Analytic Study of the Flute Works of Jacques Ibert." D.M.A. diss., University of Washington, 1980.

IMBRIE, ANDREW (b. 1921)

4011. Boykan, Martin. "Third Quartet." PNM 3, no. 1 (1964): 139–46.

4012. Brown, Whitman P. "Phrase Behavior and Cadence Formation in the First Movement of Andrew Imbrie's *Pilgrimage*." Ph.D. diss., Brandeis University, 1999.

4013. Durant, Douglas Fredrick. "Andrew Imbrie: Analysis and Speculations." Ph.D. diss., Brandeis University, 1989. [*Angle of Repose* (Act III, Scene I), String Quartet No. 4 (Movement I)]

4014. Reynolds, Christopher A. "A New Cantata by Andrew Imbrie: *Prometheus Bound*." ACR 23, no. 2 (1981): 3–10.

INDY, VINCENT D' (1851–1931)

4015. Keym, Stefan. "'L'unité dans la variété': Vincent d'Indy und das zyklische Prinzip." MTH 13, no. 3 (1998): 223–41. [Piano Sonata, op. 63; Symphony No. 2, op. 57; Violin Sonata, op. 59]

4016. M-Kniesner. [Piano Sonata, op. 63]

4017. Luck, Ray. "An Analysis of Three Variations Sets for Piano by Bizet, d'Indy and Pierné." D.M.A. diss., Indiana University, 1978.

4018. Schneider, Herbert. "Das Streichquartett Op. 45 von Vincent d'Indy als Exemplum der zyklischen Sonate." F-Finscher: 655–67.

4019. Schubert, Giselher. "'Vibrierende Gedanken' und das 'Katasterverfahren' der Analyse: Zu den Klaviersonaten von Dukas und d'Indy." F-Dahlhaus: 619–34. [Piano Sonata, op. 63]

4020. Schwartz, Manuela. "Symbolic Structures and Elements in the Opera *Fervaal* of Vincent d'Indy." CMR 17, no. 3 (1998): 43–56.

IRELAND, JOHN (1879–1962)

4021. Dickinson, A. E. F. "The Progress of John Ireland." MR 1 (1940): 343–53.

4022. Rankin, W. Donald. "The Solo Piano Music of John Ireland." D.M.A. diss., Boston University, 1970.

4023. Townsend, Nigel. "The Achievement of John Ireland." ML 24 (1943): 65–74.

4024. Yenne, Vernon Lee. "Three Twentieth-Century English Song Composers: Peter Warlock, E. J. Morran, and John Ireland." D.M.A. diss., University of Illinois, 1969. No DA listing.

IVES, CHARLES (1874–1954)

Celestial Railroad

4025. Brodhead, Thomas M. "Ives's *Celestial Railroad* and His Fourth Symphony." AMUS 12, no. 4 (1994): 389–424.

Choral Works (various; *see also* specific choral works)

4026. Kumlien, Wendell C. "The Sacred Choral Music of Charles Ives: A Study in Style Development." D.M.A. diss., University of Illinois, 1969.

Chromâtimelôdtune

4027. Lambert, J. Philip. "Aggregate Structures in Music of Charles Ives." JMT 34, no. 1 (1990): 29–55.

4028. ———. "Another View of *Chromâtimelôdtune*." JMR 1, no. 4 (1991): 237–62.

Concord Sonata. See Piano Sonata No. 2

In Re Con Moto et al.

4029. Lambert, J. Philip. "Interval Cycles as Compositional Resources in the Music of Charles Ives." MTS 12, no. 1 (1990): 43–82.

Orchestral Set No. 1: Three Places in New England

4030. Josephson, Nors S. "The Initial Sketches for Ives's 'St. Gaudens in Boston Common.'" SN 12 (1984–1985): 46–63.

4031. Kramer, Jonathan D. "Postmodern Concepts of Musical Time." ITR 17, no. 2 (1996): 21–61. ["Putnam's Camp"]

4032. Stein, Alan. "The Musical Language of Charles Ives's Three Places in New England." D.M.A. diss., University of Illinois, 1975.

Piano Sonata No. 1

4033. Greenfield, John Wolkowsky. "Charles Edward Ives and the Stylistic Aspects of His First Piano Sonata." D.M.A. diss., University of Miami, 1976.

Piano Sonata No. 2 ("Concord, Mass., 1840–1860")

4034. Albert, Thomas Russell. "The Harmonic Language of Charles Ives' *Concord Sonata*." D.M.A. diss., University of Illinois, 1974.

4035. Babcock, Michael J. "Ives's 'Thoreau': A Point of Order." ASUC 9–10 (1974–1975): 89–102.

4036. Block, Geoffrey. *Ives: Concord Sonata*. Cambridge: Cambridge University Press, 1996.

4037. Brodhead, Thomas M. "Ives's *Celestial Railroad* and His Fourth Symphony." AMUS 12, no. 4 (1994): 389–424.

4038. Clark, Sondra Rae. "The Element of Choice in Ives's *Concord Sonata*." MQ 60 (1974): 167–86.

4039. ———. "The Evolving *Concord Sonata*: A Study of Choices and Variants in the Music of Charles Ives." Ph.D. diss., Stanford University, 1972.

4040. Conen, Hermann. "'All the Wrong Notes Are Wright': Zu Charles Ives 2. Klaviersonate 'Concord, Mass. 1840–60.'" N 1 (1980): 28–42.

4041. Fischer, Fred. "Ives's *Concord Sonata*." PQ 92 (1975–1976): 23–27.

4042. ———. *Ives's Concord Sonata*. Denton, Tex.: C/G Productions, 1981.

4043. Ghandar, Ann. "Charles Ives: Organization in 'Emerson.'" MS 6 (1980): 111–27.

4044. M-Rathert.

4045. Schubert, Giselher. "Die *Concord-Sonata* von Charles Ives: Anmerkungen zur Werkstruktur und Interpretation." F-Savoff: 121–38.

4046. ———. "La sonate *Concord* de Charles Ives." Trans. Carlo Russi. CC 7 (1986): 110–28.

Psalm 90

4047. Grantham, Donald. "A Harmonic *Leitmotif* System in Ives's *Psalm 90*." ITO 5, no. 2 (1979–1981): 3–14.

Robert Browning Overture

4048. Hüsken, Renate. "Charles Ives *Robert Browning Overture*." N 1 (1980): 16–24.

4049. Kolter, Horst. "Zur Kompositionstechnik von Charles Edward Ives." NZM 113 (1972): 559–67.

Songs

4050. Argento, Dominick. "A Digest Analysis of Ives's *On the Antipodes*." SMM 6 (1975–1976): 192–200.

4051. Euteneuer-Rohrer, Ursula Henrietta. "Charles Ives *The Cage*: Eine Werkbetrachtung." N 1 (1980): 47–53.

4052. Hitchcock, H. Wiley. "'A Grand and Glorious Noise!' Charles Ives as Lyricist." AMUS 15, no. 1 (1997): 26–44.

4053. Johnson, Timothy A. "Chromatic Quotations of Diatonic Tunes in Songs of Charles Ives." MTS 18, no. 2 (1996): 236–61. [*Old Home Day*, various other songs]

4054. Lambert, J. Philip. "Interval Cycles as Compositional Resources in the Music of Charles Ives." MTS 12, no. 1 (1990): 43–82. [*On the Antipodes*]

4055. M-Lambert. [*The Cage*]

4056. Lorenz, Christof. "Das Liedschaffen Charles Ives." Ph.D. diss., University of Cologne, 1978.

4057. Newman, Philip. "The Songs of Charles Ives." Ph.D. diss., University of Iowa, 1967.

4058. M-Rathert. [*Paracelsus*]

4059. Schoffman, Nachum. "Charles Ives's Song *Vote for Names*." CM 23 (1977): 56–68.

4060. ———. "Ives: Un exemple de polyphonie complexe." Trans. Jacques Demierre. CC 7 (1986): 155–75. [*Aeschylus and Sophocles*]

4061. ———. "The Songs of Charles Ives." Ph.D. diss., Hebrew University, Jerusalem, 1977.

4062. Starr, Lawrence. "Style and Substance: *Ann Street* by Charles Ives." PNM 15, no. 2 (1977): 23–33.

4063. Velten, Klaus. "Ein Komponist zwischen den Zeiten: Traditionelle Geist und fortschrittliche Gestaltungsweise in Klavierliedern von Charles Ives." MB 15, no. 12 (1983): 11–15.

4064. ———. "Der Künstler und die Natur: Ein Interpretationsbeitrag zum Liedschaffen von Charles Ives." MB 13 (1981): 544–46.

String Quartets

4065. Budde, Elmar. "Anmerkungen zum Streichquartett Nr. 2 von Charles E. Ives." In *Bericht über den Internationalen Musikwissenschaftlichen Kongress Bonn 1970, Gesellschaft für Musikforschung*, ed. Carl Dahlhaus, 303–7, 317–19. Kassel: Bärenreiter, 1971.

4066. M-Rathert. [No. 2]

4067. Walker, Gwyneth. "Tradition and Breaking of Tradition in the String Quartets of Ives and Schoenberg." D.M.A. diss., University of Hartford, 1976.

Study No. 5 (Piano)

4068. M-Lambert.

Symphonies (various; *see also* specific symphonies)

4069. Badolato, James Vincent. "The Four Symphonies of Charles Ives: A Critical, Analytical Study of the Musical Style of Charles Ives." Ph.D. diss., Catholic University of America, 1978.

4070. Herrmann, Bernard. "Four Symphonies by Charles Ives." MM 22 (1945): 215–22.

4071. Magers, Roy Vernon. "Aspects of Form in the Symphonies of Charles E. Ives." Ph.D. diss., Indiana University, 1975.

Symphony: New England Holidays

4072. Maisel, Arthur. "'The Fourth of July' by Charles Ives: Mixed Harmonic Criteria in a Twentieth-Century Classic." TP 6, no. 1 (1981): 3–32.

4073. Nelson, Mark D. "Beyond Mimesis: Transcendentalism and Processes of Analogy in Charles Ives's 'The Fourth of July.'" PNM 22 (1983–1984): 353–84.

Symphony No. 1

4074. M-Roller. [Movement I]

Symphony No. 2

4075. Burkholder, J. Peter. "'Quotation' and Paraphrase in Ives's Second Symphony." NCM 11, no. 1 (1987): 3–25. Reprinted in *Music at the Turn of the Century*, ed. Joseph Kerman, 33–55. Berkeley: University of California Press, 1990.

4076. Charles, Sydney Robinson. "The Use of Borrowed Material in Ives's Second Symphony." MR 28 (1967): 102–11.

4077. Sterne, Colin. "The Quotations in Charles Ives's Second Symphony." ML 52 (1971): 39–45.

Symphony No. 3

4078. M-Roller. [Movement III]

Symphony No. 4

4079. Brodhead, Thomas M. "Ives's *Celestial Railroad* and His Fourth Symphony." AMUS 12, no. 4 (1994): 389–424.

4080. Brooks, William. "Unity and Diversity in Charles Ives's Fourth Symphony." Y 10 (1974): 5–49.

4081. Cyr, Gordon. "Intervallic Structural Elements in Ives's Fourth Symphony." PNM 9, no. 2–10, no. 1 (1971): 291–303.

4082. Kolter, Horst. "Zur Kompositionstechnik von Charles Edward Ives." NZM 113 (1972): 559–67.

4083. Rathert, Wolfgang. "Charles Ives: Symphony Nr. 4, 1911–1916." N 3 (1982–1983): 226–41.

4084. M-Rathert.

4085. M-Roller. [Movement I]

4086. Stone, Kurt. "Ives's Fourth Symphony: A Review." MQ 52 (1966): 1–16.

Three-Page Sonata

4087. Baron, Carol Kitzes. "Ives on His Own Terms: An Explication, a Theory of Pitch Organization, and a New Critical Edition for the *Three-Page Sonata*." Ph.D. diss., City University of New York, 1987.

Three Places in New England. See Orchestral Set No. 1

Tone Roads et al.

4088. M-Lambert. [No. 1]

Unanswered Question

4089. Enke, Heinz. "Charles Ives *The Unanswered Question*." M-Benary: 30–34. Reprinted in *Zur musikalischen Analyse*, ed. Gerhard Schumacher, 232–40. Darmstadt: Wissenschaftliche Buchgesellschaft, 1974.

4090. Hitchcock, H. Wiley, and Noel Zahler. "Just What *Is* Ives's Unanswered Question?" NOTES 44, no. 3 (1988): 437–43.

4091. Jolas, Betsy. "Sur Ives *The Unanswered Question*." MJ 1 (1970): 13–16.

Universe Symphony

4092. Lambert, J. Philip. "Interval Cycles as Compositional Resources in the Music of Charles Ives." MTS 12, no. 1 (1990): 43–82.

4093. Rathert, Wolfgang. "Paysage imaginaire et perception totale: L'idée et la forme de la symphonie *Universe*." Trans. Vincent Barras. CC 7 (1986): 129–54.

Violin Sonatas

4094. Forte, Allen. "The Diatonic Looking Glass, or an Ivesian Metamorphosis." MQ 76, no. 3 (1992): 355–82. [No. 2 (Movement II)]

4095. Gingerich, Lora L. "A Technique for Melodic Motivic Analysis in the Music of Charles Ives." MTS 8 (1986): 75–93. [No. 4 (Movement III)]

Various Works

4096. Bellamann, Henry. "Charles Ives: The Man and His Music." MQ 19 (1933): 45–58.

4097. Blum, Stephen. "Ives's Position in Social and Musical History." MQ 63 (1977): 459–82.

4098. Boatwright, Howard. "Ives's Quarter-Tone Impressions." PNM 3, no. 2 (1965): 22–31.

4099. Burkholder, J. Peter. *Charles Ives: The Ideas behind the Music*. New Haven, Conn.: Yale University Press, 1985.

4100. ———. "The Evolution of Charles Ives's Music: Aesthetics, Quotation, Technique." Ph.D. diss., University of Chicago, 1983.

4101. ———. "'Quotation' and Emulation: Charles Ives's Uses of His Models." MQ 81 (1985): 1–26.

4102. Cowell, Henry. *Charles Ives and His Music*. New York: Oxford University Press, 1955.

4103. Danner, Gregory. "Ives's Harmonic Language." JMR 5 (1984–1985): 237–49.

4104. Ellison, Mary. "Ives's Use of American 'Popular' Tunes as Thematic Material." In *Charles Edward Ives*, ed. F. W. O'Reilly, 30–34. Coral Gables, Fla.: University of Miami, 1976.

4105. Helm, Everett. "Charles Ives: Pionier der modernen Musik." MELOS 25 (1958): 119–23.

4106. Henderson, Clayton W. "Quotation as a Style Element in the Music of Charles Ives." Ph.D. diss., Washington University, 1969.

4107. ———. "Structural Importance of Borrowed Music in the Works of Charles Ives: A Preliminary Assessment." In Report of the Eleventh Congress, International Musicological Society, Copenhagen, 1972, ed. H. Glahn et al., 437. Copenhagen: Hansen, 1974.

4108. Hitchcock, H. Wiley. *Ives*. Oxford: Oxford University Press, 1977.

4109. Hutchinson, Mary Ann. "Unrelated Simultaneity as an Historical Index to the Music of Charles Ives." M.M. thesis, Florida State University, 1970.

4110. Josephson, Nors S. "Charles Ives: Intervallische Permutationen im Spätwerk." ZM 9, no. 2 (1978): 27–33.

4111. ———. "Zur formalen Struktur einiger später Orchesterwerke von Charles Ives (1874–1954)." MF 27 (1974): 57–64.

4112. Kolosick, J. Timothy. "A Computer-Assisted, Set-Theoretic Investigation of Vertical Simultaneities in Selected Piano Compositions by Charles E. Ives." Ph.D. diss., University of Wisconsin, 1981.

4113. Lambert, J. Philip. "Ives and Counterpoint." AMUS 9, no. 2 (1991): 119–48.

4114. ———. "Ives' 'Piano Drum' Chords." INT 3 (1989): 1–36.

4115. ———. "Toward a Theory of Chord Structure for the Music of Charles Ives." JMT 37, no. 1 (1993): 55–83.

4116. Marshall, Dennis. "Charles Ives's Quotations: Manner or Substance?" PNM 6, no. 2 (1968): 45–56.

4117. Maske, Ulrich. *Charles Ives in seiner Kammermusik für drei bis sechs Instrumente.* Regensburg: Bosse, 1971.

4118. Milligan, Terry G. "Charles Ives: A Survey of the Works for Chamber Ensemble which Utilize Wind Instruments (1898–1908)." JBR 18, no. 1 (1982–1983): 60–68.

4119. Montague, Stephen Rowley. "The Simple and Complex in Selected Works of Charles Ives." M.M. thesis, Florida State University, 1967.

4120. Perison, Harry. "The Quarter-Tone System of Charles Ives." CM 18 (1974): 96–104.

4121. Quackenbush, Margret Diane. "Form and Texture in the Works for Mixed Chamber Ensemble by Charles Ives." M.A. thesis, University of Oregon, 1976.

4122. Rinehart, John McLain. "Ives's Compositional Idioms: An Investigation of Selected Short Works as Microcosms of His Musical Language." Ph.D. diss., Ohio State University, 1971.

4123. Schoffman, Nachum. "Serialism in the Works of Charles Ives." TEMPO 138 (1981): 21–32.

4124. Starr, Lawrence. "Charles Ives: The Next Hundred Years: Towards a Method of Analysing the Music." MR 38 (1977): 101–11.

4125. ———. "The Early Styles of Charles Ives." NCM 7 (1983–1984): 71–81.

4126. Tick, Judith. "Ragtime and the Music of Charles Ives." CM 18 (1974): 105–13.

4127. Ward, Charles W. "Charles Ives: The Relationship of His Aesthetic Theories and Compositional Processes." Ph.D. diss., University of Texas, 1974.

– J –

JACOB, GORDON (1895–1984)

4128. Hall, Louis Oilman. "A Stylistic and Performance Analysis of Selected Solo Oboe Works of Gordon Jacob." Ed.D. diss., University of Illinois, 1979.

4129. Lee, Walter F. "Analysis of Selected Compositions by Gordon Jacob for Solo Oboe: Sonata for Oboe and Piano, Sonatina for Oboe and Harpsichord, Two Pieces for Two Oboes and Cor anglais, and Concerto No. 2 for Oboe." D.M.A. diss., Peabody Conservatory, 1978.

4130. Pusey, Robert Samuel. "Gordon Jacob: A Study of the Solo Works for Oboe and English Horn and Their Ensemble Literature." D.M.A. diss., Peabody Conservatory, 1980.

JACOBS, EDWARD (b. 1961)

4131. Jacobs, Edward. "Elements of a Style." CM 67–68 (1999): 157–66.

JANÁČEK, LEOŠ (1854–1928)

Ballad of Blaník

4132. M-Novak.

Cunning Little Vixen

4133. ASO 84 (1986).

4134. Beckerman, Michael. "Janáček and the Herbartians." MQ 69 (1983): 388–407.

4135. Josephson, Nors S. "Musikalische und dramatische Struktur in Janáčeks *Das schlaue Füchslein.*" JSIM (1996): 142–53.

Danube

4136. Knaus, Jakob. "Leoš Janáčeks *Donau*-Symphonie." OMZ 42, no. 4 (1987): 173–78.

Fiddler's Child

4137. Novak, John K. "Barthes's Narrative Codes as a Technique for the Analysis of Programmatic Music: An Analysis of Janáček's *The Fiddler's Child.*" ITR 18, no. 1 (1997): 25–64.

4138. M-Novak.

From the House of the Dead

4139. ASO 107 (1988).

Glagolithic Mass

4140. Beckerman, Michael. "Janáček and the Herbartians." MQ 69 (1983): 388–407.

4141. Hollander, Hans. "Janáčeks Glazolitische Messe." M 12 (1958): 329–33.

4142. Wingfield, Paul. *Janáček: Glagolithic Mass*. Cambridge: Cambridge University Press, 1992.

Jenůfa

4143. ASO 102 (1987).

4144. Prey, Stefan. "Diatonik bei Janáček." M 42, no. 5 (1988): 442–47. [Prelude]

4145. Ströbel, Dietmar. *Motiv und Figur in den Kompositionen der Jenufawerkgruppe Leoš Janáčeks*. Munich: Katzbichler, 1975.

4146. Wingfield, Paul. "Janáček's Speech-Melody Theory in Concept and Practice." COJ 4, no. 3 (1992): 281–301.

Káťa Kabanová

4147. ASO 114 (1988).

4148. Tyrrell, John. *Leoš Janáček: Káťa Kabanová*. Cambridge: Cambridge University Press, 1982.

4149. Wingfield, Paul. "Janáček's Speech-Melody Theory in Concept and Practice." COJ 4, no. 3 (1992): 281–301.

4150. ———. "Unlocking a Janáček Enigma: The Harmonic Origins of Kudrjáš's 'Waiting' Song." ML 75, no. 4 (1994): 561–75.

4151. Wörner, Karl H. "Katjas Tod: Die Schlussszene der Oper *Katja Kabanowa* von Leoš Janáček." SMZ 99 (1959): 91–96.

Makropulos Affair

4152. ASO 188 (1999).

4153. Beckerman, Michael. "Janáček and the Herbartians." MQ 69 (1983): 388–407.

Nursery Rhymes

4154. Novak, John K. "Janáček's *Nursery Rhymes* as a Compendium of His Compositional Style." CMS 39 (1999): 43–63.

Operas (various; *see also* specific operas)

4155. Evans, Michael. *Janáček's Tragic Operas*. London: Faber, 1977.

4156. Kneif, Tibor. *Die Bühnenwerke von Leoš Janáček*. Vienna: Universal, 1975.

4157. Schön, Eva-Maria. "Darstellung der Charaktere in Leoš Janáčeks Opern." Ph.D. diss., Halle-Salle, 1976.

4158. Shawe-Taylor, Desmond. "The Operas of Leoš Janáček." PRMA 85 (1958–1959): 49–64.

4159. Tyrrell, John R. "Janáček's Stylistic Development as an Operatic Composer as Evidenced in His Revisions of the First Five Operas." Ph.D. diss., Oxford University, 1969.

Piano Works

4160. Jiránek, Jaroslav. "Janáčeks Klavierkompositionen vom Standpunkt ihres dramatischen Charakters: Versuch einer semantischen Analyse." AM 39 (1982): 179–97.

4161. Salocks, Christopher Stephen. "Form and Interpretation in Leoš Janáček's *Po zarostlém chodníčku*." D.M.A. diss., Stanford University, 1980.

4162. Uhde, Jürgen. "Ein musikalisches Monument: Zu Leoš Janáčeks Klaviersonaten-Fragment '1.10.1905.'" ZM 6, no. 2 (1975): 89–95.

Sinfonietta

4163. Beckerman, Michael. "Janáček and the Herbartians." MQ 69 (1983): 388–407.

4164. Hollander, Hans. "Der Klassizismus in Janáčeks Sinfonietta." NZM 135 (1974): 685–87.

String Quartets

4165. Beckerman, Michael. "Janáček and the Herbartians." MQ 69 (1983): 388–407. [No. 1]

4166. Wehnert, Martin. "Anmerkungen zu Semantik in der Streichquartetten Leoš Janáček." M-Pečman: 177–97.

Taras Bulba

4167. Goren, Richard. "Janáček and *Taras Bulba*." MR 22 (1961): 302–6.

4168. M-Novak.

4169. Wehnert, Martin. "Imagination und thematisches Verständnis bei Janáček: Dargestellt an *Taras Bulba*." BM 22 (1980): 292–308.

Violin Concerto ("The Pilgrimage of a Little Soul")

4170. Knaus, Jakob. "Leoš Janáčeks Violinkonzert: Die späte Entdeckung eines bemerkenswerten Werkes." NZM 152, no. 1 (1991): 41–45.

Various Works

4171. Barvik, Miroslav. "Interpretationsprobleme der Musik von Leoš Janáček." JP 2 (1979): 170–89.

4172. Geck, Adelheid. *Der Volksliedmaterial Leoš Janáček: Analysen der Strukturen unter Einbeziehung von Janáčeks Randbemerkungen und Volksliedstudien.* Regensburg: Bosse, 1975.

4173. Gerlach, Reinhard. "Leoš Janáček und die erste und zweite Wiener Schule: Ein Beitrag zur Stilkritik seines instrumentalen Spätwerks." MF 24 (1971): 19–34.

4174. Gülke, Peter. "Protokolle des schöpferischen Prozesses zur Musik von Leoš Janáček." NZM 134 (1973): 407–12, 498–503.

4175. ———. "Versuch zur Aesthetik der Musik Leoš Janáček." DJM 12 (1967): 5–39.

4176. Helman, Zofia. "Zur Modalität im Schaffen Szymanowskis und Janáčeks." M-Pečman/J: 201–11.

4177. Hollander, Hans. "The Music of Leoš Janáček: Its Origin in Folklore." MQ 41 (1955): 171–76.

4178. Kaderavek, Milan R. "Stylistic Aspects of the Late Chamber Music of Leoš Janáček: An Analytic Study." D.M.A. diss., University of Illinois, 1970.

4179. Schönfelder, Gerd. "Einige Gesichtspunkte zu musikalischer Struktur und Bedeutung im Schaffen Leoš Janáčeks." BM 22 (1980): 280–92.

4180. Trojan, Jan. "Leoš Janáček: Entdecker und Theoretiker der harmonischen Struktur im mährischen Volkslied." M-Pečman/J: 243–50.

4181. Vetterl, Karel. "Janáček's Creative Relationship to Folk Music." M-Pečman/J: 235–42.

JARRELL, MICHAEL (b. 1958)

4182. Nieminen, Risto, ed. *Michael Jarrell.* Paris: IRCAM, 1992.

4183. Steiner, Christoph. "Eines blauflimmernd bestimmten sich errinernd: Michael Jarrells *Assonance V.*" DI 57 (1998): 26–33.

JELINEK, HANNS (1901–1969)

4184. Redlich, Hans F. "Hanns Jelinek." MR 21 (1960): 66–72.

JENEY, ZOLTÁN (b. 1943)

4185. Lück, Harmut. "Zustand, Kreis, und Continuum: Drei Aspekte der Stile; Über den ungarischen Komponisten Zoltán Jeney." MTX 10 (1985): 17–21.

JEPPESEN, KNUD (1892–1974)

4186. Mathiassen, Finn. "Jeppesen's Passacaglia." F-Jeppesen: 293–308.

JOACHIM, JOSEPH (1831–1907)

4187. Struck, Michael. "Dialog über die Variation, präzisiert: Joseph Joachims *Variationen über ein irisches Elfenlied* und Johannes Brahms' Variationenpaar Op. 21 im Licht der gemeinsamen gattungstheoretischen Diskussion." F-Floros/60: 105–54.

JOHNSON, TOM (b. 1939)

4188. Gembris, Heiner. "Musikwissen als Oper: Tom Johnsons *Riemannoper.*" MTX 25 (1988): 27–30.

4189. Litzel, Susanne. "Eine 'wahre' Oper: Tom Johnsons *Four Note Opera.*" MTX 25 (1988): 36–39.

JOHNSTON, BEN (b. 1926)

4190. Childs, Barney. "Ben Johnston: *Quintet for Groups.*" PNM 7, no. 1 (1968): 110–21.

4191. Elster, Steven. "A Harmonic and Serial Analysis of Ben Johnston's String Quartet No. 6." PNM 29, no. 2 (1991): 138–65.

4192. Fonville, John. "Ben Johnston's Extended Just Intonation: A Guide for Interpreters." PNM 29, no. 2 (1991): 106–37. [String Quartets]

4193. Gibbens, John Jeffrey. "Design in Ben Johnston's *Sonata for Microtonal Piano.*" I 18, no. 3 (1989): 161–94. [*Sonata/Grindlemusic*]

4194. Maltz, Richard. "Microtonal Techniques in the Music of Harry Partch and Ben Johnson." MRF 7 (1992): 14–37. [String Quartet No. 4 ("Ascent" [*Amazing Grace*])]

JOLAS, BETSY (b. 1926)

4195. Krastewa, Iwanka. "Betsy Jolas." SMZ 114 (1974): 342–49.

4196. Mathon, Geneviève. "D'une pratique monodique: *Caprice* de Betsy Jolas." ANM 19 (1990): 73–78. [*Caprice à 1 voix*]

JOLIVET, ANDRÉ (1905–1974)

4197. M-Kniesner. [Piano Sonata No. 1]

JOPLIN, SCOTT (1867?–1917)

4198. Perone, James E. "Chromatic Harmony in the Waltzes of Scott Joplin: Source Material for Harmonic Study." MTEA 7 (1999): 4–16.

4199. Reed, Addison Walker. "The Life and Works of Scott Joplin." Ph.D. diss., University of North Carolina, 1973.

4200. Wooldridge, Marc Charles. "Rhythmic Implications of Diatonic Theory: A Study of Scott Joplin's Ragtime Piano Works." Ph.D. diss., State University of New York at Buffalo, 1992.

JUZELIŪNAS, JULIUS (b. 1916)

4201. M-Lampsatis.

– K –

KABALEVSKY, DMITRY BORISOVICH (1904–1987)

4202. Adams, John P. "A Study of the Kabalevsky Preludes, Op. 38." Ph.D. diss., Indiana University, 1976.

KAGEL, MAURICIO (b. 1931)

Anagrama

4203. Knockaert, Yves. "An Analysis of Kagel's *Anagrama.*" I 5 (1976): 173–88.

Exotica

4204. Pelinski, Ramon. "Masques de l'identité: Réflexions sur *Exotica* de Maurice Kagel." CIR 6, no. 2 (1995): 47–59.

4205. ———. "Mauricio Kagel's *Exotica*: Aspects of Exoticism in New Music." CAUSM 3, no. 2 (1974): 1–9.

Kantrimiusik (Pastorale für Stimmen und Instrumente)

4206. Condé, Gerard. "La charrue avant les boeufs: Essai sur *Kantrimiusik.*" MJ 27 (1977): 58–71.

Match

4207. Roelcke, Eckhard. "Instrumentales Theater: Anmerkungen zu Mauricio Kagels *Match* und *Sur scène.*" HJM 10 (1988): 215–38.

4208. Schmidt, Christian Martin. "Mauricio Kagel: *Match* für drei Spieler." Stephan: 145–53.

4209. Tibbe, Monika. "Schwierigkeiten und Möglichkeiten der Analyse zeitgenossischer Musik, dargestellt an *Match* von Mauricio Kagel." ZM 3, no. 2 (1972): 18–21.

Musik für Renaissance-Instrumente

4210. Schmidt, Dörte. "Über Möglichkeiten: Zu Mauricio Kagels Musik für Renaissanceinstrumente." T 15, no. 3 (1990): 186–94.

Pas de cinq (Wandelszene)

4211. Bernager, Olivier. "Notes sur une pratique du théâtre musical: À partir de *Repertoire* et de *Pas de cinq* de Mauricio Kagel." MJ 27 (1977): 13–24.

Recitativarie

4212. Klüppelholz, Werner. "Musik als Theologie: Zu Kagels *Rezitativarie.*" Melos/NZM 3 (1977): 483–89.

Sankt-Bach-Passion

4213. Oehlschlägel, Reinhard. "Mild traditionalistische Festmusik: Zur *Sankt-Bach-Passion* von Maurice Kagel." MTX 11 (1985): 53–55.

Schall

4214. Kooij, Fred van der. "'Les sons sont quoi?' Das Prinzip der Entgrenzung in *Der Schall* von Mauricio Kagel." DI 65 (2000): 4–13.

Staatstheater (szenische Komposition)

4215. Bernager, Olivier. "Notes sur une pratique du théâtre musical: À partir de *Repertoire* et de *Pas de cinq* de Mauricio Kagel." MJ 27 (1977): 13–24.

4216. Karger, Reinhard. "Mauricio Kagels *Repertoire.*" Melos/NZM 2, (1976): 375–80.

4217. Stoianova, Ivanka. "Multiplicité, non-directionnalité et jeu dans les pratiques contemporaines du spectacle musico-theatral (I): Théâtre instrumental et impromuz; Mauricio Kagel, *Staatstheater*; Ghedalia Tazartes, *Ghédal et son double.*" MJ 27 (1977): 38–48.

4218. Zarius, Karl-Heinz. "Composition en tant qu'analyse: Destruction et construction dans *Staatstheater* de Kagel." MJ 27 (1977): 25–37.

Sur scène

4219. Roelcke, Eckhard. "Instrumentales Theater: Anmerkungen zu Mauricio Kagels *Match* und *Sur scène*." HJM 10 (1988): 215–38.

Unguis incarnatus est

4220. Decarsin, François. "Liszt's *Nuages gris* and Kagel's *Unguis incarnatus est*: A Model and Its Issue." Trans. Jonathan Dunsby. MA 4, no. 3 (1985): 259–63.

Variationen ohne Fuge

4221. Klüppelholz, Werner. "'Ohne das Wesentliche der Ideen unkenntlich zu machen': Zu Kagels *Variationen ohne Fuge*." M-Brinkmann: 114–29.

Various Works

4222. Frisius, Rudolf. "Kompositions als Kritik an Inventionen: Tendenzen in neueren Stücken von Mauricio Kagel und ihre Betdueung für den Musikunterricht." MB 9 (1977): 600–606.

4223. Klüppelholz, Werner. "Mauricio Kagel und die Tradition." M-Brinkmann: 102–13.

4224. ———. *Mauricio Kagel, 1970–1980*. Cologne: Dumont, 1981.

4225. Noller, Joachim. "Fluxus und die Musik der sechziger Jahre: Über vernachlässigte Aspekte am Beispiel Kagels und Stockhausens." NZM 146, no. 9 (1985): 14–19.

4226. Perrin, Glyn. "Mauricio Kagel." CT 15 (1976–1977): 13–16.

4227. Schmiedeke, Ulrich. *Der Beginn der neuen Orgelmusik: Die Orgelkompositionen von Hambraeus, Kagel und Ligeti*. Munich: Katzbichler, 1981.

KAHN, ERICH ITOR (1905–1956)

4228. Allende-Blin, Juan. *Erich Itor Kahn*. Munich: Text + Kritik, 1994.

KALOMIRIS, MANOLIS (1883–1962)

4229. Zack, George. "The Music Dramas of Manolis Kalomiris." Ph.D. diss., Florida State University, 1971.

KAMINSKI, HEINRICH (1886–1946)

4230. Reck, Albert von. "Mystik und Form in *Magnificat* von Heinrich Kaminski." SMZ 96 (1956): 153–60.

4231. Samson, Ingried. *Das Vokalschaffen von Heinrich Kaminski*. Franfurt am Main, 1956.

KAMPELA, ARTHUR (b. 1960)

4232. Kampela, Arthur. "A Knife All Blade: Deciding the Side Not to Take." CM 67–68 (1999): 167–93.

KARCHIN, LOUIS (b. 1951)

4233. Carl, Robert. "Three Points on the Spectrum: The Music of Louis Karchin, Lois V. Vierk, and Paul Dresher." CMR 10, no. 1 (1994): 11–31.

KARG-ELERT, SIGFRID (1877–1933)

4234. Hartmann, Günter. "Sigfrid Karg-Elerts Choralimprovisation op. 65/56." MK 57, no. 5 (1987): 234–39.

4235. Michael, Frank. "Die Einheit in der Vielfalt: Sigfrid Karg-Elerts Sonata ('Appassionata') fis-Moll." T 16, no. 2 (1991): 424–30. [*Sonata appassionata*, op. 140]

KATZER, GEORG (b. 1935)

4236. Klement, Udo. "Die Analyse: Orchesterkonzerte von Ernst Hermann Meyer, Siegfried Matthus, und Georg Katzer." MG 28 (1978): 599–603. [Concerto for Orchestra No. 1]

4237. Schneider, Frank. "'Und das Schöne blüht nur im Gesang': Zwei Versuche über Georg Katzers Komposition." MTX 7 (1984): 25–29.

KAY, ULYSSES (1917–1995)

4238. Hadley, Richard Thomas. "The Published Choral Music of Ulysses Simpson Kay, 1943–1968." Ph.D. diss., University of Iowa, 1972.

4239. Hayes, Laurence Melton. "The Works of Ulysses Kay: A Stylistic Study of Selected Works." Ph.D. diss., University of Wisconsin, 1971.

KEE, COR (1900–1997)

4240. Heusinkveld, Frances Mary. "The Psalm-Based Organ Music of Cor Kee." Ph.D. diss., University of Iowa, 1978.

KELEMEN, MILKO (b. 1924)

4241. Gligo, Nikša. "Milko Kelemen: *Passionato* für Flöte und gemischten Chor; Voraussetzungen für eine mögliche Analyse." ZM 6, no. 2 (1975): 71–75.

KELLER, MAX (b. 1947)

4242. Rüdiger, Wolfgang. "Von der subversiven Lautlosigkeit der Ameisen: Analytische Gedanken zu Max E. Kellers *Gesängen III.*" F-Knepler, vol. 3: 117–27.

KELTERBORN, RUDOLF (b. 1931)

4243. Kelterborn, Rudolf. "*Changements* pour grand orchestre (1972/73)." SMZ 117 (1977): 24–27.

4244. Mohr, Ernst. "Rudolf Kelterborn: Analytische Hinweise zu seiner *Missa* für Sopran, Tenor, Chor und Orchester." M 16 (1962): 232–36.

4245. Weber, Martin. *Die Orchesterwerke Rudolf Kelterborns.* Regensburg: Bosse, 1981.

KENINS, TALIVALDIS (b. 1919)

4246. Rapoport, Paul. "The Symphonies of Tālivaldis Ķeniņš." TEMPO 157 (1986): 13–20. [Symphonies Nos. 1–9]

KERN, MATHIAS (b. 1928)

4247. Dorfmüller, Joachim. "'Eigene Wege im Umfeld der Zeitströmungen': Zur Orgelmusik von Mathias Kern." MK 50 (1980): 68–75.

KERR, HARRISON (1897–1978)

4248. Kohlenberg, Randy Bryan. "Harrison Kerr: Portrait of a Twentieth-Century Composer." Ph.D. diss., University of Oklahoma, 1978.

KESSLER, THOMAS (b. 1937)

4249. Koblyakov, Lev. "Thomas Kesslers *Control*-Stücke." DI 24 (1990): 16–22. [*Drum Control, Flute Control, Piano Control*]

KETTING, OTTO (b. 1935)

4250. Hartsuiker, Ton. "Otto Ketting and His Time Machine." SS 57 (1974): 1–13.

4251. Leeuw, Ton de. "Otto Ketting: *Due Canzoni.*" SS 18 (1964): 10–15.

4252. Samama, Leo. "Otto Ketting's Symphony for Saxophones and Orchestra: Elements of a Technique." KN 10 (1979): 14–19.

KETTING, PIET (1904–1984)

4253. Bakker, M. Geerink. "Piet Ketting: Trio per flauto, clarinette, e fagotto." SS 22 (1965): 24–29.

KEULEN, GEERT VAN (b. 1943)

4254. Groot, Rokus de. "The Dismantling and Reconstruction of Western Harmony: An Analysis of Geert van Keulen's *Tympan.*" KN 29, no. 1 (1995): 19–23.

KHANDOSHKIN, IVAN YEVSTAFYEVICH (1747–1804)

4255. Schwarz, Boris. "Khandoshkin's Earliest Printed Work Rediscovered." F-Abraham: 81–86.

KILLMAYER, WILHELM (b. 1927)

4256. Mauser, Siegfried. "Musik als Sprache: Anmerkungen zu Wilhelm Killmayers Klavierstück I." NZM 143, no. 12 (1982): 23–26.

KILPINEN, YRJÖ (1892–1959)

4257. Pullano, Frank Louis. "A Study of the Published German Songs of Yrjö Kilpinen." D.M.A. diss., University of Illinois, 1970.

KIM, EARL (1920–1998)

4258. Barkin, Elaine. "Earl Kim: *Earthlight.*" PNM 19, no. 2 (1980–1981): 269–277. [*Narratives*]

4259. Marks, Kent. "The Interior Monologue in Earl Kim's Violin Concerto." PNM 34, no. 2 (1996): 106–31.

KIRCHNER, LEON (b. 1919)

4260. Anthony, Carl Rheinhardt. "Formal Determinants in Four Selected Compositions of Leon Kirchner." Ph.D. diss., University of Arizona, 1984. [Concerto for Violin, Cello, Ten Winds, and Percussion; Music for Orchestra; String Quartet No. 2; Toccata for Strings, Solo Winds, and Percussion]

4261. Ringer, Alexander L. "Leon Kirchner." MQ 43 (1957): 1–20.

4262. M-Schweitzer. [String Quartet No. 1]

4263. True, Nelita. "A Style Analysis of the Published Piano Works of Leon Kirchner." D.M.A. diss., Peabody Conservatory, 1976.

KIRCHNER, THEODOR (1823–1903)
4264. Kahler, Otto-Hans. "Ein Brahmszitat in Theodor Kirchners Walzer op. 86,6." BS 8 (1990): 31–33.

KJERULF, HALFDAN (1815–1868)
4265. Olson, Robert Wallace. "A Comparative Study of Selected Norwegian Romances by Halfdan Kjerulf, Edvard Grieg, and Eyvind Alnaes." Ph.D. diss., University of Illinois, 1973.
4266. Schjeldreup-Ebbe, Dag. "Modality in Halfdan Kjerulf's Music." ML 38 (1957): 238–46.

KLEBE, GISELHER (b. 1925)
4267. Lewinski, Wolf-Eberhard von. "Giselher Klebe." R 4 (1958): 89–97. [Piano Trio ("Elegia appassionata"), String Quartet No. 1]
4268. McCredie, Andrew D. "Giselher Klebe." MR 26 (1965): 220–35.

KLEIN, BERNHARD (1793–1832)
4269. Mies, Paul. "Ein Sinfonie-Fragment von Bernard Klein." F-Fellerer/60: 144–54.

KLERK, ALBERT DE (1917–1998)
4270. Visser, Piet. "Albert de Klerk: Missa *Mater Sanctae laetitiae.*" SS 23 (1965): 26–30.
4271. ———. "Ricercare for Organ, *Hommage à Sweelinck.*" SS 23 (1965): 31–35.

KLUGE, MANFRED (1928–1971)
4272. Tesche, Thomas. "'. . . von glühender Bewunderung bis zu völliger Ablehnung': Einige Gedanken zum Werk Manfred Kluges." MK 61, no. 1 (1991): 16–27.

KOCHAN, GÜNTER (1930–1995)
4273. Gerlach, Hannelore. "Günter Kochan: *Mendelssohn-Variationen* für Klavier und Orchester." MG 24 (1974): 86–90.
4274. Klement, Udo. "Die Analyse: Oratorium *Das Friedenfest* von Günter Kochan." MG 31 (1981): 213–16.
4275. Müller, Hans Peter. "*Die Asche von Birkenau*: Zu Günter Kochans neuer Solo-Kantate." MG 16 (1966): 453–62.
4276. ———. "Revision mit Konsequenz: Bemerkungen zu zwei Fassungen von Günter Kochans Sinfonie mit Chor." MG 16 (1966): 263–67.
4277. Schäfer, Hansjürgen. "Konzert für Klavier und Orchester Op. 16 von Günter Kochan." MG 9, no. 5 (1959): 22–25.
4278. ———. "Reichtum der Gedanken und Empfindungen: Bemerkungen zu Günter Kochans Sinfonietta 1960." MG 12 (1962): 286–89.
4279. Wolf, Werner. "Sinfonie für grosses Orchester mit Chor: Ein neues bedeutendes Werk von Günter Kochan." MG 14 (1964): 143–46.

KODÁLY, ZOLTÁN (1882–1967)
Annie Miller
4280. Ittzés, Mihály. "*Molnár Anna (Annie Miller)*: A Székely Folk Ballad Arranged by Zoltán Kodály for Mixed Choir." Trans. Judit Pokoly. IKSB 1986, no. 1: 23–42.

Cello Sonata, Op. 4
4281. Brewer, Linda Rae Judd. "Progressions among Non-Twelve-Tone Sets in Kodály's Sonata for Violoncello and Piano, Op. 4: An Analysis for Performance Interpretation." D.M.A. diss., University of Texas, 1978.

Choral Works (various; *see also* specific choral works)
4282. Bárdos, Lajos. "On Kodály's Children's Choruses." IKSB 1979, no. 1: 32–47; 1979, no. 2: 36–43; 1980, no. 2: 44–53; 1981, no. 1: 27–35; 1981, no. 2: 26–35; 1982, no. 1: 20–36.
4283. Ittzés, Mihály. "Variation and Refrain in Kodály's Choral Works." IKSB 1990, no. 2: 20–26.
4284. Lindlar, Heinrich. "Einige Kodály-Chöre." MZ 9 (1954): 29–32.
4285. Steen, Philip Lewis. "Zoltán Kodály's Choral Music for Children and Youth Choirs." Ph.D. diss., University of Michigan, 1970.
4286. Stevens, Halsey. "The Choral Music of Zoltán Kodály." MQ 54 (1958): 147–68.
4287. Young, Percy. "Zoltán Kodály and the Choral Tradition." ACR 8, no. 1 (1965): 1–3, 8, 10–11, 17.

Dances of Galánta
4288. Sárosi, Mint. "Instrumental Folk Music in Kodály's Works: The *Galánta* and *Marosszék Dances.*" SM 25 (1983): 23–28.

Dances of Marosszék
4289. Sárosi, Mint. "Instrumental Folk Music in Kodály's Works: The *Galánta* and *Marosszék Dances.*" SM 25 (1983): 23–28.

Háry János

4290. Blasi, Franz. "Zoltán Kodálys *Háry János.*" ME 21 (1968): 221–27.

Menuetto for String Quartet

4291. Laki, Peter G. "Minuet for String Quartet (1897): Kodály's First Surviving Composition Rediscovered." NOTES 49, no. 1 (1992): 28–38.

Missa brevis

4292. Seiber, Matyas. "Kodály: *Missa brevis.*" TEMPO 4 (1947): 3–6.

Piano Works

4293. Korody, István Paku. "Influence of French Impressionism and the Essence of the Hungarian National Character in Zoltán Kodály's Piano Music." D.M.A. diss., Ohio State University, 1978.

Psalmus hungaricus

4294. Bónis, Ferenc. "Beobachtungen zum Schaffensprozess in Kodálys *Psalmus hungaricus.*" KJ 75 (1991): 93–105.

4295. ———. "Zoltán Kodálys Weg zum *Psalmus Hungaricus.*" M 41, no. 1 (1987): 13–20.

Songs

4296. Jolly, Cynthia. "The Art Songs of Kodály." TEMPO 63 (1962): 2–12.

Symphony

4297. Breuer, János. "Zoltán Kodálys Symphonie: Ein Schweizer Auftragswerk." Trans. Michel R. Flechter. SMZ 122 (1983): 157–63.

4298. Weissman, John S. "Kodály's Symphony: A Morphological Study." TEMPO 60 (1961): 19–36.

Various Works

4299. Danis, Ferenc. "Zoltán Kodály: Der Meister der ungarischen Neoklassik." OMZ 35 (1980): 129143.

4300. Ittzés, Mihály. "The Musical World of Kodály's Instrumental Pieces for Children." IKSB 1980, no. 2: 13–23.

4301. Mellers, Wilfred H. "Kodály and the Christian Epic." ML 22 (1941): 155–61.

4302. Szöllösy, Andras. "Kodály's Melody." TEMPO 63 (1962): 12–16.

4303. Vargyas, Lajos. "Wirkung der Voiksmusikforschung auf Kodály's Schöpfungen." SM 25 (1983): 39–60.

4304. Weissman, John S. "Kodály's Later Orchestral Music." TEMPO 17 (1950): 16–23.

4305. ———. "Kodály's späte Orchesterwerke." MZ 9 (1954): 16–28.

4306. ———. "Notes to Kodály's Recent Setting of Hungarian Dances." TEMPO 32 (1954): 29–32.

KOECHLIN, CHARLES (1867–1950)

4307. Fortassier, Pierre. "La musique des choeurs de l'*Alceste* d'Euripide." RM 340–341 (1981): 73–80.

4308. Guieysse, Jules. "Charles Koechlin: L'oeuvre d'orchestre." Revised by Paul-Gilbert Langevin. RM 324–326 (1979): 147–67.

4309. Hirsbrunner, Theo. "Zur Harmonik Charles Koechlins." DI 26 (1990): 4–7. [*Paysages et marines* (Solo piano version)]

4310. Kirk, Elise Kuhl. "Art nouveau and the Melodic Style of Charles Koechlin." MMA 13 (1984): 117–29.

4311. ———. "The Chamber Music of Charles Koechlin (1867–1950)." Ph.D. diss., Catholic University of America, 1977.

4312. Koechlin, Charles. "Étude sur Charles Koechlin par lui-même." RM 340–341 (1981): 39–72.

4313. Langevin, Paul-Gilbert. "Charles Koechlin: Musicien de l'avenir." RM 324–326 (1979): 135–45.

4314. McGuire, Thomas Howard. "The Piano Works of Charles Koechlin (1867–1950)." Ph.D. diss., University of North Carolina, 1975.

4315. Orledge, Robert F. "A Study of the Composer Charles Koechlin (1867–1950)." Ph.D. diss., Cambridge University, 1973.

KOENIG, GOTTFRIED MICHAEL (b. 1926)

4316. Decroupet, Pascal. "Timbre Diversification in Serial Tape Music and Its Consequence on Form." CMR 10, no. 2 (1994): 13–23. [*Klangfiguren II*]

4317. Metzger, Heinz-Klaus, and Rainer Riehn, eds. *Gottfried Michael Koenig.* Munich: Text + Kritik, 1989. [*String Quartet 1959,* other works]

KOFFLER, JÓZEF (1896–1944)

4318. Gołąb, Maciej. "Zwölftontechnik bei Józef Koffler: Ein polnischer Beitrag zur Geschichte der Dodekaphonie in der ersten Hälfte des 20. Jahrhunderts." MO 10 (1986): 167–79.

KÖHLER, SIEGFRIED (1927–1984)

4319. Felix, Werner. "*Reich des Menschen*: Poem nach Dichtungen von Johannes R. Beicher/Musik: Siegfried Köhler." MG 18 (1968): 5–10.

4320. Schönfelder, Gerd. "Die Analyse: IV. Sinfonie von Siegfried Köhler." MG 29 (1979): 398–402.

KÖHLER, WOLFGANG (b. 1923)

4321. Hopf, Helmuth. "Zu Kompositionstechniken im Konzert für Orchester von Wolfgang Köhler." F-Boetticher: 120–29.

4322. ———. "Zu Wolfgang Köhlers Sinfonie Nr.3, Op. 42." F-Valentin: 53–60.

KOKKONEN, JOONAS (1921–1996)

4323. Jurkowski, Edward. "Joonas Kokkonen's 'Free' Dodecaphonic Composition? A Study of the Passacaglia from the String Quartet No. 2." STMO 3 (2000).

4324. ———. "The Symphonies of Joonas Kokkonen." TEMPO 208 (1999): 18–23.

KOMITAS, SOGOMON (1869–1935)

4325. Vagramian, Violet. "Representative Secular Choral Works of Gomidas: An Analytical Study and Evaluation of His Musical Style." Ph.D. diss., University of Miami, 1973.

KONDO, JO (b. 1947)

4326. Kondo, Jo. "The Art of Being Ambiguous: From Listening to Composing." CMR 2, no. 2 (1988): 7–29.

KOPYTMAN, MARK (b. 1929)

4327. Uscher, Nancy. "A Twentieth-Century Approach to Heterophony: Mark Kopytman's *Cantus II*." TEMPO 156 (1986): 19–22.

KOX, HANS (b. 1930)

4328. Geraedts, Jaap. "Hans Kox: Concerto for Violin and Orchestra." SS 21 (1964): 12–16.

4329. Rossum, Frans van. "*Dorian Gray:* An Opera to Strike Joy into a Director's Heart." KN 6 (1977): 12–18.

4330. Werker, Gerard. "*In Those Days* by Hans Kox: A Musical Memory of the Battle of Arnhem." SS 43 (1970): 24–30.

KOZELUCH, LEOPOLD (1747–1818)

4331. Hickman, Roger. "Leopold Kozeluch and the Viennese *Quatuor Concertant*." CMS 26 (1989): 42–52. [String quartets]

KRAFT, WILLIAM (b. 1923)

4332. Harbinson, William G. "Analysis: William Kraft's *Dialogues and Entertainments*." JBR 19, no. 1 (1983–1984): 16–25.

KRAMER, JONATHAN D. (1942–2004)

4333. Kramer, Jonathan D. "Coming to Terms with Music as Protest and Remembrance: One Composer's Story." CM 67–68 (1999): 195–242. [*No Beginning, No End*]

KRAMER, LAWRENCE (b. 1946)

4334. Kramer, Lawrence. "Text and Music: Some New Directions." CMR 5 (1989): 143–53. [*Jornado del Muerto*]

KRÄTZSCHMAR, WILFRIED (b. 1944)

4335. Raab, Hans-Heinrich. "Die Analyse: II. Sinfonie von Wilfried Krätzschmar." MG 31 (1981): 73–76.

KRAUS, EBERHARD (b. 1931)

4336. Stein, Franz A. "Historische Aspekte in den Zwölftonkompositionen von Eberhard Kraus." M-Beck: 193–212.

KRAUSE-GRAUMNITZ, HEINZ (1911–1979)

4337. Hennenberg, Fritz. "*An die Nachgeborenen*." MG 10 (1960): 299–301.

KREIGER, ARTHUR (b. 1945)

4338. Rosenzweig, Morris. "Contemplated Balances: A Brief View of Arthur Kreiger and Peter Lieberson." CMR 10, no. 1 (1994): 101–19.

KRENEK, ERNST (1900–1991)

Doppelt beflügeltes Band

4339. Neuwirth, Gösta. "Bemerkungen zu einigen späteren Werken Ernst Křeneks." M-Metzger/Křenek: 149–60.

Fibonacci mobile

4340. Neuwirth, Gösta. "Bemerkungen zu einigen späteren Werken Ernst Křeneks." M-Metzger/Křenek: 149–60.

Karl V

4341. Schmidt, Matthias. "Fragmente einer Sprache der Musik: Zu Schönbergs *Moses und Aron* und Kreneks *Karl V*." AM 53, no. 2 (1996): 135–59.

4342. Zenck, Claudia Maurer. "Schöne und 'scheene' Musik: Zur Entstehung von *Karl V*." M-Metzger/Křenek: 38–52.

Lamentatio Jeremiae prophetae

4343. M-Ogdon.

4344. M-Vogt: 239–48.

O Lacrymosa
4345. Cremonese, Adriano. "Rilke–*Ô Lacrimosa*–Křenek." M-Metzger/Křenek: 114–28.

Operas (various; *see also* specific operas)
4346. Rogge, Wolfgang. *Ernst Krenek: Opern.* Wolfenbüttel: Möseler; Hamburg: Vera, 1970.

Organ Works
4347. Haselböck, Martin. "Die Orgelwerke Ernst Kreneks: Eine Überschau; Zum 80. Geburtstag des Komponisten am 23 August 1980." MK 50 (1980): 114–22.

Orpheus und Eurydike
4348. Knoch, Hans. *Orpheus und Eurydike: Der antike Sagenstoff in den Opern von Darius Milhaud und Ernst Krenek.* Regensburg: Bosse, 1977.

Piano Works
4349. M-Buccheri.
4350. Houser, James D. "The Evolution of Ernst Krenek's Twelve-Tone Technique." M.A. thesis, University of Rochester, 1977. [Eight Pieces, op. 110; *Sechs Vermessene,* op. 168; *Twelve Variations in Three Movements,* op. 79]
4351. Huetteman, Albert George. "Ernst Krenek's Theories on the Sonata and the Relations to His Six Piano Sonatas." Ph.D. diss., University of Iowa, 1968.
4352. M-Ogdon. [Piano Sonata No. 3]

Sestina
4353. Krenek, Ernst. "*Sestina.*" MELOS 25 (1958): 235–38.

Songs
4354. M-Johnson. [Lieder, op. 82]
4355. Schollum, Robert. "Anmerkungen zum Liedschaffen Ernst Kreneks." OMZ 35 (1980): 446–52.

Spätlese
4356. Neuwirth, Gösta. "Bemerkungen zu einigen späteren Werken Ernst Křeneks." M-Metzger/Křenek: 149–60.

Symphonic Elegy
4357. M-Ogdon.

Transparencies
4358. M-Wennerstrom

Wechselrahmen
4359. Neuwirth, Gösta. "Bemerkungen zu einigen späteren Werken Ernst Křeneks." M-Metzger/Křenek: 149–60.

Various Works
4360. Erikson, Robert. "Krenek's Later Music (1930–1947)." MR 9 (1948): 29–43.
4361. M-Hines.
4362. Neuwirth, Gösta. "Rotas-Sator: Für Ernst Krenek zum 23. August 1980." OMZ 35 (1980): 461–72.
4363. Reich, Willi. "Ernst Kreneks Arbeit in der Zwölftontechnik." SMZ 89 (1949): 49–53.
4364. Schuh, Willi. "Zur Zwölftontechnik bei Ernst Krenek." SMZ 74 (1934): 217–23.

KREUTZER, CONRADIN (1780–1849)
4365. Peake, Luise Eitel. "Kreutzer's *Wanderlieder*: The Other *Winterreise.*" MQ 65 (1979): 83–102.

KRÖLL, GEORG (b. 1934)
4366. Gruhn, Wilfried. "Bearbeitung als kompositorische Reflexion in neuer Musik." M 28 (1974): 522–28. [*Parodia ad Perotinum*]
4367. Zelinsky, Beate, and David Smeyers. "Zum 60. Gebrutstag von Georg Kröll: *Zweigesänge* für zwei Klarinetten." T 19, no. 2 (1994): 118–22.

KROPFREITER, AUGUSTINUS FRANZ (b. 1936)
4368. Ank, Matthias. "Der Orgelstil des Augustinus Franz Kropfreiter: Eine Beschreibung." MK 59, no. 2 (1989): 74–82.

KRUYF, TON DE (b. 1937)
4369. Vermeulen, Ernst. "Pleasure in Virtuosity: *Serenata* by Ton de Kruyf." SS 40 (1969): 23–28.
4370. ———. "Ton de Kruyf: *Spinoza.*" SS 47 (1971): 1–14.

KUBIK, GAIL (1914–1984)
4371. Lyall, Max Dail. "The Piano Music of Gail Kubik." D.M.A. diss., Peabody Conservatory, 1980.

KUBIZEK, AUGUSTIN (b. 1918)
4372. Suyka, Ulf-Diether. "Augustin Kubizek: *Mater castisissima* Op. 22c/2." ME 30 (1976–1977): 70–72.

KUHLAU, FRIEDRICH (1786–1832)
4373. Busk, Gorm. "Kuhlaus klaversonater og -sonatiner." DAM 19 (1988–1991): 113–56.
4374. Mehring, Arndt. *Friedrich Kuhlau in the Mirror of His Flute Works.* Warren, Mich.: Harmonie Park, 2000.

KUNAD, RAINER (1936–1995)
4375. Hartwig, Dieter. "Rainer Kunads *Sinfonie 64*." MG 16 (1966): 816–22. [Symphony No. 1]
4376. Kneipel, Eberhard. "Klavierkonzert von Rainer Kunad." MG 21 (1971): 625–29.

KUNZEN, FRIEDRICH LUDWIG AEMILIUS (1761–1817)
4377. Abert, Anna Amalie. "*Oberon* in Nord und Süd." F-Gudewill: 51–68. [*Holger Danske*]

KURTÁG, GYÖRGY (b. 1926)
Játékok
4378. Wischmann, Claus. "Spaß am Experiment: György Kurtágs *Játékok* für Klavier." MTX 72 (1997): 51–62.

Kafka-Fragmente
4379. Kirchberg, Klaus. "Bruchstücke einer Konfession: György Kurtág und seine *Kafka-Fragmente*." NZM 149, no. 1 (1988): 23–27.
4380. Spangemacher, Friedrich. "'Der wahre Weg geht über ein Seil': Zu György Kurtágs *Kafka-Fragmenten*." MTX 27 (1988): 30–35. French trans., CC 12–13 (1990): 254–65.

Messages of the Late R. V. Troussova
4381. Lück, Hartmut. "Die Einsamkeit einer verstorbenen Dame: György Kurtágs *Die Botschaften der verewigten R. V. Trusova*." MTX 27 (1988): 26–29.

Officium breve in memoriam Andreae Szervánszky
4382. Hoffmann, Peter. "Post-Webernsche Musik? Gyorgy Kurtágs Webern-Rezeption am Beispiel seines Streichquartetts Op. 28." MTH 7, no. 2 (1992): 129–48.

Sayings of Péter Bornemisza
4383. Kroó, György. "Les *Dits de Péter Bornemisza* de György Kurtág: Concerto pour soprano et piano." Trans. Mireille T. Tóth. CC 12–13 (1990): 211–52.
4384. Willson, Rachel Beckles. "The Fruitful Tension between Inspiration and Design in György Kurtág's *The Sayings of Péter Bornemisza* Op. 7 (1963–68)." MPSS 11 (1998): 36–42.

Stele
4385. Asmus, Bernd. "Wie ein Weg in Herbst: Versuch über György Kurtágs *Stele*, Op. 33." MAS 4, no. 13 (2000): 5–17.

String Quartet, Op. 1
4386. Hoffmann, Peter. "'Die Kakerlake sucht den Weg zum Licht': Zum Streichquartett Op. 1 von György Kurtág." MF 44, no. 1 (1991): 32–48.
4387. Hohmaier, Simone. "Am Rande der Hauptströmungen: Zu Einfluß und Material in György Kurtágs Quartetto per archi opus 1 von 1959." MTX 72 (1997): 39–46.
4388. Weber, Katharina. "Material für ein Lebenswerk: Zum 1. Satz des Quartetto per archi Op. 1 von György Kurtág." DI 56 (1998): 13–18.

Various Works
4389. Spangemacher, Friedrich. "György Kurtág." NZM 143, no. 9 (1982): 28–33.
4390. Szendy, Peter. "Musique et texte dans l'œuvre de György Kurtág." CC 12–13 (1990): 266–84.
4391. Walsh, Stephen. "György Kurtág: An Outline Study." TEMPO 140 (1982): 11–21; 142 (1982): 10–19.

KURZ, SIEGFRIED (b. 1930)
4392. Gülke, Peter. "Bemerkungen zur Musik für Orchestra 1960 von Siegfried Kurz." MG 13 (1963): 198–201.
4393. Schönewolf, Karl. "Bemerkungen zur II. Sinfonie von Siegfried Kurz." MG 12 (1962): 724–27.

KURZBACH, PAUL (b. 1902)
4394. Brock, Hella. "Das Freundliche: Ein Wesenzug unserer Musik zum Violonkonzert Paul Kurzbachs." MG 20 (1970): 757–62.

KUTZVIČIUS, BRONISLOVAS (b. 1932)
4395. M-Lampsatis.

KUULA, TOIVO (1883–1918)

4396. Hillila, Ruth Ester. "The Songs of Toivo Kuula and Leevi Madetoja and Their Place in Twentieth-Century Finnish Art Song." Ph.D. diss., Boston University, 1964.

– L –

LA CASINIÈRE, YVES DE (1897–1971)

4397. M-Kniesner. [Piano Sonata, B minor]

LACHENMANN, HELMUT (b. 1935)

Accanto: Musik für einen Klarinettisten mit Orchester

4398. Ramaut, Béatrice. "*Accanto* de Hulmut Lachenmann." ENT 10 (1992): 23–30.

4399. ———. "Deux mises en scène d'une conscience de la tradition: *Opera* de Berio (1969) et *Accanto* de Lachenmann (1976)." RDM 79, no. 1 (1993): 109–41.

Air: Musik für grosses Orchester und Schlagzeug-solo

4400. Häcker, Karsten. "Versuch über den Strukturklang: *Air* von Helmut Lachenmann." MTX 67–68 (1997): 95–105.

Harmonica: Musik für grosses Orchester mit Tuba-Solo

4401. Baucke, Ludolf. "'Mensch, erkenn dich doch . . .': Anmerkungen zu Helmut Lachenmann, *Harmonica*." MTX 3 (1984): 6–9.

Mouvement (—vor der Erstarrung)

4402. Shaked, Yuval. "'Wie ein Käfer, auf dem Rücken zappelnd': Zu *Mouvement (—vor der Erstarrung)* (1982–1984) von Helmut Lachenmann." MTX 8 (1985): 9–16.

Notturno: Musik für Julia

4403. Horn, Josefine Helen. "Postserielle Mechanismen der Formgenerierung: Zur Entstehung von Helmut Lachenmanns *Notturno*." MTX 79 (1999): 14–25.

Piano Works

4404. Kabisch, Thomas. "Dialektisches Komponieren—dialektisches Hören: Zu Helmut Lachenmanns Klavierkompositionen (1956–1980)." MTX 38 (1991): 25–32.

4405. ———. "Neue Musik im Klavierunterricht: Analytische und didaktische Anmerkungen zu *Ein Kinderspiel* (1980) von Helmut Lachenmann." M 39, no. 2 (1985): 156–60.

4406. Nonnenmann, Rainer. "Das unerkannt Bekannte: Kritische Anmerkungen zum Verfremdungsgebrauch in Helmut Lachenmanns *Guero: Studie für Klavier* (1970)." MTH 15, no. 2 (2000): 111–20.

Schwankungen am Rand: Musik für Blech und Saiten

4407. Oehlschlägel, Reinhard. "Wider-Setzungen: Lachenmanns *Schwankungen am Rand*." MTX 67–68 (1997): 93–94.

String Quartet No. 2 ("Reigen seliger Geister")

4408. Kaltenecker, Martin. "Fragmente zu Lachenmanns 'Reigen seliger Geister.'" MTX 67–68 (1997): 67–74.

Tanzsuite mit Deutschlandlied

4409. Stawowy, Milena. "'Fluchtversuch in die Höhle des Löwen': Helmut Lachenmanns *Tanzsuite mit Deutschlandlied*." MTX 67–68 (1997): 77–90.

temA

4410. Nonnenmann, Karl Rainer. "Auftakt der 'instrumentalen musique concrète': Helmut Lachenmanns *temA* von 1968." MTX 67–68 (1997): 106–14.

Variationen über ein Thema von Franz Schubert

4411. Nonnenmann, Karl Rainer. "Melancholie in Franz Schuberts Walzer in cis-Moll D 643 und Helmut Lachenmanns *Schubertvariationen* (1956)." AM 54, no. 4 (1997): 247–68.

Various Works

4412. Mäckelmann, Michael. "Helmut Lachenmann oder 'Das neu zu rechtfertigende Schöne': Zum 50. Geburtstag des Komponisten." NZM 146, no. 11 (1985): 21–25.

4413. Metzger, Heinz-Klaus, and Rainer Riehn, eds. *Helmut Lachenmann*. Munich: Text + Kritik, 1988.

LACHNER, FRANZ PAUL (1803–1890)

4414. Wagner, Günter. *Franz Lachner als Liederkomponist nebst einem biographischen Teil und dem thematischer Verzeichnis sämtlicher Lieder.* Munich: Katzbichler, 1970.

LACK, THÉODORE (1846–1921)
4415. M-Kniesner. [*Sonate pastorale,* Op. 253]

LA HACHE, THEODORE VON (1822?–1869)
4416. Fields, Warren C. "The Life and Works of Theodore von la Hache." Ph.D. diss., University of Iowa, 1973.

LAJTHA, LÁSZLÓ (1892–1963)
4417. Weissman, John S. "László Lajtha: The Symphonies." MR 36 (1975): 197–214.

LALO, EDOUARD (1823–1892)
4418. ASO 65 (1984) [*Le roi d'Ys*]
4419. Macdonald, Hugh. "A Fiasco Remembered: *Fiesque* Dismembered." F-Abraham: 163–85.

LANDRÉ, GUILLAUME (1905–1968)
4420. Flothuis, Marius. "Guillaume Landré: Fourth String Quartet (1965)." SS 40 (1969): 20–22.
4421. Wouters, Jos. "Guillaume Landré." SS 15 (1963): 1–17.
4422. ———. "Guillaume Landré: Symphony No. 3." SS 20 (1964): 34–37.
4423. ———. "Guillaume Landré: *Symphonic Permutations.*" SS 8 (1961): 10–13.

LANG, DAVID (b. 1957)
4424. Mahoney, Shafer. "David Lang's *International Business Machine*: An Analysis." Ph.D. diss., University of Rochester, 1999.

LANGLAIS, JEAN (1907–1991)
4425. Krellwitz, Janet. "The Relationship of the Plainsong and the Organ Music of Jean Langlais." Ed.D. diss., New York University, 1981.
4426. Kurr, Doreen Barbara. "The Organ Works of Jean Langlais." D.M.A. diss., University of Washington, 1971.

LANNER, JOSEPH (1801–1843)
4427. Barford, Philip T. "The Early Dances of Josef Lanner." MR 21 (1960): 114–20.
4428. ———. "Joseph Lanner: A further Appraisal." MR 21 (1960): 179–85.

LANSKY, PAUL (b. 1944)
4429. Code, David Loberg. "Observations in the Art of Speech: Paul Lansky's *Six Fantasies.*" PNM 28, no. 1 (1990): 144–69.

LANZA, ALCIDES (b. 1929)
4430. Ledroit, Christien. "*Trilogy* by Alcides Lanza." EXT 9, no. 2 (1999): 42–53.

LASSEN, EDUARD (1830–1904)
4431. Marx-Weber, Magda. "Die Lieder Eduard Lassens." HJM 2 (1974): 147–85.

LAYTON, BILLY JIM (b. 1924)
4432. Browne, Richmond. "*Dance Fantasy.*" PNM 4, no. 1 (1965): 161–70.

LAZAROF, HENRI (b. 1932)
4433. Applebaum, Edward. "An Analysis of Lazarof's *Textures.*" NW 3 (1973): 26–29.

LEBOFFE, ENRICO
4434. Webster, Jesser Alfred, Jr. "The Discovery of Enrico Leboffe, Immigrant American-Italian Composer." D.M.A. diss., University of Oklahoma, 1978.

LECHTHALER, JOSEF (1891–1948)
4435. Klein, Rudolph. "Ein unbekanntes Werk von Josef Lechthaler." ME 5 (1952): 139–44. [*Orgelphantasie,* op. 31]

LEES, BENJAMIN (b. 1924)
4436. Cooke, Deryck. "Benjamin Lees' *Visions of Poets.*" TEMPO 68 (1964): 25–31.
4437. ———. "The Music of Benjamin Lees." TEMPO 51 (1959): 16–29.
4438. ———. "The Recent Music of Benjamin Lees." TEMPO 64 (1963): 11–21.
4439. Kim, Hyung Bae. "The Solo Piano Works of Benjamin Lees Published from 1956 to 1976." D.M.A. diss., Peabody Conservatory, 1981.
4440. Slonimsky, Nicolas. "Benjamin Lees In Excelsis." TEMPO 113 (1975): 14–21.
4441. Westwood, Shirley Ann. "Poetic Imagery in the Songs of Benjamin Lees." D.M.A. diss., University of Missouri, 1980.

LEEUW, REINBERT DE (b. 1938)

4442. Markus, Wim. "*Axel* or the Rejection of Life." KN 6 (1977): 19–32.

LEEUW, TON DE (1926–1996)

4443. Dominick, Lisa R. "Mode and Movement in Recent Works of Ton de Leeuw." KN 17 (1983): 15–23. [*And They Shall Reign for Ever, Birth of Music II, Car nos vignes sont en fleur, Chronos, Clair obscure, Magic of Music II, Modal Music*]

4444. Groot, Rokus de. "Aspects of Ton de Leeuw's Musical Universe." KN 23 (1986): 17–31.

4445. Leeuw, Ton de. "Ton de Leeuw: *Mouvements rétrogrades.*" SS 8 (1961): 14–15.

4446. Manneke, Daan. "Ton de Leeuw: *Music for Organ and 12 Players.*" SS 49 (1971–1972): 7–12.

4447. ———. "Ton de Leeuw: *Music for Strings.*" SS 48 (1971): 17–26.

4448. Paap, Wouter. "A New String Quartet by Ton de Leeuw." SS 25 (1965): 24–28. [String Quartet No. 2]

4449. Vermeulen, Ernst. "*Lamento pacis* by Ton de Leeuw." SS 39 (1969): 23–32.

4450. Wouters, Jos. "Ton de Leeuw." SS 19 (1964): 1–29.

LE FLEMING, CHRISTOPHER (1908–1985)

4451. Urrows, David Francis. "The Choral Music of Christopher Le Fleming." ACR 28, no. 3 (1986): 1–29.

LEHAR, FRANZ (1870–1948)

4452. ASO 45 (1982). [*Die lustige Witwe*]

LEIBOWITZ, RENÉ (1913–1972)

4453. Bowlby, Timothy J. "'In Memoriam Alban Berg?' An Analysis of René Leibowitz's Five Pieces for Clarinet and Piano, Op. 29 (1952)." EXT 7, no. 2 (1995): 78–114.

4454. Maguire, Jan. "René Leibowitz." PNM 21 (1982–1983): 241–56. [*Todos carán*]

4455. M-Ogdon: 252–311. [String Quartet No. 3]

4456. Saby, Bernard. "Un Aspect des problèmes de la thématique sérielle: A propos de la *Symphonie de chambre*, Op. 16, de René Leibowitz." POL 4 (1949): 54–63.

LEKBERG, SVEN (1899–1984)

4457. Lamb, Gordon Howard. "The Choral Music of Sven Lekberg." Ph.D. diss., University of Iowa, 1973.

LEONCAVALLO, RUGGERO (1857–1919)

4458. ASO 50 (1983). [*Pagliacci*]

LERDAHL, FRED (b. 1943)

4459. Harbison, John. "Symmetries and the 'New Tonality.'" CMR 6, no. 2 (1992): 71–79. [String Quartet No. 1]

LESSER, WOLFGANG (1923–1999)

4460. Schaefer, Hansjürgen. "'. . . gesellschaftlich Konkret': Bemerkungen zum Violinkonzert von Wolfgang Lesser." MG 14 (1964): 331–35.

LEVY, ERNST (1895–1981)

4461. Levarie, Siegmund. "La musique d'Ernst Levy." SMZ 108 (1968): 178–87.

LEWIN, DAVID (1933–2003)

4462. Levy, Burt J. "David Lewin: *Classical Variations on a Theme by Schoenberg* for Cello and Piano (1960)." PNM 7, no. 2 (1969): 167–71.

LIDHOLM, INGVAR (b. 1921)

4463. Brolsma, Bruce Edward. "The Music of Ingvar Lidholm: A Survey and Analysis." Ph.D. diss., Northwestern University, 1979.

4464. Lidholm, Ingvar. "*Poesis* for Orchestra." M-Ligeti: 55–80.

4465. ———. "*Poesis* für Orchester." MELOS 36 (1969): 63–76.

LIEBERMANN, ROLF (1910–1999)

4466. Stuckenschmidt, H. H. "Rolf Liebermann: Bildnis eines Komponisten." SMZ 92 (1952): 137–43.

LIEBERSON, PETER (b. 1946)

4467. Rosenzweig, Morris. "Contemplated Balances: A Brief View of Arthur Kreiger and Peter Lieberson." CMR 10, no. 1 (1994): 101–19.

LIER, BERTUS VAN (1906–1972)
4468. Wouters, Jos. "Bertus van Lier: Sonatina No. 2." SS 13 (1962): 9–11.

LIGETI, GYÖRGY (b. 1923)
Apparitions
4469. Bernard, Jonathan W. "Inaudible Structures, Audible Music: Ligeti's Problem, and His Solution." MA 6, no. 3 (1987): 207–36.
4470. M-Salmenhaara.

Artikulation
4471. Miereanu, Costin. "Une musique électronique et sa 'partition': *Artikulation*." MJ 15 (1974): 102–9.

Atmosphères
4472. Bayer, Francis. "*Atmosphères* de György Ligeti: Élements pour une analyse." ANM 15 (1989): 18–24.
4473. Beurmann, Andreas E., and Albrecht Schneider. "Struktur, Klang, Dynamik: Akustische Untersuchungen an Ligetis *Atmosphères*." HJM 11 (1988): 311–34.
4474. Brauneiss, Leopold. "Proportionen im ametrischen Raum: Zu Ligetis Werken *Atmosphères* und Konzert für Violoncello und Orchester." M-Brauneiss: 31–42.
4475. Kaufmann, Harold. "Strukturen im Strukturlosen." MELOS 31 (1964): 391–98.
4476. M-Roberts.
4477. M-Salmenhaara.
4478. Schneider, Sigrun. "Zwischen Statik und Dynamik: Zur formalen Analyse von Ligetis *Atmosphères*." MB 7 (1975): 507–10.
4479. Suplicki, Markus. "György Ligeti: *Atmosphères*—eine unkausale Form?" MTH 10, no. 3 (1995): 235–47.
4480. M-Vogt: 307–14.

Aventures
4481. Kaufmann, Harold. "Un cas de musique absurde: *Aventures* et *Nouvelles aventures* de Ligeti." MJ 15 (1974): 75–98.
4482. Klüppelholz, Werner. "Aufhebung der Sprache: Zu Gyorgy Ligetis *Aventures*." Melos/NZM 2 (1976): 11–15.
4483. M-Salmenhaara.

Bagatellen
4484. Benedictis, Fabio de Sanctis. "György Ligeti: Sechs Bagatellen für Bläserquintett." T 19, no. 3 (1994): 194–201.

Cello Concerto
4485. M-Bersano.
4486. Brauneiss, Leopold. "Proportionen im ametrischen Raum: Zu Ligetis Werken *Atmosphères* und Konzert für Violoncello und Orchester." M-Brauneiss: 31–42.
4487. Reverdy, Michèle. "Le Concerto pour violoncelle de György Ligeti: Matériau, mouvement et forme." ANM 6 (1987): 80–85.
4488. Schultz, Wolfgang-Andreas. "Zwei Studien über das Cello-Konzert von Ligeti." ZM 6, no. 2 (1975): 97–104.
4489. Stephan, Rudolf. "György Ligeti: Konzert für Violoncello und Orchester; Anmerkungen zur Cluster-Komposition." M-Stephan: 117–27.

Chamber Concerto
4490. Bernager, Olivier. "Autour du Concerto de chambre de Ligeti." MJ 15 (1974): 99–101.
4491. Bernard, Jonathan W. "Inaudible Structures, Audible Music: Ligeti's Problem, and His Solution." MA 6, no. 3 (1987): 207–36.
4492. Mennesson, Christine. "György Ligeti: Une approche synthétique du Kammerkonzert en vue de l'interpretation." ANM 34 (1999): 52–61.
4493. Michel, Pierre. "György Ligeti: Kammerkonzert pour treize instrumentistes (1969–70)." ANM 34 (1999): 31–51.
4494. Mountain, Rosemary. "An Investigation of Periodicity in Music, with Reference to Three Twentieth-Century Compositons." Ph.D. diss., University of Victoria, 1993.
4495. ———. "Time and Texture in Lutoslawski's Concerto for Orchestra and Ligeti's Chamber Concerto." EXT 7, no. 1 (1994): 129–90.
4496. Piencikowski, Robert. "Les points sur les i: Le concerto de chambre de Ligeti." INH 2 (1987): 211–16.
4497. Pulido, Alejandro. "Differentiation and Intergration in Ligeti's Chamber Concerto, III." SONUS 9, no. 1 (1988): 59–80. [Movement III]
4498. Roig-Francolí, Miguel A. "Harmonic and Formal Processes in Ligeti's Net-Structure Compositions." MTS 17, no. 2 (1995): 242–67. [Movement I]
4499. Searby, Michael. "Ligeti's Chamber Concerto: Summation or Turning Point?" TEMPO 168 (1989): 30–34.

Continuum

4500. Hicks, Michael. "Interval and Form in Ligeti's *Continuum* and *Coulée*." PNM 31, no. 1 (1993): 172–90.

4501. Toop, Richard. "L'illusion de la surface." Trans. Daniel Haefliger and Jacques Demierre. CC 12–13 (1990): 60–96.

4502. Urban, Uve. "Serielle Technik und barocker Geist in Ligetis Cembalo-Stück *Continuum*." MB 5 (1973): 63–70.

Double Concerto

4503. Eitan, Zohar. "Functionality within Cluster Harmony: Cadences and Primary Notes in the First Movement of Ligeti's Double Concerto (1972)." OM 11 (1993–1994): 92–123.

Etudes (Piano)

4504. Bouliane, Denys. "Imaginäre Bewegung: György Ligetis Etudes pour piano." MTX 28–29 (1989): 73–84.

4505. ———. "Six etudes pour piano de György Ligeti." CC 12–13 (1990): 98–132. [Premier livre]

4506. Floros, Constantin. "Versuch über Ligetis jüngste Werke." HJM 11 (1988): 335–48. [Premier livre]

4507. Kinzler, Hartmuth. "György Ligeti: Decision and Automatism in *Désordre*, 1re Étude, Premier livre." I 20, no. 2 (1991): 89–124. German trans., HJM 13 (1995): 337–72.

4508. Mennesson, Christine. "György Ligeti: Études pour piano (plus particulièrement *Automne à Varsovie*); Les illusions acoutiques comme matériau d'une écriture." ANM 36 (2000): 76–93.

4509. Rümenapp, Peter. "Raumkonstruktion und Zeitordnung in Ligetis sechster Klavieretüde." MTX 67–68 (1997): 40–43. [Premiere liver, no. 6]

4510. Schütz, Hannes. "Music und Chaostheorie: Gedanken zu Ligetis Klavieretüde Nr. 1–*Désordre*." M 50, no. 3 (1996): 170–76.

4511. ———. "Wiedergeburt der Ars subtilior? Eine Analyse von György Ligetis Klavieretüde Nr. 2 'Cordes vides.'" MF 50, no. 2 (1997): 205–14.

4512. Taylor, Stephen A. "Chopin, Pygmies, and Tempo Fugue: Ligeti's 'Automne a Varsovie.'" MTO 3, no. 3 (1997). [Premiere livre, no. 6]

Glissandi

4513. Camilleri, Lelio. "Metodologie e concetti analitici nello studio di musiche elettroacustiche." RIM 28 (1993): 131–74.

4514. Doati, Roberto. "Györgi Ligeti's *Glissandi*: An Analysis." I 20, no. 2 (1991): 79–87.

Grand macabre

4515. ASO 180 (1997).

4516. Fanselau, Rainer. "György Ligeti: *Le grand macabre;* Gesichtspunkte für eine Behandlung im Musikunterricht." MB 15, no. 5 (1983): 17–24.

4517. Michel, Pierre. "Les Rapports texte/musique chez György Ligeti de *Lux aeterna* au *Grand macabre*." CC 4 (1985): 128–38.

Invention

4518. Sallis, Friedemann. "La transformation d'un heritage: Bagatelle op. 6, no. 2 de Béla Bartók et *Invenció* (1948) pour piano de György Ligeti." RDM 83, no. 2 (1997): 281–93.

Lontano

4519. Boos, Michael. "Canonic Structure in György Ligeti's *Lontano*." TCM 2, no. 4 (1995): 1–3.

4520. Clendinning, Jane Piper. "Structural Factors in the Microcanonic Compositoins of György Ligeti." M-Marvin: 229–56.

4521. Dadelsen, Hans-Christian von. "Hat Distanz Relevanz: Über Kompositionstechnik und ihre musikdidaktischen Folgen; Dargestelle an György Liegtis Orchesterstück *Lontano* (1967)." MB 7 (1975): 502–6.

4522. ———. "Über die musikalischen Konturen der Entfernung: Entfernung als räumliche, historische und ästhetische Perspektive in Ligetis *Lontano*." Melos/NZM 2 (1976): 187–90.

4523. Müller, Karl-Josef. "György Ligeti (1923): *Lontano* für grosses Orchester (1967)." M-Zimmerschied: 286–308.

4524. Reiprich, Bruce. "Transformation of Coloration and Density in Gyorgy Ligeti's *Lontano*." PNM 16, no. 2 (1977–1978): 167–80.

4525. Rollin, Robert L. "The Genesis of the Technique of Canonic Sound Mass in Ligeti's *Lontano*." ITR 2, no. 2 (1978–1979): 23–33.

4526. ———. "Ligeti's *Lontano*: Traditional Canonic Technique in a New Guise." MR 41 (1980): 289–96.

4527. ———. "The Process of Textural Change and the Organization of Pitch in Ligeti's *Lontano*." D.M.A. diss., Cornell University, 1973.

Lux aeterna

4528. Bernard, Jonathan W. "Inaudible Structures, Audible Music: Ligeti's Problem, and His Solution." MA 6, no. 3 (1987): 207–36.

4529. ———. "Voice Leading as a Spatial Function in the Music of Ligeti." MA 13/2–3 (1994): 227–53.

4530. Clendinning, Jane Piper. "Structural Factors in the Microcanonic Compositoins of György Ligeti." M-Marvin: 229–56.

4531. Gottwald, Clytus. "*Lux aeterna*: Ein Beitrag zur Kompositionstechnik György Ligetis." M 25 (1971): 12–17.

4532. Jarvlepp, Jan. "Pitch and Texture Analysis of Ligeti's *Lux aeterna*." EXT 2, no. 1 (1982): 16–32.

4533. Ligeti, György. "Auf dem Weg zu *Lux aeterna*." OMZ 24 (1969): 80–88.

4534. Michel, Pierre. "Les rapports texte/musique chez György Ligeti de *Lux aeterna* au *Grand macabre*." CC 4 (1985): 128–38.

4535. Prost, Christine. "György Ligeti: *Lux aeterna,* pour chœur mixte a cappella." ANM 25 (1991): 37–51.

4536. Rummenhöller, Peter. "Möglichkeiten neuester Chormusik." In *Der Einfluss der technischen Mittler auf die Musikerziehung unserer Zeit,* 311–17. Mainz: Schott, 1968.

Magyar etüdök

4537. Aluas, Luminita. "Visible and Audible Structures: Spatio-Temporal Compromise in Ligeti's *Magyar etüdök*." TEMPO 183 (1992): 7–17.

Melodien

4538. Baca-Lobera, Ignacio. "György Ligeti's *Melodien*: A Work in Transition." I 20, no. 2 (1991): 65–78.

Monument-Selbstportrait-Bewegung

4539. Bernard, Jonathan W. "Inaudible Structures, Audible Music: Ligeti's Problem, and His Solution." MA 6, no. 3 (1987): 207–36.

4540. Febel, Reinhard. "György Ligeti: *Monument-Selbstporträt-Bewegung* (3 Stücke für 2 Klaviere)." ZM 9, no. 1 (1978): 35–51; 9, no. 2 (1978): 4–14.

4541. ———. *Musik für zwei Klaviere seit 1950 als Spiegel der Kompositionstechnik.* Herrenberg: Doring, 1978.

Nouvelles aventures

4542. Anhalt, István. "Ligeti's *Nouvelles aventures*: A Small Group as a Model for Composition." M-Anhalt: 41–92.

4543. Kaufmann, Harold. "Un cas de musique absurde: *Aventures* et *Nouvelles aventures* de Ligeti." MJ 15 (1974): 75–98.

4544. Kostakeva, Maria. "Die asemantische Semantik in der Vokalmelodik György Ligetis." MPSS 10 (1997): 15–20.

Phantasien

4545. Floros, Constantin. "Ligetis *Drei Phantasien* nach Friedrich Hölderlin (1982)." NZM 146, no. 2 (1985): 18–20.

Piano Concerto

4546. Floros, Constantin. "Versuch über Ligetis jüngste Werke." HJM 11 (1988): 335–48.

Pieces (Wind Quintet)

4547. Clendinning, Jane Piper. "Structural Factors in the Microcanonic Compositoins of György Ligeti." M-Marvin: 229–56. [No. 9]

4548. Morrison, Charles D. "Stepwise Continuity as a Structural Determinant in György Ligeti's Ten Pieces for Wind Quintet." PNM 24, no. 1 (1985): 158–82.

4549. Yannay, Yehuda. "Toward an Open-Ended Method of Analysis of Contemporary Music: A Study of Selected Works by Edgard Varèse and György Ligeti." D.M.A. diss., University of Illinois, 1974.

Ramifications

4550. Roig-Francolí, Miguel A. "Harmonic and Formal Processes in Ligeti's Net-Structure Compositions." MTS 17, no. 2 (1995): 242–67.

Requiem

4551. M-Salmenhaara.

String Quartet No. 1 ("Métamorphoses nocturnes")

4552. Jaedtke, Wolfgang. "Tradition und Transzendenz in György Ligetis Erstem Streichquartett." MTH 14, no. 1 (1999): 3–12.

String Quartet No. 2

4553. Bernard, Jonathan W. "Voice Leading as a Spatial Function in the Music of Ligeti." MA 13/2–3 (1994): 227–53. [Movement III]

4554. Borio, Gianmario. "L'eredità bartókiana nel Secondo Quartetto di G. Ligeti: Sul concetto de tradizione nella musica contemporanea." STU 13 (1984): 289–308.

4555. Kaufmann, Harold. "Ligetis zweites Streichquartett." MELOS 37 (1970): 181–86.

4556. Kyburz, Hans-Peter. "Fondement d'une interprétation: La construction numérique." Trans. Vincent Barras. CC 12–13 (1990): 133–52.

4557. Roig-Francolí, Miguel A. "Harmonic and Formal Processes in Ligeti's Net-Structure Compositions." MTS 17, no. 2 (1995): 242–67. [Movement V]

Studies (Organ)
4558. Hicks, Michael. "Interval and Form in Ligeti's *Continuum* and *Coulée*." PNM 31, no. 1 (1993): 172–90.
4559. Toop, Richard. "L'illusion de la surface." Trans. Daniel Haefliger and Jacques Demierre. CC 12–13 (1990): 60–96.

Volumina
4560. Luchese, Diane. "Levels of Infrastructure in Ligeti's *Volumina*." SONUS 9, no. 1 (1988): 38–58.

Various Works
4561. Bernard, Jonathan W. "Ligeti's Restoration of Interval and Its Significance for His Later Works." MTS 21, no. 1 (1999): 1–31.
4562. Christensen, Louis. "Introduction to the Music of György Ligeti." NW 2 (1972): 6–15.
4563. Clendinning, Jane Piper. "The Pattern-Meccanico Compositions of György Ligeti." PNM 31, no. 1 (1993): 192–234.
4564. Collins, Glena Whitman. "Avant-Garde Techniques in the Organ Works of György Ligeti." D.M.A. diss., North Texas State University, 1980.
4565. Dibelius, Ulrich. "Reflexion und Reaktion über den Komponisten György Ligeti." MELOS 37 (1970): 89–96.
4566. Dobson, E. "Illusion in the Music of György Ligeti, 1958–1968." M.M. thesis, University of Queensland, 1977.
4567. Frisius, Rudolf. "Tonal oder postseriell." MB 7 (1975): 490–501.
4568. Griffiths, Paul. *György Ligeti*. London: Robson, 1983.
4569. Gruhn, Wilfried. "Textvertonung und Sprachkomposition bei György Ligeti: Aspekte einer didaktischen Analyse zum Thema 'Musik und Sprache.'" MB 7 (1975): 511–19.
4570. Häusler, Josef. "György Ligeti oder die Netzstruktur." NZM 144, no. 5 (1983): 18–21.
4571. Hoopen, Christiane ten. "Zu Ligetis Befreiung der Musik vom Taktschlag durch präzise Notation." MTX 28–29 (1989): 68–72.
4572. Lichtenfeld, Monika. "György Ligeti oder das Ende der seriellen Musik." MELOS 39 (1972): 74–80.
4573. Ligeti, György. *György Ligeti in Conversation*. London: Eulenberg Books, 1983.
4574. Nordwall, Ore. *György Ligeti: Eine Monographie*. Mainz: Schott, 1971.
4575. Petersen, Peter. "Bartók–Lutosławski–Ligeti: Einige Bemerkungen zu ihrer Kompositionstechnik unter dem Aspekt der Tonhöhe." HJM 11 (1988): 289–309.
4576. Sabbe, Herman. *György Ligeti: Studien zur kompositorischen Phänomenologie*. Munich: Text + Kritik, 1987.
4577. Schmiedeke, Ulrich. *Der Beginn der neuen Orgelmusik: Die Orgelkompositionen von Hambraeus, Kagel, und Ligeti*. Munich: Katzbichler, 1981.

LILBURN, DOUGLAS (1915–2001)
4578. Harris, Ross. "Douglas Lilburn's Symphony No. 3 (In One Movement)." *Canzona* 2, no. 5 (1980): 3–7.

LIM, LIZA (b. 1966)
4579. Rosman, Carl. "Wie gelähmt die Zunge Fieber unter der Haut . . .: Prozesse in Liza Lims *Voodoo Child*." MAS 3, no. 11 (1999): 30–42.

LINDBERG, MAGNUS (b. 1958)
4580. Nieminen, Risto, ed. *Magnus Lindberg*. Paris: IRCAM, 1993.

LINDROTH, SCOTT (b. 1958)
4581. Wheeler, Scott. "Beyond the Flat Surface: Form and Rhetoric in Machover, Hyla, and Lindroth." CMR 10, no. 1 (1994): 75–100. [*Stomp*]

LISZT, FRANZ (1811–1886)
Album d'un voyageur
4582. Biget, Michèle. "Écriture(s) instrumentale(s): La *Vallée d'Obermann*." ANM 21 (1990): 85–95.
4583. Fowler, Andrew. "Motive and Program in Liszt's *Vallée d'Obermann*." JALS 29 (1991): 3–11.
4584. Main, Alexander. "Liszt's *Lyon*: Music and the Social Conscience." NCM 4 (1980–1981): 228–43. [Bk. I, no. 1]

An den heiligen Franziskus von Paula
4585. Sievers, Gerd. "Franz Liszts Legende *Der Heilige Franziskus von Paula* auf den Wegen schretend für Klavier in Max Regers Bearbeitung für die Orgel." HJM 2 (1976): 125–46.

Années de pèlerinage
4586. Backus, Joan. "Liszt's *Sposalizio*: A Study in Musical Perspective." NCM 12, no. 2 (1988): 173–83.
4587. Cinnamon, Howard. "Chromaticism and Tonal Coherence in Liszt's *Sonetto 104 del Petrarca*." ITO 7, no. 3 (1983–1984): 3–19.

4588. ———. "Third-Related Harmonies as Elements of Contrapuntal Prolongation in Some Works by Franz Liszt." ITO 12, nos. 5–6 (1992): 1–30.

4589. Damschroder, David Allen. "Structural Levels: A Key to Liszt's Chromatic Art." CMS 27 (1987): 46–58. ["Vallée d'Obermann"]

4590. ———. "Liszt's Composition Lessons from Beethoven (Florence, 1838–1839): 'Il penseroso.'" JALS 28 (1990): 3–19.

4591. M-Forte/L. ["Vallée d'Obermann"]

4592. Fowler, Andrew. "Franz Liszt's *Années de pèlerinage* as Megacycle." JALS 40 (1996): 113–29.

4593. ———. "Multilevel Motivic Projection in Selected Piano Works of Liszt." JALS 16 (1984): 20–34. [*Deuxième année, Italie*]

4594. Neumeyer, David. "Liszt's *Sonetto 104 del Petrarca*: The Romantic Spirit and Voice Leading." ITR 11, no. 2 (1978–1979): 2–22.

4595. Pesce, Dolores. "Liszt's *Années de pèlerinage*, Book 3: A 'Hungarian' Cycle?" NCM 13, no. 3 (1990): 207–29.

4596. Presser, Diether. "Liszts *Années de pèlerinage, Prèmiere année*: Suisse als Dokument der Romantik." *Liszt Studien 1: Kongress-Bericht, Eisenstadt 1975*, ed. Wolfgang Suppan, 137–58. Graz: Akademische Druck- & Verlagsanstalt, 1977.

4597. Way, Elizabeth. "Raphael as a Musical Model: Liszt's *Sposalizio*." JALS 40 (1996): 103–12.

4598. Wilson, Karen Sue. "A Historical Study and Stylistic Analysis of Franz Liszt's *Années de pèlerinage*." Ph.D. diss., University of North Carolina, 1977.

Blume und Duft

4599. Cinnamon, Howard. "Third-Related Harmonies as Elements of Contrapuntal Prolongation in Some Works by Franz Liszt." ITO 12, nos. 5–6 (1992): 1–30.

4600. ———. "Tonal Structure and Voice-Leading in Liszt's *Blume und Duft*." ITO 6, no. 3 (1981–1983): 12–24.

4601. M-Forte/L.

4602. Hantz, Edwin. "Motivic and Structural Unity in Liszt's *Blume und Duft*." ITO 6, no. 3 (1981–1983): 3–11.

4603. Morgan, Robert P. "Chasing the Scent: The Tonality of Liszt's *Blume und Duft*." M-Baker: 361–76.

Ce qu'on entend sur la montagne (Bergsymphonie)

4604. Dahlhaus, Carl. "Liszts *Bergsymphonie* und die Idee der symphonischen Dichtung." JSIM (1975): 96–130.

4605. M-Taruskin.

Choral Works (various; *see also* specific choral works)

4606. Cheung, Andrew Y. K. "Thematic and Motivic Transformation in Selected Sacred Choral Works of Franz Liszt." M.A. thesis, State University College, Potsdam, New York, 1979.

4607. Fudge, James Thompson. "The Male Chorus Music of Franz Liszt." Ph.D. diss., University of Iowa, 1972.

4608. Hamburger, Klára. "Program and Hungarian Idiom in the Sacred Music of Liszt." F-Walker: 239–51.

Christus

4609. Orr, Nathaniel Leon. "Liszt, *Christus,* and the Transformation of the Oratorio." JALS 9 (1981): 4–18.

4610. ———. "Liszt's *Christus* and Its Significance for Nineteenth-Century Oratorio." Ph.D. diss., University of North Carolina, 1979.

Consolations (Piano)

4611. Diercks, John. "The *Consolations*: 'Delightful Things Hidden Away.'" JALS 3 (1978): 19–24.

4612. Kielian-Gilbert, Marianne. "The Functional Differentiation of Harmonic and Transpositional Patterns in Liszt's *Consolation* No. 4." NCM 14, no. 1 (1990): 48–59.

Dante Symphony. See Symphonie zu Dantes Divina Commedia

De profundis (Psaume instrumental)

4613. Johns, Keith T. "*De profundis, psaume instrumental*: An Abandoned Concerto for Piano and Orchestra by Franz Liszt." JALS 15 (1984): 96–104.

Études de concert

4614. Bass, Richard. "Liszt's *Un sospiro*: An Experiment in Symmetrial Octave-Partitions." JALS 32 (1993): 16–37.

4615. M-Taruskin. [No. 3]

Etudes d'exécution transcendante

4616. Hunkemöller, Jürgen. "Perfektion und Perspektivenwechsel: Studien zu den drei Fassungen der *Études d'exécution transcendante* von Franz Liszt." AM 51, no. 4 (1994): 294–314.

Etudes d'exécution transcendante d'après Paganini

4617. Kabisch, Thomas. "Franz Liszt und die Tradition der 'nicht-diskursiven' Musik." SM 28 (1986): 125–36. [No. 4]

Fantasie und Fuge über den Choral "Ad nos, ad salutarem undam"

4618. Edler, Arnfried. "'In ganz neuer und freier Form geschrieben': Zu Liszts *Phantasie und Fuge über den Choral 'Ad nos ad salutarem undam.'*" MF 25 (1972): 249–58.

4619. Todd, R. Larry. "Liszt: *Fantasy and Fugue for Organ on 'Ad nos, ad salutarem undam.'*" NCM 4 (1980–1981): 250–61.

Faust-Symphonie

4620. Anderson, Lyle John. "Motivic and Thematic Transformation in Selected Works of Liszt." Ph.D. diss., Ohio State University, 1977.

4621. Brown, David. "The Introduction to Liszt's *Faust Symphony* with a Postscript on the B Minor Sonata." MR 49, no. 4 (1988): 267–71. [Movement I]

4622. Cinnamon, Howard. "Third-Related Harmonies as Elements of Contrapuntal Prolongation in Some Works by Franz Liszt." ITO 12, nos. 5–6 (1992): 1–30.

4623. De la Motte, Diether de. "Keine Geschichte: Liszts *Faust-Symphonie.*" F-Dahlhaus: 547–53.

4624. M-Forte/L.

4625. Kaplan, Richard. "Sonata Form in the Orchestral Works of Liszt: The Revolutionary Reconsidered." NCM 8 (1984–1985): 142–52.

4626. Longyear, Rey M., and Kate R. Covington. "Tonal and Harmonic Structures in Liszt's *Faust Symphony.*" SM 28 (1986): 153–71.

4627. M-Macy.

4628. Niemöller, Klaus Wolfgang. "Zur nicht-tonalen Thema-Struktur von Liszts *Faust- Symphonie.*" MF 22 (1969): 69–72.

4629. Ott, Leonard W. "The Orchestration of the *Faust Symphony.*" JALS 12 (1982): 28–37.

4630. Redepenning, Dorothea. *Franz Liszt: Faust-Symphonie.* Munich: Fink, 1988.

4631. Ritzel, Fred. "Materialdenken bei Liszt: Eine Untersuchung der 'Zwölftonthemas' der *Faust-Symphonie.*" MF 20 (1967): 289–94.

4632. Somfai, László. "Die Metamorphose der *Faust-Symphonie* von Liszt." SM 5 (1963): 283–94.

4633. ———. "Die musikalische Gestaltwandlungen der *Faust-Symphonie* von Liszt." SM 2 (1962): 87–137.

4634. M-Taruskin.

4635. Vazsonyi, Nicholas. "Liszt, Goethe, and the *Faust Symphony.*" JALS 40 (1996): 1–23.

Hamlet

4636. M-Forte/L.

4637. Murphy, Edward. "A Detailed Program for Liszt's *Hamlet.*" JALS 29 (1991): 47–60.

Harmonies poétiques et religieuses

4638. Backus, Joan. "Liszt's *Harmonies poétiques et religieuses*: Inspiration and the Challenge of Form." JALS 21 (1987): 3–21.

4639. Damschroder, David Allen. "Structural Levels: A Key to Liszt's Chromatic Art." CMS 27 (1987): 46–58. ["Funérailles"]

4640. Fowler, Andrew. "Multilevel Motivic Projection in Selected Piano Works of Liszt." JALS 16 (1984): 20–34.

4641. Kaczmarczyk, Adrienne. "The Genesis of *Funérailles*: The Connections between Liszt's *Symphonie révolutionnaire* and the Cycle *Harmonies poétiques et religieuses.*" SM 35, no. 4 (1993–1994): 361–98.

Héroïde funèbre

4642. Popovic, Linda. "Liszt's Harmonic Polymorphism: Tonal and Non-Tonal Aspects in *Héroïde Funèbre.*" MA 15, no. 1 (1996): 41–55.

Historische ungarische Bildnisse

4643. Claus, Linda W. "An Aspect of Liszt's Late Style: The Composer's Revisions for *Historische, ungarische Portäts.*" JALS 3 (1978): 3–18.

Hunnenschlacht

4644. Angerer, Manfred. "Liszts *Hunnenschlacht* und die Aporien der Symphonischen Dichtung." SZM 38 (1987): 117–34.

Ich möchte hingehn

4645. Rehding, Alexander. "Liszt und die Suche nach dem 'TrisZtan'-Akkord." ACTA 72, no. 2 (2000): 169–88.

Ideale

4646. Micznik, Vera. "The Absolute Limitations of Programme Music: The Case of Liszt's *Die Ideale.*" ML 80, no. 2 (1999): 207–40.

Introduction et variations sur une marche du Siège de Corinthe

4647. Reich, Nancy B. "Liszt's Variations on the March from Rossini's *Siège de Corinthe.*" JALS 7 (1980): 35–41.

Kennst du das Land. See Mignons Lied

Kleine Klavierstücke

4648. Wait, Mark. "Liszt, Scriabin, and Boulez: Considerations of Form." JALS 1 (1977): 9–16.

Lasst mich ruhen

4649. Roman, Zoltan. "Allegory, Symbolism, and Personification in Selected 'Night Songs' by Liszt, Mahler, and Strauss." SM 41, no. 4 (2000): 407–39.

Legende von der heiligen Elisabeth

4650. Palotai, Michael. "Liszt's Concept of Oratorio as Reflected in His Writings and in *Die Legende von der Heiligen Elisabeth.*" Ph.D. diss., University of Southern California, 1977.

Liebesträume

4651. Cook, Nicholas. "Liszt's Second Thoughts: *Liebestraum* No. 2 and Its Relatives." NCM 12, no. 2 (1988): 163–72.

4652. Wuellner, Guy. "Franz Liszt's 'Liebestraum' No. 3: A Study of 'O lieb' and Its Piano Transcription." JALS 24 (1988): 45–73.

Lugubre gondola

4653. Skoumal, Zdenek. "Liszt's Androgynous Harmony." MA 13, no. 1 (1994): 51–72.

Malédiction

4654. Johns, Keith T. "*Malédiction*: The Concerto's History, Programme, and Some Notes on Harmonic Organization." JALS 18 (1985): 29–35.

Masses

4655. Loos, Helmut. "Franz Liszts Graver Festmesse." KJ 67 (1983): 45–60.

4656. White, Charles Willis. "The Masses of Franz Liszt." Ph.D. diss., Bryn Mawr College, 1973.

Mephisto Waltzes

4657. Feofanov, Dmitry. "How to Transcribe the *Mephisto Waltz* for Piano." JALS 11 (1982): 18–27.

4658. Hunt, Mary Angela. "Franz Liszt: *The Mephisto Waltzes.*" D.M.A. diss., University of Wisconsin, 1979.

Mignons Lied (Kennst du das Land)

4659. Broeckx, Jan L., and Walter Landrieu. "Comparative Computer Study of Style, Based on Five Liedmelodies." I 1 (1972): 29–92.

4660. M-Forte/L.

4661. M-Lewis.

Nuages gris. See Trübe Wolken

Odes funèbres

4662. Stewart, Arthur Franklin. "'La notte' and 'Les Morts': Investigations into Progressive Aspects of Franz Liszt's Style." JALS 18 (1985): 67–106. 129. Psalm (*De profundis*)

4663. Eckhardt, Maria P. "Ein Spätwerk von Liszt: Der 129. Psalm." SM 18 (1976): 296–333.

4664. M-Forte/L.

Organ Works (various; *see also* specific organ works)

4665. Schwarz, Peter. *Studien zur Orgelmusik Franz Liszts: Ein Beitrag zur Geschichte der Orgelkomposition im 19. Jahrhundert.* Munich: Katzbichler, 1973.

4666. Zacher, Gerd. "Eine Fuge ist eine Fuge ist eine Fuge: Liszts B-A-C-H Komposition für Orgel." MK 47 (1977): 15–23.

Orpheus

4667. M-Taruskin.

Piano Concerto No. 1

4668. M-Taruskin.

Piano Concerto No. 2

4669. Anderson, Lyle John. "Motivic and Thematic Transformation in Selected Works of Liszt." Ph.D. diss., Ohio State University, 1977.

4670. Niemöller, Klaus Wolfgang. "Werkkonzeption im Schnittpunkt von Gattungs- und Formtraditionen: Zu Liszts 2. Klavierkonzert." F-Dahlhaus: 527–45.

Piano Sonata, B Minor

4671. Anderson, Lyle John. "Motivic and Thematic Transformation in Selected Works of Liszt." Ph.D. diss., Ohio State University, 1977.

4672. Becker, Ralf-Walter. "Formprobleme in Liszts G-Moll-Sonate: Untersuchungen zu Liszts Klaviermusik um 1850." Ph.D. diss., Universität Marburg, 1980.

4673. Brown, David. "The Introduction to Liszt's *Faust Symphony* with a Postscript on the B Minor Sonata." MR 49, no. 4 (1988): 267–71.

4674. Damschroder, David Allen. "Structural Levels: A Key to Liszt's Chromatic Art." CMS 27 (1987): 46–58.

4675. Dommel-Diény, Amy. *Schubert-Liszt*. Dommel-Diény 9. Paris: Dommel-Diény, 1976.

4676. Gourdet, Georges. "Une analyse thématique de la sonate en si mineur de Franz Liszt." ANM 7 (1987): 49–55.

4677. Grabócz, Márta. "La sonate en si mineur de Liszt: Une stratégie narrative complexe." ANM 8 (1987): 64–70.

4678. Hamilton, Kenneth. *Liszt: Sonata in B Minor*. Cambridge: Cambridge University Press, 1996.

4679. Heinemann, Michael. *Franz Liszt: Klaviersonate G-Moll*. Munich: Fink, 1993.

4680. Hering, Hans. "Franz Liszt: Grande Sonate pour le Pianoforte." JP (1981–1982): 9–17.

4681. Känski, Josef. "The Problem of Form in Franz Liszt's Sonata in B Minor." JALS 5 (1979): 4–15.

4682. Keym, Stefan. "Originalität oder Epigonentum? Zur motivisch-thematischen Struktur der B-Moll-Sonate von Julius Reubke im Vergleich mit Liszts G-Moll-Sonate." MF 51, no. 1 (1998): 34–46.

4683. Longyear, Rey M. "Liszt's B Minor Sonata: Precedents for a Structural Analysis." MR 34 (1973): 198–209.

4684. Ott, Bertrand. "An Interpretation of Liszt's Sonata in B Minor." JALS 10 (1981): 30–38; 11 (1982): 40–41.

4685. Rea, John Rocco. "Franz Liszt's 'New Path of Composition': The Sonata in B Minor as Paradigm." Ph.D. diss., Princeton University, 1978.

4686. Saffle, Michael. "Liszt's Sonata in B Minor: Another Look at the 'Double Function' Question." JALS 11 (1982): 28–39.

4687. Sandresky, Margaret Vardell. "Tonal Design in Liszt Sonata in B Minor." JALS 10 (1981): 15–29.

4688. Schläder, Jürgen. "Zur Funktion der Variantentechnik in der Klaviersonaten F-Moll von Johannes Brahms und G-Moll von Franz Liszt." HJM 7 (1984): 171–99.

4689. Szász, Tibor. "Liszt's Divine and Diabolical Symbolism: Key to the Religious Program in the Sonata in B Minor." D.M.A. diss., University of Michigan, 1985.

4690. ———. "Liszt's Symbols for the Divine and Diabolical: Their Revelation of a Program in the B Minor Sonata." JALS 15 (1984): 39–95.

4691. Tanner, Mark. "The Power of Performance as an Alternative Analytical Discourse: The Liszt Sonata in B Minor." NCM 24, no. 2 (2000): 173–92.

4692. Wilde, David. "Liszt's Sonata: Some Jungian Reflections." F-Walker: 197–224.

Piano Works (various; *see also* specific piano works)

4693. Arnold, Ben. "Recitative in Liszt's Solo Piano Music." JALS 24 (1998): 3–22.

4694. Auh, Mijai Youn. "Piano Variations by Brahms, Liszt, and Friedman on a Theme by Paganini." D.M. diss., Indiana University, 1980.

4695. Baker, James M. "The Limits of Tonality in the Late Music of Franz Liszt." JMT 34, no. 2 (1990): 145–73.

4696. Cannata, David Butler. "Perception and Apperception in Liszt's Late Piano Music." JM 15, no. 2 (1997): 178–207.

4697. Goode, William M. "The Late Piano Works of Franz Liszt and Their Influence on Some Aspects of Modern Piano Composition." Ph.D. diss., Indiana University, 1965.

4698. Grabócz, Márta. "Strategiés narratives des 'épopées philosophiques' de l'ère romantique dans l'oeuvre pianistique de F. Liszt." SM 28 (1986): 99–115.

4699. ———. "Die Wirkung des Programms auf die Entwicklung der instrumentalen Formen in Liszts Klavierwerken." SM 22 (1980): 299–325.

4700. Kokai, Rudolf. *Franz Liszt in seinen frühen Klavierwerken*. Budapest: Akadémiai Kiadó, 1969.

4701. Lee, Robert C. "Some Little Known Late Piano Works of Liszt (1869–1886): A Miscellany." Ph.D. diss., University of Washington, 1970.

4702. Lemoine, Bernard C. "Tonal Organization in Selected Late Piano Works of Liszt." Ph.D. diss., Catholic University of America, 1976.

4703. Mauser, Siegfried. "Melodische Strukturen im Spätwerk Franz Liszts." BRS (1986): 95–103.

4704. Ott, Leonard. "Closing Passages and Cadences in the Late Piano Music of Liszt." JALS 5 (1979): 64–74.

4705. Thompson, Harold Adams. "The Evolution of Whole-Tone Sound in Liszt's Original Piano Works." Ph.D. diss., Louisiana State University, 1974.

4706. Wolff, Konrad. "Beethovenian Dissonances in Liszt's Piano Works." JALS 1 (1977): 4–8.

Préludes

4707. Anderson, Lyle John. "Motivic and Thematic Transformation in Selected Works of Liszt." Ph.D. diss., Ohio State University, 1977.

4708. Bonner, Andrew. "Liszt's *Les préudes* and *Les quatre élémens:* A Reinvestigation." NCM 10, no. 2 (1986): 95–107.
4709. Haraszti, Emile. "Genèse des préludes de Liszt qui n'ont aucun rapport avec Lamertine." RDM 35 (1953): 112–13.
4710. Main, Alexander. "Liszt after Lamartine: *Les Préludes.*" ML 60 (1979): 133–48.

Prometheus
4711. Torkewitz, Dieter. "Innovation und Tradition: Zur Genesis eines Quartenakkords; Über Liszts *Prometheus*-Akkord." MF 33 (1980): 291–302.
4712. Williamson, John. "The Revision of Liszt's *Prometheus.*" ML 67, no. 4 (1986): 381–90.

Quatre élémens
4713. Bonner, Andrew. "Liszt's *Les préudes* and *Les quatre élémens:* A Reinvestigation." NCM 10, no. 2 (1986): 95–107.

R.W.–Venezia
4714. Skoumal, Zdenek. "Liszt's Androgynous Harmony." MA 13, no. 1 (1994): 51–72.
4715. Stenzl, Jürg. "L'énigme Franz Liszt: Prophéties et conventions dans les œuvres tardives; *R.W.–Venezia* (1883)." RM 405–7 (1987): 127–35.

Réminiscences de Don Juan
4716. Riethmüller, Albrecht. "Franz Liszts *Réminiscences de Don Juan.*" M-Breig: 276–91.

Réminiscences de Norma
4717. Schenkman, Walter. "Liszt's Reminiscences of Bellini's *Norma.*" JALS 9 (1981): 55–64.

Requiem
4718. Kirsch, Winfried. "Franz Liszt's 'Requiem für Männerstimmen.'" KJ 71 (1987): 93–108.

Sonetti di Petrarca
4719. Fowler, Andrew. "Franz Liszt's *Petrarch Sonnets*: The Persistent Poetic Problem." ITR 7, no. 2 (1986): 48–68. [Sonnet no. 47]

Sonetto 104 del Petrarca. See Années de pèlerinage

Songs (various; *see also* specific songs)
4720. Dart, William J. "Revisions and Reworkings in the Lieder of Franz Liszt." SMU 9 (1975): 41–53.
4721. Gibbs, Dan Paul. "A Background and Analysis of Selected Lieder and Opera Transcriptions of Franz Liszt." D.M.A. diss., North Texas State University, 1980.
4722. Montu-Berthon, Suzanne. "Un Liszt méconnu: Mélodies et Lieder, vol. I." RM 342–344 (1981): 17–184. Musical examples, RM 345–346 (1981): 5–56.
4723. Roman, Zoltan. "The Shape of the Future: Musico-Poetic and Stylistic Trends in Selected Songs by Liszt." JALS 48 (2000): 35–62.
4724. Rummenhöller, Peter. "Zur Harmonik in Franz Liszts Liedern." M 37, no. 3 (1983): 232–38.
4725. Turner, Ronald. "A Comparison of Two Sets of Liszt-Hugo Songs." JALS 5 (1979): 16–31.

Symphonic Poems (various; *see also* specific symphonic poems)
4726. Bergfeld, Joachim. *Die formale Struktur der symphonische Dichtungen Franz Liszts.* Eisenach: Kühner, 1931.
4727. Kaplan, Richard. "Sonata Form in the Orchestral Works of Liszt: The Revolutionary Reconsidered." NCM 8 (1984–1985): 142–52.

Symphonie zu Dantes Divina Commedia
4728. Barricelli, Jean-Pierre. "Liszt's Journey through Dante's Hereafter." JALS 14 (1983): 3–15.
4729. Knight, Ellen. "The Harmonic Foundation of Liszt's *Dante Symphony.*" JALS 10 (1981): 56–63.
4730. M-Taruskin.

Totentanz
4731. M-Taruskin.

Transcriptions
4732. Bellak, Richard Charles. "Compositional Technique in the Transcriptions of Franz Liszt." Ph.D. diss., University of Pennsylvana, 1976.
4733. Crockett, Barbara Allen. "Liszt's Opera Transcriptions for Piano." D.M.A. diss., University of Ilinois, 1968.
4734. Eckhardt, Mária. "Liszts Bearbeitungen von Schuberts Märschen: Formale Analyse." SM 26 (1984): 133–46.
4735. Gibbs, Dan Paul. "A Background and Analysis of Selected Lieder and Opera Transcriptions of Franz Liszt." D.M.A. diss., North Texas State University, 1980.
4736. Suttoni, Charles. "Liszt's Operatic Fantasies and Transcriptions." JALS 8 (1980): 3–14.

Trauervorspiel und Trauermarsch

4737. M-Forte/L.

4738. Torkewitz, Dieter. "Anmerkungen zu Liszts Spätstil: Das Klavierstück *Preludio funèbre* (1885)." AM 35 (1978): 231–36.

Trübe Wolken (Nuages gris)

4739. Decarsin, François. "Liszt's *Nuages gris* and Kagel's *Unguis incarnatus est*: A Model and Its Issue." Trans. Jonathan Dunsby. MA 4, no. 3 (1985): 259–63.

4740. M-Forte/L.

4741. Koykkar, Joseph. "Liszt's *Nuages gris*: An Analysis." TSP 1 (1984): 1–9.

4742. Skoumal, Zdenek. "Liszt's Androgynous Harmony." MA 13, no. 1 (1994): 51–72.

Und wir dachten der Toten

4743. Roman, Zoltan. "Allegory, Symbolism, and Personification in Selected 'Night Songs" by Liszt, Mahler, and Strauss." SM 41, no. 4 (2000): 407–39.

Unstern! Sinistre, disastro

4744. M-Forte/L.

4745. Kabisch, Thomas. "Struktur und Form im Spätwerk Franz Liszts: Das Klavierstück *Unstern* (1886)." AM 42 (1985): 178–99.

Variation über das Thema (Chopsticks)

4746. Wuellner, Guy S. "Franz Liszt's Prelude on *Chopsticks*." JALS 4 (1978): 37–44.

Variationen über das Motiv . . . von Weinen, Klagen, Sorgen, Zagen

4747. Crisp, Deborah. "Liszt's Monument to Bach: The Variations on *Weinen, Klagen, Sorgen, Zagen* for Solo Piano." MSA 21 (1998): 37–49.

4748. Tannenbaum, Michele. "Liszt and Bach: 'Invention' and 'Feeling' in the *Variations on a Motive of Bach*." JALS 41 (1997): 49–87.

Vätergruft

4749. Winkler, Gerhard J. "'Heil mir! Ich bin es wert!': Zu Liszts Vertonung der *Vätergruft*." NZM 147, nos. 7–8 (1986): 10–15.

Venezia e Napoli

4750. Schenkman, Walter. "The *Venezia e Napoli* Tarentella: Genesis and Metamorphosis." JALS 6 (1979): 10–24; 7 (1980): 42–58; 8 (1980): 44–59.

Via Crucis

4751. M-Forte/L. [Stations 5 and 8]

4752. Hill, Cecil. "Liszt's *Via Crucis*." MR 25 (1964): 202–8.

Von der Wiege bis zum Grabe

4753. Kabisch, Thomas. "Außermusikalische Implikationen des musikalischen Materials: Zum Spätwerk Franz Liszts." M 39, no. 6 (1985): 549–56.

4754. Schläder, Jürgen. "Der schöne Traum vom Ideal: Die künstlerische Konzeption in Franz Liszts letzter symphonische Dichtung." HJM 6 (1983): 47–62.

Wiegenlied (Chant du berceau)

4755. Szelényi, Laszlo. "Franz Liszt: *Wiegenlied—Chant de berceau*." M 34 (1980–1981): 19–24.

Zigeuner (Songs)

4756. Goebel, Albrecht. "Franz Liszt: *Die drei Zigeuner;* Ein Beitrag zum Balladenschaffen im 19. Jahrhundert." M 35 (1981): 241–45.

Various Works

4757. Bárdos, Lajos. "Ferenc Liszt, the Innovator." SM 17 (1975): 3–38.

4758. Dahlhaus, Carl. "Franz Liszt und die Vorgeschichte der neuen Musik." NZM 122 (1961): 387–91.

4759. Damschroder, David Allen. "The Structural Foundations of 'The Music of the Future': A Schenkerian Study of Liszt's Weimar Repertoire." Ph.D. diss., Yale University, 1981.

4760. Esteban, Julio. "On Liszt's Technical Exercises." JALS 1 (1977): 17–19.

4761. Gárdonyi, Zsolt. "Neue Tonleiter- und Sequenztypen in Liszts Frühwerken." SM 11 (1969): 169–200. Also in F-Szabolcsi: 169–99.

4762. Gut, Serge. *Franz Liszt: Les éléments du langage musical.* Paris: Klincksieck, 1975.

4763. Haraszti, Emile. "Les origines de l'orchestration de Franz Liszt." RDM 34 (1952): 81–100.

4764. Hering, Hans. "Franz Liszt und die Paraphrase." M 28 (1974): 231–34.

4765. Jiránek, Jaroslav. "Liszt and Smetana." SM 5 (1963): 139–92.

4766. Johnsson, Bengt. "Modernities in Liszt's Works." STM 46 (1964): 83–117.

4767. Mastroianni, Thomas. "The Italian Aspects of Franz Liszt." JALS 16 (1984): 6–19.

4768. Revitt, Paul J. "Franz Liszt's Harmonizations of Linear Chromaticism." JALS 13 (1983): 25–52.

4769. Rummenhöller, Peter. "Die verfremdete Kadenz: Zur Harmonik Franz Liszts." ZM 9, no. 1 (1978): 4–16.

4770. Saffle, Michael Benton. "Franz Liszt's Compositional Development: A Study of His Principal Published and Unpublished Instrumental Sketches and Revisions." Ph.D. diss., Stanford University, 1977.

4771. Satyendra, Ramon. "Conceptualizing Expressive Chromaticism in Liszt's Music." MA 16, no. 2 (1997): 219–52.

4772. ———. "Liszt's Open Structures and the Romantic Fragment." MTS 19, no. 2 (1997): 184–205.

4773. Searle, Humphrey. *The Music of Liszt.* New York: Dover, 1966.

4774. Suppan, Wolfgang, ed. *Liszt Studien 1: Kongress-Bericht, Eisenstadt 1975.* Graz: Akademische Druck- & Verlangsanstalt, 1977.

4775. Szelényi, Istvan. "Der unbekannte Liszt." SM 5 (1963): 311–31.

4776. Torkewitz, Dieter. *Harmonisches Denken im Frühwerk Franz Liszts.* Munich: Katzbichler, 1978.

4777. Walker, Alan, ed. *Franz Liszt: The Man and His Music.* London: Barrie & Jenkins, 1970.

4778. Zeke, Lajos. "'Successive Polymodality' or Different Juxtaposed Modes Based on the Same Final in Liszt's Works." SM 28 (1986): 173–85.

LITOLFF, HENRY (1818–1891)

4779. Blair, Ted M. "Henry Charles Litolff: His Life and Music." Ph.D. diss., University of Iowa, 1968.

LLOYD, JONATHAN (b. 1948)

4780. Uscher, Nancy. "Two Contemporary Viola Concerti: A Comparative Study." TEMPO 147 (1983): 23–29.

LOCKWOOD, NORMAND (1906–2002)

4781. MacDowell, John. "A Note on Some Facets of Normand Lockwood's Music." ACA 6, no. 4 (1956): 7–11.

LOEFFLER, CHARLES MARTIN (1861–1935)

4782. Colvin, Otis H. "Charles Martin Loeffler: His Life and Works." Ph.D. diss., University of Rochester, 1959.

4783. Knight, Ellen. "The Evolution of Loeffler's *Music for Four Stringed Instruments.*" AMUS 2, no. 3 (1984): 66–83.

LOEWE, CARL (1796–1869)

4784. Schleicher, Jane Ernestine. "The Ballads of Carl Loewe." D.M.A. diss., University of Illinois, 1966.

LOGAN, WENDELL (b. 1940)

4785. Wilson, Olly. "Wendell Logan: *Proportions.*" PNM 9 (1970): 135–42.

LOHSE, FRED (b. 1908)

4786. Beythien, Jürgen. "Fred Lohses Divertimento für Streichorchester." MG 15 (1965): 394–99.

4787. Raschke, Siegfried. "Charakteristik und Wirksamkeit der Prinzipien linearen Gestaltens: Untersucht und dargestellt an Kompositionen von Fred Lohse." Ph.D. diss., Karl-Marx Universität, 1969.

LOMBARDI, LUCA (b. 1945)

4788. Heister, Hanns-Werner. "Luca Lombardis Faust-Oper." DI 30 (1991): 18–23. [*Faust "Un travestimento"*]

4789. ———. "Verzweifeln und Standhalten: Zu Luca Lombardis Kantate *Majakowski.*" MG 33 (1983): 530–35.

4790. Lombardi, Luca. "Construction of Freedom." Trans. Franco Betti. PNM 22 (1983–1984): 253–64. [*Majakowski, Tui-Gesänge, Wiederkehr*]

LUCIER, ALVIN (b. 1931)

4791. DeLio, Thomas. "Der Klang als Klang: Alvin Luciers *Music for Pure Waves, Bass Drums, and Acoustic Pendulums.*" MTX 16 (1986): 36–39.

4792. ———. "The Shape of Sound: Alvin Lucier's *Music for Pure Waves, Bass Drums, and Acoustic Pendulums.*" *Percussive Notes Research Edition* 21, no. 6 (1983): 15–22. Reprint, M-DeLio: 89–105.

4793. Mumma, Gordon. "Alvin Luciers *Music for Solo Performer* 1965." S 1, no. 2 (1967): 68–69.

LUENING, OTTO (1900–1996)

4794. Neff, Severine. "Otto Luening (1900–) and the Theories of Bernhard Ziehn (1845–1912)." CM 39 (1985): 21–41.

LUTOSŁAWSKI, WITOLD (1913–1994)

Cello Concerto

4795. Huber, Alfred. "Witold Lutosławski: Cellokonzert." MELOS 40 (1973): 229–36.

Chain I–III

4796. Evans, Gerald E. "The Development and Application of the Chain Technique in the Recent Works of Witold Lutosławski." CMF 2 (1990): 35–52.

4797. Klein, Michael. "Texture, Register, and Their Formal Roles in the Music of Witold Lutosławski." ITR 20, no. 1 (1999): 37–70. [*Chain I*]

4798. Zieliński, Tadeusz. "Witold Lutosławski's *Chain I*." PM 20, nos. 1–2 (1985): 17–24.

Concerto for Orchestra

4799. Mountain, Rosemary. "An Investigation of Periodicity in Music, with Reference to Three Twentieth-Century Compositons." Ph.D. diss., University of Victoria, 1993.

4800. ———. "Time and Texture in Lutosławski's Concerto for Orchestra and Ligeti's Chamber Concerto." EXT 7, no. 1 (1994): 129–90.

4801. Paja, Jadwiga. "The Polyphonic Aspect of Lutosławski's Music." ACTA 62, nos. 2–3 (1990): 183–91.

4802. Sannemüller, Gerd. "Das Konzert für Orchester von Witold Lutosławski." SMZ 107 (1967): 258–64.

Double Concerto

4803. Lutosławki, Witold. "Interview with the Composer: Double Concerto for Oboe, Harp, and Chamber Orchestra by Witold Lutosławski." PM 15, no. 4 (1980): 7–10.

Espaces du sommeil

4804. M-Cope: 256–59.

Jeux vénitiens

4805. Thomas, Adrian. "*Jeux vénitiens*: Lutosławski at the Crossroads." CT 24 (1982): 4–7.

Livre pour orchestre

4806. Lutosławski, Witold. "*Livre pour orchestre* by Witold Lutosławski." PM 4, no. 1 (1969): 9–12.

Muzyka żałobna (Musique funèbre)

4807. Brennecke, Wilfried. "Die *Trauermusik* von Witold Lutosławski." F-Blume: 60–73. Reprint, F-Feicht: 457–71.

4808. Brumbeloe, Joseph. "Symmetry in Witold Lutosławski's *Trauermusik*." ITR 6, no. 3 (1982–1983): 3–17.

Paroles tissées

4809. Sannemüller, Gerd. "*Paroles tissées* von Witold Lutosławski." F-Gudewill: 101–10.

Piano Concerto

4810. Homma, Martina. "Nostalgie des Aufbruchs? Witold Lutosławskis Klavierkonzert; Ein Spätwerk." MTX 42 (1991): 27–35.

Poèmes d'Henri Michaux

4811. M-Anhalt: 93–147.

4812. Homma, Martina. "'Aleatorischer Kontrapunkt,' 'matière premiere,' Harmonik und Rhythmik: Zum Enstehungsprozeß von Witold Lutosławskis *Trois poèmes d'Henri Michaux* für zwanzigstimmigen Chor und Orchester (1961–1963)." MTH 14, no. 1 (1999): 13–31.

4813. ———. "Witold Lutosławski's *Trois poèmes d'Henri Michaux*: The Sketches and the Work." Trans. Michał Kubicki. PMJ 3, no. 2 (2000).

4814. Klein, Michael. "Texture, Register, and Their Formal Roles in the Music of Witold Lutosławski." ITR 20, no. 1 (1999): 37–70. [Movement III]

4815. M-Roberts.

4816. Thomas, Adrian. "A Deep Resonance: Lutosławski's *Trois Poèmes d'Henri Michaux*." SN 1 (1970): 58–70.

Preludes and Fugue

4817. Paja, Jadwiga. "The Polyphonic Aspect of Lutosławski's Music." ACTA 62, nos. 2–3 (1990): 183–91.

4818. Petersen, Peter. "Witold Lutosławski: Prelüdien und Fuge (1972)." HJM 1 (1974): 147–80.

String Quartet

4819. Gülke, Peter. "Lutosławskis Streichquartett als Kammermusik." M-Pečman: 243–49.

4820. Hansberger, Joachim. "Begrenzte Aleatorik: Das Streichquartett Witold Lutosławskis." M 25 (1971): 248–57.

4821. Schmidt, Christian Martin. "Witold Lutosławski: Streichquartett." M-Stephan: 154–62.

4822. Selleck, John. "Pitch and Duration as Textural Elements in Lutosławski's String Quartet." PNM 13, no. 2 (1974–1975): 150–61.

4823. Stucky, Steven. "The String Quartet of Witold Lutosławski." M.F.A. thesis, Cornell University, 1973.

Symphonies (various; *see also* specific symphonies)

4824. Rust, Douglas Martin. "Lutosławski's Symphonic Forms." Ph.D. diss., Yale University, 1995.

Symphony No. 1

4825. Sannemüller, Gerd. "Die 1. Sinfonie von Witold Lutosławski." MB 18 (1981): 766–72.

4826. M-Vogt: 348–57.

Symphony No. 2

4827. Dibelius, Ulrich. "Lutosławski's Second Symphony." PM 2, no. 4 (1967): 8–12.

4828. Sannemüller, Gerd. "Witold Lutosławskis 2. Sinfonie." MB 10 (1978): 588–95.

Symphony No. 3

4829. Gantchoula, Philippe. "La 3e symphonie de Lutosławski: Synthèse d'un itinéraire créateur." ANM 10 (1988): 68–74.

4830. Homma, Martina. "Unerhörtes Pathos: Witold Lutosławskis III. Sinfonie." MTX 13 (1986): 7–12.

4831. Michaely, Aloyse. "Lutosławskis III. Sinfonie: Untersuchungen zu Form und Harmonik." In *Witold Lutosławski*, ed. Heinz-Klaus Metzger and Rainer Riehn, 52–197. Munich: Text + Kritik, 1991.

Symphony No. 4

4832. Homma, Martina. "Gleichzeitigkeit des Ungleichartigen: Witold Lutosławskis Vierte Sinfonie; Synthese seines Schaffens." MTX 54 (1994): 51–56.

Trauermusik. See *Muzyka żałobna*

Various Works

4833. Casken, John. "Transition and Transformation in the Music of Witold Lutosławski." CT 12 (1975): 3–12.

4834. M-Hines.

4835. Homma, Martina. "Horizontal-Vertikal: Zur Organisation der Tonhöhe bei Witold Lutosławski." N 5 (1984–1985): 91–99.

4836. ———. *Das kompositorische Schaffen von Witold Lutosławski.* Cologne: Staatsarbeit, 1983.

4837. Kaczynski, Tadeusz. *Conversations with Witold Lutoslawki.* London: Chester, 1984.

4838. Klein, Michael Leslie. "A Theoretical Study of the Late Music of Witold Lutosławski: New Interactions of Pitch, Rhythm, and Form." Ph.D. diss., State University of New York at Buffalo, 1995.

4839. Lutosławski, Witold. "Über Rhythmik und Tonhöhenorganisation in der Kompositionstechnik unter Anwendung begrenzter Zufallswirkung." In *Witold Lutosławski*, ed. Heinz-Klaus Metzger and Rainer Riehn, 3–32. Munich: Text + Kritik, 1991.

4840. Nikolskaja, Irina. "Wiederbelebung der Melodie: Über einige Grundzüge thematischer Formung in Witold Lutosławskis Musik der achtziger Jahre." MTX 42 (1991): 51–59.

4841. Petersen, Peter. "Bartók-Lutosławski-Ligeti: Einige Bemerkungen zu ihrer Kompositionstechnik unter dem Aspekt der Tonhöhe." HJM 11 (1988): 289–309.

4842. Stucky, Steven. *Lutosławski and His Music.* Cambridge: Cambridge University Press, 1981.

4843. ———. "The Music of Witold Lutosławski: A Style-Critical Study." D.M.A. diss., Cornell University, 1978.

4844. Thomas, Adrian T. "Rhythmic Articulation in the Music of Lutosławski." M.A. thesis, University of Cardiff, 1970.

LYAPUNOV, SERGEY MIKHAYLOVICH (1859–1924)

4845. Davis, Richard. "Sergei Lyapunov (1859–1924): The Piano Works; A Short Appreciation." MR 21 (1960): 186–206.

4846. Kaiserman, David. "The Piano Works of S. M. Liapunov." JALS 3 (1978): 25–26.

– M –

MACDOWELL, EDWARD (1860–1908)

4847. Brancaleone, Francis. "Edward MacDowell and Indian Motives." AMUS 7, no. 4 (1989): 359–81.

4848. Pesce, Dolores. "New Light on the Programmatic Aesthetic of MacDowell's Symphonic Poems." AMUS 4, no. 4 (1986): 369–89. [*Lamia*, op. 29; *Lancelot und Elaine*, op. 25; *Hamlet* and *Ophelia*, op. 22]

4849. ———. "The Other Sea in MacDowell's *Sea Pieces*." AMUS 10, no. 4 (1992): 411–40.

MÂCHE, FRANÇOIS-BERNARD (b. 1935)

4850. Grabócz, Márta. "The Demiurge of Sounds and the Poeta Doctus: François-Bernard Mâche's Poetics and Music." CMR 8, no. 1 (1993): 131–82.

MACHOVER, TOD (b. 1953)

4851. Machover, Tod. "Computer Music with and without Instruments." CMR 1, no. 1 (1984–1985): 203–30. [*Electric Etudes, Fusione Fugace, Spectres parisiens*]

4852. Wheeler, Scott. "Beyond the Flat Surface: Form and Rhetoric in Machover, Hyla, and Lindroth." CMR 10, no. 1 (1994): 75–100. [*Toward the Center*]

MACKEY, STEVEN (b. 1956)

4853. Caltabiano, Ronald. "Composers Steven Mackey and Rand Steiger: An Appreciation." CMR 10, no. 1 (1994): 133–48. [*Indigenous Instruments, On All Fours*]

4854. Mackey, Steven. "Music as an Action Sport." CM 67–68 (1999): 269–88. [*Deal*]

MAC LOW, JACKSON (b. 1922)

4855. Andres, Hartmut. "'Ich war niemals nur am Klang der Worte interessiert': Zur Komposition *Winds* von Jackson Mac Low." MTX 85 (2000): 19–22. [*Winds/Instruments*]

MADERNA, BRUNO (1920–1973)

Aria da "Hyperion"

4856. Revers, Peter. "Bruno Maderna—Friedrich Hölderlin: Aspekte des Wort-Ton-Verhältnisses in Madernas *Aria da Hyperion.*" OMZ 47, no. 5 (1992): 271–79.

Fantasia e fuge

4857. Fearn, Raymond. "At the Doors of Kranichstein: Maderna's 'Fantasia' for 2 Pianos." TEMPO 163 (1987): 14–20.

Hyperion

4858. Rizzardi, Veniero. "'L'ultima serie': In margine alla genesi dell'*Hyperion* di Bruno Maderna." MPSS 6 (1993): 26–29.

Improvvisazione No. 1

4859. Verzina, Nicola. "Procedimenti di costruzione ed elaborazione del materiale in *Improvvisazione* N. 2 (1953) di Bruno Maderna." MPSS 9 (1996): 50–55.

Kranichsteiner Kammerkantate. See Vier Briefe

Oboe Concertos

4860. Verzina, Nicola. "Concezione poetica e pensiero formale nel Maderna post-seriale: Il Konzert für Oboe und Kammerensemble (1962–63)." STU 24, no. 1 (1995): 131–59. [No. 1]

4861. ———. "La dernière composition de Bruno Maderna: Le Troisième concerto pour hautbois et orchestre (1973)." DI 49 (1996): 16–22.

Serenata No. 2

4862. Fein, Markus. "Im Dialog mit dem Material: Anmerkungen zur 'Filtertechnik' in Bruno Madernas *Serenata N. 2* (1953–54/1956)." MPSS 13 (2000): 33–37.

Venetian Journal

4863. Benedictis, Angela Ida De. "'Qui forse una cadenza brillante': Viaggio nel *Venetian Journal* del Bruno Maderna." ACTA 72, no. 1 (2000): 63–105.

Vier Briefe

4864. Verzina, Nicola. "Tecnica della mutazione e tecnica seriale in *Vier Briefe* (1953) di Bruno Maderna." RIM 34 (1999): 309–45.

Various Works

4865. Fearn, Raymond. "Bruno Maderna: From the Café Pedrocchi to Darmstadt." TEMPO 155 (1985): 8–14.

4866. Weber, Horst. "Figures et Structures: Über Madernas formative Jahre um 1950." BM 34 (1992): 1–46.

MAEGAARD, JAN (b. 1926)

4867. Kullberg, Erling. "Om komponisten Jan Maegaard." F-Maegaard: 277–300.

MAGNARD, ALBÉRIC (1865–1914)

4868. Halbreich, Harry. "Magnard, le solitaire." RM 324–326 (1979): 77–86.

4869. ———. "La 4e Symphonie d'Albéric Magnard." DI 14 (1987): 4–8.

4870. Maillard, Jean. "Albéric Magnard: Les Quatre symphonies; Étude analytique." RM 324–326 (1979): 89–104.

MAGRILL, SAMUEL

4871. Magrill, Samuel. "*Dao Song*: Instructions." PNM 23, no. 1 (1984–1985): 86–97.

4872. ———. "*Dao Song*: Report to the National Endowment for the Arts." PNM 23, no. 1 (1984–1985): 134–42.

MAHLER, ALMA MARIA (1879–1964)

4873. Schollum, Robert. "Die Lieder von Alma Maria Schindler-Mahler." OMZ 34 (1979): 544–51.

MAHLER, GUSTAV (1860–1911)

Kindertotenlieder

4874. Agawu, V. Kofi. "Mahler's Tonal Strategies: A Study of the Song Cycles." JMR 6, nos. 1–2 (1986): 1–47.

4875. ———. "The Musical Language of *Kindertotenlieder* No. 2." JM 2 (1983): 81–93.

4876. Bass, Edward C. "Counterpoint and Medium in Mahler's *Kindertotenlieder.*" MR 50, nos. 3–4 (1989): 206–14.

4877. Fürbeth, Oliver. "Zu Mahlers zweitem *Kindertotenlied.*" M-Metzger/Mahler: 33–56.

4878. Grant, Parks. "Mahler's *Kindertotenlieder.*" CD 2, no. 9 (1960): 62–72.

4879. Kravitt, Edward F. "Mahler's Dirges for His Death: February 24, 1901." MQ 64 (1978): 329–53.

4880. Lespinard, Bernadette. "Les *Kindertotenlieder* de Mahler: Une apothéose du Kunstlied." ANM 18 (1990): 44–48.

Klagende Lied

4881. Diether, Jack. "Mahler's *Klagende Lied*: Genesis and Evolution." MR 29 (1968): 268–87.

4882. Klassen, Janina. "Märchenerzählung: Anmerkungen zum *Klagenden* [*sic*] *Lied.*" M-Metzger/Mahler: 8–32.

4883. Zenck, Martin. "Mahlers Streichung des 'Waldmarchens' aus dem *Klagenden Lied*: Zum Verhältnis von philologischer Erkenntnis und Interpretation." AM 38 (1981): 179–93.

Knaben Wunderhorn

4884. Ganvert, Gérard. "Trois lieder de Gustav Mahler: 'Verlor'ne Müh,' 'Das irdische Leben,' 'Revelge'; Une analyse de l'écoute à la partition." ANM 11 (1988): 66–70.

4885. Jahnke, Sabine. "Materialien zu einer Unterrichtssequenz: 'Des Antonius von Padua Fischpredigt' bei Orff–Mahler–Berio." MB 5 (1973): 615–22.

4886. Lake, William E. "Hermeneutic Musical Structures in 'Das irdische Leben' by Gustav Mahler." ITO 12, nos. 7–8 (1994): 1–14.

4887. Severtson, Kirk. "In the Spirit of the People: Mahler's Settings of Folk Poetry from *Des Knaben Wunderhorn.*" MRF 14 (1999): 1–26.

Lied von der Erde

4888. Agawu, V. Kofi. "Mahler's Tonal Strategies: A Study of the Song Cycles." JMR 6, nos. 1–2 (1986): 1–47.

4889. Baur, Uwe. "Pentatonische Melodiebildung in Gustav Mahlers *Das Lied von der Erde.*" MAU 2 (1979): 141–50.

4890. M-Carner: 52–55.

4891. Danuser, Hermann. *Gustav Mahler: Das Lied von der Erde.* Munich: Fink, 1986.

4892. ———. "Gustav Mahlers Symphonie *Das Lied von der Erde* als Problem der Gattungsgeschichte." AM 40 (1983): 276–86.

4893. ———. "Mahlers Lied 'Von der Jugend': Ein musikalisches Bild." F-Schuh: 151–69.

4894. M-Enix.

4895. Hefling, Stephen E. "*Das Lied von der Erde*: Mahler's Symphony for Voices and Orchestra—or Piano." JM 10, no. 3 (1992): 293–341.

4896. ———. *Mahler: Das Lied von der Erde.* Cambridge: Cambridge University Press, 2000.

4897. Roman, Zoltan. "Aesthetic Symbiosis and Structural Metaphor in Mahler's *Das Lied von der Erde.*" F-Blaukopf: 110–19.

4898. Tischler, Hans. "Mahler's *Das Lied von der Erde.*" MR 10 (1949): 111–14.

4899. Tuercke, Berthold. "Konzentrische Kreise: Mahlers materiales Komponieren als Kompendium einer neuen Musik." M-Metzger/Mahler: 57–99. ["Der Abschied"]

4900. Wenk, Arthur. "The Composer as Poet in *Das Lied von der Erde.*" NCM 1 (1977–1978): 33–47.

4901. Wheaton, J. Randall. "The Diatonic Potential of the Strange Sets: Theoretical Tenets and Structural Meaning in Gustav Mahler's 'Der Abschied.'" Ph.D. diss., Yale University, 1988.

Lieder (various; *see also* specific Lieder and song cycles)

4902. Borris, Siegfried. "Mahlers holzschnitthafter Liedstil." MB 5 (1973): 578–87.

4903. Dargie, Elizabeth Mary. "Music and Poetry in the Songs of Gustav Mahler." Ph.D. diss., University of Aberdeen, 1979.

4904. Gerlach, Reinhard. "Mahler, Rückert, und das Ende des Liedes: Essay über lyrisch-musikalisches Form." JSIM (1975): 7–45.

4905. Kravitt, Edward F. "Bar Form in Mahler's Songs: Omission and Misconception." *International Musicological Society, Report of the Eleventh Congress, Copenhagen 1972*, ed. Henrik Glahn, Soren Sorensen, and Peter Ryan, vol. 2, 617–22. Copenhagen: Hansen, 1974.

4906. Roman, Zoltan "The Folk Element in Mahler's Songs." CAUSM 8, no. 2 (1978): 67–84.

4907. ———. "Mahler's Songs and Their Influence on His Symphonic Thought." Ph.D. diss., University of Toronto, 1970.

4908. ———. "Structure as a Factor in the Genesis of Mahler's Songs." MR 35 (1974): 157–66.

Lieder eines fahrenden Gesellen

4909. Agawu, V. Kofi. "Mahler's Tonal Strategies: A Study of the Song Cycles." JMR 6, nos. 1–2 (1986): 1–47.

4910. Boyd, James William. "Tonality, Genre, and Form: Mahler's *Lieder eines fahrenden Gesellen*." Ph.D. diss., University of Michigan, 1994.

4911. Ringer, Alexander L. *"Lieder eines fahrenden Gesellen*: Allusion und Zitat in der musikalischen Erzählung Gustav Mahlers." F-Dahlhaus: 589–602.

4912. Roman, Zoltan. "Allegory, Symbolism, and Personification in Selected 'Night Songs' by Liszt, Mahler, and Strauss." SM 41, no. 4 (2000): 407–39. ["Die zwei blauen Augen"]

4913. ———. "The Pianoforte and Orchestral Manuscripts of Mahler's *Lieder eines fahrenden Gesellen*: Compositional Process as a Key to Chronology." M-Kühn: 402–4.

4914. Waeltner, Ernst Ludwig. "Lieder-Zyklus und Volkslied-Metamorphose: Zu den Texten der Mahlerischen Gesellenlieder." JSIM (1977): 61–95.

Lieder ("Rückert-Lieder")

4915. Jackson, Timothy L. "Die Wagnersche Umarmungs-Metapher bei Bruckner und Mahler." M-Riethmüller: 134–52.

4916. Oltmanns, Michael Johannes. "'Ich bin der Welt abhanden gekommen' und 'Der Tamboursg'sell'–Zwei Liedkonzeptionen Gustav Mahlers." AM 43, no. 1 (1986): 69–88.

4917. Roman, Zoltan. "Allegory, Symbolism, and Personification in Selected 'Night Songs' by Liszt, Mahler, and Strauss." SM 41, no. 4 (2000): 407–39. ["Um Mitternacht"]

Symphonies (various; *see also* specific symphonies)

4918. Bekker, Paul. *Gustav Mahlers Sinfonien*. Berlin: Schuster & Loeffler, 1921.

4919. Lechleitner, Gerda. "Die Rolle der Holzblasinstrumente in Scherzosätzen bei Bruckner und Mahler." BRS (1986): 119–27.

4920. McGuiness, Rosamund. "Mahler und Brahms: Gedanken zu Reminiszenzen in Mahlers Sinfonien." Melos/NZM 3 (1977): 215–24.

4921. Murphy, Edward W. "Sonata-Rondo Form in the Symphonies of Gustav Mahler." MR 36 (1975): 54–62.

4922. Roman, Zoltan. "The Chorus in Mahler's Music." MR 43 (1982): 31–43.

4923. Schmitt, Theodor. *Der langsame Symphoniesatz Gustav Mahlers: Historisch-vergleichende Studien zu Mahlers Kompositionstechnik*. Munich: Fink, 1983.

4924. Sponheuer, Bernd. *Logik des Zerfalls: Untersuchungen zum Finalproblem in den Symphonien Gustav Mahlers*. Tutzing: Schneider, 1978.

4925. Tibbe, Monika. *Über die Verwendung von Lieder und Liederelementen in instrumental Symphoniensätzen Gustav Mahlers*. Munich: Katzbichler, 1971.

4926. Vestdijk, Simon. *Gustav Mahler: Over de struckuur van zijn symfonisch oeuvre*. The Hague: Daamen, 1960.

4927. Vetter, Walther. "Gustav Mahlers sinfonische Stil: Eine Skizze." DJM 6 (1961): 7–18.

4928. Wellesz, Egon. "The Symphonies of Gustav Mahler." MR 1 (1940): 2–23.

4929. Werner, Eric. "Gustav Mahlers Symphoniethemen: Eine typologische Untersuchung der ersten vier Symphonien." MAU 7 (1987): 69–112.

Symphony No. 1

4930. Buhler, James. "'Breakthrough' as Critique of Form: The Finale of Mahler's First Symphony." NCM 20, no. 2 (1996): 125–43.

4931. Dahlhaus, Carl. "Geschichte eines Themas: Zu Mahlers erster Symphonie." JSIM (1977): 45–60.

4932. Eberle, Gottfried. "Gustav Mahler: Sinfonie Nr. 1 D-Dur." NZM 143, no. 10 (1982): 33 36.

4933. Hoyer, Michael. "Die multiperspectivische Tonalität von Mahlers 1. Symphonie." M-Stahmer: 29–116.

4934. Jones, Robert Frederick. "Thematic Development and Form in the First and Fourth Movements of Mahlers's First Symphony." Ph.D. diss., Brandeis University, 1980.

4935. Jung-Kaiser, Ute. "Die wahren Bilder und Chiffren 'tragischer Ironie' in Mahlers 'Erster.'" F-LaGrange: 101–52.

4936. Krebs, Dieter. *Gustav Mahlers Erste Symphonie: Form und Gehalt*. Munich: Katzbichler, 1997.

4937. McClatchie, Stephen. "The 1889 Version of Mahler's First Symphony: A New Manuscript Source." NCM 20, no. 2 (1996): 99–124.

4938. Osthoff, Helmuth. "Zu Gustav Mahlers erster Symphonie." AM 29 (1971): 217–27.

4939. Roman, Zoltan. "Connotative Irony in Mahler's Todtenmarsch in 'Callots Manier.'" MQ 59 (1973): 207–22.

4940. Sponheuer, Bernd. "Der Durchbruch Gustav Mahlers: Eine Untersuchung zum Finalproblem der I. Symphonie." M-Stahmer: 117–64.

Symphony No. 2

4941. Hefling, Stephen E. "Mahler's 'Todtenfeier' and the Problem of Program Music." NCM 12, no. 1 (1988): 27–53. [Movement I]

4942. Murphy, Edward W. "The Dominant Complex/Climax in Selected Works of the Late Nineteenth Century." MR 55, no. 2 (1994): 104–18. [Movement I]

4943. Palmer, John Robert. "Program and Process in the Second Symphony of Gustav Mahler." Ph.D. diss., University of California, Davis, 1996.

4944. Reilly, Edward R. "Die Skizzen zu Mahlers zweiter Symphonie." OMZ 34 (1979): 266–85.

4945. Stephan, Rudolf. *Gustav Mahler: II. Sinfonie C-Moll.* Munich: Fink, 1979.

4946. Zenck, Claudia Maurer. "Technik und Gehalt im Scherzo von Mahlers zweiter Symphonie." Melos/NZM 2 (1976): 179–84.

Symphony No. 3

4947. Danuser, Hermann. "Schwierigkeiten der Mahler-Interpretation: Ein Versuch am Beispiel der ersten Satzes der dritten Symphonie." SBM 3 (1978): 165–81.

4948. Franklin, Peter. *Mahler: Symphony No. 3.* Cambridge: Cambridge University Press, 1991.

4949. Greene, David B. *Mahler, Consciousness and Temporality.* New York: Gordon & Breach, 1984.

4950. Johnson, Steven Philip. "Thematic and Tonal Processes in Mahler's Third Symphony." Ph.D. diss., University of California, Los Angeles, 1989.

4951. Schnebel, Dieter. "Sinfonie und Wirklichkeit am Beispiel von Mahlers Dritter." M-Kolleritsch: 103–17.

4952. ———. "Über Mahlers Dritte." NZM 135 (1974): 283–88.

4953. Solvik, Morten. "Biography and Musical Meaning in the Posthorn Solo of Mahler's Third Symphony." F-LaGrange: 339–60.

4954. Williamson, John. "Mahler's Compositional Process: Rejections of an Early Sketch for the Third Symphony's First Movement." ML 61 (1980): 338–45.

Symphony No. 4

4955. Knapp, Raymond. "Suffering Children: Perspectives on Innocence and Vulnerability in Mahler's Fourth Symphony." NCM 22, no. 3 (1999): 233–67.

4956. Stephan, Rudlof. *Gustav Mahler: 4. Symphonie G-dur.* Munich: Fink, 1966.

4957. Zychowicz, James L. *Mahler's Fourth Symphony.* Oxford: Oxford University Press, 2000.

Symphony No. 5

4958. Abravaya, Niza. "Traditional Forms and Structural Interrelations in Mahler's *Trilogy* Symphonies." OM 12 (1998): 11–25.

4959. Barry, Barbara R. "The Hidden Program in Mahler's Fifth Symphony." MQ 77, no. 1 (1993): 47–66.

4960. Baxendale, Carolyn. "The Finale of Mahler's Fifth Symphony: Long-Range Musical Thought." JRMA 112, no. 2 (1986–1987): 257–79.

4961. Forte, Allen. "Middleground Motives in the Adagietto of Mahler's Fifth Symphony." NCM 8 (1984–1985): 153–63.

4962. Grant, Parks. "Mahler's Fifth Symphony." CD 2, no. 10 (1963): 125–37.

4963. Greene, David B. *Mahler, Consciousness and Temporality.* New York: Gordon & Breach, 1984.

4964. Jackson, Timothy L. "Die Wagnersche Umarmungs-Metapher bei Bruckner und Mahler." M-Riethmüller: 134–52.

4965. Micznik, Vera. "Textual and Contextual Analysis: Mahler's Fifth Symphony and Scientific Thought." IRASM 27, no. 1 (1996): 13–29.

4966. Murphy, Edward. "Unusual Forms in Mahler's Fifth Symphony." MR 47, no. 2 (1986–1987): 101–9.

Symphony No. 6

4967. Abravaya, Niza. "Traditional Forms and Structural Interrelations in Mahler's *Trilogy* Symphonies." OM 12 (1998): 11–25.

4968. Andraschke, Peter. "Struktur und Gehalt im ersten Satz von Gustav Mahlers sechster Symphonie." AM 35 (1978): 275–96.

4969. Carapezza, Paolo Emilio. "Chopin's Nocturne Op. 32, No. 1: The Source of Mahler's Sixth Symphony?" CS 5 (1995): 126–44.

4970. Del Mar, Norman. *Mahler's Sixth Symphony.* New York: Da Capo, 1982.

4971. Jaschinski, Andreas. "Gustav Mahler: Sinfonie Nr. 6 A-Moll." NZM 147, no. 9 (1986): 39–43.

4972. Jülg, Hans-Peter. *Gustav Mahlers Sechste Symphonie.* Munich: Katzbichler, 1986.

4973. Oechsle, Siegfried. "Strukturen der Katastrophe: Das Finale der VI. Symphonie Mahlers und die Endzeit der Gattung." MF 50, no. 2 (1997): 162–82. [Movement IV]

4974. Ratz, Erwin. "Musical Form in Gustav Mahler: An Analysis of the Finale of the Sixth Symphony." MR 29 (1968): 34–48.

4975. ———. "Zum Formproblem bei Gustav Mahler: Eine Analyse des Finales der VI. Symphonie." MF 9 (1956): 156–71.

4976. Redlich, Hans. "Mahler's Enigmatic Sixth." F-Deutsch: 250–56.

4977. Rosenberg, Wolf. "Zur Sechsten Symphonie." In *Gustav Mahler: Der unbekannte Bekannte*, ed. Heinz-Klaus Metzger and Rainer Riehn, 14–33. Munich: Text + Kritik, 1996.

4978. Samuels, Robert. *Mahler's Sixth Symphony: A Study in Musical Semiotics*. Cambridge: Cambridge University Press, 1995.

Symphony No. 7

4979. Abravaya, Niza. "Traditional Forms and Structural Interrelations in Mahler's *Trilogy* Symphonies." OM 12 (1998): 11–25.

4980. Agawu, Kofi. "The Narrative Impulse in the Second *Nachtmusik* from Mahler's Seventh Symphony." M-Ayrey: 226–41.

4981. M-De la Motte: 107–14.

4982. Kramer, Jonathan D. "Postmodern Concepts of Musical Time." ITR 17, no. 2 (1996): 21–61. [Movement V]

4983. Scherzinger, Martin. "The Finale of Mahler's Seventh Symphony: A Deconstructive Reading." MA 14, no. 1 (1995): 69–88.

4984. Williamson, John. "Deceptive Cadences in the Last Movement of Mahler's Seventh Symphony." SN 9 (1982): 87–96.

4985. ———. "The Structural Premises of Mahler's Introductions: Prolegomena to an Analysis of the First Movement of the Seventh Symphony." MA 5, no. 1 (1986): 29–58.

Symphony No. 8

4986. Greene, David B. *Mahler, Consciousness and Temporality*. New York: Gordon & Breach, 1984.

4987. Kneif, Tibor. "Collage oder Naturalismus? Anmerkungen zu Mahlers 'Nachtmusik I.'" NZM 134 (1973): 623–28. [Movement II]

4988. Landmann, Ortun. "Vielfalt und Einheit in der achten Sinfonie Gustav Mahlers: Beobachtungen zu den Themen und zur Formgestalt des Werkes." BM 17 (1975): 29–43.

Symphony No. 9

4989. Andraschke, Peter. *Gustav Mahlers IX. Symphonie: Kompositionsprozess und Analyse*. Wiesbaden: Franz Steiner, 1976.

4990. Dahlhaus, Carl. "Form und Motiv in Mahlers neunter Symphonie." NZM 135 (1974): 296–99.

4991. DeFotis, William. "Mahler's Symphony No. 9: An Analytic Sketch in the Form of a Conductor's Guide." MQ 80, no. 2 (1996): 276–301.

4992. De la Motte, Diether. "Das komplizierte Einfache: Zum ersten Satz der 9. Sinfonie von Gustav Mahler." M-Kolleritsch: 52–67. Reprint, MB 10 (1978): 145–51.

4993. Diether, Jack. "The Expressive Content of Mahler's Ninth: An Interpretation." CD 2, no. 10 (1963): 69–107.

4994. Fischer, Kurt von. "Die Doppelschlagfigur in den zwei letzten Sätzen von Gustav Mahlers 9. Symphonie: Versuch einer Interpretation." AM 32 (1975): 99–105.

4995. Greene, David B. *Mahler, Consciousness and Temporality*. New York: Gordon & Breach, 1984.

4996. Johnson, Julian. "The Status of the Subject in Mahler's Ninth Symphony." NCM 18, no. 2 (1994): 108–20.

4997. Lewis, Christopher Orlo. *Tonal Coherence in Mahler's Ninth Symphony*. Ann Arbor, Mich.: UMI Research Press, 1984.

4998. Micznik, Vera. "Mahler and 'The Power of Genre.'" JM 12, no. 2 (1994): 117–51. [Movement II]

4999. Ratz, Erwin. "Zum Formproblem bei Gustav Mahler: Eine Analyse des I. Satzes der IX. Symphonie." MF 8 (1955): 169–77.

5000. ———. "Le problème de la forme chez Gustav Mahler: Une analyse du 1er mouvement de la 9e symphonie." ANM 11 (1988): 71–77.

5001. Revers, Peter. "Liquidation als Formprinzip: Die formprägende Bedeutung des Rhythmus für das Adagio der 9. Symphonie von Gustav Mahler." OMZ 33 (1978): 527–33.

5002. Rothkamm, Jörg. "'Kondukt' als Grundlage eines Formkonzepts: Eine Charakteranalyse des ersten Satzes der IX. Symphonie Gustav Mahlers." AM 54, no. 4 (1997): 269–83.

5003. Schenk, Rüdiger. "Zur neunten Symphonie Gustav Mahlers." M-Stahmer: 165–21.

5004. Spinnler, Burkhard. "Zur Angemessenheit traditioneller Formbegriffe in der Analyse mahlerscher Symphonik: Eine Untersuchung des ersten Satzes der neunten Symphonie." M-Stahmer: 223–76.

Symphony No. 10

5005. Agawu, V. Kofi. "Tonal Strategy in the First Movement of Mahler's Tenth Symphony." NCM 9, no. 3 (1986): 222–33.

5006. Bergquist, Peter. "The First Movement of Mahler's Tenth Symphony: An Analysis and an Examination of the Sketches." MFO 5 (1980): 335–94.

5007. Bruns, Steven Michael. "Mahler's Motivically Expanded Tonality: An Analytical Study of the Adagio of the Tenth Symphony." Ph.D. diss., University of Wisconsin, Madison, 1989.

5008. Cooke, Deryck. "The Facts Concerning Mahler's Tenth Symphony." CD 2, no. 10 (1963): 3–27.

5009. Kaplan, Richard A. "The Interaction of Diatonic Collections in the Adagio of Mahler's Tenth Symphony." ITO 6, no. 1 (1981–1982): 29–39.

5010. ———. "Interpreting Surface Harmonic Connections in the Adagio of Mahler's Tenth Symphony." ITO 4, no. 2 (1978): 32–44.

5011. Klemm, Eberhardt. "Über ein Spätwerk Gustav Mahlers." DJM 6 (1961): 19–32.

5012. Ratz, Erwin. "Gustav Mahlers X. Symphonie." NZM 125 (1964): 307–8.

5013. Reid, Charles. "Mahler's Tenth." MR 26 (1965): 318–25.

5014. Rohland, Tyll. "Zum Adagio aus der X. Symphonie von Gustav Mahler." MB 6 (1973): 605–15.

5015. Zenck, Martin. "Ausdruck und Construcktion im Adagio der 10. Sinfonie Gustav Mahlers." In *Beitrage zur musikalischen Hermeneutik*, ed. Carl Dahlhaus, 205–22. Regensburg: Bosse, 1975.

Various Works

5016. Banks, Paul. "An Early Symphonic Prelude by Mahler?" NCM 3 (1979–1980): 141–49.

5017. Barford, Philip T. "Mahler: A Thematic Archetype." MR 21 (1960): 297–316.

5018. Birtel, Wolfgang. "'Eine ideale Darstellung des Quartetts': Zu Gustav Mahlers Bearbeitung des Streichquartetts d-Moll D. 810 von Schubert." NZM 149, no. 2 (1988): 13–17.

5019. Cardus, Neville. *Gustav Mahler: His Mind and His Music*. London: Gollancz, 1965.

5020. Danuser, Hermann. "Versuch über Mahlers Ton." JSIM (1975): 46–79.

5021. Diether, Jack. "Notes on Some Mahler Juvenalia." CD 3, no. 1 (1969): 3–100.

5022. Eggebrecht, Hans Heinrich. *Die Musik Gustav Mahlers*. Munich: Piper, 1982.

5023. Filler, Susan M. "Mahler's Sketches for a Scherzo in C Minor and a Presto in F Major." CMS 24 (1984): 69–80.

5024. Grant, Parks. "Bruckner and Mahler: The Fundamental Dissimilarity of Their Styles." MR 32 (1971): 35–55.

5025. Hansen, Mathias. "Zur Funktion von Volksmusikelementen in Kompositionstechniken Gustav Mahlers." BM 23 (1981): 31–35.

5026. Hopkins, Robert G. *Closure and Mahler's Music: The Role of Secondary Parameters*. Philadelphia: University of Pennsylvania Press, 1990.

5027. James, Burnett. *The Music of Gustav Mahler*. Rutherford, N.J.: Fairleigh Dickinson University Press, 1985.

5028. Metzger, Heinz-Klaus, and Rainer Riehn, eds. *Gustav Mahler*. Munich: Text + Kritik, 1989.

5029. Mitchell, Donald. "Gustav Mahler . . . Prospect and Retrospect." PRMA 87 (1960–1961): 83–97.

5030. ———. *Gustav Mahler: The "Wunderhorn" Years: Chronicles and Commentaries*. London: Faber, 1975.

5031. ———. *Mahler: The Early Years*. Rev. and ed. Paul Banks and David Matthews. Berkeley: University of California Press, 1980.

5032. Newlin, Dika. *Bruckner, Mahler, Schoenberg*. New York: King's Crown, 1947.

5033. Ratz, Erwin. "Zum Formproblem." In *Gustav Mahler*, 90–141. Tübingen: R. Wunderlich, 1966.

5034. Redlich, Hans. *Bruckner and Mahler*. Rev. ed. London: J. M. Dent, 1963.

5035. Schnebel, Dieter. "Das Spätmusik als neue Musik." In *Gustav Mahler*, 157–88. Tübingen: R. Wunderlich, 1966.

5036. Schoenberg, Arnold. "Gustav Mahler." *Style and Idea*, 7–36. New York: Philosophical Library, 1950.

5037. Smith, Warren Storey. "The Cyclic Principle in Musical Design and the Use of It by Bruckner and Mahler." CD 2, no. 9 (1960): 3–22.

5038. Stahmer, Klaus Hinrich. "Mahlers Frühwerk: Eine Stiluntersuchung." M-Stahmer: 9–28.

5039. Tischler, Hans. "Mahler's Impact on the Crisis of Tonality." MR 12 (1951): 113–21.

5040. ———. "Musical Form in Gustav Mahler's Works." MU 2 (1948–1949): 231–42.

5041. Truscott, Harold. "Some Aspects of Mahler's Tonality." MMR 87 (1957): 203–8.

5042. Vill, Susanne. *Vermittlungsformen verbalisierte und musikalische Inhalte in der Musik Mahlers*. Tutzing: Schneider, 1979.

5043. Werbeck, Walter. "Tempo und Form bei Mahler und Strauss." JSIM (1998): 210–24.

5044. Whaples, Miriam K. "Mahler and Schubert's A Minor Sonata D. 784." ML 65 (1984): 255–63.

MAIGUASHCA, MESÍAS (b. 1938)

5045. Maiguashca, Masias. "Zu *FMelodies*." N 5 (1984–1985): 288–96.

MAILMAN, MARTIN (1932–2000)

5046. Speck, Frederick. "Martin Mailman's *For Precious Friends Hid in Death's Dateless Night.*" JBR 26, no. 1 (1990): 14–29.

MALIPIERO, GIAN FRANCESCO (1912–1973)

5047. Bontempelli, Massimo. *Gian Francesco Malipiero.* Milano: Bompiani, 1942.

MALONE, KEVIN (b. 1958)

5048. Nash, Pamela, and Kevin Malone. "One Man's Noise Is Another Man's Music: The Demise of Pitch in Kevin Malone's *Noise Reduction.*" CMR 19, no. 4 (2000): 105–13.

MAN, RODERICK DE (b. 1941)

5049. Man, Roderik de. "*Miden Agan* for String Quartet." KN 31, no. 2 (1997): 18–21.

MANOURY, PHILIPPE (b. 1952)

5050. Manoury, Philippe. "The Arrow of Time." Trans. Tod Machover and Nigel Osborne. CMR 1, no. 1 (1984–1985): 131–44. [*Zeitlauf*]

5051. Nieminen, Risto, ed. *Philippe Manoury.* Paris: IRCAM, 1995.

5052. Simon, Yannick. "*La partition du ciel et de l'enfer* de Philippe Manoury." INH 7 (1990): 257–79.

MARBE, MYRIAM (1931–1997)

5053. Dănceanu, Liviu. "Myriam Marbe Porträt." N 4 (1983–1984): 68–78.

MARKEVITCH, IGOR (1912–1983)

5054. Bennett, Clive. "*Icare.*" TEMPO 133–134 (1980): 44–51.

5055. De Graeff, Alex. "Partita for Piano and Small Orchestra." TEMPO 133–134 (1980): 39–43.

5056. Mavrodin, Alice. "*Variations, Fugue, and Envoi on the Theme of Handel.*" TEMPO 133–134 (1980): 61–67.

MARSCHNER, HEINRICH AUGUST (1795–1861)

5057. Palmer, Allen Dean. "Heinrich August Marschner (1795–1861) and His Stage Works." Ph.D. diss., University of California, Los Angeles, 1978.

MARTIN, FRANK (1890–1974)

5058. Billeter, Bernhard. *Die Harmonik bei Frank Martin: Untersuchungen zur Analyse neuerer Musik.* Bern; Stuttgart: Haupt, 1971.

5059. ———. "Die letzten Vokalwerke von Frank Martin." SMZ 116 (1976): 344–51.

5060. Dreher, Simone. "Frank Martin: Ballade für Flöte und Klavier." T 16, no. 1 (1991): 347–57.

5061. Fischer, Kurt von. "Frank Martin: Überblick über Werk und Stil." SMZ 91 (1951): 91–96.

5062. M-Hines: 152–65.

5063. Menasce, Jacques de. "Current Chronicle." MQ 34 (1948): 271–78.

5064. Regamey, Constantin. "Les éléments flamenco dans les dernières oeuvres de Frank Martin." SMZ 116 (1976): 351–59.

5065. Rochester, Marc Andrew. "Frank Martin at Golgotha: Frank Martin's Compositional Technique as Shown by His Passion Oratorio *Golgotha.*" M.A. thesis, University of Wales, 1976.

5066. Seedorf, Thomas. "'Porträt der literarischen Form': Rilkes *Cornet* in der Vertonung von Frank Martin." MF 46, no. 2 (1993): 254–67.

5067. Tupper, Janet E. "Stylistic Analysis of Selected Works by Frank Martin." Ph.D. diss., Indiana University, 1964.

MARTINČEK, DUŠAN (b. 1936)

5068. Babcock, David. "Dušan Martinček: An Introduction to His Music." TEMPO 179 (1991): 23–27.

MARTINO, DONALD (1931–2005)

5069. Boros, James. "Donald Martino's *Fantasy Variations*: The First Three Measures." PNM 29, no. 2 (1991): 280–93.

5070. Brody, Martin. "MSHJ: Faith and Deeds in *The White Island.*" PNM 29, no. 2 (1991): 294–311.

5071. Klumpenhouwer, Henry. "Aspects of Row Structure and Harmony in Martino's Impromptu Number 6." PNM 29, no. 2 (1991): 318–54.

5072. Krims, Adam. "Some Analytical Comments on Text and Music in Martino's 'Alone.'" PNM 29, no. 2 (1991): 356–80.

5073. Rothstein, William. "Linear Structure in the Twelve-Tone System: An Analysis of Donald Martino's *Pianississimo.*" JMT 24 (1980): 129–65.

5074. Stadelman, Jeffrey. "A Symmetry of Thought." PNM 29, no. 2 (1991): 402–39. [*Quodlibets II*]

5075. Vishio, Anton. "An Investigation of Structure and Experience in Martino Space." PNM 29, no. 2 (1991): 440–76. [*Fantasies and Impromptus* (Fantasy No. 1)]

MARTINŮ, BOHUSLAV (1890–1959)

5076. Březina, Aleš. "*Das Klaviertrio mit Streichorchester* H. 231 von Bohuslav Martinů." MPSS 4 (1991): 37–41. [*Concertino*]

5077. Cable, Susan Lee. "The Piano Trios of Bohuslav Martinů (1890–1959)." D.A. diss., University of Northern Colorado, 1984.

5078. Clapham, John. "Martinů's Instrumental Style." MR 24 (1963): 158–67.

5079. Evans, Peter. "Martinů the Symphonist." TEMPO 55–56 (1960): 19–33.

5080. Hirsbrunner, Theo. "Bohuslav Martinů: Die Soloklavierwerke der dreissiger Jahre." AM 39 (1982): 64–77.

5081. Perry, Richard Kent. "The Violin and Piano Sonatas of Bohuslav Martinů." D.M.A. diss., University of Illinois, 1973.

5082. Pettway, B. Keith. "The Solo and Chamber Compositions for Flute by Bohuslav Martinů." D.M.A. diss., University of Southern Mississippi, 1980.

5083. Safránek, Milos. "Bohuslav Martinů." MQ 29 (1943): 329–54.

MARTIRANO, SALVATORE (1927–1995)

5084. Brock, Gordon Ray. "Salvatore Martirano: A Study of His Mass." D.M.A. diss., University of Illinois, 1978.

MARX, JOSEPH (1882–1964)

5085. Meyers, Joseph Kenneth. "The Songs of Joseph Marx." D.M.A. diss., University of Missouri, 1972.

5086. Paxinos, Socrates. "Late Romantic Harmony and Counterpoint in the Music of Joseph Marx (1882–1964)." Ph.D. diss., University of South Africa, 1976.

MARX, KARL (1897–1985)

5087. Doppelbauer, Josef Friedrich. "Die *a cappella* Chorwerke von Karl Marx." F-Marx: 18–41.

5088. ———. "*Missa psalmodica.*" F-Marx: 94–97.

5089. Gümbel, Martin. "Marginalien zur Hölderinkantate, Opus 52." F-Marx: 42–56.

5090. Karkoschka, Erhard. "Über späte Instrumentalwerke von Karl Marx." M 26 (1972): 542–47.

5091. Wöhler, Willi. "Anmerkungen zur Instrumentation Marxcher Orchesterwerke." F-Marx: 74–76.

MASCAGNI, PIETRO (1863–1945)

5092. ASO 50 (1983). [*Cavalliera rusticana*]

MASON, DANIEL GREGORY (1873–1953)

5093. Lewis, Ralph B. "The Life and Music of Daniel Gregory Mason." Ph.D. diss., University of Rochester, 1959.

5094. McDonald, Gail Faber. "The Piano Music of Daniel Gregory Mason: A Performance-Tape and Study of His Original Works for Piano Solo and Two Pianos." D.M.A. diss., University of Maryland, 1977.

MASSENET, JULES (1842–1912)

5095. ASO 61 (1984). [*Werther*]

5096. ASO 93 (1986). [*Don Quichotte*]

5097. ASO 109 (1988). [*Thaïs*]

5098. ASO 123 (1989). [*Manon*]

5099. ASO 148 (1992). [*Esclarmonde, Grisélidis*]

5100. ASO 161 (1994). [*Le Cid, Panurge*]

5101. ASO 187 (1998). [*Hérodiade, Le roi de Lahore*]

5102. Dorminy, Wendell Larry. "The Song Cycles of Jules Massenet." D.M.A. diss., Indiana University, 1977.

5103. John, Nicholas, ed. *Massenet: Manon.* London: Calder, 1984.

MATHER, BRUCE (b. 1939)

5104. Evangelista, José. "Une analyse de *Madrigal III* de Bruce Mather." CCM 6 (1973): 81–109.

MATHIAS, WILLIAM (1934–1992)

5105. Forbes, Elliot. "The Choral Music of William Mathias." ACR 21, no. 4 (1979): 1–32.

MATHIEU, RODOLPHE (1890–1962)

5106. Bourassa-Trépanier, Juliette. "La langue musicale de Rodolphe Mathieu." CCM 5 (1972): 19–30.

MATTHUS, SIEGFRIED (b. 1934)

5107. Hansen, Mathias. "Die Analyse: Violoncellokonzerte von Paul-Heinz Dittrick, Siegfried Matthus, und Christfried Schmidt." MG 29 (1979): 591–99.

5108. Klement, Udo. "Die Analyse: Orchesterkonzerte von Ernst Hermann Meyer, Siegfried Matthus, und George Katzer." MG 28 (1978): 599–603. [*Responso*]

5109. Matthus, Siegfried. "Über die Harmonik meiner *Cornet*-Oper." MG 37 (1987): 404–7. [*Die Weise von Liebe und Tod des Cornets Christoph Rilke*]

5110. Schaefer, Hansjürgen. "Anmerkungen zu *Noch einen Löffel Gift, Liebling?*" MG 23 (1973): 535–39.

5111. ———. "*Jede Stunde deines Lebens*: Bemerkungen zum Fernsehspiel von Armin Müller und Siegfried Matthus." MG 19 (1969): 845–48.

5112. ———. "*Lazarillo vom Tormes*: Bemerkungen zur Oper von Siegfried Matthus und Horst Seeger." MG 15 (1965): 579–86.

5113. Vogt: 381–91. [*Der letzte Schuss*]

MAW, NICHOLAS (b. 1935)

5114. Payne, Anthony. "The Music of Nicholas Maw." TEMPO 68 (1964): 2–13.

5115. ———. "Nicholas Maw's *One Man Show*." TEMPO 71 (1964–1965): 2–14.

5116. ———. "Nicholas Maw's String Quartet." TEMPO 74 (1965): 5–11.

5117. Walsh, Stephen. "Nicholas Maw's New Opera." TEMPO 92 (1970): 2–15. [*The Rising of the Moon*]

5118. Whittall, Arnold. "The Instrumental Music of Nicholas Maw: Questions of Tonality." TEMPO 106 (1973): 26–33.

5119. ———. "Maw's *Personae*: Chromaticism and Tonal Allusion." TEMPO 125 (1978): 2–5.

MAYR, SIMON (1763–1845)

5120. M-Carner: 148–71. [*L'amor coniugale*]

McGUIRE, JOHN (b. 1942)

5121. Henck, Herbert. "Skizzen zu John McGuires *Cadence Music*." N 5 (1984–1985): 302–13.

5122. McGuire, John. "Über *Pulse Music III*." N 3 (1982–1983): 252–67.

McPHEE, COLIN (1901–1964)

5123. Cowell, Henry. "Current Chronicle." MQ 34 (1948): 410–15. [*Tabuh-tabuhan*]

5124. Mueller, Richard. "Bali, *Tabuh-Tabuhan*, and Colin McPhee's Method of Intercultural Composition." JMR 10, nos. 3–4 (1991): 127–75; 11, nos. 1–2 (1991): 67–92.

McQUEEN, IAN (b. 1954)

5125. McQueen, Ian. "På Svenska, eller vad som helst: The Opera Composer Today (In Swedish, or Whatever. . . .)." CMR 5 (1989): 215–24. [*Line of Terror*]

MEAD, ANDREW (b. 1952)

5126. Mead, Andrew. "Twelve-Tone Organizational Strategies: An Analytical Sampler." INT 3 (1989): 93–169. [Chamber Symphony]

MEALE, RICHARD (b. 1932)

5127. Ghandar, Ann. "Pitch and Time Structure in *Clouds Now and Then* of Richard Meale." MMA 10 (1979): 82–92.

5128. Laubenthal, Annegrit. "Hörvergnügen als ästhetisches Gesetz: Der australische Komponist Richard Meale." NZM 146, no. 9 (1985): 21–24.

MEDETOJA, LEEVI (1887–1947)

5129. Hillila, Ruth Ester. "The Songs of Toivo Kuula and Leevi Medetoja and Their Place in Twentieth-Century Finnish Art Song." Ph.D. diss., Boston University, 1964.

MEDTNER, NICOLAS (1880–1951)

5130. Elmore, Cenieth Catherine. "Some Stylistic Considerations in the Piano Sonatas of Nikolai Medtner." Ph.D. diss., University of North Carolina, 1972.

5131. Keller, Charles William. "The Piano Sonatas of Nicolas Medtner." Ph.D. diss., Ohio State University, 1971.

5132. Loftis, Bobby Hughes. "The Piano Sonatas of Nicolai Medtner." Ph.D. diss., University of West Virginia 1970.

5133. Truscott, Harold. "Medtner's Sonata in G Minor, Op. 22." MR 22 (1961): 112–23.

MÉHUL, ETIENNE NICHOLAS (1763–1817)

5134. Grace, Michael D. "Méhul's *Ariodant* and the Early Leitmotif." F-Seay: 173–97.

5135. Ringer, Alexander L. "A French Symphonist at the Time of Beethoven: Etienne Nicholas Méhul." MQ 37 (1951): 543–65.

MENDELSSOHN, FANNY (1805–1847)

5136. Brickman, Scott Thomas. "Analysis and Interpretation of Fanny Hensel's *Italien, Notturno,* and Piano Trio (First Movement)." Ph.D. diss., Brandeis University, 1996.

5137. Cai, Camilla. "Fanny Hensel's 'Songs for the Pianoforte' of 1836–37: Stylistic Interaction with Felix Mendelssohn." JMR 14, nos. 1–2 (1994): 55–76.

5138. De la Motte, Diether. "Tre dichiarazioni d'amore per Fanny Hensel." Trans. Giuseppina La Face Bianconi. RIM 24, no. 1 (1989): 67–73. [*Das Heimweh, Die Nonne,* String Quartet (Movement III)]

5139. Nubbermeyer, Annette. "Zweifel und Bekenntnis: Fanny Hensels Kantate *Hiob;* Entstehungsgeschichte und Werkanalyse." MK 67, no. 5 (1997): 286–95.

MENDELSSOHN, FELIX (1809–1847)

Cello Sonata No. 2, Op. 58

5140. Wick, Norman L. "Shifted Downbeats in Classic and Romantic Music." ITR 15, no. 2 (1994): 73–87. [Movement III]

Choral Works (various; *see also* specific choral works)

5141. Chamber, Robert Ben. "The Shorter Choral Works with Sacred Text of Felix Mendelssohn-Bartholdy." D.M.A. diss., Southwestern Baptist Theological Seminary, 1984.

5142. Jessop, Craig Don. "An Analytical Survey of the Unaccompanied Choral Works for Mixed Voices by Felix Mendelssohn-Bartholdy." D.M.A. diss., Stanford University, 1981.

5143. Pritchard, Brian W. "Mendelssohn's Chorale Cantatas: An Appraisal." MQ 62 (1976): 1–24.

Elijah, Op. 70

5144. Ellison, Ross Wesley. "Unity and Contrast in Mendelssohn's *Elijah.*" Ph.D. diss., University of North Carolina, 1978.

5145. Plank, Steven E. "Mendelssohn and Bach: Some New Light on an Old Partnership." ACR 32, nos. 1–2 (1990): 23–28.

5146. Reimer, Erich. "Regenwunder und Witwenszene: Zur Szenengestaltung in Mendelssohns *Elias.*" MF 49, no. 2 (1996): 152–71.

5147. Werner, Jack. *Mendelssohn's "Elijah": A Historical and Analytical Guide to the Oratorio.* London: Chappell, 1965.

Erste Walpurgisnacht, Op. 60

5148. Campbell, Robert M. "Mendelssohn and Goethe: *The First Walpurgis Night.*" ACR 33, no. 1 (1991): 14–22.

5149. Dahlhaus, Carl. "Hoch symbolisch intentioniert: Zu Mendelssohns *Erster Walpurgisnacht.*" OMZ 36 (1981): 290–97.

5150. Szeskus, Reinhard. "*Die erste Walpurgisnacht,* Op. 60, von Felix Mendelssohn Bartholdy." BM 17 (1975): 171–80.

Hebriden (Fingalshöhle), Op. 26

5151. Eichhorn, Andreas. *Felix Mendelssohn-Bartholdy: "Die Hebriden," Ouvertüre für Orchester, Op. 26.* Munich: Fink, 1998.

5152. Kielian, Marianne. "Sketches after an Overture: Presented Musical Spans as Structural Models in Mendelssohn's *Hebrides Overture.*" ITO 1 (1975): 6–10.

5153. Todd, R. Larry. "Of Sea Gulls and Counterpoint: The Early Versions of Mendelssohn's *Hebrides Overture.*" NCM 2 (1979): 197–213.

5154. M-Todd.

Jesu, meine Freude

5155. Jonas, Oswald. "An Unknown Mendelssohn Work." ACR 9, no. 2 (1967): 16–22.

Lieder ohne Worte, Opp. 19b and 30

5156. M-De la Motte: 125–30. [*Venetianisches Gondellied,* op. 30, no. 6]

5157. Pessina, Marino. "I *Lieder ohne Worte* di Felix Mendelssohn: Una ricognizione analitica." ANL 28 (1999): 12–23.

5158. Tischler, Louise H., and Hans Tischler. "Mendelssohn's *Songs Without Words.*" MQ 33 (1947): 1–16.

5159. ———. "Mendelssohn's Style: The Songs Without Words." MR 8 (1947): 256–73.

Meeresstille und glückliche Fahrt, Op. 27

5160. M-Kramer: 122–42.

5161. M-Todd.

Melusine. See Ouverture zum Märchen von der schönen Melusine

O Haupt voll Blut und Wunden

5162. Todd, R. Larry. "A Passion Cantata by Mendelssohn." ACR 25, no. 1 (1983): 3–17.

Octet, Op. 20

5163. Gerlach, Reinhard. "Mendelssohns schöpferische Erinnerung: Der 'Jugendzeit'; Die Beziehungen zwischen den Violinkonzert Op. 64 und dem Oktett für Streicher, Op. 20." MF 25 (1972): 142–52.

5164. Vitercik, Greg. "Mendelssohn the Progressive." JMR 8, nos. 3–4 (1989): 333–74. [Movement III]

Organ Works (various; *see also* specific organ works)

5165. Butler, Douglas Lamar. "The Organ Works of Felix Mendelssohn-Bartholdy." Ph.D. diss., University of Oregon, 1973.

Ouverture zum Märchen von der schönen Melusine (*Die schöne Melusine*), **Op. 32**

5166. Mintz, Donald. "*Melusine*: A Mendelssohn Draft." MQ 43 (1957): 480–99.

Preludes and Fugues, Op. 37

5167. Bötel, Friedhold. "Felix Mendelssohn Bartholdys Präldien und Fugen für Orgel Op. 37: Studien zur Orgelmusik Mendelssohns unter Berücksichtigung ihrer gattungsgeschichtlichten Stellung." Ph.D. diss., Heidelberg, 1982.

Rondo brillant, **Op. 29**

5168. Konold, Wulf. "Felix Mendelssohn Bartholdys *Rondo brillant* Op. 29: Ein Beitrag zur Geschichte des einsätzigen Konzertstücks im 19. Jahrhundert." MF 38 (1985): 169–83.

Saint Paul (*Paulus*), **Op. 36**

5169. Reimer, Erich. "Mendelssohns 'edler Gesang': Zur Kompositionsweise der Sologesänge im *Paulus*." AM 50, no. 1 (1993): 44–70.

5170. ———. "Textanlage und Szengestaltung in Mendelssohns *Paulus*." AM 46, no. 1 (1989): 42–69.

Sommernachtstraum, **Op. 21**

5171. M-Todd.

Songs

5172. Lewis, Christopher. "Text, Time, and Tonic: Aspects of Patterning in the Romantic Cycle." INT 2 (1988): 37–73. [Lieder, op. 9]

5173. Stoner, Thomas Alan. "Mendelssohn's Published Songs." Ph.D. diss., University of Maryland, 1972.

5174. Thym, Jürgen, and Ann Clark Fehn. "Sonnet Structure and the German Lied: Shackles or Spurs?" JALS 32 (1993): 3–15. ["Die Liebende schreibt," op. 86, no. 3]

String Quartets

5175. Kohlhase, Hans. "Studien zur Form in den Streichquartetten von Felix Mendelssohn Bartholdy." HJM 2 (1976): 75–104.

5176. Schuhmacher, Gerhard. "Zwischen Autograph und Erstveröffentlichung: Zu Mendelssohns Kompositionsweise, dargestellt an den Streichquartetten Op. 44." BM 15 (1973): 253–62.

String Quintet No. 1, Op. 18

5177. Vitercik, Greg. "Mendelssohn the Progressive." JMR 8, nos. 3–4 (1989): 333–74.

Symphonies (various; *see also* specific symphonies)

5178. Filosa, Albert J. "The Early Symphonies and Chamber Music of Felix Mendelssohn-Bartholdy." Ph.D. diss., Yale University, 1970.

5179. Konold, Wulf. "Mendelssohns Jugendsymphonien: Eine analytische Studie." AM 46, no. 1 (1989): 1–41; 46, no. 2 (1989): 155–83.

Symphony No. 2, Op. 52 ("Lobgesang")

5180. Steinbeck, Wolfram. "Die Idee der Vokalsymphonie: Zu Mendelssohns 'Lobgesang.'" AM 53, no. 3 (1996): 222–33.

Symphony No. 4, Op. 90 ("Italian")

5181. Cooper, John Michael. "'Aber eben dieser Zweifel': A New Look at Mendelssohn's 'Italian' Symphony." NCM 15, no. 3 (1992): 169–87.

5182. Konold, Wulf. *Felix Mendelssohn Bartholdy: Symphonie Nr. 4 A-Dur Op. 90, "Die Italienische."* Munich: Fink, 1987.

5183. Weiss, Günther. "Eine Mozartspur in Felix MendelssohnBartholdys Sinfonie A-Dur Op. 90 ('Italienische')." In *Mozart: Klassik für die Gegenwart,* 87–89. Oldenburg: Stalling-Druck, 1978.

Symphony No. 5, Op. 107 ("Reformation")

5184. Wüster, Ulrich. "'Ein gewisser Geist': Zu Mendelssohns *Reformations-Symphonie*." MF 44, no. 4 (1991): 311–30. [Movements III–IV]

Violin Concerto, Op. 64

5185. Gerlach, Reinhard. "Mendelssohns schöpferische Erinnerung: Der 'Jugendzeit'; Die Beziehungen zwischen den Violinkonzert Op. 64 und dem Oktett für Streicher, Op. 20." MF 25 (1972): 142–52.

Various Works

5186. Dahlhaus, Carl. *Das Problem Mendelssohn.* Regensburg: Bosse, 1974.

5187. Filosa, Albert J. "The Early Symphonies and Chamber Music of Felix Mendelssohn-Bartholdy." Ph.D. diss., Yale University, 1970.

5188. Friedrich, Gerda Bertram. "Die Fugenkomposition in Mendelssohns Instrumentalwerk." Ph.D. diss., Rheinische Friedrich-Wilhelms Universität, Bonn, 1969.

5189. Godwin, Joscelyn. "Early Mendelssohn and Late Beethoven." ML 55 (1974): 272–85.

5190. Hoshino, Hiromi. "Mendelssohns geistliche Vokalmusik." MK 69, no. 1 (1999): 31–41.

5191. Jordahl, Robert. "A Study of the Use of the Chorale in the Works of Mendelssohn, Brahms, and Reger." Ph.D. diss., University of Rochester, 1965.

5192. Krummacher, Friedhelm. *Mendelssohn: Der Komponist; Studien zur Kammermusik für Streichen.* Munich: Fink, 1978.

5193. McDonald, John A. "The Chamber Music of Felix Mendelssohn-Bartholdy." Ph.D. diss., Northwestern University, 1970.

5194. Reiningdaus, Frieder. "Zwischen Historismus und Poesie: Über die Notwendigkeit umfassender Musikanalyse und ihre Erprobung an Klavierkammermusik von Felix Mendelssohn Bartholdy und Robert Schumann." ZM 4, no. 2 (1973): 22–29; 5, no. 1 (1974): 34–44.

5195. Rummenhöller, Peter. "Die 'vierstimmige Choralgeschicklichkeit': Bemerkungen zur Harmonik Mendelssohns." M 39, no. 1 (1985): 18–25.

5196. Schönfelder, Gerd. "Zur Frage des Realismus bei Mendelssohn." BM 14 (1972): 169–84.

5197. Schuhmacher, Gerhard, ed. *Felix Mendelssohn-Bartholdy.* Darmstadt: Wissenschaftliches Buchgesellschaft, 1982.

5198. Thomas, Mathias. *Das Instrumentalwerk Felix MendelssohnBartholdys: Ein systematische Untersuchung unter besonderer Berücksichtigung der zeitgenossischen Musiktheorie.* Göttinger musikwissenschaftliche Arbeiten 4. Kassel: Bärenreiter, 1972.

5199. Todd, Ralph Larry. "The Instrumental Music of Felix Mendelssohn-Bartholdy: Selected Studies Based on Primary Sources." Ph.D. diss., Yale University, 1979.

5200. ———. "An Unfinished Piano Concerto by Mendelssohn." MQ 68 (1982): 80-101.

5201. ———. "An Unfinished Symphony by Mendelssohn." ML 61 (1980): 293–309.

MENGAL, MARTIN JOSEPH (1784–1851)

5202. Andrews, Ralph E. "The Woodwind Quartets of Martin Joseph Mengal." Ph.D. diss., Florida State University, 1970.

MENGELBERG, MISHA (b. 1935)

5203. Vermeulen, Ernst. "Misha Mengelberg: *Anatoloose.*" SS 48 (1971): 9–16.

MENNIN, PETER (1923–1983)

5204. Goldman, Richard Franko. "Current Chronicle." MQ 35 (1949): 111–15. [Symphony No. 3]

5205. Rhoads, Mary Ruth Schneyer. "Influences of Japanese *hogaku* Manifest in Selected Compositions by Peter Mennin and Benjamin Britten." Ph.D. diss., Michigan State University, 1969.

MERCADANTE, SAVERIO (1795–1870)

5206. Mioli, Pero. "Tradizione melodrammatica e crisi di forme nelle *Due illustri rivali* di Saverio Mercadante." STU 9 (1980): 317–28.

MERIKANTO, AARRE (1893–1958)

5207. Mäkelä, Tomi. "Zwischen Inspiration und Imitation: Max Regers Streichsextett Opus 118 und das *Schott-Konzert* des Reger-Schülers Aarre Merikanto (1893–1958) im Vergleich." MF 48, no. 4 (1995): 369–94.

MESSIAEN, OLIVIER (1908–1992)

Ascension

5208. Ameringen, Sylvia van. "Olivier Messiaens *Ascension.*" M 6 (1952): 500–3.

Catalogue d'oiseaux

5209. Hold, Trevor. "Messiaen's *Birds.*" ML 52 (1971): 113–22.

5210. Philips, John Douglass. "The Modal Language of Olivier Messiaen: Principles of *Technique de mon langage musical* Reflected in *Catalogue d'oiseaux.*" D.M.A. diss., Peabody Conservatory, 1977.

Chants de terre et de ciel

5211. Ross, Mark Alan. "The Perception of Multitonal Levels in Olivier Messiaen's *Quatuor pour la fin du temps* and Selected Vocal Compositions." Ph.D. diss., University of Cincinnati, 1977.

Chronochromie

5212. M-Bersano. ["Antistrophe I"]

5213. M-Gallatin.

Corps glorieux

5214. Michaely, Aloyse. "Messiaens Trinitätstraktate." MK 69, no. 2 (1999): 90–98. [No. 7]

Couleurs de la Cité Céleste

5215. Quilling, Howard Lee. "An Analysis of Olivier Messian's *Couleurs de la Cité Céleste*." Ph.D. diss., University of California, Santa Barbara, 1984.

5216. Shepard, Brian K. "The Symbolic Elements of Messiaen's Work for Wind Ensemble, *Couleurs de la Cité Céleste*." JBR 18, no. 1 (1982–1983): 52–59.

Études de rythme

5217. M-Kirchmeyer: 175–79. ["Mode de valeurs et d'intensités"]

5218. Lee, John Madison. "Harmonic Structures in the *Études rythmiques* of Olivier Messiaen." Ph.D. diss., Florida State University, 1972.

5219. Riotte, André. "La mise en évidence de régularités locales, une étape obligée pour la modélisation formelle: L'exemple du *Mode de valeurs et d'intensités* de Messiaen." ANM 32 (1993): 54–57.

5220. Schweizer, Klaus. "Olivier Messiaens Klavieretude 'Mode de valeurs et d'intensités.'" AM 30 (1973): 128–46.

5221. Toop, Richard. "Messiaen/Goeyvaerts, Fano/Stockhausen, Boulez." PNM 13, no. 1 (1974–1975): 141–49.

Fauvette des jardins

5222. Fabbi, Roberto. "Olivier Messiaen e lo 'charme des impossibilités': *La fauvette des jardins*." RIM 24, no. 1 (1989): 153–84.

Livre d'orgue

5223. Frischknecht, Hans Eugen. "Rhythmen und Dauerwerte im *Livre d'orgue* von Olivier Messiaen." *Musik und Gottesdienst* 1 (1968): 1–12.

5224. Heiss, Hellmut. "Analysen aus dem *Livre d'orgue* von Olivier Messiaen, 1951." ZM 1, no. 2 (1970): 32–38.

5225. ———. "Struktur und Symbolik in 'Les yeux dans les roues' aus Olivier Messiaens *Livre d'orgue*." ZM 3, no. 2 (1972): 22–27.

5226. Kemmelmeyer, Karl-Jürgen. "Olivier Messiaen: *Livre d'orgue* I." MB 7 (1975): 448–53. ["Reprises par interversion"]

5227. Trawick, Eleanor F. "Serialism and Permutation Techniques in Olivier Messiaen's *Livre d'orgue*." MRF 6 (1991): 15–35.

Méditations sur le mystère de la Sainte Trinité

5228. M-Gallatin.

5229. Gilmer, Carl DuVall, III. "Messiaen's Musical Language in *Méditations sur le mystère de la Sainte Trinité*." D.M.A. diss., Memphis State University, 1978.

5230. Michaely, Aloyse. "Messiaens Trinitätstraktate." MK 69, no. 2 (1999): 90–98. [No. 5]

5231. Shenton, Andrew. "The Unspoken Word: Olivier Messiaen's *langage communicable*." Ph.D. diss., Harvard University, 1998.

5232. Weir, Gillian. "Messiaen's Musical Language: A Review of His *Méditations sur le mystère de la Sainte Trinité* for Organ." SMU 13 (1979): 66–76.

Messe de la Pentecôte

5233. Hohlfeld-Ufer, Ingrid, and Almut Rössler. *Die musikalische Sprache Olivier Messiaens dargestellt an dem Orgelzyklus "Die Pfingstmesse."* Duisburg: Gilles & Francke, 1978.

5234. Raiss, Hans-Peter. "Olivier Messiaen: *Messe de la Pentecôte* für Orgel (1950)." M-Vogt: 249–53.

Nativité du Seigneur

5235. Ernst, Karin. "Olivier Messiaen: *La Nativité du Seigneur* für Orgel (1935)." NZM 146, no. 12 (1985): 37–39.

5236. Hochreither, Karl. "Olivier Messiaen: *La Nativité du Seigneur*." F-Schneider: 64–78.

Offrandes oubliées

5237. Klassen, Janina. "Theologischer Regenbogen: *Les offrandes oubliées* von Olivier Messiaen." JSIM (1998): 268–76.

Oiseaux exotiques

5238. Bessiére, Marie. "*Oiseaux exotiques* d'Olivier Messiaen: De la nature à l'œuvre musicale." ANM 7 (1987): 62–67.

5239. Šimundža, Mirjana. "Messiaen's Rhythmical Organisation and Classical Indian Theory of Rhythm (II)." IRASM 19, no. 1 (1988): 53–73.

Organ Works (various; *see also* specific organ works)

5240. Adams, Beverly Decker. "The Organ Compositions of Olivier Messiaen." Ph.D. diss., University of Utah, 1969.

5241. Ahrens, Sieglind, Hans-Dieter Möller, and Almut Rössler. *Das Orgelwerk Messiaens*. Duisberg: Gilles & Francke, 1976.

5242. Ernst, Karin. *Der Beitrag Olivier Messiaens zur Orgelmusik des 20. Jahrhunderts*. Friburg: Hochschulverlag, 1980.

5243. Gárdonyi, Zsolt. "Zur Harmonik Olivier Messiaens: Versuch einer Handreichung zur Einstudierung seiner Orgelmusik." MK 48 (1978): 217–27.

5244. Holloway, Clyde. "The Organ Works of Olivier Messiaen and Their Importance in His Total Oeuvre." S.M.D. diss., Union Theological Seminary, 1974.

5245. Kemmelmeyer, Karl-Jürgen. *Die gedrückten Orgelwerke Olivier Messiaens bis zum "Verset pour la fête de la dédicace."* Regensburg: Bosse, 1974.

5246. Thissen, Paul. "Zahlensymbolik im Orgelwerk von Olivier Messiaen." KJ 80 (1996): 115–31.

Petites liturgies de la Présence Divine

5247. M-Gallatin.

5248. Günther, Siegfried. "Olivier Messiaen: *Trois petites liturgies de la Présence Divine.*" MK 28 (1959): 153–59.

Piano Works (various; *see also* specific piano works)

5249. Goebels, Franzpeter. "Bemerkungen und Materialen zum Studium neuer Klaviermusik." SMZ 113 (1973): 265–68, 336–40.

5250. Reverdy, Michele. *L'oeuvre pour piano d'Olivier Messiaen*. Paris: Leduc, 1978.

Poèmes pour Mi

5251. M-Gallatin.

5252. Ross, Mark Alan. "The Perception of Multitonal Levels in Olivier Messiaen's *Quatuor pour la fin du temps* and Selected Vocal Compositions." Ph.D. diss., University of Cincinnati, 1977.

Preludes (Piano)

5253. M-Gallatin.

5254. Hirsbrunner, Theo. "Die Préludes für Klavier von Olivier Messiaen." M 42, no. 4 (1988): 361–65.

5255. Lee, John M. "A Look at Olivier Messiaen: The Man, His Philosophy, and His Piano Preludes." PQ 128 (1984–1985): 52–56.

Quatuor pour la fin du temps

5256. Bernstein, David Stephen. "Messiaen's *Quatuor pour la fin du temps*: An Analysis Based upon Messiaen's Theory of Rhythm and His Use of Modes of Limited Transposition." D.M.A. diss., Indiana University, 1974.

5257. Farrell, Kandace L. "Unification in Olivier Messiaen's *Quatour pour la fin du temps*: A Scalar Analysis of Movements 4, 5, and 8." TSP 4 (1987): 25–40.

5258. Koozin, Timothy. "Spiritual-Temporal Imagery in Music of Olivier Messiaen and Toru Takemitsu." CMR 7, no. 2 (1993): 185–202.

5259. Morris, David. "A Semiotic Invesigation of Messiaen's 'Abîme des oiseaux.'" MA 8, nos. 1–2 (1989): 125–58.

5260. Pople, Anthony. *Messiaen: Quatuor pour la fin du temps*. Cambridge: Cambridge University Press, 1998.

5261. Ross, Mark Alan. "The Perception of Multitonal Levels in Olivier Messiaen's *Quatuor pour la fin du temps* and Selected Vocal Compositions." Ph.D. diss., University of Cincinnati, 1977.

5262. Šimundža, Mirjana. "Messiaen's Rhythmical Organisation and Classical Indian Theory of Rhythm (I)." IRASM 18, no. 1 (1987): 117–44.

Rechants

5263. M-Gallatin.

5264. Prost, Christine. "Questions de rhythme et d'interpretation: *Le printemps* de Claude Le Jeune, *Cinq rechants* d'Olivier Messian." ANM 9 (1987): 33–42.

Saint François d'Assise: scènes franciscaines

5265. Guiberteau, Francine. "*Le Saint-François d'Assise* d'Olivier Messiaen: Événement et avènement." ANM 1 (1985): 61–83.

Transfiguration de Notre Seigneur Jésus-Christ

5266. Messiaen, Olivier. "Gedanken zu meiner *Transfiguration*." BOGM (1974–1975): 23–28.

Turangalîla-symphonie

5267. Burkat, Leonard. "Current Chronicle." MQ 36 (1950): 259–68.

5268. Hook, Julian L. "Rhythm in the Music of Messiaen: An Algebraic Study and an Application in the *Turangalîla Symphony*." MTS 20, no. 1 (1998): 97–120.

5269. Schweizer, Klaus. *Olivier Messiaen: Turangalîla-symphonie.* Munich: Fink, 1982.

5270. Šimundža, Mirjana. "Messiaen's Rhythmical Organisation and Classical Indian Theory of Rhythm (I)." IRASM 18, no. 1 (1987): 117–44.

Vingt regards sur l'Enfant-Jésus

5271. Bruhn, Siglind. "The Exchange of Natures and the Nature(s) of Time: Another of Messiaen's 'créatures immatérielles et symboliques'; *Looking upon the Infant Jesus.*" TCM 2, no. 10 (1995): 7–12. ["Regard du temps"]

5272. ———. "The Exchange of Natures and the Nature(s) of Time: One of Messiaen's 'créatures immatérielles et symboliques'; *Looking upon the Infant Jesus.*" TCM 2, no. 9 (1995): 1–5. ["L'échange"]

5273. Carl, Beate. "Rhythmus, Metrum und die Verknüpfung von Tondauer und -höhe in Olivier Messiaens Klavierzyklus *Vingt regards sur l'Enfant-Jésus.*" MF 49, no. 4 (1996): 383–402.

5274. Ennis, Paula. "A Study of Coherence and Unity in Messiaen's Cycle *Vingt regards sur l'Enfant-Jésus.*" Ph.D. diss., Indiana University, 1979.

5275. Marie, Jean-Etienne. "Inverse Function: Differentiation and Integration in Messiaen and Boulez." SONUS 2, no. 1 (1981): 26–33.

5276. Michaely, Aloyse. "Verbum caro: Die Darstellung des Mysteriums der Inkarnation in Olivier Messiaens *Vingt regards sur l'Enfant-Jésus.*" HJM 6 (1983): 225–346.

5277. Morris, Betty Ann Walker. "Symbolism and Meaning in *Vingt regards sur l'Enfant-Jésus* by Olivier Messiaen." D.M.A. diss., North Texas State University, 1978.

5278. Walker, Rosemary. "Modes and Pitch-Class Sets in Messiaen: A Brief Discussion of 'Première Communion de la Vierge.'" MA 8, nos. 1–2 (1989): 159–68.

Various Works

5279. Angermann, Klaus. "Die Wollust der Ordnung: Messiaens konstruktive Sinnlichkeit." NZM 149, no. 9 (1988): 11–17.

5280. Bell, Carl Huston. *Olivier Messiaen.* Boston: Twayne, 1984.

5281. ———. "A Structural and Stylistic Analysis of Representative Works by Olivier Messiaen." D.M.A. diss., Columbia University, 1976.

5282. Bernard, Jonathan W. "Messiaen's Synaesthesia: The Correspondence between Color and Sound Structure in His Music." MP 4, no. 1 (1986): 41–68.

5283. Borris, Siegfried. "Olivier Messiaen: Der pater gloriosus der Neuen Musik." M 38, no. 4 (1984): 331–35.

5284. Drew, David. "Messiaen: A Provisional Study." SCORE 10 (1954): 33–49; 13 (1955): 59–73; 14 (1955): 41–61.

5285. Forster, Max. *Technik modaler Komposition bei Olivier Messiaen.* Tübinger Beiträge zur Musikwissenschaft 4. Neuhausen-Stuttgart Hänssler, 1976.

5286. Fremiot, Marcel. "Le rythme dans le langage d'Olivier Messiaen." POL 2 (1948): 58–64.

5287. Griffiths, Paul. *Olivier Messiaen and the Music of Time.* Ithaca, N.Y.: Cornell University Press, 1985.

5288. Gunden, Heidi Cecilia von. "Timbre as Symbol in Selected Works of Olivier Messiaen." Ph.D. diss., University of California at San Diego, 1977.

5289. Hirsbrunner, Theo. "Motivvarianten bei Olivier Messiaen." DI 18 (1988): 4–8.

5290. Hold, Trevor. "Messiaen's *Birds.*" ML 52 (1971): 113–22.

5291. Johnson, Robert Sherlaw. *Messiaen.* Berkeley: University of California Press, 1975.

5292. Krastewa, Iwanka. "Le langage rythmique d'Olivier Messiaen et la métrique ancienne grecque." SMZ 112 (1972): 79–86.

5293. Messiaen, Olivier. *La technique de mon langage musical.* Paris: Leduc, 1956.

5294. Michaely, Aloyse. *Die Musik Olivier Messiaens: Untersuchungen zum Gesamtschaffen.* Hamburg: Verlag der Musikalienhandlung K. D. Wagner, 1987.

5295. Nelson, David Lowell. "An Analysis of Olivier Messiaen's Chant Paraphrases." Ph.D. diss., Northwestern University, 1992.

5296. Nichols, Roger. *Messiaen.* Oxford: Oxford University Press, 1975.

5297. Peterson, Larry Wayne. "Messiaen and Rhythm: Theory and Practice." Ph.D. diss., University of North Carolina, 1973.

5298. Piencikowski, Robert. "Fonction relative du timbre dans la musique contemporaine: Messiane, Carter, Boulez, Stockhausen." ANM 3 (1986): 51–53.

5299. Rostand, Claude. "Messiaen et ses trois styles." SMZ 97 (1957): 133–39.

5300. Schlee, Thomas Daniel. "Hommage à Olivier Messiaen." OMZ 34 (1979): 28–40.

5301. Schweizer, Klaus. "Dokumentarische Materialen bei Olivier Messiaen." Melos/NZM 4 (1978): 477–85.

5302. Trawick, Eleanor F. "Order, Progression, and Time in the Music of Messiaen." EXT 9, no. 2 (1999): 64–76.

5303. Tremblay, Gilles. "Oiseau, nature, Messiaen, musique." CCM 1 (1970): 15–40.

MEYER, ERNST HERMANN (1905–1988)

5304. Hennenberg, Fritz. "Vielschichtigkeit von Form und Inhalt: Bemerkungen zu Ernst Hermann Neyers *Poem für Viola und Orchester.*" MG 15 (1965): 804–8.

5305. Klement, Udo. "Die Analyse: Orchesterkonzerte von Ernst Hermann Meyer, Siegfried Matthus, und Georg Katzer." MG 28 (1978): 599–603. [Concerto for Orchestra]

5306. Markowski, Liesel. "Biennale-Eregnis: Meisterliches Kammermusikspiel: Das Berliner Streichquartett spielt Ernst Hermann Meyer." MG 19 (1969): 313–16.

5307. ———. "Ernst Hermann Meyers 3. Streichquartett." MG 19 (1969): 451–56.

5308. Niemann, Konrad. "'Ich denke und fühle im Lied . . .': Ernst Hermann Meyers Vertonungen von Fürnbergs Dichtungen." MG 39 (1989): 512–16.

5309. Rienäcker, Gerd. "*Reiter der Nacht*: Analytischen Bemerkungen zur Oper von Ernst Hermann Meyer." MG 24 (1974): 525–30.

5310. Schaefer, Hansjürgen. "Bemerkungen zu Ernst Hermann Meyers Streichsinfonie." MG 11 (1961): 656–60.

5311. ———. ". . . *dass kein Unheil komme über unser Erden*: Ein neuer Liederzyklus von Ernst Hermann Meyer." MG 15 (1965): 809–11.

5312. ———. "Ernst Hermann Meyers Violinkonzert." MG 15 (1965): 330–32.

5313. Schönewolf, Karl. "Ardens sed virens: Zwei Streichquartette von Ernst Hermann Meyer." MG 9, no. 10 (1959): 3–7; 9, no. 11 (1959): 13–15.

MEYERBEER, GIACOMO (1791–1864)

5314. ASO 76 (1985). [*Robert le diable*]

5315. ASO 134 (1990). [*Les Huguenots*]

5316. Frese, Christhard. *Dramaturgie der grossen Opern Giacomo Meyerbeers.* Berlin-Lichterfelde: Lienau, 1970.

5317. Gibson, Robert Wayne. "Meyerbeer's *Le prophète*: A Study in Operatic Style." Ph.D. diss., Northwestern University, 1972.

MICHAEL, DAVID MORITZ (1751–1827)

5318. Roberts, Dale Alexander. "The Sacred Vocal Music of David Moritz Michael: An American Moravian composer." D.M.A. diss., University of Kentucky, 1978.

MIDDELSCHULTE, WILHELM (1863–1943)

5319. Belcher, Euel H., Jr. "The Organ Music of Wilhelm Middelschulte." Ph.D. diss., Indiana University, 1975.

MIGNONE, FRANCISCO (1897–1986)

5320. Verhaalen, Sister Marion. "Francisco Mignone: His Music for Piano." IAMB 79 (1970–1971): 1–36.

MIHALOVICH, ÖDÖN (1842–1929)

5321. Szerzo, Katalin. "Eine Oper der ungarischen Wagner-Schule: Edmund von Mihalovich, *Eliane.*" SM 19 (1977): 109–60.

MIKI, MINORU (b. 1930)

5322. Nuss, Steven. "Western Instruments, Japanese Music: Issues of Texture and Harmony in Minoru Miki's *Jo no kyoku.*" TP 21 (1996): 167–87. [*Eurasian Trilogy* No. 1]

MILHAUD, DARIUS (1892–1974)

Chamber Symphony No. 2 ("Pastorale")

5323. Harrison, Daniel. "Bitonality, Pentatonicism, and Diatonicism in a Work by Milhaud." M-Baker: 393–408.

Choral Works

5324. Hodgson, Kenneth Dorsey. "An Examination of the Compositions by Darius Milhaud for Unaccompanied Mixed Voices." D.M.A. diss., University of Illinois, 1979.

5325. M-Larson.

Operas

5326. Knoch, Hans. *Orpheus und Eurydike: Der antike Sagenstoff in den Opern von Darius Milhaud und Ernst Krenek.* Regensburg: Bosse, 1977.

5327. Rosteck, Jens. "Die lapidare Schönheit des Alltags: Darius Milhauds erste Oper *La brebis égarée.*" NZM 153, no. 5 (1992): 20–26.

Organ Works

5328. Goetze, Wilhelm Albin Arthur. "An Analytical Study of Milhaud's *Neuf préludes* for organ." Ed.D. diss., Columbia University, 1976.

5329. Schaeffer, Stephen Gleim. "The Organ Works of Darius Milhaud." D.M.A. diss., University of Cincinnati, 1977.

Piano Works

5330. Ehrler, Hanno. *Untersuchungen zur Klaviermusik von Francis Poulenc, Arthur Honegger, und Darius Milhaud.* Tutzing: Schneider, 1990.

5331. M-Forte: 39–47. [*Une journée* ("Midi")]

5332. M-Kniesner. [Piano Sonata No. 1]

Songs

5333. Noble, Natoma Nash. "The Neoclassic Aesthetic in Two Early Song Cycles by Darius Milhaud." D.M.A. diss., University of Texas, 1981. [*Poèmes juifs, Six chants populaires hébraïques*]

String Quartets

5334. Cherry, Paul Wyman. "The String Quartets of Darius Milhaud." Ph.D. diss., University of Colorado, 1980.

5335. Helm, Everett. "Milhaud: XIV + XV = Oktett." MELOS 22 (1955): 71–75.

5336. Rosteck, Jens. "Das 'nette Spiel' der Polytonalität: Zur Wahlverwandschaft zwischen Darius Milhaud und Paul Hindemith." MF 46, no. 3 (1993): 268–84. [Nos. 4, 6]

String Septet

5337. Purrone, Kevin. "The Septuor à cordes of Darius Milhaud." ITR 3, no. 3 (1979–1980): 36–61.

Symphonies. *See also* Chamber Symphony No. 2

5338. Swickard, Ralph James. "The Symphonies of Darius Milhaud: An Historical Perspective and Critical Study of Their Musical Content, Style, and Form." Ph.D. diss., University of California, Los Angeles, 1973.

Various Works

5339. Bauer, Marion. "Darius Milhaud." MQ 29 (1942): 139–59.

5340. Daniel, Keith W. "A Preliminary Investigation of Pitch-Class Set Analysis in the Atonal and Polytonal Works of Milhaud and Poulenc." ITO 6, no. 6 (1981–1983): 22–48.

5341. Laughton, John Charles. "The Woodwind Music of Milhaud." D.M.A. diss., University of Iowa, 1980.

5342. MacKenzie, Nancy Mayland. "Selected Clarinet Solo and Chamber Music of Darius Milhaud." Ph.D. diss., University of Wisconsin, 1984.

5343. McCarthy, Peter J. "The Sonatas of Darius Milhaud." Ph.D. diss., Catholic University of America, 1972.

5344. Mason, Colin. "The Chamber Music of Milhaud." MQ 43 (1957): 326–41.

5345. Petrella, Robert Louis. "The Solo and Chamber Music for Clarinet by Darius Milhaud." D.M.A. thesis, University of Maryland, 1979.

5346. Trickey, Samuel Miller. "*Les Six.*" Ph.D. diss., North Texas State University, 1955.

MOE, DANIEL (b. 1926)

5347. Erickson, Karle Joseph. "The Choral Music of Daniel Moe (1926–) Written between 1952 and 1967." Ed.D. diss., University of Illinois, 1970.

MOERAN, E. J. (1894–1950)

5348. M-Curtis.

5349. Statham, Heathcote. "Moeran's Symphony in G Minor." MR 1 (1940): 245–54.

5350. Yenne, Vernon Lee. "Three Twentieth-Century English Song Composers: Peter Warlock, E. J. Moeran, and John Ireland." D.M.A. diss., University of Illinois, 1969.

MOEVS, ROBERT (b. 1920)

5351. Boros, James. "The Systematic Chromaticism of Robert Moevs." PNM 28, no. 1 (1990): 294–322.

5352. Wilkinson, Carlton. "Robert Moev's *Heptáchronon* for Solo Cello." PNM 35, no. 1 (1997): 231–61.

MOLCHANOV, KIRILL VLADIMIROVICH (1922–1982)

5353. Taruskin, Richard. "Current Chronicle." MQ 62 (1976): 105–15. [*The Dawns Here Are Calm*]

MONIUSZKO, STANISIAW (1819–1872)

5354. ASO 83 (1986). [*The Haunted Manor*]

5355. Abraham, Gerald. "The Operas of Stanisław Moniuszko." M-Abraham: 156–71.

5356. Hunt, R. E. "Moniuszko's Musical Treatment of Poems by Mickiewica." Ph.D. diss., London, 1980.

MONK, MEREDITH (b. 1942)

5357. Lassetter, Leslie. "Opera from Elsewhere: Meredith Monk's *Atlas.*" MRF 8 (1993): 20–37.

MONNIKENDAM, MARIUS (1896–1977)

5358. Schouten, Jan. "Marius Monnikendam: *Via sacra.*" SS 55 (1974): 29–36.

MOÓR, EMMANUEL (1863–1931)

5359. Truscott, Harold. "The Piano Concertos of Emmanuel Moir." MR 21 (1960): 121–29.

MOORE, DOUGLAS S. (1893–1969)

5360. Reagan, Donald Joseph. "Douglas Moore and His Orchestral Works." Ph.D. diss., Catholic University of America, 1972.

5361. Weitzel, Harold. "A Melodic Analysis of Selected Vocal Solos in the Operas of Douglas Moore." Ph.D. diss., New York University, 1971.

MOORE, UNDINE SMITH (1904–1989)

5362. Jones, John Robert Douglas. "The Choral Works of Undine Smith Moore: A Study of Her Life and Work." Ed.D. diss., New York University, 1980.

MORRIS, ROBERT (b. 1943)

5363. Hanninen, Dora A. "A General Theory for Context-Sensitive Music Analysis: Applications to Four Works for Piano by Contemporary American Composers." Ph.D. diss., University of Rochester, 1996. [*Canonic Variations*]

5364. Morris, Robert. "Some Remarks on *Odds and Ends*." PNM 35, no. 2 (1997): 237–45.

MOSCHELES, IGNAZ (1794–1870)

5365. Heussner, Ingeborg. "Formale Gestaltungsprinzipe bei Ignaz Moscheles." F-Engel/H: 155–65.

MOSER, ROLAND (b. 1943)

5366. Brotbeck, Roman. "Roland Mosers *Brentanophantasien*." DI 47 (1996): 24–27.

MOSOLOV, ALEKSANDR VASIL'YEVICH (1900–1973)

5367. Barsova, Inna. "Das Frühwerk von Alekandr Mosolov." JP 2 (1979): 117–69.

MOSS, LAWRENCE K. (b. 1927)

5368. Barkin, Elaine. "Lawrence K. Moss: Three Rilke Songs from *Das Studenbuch* (1963)." PNM 6, no. 1 (1967): 144–52.

5369. Kelley, Danny Roy. "The Solo Piano Works of Lawrence K. Moss." D.M.A. diss., Peabody Conservatory, 1985.

MUL, JAN (1911–1971)

5370. Mul, Jan. "Jan Mul: Sinfonietta." SS 12 (1962): 14–16.

MURAIL, TRISTAN (b. 1947)

5371. Anderson, Juliana. "Dans le contexte." Trans. Jean-Philippe Guye. ENT 8 (1989): 13–23.

5372. ———. "*De Sable* a *Vues aeriennes*: Le developpement d'un style." Trans. Louis Murail. ENT 8 (1989): 123–37.

5373. Dalbavie, Marc-André. "Notes sur *Gondwana*." ENT 8 (1989): 139–45.

5374. Humbertclaude, Eric. "Les modèles perceptuels par simulation instrumentale dan les œuvres de Tristan Murail." DI 11 (1987): 8–11.

5375. Murail, Tristan. "Spectra and Pixies." CMR 1, no. 1 (1984–1985): 157–70. [*Désintégrations*]

5376. Rose, François. "Introduction to the Pitch Organization of French Spectral Music." PNM 34, no. 2 (1996): 6–39.

5377. Schœller, Phillippe. "Mutation de l'écriture: *Éclat, Stria, Désintégrations*." INH 1 (1986): 197–208.

MUSGRAVE, THEA (b. 1928)

5378. Freedman, Deborah. "Thea Musgrave's Opera *Mary, Queen of Scots*." D.M.A. diss., Peabody Conservatory, 1985.

5379. McDonald, Kenneth Allan. "Dramatic Concerto Elements as Manifested in Thea Musgrave's Concerto for Orchestra." D.M.A. diss., University of Washington, 1979.

5380. McGregor, R. E. "An Analysis of Thea Musgrave's Compositional Style from 1958 to 1967." Ph.D. diss., Liverpool, 1980.

5381. Roma, Catherine. "The Choral Music of Thea Musgrave." ACR 31, no. 1 (1989): 13.

5382. ———. "The Choral Music of Thea Musgrave." MRF 2, no. 1 (1987): 23–67.

MUSORGSKY, MODEST PETROVICH (1839–1881)

Boris Godunov

5383. ASO 27–28 (1980).

5384. ASO 191 (1999).

5385. Carr, Maureen Ann. "Keys and Modes, Functions and Progressions in Mussorgsky's *Boris Godounov*." Ph.D. diss., University of Wisconsin, 1972.

5386. Forte, Allen. "Musorgsky as Modernist: The Phantasmic Episode in *Boris Gudunov*." MA 9, no. 1 (1990): 3–45.

5387. Hoffmann-Erbrecht, Lothar. "Die russischen Volklieder in Mussorgskis *Boris Godunov.*" F-Wiora: 458–65.

5388. John, Nicholas, ed. *Mussorgsky: Boris Godunov.* London: Calder, 1982.

5389. Le Roux, Maurice. *Moussorgski: Boris Godounov.* Paris: Aubier Montaigne, 1980.

5390. Oldani, Robert W. "New Perspectives on Mussorgsky's *Boris Godunov.*" Ann Arbor, Mich.: UMI Research Press, 1979.

5391. Taruskin, Richard. "Musorgsky vs. Musorgsky: The Versions of *Boris Godunov.*" NCM 8, no. 2 (1984): 91–118; 8, no. 3 (1985): 245–72.

5392. M-Taruskin. [Prologue; *see also* 5393]

5393. Van den Toorn, Pieter C. "Taruskin's Angle." ITO 10, no. 3 (1987): 27–46.

Khovanshchina

5394. ASO 57–58 (1983).

Nursery

5395. Agawu, V. Kofi. "Pitch Organizational Procedures in Mussorgsky's *Nursery.*" ITR 5, no. 1 (1981–1982): 23–59.

5396. Russ, Michael. "The Mysterious Thread in Mussorgsky's *Nursery.*" MA 9, no. 1 (1990): 47–65.

Piano Works (various; *see also Pictures at an Exhibition*)

5397. Angerer, Manfred. "Genrestück und Expressivität: Zu Mussorgskys kleinen Klavierstücken." OMZ 36 (1981): 298–303.

Pictures at an Exhibition

5398. Hübsch, Lini. *Modest Mussorgskij: Bilder einer Ausstellung.* Munich: Fink, 1990.

5399. Lehmann, Dieter. "Charakter und Bedeutung der 'Promenaden' in Mussorgskis *Bilder einer Ausstellung.*" SM 4 (1963): 235–55.

5400. Mayer-Rosa, Eugen. "Das 'Grosse Tor von Kiew' im Bild und in der Musik." ME 24 (1971): 117–22.

5401. McQuere, Gordon D. "Analyzing Musorgsky's 'Gnome.'" ITR 13, no. 1 (1992): 21–40.

5402. Perry, Simon. "Rummaging Through the 'Catacombs': Clues in Musorgsky's Pitch Notations." MA 14, nos. 2–3 (1995): 221–55. [Also: "Con mortuis in lingua mortua"]

5403. Puffett, Derrick. "A Graphic Analysis of Musorgsky's 'Catacombs.'" MA 9, no. 1 (1990): 67–78.

Songs (various; *see also* specific songs)

5404. Fox, Andrew Criddle. "Evolution of Style in the Songs of Modest Mussorgsky." Ph.D. diss., Florida State University, 1974.

5405. Lehmann, Dieter. "Satire und Parodie in den Liedern Modest Mussorgskis." BM 9 (1967): 105–11.

5406. Sydow, Brigitte. "Untersuchungen über die Klavierlieder M. P. Mussorgskis." Ph.D. diss., Göttingen, 1974.

5407. Weber-Bockholdt, Petra. *Die Lieder Mussorgskijs: Herkunft und Erscheinungsform.* Munich: Fink, 1982.

Sunless

5408. Friehl, Heather McMaster. "A Study of Mussorgsky's Use of Declamation in the Song Cycle *Without Sun.*" M.A. diss., Brigham Young University, 1978.

5409. Russ, Michael. "'Be Bored': Reading a Mussorgsky Song." NCM 20, no. 1 (1996): 27–45.

Various Works

5410. Josephson, Nors S. "Westeuropäische Stilmerkmale in der Musik Mussorgskis." BM 31, no. 2 (1989): 95–111.

5411. Leyda, Jay, and Sergie Bertensen, eds. *The Mussorgsky Reader.* New York: Norton, 1947.

5412. Taruskin, Richard. "Serov and Musorgsky." F-Abraham: 139–61.

5413. Will, Roy T. "A Stylistic Analysis of the Works of Moussorgsky." Ph.D. diss., University of Rochester, 1949.

MYASKOVSKY, NIKOLAY YAKOVLEVICH (1881–1950)

5414. Foreman, George Calvin. "The Symphonies of Nikolai Yakovlevich Miaskovsky." Ph.D. diss., University of Kansas, 1981.

MYHILL, JOHN (1923–1987)

5415. Hiller, Lejaren, and Charles Ames; graphics by Robert Franki. "Automated Composition: An Installation at the 1985 International Exhibition in Tsukuba, Japan." PNM 23, no. 2 (1984–1985) 196–215. [*Toy Harmonium*]

– N –

NANCARROW, CONLON (1912–1997)

5416. DeVisscher, Eric. "Temps, texture, et timbre chez Conlon Nancarrow." ENT 9 (1990): 35–49. [Various Studies for Player Piano]

5417. Fürst-Heidtmann, Monika. "Time Is the Last Frontier in Music: Les etudes pour player piano de Conlon Nancarrow." Trans. Simone Hardt and Vincent Barras. CC 6 (1986): 50–74.

5418. Gann, Kyle. *The Music of Conlon Nancarrow.* Cambridge: Cambridge Univeristy Press, 1995.

5419. Hocker, Jürgen. "Die Zeit als dritte Dimension: Zur Anatomie von Conlon Nancarrows Study No. 36 for Player Piano." MTX 31 (1989): 50–56.

5420. Jarvlepp, Jan. "Conlon Nancarrow's Study Nr. 27 for Player Piano Viewed Analytically." PNM 22 (1983–1984): 218–22.

5421. Phleps, Thomas. "'Complex, but Simple': Conlon Nancarrows tempo-dissonierende Boogie-Woogies und Canons für Player Piano." HJM 17 (2000): 177–208. [Studies for Player Piano Nos. 3, 21, 31]

5422. Thomas, Margaret. "Nancarrow's Canons: Projections of Temporal and Formal Structures." PNM 38, no. 2 (2000): 106–33. [Various Studies for Player Piano]

5423. ———. "Nancarrow's 'Temporal Dissonance': Issues of Tempo Proportions, Metric Synchrony, and Rhythmic Strategies." INT 14, no. 15 (2000–2001): 137–80. [Study for Player Piano No. 41, various other studies]

5424. Vayo, David. "Timbre in Nancarrow's Studies for Player Piano." CMF 5–6 (1993–1994): 1–4.

NAYLOR, BERNARD (1907–1986)

5425. Baerg, William John. "A Study of Selected Choral Works of Bernard Naylor." D.M.A. diss., Peabody Conservatory, 1979.

NEIDHÖFER, CHRISTOPH (b. 1967)

5426. Haefeli, Anton. "'Immer wieder ausbrechen': Ein Porträt des Komponisten Christoph Neidhöfer." DI 64 (2000): 28–35.

NEILL, BEN (b. 1957)

5427. Gann, Kyle. "Downtown Beats for the 1990s: Rhys Chatham, Mikel Rouse, Michael Gordon, Larry Polansky, Ben Neill." CMR 10, no. 1 (1994): 33–49.

NELSON, RON (b. 1929)

5428. Chesnutt, Rod. "An Analysis of Ron Nelson's Passacaglia." JBR 31, no. 1 (1995): 70–94.

5429. Cox, Dennis Keith. "Aspects of the Compositional Styles of Three Selected Twentieth-Century American Composers of Choral Music: Alan Hovhaness, Ron Nelson, and Daniel Pinkham." D.M.A. diss., University of Missouri, 1978.

NEWCATER, GRAHAM (b. 1941)

5430. Rorich, Mary Elizabeth. "Graham Newcater's Orchestral Works: Case Studies in the Analysis of Twelve-Tone Music." Ph.D. diss., University of the Witwatersrand, Johannesburg, 1985.

NIBLOCK, PHILL (b. 1933)

5431. Groneymer, Gisela. "Ein radikale Minimalist: Ein Porträt des amerikanischen Klang-Technikers Phill Niblock." MTX 12 (1985): 14–17.

NIELSEN, CARL (1865–1931)

5432. Fanning, David. *Nielsen: Symphony No. 5.* Cambridge: Cambridge University Press, 1997.

5433. Hiatt, James Smith. "Form and Tonal Organization in the Late Instrumental Works of Carl Nielsen." Ph.D. diss., Indiana University, 1986.

5434. Jones, William Isaac. "A Study of Tonality in the Symphonies of Carl Nielsen." Ph.D. diss., Florida State University, 1973.

5435. Konold, Wulf. "Carl Nielsens Violinkonzert Op. 33: Ein analytischer Versuch." F-Gudewill: 91–100.

5436. Miller, Mina Florence. "The Solo Piano Music of Carl Nielsen: An Analysis for Performance." Ph.D. diss., New York University, 1978.

5437. ———. "Some Thoughts upon Editing the Music of Carl Nielsen." CM 34 (1982): 64–74.

5438. Simpson, Robert. *Carl Nielsen, Symphonist.* Rev. ed. London: Kahn & Averill, 1979.

5439. Thomas, Stephen R. "Carl Nielsen's *Piano Music for Young and Old,* Opus 53: Miniature Etudes in Musicianship." TCM 6, no. 5 (1999): 8–16.

5440. Waterhouse, John C. G. "Nielsen Reconsidered." MT 106 (1965): 425–27, 514–17, 593–95.

5441. Wilson, Dean C. "An Analytical and Statistical Study of the Harmony in Carl Nielsen's Six Symphonies." Ph.D. diss., Michigan State University, 1967.

NIXON, ROGER (b. 1921)

5442. Nixon, Roger. "*Fiesta del Pacifico.*" JBR 3, no. 1 (1966–1967): 29–32.

5443. ———. "*Reflections.*" JBR 4, no. 1 (1967–1968): 53–60.

NOBRE, MARLOS (b. 1939)

5444. Nobre, Maria Luiza Corker. "*Sonancias III,* Opus 49 de Marlos Nobre." LAMR 15, no. 2 (1994): 226–43.

NONO, LUIGI (1924–1990)

A Carlo Scarpa architetto, ai suoi infiniti possibili

5445. Drees, Stefan. "Transformation des Todes: Luigi Nonos *A Carlo Scarpa, architetto, ai suoi infiniti possibili* per orchestra a microintervali." MTX 69–70 (1997): 24–35.

5446. Huber, Nicolaus A. "Nuclei and Dispersal in Luigi Nono's *A Carlo Scarpa architetto, ai suoi infiniti possibili* per orchestra a microintervalli." CMR 18, no. 2 (1999): 19–35.

A Pierre

5447. Davismoon, Stephen. "Marking Time." CMR 18, no. 1 (1999): 81–98.

Al gran sole carico d'amore

5448. Schomerus, Ute. "'Lenin 71–17': Zur Verknüpfung historischer Kontexte in Luigi Nonos *Al gran sole carico d'amore.*" HJM 17 (2000): 259–77.

5449. Vogt, Harry. "*Al gran solo* carico d'autocitazione, oder, zwischen Patchwork und Pasticcio: Zur dramaturgisch-musikalischen Gestaltung der 2. szenischen Aktion *Al gran sole carico d'amore* von Luigi Nono." N 5 (1984–1985): 125–39.

Canti di vita e d'amore: Sul ponte di Hiroshima

5450. Irvine, John. "Luigi Nono's *Canti di vita e d'amore*: New Phases of Development 1960–62." CMR 18, no. 2 (1999): 87–109.

Canto sospeso

5451. Bailey, Kathryn. "'Work in Progress': Analysing Nono's *Il canto sospeso.*" MA 11, nos. 2–3 (1992): 279–334.

5452. Feneyrou, Laurent. "*Il canto sospeso* de Luigi Nono: Esquisse analytique." ANM 31 (1993): 53–63.

5453. Fox, Christopher. "Luigi Nono and the Darmstadt School: Form and Meaning in the Early Works (1950–1959)." CMR 18, no. 2 (1999): 111–30.

5454. Hercher, Christiane. "Ein Geheimnis des L. N.: Zum V. Satz des von Luigi Nono." F-Knepler, vol. 3: 29–45.

5455. Raiss, Hans-Peter. "Luigi Nono: *Il canto sospeso* (1956)." M-Vogt: 287–91.

5456. Stockhausen, Karlheinz. "Music and Speech." R 6 (1964): 40–64.

5457. M-Stockhausen: 157–65.

Con Luigi Dallapiccola

5458. Davismoon, Stephen. "Marking Time." CMR 18, no. 1 (1999): 81–98.

Fabbrica illuminata

5459. Flammer, Ernst Helmuth. "Form und Gehalt: Eine Analyse von Luigi Nonos *La fabbrica illuminata.*" Melos/NZM 3 (1977): 401–11.

5460. Gruhn, Wilfried. "Didaktische Reflexionen zu Luigi Nonos *La fabbrica illuminata.*" MB 9 (1977): 285–91.

Fragmente-Stille, an Diotima

5461. Frobenius, Wolf. "Luigi Nonos Streichquartett *Fragmente-Stille, an Diotima.*" AM 54, no. 3 (1997): 177–93.

5462. Haas, Georg Friedrich. "*Fragmente-Stille, an Diotima*: Indagini iconografiche sul quartetto per archi di Luigi Nono." ANL 9 (1992): 3–19.

5463. Müller, Gerhard. "*Fragmente-Stille, an Diotima* per quartetto d'archi von Luigi Nono: Eine Werkbetrachtung." MG 40 (1990): 352–60.

5464. Nielinger-Vakil, Carola. "Quiet Revolutions: Hölderlin Fragments by Luigi Nono and Wolfgang Rihm." ML 81, no. 2 (2000): 245–74.

Incontri

5465. Piencikowski, Robert. "Règlement de comptes: *Incontri* de Luigi Nono." DI 15 (1988): 14–17.

5466. Stenzl, Jürg. "Nonos *Incontri.*" MELOS 39 (1972): 150–53.

5467. M-Wennerstrom.

Intolleranza 1960/1971

5468. Gilbert, Janet Monteith. "Dialectic Music: An Analysis of Luigi Nono's *Intolleranza.*" D.M.A. diss., University of Illinois, 1979.

Polifonica–monodia–ritmica

5469. Fox, Christopher. "Luigi Nono and the Darmstadt School: Form and Meaning in the Early Works (1950–1959)." CMR 18, no. 2 (1999): 111–30.

Prometeo

5470. Jeschke, Lydia. *Prometeo: Geschichtskonzeptionen in Luigi Nonos Hörtragödie.* Stuttgart: F. Steiner, 1997.

5471. Oehlschlägel, Reinhard. "Klanginstallation und Wahrnehmungskomposition: Zur Nuova Versione von Luigi Nonos *Prometeo.*" MTX 12 (1985): 10–13.

Sofferte onde serene

5472. Davismoon, Stephen. "Marking Time." CMR 18, no. 1 (1999): 81–98.

Varianti

5473. Kolisch, Rudolf. "Nonos *Varianti.*" MELOS 24 (1957): 292–96.

Variazioni canoniche sulla serie dell'Op. 41 di A. Schönberg

5474. Fox, Christopher. "Luigi Nono and the Darmstadt School: Form and Meaning in the Early Works (1950–1959)." CMR 18, no. 2 (1999): 111–30.

Various Works

5475. Carvalho, Mário Vieira de. "Towards Dialectic Listening: Quotation and Montage in the Work of Luigi Nono." CMR 18, no. 2 (1999): 37–85.

5476. Gentilucci, Armando. "La tecnica corale di Luigi Nono." RIM 2 (1967): 111–29.

5477. Kramer, Jonathan. "The Fibonacci Series in Twentieth-Century Music." JMT 17 (1973): 110–48.

5478. Lachenmann, Helmut. "Luigi Nono oder Rückblick auf die serielle Musik." MELOS 38 (1971): 225–30.

5479. Poné, Gundaris. "Webern and Luigi Nono: The Genesis of a New Compositional Morphology and Syntax." PNM 10, no. 2 (1972): 111–19.

5480. Riede, Bernd. *Luigi Nonos Kompositionen mit Tonband: Ästhetik des musikalischen Materials—Werkanalysen—Werkverzeichnis.* Munich: Katzbichler, 1986.

5481. Spangemacher, Friedrich. *Luigi Nono: Die elektronische Musik; Historische Kontext, Entwicklung, Kompositionstechnik.* Regensburg: Bosse, 1983.

5482. Stenzl, Jürg, ed. *Luigi Nono: Texte; Studien zu seiner Musik.* Zurich: Atlantis, 1975.

NORDHEIM, ARNE (b. 1931)

5483. Rickards, Guy. "Shadows and Acclamations: The Cello Music of Arne Nordheim." TEMPO 181 (1992): 8–14.

NØRGÅRD, PER (b. 1932)

5484. Beyer, Anders. "Ausdruck und Konstruktion: Mehrdeutigkeit im dritten Satz von Per Nørgårds Violinkonzert *Helle Nacht.*" MTX 50 (1993): 37–46.

5485. Nørgård, Per. "Inside a Symphony." NW 8 (1975): 4–16. [Symphony No. 3]

NØRHOLM, IB (b. 1931)

5486. Andersen, Mogens. "Tonaliteter: Om struktur og betydning i Ib Nørholms symfonier og om tonalitet som fænomen og begreb." DAM 23 (1995): 39–62.

NUFFEL, JULES VAN (1883–1953)

5487. Chase, Robert Allen. "Jules van Nuffel and His Music." Ph.D. diss., Columbia University Teachers College, 1978.

NUNES, EMMANUEL (b. 1941)

5488. Rafael, João. "The Fertile Development: An Analysis of *Wandlungen* of Emmanuel Nunes." EXT 8, no. 2 (1997): 33–55.

5489. Szendy, Peter, ed. *Emmanuel Nunes.* Paris: IRCAM: 1998.

NYMAN, MICHAEL (b. 1944)

5490. Millard Daugherty, Florence. "Narrative and Nonnarrative Structures in the Film Music of Michael Nyman." Ph.D. diss., Florida State University, 1997.

NYSTEDT, KNUT (b. 1915)

5491. Spicher, Linda Krakowski. "An Analysis of Selected Choral Works by Knut Nystedt." M.A. thesis, University of Iowa, 1974.

NYSTROEM, GÖSTA (1890–1966)

5492. Christenson, Peter Louis. "The Orchestral Works of Gösta Nystroem: A Critical Study." Ph.D. diss., University of Washington, 1961.

– O –

OFFENBACH, JACQUES (1819–1880)
5493. ASO 25 (1980). [*Les contes d'Hoffmann*]
5494. ASO 66 (1984). [*La Périchole*]
5495. ASO 125 (1989). [*La belle Hélène*]
5496. ASO 185 (1998). [*Orphée aux enfers*]
5497. Lyon, Raymond, and Louis Saguer. *Les contes d'Hoffmann: Étude et analyse.* Paris: Mellottée, 1948.

OHANA, MAURICE (1913–1992)
5498. Marcel, Odile. "'L'Ibérisme' de Maurice Ohana." RM 351–52 (1982): 11–26.
5499. Prost, Christine. "*Minotaure aux miroirs*: Analyse." RM 391–93 (1986): 129–47.
5500. ———. "Poétique musicale de Maurice Ohana: Statisme et dynamisme." RM 391–93 (1986): 107–27.
5501. Reibel, Guy. "La musique de vocale et chorale de Maurice Ohana." RM 391–93 (1986): 71–85.
5502. Roberts, Paul. "La musique de piano de Mauric Ohana." RM 391–93 (1986): 27–50.

OLIVEROS, PAULINE (b. 1932)
5503. Madsen, Pamela A. "Toward a Feminine Form in Music: Pauline Oliveros's *Rose Moon*." CMF 5–6 (1993–1994): 5–14.
5504. Von Gunden, Heidi. *The Music of Pauline Oliveros.* Metuchen, N.J.: Scarecrow, 1983.
5505. ———. "The Theory of Sonic Awareness in *The Greeting* by Pauline Oliveros." PNM 19, no. 2 (1980–1981): 409–15.

ORFF, CARL (1895–1982)
Antigonae
5506. Ptak, Milos O. "Current Chronicle." MQ 36 (1950): 105–9.
5507. Stäblein, Bruno. "Schöpferische Tonalität: Zum Grossaufbau von Orffs *Antigonae*." M 6 (1962): 145–48.

Carmina Burana
5508. Schlager, Karlheinz. "Carl Orff und das Mittelalter." F-Göller: 405–18.

De temporum fine comoedia
5509. Thomas, Werner, and Rudolf Klein. "Zu Carl Orffs *De temporum fine comoedia*." OMZ 28 (1973): 290–300.

Gisei, das Opfer
5510. Revers, Peter. "Carl Orff und der Exotismus: Zur Ostasienrezeption in seiner fruhen *Oper Gisei, das Opfer*." F-Floros/60: 233–59.

Prometheus desmotes
5511. Kaufmann, Harold. "Carl Orffs Musik heute: An Beispielen aus *Prometheus* verdeutlicht." NZM 134 (1973): 421–26.

Various Works
5512. Helm, Everett. "Carl Orff." MQ 41 (1955): 285–304.
5513. Jahnke, Sabine. "Materialien zu einer Unterrichtssequenz: Des Antonius von Padua Fischpredigt bei Orff-Mahler-Berio." MB 5 (1973): 615–22.
5514. Keller, Wilhelm. "Wie komponiert Karl Orff?" OMZ 17 (1962): 431–43.
5515. Kiekert, Ingeborg. *Die musikalische Form in den Werken Carl Orffs.* Regensburg: Bosse, 1957.
5516. Liess, Andreas. "Die musiké techni Carl Orffs." M 9 (1955): 305–9.
5517. Seifert, Wolfgang. "Die humanistische Botschaft eines zeitgemässen Unzeitgemässen: Kleines und grosses Welttheater." NZM 143, no. 5 (1982): 4–15.

ORNSTEIN, LEO (1893–2002)
5518. Darter, Thomas Eugene, Jr. "The Futurist Piano Music of Leo Ornstein." D.M.A. diss., Cornell University, 1979.

ORR, C. W. (1893–1976)
5519. M-Curtis.
5520. Rawlins, Joseph Thomas. "The Songs of Charles Wilfred Orr with Special Emphasis on His Houseman Settings." D.M.A. diss., Louisiana State University, 1972.

ORREGO-SALAS, JUAN (b. 1919)
5521. Curtis, Brandt B. "Rafael Alberti and Chilean Composers." D.M.A. diss., Indiana University, 1977. [*El alba del Alhelí*].

ORTHEL, LÉON (1905–1985)
5522. Geraedts, Jaap. "Léon Orthel: Scherzo No. 2." SS 25 (1965): 20–23.
5523. Wouters, Jos. "Léon Orthel: *Piccola sinfonia.*" SS 6 (1961): 20–25.

OTTE, HANS (b. 1926)
5524. Baucke, Ludolf. "'Ich mein's immer sehr wörtlich . . .': Notizen zu Hans Ottes *philharmonie.*" MTX 17 (1986): 21–24.
5525. ———. "In Augenblicken Verweilen: Anmerkungen zu Hans Ottes *Das Buch der Klänge.*" N 5 (1984–1985): 140–45.
5526. Oehlschlägel, Reinhard. "Wahrnehmungsritual: Zu Hans Ottes *arbeit.*" MTX 17 (1986): 47–51.

OTTERLOO, WILLEM VAN (1907–1978)
5527. Flothuis, Marius. "Willem van Otterloo: Sinfonietta for 16 Wind Instruments." SS 16 (1963): 20–23.

– P –

PAGH-PAAN, YOUNGHI (b. 1945)
5528. Pagh-Paan, Younghi. "Unterwegs: Reflexionen über meine Tätigkeit als Komponisten." N 4 (1983–1984): 20–37.
5529. Rosch, Charlotte. "Die Komposition *Flammenzeichen* von Younghi Pagh-Paan: Eine musikalische Begegnung mit einem 'ganz anderen Deutschland.'" HJM 15 (1998): 387–96.

PAINE, JOHN KNOWLES (1839–1906)
5530. Schmidt, John Charles. "The Life and Works of John Knowles Paine." Ph.D. diss., New York University, 1979.

PAISIELLO, GIOVANNI (1740–1816)
5531. Hunt, Jno Leland. "The Life and Keyboard Works of Giovanni Paisiello (1740–1816)." Ph.D. diss., University of Michigan, 1973.
5532. Lippmann, Friedrich. "'Il mio ben quando verrà': Paisiello creatore di una nuova semplicità." STU 19, no. 2 (1990): 385–405. [Various operas]
5533. Russo, Francesco Paolo. "I libretti di Giambattista Lorenzi e le opere di Giovanni Paisiello: Da *Il furbo malaccorto* a *Le vane gelosie* (1767–1790)." STU 20, no. 2 (1991): 267–315.

PALMER, ROBERT (b. 1915)
5534. Austin, William. "The Music of Robert Palmer." MQ 42 (1956): 35–50.
5535. M-Chihara.

PANUFNIK, ANDRZEJ (1914–1991)
5536. Hall, Barrie. "Andrzej Panufnik and His *Sinfonia sacra.*" TEMPO 71 (1964–1965): 14–22.
5537. Panufnik, Andrezj. "About My *Autumnal Music* and *Universal Prayer.*" TEMPO 96 (1971): 11–15.
5538. Truscott, Harold. "The Achievement of Andrzej Panufnik." TEMPO 163 (1987): 7–12.
5539. ———. "Andrzej Panufnik." TEMPO 55–56 (1960): 13–18.
5540. Walsh, Stephen. "The Music of Andrjez Panufnik." TEMPO 111 (1974): 7–14.

PAPINEAU-COUTURE, JEAN (1916–2000)
5541. Beckwith, John. "Jean Papineau-Couture." CMJ 3, no. 2 (1958): 4–20.
5542. Dixon, Gail. "The *Pièces concertantes* Nos. 1, 2, 3, and 4 of Jean Papineau-Couture." SMUWO 9 (1984): 93–123.

PARKER, HORATIO (1863–1919)
5543. Kearns, William Kay. "Horatio Parker (1863–1919): A Study of His Life and Music." Ph.D. diss., University of Illinois, 1965.
5544. ———. "Horatio Parker's Oratorios: A Measure of the Changing Genre at the Turn of the Century." IAMR 11, no. 2 (1991): 65–73.

PARRIS, ERICK
5545. Parris, Erick. "An Analysis of Piece for Solo Cello: A Semiotic Approach." EXT 9, no. 2 (1999): 1–19.

PARROTT, IAN (b. 1916)
5546. Thomas, A. F. Leighton. "A Note on Parrott's *Jubilate Deo.*" *Welsh Music* 3, no. 3 (Summer 1968): 20–23.

PÄRT, ARVO (b. 1935)
5547. Bradshaw, Susan. "Arvo Pärt." CT 26 (1983): 25–28.

5548. Brauneiss, Leopold. "Die Rationalität des Heiligen Geistes: Analytische Annäherungen an Arvo Pärt." M-Brauneiss: 9–30. [*Berliner Messe, Summa*]

5549. Chiesa, Silvana. "Un progetto di analisi stilistica dello Stabat mater di Arvo Pärt." ANL 18 (1995): 12–21.

5550. Eichert, Randolph G. "Satztechnik, Form und Harmonik in der Musik von Arvo Pärt." MTH 14, no. 1 (1999): 47–63.

5551. Fischer, Kurt von. "Zur *Johannes-Passion* von Arvo Pärt." KJ 75 (1991): 133–38.

5552. Hess, Frauke M., and Christina Frink. "Die tönende Stille der Glocken: Arvo Pärts Tintinnabuli-Stil; Emanation oder Technik?" NZM 158, no. 3 (1997): 38–41. [*Cantus in memoriam Benjamin Britten*]

5553. Mellers, Wilfrid. "Arvo Pärt, God, and Gospel: *Passio Domini Nostri Iesu Christi Secundum Iohannem* (1982)." CMR 12, no. 2 (1995): 35–48. [*St. John Passion*]

5554. Quinn, Peter. "Out With the Old and In With the New: Arvo Pärt's Credo." TEMPO 211 (2000): 16–20.

5555. Ramaut-Chevassus, Béatrice. "La postmodernité musicale: Points forts d'un phénomène aux multiples facettes (Pärt, Bryars, Adams)." ANM 33 (1998): 94–103. [*Fratres*]

PARTCH, HARRY (1901–1974)

5556. Earls, Paul. "Harry Partch: Verses in Preparation for *Delusion of the Fury.*" Y 3 (1967): 1–32.

5557. Gilmore, William Robert. "Harry Partch: The Early Vocal Works, 1930–1933." Ph.D. diss., Queen's University of Belfast, 1992.

5558. ———. "On Harry Partch's *Seventeen Lyrics by Li Po.*" PNM 30, no. 2 (1992): 22–58.

5559. Hackbarth, Glenn Allen. "An Analysis of Harry Partch's *Daphne of the Dunes.*" D.M.A. diss., University of Illinois, 1979.

5560. Maltz, Richard. "Microtonal Techniques in the Music of Harry Partch and Ben Johnson." MRF 7 (1992): 14–37. [*And on the Seventh Day Petals Fell in Petaluma*]

5561. Stahnke, Manfred. "Zwei Blumen der reinen Stimmung im 20. Jahrhundert: Harry Partch und Gérard Grisey." HJM 17 (2000): 369–89.

5562. Woodbury, Arthur. "Harry Partch: Corporeality and Monophony." S 1, no. 2 (1967): 91–93.

PARTOS, OEDOEN (1907–1977)

5563. Bahat, Avner. "Traditional Elements and Dodecaphonic Technique in the Music of Oedoen Partos (1907–1977)." ISM 1 (1978): 175–91.

5564. Ron, Yohanan. "Expression of the Twelve-Tone Row in the Works of Oedoen Partos and Josef Tal." OM 11 (1993–1994): 81–91. [String Quartet No. 2]

PAYNE, ANTHONY (b. 1936)

5565. Bradshaw, Susan, and Richard Rodney Bennett. "Anthony Payne and His *Paean.*" TEMPO 100 (1972): 40–44.

PAZ, JUAN CARLOS (1901–1972)

5566. Sargent, David H. "The Twelve-Tone Row Technique of Juan Carlos Paz." Y 11 (1975) 82–105.

5567. Tabor, Michelle. "Juan Carlos Paz: A Latin American Supporter of the International Avant Garde." LAMR 9, no. 2 (1988): 207–32.

PEIXINHO, JORGE (1940–1995)

5568. MacKay, John. "Concerto for Harp and Orchestra by Jorge Peixinho: Commentary with Graphic Analysis." EXT 8, no. 2 (1997): 9–15.

PELES, STEPHEN (b. 1950)

5569. M-Hanninen. [Phantasy]

PENDERECKI, KRZYSZTOF (b. 1933)

Anaklasis

5570. Huber, Alfred. "Pendereckis *Anaklasis* für Streicher und Schlagzeuggruppen." MELOS 38 (1971): 87–91.

5571. Müller, Karl-Joseph. "Krzysztof Penderecki (1933): *Anaklasis* (1959–1960) für Streicher und Schlagzeuggruppen." M-Zimmerschied: 215–33.

Capriccio for Violin and Orchestra

5572. M-Cope: 78–81.

De natura sonoris

5573. Albers, Bradley Gene. "*De natura sonoris I* and *II* by Krzysztof Penderecki: A Comparative Analysis." D.M.A. diss., University of Illinois, 1978.

5574. Butcher, Eric A. "Quantitative Parameters of Spatial Dynamics in Musical Space." ITR 18, no. 1 (1997): 1–24. [*De natura sonoris I]*

5575. M-Roberts.

Devils of Loudun

5576. Jahnke, Sabine. "Musikdramatischer Exorzismus in Pendereckis Oper *Die Teufel von Loudun.*" MB 7 (1975): 615–17.

5577. Kellner, Hans. "Devils and Angels: A Study of the Demonic in Three Twentieth-Century Operas." JMR 2 (1976–1978): 255–72.

Dimensions of Time and Silence

5578. Müller, Karl-Joseph. "Pendereckis Musik im 'mobilen Netz trigonometrischer Punkte.'" MB 7 (1975): 622–29.

Fluorescencje

5579. M-Bersano.

Passio et mors domini nostri Jesu Christi secundum Lucam

5580. Kaack, Brunhilde. "Pendereckis Zwölftonreihe." M 29 (1975): 9–15.

5581. Müller, Karl-Joseph. *Informationen zu Pendereckis Lukas-Passion.* Frankfurt am Main: M. Diesterweg, 1973.

5582. Robinson, Ray, and Allen Winold. *A Study of the Penderecki St. Luke Passion.* Celle: Moeck; Totowa, N.J.: European American Music Distributors, 1982.

5583. Schuler, Manfred. "Das B-A-C-H Motiv in Pendereckis *Lukaspassion.*" KJ 65 (1981): 105–11.

5584. ———. "Tonale Phänomene in Pendereckis *Lukaspassion.*" Melos/NZM 1 (1976): 457–60.

5585. Stroh, Wolfgang Martin. "Penderecki und das Hören erfolgreicher Musik." MELOS 37 (1970): 452–60.

5586. M-Vogt: 358–71.

Pittsburgh Overture

5587. Tyra, Thomas. "An Analysis of Penderecki's *Pittsburgh Overture.*" JBR 10, no. 1 (1973–1974): 37–38; 10, no. 2 (1973–1974): 5–12.

Polskie requiem

5588. Chłopick, Regina. "Krysztof Penderecki's *The Polish Requiem.*" MTEA 3 (1994): 23–26.

5589. Delisi, Daniel J. "Penderecki's *Polish Requiem*: Some Notes on Texture and Form." ACR 30, no. 1 (1988): 14–16.

Polymorphia

5590. Meister, Christopher. "Convergence as a Mode of Musical Organization: Comparing Vareses's *Hyperprism* and Penderecki's *Polymorphia.*" EXT 7, no. 1 (1994): 110–28.

Psalmy Dawida

5591. Müller, Karl-Joseph. "Krzysztof Penderecki (1933): Aus den *Psalmen Davids* für gemischten Chor und Instrumentalensemble (1958)." M-Zimmerschied: 201–14.

St. Luke Passion. *See Passio et mors domini nostri Jesu Christi secundum Lucam*

Stabat mater

5592. Unverricht, Hubert. "Penderecki's Stabat mater." KJ 75 (1991): 127–31.

Threnody "To the Victims of Hiroshima"

5593. Butcher, Eric A. "Quantitative Parameters of Spatial Dynamics in Musical Space." ITR 18, no. 1 (1997): 1–24.

5594. Gruhn, Wilfried. "Strukturen und Klangmodelle in Pendereckis *Threnos.*" MELOS 38 (1971): 409–11.

5595. Reiter, R. Burkhardt. "Influences of the Arch Form in Relation to the Properties of Pitch Structure and Formal Design Found within Krystof Penderecki's *Threnody for the Victims of Hiroshima.*" MTEA 6 (1997): 19–24.

Unterbrochene Gedanke

5596. Jammermann, Marco. "Zu Krzysztof Pendereckis Streichquartettstück *Der unterbrochene Gedanke* (1988)." MTH 14, no. 1 (1999): 33–44.

Various Works

5597. Brauneiss, Leopold. "Kontinuität und Wandel im Werk Krzysztof Pendereckis." OMZ 47, no. 10–11 (1993): 530–36.

5598. Robinson, Ray. "Krysztof Penderecki's Orchestra." MTEA 7 (1999): 17–26.

5599. Schuler, Manfred. "Traditionelle Satztechniken im geistlichen Schaffen Pendereckis." KJ 75 (1991): 119–25.

5600. Schwinger, Wolfram. *Penderecki: Begegnung, Lebensdaten, Werkkommentare.* Stuttgart: Deutsche Verlags-Anstalt, 1979.

5601. Zielinski, Tadeusz A. "Der einsame Weg des Krzysztof Penderecki." MELOS 29 (1962): 318–23.

PENTLAND, BARBARA (1912–2000)

5602. Eastman, Sheila, and Timothy McGee. *Barbara Pentland.* Toronto: University of Toronto Press, 1983.

5603. McGee, Timothy J. "Barbara Pentland in the 1950s: String Quartet No. 2 and *Symphony for Ten Parts*." SMUWO 9 (1984): 133–52.

5604. Turner, Robert. "Barbara Pentland." CMJ 2, no. 4 (1958): 15–26.

PÉPIN, CLERMONT (b. 1926)

5605. Schuster, John. "Compositional Process in Clermont Pépin's *Quasars*." SONUS 12, no. 2 (1992): 28–43. [Symphony No. 3]

PEPPING, ERNST (1901–1981)

Liederbuch nach Gedichten von Paul Gerhard

5606. Blankenburg, Walter. "Ernst Peppings *Liederbuch nach Gedichten von Paul Gerhart* in geschichtlicher Beleuchtung." F-Pepping: 147–57.

Organ Works

5607. Hochreither, Karl. "Ernst Peppings Toccata und Fuge *Mitten wir im Leben sind*." F-Pepping: 116–46.

5608. Manicke, Dietrich. "Ernst Peppings Orgelwerke." F-Pepping: 105–15.

5609. Weeks, William B. "The Use of the Chorale in the Organ Works of Ernst Pepping." D.M.A. diss., University of Arizona, 1970.

Piano Works

5610. Blume, Friedrich. "Ernst Pepping: Sonatine für Klavier." F-Pepping: 46–47.

5611. Hamm, Walter. *Studien über Ernst Peppings drei Klaviersonaten*. Würzburg: K. Triltsch, 1955.

Sacred Choral Works

5612. Adrio, Adam. "Zu Ernst Peppings *A-capella-Messe*." M 5 (1951): 203–10.

5613. Grote, Gottfried. "Der Weg zum *Passionsbericht des Matthaus* von Ernst Pepping: Strukturelle Untersuchungen." F-Pepping: 57–83.

5614. Poos, Heinrich. "Ernst Peppings Liedmotetten nach Weisen der böhmischen Brüder." MK 51 (1981): 67–82, 177–89.

5615. ———. "Ernst Peppings Prediger-Motette." MK 38 (1968): 176–82.

5616. Witte, Gerd. "Die *Weihnachtsgeschichte des Lukas* in der Fassung Ernst Peppings: Ein Beitrag zum Verhältnis von Sprache und Musik in Ernst Peppings Vokalmusik." F-Pepping: 84–104.

Secular Choral Works

5617. Poos, Heinrich. "Ernst Peppings Chorlied 'Anakreons Grab': In Memoriam." NZM 142 (1981): 252–58. [*Heut und ewig*]

5618. ———. *Ernst Peppings Liederkreis für Chor nach Gedichten von Goethe "Heut und Ewig": Studien zum Personstil Peppings*. Berlin: Merseburger, 1965.

Various Works

5619. Adrio, Adam. "Junge Komponisten: 4. Ernst Pepping." F-Pepping: 38–45.

5620. ———. "Die Welsen der bömischen Brüder im Werk Ernst Peppings." F-Fellerer/70: 23–34.

5621. Baumgärtel, Lothar. "Lebendige Aussage: Ernst Pepping (geboren 12–9–1901)." F-Mauersberger: 127–34.

5622. Dürr, Alfred. "Gedanken zum Kirchen-Musikschaffen Ernst Peppings." MK 31 (1961): 145–72.

PERLE, GEORGE (b. 1915)

5623. Carrabre, Thomas Patrick. "Twelve-Tone Tonality and the Music of George Perle." Ph.D. diss., City University of New York, 1993.

5624. Custer, Arthur. "Current Chronicle." MQ 53 (1967): 252–54. [Wind Quintet No. 2]

5625. Kraft, Leo. "The Music of George Perle." MQ 57 (1971): 444–65.

5626. Perle, George. "Symmetry, the Twelve-Tone Scale, and Tonality." CMR 6, no. 2 (1992): 81–96. [Sinfonietta I]

5627. Rosenhaus, Steven L. "Harmonic Motion in George Perle's Wind Quintet No. 4." Ph.D. diss., New York University, 1995.

5628. Saylor, Bruce. "Current Chronicle: A New Work by George Perle." MQ 61 (1975): 471 75. [*Songs of Praise and Lamentation*]

5629. Swift, Richard. "A Tonal Analog: The Tone-Centered Music of George Perle." PNM 21 (1982–1983): 257–84.

5630. Weinberg, Henry. "The Music of George Perle." ACA 10, no. 3 (1962): 6–11.

PERSICHETTI, VINCENT (1915–1987)

5631. Ashizawa, Theodore Fumio. "The Choral Music of Vincent Persichetti (b.1915)." D.M.A. diss., University of Washington, 1977.

5632. Barnard, Jack Richard. "The Choral Music of Vincent Persichetti: A Descriptive Analysis." Ph.D. diss., Florida State University, 1974.

5633. Evett, Robert. "The Music of Vincent Persichetti." JR 2, no. 2 (1955): 15–30.
5634. Farrell, Laurence. "Vincent Persichetti's Piano Sonatas from 1943 to 1965." Ph.D. diss., University of Rochester, 1976.
5635. Hilfiger, John Jay. "A Comparison of Some Aspects of Style in the Band and Orchestra Music of Vincent Persichetti." Ph.D. diss., University of Iowa, 1985.
5636. M-Hines.
5637. M-Jeter. [Sonata for Two Pianos]
5638. Mullins, Joe Barry. "A Comparative Analysis of Three Symphonies for Band." JBR 6, no. 1 (1969–1970): 17–28. [Symphony for Band (Symphony No. 6)]
5639. Persichetti, Vincent. "Symphony No. 6 for Band." JBR 1, no. 1 (1964–1965): 17–20.

PETERSON-BERGER, WILHELM (1867–1942)
5640. Scriven, Marianne Sjoren. "The Art Songs of Wilhelm Peterson-Berger." D.M.A. diss., University of Missouri, 1973.

PETRASSI, GOFFREDO (b. 1904)

Concertos for Orchestra Nos. 1–6
5641. Vlad, Roman. "Goffredo Petrassi Orchesterkonzerte." MELOS 26 (1959): 174–78.

Estri
5642. Weissman, John S. "Current Chronicle." MQ 61 (1975): 588–94.

Inventions (Piano)
5643. Stone, Olga. "Petrassi's Eight Inventions for Piano." MR 33 (1972): 21–27.

Piano Concerto
5644. Stone, Olga. "Goffredo Petrassi's Concerto for Pianoforte and Orchestra: A Study of Twentieth-Century Neo-Classic Style." MR 39 (1978): 240–57.

Serenata
5645. Bortolotto, Mario. "Zwei neue Werke von Goffredo Petrassi." MELOS 30 (1963): 114–17.

Sonata da camera
5646. Stone, Olga. "Petrassi's *Sonata da camera* for Harpsichord and Ten Instruments: A Study of Twentieth-Century Linear Style." MR 37 (1976): 283–94.

String Quartet
5647. Bortolotto, Mario. "Zwei neue Werke von Goffredo Petrassi." MELOS 30 (1963): 114–17.

Tre per sette
5648. Weissman, John S. "Current Chronicle." MQ 61 (1975): 588–94.

Various Works
5649. Bonelli, Anthony Eugene. "Serial Techniques in the Music of Goffredo Petrassi: A Study of His Compositions from 1950 to 1959." Ph.D. diss., University of Rochester, 1970.
5650. Bortolotto, Mario. "Petrassi Stil 1960." MELOS 33 (1966): 48–50.
5651. Pinzauti, Leonardo. "Petrassi Sacro." CHI 3 (1966): 297–303.
5652. Weissman, John S. "Goffredo Petrassi and His Music." MR 22 (1961): 198–211.

PETTERSSON, ALLAN (1911–1980)
5653. Revers, Peter. "'Blühende Weizenwelten', erwachsen am 'Baum des Martyriums': Zur Neruda-Rezeption in Allan Pettersons 12. Symphonie *Die Toten auf dem Marktplatz* und der Kantate *Vox humana*." HJM 17 (2000): 241–57.

PFITZNER, HANS (1869–1949)

Arme Heinrich
5654. Hirtler, Franz. *Hans Pfitzners "Armer Heinrich" in seiner Stellung zur Musik des ausgehender 19. Jahrhunderts.* Würzburg: Triltsch, 1940.

Cello Concerto, Op. 42
5655. Osthoff, Wolfgang. "Jugendwerk, Früh-, Reife-, und Alterstil: Zum langsamen Satz des Cellokonzerts in A-Moll Op. 52 von Hans Pfitzner." AM 33 (1976): 89–118.

Fantasie, Op. 56
5656. Mohr, Wilhelm. "Hans Pfitzners Phantasie für Orchester Opus 56." MHPG 10 (1962): 4–12.

Lethe
5657. Ringger, Rolf Urs. "*Lethe*: Hans Pfitzners Orchesterlied Op. 37." MHPG 43 (1981): 91–98.

Lieder, Op. 29
5658. Mohr, Wilhelm. "Von Pfitzners 'Abbitte' in einer Sammlung von Hölderlin-Vertongungen." MHPG 24 (1969): 8–10.

Palestrina
5659. Fleury, Albert. "Historische und stilgeschichtliche Probleme in Pfitzners *Palestrina*." F-Osthoff/70: 229–40.
5660. Henderson, Donald Gene. "Hans Pfitzner's *Palestrina*: A Twentieth-Century Allegory." MR 31 (1970): 32–42.
5661. Kleinknecht, Friedrich. "Der Kontrapunkt in Pfitzners *Palestrina*." MHPG 41 (1981): 20–27.
5662. Osthoff, Wolfgang. "Eine neue Quelle zu Palestrinazitat und Palestrinasatz in Pfitzners musikalischer Legende." F-Osthoff/80: 185–209.
5663. Rectanus, Hans. "Die musikalische Zitate in Hans Pfitzners *Palestrina*." F-Pfitzner: 22–27.
5664. Stein, Herbert von. "Äusserungen Hans Pfitzners über eine thematische Analyse zu *Palestrina*." MHPG 28 (1972): 2–11.

Sextet, Op. 55
5665. Mohr, Wilhelm. "Hans Pfitzners Sextett Opus 55." MHPG 7 (1960): 2–12.

Songs, Op. 53
5666. Vogel, Johann Peter. "Pfitzners drei Männerchöre Op. 53." M 41, no. 6 (1987): 514–19.

Songs (various; *see also* specific collections of Lieder and songs)
5667. Diez, Werner. *Hans Pfitzners Lieder: Versuch einer Stilbetrachtung.* Regensburg: Bosse, 1968.
5668. Habelt, Hans-Jürgen. "Hans Pfitzners Lieder auf Texte von Heinrich Heine." MHPG 46 (1984): 3–17.
5669. Lindlar, Heinrich. *Hans Pfitzner Klavierlied.* Würzburg: K. Triltsch, 1940.

String Quartet (1886)
5670. Mohr, Wilhelm. "Pfitzners Streichquartett in D-Moll (1886): Eine Analyse." M 27 (1973): 483–85.

String Quartet No. 1
5671. Pfitzner, Hans. "Streichquartett in D-Dur, Op. 13." MHPG 53 (1993): 51–55.

String Quartet No. 2
5672. Vogel, Johann Peter. *Hans Pfitzner: Streichquartett Cis-Moll Op. 36.* Munich: Fink, 1991.

Studies, Op. 51
5673. Medek, Tilo. "Gedanken zu den Sechs Studien Op. 51 für Klavier von Hans Pfitzner." MHPG 56 (1996): 34–41.

Violin Concerto, Op. 34
5674. Osthoff, Wolfgang. "Pfitzner in der aktuellen Musikliteratur XVI: Eine Analyse des Violinkonzerts." MHPG 53 (1993): 35–40.

Various Works
5675. Abendroth, Walter. *Deutsche Musik der Zeitwende: Eine Kulturphilosophische Persönlichkeitstudie über Anton Bruckner und Hans Pfitzner.* Hamburg: Haneseatische Verlagsanstalt, 1937.
5676. Henderson, Donald Gene. "Hans Pfitzner: The Composer and His Instrumental Works." Ph.D. diss., University of Michigan, 1963.
5677. Seebohm, Reinhard. "'Eine leichte Art des Ernstes': Betrachtungen zu Pfitzners späten Instrumentalwerken." MHPG 49 (1988): 27–40.
5678. ———. "Pfitzners Verhältnis zu Joseph Haydn." MHPG 34 (1975): 34–54.
5679. Truscott, Harold. "Pfitzner's Orchestral Music." TEMPO 104 (1973): 2–10.

PHILIPP, FRANZ (1890–1972)
5680. Rahner, Hugo Ernst. [Essay on various works.] F-Philipp: 124–44.
5681. Steinert, Bernhard. "*Zwischen Zeit und Ewigkeit*." F-Philipp: 103–9.

PIERNÉ, GABRIEL (1863–1937)
5682. Luck, Ray. "An Analysis of Three Variation Sets for Piano by Bizet, d'Indy and Pierné." D.M.A. diss., Indiana University, 1978.

PIJPER, WILLEM (1894–1947)
5683. Clardy, Mary Karen King. "Compositional Devices of Willem Pijper (1894–1947) and Henk Badings (b. 1907) in Two Selected Works: Pijper's Sonata per flauto e pianoforte (1925) and Badings' Concerto for Flute and Wind Symphony Orchestra (1963)." D.M.A. diss., North Texas State University, 1980.

5684. Dickinson, Peter. "The Instrumental Music of Willem Pijper (1894–1947)." MR 24 (1963): 327–32.
5685. Hoogerwerf, Frank W. "The Chamber Music of Willem Pijper (1894–1947)." Ph.D. diss., University of Michigan, 1974.
5686. ———. "The String Quartets of Willem Pijper." MR 38 (1977): 44–64.
5687. Ringer, Alexander L. "Willem Pijper and the Netherlands School of the Twentieth Century." MQ 41 (1955): 427–45.
5688. Ritsema, Herbert. "The Germ Cell Principle in the Works of Willem Pijper (1894–1947)." Ph.D. diss., University of Iowa, 1974.
5689. Ryker, Harrison Clinton. "The Symphonic Music of Willem Pijper (1894–1947)." Ph.D. diss., University of Washington, 1972.
5690. Wouters, Jos. "Willem Pijper." SS 30 (1967): 1–38.

PINKHAM, DANIEL (1923–2006)
5691. Corzine, Michael Loyd. "The Organ Works of Daniel Pinkham." D.M.A. diss., University of Rochester, 1979.
5692. Cox, Dennis Keith. "Aspects of the Compositional Styles of Three Selected Twentieth-Century American Composers of Choral Music: Alan Hovhaness, Ron Nelson, and Daniel Pinkham." D.M.A. diss., University of Missouri, 1978.
5693. Johnson, Marlowe W. "The Choral Music of Daniel Pinkham." Ph.D. diss., University of Iowa, 1968.
5694. ———. "The Choral Writing of Daniel Pinkham." ACR 8, no. 4 (1966): 1, 12, 14–16.

PISK, PAUL A. (1893–1990)
5695. Collins, Thomas William. "The Instrumental Music of Paul A. Pisk." D.M.A. diss., University of Missouri, 1972.
5696. Kennen, Kent. "Paul A. Pisk." ACA 9, no. 1 (1959): 7–16.

PISTON, WALTER (1894–1976)
5697. Archibald, Bruce. "Current Chronicle." MQ 59 (1973): 121–25. [Flute Concerto]
5698. Austin, William. "Piston's Fourth Symphony: An Analysis." MR 16 (1955): 120–37.
5699. Carter, Elliott. "Walter Piston." MQ 32 (1946): 354–75.
5700. Donahue, Robert Laurence. "Comparative Analysis of Phrase Structure in Selected Movements of the String Quartets of Béla Bartók and Walter Piston." D.M.A. diss., Cornell University, 1964.
5701. Pollack, Howard Joel. "Walter Piston and His Music." Ph.D. diss., Cornell University, 1981.
5702. Taylor, Clifford. "Walter Piston: For His Seventieth Birthday." PNM 3, no. 1 (1964): 102–14.

PLATZ, ROBERT H. P. (b. 1951)
5703. Allende-Blin, Juan. "Eine Musik, die ständig unterwegs ist: *Chlebnikov* von Rober H.P. Platz." MTX 17 (1986): 14–16.
5704. Morawska-Büngeler, Marietta. "Wie der Klang zum Raum wird: Zu Requiem und *Andere Räume* von Robert H. P. Platz." MTX 75 (1998): 21–24.
5705. Platz, Robert H. P. "Mehr als nur Noten." DBNM 20 (1994): 87–94.
5706. ———. "Über *Schwelle* (1973–1978)." N 1 (1980): 87–94.
5707. Toop, Richard. "Immer weiter: 'Formal Polyphonie' und Robert H.P. Platz' Donaueschinger Zyklus." MAS 2, no. 6 (1998): 61–76. [*Andere Räume, Echo II, Nerv II, Turm/Weiter*]
5708. Van den Hoogen, Eckhardt. "Raumform: Formpolyphonie von Robert H. P. Platz." M 5 (1984–1985): 220–25.

POLANSKY, LARRY (b. 1954)
5709. Gann, Kyle. "Downtown Beats for the 1990s: Rhys Chatham, Mikel Rouse, Michael Gordon, Larry Polansky, Ben Neill." CMR 10, no. 1 (1994): 33–49.
5710. Polansky, Larry. "*Bedhaya Guthrie/Bedhaya Sadra* for Voices, Kemanak, Melody Instruments, and Accompanimental Javanese Gamelan." PNM 34, no. 1 (1996): 28–55.

POLDOWSKI (1879–1932)
5711. Brand, Myra Jean. "Poldowski (Lady Dean Paul): Her Life and Her Song Settings of French and English Poetry." D.M.A. diss., University of Oregon, 1979.

PONCHIELLI, AMILCARE (1834–1886)
5712. Polignano, Antonio. "Costanti stilistiche ed elementi di drammaturgia musicale nelle due versioni del finale d'atto della *Gioconda* di Ponchielli (1876–1879)." RIM 27 (1992): 327–50.

PONSE, LUCTOR (1914–1998)
5713. Wouters, Jos. "Luctor Ponse: *Concerto da camera* with Solo Bassoon." SS 19 (1964): 32–34.

POOLE, GEOFFREY (b. 1949)
5714. Burn, Andrew. "Geoffrey Poole: An Introductory Note on His Music." TEMPO 145 (1983): 12–18.

POPE, STEPHEN TRAVIS (b. 1955)
5715. Pope, Stephen Travis. "Producing *Kombination XI*: Using Modern Hardware and Software Systems for Composition." LMJ 2, no. 1 (1992): 23–28.

PORCELIJN, DAVID (b. 1947)
5716. Vermeulen, Ernst. "David Porcelijn: *Cybernetica* for Orchestra." SS 49 (1971–1972): 13–22.

PORTER, COLE (1891–1964)
5717. Siebert, Lynn Laitman. "Cole Porter: An analysis of Five Musical Comedies and a Thematic Catalogue of the Complete Works." Ph.D. diss., City University of New York, 1975.

PORTER, QUINCY (1897–1966)
5718. Frank, Robert Eugene. "Quincy Porter: A Survey of the Mature Style and a Study of the Second Sonata for Violin and Piano." D.M.A. diss., Cornell University, 1973.

PORTER, TIM
5719. Head, Raymond. "Tim Porter's *The Irish Blackbird*." TEMPO 155 (1985): 36–38.

POULENC, FRANCIS (1899–1963)
Choral Works
5720. Almond, Frank Ward. "Melody and Texture in the Choral Works of Francis Poulenc." Ph.D. diss., Florida State University, 1970.
5721. Browning, John. "Poulenc and Text." TCM 2, no. 9 (1995): 8–9. [Works with Latin texts]
5722. Daniel, Keith. "The Choral Music of Francis Poulenc." ACR 24, no. 1 (1982): 5–36.
5723. Ebensberger, Gary Lee. "The Motets of Francis Poulenc." Ph.D. diss., University of Texas, 1970.

Concert champêtre
5724. Blay, Philippe. "Francis Poulenc: Le *Concert champêtre*." ANM 21 (1990): 37–44.

Dialogues des Carmélites
5725. ASO 52 (1983).

Organ Concerto
5726. Shaw, Richard E. "The Areas of Tonicization in Francis Poulenc's *Concerto en sol mineur pour orgue, orchestre à cordes et timbales*." MTEA 3 (1994): 45–57.

Piano Works
5727. Davies, Laurence. "The Piano Music of Poulenc." MR 33 (1972): 194–203.
5728. Ehrler, Hanno. *Untersuchungen zur Klaviermusik von Francis Poulenc, Arthur Honegger, und Darius Milhaud.* Tutzing: Schneider, 1990.
5729. Nelson, Jon Ray. "The Piano Music of Francis Poulenc." Ph.D. diss., University of Washington, 1978.
5730. Romain, Edwin Philip. "A Study of Francis Poulenc's Fifteen Improvisations for Piano Solo." D.M.A. diss., University of Southern Mississippi, 1978.

Songs
5731. Hargrove, Guy Arnold, Jr. "Francis Poulenc's Settings of Guillaume Apollinaire and Paul Eluard." Ph.D. diss., University of Iowa, 1971.
5732. Weide, Marion. "Style and Imagery in the Song Cycles of Poulenc." Ph.D. diss., University of California, Santa Barbara, 1976.
5733. Wood, Vivian Poates. "Francis Poulenc's Songs for Voice and Piano." Ph.D. diss., Washington University, 1973.

Various Works
5734. Brandt, Regina. "Die religiöse Musik von Francis Poulenc: Eine Werkübersicht." KJ 73 (1989): 97–117.
5735. Daniel, Keith W. *Francis Poulenc: A Study of His Artistic Development and His Musical Style.* Ann Arbor, Mich.: UMI Research Press, 1982.
5736. ———. "A Preliminary Investigation of Pitch-Class Set Analysis in the Atonal and Polytonal Works of Milhaud and Poulenc." ITO 6, no. 6 (1981–1983): 22–48.
5737. Poulin, Pamela L. "Three Styles in One: Poulenc's Chamber Works for Wind Instruments." MR 50, nos. 3–4 (1989): 270–80.
5738. ———. "Three Stylistic Traits in Poulenc's Chamber Works for Wind Instruments." Ph.D. diss., University of Rochester, 1983.
5739. Werner, Warren Kent. "The Harmonic Style of Francis Poulenc." Ph.D. diss., University of Iowa, 1966.

POUSSEUR, HENRI (b. 1929)

5740. Decroupet, Pascal. "À la recherche de l'harmonie perdue: Regards analytiques sur le 'Prologue dans le ciel' de *Votre Faust* de Henri Pousseur." RBM 43 (1989): 87–100.

5741. Jost, Peter. "Komponieren mit Schumann: Henri Pousseurs *Dichterliebesreigentraum.*" MTH 15, no. 2 (2000): 121–36.

5742. Lee, Marjorie Huffman. "The Piano Cmpositions of Henri Pousseur." D.M.A. diss., University of Maryland, 1977.

5743. Metzger, Heinz-Klaus, and Rainer Riehn, eds. *Henri Pousseur.* Munich: Text + Kritik, 1990.

5744. Pousseur, Henri. "Der Jahrmarkt von *Votre Faust.*" BOGM (1968–1969): 25–40.

5745. ———. "Une mémoire obstinément prospective." RBM 43 (1989): 21–34. [*Mnémosyne doublement obstinée*]

5746. Witts, Dick. "Pousseur's *L'effacement du Prince Igor.*" TEMPO 122 (1977): 10–17.

5747. ———. "Report on Henri Pousseur." CT 13 (1976): 13–22. [*Die Erprobung des Petrus Hebraicus*]

POWELL, MEL (1923–1998)

5748. Melbinger, Timothy Gordon. "An Analysis of Mel Powell's *Piano Trio '94.*" Ph.D. diss., Brandeis University, 1999.

5749. Sollberger, Harvey. "Haiku Settings." PNM 3, no. 1 (1964): 147–55.

5750. Thimmig, Leslie. "The Music of Mel Powell." MQ 55 (1969): 31–44.

PRAEGER, FERDINAND (1815–1891)

5751. Ryberg, James Stanley. "Four String Quartets by Ferdinand Praeger: An Analytical Study." Ph.D. diss., Northwestern University, 1978.

PRÉVOST, ANDRÉ (1934–2001)

5752. Loranger, Pierre. "André Prévost: *Évanescence.*" CCM 4 (1972): 168–72.

5753. Prévost, André. "Formulation et conséquences d'une hypothèse." CCM 1 (1970): 67–79. [*Terre des hommes*]

PROKOFIEV, SERGEY (1891–1953)

Cello Concerto, Op. 58

5754. Henderson, Lyn. "A Comparative Study of Prokofiev's Cello Concerto, Op. 58 and Sinfonia concertante, Op. 125." MR 52, no. 2 (1991): 123–36.

Fiery Angel, Op. 37

5755. Henderson, Lyn. "How *The Flaming Angel* Became Prokofiev's Third Symphony." MR 40 (1979): 49–52.

5756. Kellner, Hans. "Devils and Angels: A Study of the Demonic in Three Twentieth-Century Operas." JMR 2 (1976–1978): 255–72.

5757. Loos, Helmut. "Form und Ausdruck bei Prokofjew: Die Oper *Der feurige Engel* und die Dritte Symphonie." MF 43, no. 2 (1990): 107–24.

5758. Swarsenski, Hans. "Sergeii Prokofieff: *The Flaming Angel.*" TEMPO 39 (1956): 16–27.

Flute Sonata, Op. 94

5759. Kaufman, Rebecca S. "Tonal Determinants in Prokofiev's Sonata for Flute and Piano, Op. 94." TSP 5 (1988): 1–13.

Gambler, Op. 24

5760. Robinson, Harlow. "Dostoevsky and Opera: Prokofiev's *The Gambler.*" MQ 70 (1984): 96–106.

Love for Three Oranges, Op. 33

5761. ASO 133 (1990).

Operas (various; *see also* specific operas)

5762. McAllister, Margaret Notman. "The Operas of Sergei Prokofiev." Ph.D. diss., New Hall, Cambridge, 1970.

Piano Concertos

5763. Henderson, Lyn. "Prokofiev's Fifth Piano Concerto." MR 47, no. 4 (1986–1987): 267–82.

5764. ———. "Prokofiev's Fouth Piano Concerto." MR 51, no. 1 (1990): 46–55.

Piano Sonatas (various; *see also* specific piano sonatas)

5765. Chaikin, Lawrence. "The Prokofieff Sonatas: A Psychograph." PQ 86 (1974): 8–19.

5766. Kinsey, David Leslie. "The Piano Sonatas of Serge Prokofiev: A Critical Study of the Elements of Their Style." M.A. thesis, Columbia University, 1959.

5767. Vlahcevic, Sonia Klosek. "Thematic-Tonal Organization in the Piano Sonatas of Sergei Prokofiev." Ph.D. diss., Catholic University of America, 1975.

Piano Sonata No. 7, Op. 83

5768. Karl, Gregory. "Organic Methodologies and Non-Organic Values: The *Andante caloroso* of Prokofiev's Seventh Piano Sonata." JMR 18, no. 1 (1988): 31–62.

5769. M-Mathes.

Piano Sonata No. 8, Op. 84

5770. Brown, Malcolm. "Prokofiev's Eighth Piano Sonata." TEMPO 70 (1964): 9–15.

Piano Works (various; *see also* specific piano works)

5771. Ashley, Patricia Ruth. "Prokoviev's Piano Music: Line, Chord and Key." Ph.D. diss., University of Rochester, 1963.

5772. Forner, Johannes. "Tradition und veränderte Struktur: Gestaltungsprinzipien im Klavierschaffen des jungen Prokofjew (geb. am 23.4.1891)." MG 16 (1966): 273–79.

5773. Thibodeau, Michael James. "An Analysis of Selected Piano Works by Sergey Prokofiev Using the Theories of B. L. Yavorsky." Ph.D. diss., Florida State University, 1993.

Romeo and Juliet

5774. Stephenson, Ken. "Melodic Tendencies in Prokofiev's *Romeo and Juliet.*" CMS 37 (1997): 109–28.

5775. ———. "Painting the Phantom Text: Hidden Correspondences between Prokofiev's *Romeo i Dzhul'yetta* and Shakespeare's *Romeo and Juliet.*" MTEA 5 (1996): 12–22.

Symphonies (various; *see also* specific symphonies)

5776. Brown, Malcolm. "The Symphonies of Sergei Prokofiev." Ph.D. diss., Florida State University, 1967.

5777. Streller, Friedbert. "Die frühen Sinfonien Sergej Prokofjews: Ein Beitrag zu semantischer Analyse von Musik." Ph.D. diss., Berlin, 1972.

Symphony No. 3, Op. 44

5778. Henderson, Lyn. "How *The Flaming Angel* Became Prokofiev's Third Symphony." MR 40 (1979): 49–52.

5779. Loos, Helmut. "Form und Ausdruck bei Prokofjew: Die Oper *Der feurige Engel* und die Dritte Symphonie." MF 43, no. 2 (1990): 107–24.

Symphony No. 5, Op. 100

5780. Austin, William W. "Prokofiev's Fifth Symphony." MR 17 (1956): 205–20.

Symphony No. 7, Op. 131

5781. Lockspeiser, Edward. "Prokofieff's Seventh Symphony." TEMPO 37 (1955): 24–27.

Symphony-Concerto, Op. 125

5782. Henderson, Lyn. "A Comparative Study of Prokofiev's Cello Concerto, Op. 58 and *Sinfonia concertante,* Op. 125." MR 52, no. 2 (1991): 123–36.

***Things in Themselves,* Op. 45**

5783. Eidschun, Robert Walter. "Sergei Prokofiev's 'Chose en soi b' (Op. 45b): Analysis." Ph.D. diss., University of Rochester, 1998.

Violin Concertos

5784. Henderson, Lyn. "The Violin Concertos of Prokofiev." MR 54, nos. 3–4 (1993): 257–64.

Violin Sonata No. 2, Op. 94 bis. *See* Flute Sonata, Op. 94

***War and Peace,* Op. 91**

5785. ASO 194 (2000).

Various Works

5786. Bass, Richard. "Prokofiev's Technique of Chromatic Displacement." MA 7/ (1988): 197–214.

5787. Berka, Zdenka. "Themes of Prokofiev's Early Period: A Melodic Analysis." M.M. thesis, University of Alberta, 1976.

5788. Cholopov, Juri N. "Der russische Neoklassizismus bei Sergej Prokof'ev und Dimitrij Šostakovič." JP 3 (1980): 170–99.

5789. Cholopowa, W. "Zur Rhythmik Prokofjews." MG 20 (1970): 372–81.

5790. Jahn, Renate. "Zum 70. Geburtstag Serge Prokofjews: Vom 'Spieler' zur 'Erzählung vom wahren Mensch.'" MG 11 (1961): 232–38.

5791. Kaufman, Rebecca Sue. "Expanded Tonality in the Late Chamber Works of Sergei Prokofiev." Ph.D. diss., University of Kansas, 1987.

5792. Minturn, Neil Borden. "An Integral Approach to the Music of Sergei Prokofiev Using Tonal and Set Theoretic Analytical Techniques." Ph.D. diss., Yale University, 1988.

5793. ———. *The Music of Sergei Prokofiev.* New Haven, Conn.: Yale University Press, 1997.

5794. MZ 5 (1953). [Special issue]

5795. Samuel, Claude. *Prokofiev.* Paris: Seuil, 1960.

5796. Streller, Friedbert. *Serge Prokofiev.* Leipzig: Breitkopf & Härtel, 1960.

5797. Swarsenski, Hans. "Prokofieffs Orchesterwerke." MZ 5 (1953): 41–49.

5798. ———. "Prokofieffs Orchestral Works." TEMPO 11 (1949): 10–25.

PUCCINI, GIACOMO (1858–1924)

Bohème

5799. ASO 20 (1979).

5800. Groos, Arthur. *Giacomo Puccini: La bohème.* Cambridge: Cambridge University Press, 1986.

5801. John, Nicholas, ed. *Puccini: La bohème.* London: Calder, 1983.

Fanciulla del West

5802. ASO 165 (1995).

Gianni Schicchi

5803. ASO 82 (1985).

Madama Butterfly

5804. ASO 56 (1983).

5805. Atlas, Allan W. "Crossed Stars and Crossed Tonal Areas in Puccini's *Madama Butterfly.*" NCM 14, no. 2 (1990): 186–96.

5806. Berg, Karl Georg Maria. "Das Liebesduett aus *Madame Butterfly*: Überlegungen zur Szenendramaturgie bei Giacomo Puccini." MF 38 (1985): 183–94.

5807. John, Nicholas, ed. *Puccini: Madam Butterfly.* London: Calder, 1984.

5808. Krohn, Ilmari. "Puccini: *Butterfly.*" F-Scheurleer: 181–90.

Manon Lescaut

5809. ASO 137 (1991).

Suor Angelica

5810. Greenwald, Helen M. "Verdi's Patriarch and Puccini's Matriarch: 'Through the Looking-Glass and What Puccini Found There.'" NCM 17, no. 3 (1994): 220–36.

Tosca

5811. ASO 1 (1977).

5812. Burton, Deborah Ellen. "An Analysis of Puccini's *Tosca*: A Heuristic Approach to the Unifying Elements of the Opera." Ph.D. diss., University of Michigan, 1995.

5813. Carner, Mosco. *Giacomo Puccini: Tosca.* New York: Cambridge University Press, 1985.

5814. Courtin, Michèle. *"Tosca" de Giacomo Puccini.* Paris: Aubier, 1983.

5815. John, Nicholas, ed. *Puccini: Tosca.* London: Calder, 1982.

5816. M-Leibowitz/F: 259–74.

5817. Schoffman, Nachum. "Puccini's *Tosca*: An Essay in Wagnerism." MR 53, no. 4 (1992): 268–90.

5818. Winterhoff, Hans-Jürgen. *Analytische Untersuchungen zu Puccinis "Tosca."* Regensburg: Bosse, 1973.

Trittico

5819. ASO 190 (1999).

5820. Leukel, Jürgen. *Studien zu Puccinis "Il Trittico: Il Tabarro–Suor Angelica–Gianni Schicchi."* Munich: Katzbichler, 1983.

Turandot

5821. ASO 33 (1981).

5822. Girardi, Michele. "*Turandot*: Il futuro interrotto del melodramma italiano." RIM 17 (1982): 155–81.

5823. John, Nicholas, ed. *Puccini: Turandot.* London: Calder, 1984.

5824. Revers, Peter. "Analytische Betrachtungen zu Puccinis *Turandot.*" OMZ 34 (1979): 342–51.

Various Works

5825. Ashbrook, William. *The Operas of Puccini.* Ithaca, N.Y.: Cornell University Press, 1985.

5826. Carner, Mosco. "Debussy and Puccini." M-Carner: 139–47.

5827. Christen, Norbert. *Giacomo Puccini: Analytische Untersuchungen der Melodik, Harmonik und Instrumentation.* Hamburg: Verlag der Musikalienhandlung Wagner, 1978.

5828. D'Ecclesiis, Rev. Gennaro A. "The Aria Technique of Giacomo Puccini: A Study in Musico-Dramatic Style." Ph.D. diss., New York University, 1961.

5829. Valente, Richard. *The Verismo of Giacomo Puccini: From Scapigliatura to Expressionism.* Ann Arbor: Braun-Blumfield, 1971.

– R –

RACHMANINOFF, SERGE (1873–1943)

Aleko

5830. Norris, Geoffrey. "Rakhmaninov's Student Opera." MQ 59 (1973): 441–48.

All-Night Vigil, **Op. 37**

5831. Loftis, Eric Kenneth. "An Investigation of the Textural Contrasts in Sergei Rachmaninov's *Night Vigil,* Opus 37." Ph.D. diss., University of Southern Mississippi, 1980.

5832. Prussing, Stephen Henry. "Compositional Techniques in Rachmaninoff's Vespers, Op. 37." Ph.D. diss., Catholic University of America, 1980.

Piano Concertos (various; *see also* specific piano concertos)

5833. Coolidge, Richard. "Architectonic Technique and Innovation in the Rakhmaninov Piano Concertos." MR 40 (1979): 176–216.

Piano Concerto No. 1, Op. 1

5834. Butzbach, Fritz. *Studien zum Klavierkonzert Nr. 1 Fis-Moll Op. 1 von Rachmaninov.* Regensburg: Bosse, 1979.

Piano Concerto No. 3, Op. 30

5835. Karl, Gregory. "Cyclic Structure in Two Works of Rakhmaninov." MRF 3, no. 1 (1988): 5–22.

5836. Yasser, Joseph. "The Opening Theme of Rachmaninoff's Third Piano Concerto and Its Liturgical Prototype." MQ 55 (1969): 313–28.

Piano Concerto No. 4, Op. 40

5837. Redepenning, Dorothea. "'Das undurchdringliche Schweigen erstarrter Erinnerungen': Anmerkungen zu Sergej Rachmaninovs Werken der Emigration." HJM 13 (1995): 253–69.

Preludes, Op. 32

5838. Baca, Richard. "A Style Analysis of the Thirteen Preludes, Opus 32, of Sergei Rachmaninoff." D.M.A. diss., Peabody Conservatory, 1975.

5839. Rummenhöller, Peter. "Zum Warencharakter in der Musik: Analyse von Sergej Rachmaninovs Prelude Op. 32, Nr. 1." ZM 4, no. 2 (1973): 30–36.

Songs, Op. 38

5840. Simpson, Anne. "Dear Re: A Glimpse into the Six Songs of Rachmaninoff's Opus 38." CMS 24, no. 1 (1984) 97–106.

Symphonic Dances, **Op. 45**

5841. Burba, Otto-Jürgen. "Rückblick und Abschied: Thematisch-motivische Prozesse in Rachmaninows später Symphonik." M 49, no. 3 (1995): 154–58.

5842. Redepenning, Dorothea. "'Das undurchdringliche Schweigen erstarrter Erinnerungen': Anmerkungen zu Sergej Rachmaninovs Werken der Emigration." HJM 13 (1995): 253–69.

Symphony No. 1, Op. 13

5843. Collins, Dana Livingston. "Form, Harmony, and Tonality in S. Rakhmaninov's Three Symphonies." Ph.D. diss., University of Arizona, 1988.

5844. Drude, Matthias. "Entdeckung Rachmaninow: Versuch über die 1. Sinfonie." M 49, no. 3 (1995): 159–62.

Symphony No. 2, Op. 27

5845. Collins, Dana Livingston. "Form, Harmony, and Tonality in S. Rakhmaninov's Three Symphonies." Ph.D. diss., University of Arizona, 1988.

5846. Karl, Gregory. "Cyclic Structure in Two Works of Rakhmaninov." MRF 3, no. 1 (1988): 5–22.

5847. Rubin, David. "Transformations of the *Dies Irae* in Rachmaninov's Second Symphony." MR 23 (1962): 132–36.

Symphony No. 3, Op. 44

5848. Burba, Otto-Jürgen. "Rückblick und Abschied: Thematisch-motivische Prozesse in Rachmaninows später Symphonik." M 49, no. 3 (1995): 154–58.

5849. Collins, Dana Livingston. "Form, Harmony, and Tonality in S. Rakhmaninov's Three Symphonies." Ph.D. diss., University of Arizona, 1988.

5850. Redepenning, Dorothea. "'Das undurchdringliche Schweigen erstarrter Erinnerungen': Anmerkungen zu Sergej Rachmaninovs Werken der Emigration." HJM 13 (1995): 253–69.

Various Works

5851. Walsh, Stephen. "Sergei Rachmaninoff 1873–1943." TEMPO 195 (1973): 12–21.

5852. Yasser, Joseph. "Progressive Tendencies in Rachmaninoff's Music." MU 2 (1948–1949): 1–22.

RADULESCU, HORATIU (b. 1942)

5853. Heaton, Roger. "Horatiu Radulescu: *Sound Plasma.*" CT 26 (1983): 23–24.

RAFF, JOACHIM (1822–1882)

5854. Wiegandt, Matthias. "Shakespeare, Mendelssohn, Raff–und ein verkappter 'Sommernachtstraum'?" MTH 9, no. 3 (1994): 195–209. [Symphony No. 9]

RANDALL, JAMES K. (b. 1929)

5855. Capalbo, Marc. "Charts." PNM 19, no. 2 (1980–1981): 309–33. [*8va, Greek Nickle Pieces, Mead, Sound Scroll*]

RANDS, BERNARD (b. 1934)

5856. Boss, Jack. "The 'Continuous Line' and Structural and Semantic Text-Painting in Bernard Rands's *Canti d'Amor.*" PNM 36, no. 2 (1998): 143–85.

RASMUSSEN, KARL AAGE (b. 1947)

5857. Sørensen, Søren Møller. "Ny musik, men ikke modernisme: To unge komponister i de danske 1970ere–Karl Aage Rasmussen og Hans Abrahamsen." DAM 26 (1998): 35–57.

RATHAUS, KAROL (1895–1954)

5858. Schwarz, Boris. "Karol Rathaus." MQ 41 (1955): 481–95.

RAUTAVAARA, EINOJUHANI (b. 1928)

5859. Sivuoja-Gunaratnam, Anne. "Nature Versus Culture in Einojuhani Rautavaara's *Thomas.*" ITR 13, no. 2 (1992): 89–106.

RAVEL, MAURICE (1875–1937)

Berceuse sur le nom de Gabriel Fauré

5860. Mies, Paul. "Widmungsstücke mit Buchstaben-Motto bei Debussy und Ravel." SZM 25 (1962): 363–68.

Bolero

5861. Gut, Serge. "Le phénomène répétitif chez Maurice Ravel: De l'obsession à l'annihilation incantatoire." IRASM 21, no. 1 (1990): 29–46.

Daphnis et Chloé

5862. Sannemüller, Gerd. *Maurice Ravel: Daphnis und Chloé, 1. und 2. Suite.* Munich: Fink, 1983.

5863. M-Schultz: 58–60.

Enfant et les sortilèges

5864. ASO 127 (1990).

5865. Green, Marcia S. "Ravel and Krenek: Cosmic Music Makers." CMS 24, no. 2 (1984): 96–104.

5866. Kaminsky, Peter. "Of Children, Princesses, Dreams, and Isomorphisms: Text-Music Transformation in Ravel's Vocal Works." MA 19, no. 1 (2000): 29–68.

5867. Lassus, Marie-Pierre. "Ravel, l'enchanteur." ANM 26 (1992): 40–47.

5868. Prost, Christine. "Maurice Ravel: *L'enfant et les sortilèges.*" ANM 21 (1990): 65–81.

Gaspard de la nuit

5869. Hirsbrunner, Theo. "*Gaspard de la nuit* von Maurice Ravel." AM 44, no. 4 (1987): 268–81.

5870. Pohl, Norma Davis. "*Gaspard de la nuit* by Maurice Ravel: A Theoretical and Performance Analysis." Ph.D. diss., Washington University, 1978.

Heure espagnole

5871. Clifton, Keith E. "Maurice Ravel's *L'heure espagnole*: Genesis, Sources, Analysis." Ph.D. diss., Northwestern University, 1998.

Jeux d'eau

5872. Light, Edwin Hamilton. "Ravel's *Jeux d'eau.*" D.M.A. diss., Boston University, 1983.

Ma mère l'oye

5873. Sannemüller, Gerd. "*Ma mère l'oye* von Maurice Ravel: Fünf Stücke für Kinder." MB 6 (1974): 174–78.

Mélodies populaires grecques

5874. Gut, Serge. "Permanence et transformation des structures mélodiques grecques antiques: Dans les *Mélodies populaires grecques* de Maurice Ravel." RDM 84, no. 2 (1998): 263–76.

Menuet sur le nom d'Haydn

5875. Mahlert, Ulrich. "Gebannte Improvisation und Maskentanz: Die 'Haydn'-Stücke von Claude Debussy und Maurice Ravel." MB 19, no. 12 (1987): 912–19.

5876. Mies, Paul. "Widmungsstücke mit Buchstaben-Motto bei Debussy und Ravel." SZM 25 (1962): 363–68.

Miroirs

5877. Howat, Roy. "Debussy, Ravel, and Bartók: Towards Some New Concepts of Form." ML 58 (1977): 285–93. [*Oiseaux tristes*]

5878. ———. "Ravel, Rhythm, and Form." MSA 16 (1993): 39–47. [*Alborada del gracioso*]

Piano Concerto

5879. M-Pfann.

5880. Prost, Christine. "Maurice Ravel: Le concerto en sol pour piano et orchestre; Analyse descriptive et problématique musicale." ANM 11 (1988): 78–83.

Piano Concerto for the Left Hand

5881. Dorival, Jérôme. "Ravel: Trois regards sur le *Concerto pour la main gauche*." ANM 33 (1998): 79–91.

5882. Kefferstan, Christine. "Maurice Ravel's *Concerto pour la main gauche*." PQ 145 (1989): 43–47.

5883. M-Pfann.

Piano Works (various; *see also* specific piano works)

5884. Keil, Werner. *Untersuchungen zur Entwicklung des frühen Klaveristils von Debussy und Ravel*. Wiesbaden: Breitkopf & Härtel, 1982.

Poèmes de Stéphane Mallarmé

5885. Ette, Wolfram, and Eckehard Kim. "Surgi de la croupe et du bond: Stéphane Mallarmé–Maurice Ravel." MAS 1, nos. 1–2 (1997): 35–74.

5886. Gronquist, Robert. "Ravel's *Trois poèmes de Stéphane Mallarmé*." MQ 64 (1978): 507–23.

5887. Hirsbrunner, Theo. "Zu Debussys und Ravels Malarmé-Vertonungen." AM 35 (1978): 81–103.

Rapsodie espagnole

5888. Sannemüller, Gerd. "Die *Rapsodie espagnole* von Maurice Ravel." MB 11 (1979): 675–82.

Shéhérazade

5889. M-Schultz: 45–48. [*Asie*]

Sonata for Violin and Cello

5890. Fruehwald, Edwin Scott. "Harmonic Organization in the Large-Scale Instrumental Chamber Works of Maurice Ravel's 'style pépouillé.'" M.A. thesis, University of North Carolina, 1979.

5891. M-Pfann.

5892. Sannemüller, Gerd. "Die Sonate für Violine und Violoncello von Maurice Ravel." MF 28 (1975): 408–19.

Sonatine

5893. Dommel-Diény, Amy. "L'harmonie de Ravel vue à travers le second mouvement de la Sonatine." SMZ 117 (1977): 4–10.

Songs (various; *see also* specific song cycles)

5894. Kaminsky, Peter. "Of Children, Princesses, Dreams, and Isomorphisms: Text-Music Transformation in Ravel's Vocal Works." MA 19, no. 1 (2000): 29–68.

5895. Orenstein, Arbie. "The Vocal Works of Maurice Ravel." Ph.D. diss., Columbia University, 1968.

5896. Sachs, Klaus-Jürgen. "Maurice Ravels *Sainte* (1896) nach Stéphane Mallarmé." AM 54, no. 2 (1997): 95–119.

Tombeau de Couperin

5897. Goebels, Franzpeter. "*Le tombeau de Couperin*: Bemerkungen und Anregungen zu Ravels Klavierwerk." M 41, no. 4 (1987): 319–22.

5898. Howat, Roy. "Ravel, Rhythm, and Form." MSA 16 (1993): 39–47.

Valses nobles et sentimentales

5899. Kabisch, Thomas. "Franz Liszt und die Tradition der 'nicht-diskursiven' Musik." SM 28 (1986): 125–36. [No. 3]

5900. McCrae, Elizabeth. "Ravel's *Valses nobles et sentimentales*: Analysis, Stylistic Considerations, Performance Problems." D.M.A. diss., Boston University, 1974.

5901. Pepin, M. Natalie. "Dance and Jazz Elements in the Piano Music of Maurice Ravel." D.M.A. diss., Boston University, 1972.

Violin Sonata

5902. Fruehwald, Edwin Scott. "Harmonic Organization in the Large-Scale Instrumental Chamber Works of Maurice Ravel's 'style pépouillé.'" M.A. thesis, University of North Carolina, 1979.
5903. M-Pfann.

Various Works

5904. Baur, Steven. "Ravel's 'Russian' Period: Octatonicism in His Early Works, 1893–1908." JAMS 52, no. 3 (1999): 531–92.
5905. Braun, Jürgen. *Die Thematik in dem Kammermusikwerken von Maurice Ravel.* Regensburg: Bosse, 1966.
5906. Hopkins, James F. "Ravel's Orchestral Transcription Technique." Ph.D. diss., Princeton University, 1969.
5907. Kabisch, Thomas. "Oktatonik, Tonalität und Form in der Musik Maurice Ravels." MTH 5, no. 2 (1990): 117–36.
5908. Landormy, Paul. "Maurice Ravel (1875–1937)." MQ 25 (1939): 430–31.
5909. Mawer, Deborah, ed. *The Cambridge Companion to Ravel.* Cambridge: Cambridge University Press, 2000.
5910. Mueller, Robert Earl. "The Concept of Tonality in Impressionist Music, Based on the Works of Debussy and Ravel." Ph.D. diss., Indiana University, 1954.
5911. Orenstein, Arbie. "Maurice Ravel's Creative Process." MQ 53 (1967): 467–81.
5912. Weiss-Aigner, Günter. "Eine Sonderform der Skalenbildung in der Musik Ravels." MF 25 (1972): 323–26.
5913. Wilson, Eugene N. "Form and Texture in the Chamber Music of Debussy and Ravel." Ph.D. diss., University of Washington, 1968.

RAWSTHORNE, ALAN (1905–1971)

5914. Allison, Rees Stephen. "The Piano Works of Alan Rawsthorne (until 1968)." Ph.D. diss., Washington University, 1970.
5915. Cooper, Martin. "Current Chronicle." MQ 35 (1949): 305–11.
5916. Dickinson, A. E. F. "The Progress of Alan Rawsthorne." MR 12 (1951): 87–104.

REA, JOHN (b. 1944)

5917. Gonneville, Michel. "Le charme étrange des espaces familiers: Périple analytique dans *Treppenmusik* de John Rea." CIR 11, no. 1 (2000): 9–32.

READ, THOMAS L. (b. 1938)

5918. Read, Thomas L. ". . . Whence Freedom." CM 67–68 (1999): 327–43.

REBIKOV, VLADIMIR IVANOVICH (1866–1920)

5919. Dale, William Henry. "A Study of the Musico-Psychological Dramas of Vladimir Ivanovitch Rebikov." Ph.D. diss., University of Southern California, 1955.

REDA, SIEGFRIED (1916–1968)

5920. Hattlestad, Roger Merle. "Siegfried Reda's *Vorspiele zu den Psalm-Liedern.*" D.M.A. diss., University of Iowa, 1974.

REDGATE, ROGER (b. 1958)

5921. Barrett, Richard. "Critical/Convulsive: The Music of Roger Redgate." CMR 13, no. 1 (1995): 133–46.

REGER, MAX (1873–1916)

Aus meinem Tagebuch, Op. 82

5922. Lissa, Zofia. "Max Regers Metamorphosen der Berceuse Op. 57 von Frédéric Chopin." F-Federov/65: 79–83. Reprint, F-Wiener: 35–40. [No. 12]

Choral Works

5923. Troskie, Albert J. J. "Die Tonsymbolik in Regers Chorwerken." F-Schreiber: 119–25.

Chorale Fantasias, Op. 52

5924. Siemens, Hayko. "Max Regers Phantasie über den Choral *Wachet auf, ruft uns die Stimme,* Op. 52/2: Die Vollen-dung der symphonischen Cantus-Firmus-Form." MK 57, no. 5 (1987): 215–33.

Clarinet Quintet

5925. Häfner, Roland. *Max Reger: Klarinettenquintett, Op. 146.* Munich: Fink, 1982.
5926. Kühn, Hellmut. "Sang und Gegensang: Zu Regers Klarinettenquintett Opus 146." NZM 134 (1973): 141–43. Also in MB 5 (1973): 670–72.

Fantasia and Fugue, Op. 135b

5927. Haupt, Helmut. "Max Regers letztes Orgelwerk Op. 135b." *Mitteilungen des Max-Regers-Instituts* 17 (1968): 6–12.

Intermezzi, Op. 45

5928. Harrison, Daniel. "Max Reger's Motivic Technique: Harmonic Innovations at the Borders of Atonality." JMT 35, nos. 1–2 (1991): 61–92. [No. 5]

***Introduction, Passacaglia and Fugue*, Op. 127**

5929. Haupt, Helmut. "Max Regers symphonisches Orgelschaffen: *Introduktion, Passacaglia und Fugue* Op. 127." MK 47 (1977): 225–32.

Organ Works (various; *see also* specific organ works)

5930. Barker, John Wesley. "The Organ Works of Max Reger." MMA 1 (1966): 56–73. Also in F-Bishop: 56–73.

5931. Drude, Matthias. "Stichworte und Randbemerkungen zu Regers Harmonik." MTH 11, no. 2 (1996): 111–23.

5932. Kalkoff, Artur. *Das Orgelschaffen Max Regers im Lichte der deutschen Orgelneurungsbewegung.* Kassel: Bärenreiter, 1950.

5933. Manz, André. "Max Reger als Orgelkomponist: 'Extremer Fortschrittsmann'?" F-Schreiber: 105–17.

5934. Sievers, Gerd. "Franz Liszts Legende *Der Heilige Franziskus von Paul auf den Wogen schreitend* für Klavier in Max Regers Bearbeitung für die Orgel." F-Schreiber: 9–27.

5935. Walter, Rudolf. "Max Regers Choralvorspiele." KJ 40 (1956): 127–38.

Piano Trio, Op. 102

5936. Fischer, Kurt von. "Bemerkungen zum ersten Satz des Klaviertrios Op. 102 von Max Reger." STU 9 (1980): 151–59.

Piano Works (various; *see also* specific piano works)

5937. Hopkins, William Thomas. "The Short Piano Compositions of Max Reger (1873–1916)." Ph.D. diss., Indiana University, 1971.

Requiem

5938. Shigihara, Susanne. "Spannungsfelder: Max Regers Requiemkompositionen im Kontext der Gattungsgeschichte." KJ 75 (1991): 29–62.

Sextet, Op. 118

5939. Mäkelä, Tomi. "Zwischen Inspiration und Imitation: Max Regers Streichsextett Opus 118 und das *Schott-Konzert* des Reger-Schülers Aarre Merikanto (1893–1958) im Vergleich." MF 48, no. 4 (1995): 369–94.

Songs

5940. Wehmeyer, Grete. *Max Reger als Liederkomponist: Ein Beitrag zum Problem der Wort-Ton-Beziehung.* Regensburg: Bosse, 1955.

5941. Zimmermann, Petra. "'Erlaubt sich der Komponist einen üblen Scherz?': Fragen an Max Regers Klavierlied *Ein Drängen* (Op. 97, Nr. 3)." JSIM (1999): 137–52.

String Quartets

5942. Wilke, Rainer. *Brahms, Reger, Schönberg, Streichquartette: Motivisch-thematische Prozesse und formale Gestalt.* Hamburg: Wagner, 1980.

***Symphonic Fantasia and Fugue*, Op. 57**

5943. Haupt, Helmut. "*Symphonische Phantasie und Fugue* Op. 57: Ein Markstein in Max Regers Orgelschaffen." MK 49 (1979): 120–26.

5944. Wuensch, Gerhard. "Max Regers *Symphonische Phantasie und Fuge* Opus 57: Betrachtungen zum musikalischen Hörerlebnis." F-Schenk: 237–54.

***Träume am Kamin*, Op. 143**

5945. Harrison, Daniel. "Max Reger's Motivic Technique: Harmonic Innovations at the Borders of Atonality." JMT 35, nos. 1–2 (1991): 61–92. [No. 1]

5946. Lissa, Zofia. "Max Regers Metamorphosen der Berceuse Op. 57 von Frédéric Chopin." F-Federov/65: 79–83. Reprint, F-Wiener: 35–40. [No. 9]

***Variations and Fugue on a Theme of Beethoven*, Op. 86**

5947. Kranz, Maria Hinrichs. "Max Reger's Piano Variations on Themes of Bach, Beethoven, and Telemann." D.M.A. diss., American Conservatory of Music, 1985.

***Variations and Fugue on a Theme of G. P. Telemann*, Op. 134**

5948. Holliman, Janesetta. "A Stylistic Study of Max Reger's Solo Piano Variations and Fugues on Themes by Johann Sebastian Bach and Georg Philipp Telemann." Ph.D. diss., New York University, 1973.

5949. Kranz, Maria Hinrichs. "Max Reger's Piano Variations on Themes of Bach, Beethoven, and Telemann." D.M.A. diss., American Conservatory of Music, 1985.

Variations and Fugue on a Theme of J. S. Bach, **Op. 81**

5950. Holliman, Janesetta. "A Stylistic Study of Max Reger's Solo Piano Variations and Fugues on Themes by Johann Sebastian Bach and Georg Philipp Telemann." Ph.D. diss., New York University, 1973.

5951. Kranz, Maria Hinrichs. "Max Reger's Piano Variations on Themes of Bach, Beethoven, and Telemann." D.M.A. diss., American Conservatory of Music, 1985.

Variations and Fugue on a Theme of Mozart, **Op. 132**

5952. Ehrenforth, Karl Heinrich. "Max Reger: *Variationen und Fuge über ein Thema von W. A. Mozart* für grosses Orchester, Op. 132 (1914)." MB 5 (1973): 673–76.

5953. Weiss-Aigner, Günter. *Max Reger: Mozart-Variationen Op. 132.* Munich: Fink, 1989.

Variations and Fugue on an Original Theme, **Op. 73**

5954. Harrison, Daniel. "Max Reger's Motivic Technique: Harmonic Innovations at the Borders of Atonality." JMT 35, nos. 1–2 (1991): 61–92.

Violin Concerto, Op. 101

5955. Weiss-Aigner, Günter. "Max Reger und die Tradition: Zum Violinkonzert A-Dur Op. 101." NZM 135 (1974): 614–20.

Various Works

5956. Andraschke, Peter. "Regers Chopin-Bearbeitungen." CS 4 (1994): 72–85. [*Spezialstudien*]

5957. Gatscher, Emanuel. *Die Fugentechnik Max Regers in ihrer Entwicklung.* Stuttgart: J. Engelhorns Nachfolge, 1925.

5958. Grabner, Hermann. *Regers Harmonik.* 2d ed. Wiesbaden: Breitkopf & Härtel, 1961.

5959. Harrison, Daniel. "A Theory of Harmonic and Motivic Structure for the Music of Max Reger." Ph.D. diss., Yale University, 1986.

5960. Herbst, Wolfgang. *"Ben marcato*: Max Regers Bemühungen um die Erkennbarkeit musikalischer Strukturen." F-Walcha: 107–13.

5961. Kaufmann, Harold. "Ausholung der Tonalität bei Reger." NZM 128 (1967): 28–33.

5962. Möller, Martin. *Untersuchungen zur Satztechnik Max Regers: Studien an den Kopfsätzen der Kammermusikwerke.* Wiesbaden: Breitkopf & Härtel, 1980.

5963. Schaffer, Mark Andrew. "The Use of Variation Principle in the Works of Max Reger." Ph.D. diss., Univeristy of Cincinnati, 1989.

5964. Sievers, Gerd. "Die Harmonik im Werk Max Regers." F-Reger: 55–82.

5965. Zingerle, Hans. "Chromatische Harmonik bei Brahms und Reger: Ein Vergleich." SZM 27 (1966): 151–85.

REICH, STEVE (b. 1936)

City Life

5966. Guillot, Matthieu. "Steve Reich: *City Life,* l'urbanité comme modèle sonore." ANM 33 (1998): 51–59.

Clapping Music

5967. Saltini, Roberto Antonio. "Structural Levels and Choice of Beat-Class Sets in Steve Reich's Phase-Shifting Music." INT 7 (1993): 149–78.

5968. Shankovich, Robert. "Minimalism: A Retrospective and Prospective Definition." MTEA 1 (1992): 40–49.

Come Out

5969. Schwarz, David. "Listening Subjects: Semiotics, Psychoanalysis, and the Music of John Adams and Steve Reich." PNM 31, no. 2 (1993): 24–56.

Desert Music

5970. Bennett, Mark Stephen. "A Brief History of Minimalism: Its Aesthetic Concepts and Origins and a Detailed Analysis of Steve Reich's Desert Music." D.M.A. doc., University of Illinois, 1993.

5971. Coronti, Joseph A., Jr. "Scoring the 'Absolute Rhythm' of William Carlos Williams: Steve Reich's *The Desert Music.*" In *Poetry as Text in Twentieth-Century Vocal Music: From Stravinsky to Reich,* 19–34. Lewiston, N.Y.: Mellen, 1992.

5972. Horlacher, Gretchen. "Multiple Meters and Metrical Processes in the Music of Steve Reich." INT 14–15 (2000–2001): 265–97.

5973. Quinn, Ian. "Fuzzy Extensions to the Theory of Contour." MTS 19, no. 2 (1997): 232–63.

Different Trains

5974. Cumming, Naomi. "The Horrors of Identificaton: Reich's *Different Trains.*" PNM 35, no. 1 (1997): 129–52.

5975. Dadelsen, Hans-Christian von. "Diesseits und jenseits von Raum und Zeit: Steve Reichs *Different Trains.*" In *Nähe und Distanz: Nachgedachte Musik der Gegenwart,* ed. Wolfgang Gratzer. Vol. 1, 235–46. Hofheim: Wolke, 1996.

Drumming

5976. McGuire, John. "Steve Reich, *Drumming*: Ein Werkkommentar." N 1 (1980): 142–48.

It's Gonna Rain

5977. Schwarz, David. "Listening Subjects: Semiotics, Psychoanalysis, and the Music of John Adams and Steve Reich." PNM 31, no. 2 (1993): 24–56.

Music for Eighteen Musicians

5978. Christensen, Erik. *The Musical Timespace: A Theory of Musical Listening.* Aalberg: Aalberg University Press, 1996.

5979. Raab, Claus. "Music der Allmählichkeit und des Präsens: Graduelle Verfahren in *Music for 18 Musicians* von Steve Reich." In *Reflexionen über Musik heute: Texte und Analyses*, ed. Wilfried Gruhn, 169–84. Mainz: Schott, 1981.

Octet

5980. Heisinger, Brent. "Compositional Devices in Steve Reich's Octet." EXT 5, no. 2 (1991): 29–46.

5981. McGuire, John. "Steve Reich, Octet: Ein Werkkommentar." N 1 (1980): 149–55.

Phase Patterns

5982. Cohn, Richard. "Transpositional Combination of Beat-Class Sets in Steve Reich's Phase-Shifting Music." PNM 30, no. 2 (1992): 146–77.

5983. Saltini, Roberto Antonio. "Structural Levels and Choice of Beat-Class Sets in Steve Reich's Phase-Shifting Music." INT 7 (1993): 149–78.

Piano Phase

5984. Epstein, Paul. "Pattern Structure and Process in Steve Reich's *Piano Phase.*" MQ 72, no. 4 (1986): 494–502.

5985. Horlacher, Gretchen. "Multiple Meters and Metrical Processes in the Music of Steve Reich." INT 14–15 (2000–2001): 265–97.

5986. Wilson, Stephanie Elizabeth. "Pattern Perception and Temporality in the Music of Steve Reich: An Interdisciplinary Approach." Ph.D. diss., University of New South Wales, 2000.

Sextet

5987. Warburton, Daniel. "Aspects of Organization in the Sextet of Steve Reich." Ph.D. diss., University of Rochester, 1988.

Tehillim

5988. Dadelsen, Hans-Christian von. "Maskierter Kult und demaskierte Kultur: Steve Reich, *Tehillim,* ein Analyse-Essay zwischen Mars und Minimal." NZM 49, no. 1 (1987): 21–49.

5989. Gronemeyer, Gisela. "'I Want to Do Just Steve Reich Individual': Zu Steve Reich's Psalmkomposition *Tehillim.*" MTX 2 (1983): 22–25.

Violin Phase

5990. Cohn, Richard. "Transpositional Combination of Beat-Class Sets in Steve Reich's Phase-Shifting Music." PNM 30, no. 2 (1992): 146–77.

Various Works

5991. Hascher, Werner. "Steve Reich." Ph.D. diss., Universität Wien, 1991.

5992. M-Mertens: 47–66.

5993. Pardey, Wolfgang. "Repetitive Musik von Steve Reich: Analysen, Interpretation, und didaktische Ansätze." MB 14, no. 3 (1982): 153–62.

5994. Potter, Keith. "The Recent Phases of Steve Reich." CT 29 (1985): 28–34.

5995. M-Potter.

5996. Reich, Steve. *Writings on Music, 1965–2000.* Oxford: Oxford University Press, 2002.

5997. Schwarz, K. Robert. "Steve Reich: Music as a Gradual Process." PNM 19, nos. 1–2 (1980–1981): 373–392; 20, nos. 1–2 (1981–1982): 225–86.

5998. Scott, Stephen. "The Music of Steve Reich." NW 6 (1974): 21–28.

REICHA, ANTOINE (1770–1836)

5999. Bulley, Michael. "Reicha's 13th Fugue." MR 46, no. 3 (1985): 163–69. [36 Fugues (1803); discusses most with emphasis on No. 13]

6000. Laing, Millard M. "Anton Reicha's Quintets for Flute, Oboe, Clarinet, Horn and Bassoon." Ed.D. diss., University of Michigan, 1952.

6001. Morris, Mellasenah Young. "A Style Analysis of the Thirty-Six Fugues for Piano, Opus 36, by Anton Reicha." D.M.A. diss., Peabody Conservatory, 1980.

REIMANN, ARIBERT (b. 1936)

6002. Riemer, Franz. "Aribert Reimann: *Nunc dimittis, Canticum Simeonis* für Baßflöte, Bariton und gemischten Chor: Ein Beitrag zum kirchenmusikalischen Schaffen der Gegenwart." MK 57, no. 2 (1987): 69–83.

RENNER, JOSEPH (1868–1934)

6003. Kraus, Eberhard. "Der gregorianische Choral im Orgelschaffen der Regensburg Domorganisten Joseph Hanisch (1812–1892) und Joseph Renner (1868–1934)." F-Haberl: 151–67.

REUBKE, JULIUS (1834–1858)

6004. Chorzempa, Daniel Walter. "Julius Reubke: Life and Works." Ph.D. diss., University of Minnesota, 1971.

6005. Keller, Hermann. "Der Orgelkomponist Julius Reubke." MK 29 (1959): 35–39.

6006. Keym, Stefan. "Originalität oder Epigonentum? Zur motivisch-thematischen Struktur der B-Moll-Sonate von Julius Reubke im Vergleich mit Liszts G-Moll-Sonate." MF 51, no. 1 (1998): 34–46.

6007. Songayllo, Raymond. "A Neglected Masterpiece." JALS 18 (1985): 122–28. [Piano Sonata in B-Flat Minor]

REUTER, FRITZ (1896–1963)

6008. Wichtmann, Kurt. "Fritz Reuters *Sechs Lieder auf Gedichte von Louis Fürnberg.*" MG 13 (1963): 169–71.

REUTTER, HERMANN (1900–1985)

6009. Reutter, Hermann. "Meine Lieder-Zyklen auf Gedichte von Lorca." MELOS 30 (1963): 283–91.

REVUELTAS, SILVESTRE (1899–1940)

6010. Zohn-Muldoon, Ricardo. "The Song of the Snake: Silvestre Revueltas' *Sensemayá.*" LAMR 19, no. 2 (1998): 133–59.

REYNOLDS, ROGER (b. 1934)

6011. Loucky, David. "Contemporary Notation and Limited Indeterminacy: Roger Reynolds' *from behind the unreasoning mask.*" EXT 5, no. 2 (1991): 47–61.

6012. Reynolds, Roger. "A Perspective on Form and Experience." CMR 2, no. 1 (1987): 277–308. [*Archipelago*]

6013. Vérin, Nicolas. "*Archipelago* de Roger Reynolds." INH 8–9 (1991): 178–205.

RHEINBERGER, JOSEPH (1839–1901)

6014. Hunsberger, David Ritchie. "Fugal Style in the Organ Sonatas and Fughettas of Josef Rheinberger." Ph.D. diss., Washington University, 1979.

RIDOUT, GODFREY (1918–1984)

6015. Gilpin, Wayne George William. "Godfrey Ridout: Choral Music with Orchestra." M.M. thesis, University of Alberta, 1978.

RIEDL, JOSEF ANTON (b. 1927/1929)

6016. Frisius, Rudolf. "Variable Lautkonstellationen, variable Kompositionen: Kompositorische und metakompositorische Tendenzen bei Josef Anton Riedl; Anmerkungen zu seinen Lautgedichten." N 5 (1984–1985): 169–85.

6017. Zeller, Hans Rudolf. "Experimentelle Klangerzeugung und Instrument: Versuch über Joseph Anton Riedl." MTX 3 (1984): 46–57.

6018. ———. "Soli für Schlagzeug: Unbekannte(re)s von Josef Anton Riedl." N 5 (1984–1985): 151–68.

RIEGGER, WALLINGFORD (1885–1961)

6019. Buccheri, Elizabeth C. "The Piano Chamber Music of Wallingford Riegger." D.M.A. diss., University of Rochester, 1978.

6020. Freeman, Paul D. "The Compositional Technique of Wallingford Riegger as Seen in Seven Major Twelve-Tone Works." Ph.D. diss., University of Rochester, 1963.

6021. Gatewood, Dwight Dean, Jr. "Wallingford Riegger: A Biography and Analysis of Selected Works." Ph.D. diss., George Peabody College for Teachers, 1970.

6022. Goldman, Richard Franko. "Current Chronicle." MQ 34 (1948): 594–99. [Symphony No. 3]

6023. ———. "The Music of Wallingford Riegger." MQ 36 (1950): 39–61.

6024. Ott, Leonard William. "An Analysis of the Later Orchestral Style of Wallingford Riegger." Ph.D. diss., Michigan State University, 1970.

6025. Savage, Newell Gene. "Structure and Cadence in the Music of Wallingford Riegger." Ph.D. diss., Stanford University, 1972.

6026. Schmoll, Joseph Benjamin. "An Analytical Study of the Principal Instrumental Compositions of Wallingford Riegger." Ph.D. diss., Northwestern University, 1954.

RIEHM, ROLF (b. 1937)

6027. Großmann-Vendrey, Susanna. "Du könntest anders horen!: Musik von Rolf Riehm." MTH 8, no. 3 (1993): 263–83. [*"Ich denk viel."/Mr.President/pizz/13*]

6028. Whybrow, Julia. "Eine Einführung in das Blockflötenstück *Weeds in Ophelia's Hair* von Rolf Riehm." T 20, no. 1 (1995): 357–61.

RIES, FERDINAND (1784–1838)

6029. Darbellay, Étienne. "Epigonalité ou originalité? Les Sonates pour piano seul de Ferdinand Ries (1784–1838)." SBM 4 (1980): 51–101.

RIESCO, CARLOS (b. 1925)

6030. Curtis, Brandt B. "Rafael Alberti and Chilean Composers." D.M.A. diss., Indiana University, 1977. [*Sobre los angeles*]

RIHM, WOLFGANG (b. 1952)

6031. Andraschke, Peter. "Traditionsmomente in Kompositionen von Christobal Halffter, Klaus Huber, und Wolfgang Rihm." M-Brinkmann: 130–52.

6032. Brügge, Joachim. "Zur Form und Ästhetik in Wolfgang Rihms drittem Steichquartett *Im Innersten* (1976)." MF 52, no. 2 (1999): 178–89. [String Quartet No. 3]

6033. Frisius, Rudolf. "Werk und Werkzyklus: Bemerkungen zum *Chiffre-Zyklus* von Wolfgang Rihm." MTX 11 (1985): 17–20.

6034. Heister, Hanns-Werner. "Sackgasse oder Ausweg aus dem Elfenbeinturm? Zur musikalischen Sprache in Wolfgang Rihms *Jakob Lenz.*" BM 24 (1982): 3–16.

6035. Nielinger-Vakil, Carola. "Quiet Revolutions: Hölderlin Fragments by Luigi Nono and Wolfgang Rihm." ML 81, no. 2 (2000): 245–74. [*Hölderlin-Fragmente*]

6036. Schmierer, Elisabeth. "Wolfgang Rihm: Klavierstück Nr. 5 (*Tombeau*)." N 1 (1980): 110–13.

RILEY, TERRY (b. 1935)

6037. Holm-Hudson, Kevin. "Just Intonation and Indian Aesthetic in Terry Riley's *The Harp of New Albion.*" EXT 10, no. 1 (2000): 97–117.

6038. M-Mertens: 35–46.

6039. M-Potter.

6040. Welch, Allison. "Meetings Along the Edge: *Svara* and *Tāla* in American Minimal Music." AMUS 17, no. 2 (1999): 179–99. [*Mythic Birds Waltz, A Rainbow in Curved Air*]

RIMSKY-KORSAKOV, NIKOLAY ANDREYEVICH (1844–1908)

6041. Abraham, Gerald. "*Pskovityanka*: The Original Version of Rimsky-Korsakov's First Opera." MQ 54 (1968): 58–73. Reprint, M-Abraham: 68–82.

6042. ———. "Rimsky-Korsakov's Gogol Operas." ML 12 (1931): 242–52.

6043. ASO 162 (1994). [*Legend of the Invisible City of Kitezh and the Maiden Fevroniya, Sadko*]

6044. Feinberg, Saul. "Rimsky-Korsakov's Suite from *Le coq d'or.*" MR 30 (1969): 47–64.

6045. Griffiths, Steven A. K. "A Critical Study of the Music of Rimsky-Korsakov up to 1890." Ph.D. diss., University of Sheffield, 1982.

6046. Lischké, André. "Les Leitmotive de *Snegourotchka* analysés par Rimsky-Korsakov." RDM 65 (1979): 51–75. [*The Snow Maiden*]

6047. Neff, Lyle K. "Close to Prose or Worse Than Verse? Rimsky-Korsakov's Intermediate Type of Opera Text." OQ 15, no. 2 (1999): 238–50.

6048. Schuster-Craig, John. "'Bizarre Harmony and the So-Called Newest Style': The Harmonic Language of Rimsky-Korsakov's *Le coq d'or.*" JALS 43 (1998): 45–55.

6049. Slonimskij, S. "Die lebendige, moderne Kunst Rimski-Korsakows." *Kunst und Literatur* 17, no. 12 (1969): 1307–16.

6050. M-Taruskin.

RISSET, JEAN-CLAUDE (b. 1938)

6051. M-Cope: 198–202. [*Inharmonique*]

6052. Di Scipio, Agostino. "An Analysis of Jean-Claude Risset's *Contours.*" JNMR 29, no. 1 (2000): 1–21.

6053. Koblyakov, Lev. "Jean-Claude Risset: *Songes* (1979) (9')." CMR 1, no. 1 (1984–1985): 171–73.

6054. Lorrain, Denis. *"Inharmoniques": Analyse de la bande magnetique de l'oeuvre de Jean-Claude Risset.* Rapports IRCAM 26/80. Paris: Centre Georges Pompidou, 1980.

6055. Risset, Jean-Claude. "Composing Sounds, Bridging Gaps: The Musical Role of the Computer in My Music." In *Musik und Technik*, ed. Helga da la Motte-Haber and Rudolf Frisius, 152–81. Mainz: Schott, 1996.

RITTER, PETER (1763–1846)

6056. Elsen, Josephine C. "The Instrumental Works of Peter Ritter (1763–1846)." Ph.D. diss., Northwestern University, 1967.

6057. Jessel, Sister Mary Lisa, O. P. "The Vocal Works of Peter Ritter (1763–1846)." Ph.D. diss., Catholic University of America, 1962.

ROCHBERG, GEORGE (1918–2005)

6058. M-Buccheri.

6059. Copenhaver, Lee R. "The Symphonies of George Rochberg." Ph.D. diss., University of Iowa, 1987.

6060. M-Johnson. [*Blake Songs*]

6061. Reise, Jay. "Rochberg the Progressive." PNM 19, no. 2 (1980–1981): 395–407. [String Quartet No. 3]

6062. Ringer, Alexander L. "Current Chronicle." MQ 58 (1972): 128–32. [*David, the Psalmist; Sacred Song of Reconciliation; Songs in Praise of Krishna;* Symphony No. 3]

6063. ———. "The Music of George Rochberg." MQ 52 (1966): 409–30.

6064. Sams, Carol Lee. "Solo Vocal Writing in Selected Works of Berio, Crumb, and Rochberg." D.M.A. diss., University of Washington, 1975.

6065. Smith, Joan Templar. "The String Quartets of George Rochberg." Ph.D. diss., University of Rochester, 1976.

RODGERS, RICHARD (1902–1979)

6066. Kaye, Milton. "Richard Rodgers: A Comparative Melody Analysis of His Songs with Hart and Hammerstein Lyrics." Ed.D. diss., New York University, 1969.

ROGERS, BERNARD (1893–1968)

6067. Diamond, David. "Bernard Rogers." MQ 33 (1947): 207–27.

6068. Fox, Charles Warren. "Current Chronicle." MQ 34 (1948): 415–17. [Symphony No. 4]

6069. Intili, Dominic Joseph. "Text-Music Relationships in the Large Choral Works of Bernard Rogers." Ph.D. diss., Case Western Reserve University, 1977.

ROMBERG, ANDREAS JAKOB (1767–1821)

6070. Werner, Klaus G. "Zwischen Emanuel Bach und Louis Spohr: Kontrapunkt und lyrischer Ton in den Sinfonien Andreas Rombergs." MF 53, no. 2 (2000): 158–75.

ROPARTZ, JOSEPH GUY (1864–1955)

6071. Maillard, Jean. "Guy Ropartz, chantre d'armor." RM 324–326 (1979): 107–13.

6072. ———. "Guy Ropartz: Les six symphonies; Étude analytique." RM 324–326 (1979): 118–32.

6073. ———. "Guy Ropartz: Un drame de l'exil; *Le pays* (1912)." RM 324–326 (1979): 114–17.

ROREM, NED (b. 1923)

6074. Davis, Deborah Louise Bodwin. "The Choral Works of Ned Rorem." Ph.D. diss., Michigan State University, 1978.

6075. Griffiths, Richard Lyle. "Ned Rorem: Music for Chorus and Orchestra." D.M.A. diss., University of Washington, 1979.

6076. Johnson, Bret. "Still Sings the Voice: A Portrait of Ned Rorem." TEMPO 153 (1985): 7–12.

6077. Miller, Philip Lieson. "The Songs of Ned Rorem." TEMPO 127 (1978): 25–81.

6078. North, William Sills. "Ned Rorem as a Twentieth-Century Song Composer." D.M.A. diss., University of Illinois, 1965.

6079. Pilar, Lillian Nobleza. "The Vocal Style of Ned Rorem in the Song Cycle *Poems of Love and the Rain*." Ph.D. diss., Indiana University, 1972.

ROSENBERG, HILDING (1892–1985)

6080. Broman, Per Olov. *Kakofont storhetsvansinne eller uttryck för det djupast liv? Om ny musik och musikåskådning i svenskt 1920-tal, med särskild tonvikt på Hilding Rosenberg.* Uppsala: Uppsala University, 2000.

6081. Karlsson, Henrik. "Hilding Rosenbergs beredskapsoratorium." STM 74, no. 2 (1992): 61–77. [*Svensk lagsaga*]

ROSENBLUM, MATHEW (b. 1954)

6082. Moe, Eric. "Beyond Right and Wrong Ways to Write Music: Tsontakis, Rosenblum, and Diesendruck." CMR 10, no. 1 (1994): 149–95. [*Circadian Rhythms*]

ROSENFELD, GERHARD (1931–2003)

6083. Kneipel, Eberhard. "Cellokonzert von Gerhard Rosenfeld." MG 20 (1970): 186–91.

ROSSINI, GIOACHINO (1792–1868)

Aureliano in Palmira

6084. Linder, Thomas. "Rossini's *Aureliano in Palmira*: A Descriptive Analysis." OQ 15, no. 1 (1999): 18–32.

Barbiere di Siviglia
6085. ASO 37 (1981).
6086. Natale, Marco de. "L'analisi dell'opera in musica: Un problema incombente." ANL 11 (1993): 6–25.

Cenerentola, ossia La bontà in trionfo
6087. ASO 85 (1985).
6088. John, Nicholas, ed. *Rossini: La Cenerentola.* London: Calder, 1981.

Comte Ory
6089. ASO 140 (1991).

Gazza ladra
6090. ASO 110 (1988).

Guillaume Tell
6091. ASO 118 (1989).
6092. Gerhard, Anselm. "L'eroe titubante e il finale aperto: Un dilemma insolubile nel *Guillaume Tell* di Rossini." RIM 19 (1984): 113–30.
6093. Tegen, Martin. "Från formel till ledmotiv: Några funderingar kring Rossinis *Guillaume Tell.*" M-Lönn: 163–73.

Italiana in Algeri
6094. ASO 157 (1994).

Moïse et Pharaon, ou Le passage de la Mer Rouge
6095. Conati, Marcello. "Between Past and Future: The Dramatic World of Rossini in *Mosè in Egitto* and *Moïse et Pharaon.*" NCM 4 (1980): 32–48.

Mosè in Egitto
6096. Conati, Marcello. "Between Past and Future: The Dramatic World of Rossini in *Mosè in Egitto* and *Moïse et Pharaon.*" NCM 4 (1980): 32–48.

Otello, ossia Il moro di Venezia
6097. Liebscher, Julia. "Introduktion und Exposition in der Oper: Eine musikdramaturgische Untersuchung am Beispiel des *Otello* (1816) von Gioacchino Rossini." MF 44, no. 2 (1991): 105–29.

Semiramide
6098. ASO 184 (1998).

Siège de Corinthe
6099. ASO 81 (1985).

Tancredi
6100. Gossett, Philip. "The 'candeur virginale' of *Tancredi.*" MT 172 (1971): 326–29.

Turco in Italia
6101. ASO 169 (1996).

Viaggio a Reims, ossia L'albergo del giglio d'oro
6102. ASO 140 (1991).

Various Works
6103. Balthazar, Scott L. "Rossini and the Development of the Mid-Century Lyric Form." JAMS 41, no. 1 (1988): 102–25.
6104. Colas, Damien. "Anamorphoses et métamorphoses dans l'arabesque rossinienne: Étude stylistique des variantes ornementales." ANM 17 (1989): 38–45.
6105. Gossett, Philip. "The Overtures of Rossini." NCM 3 (1979–1980): 3–31.
6106. Tartak, Marvin H. "The Italian Comic Operas of Rossini." Ph.D. diss., University of California at Berkeley, 1968.

ROTT, HANS (1858–1884)
6107. Litterscheid, Frank. "Die E-Dur-Sinfonie von Has Rott: Analytische Betrachtungen." In *Hans Rott: Der Begründer der neuen Symhonie,* ed. Heinz-Klaus Metzger and Rainer Riehn,15–44. Munich: Text + Kritik, 1999.

ROUSE, MIKEL (b. 1957)
6108. Gann, Kyle. "Downtown Beats for the 1990s: Rhys Chatham, Mikel Rouse, Michael Gordon, Larry Polansky, Ben Neill." CMR 10, no. 1 (1994): 33–49.

ROUSSEL, ALBERT (1869–1937)

6109. Doskey, Henry. "The Piano Music of Albert Roussel." D.M. diss., Indiana University, 1980.

6110. Eddins, John M. "The Symphonic Music of Albert Roussel." Ph.D. diss., Florida State University, 1967.

6111. Feller, Elisabeth. "Gedanken zu *Joueure de flûte* von Albert Roussel (1869–1937)." T 13, no. 2 (1988): 84–91.

6112. Kawka, Daniel. "Albert Roussel: Sinfonietta, opus 52." ANM 33 (1998): 36–49.

6113. Miller, Catherine. "La musique vocale: Branche de la recherche musico-littéraire? Un exemple d'analyse; Les mélodies d'Albert Roussel (1869–1937) composées sur des poèmes de René Chalupt (1885–1957)." RBM 53 (1999): 197–218. ["Le bachelier de Salamanque," op. 20, no. 1; "Coeur en peril," op. 50, no. 1]

6114. Stevens, James William. "The Complete Songs for Voice and Piano of Albert Roussel." D.M.A. diss., University of Maryland, 1976.

ROUTH, FRANCIS (b. 1927)

6115. Routh, Francis. "A Sacred Tetralogy." TEMPO 119 (1976): 23–29.

RÓZSA, MIKLÓS (1907–1995)

6116. M-Larson.

RUBBRA, EDMUND (1901–1980)

6117. Dawney, Michael. "Edmund Rubbra and the Piano." MR 31 (1970): 241–48.

6118. Hutchings, Arthur. "Rubbra's Third Symphony: A Study of Its Texture." MR 2 (1941): 14–28.

6119. Lyne, Gregory Kent. "The Choral Works of Edmund Rubbra." D.M.A. diss., University of Northern Colorado, 1976.

6120. Mason, Colin. "Rubbra's Four Symphonies." MR 8 (1947): 131–39.

6121. Mellers, W. H. "Rubbra and the Dominant Seventh: Notes on an English Symphony." MR 4 (1943): 145–56.

6122. Payne, Elsie. "Rubbra's Contrapuntal Textures." MMR 84 (1954): 143–50.

6123. ———. "Rubbra's Sixth Symphony." MMR 85 (1955): 201–7.

6124. ———. "Some Aspects of Rubbra's Style." MR 16 (1955): 198–217.

6125. Rubbra, Edmund. "String Quartet No. 2 in E Flat, Op 73." MR 14 (1953): 36–44.

6126. ———. "Symphony No. 5 in B Flat, Op. 63." MR 10 (1949): 26–35.

RUBIN, MARCEL (1905–1995)

6127. Krones, Hartmut. "Die Harmonik im Oeuvre Marcel Rubins." OMZ 45, no. 5 (1990): 245–54.

RUBINSTEIN, ANTON GRIGOR'YEVICH (1829–1894)

6128. Norris, Jeremy. "The Piano Concertos of Anton Rubinstein." MR 46, no. 4 (1985): 241–83.

RUDIN, ANDREW (b. 1939)

6129. Chittum, Donald. "Current Chronicle." MQ 55 (1969): 99–102. [*Tragoedia*]

RUGGLES, CARL (1876–1971)

Angels

6130. Babcock, David. "Carl Ruggles: Two Early Works and *Sun-Treader*." TEMPO 135 (1980): 3–12.

6131. Dombek, Stephen. "A Study of Harmonic Interrelationships and Sonority Types in Carl Ruggles' *Angels*." ITR 4, no. 1 (1980–1981): 29–44.

6132. Ziffrin, Marilyn J. "*Angels*: Two Views." MR 29 (1968): 184–96.

Evocations (Piano)

6133. Chapman, Alan. "A Theory of Harmonic Structures for Non-Tonal Music." Ph.D. diss., Yale University, 1978.

6134. Gilbert, Steven E. "Carl Ruggles (1876–1971): An Appreciation." PNM 11, no. 1 (1972): 224–32.

6135. ———. "The 'Twelve-Tone' System of Carl Ruggles: A Study of the *Evocations* for Piano." JMT 14, no. 1 (1970): 68–91.

6136. Slottow, Stephen. "Fifths and Semitones: A Ruggles Compositional Model and Its Unfoldings." TP 25 (2000): 87–103. [No. 4]

Men and Mountains

6137. Babcock, David. "Carl Ruggles: Two Early Works and *Sun-Treader*." TEMPO 135 (1980): 3–12.

Organum

6138. Gilbert, Steven E. "Carl Ruggles (1876–1971): An Appreciation." PNM 11, no. 1 (1972): 224–32.

Sun-Treader

6139. Babcock, David. "Carl Ruggles: Two Early Works and Sun-Treader." TEMPO 135 (1980): 3–12.

6140. Carl, Robert. "'A Fearful Symmetry': Micro/Macro Structure in Carl Ruggles' *Sun-Treader*." SONUS 15, no. 2 (1995): 25–53.

6141. Gilbert, Steven E. "Carl Ruggles (1876–1971): An Appreciation." PNM 11, no. 1 (1972): 224–32.

6142. ———. "Carl Ruggles and Total Chromaticism." Y 7 (1971): 43–50.

Various Works

6143. Harrison, Lou. "Carl Ruggles." SCORE 12 (1955): 15–26.

6144. Kirkpatrick, John. "The Evolution of Carl Ruggles." PNM 6, no. 2 (1968): 144–66.

6145. Peterson, Thomas E. "The Music of Carl Ruggles." Ph.D. diss., University of Washington, 1967.

6146. Tenney, James. "The Chronological Development of Carl Ruggles' Melodic Style." PNM 16, no. 1 (1977): 36–69.

6147. Woo, Wha-Kyoung. "The Music of Carl Ruggles: A Study of Compositional Procedures and Harmonic Organization in His Eight Published Works." Ph.D. diss., Michigan State University, 1993.

RUSSELL, ARMAND (b. 1932)

6148. Russell, Armand. "*Themes and Fantasia* (Armand Russell): Analysis by the Composer, Edited by Dr. James Neilson." JBR 14, no. 1 (1978–1979): 50–53.

RUZICKA, PETER (b. 1948)

6149. Schäfer, Thomas. "*. . . Über ein Verschwinden*—'Musik über Musik': Peter Ruzickas 3. Streichquartett im Kontext." MTH 9, no. 3 (1994): 227–44.

6150. ———. "'Verschwiegene Lieder': Ein instrumentales 'Requiem' für Paul Celan; Anmerkungen zu Peter Ruzickas zweitem Streichquartett . . . *fragment* . . . ." MF 50, no. 3 (1997): 295–318.

RZEWSKI, FREDERIC (b. 1938)

6151. M-Cope. [*Coming Together*]

6152. Oehlschlägel, Reinhard. "Ein Anti-Kriegstuck: *Les perses* von Frederic Rzewski." MTX 11 (1985): 28–31. [*The Persians*]

6153. Sherr, Larry. "Vereinigung der Vielfalt: *The People United Will Never Be Defeated!* von Frederic Rzewski." MTX 1 (1985): 38–48.

6154. Wason, Robert W. "Tonality and Atonality in Frederic Rzewski's *Variations on 'The People United Will Never Be Defeated!'*" PNM 26, no. 1 (1988): 108–43.

– S –

SAARIAHO, KAIJA (b. 1952)

6155. Nieminen, Risto, ed. *Kaija Saariaho*. Paris: IRCAM, 1994.

6156. Saariaho, Kaija. "Timbe and Harmony: Interpolations of Timbral Structures." CMR 2, no. 1 (1987): 93–133.

SAINT-SAËNS, CAMILLE (1835–1921)

6157. ASO 15 (1978). [*Samson et Dalila*]

6158. Fallon, Daniel. "The Symphonies and Symphonic Poems of Camille Saint-Saëns." Ph.D. diss., Yale University, 1973.

6159. Pollei, Paul C. "Lisztian Piano Virtuoso Style in the Piano Concerti of Camille Saint-Saëns." JALS 7 (1980): 59–79.

6160. Scherperel, Loretta Fox. "The Solo Organ Works of Camille Saint-Saëns." D.M.A. diss., University of Rochester, 1978.

6161. Stegemann, Michael. "Die Solokonzertwerke von Camille Saint-Saëns." Ph.D. diss., Münster, 1981.

6162. Tubergen, David Gene. "A Stylistic Analysis of Selected Violin and Piano Sonatas of Fauré, Saint-Saëns, and Franck." Ph.D. diss., New York University, 1985. [Violin Sonata no. 1, op. 75]

SALIERI, ANTONIO (1750–1825)

6163. Hettrick, Jane Schatkin. "Antonio Salieri's Mass in B Flat (1809)." SZM 39 (1988): 141–57.

SAMINSKY, LAZARE (1882–1959)

6164. Slonimsky, Nicolas. "Lazare Saminsky." MM 12 (1935): 69–72.

SANDBERG, MORDECAI (1897–1973)

6165. Brotbeck, Roman. "Völkerverbindende Tondifferenzierung: Mordecai Sandberg, ein verkannter Pionier der Mikrotonalität." NZM 152, no. 4 (1991): 38–44.

SANDI, LUIS (b. 1905)

6166. Gomez, Leslie M. "The Choral Music of Luis Sandi (1905–)." D.M.A. diss., Southwestern Baptist Theological Seminary, 1984.

SATIE, ERIK (1866–1925)

Fils des étoiles
6167. Austin, William W. "The Rhythm of Satie and 'Oriental Timelessness'." MMA 13 (1984): 97–111.
6168. Gillmor, Alan. "Satie, Cage, and the New Asceticism." CAUSM 5, no. 2 (1975): 47–66. Reprint, CT 25 (1982): 15–20.

Mercure
6169. Orledge, Robert. "Erik Satie's Ballet *Mercure* (1924): From Mount Etna to Montmartre." JRMA 123, no. 2 (1998): 229–49.

Musique d'ameublement
6170. Blickhan, Charles Timothy. "Erik Satie: *Musique d'ameublement.*" D.M.A. diss., University of Illinois, 1976.

Parade
6171. DeLio, Thomas. "Time Transfigured: Erik Satie's *Parade.*" CMR 7, no. 2 (1993): 141–62.

Piano Works
6172. Austin, William W. "The Rhythm of Satie and 'Oriental Timelessness'." MMA 13 (1984): 97–111. [*Gnossienne* No. 3]
6173. Boaz, Mildred Meyer. "T. S. Eliot and Music: A Study of the Development of Musical Structures in Selected Poems by T. S. Eliot and Music by Erik Satie, Igor Stravinsky, and Béla Bartók." Ph.D. diss., University of Illinois, 1977. [*Gymnopédies*]
6174. Geeraert, Nicole. "Erik Satie: *3 gymnopédies.*" NZM 146, no. 4 (1985): 32–35.
6175. Gillmor, Alan. "Satie, Cage, and the New Asceticism." CAUSM 5, no. 2 (1975): 47–66. Reprint, CT 25 (1982): 15–20. [*Vexations*]
6176. Koon, Margery A. "Aspects of Harmonic Structure in Piano Works of Erik Satie." D.M.A. diss., University of Wisconsin, 1974.
6177. Orledge, Robert. "Satie's Sarabandes and Their Importance to His Composing Career." ML 77, no. 4 (1996): 555–65.
6178. ——. "Understanding Satie's *Vexations.*" ML 79, no. 3 (1998): 386–95.
6179. Porter, David H. "Recurrent Motifs in Erik Satie's *Sports et divertissements.*" MR 39 (1978): 227–30.

Porte héroïque du ciel
6180. Austin, William W. "The Rhythm of Satie and 'Oriental Timelessness'." MMA 13 (1984): 97–111. [Prelude]

Sonneries de la Rose+Croix
6181. Gowers, Patrick. "Satie's *Rose Croix* music (1891–1895)." PRMA 92 (1965–1966): 1–25.

Uspud
6182. Austin, William W. "The Rhythm of Satie and 'Oriental Timelessness'." MMA 13 (1984): 97–111.
6183. Orledge, Robert. "Satie, Koechlin and the Ballet *Uspud.*" ML 68, no. 1 (1987): 26–41.

Various Works
6184. Adams, Courtney S. "Erik Satie and Golden Section Analysis." ML 77, no. 2 (1996): 242–52.
6185. Dickinson, Peter. "Erik Satie (1866–1925)." MR 28 (1967): 139–46.
6186. Orledge, Robert. "Satie's Approach to Composition in His Later Years (1913–24)." PRMA 111 (1984–1985): 155–79.
6187. ——. *Satie the Composer.* Cambridge: Cambridge University Press, 1990.
6188. Wehmeyer, Grete. *Erik Satie.* Regensburg: Bosse, 1974.
6189. ——. "Saties Instantaneismus." F-Fellerer/70: 626–39.

SAUGUET, HENRI (1901–1989)
6190. Bril, France-Yvonne. "Henri Sauguet et la musique lyrique." RM 361–63 (1983): 139–49.
6191. Hofmann, André. "Les ballets." RM 361–63 (1983): 155–69.
6192. Holstein, Jean-Paul. "Les symphonies." RM 361–63 (1983): 185–210.
6193. M-Kniesner. [Piano Sonata]
6194. Mari, Pierrette. "Aperçu esthétique." RM 361–63 (1983): 131–37.
6195. Robert, Frederic. "Les mélodies d'Henri Sauguet." RM 361–63 (1983): 173–83.

SCELSI, GIACINTO (1905–1988)
6196. Freeman, Robin. "Tanmatras: The Life and Work of Giacinto Scelsi." TEMPO 176 (1991): 8–19.
6197. Halbreich, Harry. "Analyse de *KONX-OM-PAX* de Giacinto Scelsi." DI 19 (1989): 14–20.
6198. Menke, Johannes. "Esaltazione serena: Zum dritten Stück der *Tre canti sacri* von Giacinto Scelsi." MAS 4, no. 15 (2000): 44–54.
6199. Zenck, Martin. "Die andere Avantgarde des Giacinto Scelsi: Analytisch-ästhetische Reflexionen zum Klavierwerk." MTX 26 (1988): 41–48.

SCHACHT, THEODOR, FREIHERR VON (1748–1823)

6200. Färber, Sigfrid. "Der fürstlich Thorn und taxissche Hofkomponist Theodor von Schacht und seine Opernwerke." In *Studien zur Musikgeschichte der Stadt Regensburg I*, ed. Hermann Beck, 11–122. Regensburg: Bosse, 1979.

SCHAEFFER, BOGUSŁAW (b. 1929)

6201. Fessmann, Klaus. "Bergson zu Klang gebracht: Beobachtungen zur *Bergsoniana* von Bogusław Schäffer." Melos/NZM 3 (1977): 28–32.

6202. Hubisz, Boguslawa. "Bogusław Schäffer's New Composition." PM 12, no. 2 (1977): 5–10. [*Missa elettronica*]

SCHAEFFER, PIERRE (1910–1995)

6203. Wehinger, Rainer. "Belebte Klänge: Analytische Skizze von P. Schaeffers *Étude aux sons animés.*" MB 11 (1979): 746–51.

SCHAFER, R. MURRAY (b. 1933)

6204. Adams, Stephen. *R. Murray Schafer.* Toronto: University of Toronto Press, 1983.

6205. M-Anhalt: 247–52. [*In Search of Zoroaster*]

6206. Mather, Bruce. "Notes sur *Requiems for the Party Girl* de Schafer." CCM 1 (1970): 91–97.

6207. Schafer, R. Murray, and Olga Ranzenhofer. "Îles de la Nuit: Parcours dans l'œuvre pour quatuor à cordes de R. Murray Schafer." CIR 11, no. 2 (2000): 15–52.

6208. Schafer, R. Murray. "Notes for the Stage Work *Loving* (1965)." CCM 8 (1974): 9–26.

SCHAT, PETER (1935–2003)

6209. Baaren, Kees van. "Peter Schat: *Entelechy* No. 1 for 5 Groups of Instruments." SS 9 (1961): 8–12.

6210. Douw, André. "Peter Schat's Tone Clock." KN 26, no. 2 (1992): 8–14.

6211. Samama, Leo. "Symphony No. 1: A Short Analysis." KN 9 (1979): 34–42.

6212. Schat, Peter. "*Monkey Subdues the White-Bone Demon*: The Development of Characters Composed." KN 12 (1980): 17–30.

6213. ———. "Peter Schat's Symphony No. 1." KN 9 (1979): 31–34.

6214. Schuyt, Nico. "Peter Schat: *Improvisations and Symphonies for Wind Quintet.*" SS 7 (1961): 12–19.

SCHENKER, FRIEDRICH (b. 1942)

6215. Petersen, Peter, and Hans-Gerd Winter. "*Büchner* auf der Bühne: Friedrich Schenkers Versuch einer 'biographischen Oper.'" HJM 14 (1997): 245–70.

6216. Schneider, Frank. "Analyse: *Epitaph für Neruda* von Friedrich Schenker." MG 25 (1975): 269–74.

6217. ———. "'Durch neuen Klang Leben sichern': Zur *Michelangelo-Sinfonie* von Friedrich Schenker." MTX 30 (1989): 21–24.

6218. ———. "Ein Appell zur Wachsamkeit: Friedrich Schenkers *Fanal Spanien 1936.*" MTX 12 (1985): 4–6.

SCHIELEIN, DODO (b. 1968)

6219. Beth, Kerstin. "Mal was anderes: Zur Musik Dodo Schieleins." HJM 15 (1998): 413–25.

SCHMIDT, CHRISTFRIED (b. 1932)

6220. Hansen, Mathias. "Die Analyse: Violoncellokonzerte von Paul-Heinz Dietrich, Siegfried Matthus, und Christfried Schmidt." MG 29 (1979): 591–99.

SCHMIDT, FRANZ (1874–1939)

Buch mit sieben Siegeln

6221. Blasi, Franz. "Das Buch mit sieben Siegeln von Franz Schmidt." ME 18 (1964): 63–67, 107–15, 157–64, 210–15.

6222. Wickes, Lewis. "Franz Schmidt's Oratorio *The Book with Seven Seals.*" MMA 1 (1966): 37–55. Also published in F-Bishop: 37–55.

Organ Works

6223. Nemeth, Carl. "Studien zur Tokkata und Fuge As-Dur von Franz Schmidt." ME 12 (1958): 79–87.

6224. Rapf, Kurt. "Franz Schmidt und die Orgel." ME 28 (1974–1975): 3–8.

6225. Scholz, Rudolf. "Die Orgeltoccata in C-Dur von Franz Schmidt." ME 22 (1968): 155–60; 25 (1969): 206–10.

6226. ———. *Die Orgelwerke von Franz Schmidt: Strukturelle und kompositions-technische Untersuchungen an seinen Orgelwerken mit Fugen.* Vienna: Notring, 1971.

String Quartets

6227. Grote, Adalbert. "Elemente 'logischen' Komponierens in den Streichquartetten Franz Schmidts." OMZ 44, no. 1 (1989): 11–16.

Symphonies

6228. Ottner, Carmen. "Franz Schmidt: Vierte Symphonie, 'Ein Requiem für meine Tochter.'" OMZ 51, no. 8 (1996): 531–38.

6229. Wildner, Johannes. "Die Symphonien von Franz Schmidt." Ph.D. diss., Universität Wien, 1979.

Variationen über ein Husarenlied

6230. Neuman, Konrad. "Folkloristischen Einflüsse in den Werken Franz Schmidts." OMZ 24 (1969): 26–30.

Various Works

6231. Corfield, T. B. "Hungarian and Gypsy Elements in the Music of Franz Schmidt." MR 47, no. 2 (1986–1987): 110–18.

6232. Herrmann, Hellmut. "Franz Schmidts Harmonik." OMZ 29 (1974): 534–40.

6233. OMZ 29, no. 11 (1974). [Special issue]

SCHMITT, FLORENT (1870–1958)

6234. Rife, Jerry Edwin. "A Study of the Early Twentieth-Century Compositional Style of Florent Schmitt Based on an Examination of *Psaume XLVII* and *La tragédie de Salomé.*" Ph.D. diss., Michigan State University, 1986.

SCHNABEL, ARTUR (1882–1951)

6235. Dümling, Albrecht. "Der Komponist Artur Schnabel." DI 12 (1987): 10–19.

SCHNEBEL, DIETER (b. 1930)

Choralvorspiele I/II

6236. Zeller, Hans Rudolf. "Choralbearbeitung als Arbeitsprozess." MELOS 40 (1973): 79–103.

Compositio

6237. Ruzicka, Peter. "*Compositio.*" MTX 57–58 (1995): 83–84.

Für Stimmen (. . . missa est): dt 31,6

6238. Rummenhöller, Peter. "Möglichkeiter neuster Chormusik." In *Der Einfluss der technischen Mittler auf die Musikerziehung unserer Zeit*, 311–17. Mainz: Schott, 1968.

6239. Stoianowa, Iwanka. "Verbe et son: 'Centre et absence': Sur *Cummings ist der Dichter* de Boulez, *O King* de Berio, et *Für Stimmen . . . missa est* de Schnebel." MJ 16 (1974): 79–102.

Jowaegerli (Tradition IV₁)

6240. Dibelius, Ulrich. "Vision zum Weltenbrand: Zu Dieter Schnebel *Jowaegerli.*" MTX 1 (1983): 6–8.

Körper-Sprache

6241. Oehlschlägel, Reinhard. "*Körper-Sprache.*" MTX 57–58 (1995): 53–56.

Missa (*Tradition V*)

6242. Wilkening, Martin. "Missa." MTX 57–58 (1995): 45–48.

Mo-no (Musik zum Lesen)

6243. Karkoschka, Erhard. "Schnebels *Musik zum Lesen.*" MELOS 41 (1974): 350–64.

Piano Quintet, B-Flat Major (*Tradition II₁*)

6244. Gronemeyer, Gisela. "B-Dur-Quintett." MTX 57–58 (1995): 65–68.

Sinfonie X (*Tradition VI*)

6245. Dibelius, Ulrich. "Sinfonie X." MTX 57–58 (1995): 41–44.

Sinfonie-Stücke (Tradition III₂)

6246. Heister, Hanns-Werner. "*Sinfonie-Stücke.*" MTX 57–58 (1995): 49–52.

Urteil

6247. Nauck, Gisela. *Musik im Raum, Raum in der Musik*, 154–67. Stuttgart: F. Steiner, 1997.

SCHNITTKE, ALFRED (1934–1998)

6248. Eberle, Gottfried. "Figur und Struktur von Kreuz und Kreis am Beispiel von Alfred Schnittkes Klavierquintett." F-Schnittke: 46–54.

6249. ———. "Utopie von der Universalreligion: Zu Alfred Schnittkes 4. Sinfonie." MTX 30 (1989): 35–42.

6250. Lesle, Lutz. "Alfred Schnittke, Requiem: Eine Werkeinführung." F-Floros/60: 387–98.

6251. Peterson, Kirsten. "Structural Threads in the Patchwork Quilt: Polystylistics and Motivic Unity in Selected Works by Alfred Schnittke." Ph.D. diss., University of Connecticut, 2000.

SCHNYDER VON WARTENSEE, XAVER (1786–1868)

6252. Schneider, Peter Otto. "Zur Militärsinfonie von Schnyder von Wartensee." SMZ 104 (1964): 11–21.

SCHOECK, OTHMAR (1886–1957)

Festlicher Hymnus

6253. Vogel, Werner. "Othmar Schoecks *Festlicher Hymnus*." SMZ 91 (1951): 237–42.

Penthesilea

6254. Eidenbenz, Richard. "Über Harmonik und tonale Einheit in Othmar Schoecks *Penthesilea*." SJM 4 (1929): 94–130.

6255. Schuh, Willi. "Marginalien zu Othmar Schoecks *Penthesilea*-Melodik." SMZ 108 (1968): 167–73.

Ritornelle und Fughetten

6256. Andreae, Hans. "Othmar Schoecks *Ritornelle und Fughetten*: Eine pädagogische Parallel zu Bach's *Wohltempierten Klavier*." SMZ 101 (1961): 222–28.

Schloss Dürande

6257. Schuh, Willi. "Idee und Tongestalt in Schoecks *Schloss Dürande*." SMZ 83 (1943): 74–83.

Songs

6258. Mohr, Ernst. "Das Problem der Form in Schoecks Liederzyklen." SMZ 83 (1953): 85–91.

6259. Puffett, Derrick. "The Song Cycles of Othmar Schoeck: A Critical Survey." Ph.D. diss., Wolfson College, Oxford, 1976.

6260. ———. *The Song Cycles of Othmar Schoeck*. Bern: Haupt, 1982.

6261. Tiltmann-Fuchs, Stefanie. *Othmar Schoecks Liedzyklen für Singstimme und Orchester: Studien zum Wort-Ton-Verhältnis*. Regensburg: Bosse, 1976.

6262. Vogel, Werner. "Wesenzüge Schoeckscher Lyrik (Eine Studie)." SMZ 86 (1946): 314–20.

6263. ———. *Wesenzüge von Othmar Schoecks Liedkunst*. Zurich: Juris, 1950.

6264. Walton, Chris. "Ein unveröffentlichtes Lied von Othmar Schoeck." DI 19 (1989): 12–14. [*Sommerabend*]

Wandersprüche

6265. Walton, Chris. "Metrische Modulation in Othmar Schoecks *Wandersprüchen*." DI 19 (1987): 8–11.

Various Works

6266. Arnold, Willy. "Othmar Schoecks Harmonik." Ph.D. diss., Zürich, 1971.

6267. Hirsbrunner, Theo. "Othmar Schoeck: Zwischen Romantik und Moderne." M 35 (1981): 246–49.

SCHOENBERG, ARNOLD (1874–1951)

Balladen, Op. 12

6268. Harbinson, William G. "Rhythmic Structure in Schoenberg's 'Jane Grey.'" JASI 7, no. 2 (1983): 222–37.

6269. Martin, Henry. "A Structural Model for Schoenberg's 'Der verlorene Haufen,' Op. 12/2." ITO 3, no. 3 (1977): 4–22.

Begleitungsmusik zu einer Lichtspielszene, Op. 34

6270. Hush, David. "Modes of Continuity in Schoenberg's *Begleitungsmusik,* Op. 34." JASI 8, no. 1 (1984), supplement: 1–45.

6271. Neumeyer, David P. "Schoenberg at the Movies: Dodecaphony and Film." MTO 0, no. 1 (1993).

Buch der hängenden Gärten, Op. 15

6272. Brinkmann, Reinhold. "Schönberg und George: Interpretation eines Liedes." AM 26 (1969): 1–28.

6273. Brown, Julie. "Schoenberg's Musical Prose as Allegory." MA 14, nos. 2–3 (1995): 161–91. [No. 1]

6274. Dahlhaus, Carl. "Musikalische Prosa." NZM 125 (1964): 176–82.

6275. ———. "Schönberg's Lied 'Streng ist uns das Glück und Spröde.'" M-Abraham/L: 45–52.

6276. Dean, Jerry Mac. "Evolution and Unity in Schoenberg's George Songs, Op. 15." Ph.D. diss., University of Michigan, 1971.

6277. De Zeeuw, Anne Marie. "A Numerical Metaphor in a Schoenberg Song, Op. 15, No. XI." JM 11, no. 3 (1993): 396–410.

6278. Dill, Heinz J. "Schoenberg's George-Lieder: The Relationship between Text and Music in Light of Some Expressionist Tendencies." CM 17 (1974): 91–95.

6279. Domek, Richard. "Some Aspects of Organization in Schoenberg's *Book of the Hanging Gardens,* Opus 15." CMS 19 (1979): 111–28.

6280. Dümling, Albrecht. *Die fremden Klänge der hängenden Gärten.* Munich: Kindler, 1981.

6281. ———. "Öffentliche Einsamkeit: Untersuchungen zur Situation von Lied und Lyrik um 1900 am Beispiele des *Buches der hängenden Gärten* von Stephan George und Arnold Schönberg." Ph.D. diss., Technische Universität, Berlin, 1978.

6282. Ehrenforth, Karl Heinrich. *Ausdruck und Form: Schönbergs Druchbruch zur Atonalität in den George-Liedern, Op. 15.* Bonn: Bouvior, 1963.

6283. ———. "Schönberg und Webern: Das XIV. Lied aus Schönbergs George-Liedern Op. 15." NZM 126 (1965): 102–5.

6284. Falck, Robert. "Fear and Hope: Schoenberg's Opus 15, No. VII." CAUSM 7 (1977): 91–105.

6285. Fisher, George. "Text and Music in Song VIII of *Das Buch der hängenden Gärten.*" ITO 6, no. 2 (1981–1983): 3–16.
6286. Forte, Allen. "Concepts of Linearity in Schoenberg's Atonal Music: A Study of the Opus 15 Song Cycle." JMT 36, no. 2 (1992): 285–382.
6287. Jacobs, Jann B. "Grundgestalt analysis." M.A. thesis, Northwestern University, 1979. [Nos. 2, 5]
6288. Kaufmann, Harold. "Struktur in Schönberg's Georgeliedern." M-Abraham/L: 53–61.
6289. Krebs, Harald. "Three Versions of Schoenberg's Op. 15, No. 14: Obvious Differences and Hidden Similarities." JASI 8, no. 2 (1984): 131–40.
6290. Larson, Steve. "A Tonal Model of an 'Atonal' Piece: Schönberg's Opus 15, Number 2." PNM 25 (1987): 418–33.
6291. Lewin, David. "Toward the Analysis of a Schoenberg Song (Op. 15, No. XI)." PNM 12 (1973–1974): 43–86.
6292. ———. "A Way into Schoenberg's Opus 15, Number 7." ITO 6, no. 1 (1981–1982): 3–24.
6293. Schäfer, Thomas. "Wortmusik–Tonmusik: Ein Beitrag zur Wagner-Rezeption von Arnold Schönberg und Stefan George." MF 47, no. 3 (1994): 252–73.
6294. Schwab, Heinrich W. ". . . in einer Art psalmodischem Ton angeblicher Lieder': Zur Struktur der Vertonung in Schönbergs Op. 15." F-Maegaard: 81–96.
6295. Silverton, Jann Jacobs. "A Grundgestalt Analysis of Op. 15, *Das Buch der hängenden Gärten* by Arnold Schoenberg on Poems of Stefan George." Ph.D. diss., Northwestern University, 1986.
6296. Smith, Glenn Edward. "Schoenberg's *Book of the Hanging Gardens*: An Analysis." D.M.A. diss., Indiana University, 1973.
6297. M-Straus: 47–53. [No. 11]
6298. Stroh, Wolfgang Martin. "Schoenberg's Use of Text: The Text as a Musical Control in the 14th Georgelied, Op. 15." PNM 6, no. 2 (1968): 34–44.

Choral Works (various; *see also* specific choral works)
6299. Specht, Robert John, Jr. "Relationships between Text and Music in the Choral Works of Arnold Schoenberg." Ph.D. diss., Case Western Reserve University, 1976.

Concerto for String Quartet and Orchestra
6300. Floreen, John Eric. "Arnold Schoenberg's Concerto for String Quartet and Orchestra after the Concerto Grosso, Op. 6, No. 7 by G. F. Handel: Transcription, Arrangement, and Recomposition." D.M.A. diss., University of Iowa, 1980.
6301. Hübler, Klaus K. "Schönberg und Händel: Über systembedingtes Unverständnis." MB 14, no. 12 (1982): 791–800.
6302. Straus, Joseph N. "Recompositions by Schoenberg, Stravinsky, and Webern." MQ 72, no. 3 (1986): 301–28.

***Dreimal tausend Jahre*, Op. 50a**
6303. André, Naomi. "Returning to a Homeland: Religion and Political Context in Schoenberg's *Dreimal tausend Jahre.*" M-Cross/P: 259–306.
6304. Hufschmidt, Wolfgang. "Sprache und 'Sprachgebrauch' bei Schönberg." ZM 5, no. 1 (1974): 11–20.

***Erwartung*, Op. 17**
6305. Buchanan, Herbert H. "A Key to Schoenberg's *Erwartung* (Op. 17)." JAMS 20 (1967): 434–49.
6306. Budde, Elmar. "Arnold Schönbergs Monodram *Erwartung*: Versuch einer Analyse des ersten Satzes." AM 36 (1979): 1–20.
6307. Hoffman, Michael. "Schoenberg's *Erwartung*: An Overview Analysis." TCM 6, no. 9 (1999): 6–13.
6308. Laborda, José Maria Garcia. *Studien zu Schonbergs Monodram "Erwartung," Op. 17.* Laaber: Laaber, 1981.
6309. Mauser, Siegfried. *Das expressionistische Musiktheater der Wiener Schule: Stilistische und entwicklungsgeschichtliche Untersuchungenen zu Arnold Schönbergs "Erwartung" und "Die glückliche Hand" und Alban Bergs "Wozzeck."* Regensburg: Bosse, 1982.
6310. Penney, Diane Holloway. "Schonberg's Janus-Work *Erwartung*: Its Musico-Dramatic Structure and Relationship to the Melodrama and Lied Traditions." Ph.D. diss., University of North Texas, 1989.
6311. M-Schultz: 108–11.
6312. Suderburg, Robert Charles. "Tonal Cohesion in Schoenberg's Twelve-Tone Music." Ph.D. diss., University of Pennsylvania, 1966.

***Glückliche Hand*, Op. 18**
6313. Albèra, Philippe. "A propos de *Die glückliche Hand.*" CC 1 (1984): 156–66.
6314. Auner, Joseph H. "In Schoenberg's Workshop: Aggregates and Referential Collections in *Die glückliche Hand.*" MTS 18, no. 1 (1996): 77–105.
6315. Beck, Richard Thomas. "The Sources and Significance of *Die glückliche Hand.*" M-Kühn: 427–29.
6316. Crawford, John C. "*Die glückliche Hand*: Schoenberg's Gesamtkunstwerk." MQ 60 (1974): 583–601.
6317. Demierre, Jacques. "Repères analytiques." CC 2 (1984): 167–77.

6318. Krebs, Harald. "Tonal Allusions in Schoenberg's *Die glückliche Hand.*" SMUWO 13 (1991): 49–67.

6319. Latham, Edward D. "Physical Motif and Aural Salience: Sounds and Symbols in *Die glückliche Hand,* Op. 18." M-Cross/S: 179–202.

6320. Mäckelmann, Michael. "*Die glückliche Hand*: Eine Studie zu Musik und Inhalt von Arnold Schönbergs 'Drama mit Musik.'" HJM 10 (1988): 7–36.

6321. Mauser, Siegfried. *Das expressionistische Musiktheater der Wiener Schule: Stilistische und entwicklungsgeschichtliche Untersuchungen zu Arnold Schönbergs "Erwartung" und "Die glückliche Hand" und Alban Bergs "Wozzeck."* Regensburg: Bosse, 1982.

6322. Rodean, Richard William. "An Analysis of Structural Elements and Performance Practice in Arnold Schoenberg's *Die glückliche Hand,* Op. 18." Ph.D. diss., Texas Tech University, 1980.

6323. M-Schultz: 112–22.

6324. Stadien, Peter. "Schoenberg's Speech-Song." ML 62 (1981): 1–11.

6325. Truman, Philip. "Synaesthesia and *Die glückliche Hand.*" I 12 (1983): 481–503.

Gurre-Lieder

6326. Berg, Alban. *Arnold Schönberg: "Gurrelieder" Führer.* Vienna: Universal, n.d. English translation by Mark Devoto, JASI 16 (1993): 24–235.

6327. Campbell, Brian G. "*Gurrelieder* and the Fall of the Gods: Schoenberg's Struggle with the Legacy of Wagner." M-Cross/S: 31–63.

6328. Schubert, Giselher. *Schönbergs frühe Instrumentation: Untersuchungen zu den "Gurrelieder" zu Op. 5 und Op. 8.* Baden-Baden: Koerner, 1975.

6329. Stadien, Peter. "Schoenberg's Speech-Song." ML 62 (1981): 1–11.

Herzgewächse, **Op. 20**

6330. Carlson, David. "*Exempli gratia*: Two Instances of 'Bilingual Text-Painting' in Schoenberg's *Herzgewächse,* Op. 20." ITO 6, no. 1 (1981–1982): 25–28.

6331. Clifton, Thomas. "On Listening to *Herzgewächse.*" PNM 11, no. 2 (1975): 87–103.

6332. Diettrich, Eva. "Schönbergs *Herzgewächse.*" F-Wessely: 103–12.

6333. Hough, Bonny Ellen. "Schoenberg's *Herzgewächse,* Op. 20: An Integrated Approach to Atonality through Complementary Analyses." Ph.D. diss., Washington University, 1982.

6334. Ruf, Wolfgang. "Arnold Schönbergs Lied *Herzgewächse.*" AM 41 (1984): 257–73.

6335. Wood, Jeffrey. "Tetrachordal and Inversional Structuring in Arnold Schoenberg's *Herzgewächse,* Op. 20." ITO 7, no. 3 (1983–1984): 23–34.

Israel Exists Again

6336. Mäckelmann, Michael. "*Israel Exists Again*: Anmerkungen zu Arnold Schönbergs Entwurf einer Israel-Hymne." MF 39, no. 1 (1986): 18–29.

Jakobsleiter

6337. Christensen, Jean Marie. "Arnold Schoenberg's Oratorio *Die Jakobsleiter.*" Ph.D. diss., University of California, Los Angeles, 1979.

6338. ———. "Schoenberg's Sketches for *Die Jakobsleiter*: A Study of a Special Case." JASI 2 (1978): 112–21.

6339. Goehr, Alexander. "Schoenberg and Karl Kraus: The Idea behind the Music." MA 4, nos. 1–2 (1985): 59–71.

6340. Ringer, Alexander L. "Faith and Symbol: On Arnold Schoenberg's Last Musical Utterance." JASI 6, no. 1 (1982): 80–95.

6341. Shaw, Jennifer. "Rethinking Schoenberg's Composition of *Die Jakobsleiter.*" TP 18 (1993): 87–108.

6342. Zillig, Winfried. "Arnold Schönbergs *Jakobsleiter.*" OMZ 16 (1961): 193–204.

6343. ———. "Bericht über Arnold Schönbergs *Jakobsleiter.*" NMD 4 (1960–1961): 29–40.

6344. ———. "Notes on Arnold Schoenberg's Unfinished Oratorio *Die Jakobsleiter.*" SCORE 25 (1959): 7–16.

Kammersymphonie No. 1, Op. 9

6345. Berg, Alban. *Arnold Schönberg Kammersymphonie Op. 9: Thematische Analyse.* Vienna: Universal, n.d. Translated by Mark DeVoto under the title "Chamber Symphony Guide," JASI 16 (1993): 236–68.

6346. M-Leibowitz: 65–66.

Kammersymphonie No. 2, Op. 38

6347. Dale, Catherine. "The 'Skeleton in Schoenberg's Musical Closet': The Chequered Compositional History of Schoenberg's Second Chamber Symphony." JRMA 123, no. 1 (1998): 68–104.

6348. Hinrichsen, Hans-Joachim. "'Eines der dankbarsten Mittel zur Erzielung musikalischer Formwirkung': Zur Funktion der Tonalität im Frühwerk Arnold Schönbergs." AM 57, no. 4 (2000): 340–61.

Klavierstücke, Op. 11

6349. Brinkmann, Reinhold. *Arnold Schönberg: Drei Klavierstuck Op. 11: Studien zur frühen Atonalität bei Schönberg.* Wiesbaden: F. Steiner, 1969.
6350. Brower, Candace. "Dramatic Structure in Schoenberg's Opus 11, Number 1." MRF 4, no. 1 (1989): 25–52.
6351. Christensen, Thomas. "Schoenberg's Opus 11, No. 1: A Parody of Pitch Cells from Tristan." JASI 10, no. 1 (1987): 38–44.
6352. Cinnamon, Howard. "Tonal Elements and Unfolding Nontriadic Harmonies in the Second of Schoenberg's Drei Klavierstücke, Opus 11." TP 18 (1993): 127–70.
6353. Forte, Allen. "The Magical Kaleidoscope: Schoenberg's First Atonal Masterwork, Opus 11, No. 1." JASI 5, no. 2 (1981): 127–68.
6354. Gostomsky, Dieter. "Tonalität-Atonalität: Zur Harmonik von Schönbergs Klavierstück Op. 11, Nr. 1." ZM 7, no. 1 (1976): 54–71.
6355. Lewin, David. "Some Notes on Schoenberg's Op. 11." ITO 3, no. 1 (1977–1978): 3–7.
6356. ———. "A Tutorial on Klumpenhouwer Networks, Using the Chorale in Schoenberg's Opus 11, No. 2." JMT 38, no. 1 (1994): 79–101.
6357. Ogdon, Will. "How Tonality Functions in Schoenberg's Opus 11, No. 1." JASI 5, no. 2 (1981): 169–81.
6358. M-Perle: 10–15.
6359. Reible, John Joseph, III. "Tristan-Romanticism and the Expressionism of the Three Piano Pieces, Opus 11 of Arnold Schoenberg." Ph.D. diss., Washington University, 1980.
6360. Revault d'Allonnes, Olivier. "Les trois pièces pour piano de Schönberg ou comment oublier." INH 4 (1988): 171–80.
6361. M-Schultz: 106–7.
6362. M-Schultz/D. [No. 2]
6363. Wittlich, Gary. "Interval Set Structure in Schoenberg's Op. 11, No. 1." PNM 13, no. 1 (1974–1975): 41–55.

Klavierstücke, Op. 23

6364. Bailey, Kathryn. "Transitional Aspects of Schoenberg's Opus 23, No. 2." CAUSM 2, no. 2 (1972): 24–30.
6365. Barkin, Elaine. "Pitch-Time Structure in Arnold Schoenberg's Opus 23, No. 1: A Contribution toward a Theory of Notational Music." Ph.D. diss., Brandeis University, 1971.
6366. ———. "Registral Procedures in Schoenberg's Op. 23/1." MR 34 (1973): 141–45.
6367. ———. "A View of Schoenberg's Op. 23/1." PNM 12 (1973–1974): 99–127.
6368. Friedmann, Michael. "Schoenberg's Waltz, Opus 23, No. 5: Multiple Mappings in Form and Row." TP 18 (1993): 57–86.
6369. Graziano, John. "Serial Procedures in Schoenberg's Op. 23." CM 13 (1972): 58–63.
6370. Hasty, Christopher. "Segmentation and Process in Post-Tonal Music." MTS 3 (1981): 54–73.
6371. Holtmeier, Ludwig. "Arnold Schönbergs Klavierstück Op. 23, II." MAS 3, no. 12 (1999): 40–51.
6372. Lefkowitz, David S. "Listening Strategies and Hexachordal Combinatorial 'Functions' in Schoenberg's Op. 23, No. 4." MA 16, no. 3 (1997): 309–48.
6373. ———. "Schoenberg and His Op. 23, No. 4: A Functional Analysis." MA 18, no. 3 (1999): 375–80.
6374. Morris, Robert D. "Modes of Coherence and Continuity in Schoenberg's Piano Piece, Opus 23, No. 1." TP 17 (1992): 5–34.
6375. Oesch, Hans. "Schönberg im Vorfeld der Dodekaphonie: Zur Bedeutung des dritten Satzes aus Opus 23 für die Herausbildung der Zwölfton-Technik." ZM 5, no. 1 (1974): 2–10. Also in MELOS 41 (1974): 330–38.
6376. M-Perle: 42–52.

Klavierstücke, Op. 33

6377. Alegant, Brian. "Unveiling Schoenberg's Op. 33b." MTS 18, no. 2 (1996): 143–66.
6378. Bailey, Kathryn. "Row Anomalies in Opus 33: An Insight into Schoenberg's Understanding of the Serial Procedure." CM 22 (1976): 42–66.
6379. Doebel, Wolfgang. "Das Klavierstück Op. 33b von Arnold Schönberg: Kompositorische Struktur und biographisch-ästhetisches Umfeld." F-Floros/70: 213–26.
6380. Friedmann, Michael L. "Motive, Meter, and Row: Conflicting Imperatives to the Performer in Schoenberg's Klavierstück Op. 33b." EXT 6, no. 2 (1993): 29–49.
6381. Glofcheskie, John. "'Wrong' Notes in Schoenberg's Op. 33a." SMU 1 (1976): 88–104.
6382. Graebner, Eric. "An Analysis of Schoenberg's Klavierstück, Op. 33a." PNM 12 (1973–1974): 128–40.
6383. Lefkowitz, David S. "Perspectives on Order, Disorder, Combinatoriality, and Tonality in Schoenberg's Opus 33a and 33b Piano Pieces." INT 11 (1997): 67–134.

6384. MacKay, John. "Series, Form, and Function: Comments on the Analytical Legacy of René Leibowitz and Aspects of Tonal Form in the Twelve-Tone Music of Schoenberg and Webern." EXT 8, no. 1 (1996): 92–131. [Op. 33b]

6385. M-Perle: 111–16.

6386. Puzan, Matthew Davis. "Dynamic Symmetry in the Music of George Gershwin and Arnold Schoenberg." TCM 2, no. 12 (1995): 1–4. [Op. 33a]

6387. Schoffman, Nachum. "Schoenberg Opus 33a Revisited." TEMPO 146 (1983): 31–42.

6388. M-Straus: 173–79.

Kleine Klavierstücke, **Op. 19**

6389. Baker, James M. "Voice Leading in Post-Tonal Music: Suggestions for Extending Schenker's Theory." MA 9, no. 2 (1990): 177–200.

6390. Boge, Claire Louise. "The Dyad as Voice in Schoenberg's Opus 19: Pitch and Interval Prolongations, Voice-Leading, and Relational Systems." Ph.D. diss., University of Michigan, 1985.

6391. M-Cohn. [No. 2]

6392. Cooper, Grosvenor, and Leonard Meyer. *The Rhythmic Structure of Music.* Chicago: University of Chicago Press, 1960.

6393. DeLio, Thomas. "Language and Form in An Early Atonal Composition: Schoenberg's Op. 19, No. 2." ITR 15, no. 2 (1994): 17–40.

6394. Demske, Tom. "Registral Centers of Balance in Atonal Works by Schoenberg and Webern." ITO 9, nos. 2–3 (1986): 60–76. [No. 4]

6395. First, Craig P. "Toward a Theory of Compositional Processes in Schoenberg's Op. 19/2." TSP 6 (1989): 1–21. Reprinted in TSP 7 (1992): 1–27.

6396. Forte, Allen. "Context and Continuity in an Atonal Work: A Set-Theoretic Approach." PNM 1, no. 2 (1963): 72–82.

6397. Grandjean, Wolfgang. "Form in Schönbergs Op. 19, 2." ZM 8, no. 1 (1977): 15–18.

6398. Isaacson, Eric J. "Issues in the Study of Similarity in Atonal Music." MTO 2, no. 7 (1996). [No. 4]

6399. Kasztelan, Helen. "Simple and Complex Games in Bartók's Studies, Op. 18." F-Melbourne: 365–79. [No. 2]

6400. Lewin, David. "Transformational Techniques in Atonal and Other Music Theories." PNM 21 (1982–1983): 312–71. [No. 6]

6401. Lubet, Alex. "Vestiges of Tonality in a Work of Arnold Schoenberg." ITR 5, no. 3 (1981–1982): 11–21. [No. 3]

6402. Massow, Albrecht von. "Abscheid und Neuorientierung: Schönbergs Klavierstück Op. 19,6." AM 50, no. 2 (1993): 187–95.

6403. Morrison, Charles D. "Syncopation as Motive in Schoenberg's Op. 19, Nos. 2, 3, and 4." MA 11, no. 1 (1992): 75–93.

6404. Phipps, Graham H. "The Tritone as an Equivalency: A Contextual Perspective for Approaching Schoenberg's Music." JM 4 (1985–1986): 51–69.

6405. Spindler, Matthias. "Metamorphose per Anamorphose: Zur Emanzipation der Terz in Schönbergs Klavierstück Op. 19, 2." F-Floros/70: 199–212.

6406. Stein, Deborah. "Schoenberg's Opus 19, No. 2: Voice-Leading and Overall Structure." ITO 2, no. 7 (1976): 27–43.

6407. Stuckenschmidt, H. H. "Opus 19, Nummer 3: Eine Schönberg-Analyse." OM 1 (1971–1972): 88–90.

6408. Travis, Roy. "Directed Motion in Schoenberg and Webern." PNM 4, no. 2 (1966): 85–89.

6409. Väisälä, Olli. "Concepts of Harmony and Prolongation in Schoenberg's Op. 19/2." MTS 21, no. 2 (1999): 230–59.

6410. Vlad, Roman. "Una pagina di Schoenberg." STU 14 (1985): 171–92.

6411. Williams, Edgar Warren, Jr. "A View of Schoenberg's Opus 19, No. 2." CMS 25 (1985): 144–51.

Kol nidre, **Op. 39**

6412. Mäckelmann, Michael. "Ein Gebet für Israel, als die Synagogen brannten: Über Schönbergs *Kol nidre*, zum Gedenken an den Pogrom der Kristallnacht 1938." NZM 149, no. 11 (1988): 3–8.

6413. Zahn, Dieter. "Arnold Schönbergs *Kol nidre*, Op. 39: Eine Analyse." MK 57, no. 2 (1987): 57–69.

Lieder (various; *see also* specific collections and song cycles)

6414. Bailey, Walter B. "Prophetic Aspects of Musical Style in the Early Unpublished Songs of Arnold Schoenberg." MQ 74, no. 4 (1990): 491–520.

6415. M-Broekema.

6416. Crawford, John. "The Relationship of Text and Music in the Vocal Works of Schoenberg, 1908–1924." Ph.D. diss., Harvard University, 1963.

6417. Venus, Dankmar. *Vergleichende Untersuchung zur melodischen Struktur der Singstimmen in den Liedern von Arnold Schönberg, Alban Berg, Anton Webern, und Paul Hindemith.* Göttingen, 1965.

Lieder, Op. 2

6418. Just, Martin. "Schönbergs 'Erwartung,' Op. 2, Nr.1." M-Kühn: 425–27.

Lieder, Op. 6

6419. Cratty, William S. "The Role of Vagrant Harmonies in Selected Lieder by Wolf, Strauss, and Schoenberg." EXT 4, no. 2 (1987–1988): 68–79. [No. 5]

6420. Jalowetz, Heinrich. "On the Spontaneity of Schoenberg's Music." MQ 30 (1944): 388–90.

6421. Lewis, Christopher. "Mirrors and Metaphors: Reflections on Schoenberg and Nineteenth-Century Tonality." NCM 11, no. 1 (1987): 26–42. Reprinted in *Music at the Turn of the Century*, ed. Joseph Kerman, 15–31. Berkeley: University of California Press, 1990. [Nos. 1, 7]

6422. Neff, Severine. "Reinventing the Organic Artwork: Schoenberg's Changing Images of Tonal Form." M-Cross/S: 275–308. [No. 7]

6423. Street, Alan. "'The Ear of the Other': Style and Identity in Schoenberg's Eight Songs, Op. 6." M-Cross/S: 103–37.

Lieder, Op. 14

6424. Cinnamon, Howard. "Some Elements of Tonal and Motivic Structure in 'In diesen Wintertagen,' Op. 14, No. 2, by Arnold Schoenberg: A Schoenbergian-Schenkerian Study." ITO 7, nos. 7–8 (1983–1984): 23–49.

6425. Hauer, Christian. "La crise d'identité de Schönberg et la rencontre avec un texte de Stefan George: Le lied op. 14, no. 1 comme œuvre-clé." DI 47 (1996): 4–8.

6426. Jackson, Timothy L. "Schoenberg's Op. 14 Songs: Textual Sources and Analytical Perception." TP 14–15 (1989–1990): 35–58.

6427. Neff, Severine. "Ways to Imagine Two Successive Pieces of Schoenberg: The Second String Quartet, Opus 10, Movement One; The Song 'Ich darf nicht dankend,' Opus 14, No. 1." Ph.D. diss., Princeton University, 1979.

Lieder, Op. 22 (*Orchestral Songs*)

6428. Boss, Jack Forrest. "An Analogue to Developing Variation in a Late Atonal Song of Arnold Schoenberg." Ph.D. diss., Yale University, 1991. ["Seraphita"]

6429. ———. "Schoenberg's Op. 22 Radio Talk and Developing Variation in Atonal Music." MTS 14, no. 2 (1992): 125–49. ["Seraphita"]

6430. ———. "The 'Musical Idea' and Global Coherence in Schoenberg's Atonal Serial Music." INT 14–15 (2000–2001): 209–64. ["Seraphita"]

6431. Dunsby, Jonathan M. "Schoenberg's 'Premonition,' Op. 22, No. 4, in Retrospect." JASI 1 (1976–1977): 137–49.

6432. Falck, Robert. "Schoenberg's (and Rilke's) 'Alle, welche dich suchen.'" PNM 12 (1973–1974): 87–98.

6433. Hill, Richard S. "Schoenberg's Tone-Rows and the Tonal System of the Future." MQ 22 (1936): 14–37.

6434. Schoenberg, Arnold. "Une analyse des Lieder avec orchestre d'Arnold Schoenberg par le compositeur." MJ 16 (1974): 43–53.

6435. ———. "Analysis of the *Four Orchestral Songs,* Opus 22." PNM 3, no. 2 (1965): 1–21.

Moses und Aron

6436. ASO 167 (1995).

6437. Cherlin, Michael. "Dramaturgy and Mirror Imagery in Schönberg's *Moses und Aron*: Two Paradigmatic Interval Palindromes." PNM 29, no. 2 (1991): 50–71.

6438. ———. "The Formal and Dramatic Organization of Schoenberg's *Moses und Aron*." Ph.D. diss., Yale University, 1983.

6439. ———. "Schoenberg's Representation of the Divine in *Moses und Aron*." JASI 9, no. 2 (1986): 210–16.

6440. Fleischer, Robert Jay. "Schoenberg, Dualism, and *Moses und Aron*." D.M.A. diss., University of Illinois, 1980.

6441. Goehr, Alexander. "Schoenberg and Karl Kraus: The Idea behind the Music." MA 4, nos. 1–2 (1985): 59–71.

6442. Hair, Graham. "Schoenberg's *Moses and Aron*." Ph.D. diss., Sheffield, 1973.

6443. Keller, Hans. "Schoenberg: *Moses and Aron*." SCORE 21 (1957): 30–45.

6444. Latham, Edward D. "The Prophet and the Pitchman: Dramatic Structure and Its Musical Elucidation in *Moses und Aron*, Act 1, Scene 2." M-Cross/P: 131–58.

6445. Lewin, David. "*Moses and Aron*: Some General Remarks and Analytic Notes for Act I, Scene I." PNM 6, no. 1 (1967): 1–17.

6446. Newlin, Dika. "The Role of the Chorus in Schoenberg's *Moses and Aaron*." ACR 9, no. 1 (1966): 1–4, 18.

6447. Schmidt, Matthias. "Fragmente einer Sprache der Musik: Zu Schönbergs *Moses und Aron* und Kreneks *Karl V*." AM 53, no. 2 (1996): 135–59.

6448. Simpson, Reynold. "Schoenberg's *Moses und Aron* and the Nineteenth-Century Tradition of Operatic Innovation." ITR 13, no. 2 (1992): 23–39.

6449. Stadien, Peter. "Schoenberg's Speech-Song." ML 62 (1981): 1–11.

6450. Stuckenschmidt, H. H. "An Introduction to Schoenberg's Opera *Moses and Aron*." F-Pisk: 243–56.

6451. M-Vogt: 229–38.

6452. White, Pamela C. *Schoenberg and the God-Idea: The Opera "Moses and Aron."* Ann Arbor, Mich.: UMI Research Press, 1985.

6453. Wörner, Karl H. *Gotteswort und Magie: Die Oper "Moses und Aron" von Arnold Schönberg.* Heidelberg: Schneider, 1959.

6454. ———. "Polyphonie der Symbole: Die 39 Schlusstakte von Schönberg's *Moses und Aron.*" MELOS 24 (1957): 350–52.

6455. ———. *Schoenberg's "Moses and Aron."* New York: St. Martin's, 1963.

Ode to Napoleon, Op. 41

6456. List, Kurt. "*Ode to Napoleon.*" MM 21 (1944): 139–45.

6457. M-Milstein.

Orchester-Lieder, Op. 8

6458. Lewis, Christopher. "Mirrors and Metaphors: Reflections on Schoenberg and Nineteenth-Century Tonality." NCM 11, no. 1 (1987): 26–42. Reprinted in *Music at the Turn of the Century*, ed. Joseph Kerman, 15–31. Berkeley: University of California Press, 1990. [No. 5]

6459. Schubert, Giselher. *Schönbergs frühe Instrumentation: Untersuchungen zu den "Gurrelieder" zu Op. 5 und Op. 8.* Baden-Baden: Koerner, 1975.

Orchesterstücke, Op. 16

6460. Avshalomov, David. "Arnold Schoenberg's Five Pieces for Orchestra, Op. 16: The Story of the Music and Its Revisions, with a Critical Study of His 1949 Revision." D.M.A. diss., University of Washington, 1976.

6461. Benjamin, William E. "Abstract Polyphonies: The Music of Schoenberg's Nietzschean Moment." M-Cross/P: 1–39. [No. 5]

6462. Burkhart, Charles. "Schoenberg's *Farben*: An Analysis of Op. 16, No. 3." PNM 12 (1973–1974): 141–72.

6463. Cogan, Robert. "Reconceiving Theory: The Analysis of Tone Color." CMS 15 (1975): 52–69.

6464. Dineen, Murray. "Schoenberg's 'Vergangenes,' Op. 16, No. 2: Social Critique and Analysis." EXT 8, no. 1 (1996): 132–50.

6465. Doflein, Erich. "Schönbergs Opus 16 Nr. 3: Der Mythos der Klangfarbenmelodie." MELOS 36 (1969): 203–5.

6466. ———. "Schönbergs Op. 16 Nr. 4: Geschichte einer Überschrift." MELOS 36 (1969): 206–9.

6467. Förtig, Peter. "Analyse des Opus 16, Nr. 4 von Arnold Schönberg." MELOS 36 (1969): 206–9.

6468. Lansky, Paul. "Pitch-Class Consciousness." PNM 13, no. 2 (1974–1975): 30–56.

6469. Mäckelmann, Michael. *Arnold Schönberg: Fünf Orchesterstücke Op. 16.* Munich: Fink, 1987.

6470. Mastropasqua, Mauro. "Analisi della Klangfarbenmelodie: Schönberg, Op. 16, III–*Farben (Sommermorgen am See)*." ANL 3 (1990): 12–25.

6471. M-Rahn: 59–73. [No. 3]

6472. Rufer, Josef. "Noch einmal Schönbergs Op. 16." MELOS 36 (1969): 366–68.

6473. Tsang, Lee. "Musical Timbre in Context: The Second Viennese School, 1909–1925." Ph.D. diss., University of Southhampton, 2000. [No. 3]

Orchestral Songs, Op. 22. *See* Lieder, Op. 22

Passacaglia (Orchestra)

6474. Haimo, Ethan. "Redating Schoenberg's Passacaglia for Orchestra." JAMS 40, no. 3 (1987): 471–94.

Pelleas und Melisande, Op. 5

6475. Ackermann, Peter. "Schönbergs *Pelleas und Melisande* und die Tradition der Symphonischen Dichtung." AM 49, no. 2 (1992): 146–56.

6476. Berg, Alban. *Arnold Schönbergs "Pelleas und Melisande": Kurze thematische Analyse.* Vienna: Universal, n.d. Translated by Mark DeVoto under the title "*Pelleas and Melisande* Guide," JASI 16 (1993): 270–92.

6477. Harvey, Jonathan. "Schoenberg: Man or Woman?" ML 56 (1975): 371–85.

6478. Puffett, Derrick. "'Music That Echoes within One' for a Lifetime: Berg's Reception of Schoenberg's *Pelleas und Melisande.*" ML 76, no. 2 (1995): 209–64.

6479. Schubert, Giselher. *Schönbergs frühe Instrumentation: Untersuchungen zu den "Gurrelieder" zu Op. 5 und Op. 8.* Baden-Baden: Koerner, 1975.

6480. M-Schultz: 98–105.

6481. Staempfli, Edward. "*Pelleas und Melisande:* Eine Gegenüberstellung der Werke von Claude Debussy und Arnold Schonberg." SMZ 112 (1972): 65–72.

Phantasy for Violin and Piano, Op. 47

6482. Boss, Jack. "The 'Musical Idea' and Global Coherence in Schoenberg's Atonal Serial Music." INT 14–15 (2000–2001): 209–64.

6483. M-Forte: 110–27.

6484. Friedmann, Michael L. "A Methodology for the Discussion of Contour: Its Application to Schoenberg's Music." JMT 29, no. 2 (1985): 223–47.

6485. Hasty, Christopher F. "Form and Idea in Schoenberg's Phantasy." M-Baker: 459–79.

6486. Lewin, David. "A Study of Hexachord Levels in Schoenberg's *Violin Fantasy.*" PNM 6, no. 1 (1967): 18–32.

6487. Polansky, Larry. "History and the Word: Form and Tonality in Schoenberg's Phantasy for Violin with Piano Accompaniment." EXT 3, no. 1 (1985): 29–40.

6488. Raab, Claus. "*Fantasia quasi una sonata*: Zu Schönbergs *Phantasy for Violin with Piano Accompaniment,* Op. 47." Melos/NZM 2 (1976): 191–96.

6489. Whittall, Arnold. "The *Violin Fantasy*: Schoenberg's Serial Scaffolding." CT 6 (1973): 3–6.

Piano Concerto, Op. 42

6490. Bishop, David M. "Schoenberg's Concerto for Piano and Orchestra, Op. 42: A Reexamination of the Evolution of the Series in the Sketches." JASI 14, no. 1 (1991): 134–49.

6491. Garst, Marilyn M. "The Early Twentieth-Century Piano Concerto as Formulated by Stravinsky and Schoenberg." Ph.D. diss., Michigan State University, 1972.

6492. Jalowetz, Heinrich. "On the Spontaneity of Schoenberg's Music." MQ 30 (1944): 394–408.

6493. Johnson, Paul. "Rhythm and Set Choice in Schoenberg's Piano Concerto." JASI 11, no. 1 (1988): 38–51.

6494. Leibowitz, René. "Schönbergs Klavierkonzert, Op. 42." MELOS 16 (1949): 44–48.

6495. Litwin, Stefan. "Musik als Geschichte, Geschichte als Musik: Zu Arnold Schonbergs Klavierkonzert Op. 42 (1942)." DI 59 (1999): 12–17.

6496. Mäkelä, Tomi. "Schönbergs Klavierkonzert Opus 42—Ein romantisches Virtuosenkonzert? Ein Beitrag zu Analyse der kompositorischen Prinzipien eines problematischen Werkes." MF 45, no. 1 (1992): 1–20.

6497. Mead, Andrew. "Twelve-Tone Organizational Strategies: An Analytical Sampler." INT 3 (1989): 93–169.

6498. Newlin, Dika. "Secret Tonality in Schoenberg's Piano Concerto." PNM 13, no. 1 (1974–1975): 137–39.

6499. Wall, Byron E. "A Comparison of Two Great Piano Concertos: Mozart's in C Minor and Schoenberg's." D 1, no. 1 (1969): 8–20.

Piano Works (various; *see also* specific piano works)

6500. M-Buccheri.

6501. Carpenter, Patricia. "The Piano Music of Arnold Schoenberg." PQ 41 (1962): 26–31; 42 (1962–1963): 23–29.

6502. Friedburg, Ruth. "The Solo Keyboard Works of Arnold Schoenberg." MR 23 (1962): 39–43.

6503. Ganter, Claus. *Ordnungsprinzip oder Konstruktion? Die Entwicklung der Tonsprache Arnold Schönbergs am Beispiel seiner Klavierwerke.* Munich: Katzbichler, 1997.

6504. Kraus, Elsie C. "Schönbergs Klavierwerk steht lebendig vor mir." MELOS 41 (1974): 134–39.

6505. Krieger, Georg. *Schönbergs Werke für Klavier.* Göttingen: Vandenhoeck & Ruprecht, 1968.

6506. Newlin, Dika. "The Piano Music of Arnold Schoenberg." PQ 105 (1979): 38–43.

6507. Rogge, Wolfgang. *Das Klavierwerk Arnold Schönbergs.* Regensburg: Bosse, 1964.

6508. Tuttle, T. Temple. "Schoenberg's Compositions for Piano Solo." MR 18 (1957): 301–4.

6509. Wee, A. DeWayne. "The Twelve-Tone Piano Compositions of Arnold Schoenberg." D.M. diss., Indiana University, 1968.

***Pierrot lunaire,* Op. 21**

6510. Asarnow, Elliot Bruce. "Arnold Schoenberg's 'Heimweh' from *Pierrot lunaire*: Registral Partitioning of the Harmonic Structure." Ph.D. diss., Brandeis University, 1979.

6511. Bailey, Kathryn. "Formal Organization and Structural Imagery in Schoenberg's *Pierrot lunaire.*" SMUWO 2 (1977): 93–107.

6512. Beiringer, Gene. "Musical Metaphors in Schoenberg's 'Der kranke Mond' (*Pierrot lunaire,* No. 7)." ITO 8, no. 7 (1984–1985): 3–14.

6513. Berkovitz, Darlene Rae. "Arnold Schoenberg's *Pierrot lunaire*: A Study of the Music and Text." Ph.D. diss., Yale University, 1986.

6514. Cohen, John. "Gloses sur le *Pierrot lunaire*: Forme et expression." ANM 9 (1987): 29–32.

6515. Dreyer, Martin. "Pierrot's Voice: New Monody or Old Prosody." CT 10 (1974–1975): 15–20.

6516. Dunsby, Jonathan. *Schoenberg: Pierrot Lunaire.* Cambridge: Cambridge University Press, 1992.

6517. Gilbert, Jan. "Schoenberg's Harmonic Visions: A Study of Text Painting in 'Die Kreuze.'" JASI 8, no. 2 (1984): 117–30.

6518. Gillespie, Jeffrey L. "Motivic Transformations and Networks in Schoenberg's 'Nacht' from *Pierrot Lunaire.*" INT 6 (1992): 34–65.

6519. Lessem, Alan. "Text and Music in Schoenberg's *Pierrot lunaire.*" CM 19 (1975): 103–12.

6520. Lewin, David. "Some Notes on *Pierrot lunaire.*" M-Baker: 433–57.

6521. Lewin, Harold F. "Schoenberg's *Pierrot lunaire*: The Rhythmic Relation between Sprechstimme and Instrumental Writing in 'Eine blasse Wäscherin.'" TP 5, no. 1 (1980): 25–39.

6522. Perle, George. *"Pierrot lunaire."* F-Sachs/C: 307–12.

6523. Roeder, John. "Interacting Pulse Streams in Schoenberg's Atonal Polyphony." MTS 16, no. 2 (1994): 231–49. ["Mondestrunken," "Columbine"]

6524. Schmidt, Matthias. "Musik ohne Noten: Arnold Schönbergs *Pierrot lunaire* und Karl Kraus." SZM 47 (1999): 365–93.

6525. Smyth, David H. "The Music of *Pierrot lunaire*: An Analytic Approach." TP 5, no. 1 (1980): 5–24.

6526. Stadien, Peter. "Schoenberg's Speech-Song." ML 62 (1981): 1–11.

6527. Sterne, Colin C. "Pythagoras and Pierrot: An Approach to Schoenberg's Use of Numerology in the Construction of *Pierrot lunaire.*" PNM 21 (1982–1983): 506–34.

6528. M-Straus: 22–25. ["Nacht"]

6529. Youens, Susan. "Excavating an Allegory: The Texts of *Pierrot lunaire.*" JASI 8, no. 2 (1984): 95–115.

Prelude "Genesis," Op. 44

6530. Dahlhaus, Carl. "Die Fuge als Präludium: Zur Interpretation von Schönbergs *Genesis*-Komposition Opus 44." M 37, no. 6 (1983): 522–24.

6531. Leibowitz, René. "Aspects récents de la technique de douze sons." POL 4 (1949): 32–53.

Satiren, Op. 28

6532. Konold, Wulf. "Schönbergs Kantate *Der neue Klassizismus.*" M 29 (1975): 388–93.

Serenade, Op. 24

6533. Lester, Joel. "Pitch Structure Articulation in the Variations of Schoenberg's Serenade." PNM 6, no. 2 (1968): 22–34.

6534. ———. "A Theory of Atonal Prolongations as Used in an Analysis of the Serenade, Op. 24, by Arnold Schoenberg." Ph.D. diss., Princeton University, 1970.

String Quartets (various; *see also* specific string quartets)

6535. Kelly, Claire Bennett. "Declaration, Dissolution, and Reassembly: A Creative Principle in the String Quartets of Arnold Schoenberg." M.M. thesis, Florida State University, 1970.

6536. Morgan, Robert P. "Schoenberg and the Musical Tradition: The Four String Quartets." MN 1, no. 4 (1971): 3–10.

6537. M-Pütz.

6538. Rauchhaupt, Ursula van, compiler. *Die Streichquartette der Wiener Schule, Schönberg, Berg,Webern: Eine Dokumentation.* Munich: Ellermann, 1971.

6539. Schmidt, Erich. "Studie über Schönbergs Streichquartette." SMZ 74 (1934): 1-8, 84–91, 155–63.

6540. Walker, Gwyneth. "Tradition and Breaking of Tradition in the String Quartets of Ives and Schoenberg." D.M.A. diss., University of Hartford, 1976.

6541. Wilke, Rainer. *Brahms, Reger, Schönberg Streichquartette: Motivisch-thematische Prozesse und formale Gestalt.* Hamburg: Wagner, 1980.

String Quartet, D Major

6542. Boestfleisch, Rainer. *Arnold Schönbergs frühe Kammermusik: Studien unter besonderer Berücksichtigung der ersten beiden Streichquartette.* Frankfurt am Main: Lang, 1990.

6543. Gerlach, Reinhard. "War Schönberg von Dvořák beeinflusst? Zu Arnold Schönbergs Streichqartett D-Dur." NZM 133 (1972): 122–27.

6544. Maegaard, Jan. "Arnold Schönbergs Scherzo in F-Dur für Streichquartett." DAM 14 (1983): 133–40.

6545. Musgrave, Michael Graham. "Schoenberg and Brahms: A Study of Schoenberg's Response to Brahms's Music as Revealed in His Didactic Writings and Selected Early Compositions." Ph.D. diss., King's College, London, 1980.

String Quartet No. 1, Op. 7

6546. Benson, Mark. "Schoenberg's Private Program for the String Quartet in D Minor, Op. 7." JM 11, no. 3 (1993): 374–95.

6547. Boestfleisch, Rainer. *Arnold Schönbergs frühe Kammermusik: Studien unter besonderer Berücksichtigung der ersten beiden Streichquartette.* Frankfurt am Main: Lang, 1990.

6548. Frisch, Walter. "Thematic Form and the Genesis of Schoenberg's D-Minor Quartet, Opus 7." JAMS 41, no. 2 (1988): 289–314.

6549. Hinrichsen, Hans-Joachim. "'Eines der dankbarsten Mittel zur Erzielung musikalischer Formwirkung': Zur Funktion der Tonalität im Frühwerk Arnold Schönbergs." AM 57, no. 4 (2000): 340–61.

6550. M-Leibowitz: 61–65.

6551. Musgrave, Michael Graham. "Schoenberg and Brahms: A Study of Schoenberg's Response to Brahms's Music as Revealed in His Didactic Writings and Selected Early Compositions." Ph.D. diss., King's College, London, 1980.

6552. Neff, Severine. "Aspects of Grundgestalt in Schoenberg's First String Quartet, Op. 7." TP 9 (1984): 7–56.

6553. Schmidt, Christian Martin. "Schonbergs Analytische Bemerkungen zum Streichquartett Op. 7." OMZ 39 (1984): 296–300.

6554. Schubert, Peter. "'A New Epoch of Polyphonic Style': Schoenberg on Chords and Lines." MA 12, no. 3 (1993): 289–319.

String Quartet No. 2, Op. 10

6555. Bleek, Tobias. "Entrückung: Text und musikalische Struktur im Schluss-satz von Arnold Schönbergs II. Streichquartett." AM 57, no. 4 (2000): 362–88. [Movement IV]

6556. Breig, Werner. "Agogik und Sonatenform: Zum Kopfsatz von Arnold Schönbergs Streichquartett Fis-Moll op. 10." JSIM (1999): 102–17. [Movement I]

6557. ———. "Schönbergs 'Litanei.'" M-Breig: 361–76. [Movement III]

6558. Dale, Catherine. "Foreground Motif as a Determinant of Formal and Tonal Structure in the First Movement of Schönberg's Second String Quartet." MR 52, no. 1 (1991): 52–63.

6559. ———. "Schoenberg's Concept of Variation Form: A Paradigmatic Analysis of *Litanei* from the Second String Quartet, Op. 10." JRMA 118, no. 1 (1993): 94–120.

6560. Neff, Severine. "Ways to Imagine Two Successive Pieces of Schoenberg: The Second String Quartet, Opus 10, Movement One; The Song 'Ich darf nicht dankend,' Opus 14, No. 1." Ph.D. diss., Princeton University, 1979.

6561. Pfisterer, Manfred. "Zur Frage der Satztechnik in den atonalen Werken von Arnold Schonberg." ZM 2, no. 1 (1971): 4–13.

6562. Zemlinsky, Alexander von. "Arnold Schoenberg's F-Sharp Minor Quartet: A Technical Analysis." Trans. Mark DeVoto. JASI 16 (1993): 293–321.

String Quartet No. 3, Op. 30

6563. Dietrich, Norbert. *Arnold Schönbergs drittes Streichquartett Op. 30.* Munich: Katzbichler, 1983.

6564. Möllers, Christian. *Reihentechnik und musikalische Gestalt bei Arnold Schonberg: Eine Untersuchung zum III. Streichquartett Op. 30.* Wiesbaden: Steiner, 1977.

6565. Niemöller, Klaus Wolfgang. "Klassische Formsynthese im 1. Satz von Schonbergs 3. Streichquartett." M-Kühn: 429–32.

6566. Odegard, Peter Sigurd. "Schoenberg's Variations: An Addendum." MR 27 (1966): 102–21.

6567. Peles, Stephen V. "Interpretations of Sets in Multiple Dimensions: Notes on the Second Movement of Arnold Schoenberg's String. Quartet No. 3." PNM 22 (1983–1984): 303–52.

6568. Phipps, Graham H. "The Tritone as an Equivalency: A Contextual Perspective for Approaching Schoenberg's Music." JM 4 (1985–1986): 51–69.

6569. Stein, Erwin. "Schoenberg's New Structural Form." MM 7, no. 4 (1929): 3–10.

String Quartet No. 4, Op. 37

6570. Cherlin, Michael. "Schoenberg and *Das Unheimliche*: Spectres of Tonality." JM 11, no. 3 (1993): 357–73. [Movement III]

6571. Cubbage, John Rex. "Directed Pitch Motion and Coherence in the First Movement of Arnold Schoenberg's Fourth String Quartet." Ph.D. diss., Washington University, 1979.

6572. Drude, Matthias. "'Eine reine Familienangelegenheit'? Entwickelnde Variation und Zwölftontechnik in Schönbergs 4. Streichquartett Op. 37 (1936)." M 48, no. 2 (1994): 78–82.

6573. Gradenwitz, Peter. *Arnold Schönberg: Streichquartett Nr. 4, Op. 37.* Munich: Fink, 1986.

6574. ———. "Beethoven Op. 131, Schönberg Op. 37." M-Kühn: 369–72.

6575. Haimo, Ethan. "Aspects of Set-Structure in Schoenberg's Opp. 36 and 37." ISM 5 (1990): 131–45.

6576. Klemm, Eberhardt. "Zur Theorie der Reihenstruktur und Reihendisposition in Schönbergs 4. Streichquartett." BM 8 (1966): 27–49.

6577. Lake, William E. "Structural Functions of Segmental Interval-Class 1 Dyads in Schoenberg's Fourth Quartet, First Movement." ITO 8, no. 2 (1984–1985): 21–29.

6578. M-Milstein. [Movement III]

6579. Neighbour, Oliver. "A Talk on Schoenberg for Composer's Concourse." SCORE 16 (1956): 19–28.

6580. Vilar-Paya, Maria Luisa. "Arnold Schoenberg's Fourth String Quartet and Milton Babbitt: Reconsidering an American Analytical Legacy." Ph.D. diss., University of California, Berkeley, 1999. [Movement IV]

6581. Winham, Godfrey. "Schoenberg's Fouth String Quartet: Vertical Order of the Opening." TP 17 (1992): 59–65.

String Trio, Op. 45

6582. Cherlin, Michael. "Memory and Rhetorical Trope in Schoenberg's String Trio." JAMS 51, no. 3 (1998): 559–602.

6583. Hymanson, William. "Schoenberg's String Trio (1946)." MR 11 (1950): 184–94.

6584. Jordan, Roland Carroll, Jr. "Schoenberg's String Trio, Op. 45: An Analytical Study." Ph.D. diss., Washington University, 1973.

6585. Leibowitz, René. "Aspects récents de la technique de douze sons." POL 4 (1949): 32–53.

6586. Lewin, David. "Generalized Interval Systems for Babbitt's Lists, and for Schoenberg's String Trio." MTS 17, no. 1 (1995): 81–118.

6587. Peel, John M. "On Some Celebrated Measures of the Schoenberg String Trio." PNM 14, no. 2–15, no. 1 (1976): 260–79.

6588. Staempfli, Edward. "Das Streichtrio Op. 45 von Arnold Schönberg." MELOS 37 (1970): 35–39.

Suite, Op. 25 (Piano)

6589. Flammer, Ernst Helmuth. "Zur Schönberg-Deutung in Adornos Philosophie der neuen Musik: Was ist Fortschritt?" BM 32, no. 1 (1990): 56–62.

6590. Klumpenhouwer, Henry. "An Instance of Parapraxis in the Gavotte of Schoenberg's Opus 25." JMT 38, no. 2 (1994): 217–48.

6591. Kurth, Richard. "Dis-Regarding Schoenberg's Twelve-Tone Rows: An Alternative Approach to Listening and Analysis for Twelve-Tone Music." TP 21 (1996): 79–122. [Minuet]

6592. ———. "Mosaic Polyphony: Formal Balance, Imbalance, and Phrase Formation in the Prelude of Schoenberg's Suite, Op. 25." MTS 14, no. 2 (1992): 188–208.

6593. MacKay, John. "Series, Form, and Function: Comments on the Analytical Legacy of René Leibowitz and Aspects of Tonal Form in the Twelve-Tone Music of Schoenberg and Webern." EXT 8, no. 1 (1996): 92–131. [Minuet]

6594. Phipps, Graham H. "The Tritone as an Equivalency: A Contextual Perspective for Approaching Schoenberg's Music." JM 4 (1985–1986): 51–69.

6595. M-Straus: 136–42. [Gavotte]

Suite, Op. 29 (Septet)

6596. Hyde, Martha M. *Schoenberg's Twelve-Tone Harmony: The Suite Op. 29 and the Compositional Sketches.* Ann Arbor, Mich.: UMI Research Press, 1982.

6597. Milstein, Silvina. "Schoenberg's Serial Odyssey." ML 73, no. 1 (1992): 62–79. [Movement I]

6598. M-Milstein. [Movement I]

Survivor from Warsaw, Op. 46

6599. Föllmi, Beat A. "'I Cannot Remember Ev'rything': Eine narratologische Analyse von Arnold Schönbergs Kantate *A Survivor from Warsaw, Op. 46.*" AM 55, no. 1 (1998): 28–56.

6600. Gruhn, Wilfried. "Arnold Schönberg (1874–1951): *Ein Überlebender aus Warschau, Op. 46.*" M-Zimmerschied: 128–52.

6601. ———. "Zitat und Reihe in Schönbergs *Ein Überlebender aus Waschau.*" ZM 5, no. 1 (1974): 29–33.

6602. Heller, Charles. "Traditional Jewish Material in Schoenberg's *A Survivor from Warsaw, Op. 46.*" JASI 3 (1979): 69–74.

6603. Leibowitz, René. "Aspects récents de la technique de douze sons." POL 4 (1949): 32–53.

6604. Schmidt, Christian Martin. "Schönbergs Kantate *Ein Überlebender aus Warschau, Op. 46.*" AM 33 (1976): 174–88, 261–77.

6605. Schweizer, Klaus. "*Ein Überlebender aus Warschau* für Sprecher, Männerchor und Orchester von Arnold Schönberg." MELOS 41 (1974): 365.

Theme and Variations, Op. 43a

6606. Nail, James Isaac. "The Concept of Developing Variations as a Means of Producing Unity and Variety in Schoenberg's Theme and Variations, Op. 43a." D.M.A. diss., University of Texas, 1978.

6607. Schmidt-Brunner, Wolfgang. "Arnold Schönbergs 'pädagogische' Musik: Suite für Streichorchester (1934) und Thema und Variationen für Bläserorchester Op. 43a (1943)." F-Valentin: 215–24.

Variationen für Orchester, Op. 31

6608. Cholopow, Juri. "Der Wert des Webernschen Schaffens." BM 32, no. 1 (1990): 11–18.

6609. Covach, John. "Schoenberg's 'Poetics of Music,' the Twelve-Tone Method, and the Musical Idea." M-Cross/S: 309–46.

6610. Dahlhaus, Carl. *Schönberg: Variationen für Orchester.* Munich: Fink, 1968.

6611. Engelmann, Hans Ulrich. "Schönbergs *Variationen für Orchester.*" MELOS 33 (1966): 396–400.

6612. Hicken, Kenneth Lambert. "Schoenberg's Atonality: Fused Bitonality?" TEMPO 109 (1974): 27–36.

6613. ———. "Structure and Prolongation: Tonal and Serial Organization in the Introduction of Schoenberg's *Variations for Orchestra.*" Ph.D. diss., Brigham Young University, 1970.

6614. Koivisto, Tiina. "Musical Continuities in Schoenberg's *Variations for Orchestra* Op. 31." TP 20 (1995): 57–90.

6615. Leibowitz, René. *Introduction à la musique de douze sons: Les Variations pour orchestre, Op. 31 d'Arnold Schoenberg.* Paris: L'Arche, 1949.

6616. Phipps, Graham Howard. "Schoenberg's Grundgestalt Principle: A New Approach with Particular Application to the *Variations for Orchestra.*" Ph.D. diss., University of Cincinnati, 1976.

6617. Pousseur, Henri. "La polyphonie en question (à propos de Schoenberg, Opus 31)." *Jaarboek I.P.E.M.* (1969): 47–80. Reprinted in *Musique, semantique, société,* 27–77. Tournai: Casterman, 1972.

6618. Schoenberg, Arnold. "La composition à douze sons." POL 4 (1949): 7–31.

6619. ———. "The *Orchestral Variations,* Op. 31." SCORE 27 (1960): 27–40.

Variations on a Recitative, Op. 40

6620. Radulescu, Michael. "Arnold Schönbergs *Variationen über ein Rezitativ,* Op. 40: Versuch einer Deutung." MK 52 (1982): 175–83.

6621. Traber, Jürgen Habakuk. "Versuch über ein 'Nebenwerk': Zu Arnold Schönbergs *Variations on a Recitative,* Op. 40." ZM 5, no. 2 (1974): 29–41.

6622. Watkins, Glenn E. "Schoenberg and the Organ." PNM 4, no. 1 (1965): 119–35.

Verklärte Nacht, Op. 4

6623. Heinz, Rudolf. "Das Sujet der *Verklärten Nacht*: Eine Interpretation des Dehmelschen Gedichts." ZM 5, no. 1 (1974): 21–28.

6624. Lewin, David. "On the 'Ninth-Chord in Fourth Inversion' from *Verklärte Nacht.*" JASI 10, no. 1 (1987): 45–64.

6625. Musgrave, Michael Graham. "Schoenberg and Brahms: A Study of Schoenberg's Response to Brahms's Music as Revealed in His Didactic Writings and Selected Early Compositions." Ph.D. diss., King's College, London, 1980.

6626. Pfannkuch, Wilhelm. "Zu Thematik und Form in Schönbergs Streichsextett." F-Blume: 258–71.

6627. M-Schultz: 93–97.

6628. Swift, Richard. "1/XII/99: Tonal Relations in Schoenberg's *Verklärte Nacht.*" NCM 1, no. 1 (1977): 3–14. Reprinted in *Music at the Turn of the Century,* ed. Joseph Kerman, 3–14. Berkeley: University of California Press, 1990.

Violin Concerto, Op. 36

6629. Haimo, Ethan. "Aspects of Set-Structure in Schoenberg's Opp. 36 and 37." ISM 5 (1990): 131–45.

6630. Hall, Anne C. "A Comparison of Manuscript and Printed Scores of Schoenberg's Violin Concerto." PNM 14, no. 1 (1975): 182–96.

6631. M-Hall.

6632. Leibowitz, René. "Le Concerto pour violon et orchestre d'Arnold Schoenberg." *Le compositeur et son double: Essais sur l'interprétation musicale,* 210–22. Paris: Gallimard, 1971.

6633. Mead, Andrew. "'The Key to the Treasure . . . .'" TP 18 (1993): 29–56.

6634. ———. "Large-Scale Strategy in Arnold Schoenberg's Twelve-Tone Music." PNM 24, no. 1 (1985): 120–57. [Movement I]

6635. Perle, George, and Milton Babbitt. "Babbitt, Lewin, and Schoenberg: A Critique." PNM 2, no. 1 (1963): 120–32.

6636. Pfau, Marianne Richert. "The Potential and the Actual: Process Philosophy and Arnold Schoenberg's Violin Concerto, Op. 36." TP 14–15 (1989–1990): 123–37.

6637. Suderburg, Robert Charles. "Tonal Cohesion in Schoenberg's Twelve-Tone Music." Ph.D. diss., University of Pennsylvania, 1966.

Von heute auf morgen, Op. 32

6638. Davison, Stephen. "Of Its Time, or Out of Step? Schoenberg's Zeitoper, *Von heute auf morgen.*" JASI 14, no. 2 (1991): 271–98.

6639. ———. "*Von heute auf morgen*: Schoenberg as Social Critic." M-Cross/P: 85–110.

6640. Fritz, Rebecca. *Text and Music in German Operas of the 1920s.* Frankfurt am Main: Lang, 1998.

6641. Geiger, Friedrich. "Mode und Schöpfer: Arnold Schönbergs Oper *Von heute auf morgen* als musikästhetische Polemik." HJM 17 (2000): 101–22.

6642. Keller, Hans. "Schoenberg's Comic Opera." SCORE 23 (1958): 27–36.

Wind Quintet, Op. 26

6643. Boss, Jack. "The 'Musical Idea' and Global Coherence in Schoenberg's Atonal Serial Music." INT 14–15 (2000–2001): 209–64.

6644. Butz, Rainer. "Untersuchungen zur Reihentechnik in Arnold Schönbergs Bläserquintett Op. 26." AM 45, no. 4 (1988): 251–85.

6645. Corson, Langdon. *Arnold Schoenberg's Woodwind Quintet, Op. 26: Background and Analysis.* Ed. Roy Christensen. Nashville, Tenn.: Gasparo, 1984.

6646. Maxwell, John. "Symmetrical Partitioning of the Row in Schoenberg's Wind Quintet, Op. 26." ITR 5, no. 2 (1981–1982): 1–15.

6647. Mead, Andrew. "Large-Scale Strategy in Arnold Schoenberg's Twelve-Tone Music." PNM 24, no. 1 (1985): 120–57. [Movement III]

6648. ———. "'Tonal' Forms in Arnold Schoenberg's Twelve-Tone Music." MTS 9 (1987): 67–92. [Movements I, IV]

6649. Stephan, Rudolf. "Gedanken zu A. Schönbergs Bläserquintett Op. 26." M-Benary: 42–49.

Various Works

6650. Adams, Courtney S. "Techniques of Rhythmic Coherence in Schoenberg's Atonal Instrumental Works." JM 11, no. 3 (1993): 330–56.

6651. Adorno, Theodor W. *Klangfiguren: Musikalische Schriften I,* 94–120. Berlin: Verlag, 1959.

6652. Ashforth, Alden Banning. "Linear and Textural Aspects of Schoenberg's Cadences." PNM 16, no. 2 (1977–1978): 195–224.

6653. ———. "Schoenberg's Cadential Devices." Ph.D. diss., Princeton University, 1971.

6654. Babbitt, Milton. "Since Schoenberg." PNM 12 (1973–1974): 3–28.

6655. Bailey, Walter B. *Programmatic Elements in the Works of Schoenberg.* Ann Arbor, Mich.: UMI Research Press, 1984.

6656. Ballan, Harry Reuben. "Schoenberg's Expansion of Tonality, 1899–1908." Ph.D. diss., Yale University, 1986.

6657. Berg, Alban. "Why Is Schoenberg's Music So Hard to Understand?" MR 13 (1952): 187–96.

6658. Buchanan, Herbert Herman. "An Investigation of Mutual Influences among Schoenberg, Webern, and Berg (with an Emphasis on Schoenberg and Webern, ca. 1904–1908)." Ph.D. diss., Rutgers University, 1974.

6659. Clifton, Thomas James. "Types of Ambiguity in Tonal Compositions of Arnold Schoenberg." Ph.D. diss., 1966. [Opp. 1–10]

6660. Cone, Edward T. "Sound and Syntax: An Introduction to Schoenberg's Harmony." PNM 13, no. 1 (1974–1975): 21–40.

6661. Dean, Jerry. "Schoenberg's Vertical-Linear Relationships in 1908." PNM 12 (1973–1974): 173–79.

6662. Emsley, Richard. "Schoenberg as Rhythmic Innovator." CT 8 (1974): 3–9.

6663. Epstein, David M. "Schoenberg's Grundgesalt and Total Serialism: Their Relevance to Homophonic Analysis." Ph.D. diss., Princeton University, 1968.

6664. Forte, Allen. "Schoenberg's Creative Evolution: The Path to Atonality." MQ 64 (1978): 133–76.

6665. ———. "Sets and Nonsets in Schoenberg's Atonal Music." PNM 11, no. 1 (1972): 43–64.

6666. Friedheim, Philip Alan. "Rhythmic Structure in Schoenberg's Atonal Compositions." JAMS 19 (1966): 60–62.

6667. ———. "Tonality and Structure in the Early Works of Schoenberg." Ph.D. diss., New York University, 1963. [Opp. 1–15]

6668. Godwin, Paul Milton. "A Study of Concepts of Melody, with Particular Reference to Some Music of the Twentieth Century and Examples from the Compositions of Schoenberg, Webern, and Berg." Ph.D. diss., Ohio State University, 1972.

6669. Gradenwitz, Peter. "The Idiom and Development in Schoenberg's Quartets." ML 26 (1945): 123–42.

6670. Hansen, Mathias. "Arnold Schönbergs Kompositionsverständnis und seine Auseinandersetzung mit neoklassizistischen Tendenzen in den zwanzigen Jahren." JP 3 (1980): 66–85.

6671. Hyde, Martha MacLean. "The Roots of Form in Schoenberg's Sketches." JMT 24 (1980): 1–36.

6672. ———. "The Telltale Sketches: Harmonic Structure in Schoenberg's Twelve-Tone Method." MQ 66 (1980): 560–80.

6673. ———. "A Theory of Twelve-Tone Meter." MTS 6 (1984): 14–51. [Opp. 25, 27, 29, 30, 37, 45]

6674. Johnson, P. "Studies in Atonality: Non-Thematic Structural Processes in the Early Atonal Music of Schoenberg and Webern." Ph.D. diss., Worchester, Oxford, 1978.

6675. Kassler, Michael. "A Trinity of Essays: Toward a Theory That Is the Twelve-Note Class System; Toward Development of a Constructive Tonality Theory Based on Writing by Heinrich Schenker; Toward a Simple Programming Language for Musical Information Retrieval." Ph.D. diss., Princeton University, 1967.

6676. Lack, Rudolf. "Arnold Schönberg und das deutsche Volkslied." NZM 124 (1963): 86–91.

6677. Leibowitz, René. "Les oeuvres d'Arnold Schoenberg ou la conscience du drame futur dans la musique contemporaine." POL 1 (1947): 84–104.

6678. Lessem, Alan Philip. "Music and Text in the Works of Arnold Schoenberg: The Critical Years, 1908–1922." Ph.D. diss., University of Illinois, 1973.

6679. Lewin, David. "The Intervallic Content of a Collection of Notes, Intervallic Relations between a Collection of Notes and Its Complement: An Application to Schoenberg's Hexachordal Pieces." JMT 4 (1960): 98–100.

6680. ——. "Inversional Balance as an Organizing Force in Schoenberg's Music and Thought." PNM 6, no. 2 (1968): 1–21.

6681. ——. "Vocal Meter in Schoenberg's Atonal Music, with a Note on a Serial Hauptstimme." ITO 6, no. 4 (1981–1983): 12–26. [Op. 15, no. 5; Op. 20; Op. 21, no. 2]

6682. Lichtenfeld, Monika. "Schönberg und Hauer." MELOS 32 (1965): 118–21.

6683. Lohman, Peter Nathan. "Schoenberg's Atonal Procedures: A Non-Serial Analytic Approach to the Instrumental Works, 1908–1921." Ph.D. diss., Ohio State University, 1981.

6684. Maegaard, Jan. "Schönberg's Zwölftonreihen." MF 29 (1976): 385–424.

6685. ——. *Studien zur Entwicklung des dodekaphonen Satzes bei Arnold Schönberg.* Copenhagen: Hansen, 1972.

6686. Naumann, Peter. "Untersuchungen zum Wort-Ton-Verhältnis in der Einaktern Arnold Schönbergs." Ph.D. diss., University of Cologne, 1972.

6687. Neighbour, O. W. "In Defense of Schoenberg." ML 33 (1952): 10–27.

6688. Nelson, Robert U. "Schoenberg's Variation Seminar." MQ 50 (1964): 143–63. [Opp. 10, 21, 24, 29, 31, 40, 43]

6689. Odegard, Peter Sigurd. "The Variation Sets of Arnold Schoenberg." Ph.D. diss., University of California, Berkeley, 1964.

6690. M-Ogdon.

6691. Paz, Juan Carlos. *Arnold Schoenberg: O el fin de la era tonal.* Buenos Aires: Nueva Vision, 1958.

6692. Perle, George. "Schoenberg's Late Style." MR 13 (1952): 274–82.

6693. Pfisterer, Manfred. *Studien zur Kompositionstechnik in den frühen atonalen Werken von Arnold Schönberg.* Neuhausen-Stuttgart: Hänssler, 1978.

6694. Pillin, Boris William. *Some Aspects of Counterpoint in Selected Works of Arnold Schoenberg.* Los Angeles: Western International Music, 1971.

6695. Reich, Willi. *Schoenberg: A Critical Biography.* Trans. Leo Black. New York: Praeger, 1971.

6696. Rexroth, Dieter. "Arnold Schönberg als Theoretiker der tonalen Harmonik." Ph.D. diss., Rheinischer Friedrich-Wilhelms-Universität, 1971.

6697. Richter, Lukas. "Schönbergs Harmonielehre und die freie Atonalität." DJM (1968): 43–71. Reprint, M-Pečman/J: 339–54.

6698. Rosen, Charles. *Arnold Schoenberg.* New York: Viking, 1975.

6699. Rufer, Josef. *Composition with Twelve Notes Related Only to One Another.* London: Rockcliff, 1954.

6700. ——. *Das Werk Arnold Schönbergs.* Kassel: Bärenreiter, 1974 (1959).

6701. Sadai, Yizhak. "De quelques empreintes stylistiques dean les premières œuvres de Schönberg." ANM 26 (1992): 48–54.

6702. Samson, Jim. "Schoenberg's 'Atonal' Music." TEMPO 109 (1974): 16–25.

6703. Schmidt, Christian Martin. "Ansätze zu einem harmonischen System in späten tonalen Kompositionen Schönbergs." MF 29 (1976): 425–30.

6704. Schmidt, Wolfgang. *Gestalt und Funktion rhythmischer Phänomene in der Musik Arnold Schönbergs.* Erlangen, 1973.

6705. Schneider, Frank. "Schönberg und die tschechische Musik." BM 23 (1981): 26–30.

6706. Schoenberg, Arnold. "My Evolution." MQ 38 (1952): 517–27.

6707. ——. "Problems of Harmony." MM 11 (1934): 167–87.

6708. Schollum, Robert. *Die Wiener Schule, Schonberg-Berg-Webern: Entwicklung und Ergebnis.* Vienna: Lafite, 1969.

6709. Schubli, Sigfried. "Ein Stück praktisch gewordener Ideologie: Zum Problem der Komplexen einsätzigen Form in Frühwerken Arnold Schönbergs." AM 41 (1984): 274–94.

6710. SCORE 6 (1952): 3–43. [Special issue]

6711. Spies, Claudio. "The Organ Supplanted: A Case for Differentiations." PNM 11, no. 2 (1975): 24–25. [Transcriptions of Bach]

6712. Spring, Glenn Ernest, Jr. "Determinants of Phrase Structure in Selected Works of Schoenberg, Berg, and Webern." D.M.A. diss., University of Washington, 1972.

6713. Steiner, Ena. "Suchen um des Suchens Willen: Neuentdeckte Jugendwerke Arnold Schönbergs." OMZ 29 (1974): 279–91.

6714. Stephan, Rudolf. "Schönberg als Symphoniker." OMZ 29 (1974): 267–78.

6715. Suderberg, Robert Charles. "Tonal Cohesion in Schoenberg's Twelve-Tone Music." Ph.D. diss., University of Pennsylvania, 1966.

6716. Thieme, Ulrich. *Studien zum Jugendwerk Arnold Schönbergs.* Regensburg: Bosse, 1979.

6717. Thomson, William. *Schoenberg's Error.* Philadelphia: University of Pennsylvania Press, 1991.

6718. Velten, Klaus. "Das Prinzip der entwickelnden Variation bei Johannes Brahms und Arnold Schönberg." MB 6 (1974): 547–55.

6719. Walker, Alan. "Back to Schoenberg." MR 21 (1960): 140–47.

6720. ———. "Schoenberg's Classical Background." MR 19 (1958): 283–89.
6721. Watkins, Glenn. "Schoenberg Re-Cycled." F-Fox: 72–81.
6722. Webern, Anton. "Schonbergs Musik." In *Arnold Schonberg*, 22–48. Munich: Piper, 1912.
6723. Wellesz, Egon. "Schoenberg and Beyond." MQ 2 (1916): 76–95.
6724. Whittall, Arnold. *Schoenberg Chamber Music*. BBC Music Guides, 21. Seattle: University of Washington Press, 1972.
6725. Williams, Roger B. "The Early Development of Arnold Schoenberg: 1897–1905." Ph.D. diss., Cambridge University, 1976.
6726. Yasser, Joseph. "A Letter from Arnold Schoenberg." JAMS 6 (1953): 53–62.
6727. Zenck, Claudia Maurer. "Gegenprobe: Das Überleben traditionellen Formdenkens bei Schönberg." JSIM (1998): 245–67.

SCHOLLUM, ROBERT (1913–1987)
6728. Schollum, Robert. "Mein *Mosaik*: Versuch einer Werkeinführung" ME 31 (1977–1978): 60–63.

SCHOOF, MANFRED (b. 1936)
6729. Krumpf, Hans H. "*Ode* von Manfred Schoof." MB 9 (1977): 532–35.

SCHREKER, FRANZ (1878–1934)

Ferne Klang
6730. Neuwirth, Gösta. *Die Harmonik in der Oper "Der Ferne Klang" von Franz Schreker*. Regensburg: Bosse, 1972.

Gezeichneten
6731. Granzow, Peter. "Franz Schrekers Kompositionstil in seiner Oper *Die Gezeichneten*." Ph.D. diss., University of Innsbruck, 1972.
6732. Krebs, Wolfgang. "Terzenfolgen und Doppelterzklänge in den *Gezeichneten* von Franz Schreker: Versuch einer energetisch-psychoanalytischen Betrachtungsweise." MF 47, no. 4 (1994): 365–83.
6733. Molkow, Wolfgang. "Untergang der Transzendenz Franz Schrekers Oper *Die Gezeichneten*." Melos/NZM 4 (1978): 304–11.
6734. Neuwirth, Gösta. "Musik um 1900." F-Schuh: 89–134.
6735. Powils-Okano, Kimiyo. "Tonnetz und Konsonanzgradberechnung am Beispiel des Vorspiels der Oper *Die Gezeichneten* von Franz Schreker." F-Vogel: 121–38.
6736. Wickes, Lewis. "A *Jugendstil* Consideration of the Opening and Closing Sections of the *Vorspiel* to Schreker's Opera *Die Gezeichneten*." MMA 13 (1984): 203–22.

Kammersinfonie
6737. Brinkmann, Reinhold. "Franz Schreker: In ferner Klang? Bemerkungen zur Forschungslag und Anhand der Kammersinfonie." M-Budde: 27–36.

Schatzgräber
6738. Brzoska, Matthias. *Franz Schrekers Oper Der Schatzgräber*. Stuttgart: Steiner, 1988.

Songs
6739. Budde, Elmar. "Über Metrik und Deklamation in den *Fünf Gesangen für tiefe Stimme*." M-Budde: 37–48.
6740. Danuser, Hermann. "Über Franz Schrekers *Whitman-Gesänge*." M-Budde: 49–73.

Vorspiel zu einem Drama
6741. Stephan, Rudolf. "Zu Franz Schrekers *Vorspiel zu einem Drama*." M-Schreker: 115–21.

Various Works
6742. Chadwick, Nicholas. "Franz Schreker's Orchestral Style and Its Influence on Alban Berg." MR 35 (1974): 29–46.
6743. Hoogen, Eckhardt van der. "Die Orchesterwerke Franz Schrekers in ihrer Zeit." Ph.D. diss., University of Cologne, 1980.
6744. ———. *Die Orchesterwerke Franz Schrekers in ihrer Zeit: Werkanalytische Studien*. Regensburg: Bosse, 1981.

SCHROEDER, HERMANN (1904–1984)
6745. Campbell, John Coleman. "Musical Style in the Three Organ Sonatas of Hermann Schroeder." D.M.A. diss., University of Rochester, 1975.
6746. Keusen, Raimund. *Die Orgel- und Vokalwerke von Hermann Schroeder*. Cologne: Volk, 1974.
6747. Schulze, Frederick Bennett. "The Organ Works of Hermann Schroeder." D.M.A. diss., University of Washington, 1970.

SCHUBAUR, JOHANN LUKAS (1749–1815)
6748. Sieber, Wolfgang. "Johann Lukas Schubaur als Sinfonie-Komponist." *Operpfälzer Documente der Musikgeschichte*, ed. Hermann Beck, 129–200. Regensburg: Bosse, 1976.

SCHUBERT, FRANZ (1797–1828)

Alinde, **D. 904**

6749. Gramit, David. "Lieder, Listeners, and Ideology: Schubert's *Alinde* and Opus 81." CM 58 (1995): 28–60.

Allegro, D. 947, A Minor ("Lebensstürme")

6750. Levenson, Irene Montefiore. "Smooth Moves: Schubert and Theories of Modulation in the Nineteenth Century." ITO 7, nos. 5–6 (1983–1984): 35–53.

6751. Shamgar, Beth. "Drei Klavierstücke und Allegro A-Moll von Schubert: Zwei vernachlässigte Klavierwerke von 1828." MF 44, no. 1 (1991): 49–56.

Allmacht, **D. 852**

6752. Maier, Michael. "Franz Schuberts 'Gasteiner Lieder' Op. 79 nach Texten des Patriarchen von Venedig, Ladislaus Pyrker." AM 55, no. 4 (1998): 332–53.

An die Entfernte, **D. 765**

6753. Gerhard, Anselm. "Entfernte Harmonien und fehlende Gegenwart: Anmerkungen zu Franz Schuberts Goethe-Lied *An die Entfernte* von 1822." MTH 13, no. 2 (1998): 123–30.

An die Laute, **D. 905**

6754. Gramit, David. "Lieder, Listeners, and Ideology: Schubert's *Alinde* and Opus 81." CM 58 (1995): 28–60.

Arpeggione Sonata, D. 821

6755. Geiringer, Karl. "Schubert's Arpeggione Sonata and the Super Arpeggio." MQ 65 (1979): 513–23.

Auf dem See, **D. 543**

6756. Seebass, Tilman. "Classical and Romantic Principles in Schubert's Lieder: *Auf dem See* and *Des Fischers Liebesglück.*" F-LaRue: 481–504.

Auf dem Strom, **D. 943**

6757. Hallmark, Rufus. "Schubert's *Auf dem Strom.*" M-Badura-Skoda: 25–46.

Choral Works (various; *see also* specific choral works)

6758. Cox, Richard G. "Choral Texture in the Music of Franz Schubert." Ph.D. diss., Northwestern University, 1963.

6759. Heider, Anne Harrington. "A Survey of Schubert's Part-Songs for Mixed Voices." ACR 22, no. 3 (1980): 3–17.

Dass sie hier gewesen, **D. 775**

6760. Agawu, V. Kofi. "Schubert's Harmony Revisited: The Songs 'Du liebst mich nicht' and 'Dass sie hier gewesen.'" JMR 9, no. 1 (1989): 23–42.

6761. Lek, Robbert van der. "Zum Verhältnis von Text und Harmonik in Schuberts 'Dass sie hier gewesen.'" AM 53, no. 2 (1996): 124–34.

6762. Schachter, Carl. "Motive and Text in Four Schubert Songs." M-Schachter: Chap. 8.

Des Fischers Liebesglück, **D. 933**

6763. Seebass, Tilman. "Classical and Romantic Principles in Schubert's Lieder: *Auf dem See* and *Des Fischers Liebesglück.*" F-LaRue: 481–504.

Deutscher, **D. 643**

6764. Nonnenmann, Karl Rainer. "Melancholie in Franz Schuberts Walzer in Cis-Moll D 643 und Helmut Lachenmanns *Schubertvariationen* (1956)." AM 54, no. 4 (1997): 247–68.

Divertissement sur des motifs originaux français, **D. 823**

6765. Zipp, Friedrich. "Bemerkungen zu einem zyklischen Klavierwerk zu vier Händen von Franz Schubert." M 32 (1978–1979): 18–22. [Movements II and II]

Du liebst mich nicht, **D. 756**

6766. Agawu, V. Kofi. "Schubert's Harmony Revisited: The Songs 'Du liebst mich nicht' and 'Dass sie hier gewesen.'" JMR 9, no. 1 (1989): 23–42.

6767. Youens, Susan. "Schubert and the Poetry of Graf August von Platen-Hallermünde." MR 46, no. 1 (1985): 19–34.

Erlkönig, **D. 328**

6768. Düring, Werner-Joachim. *Erlkönig-Vertonungen: Eine historische und systematische Untersuchung.* Regensburg: Bosse, 1972.

6769. Krebs, Harald. "Some Addenda to McNamee's Remarks on 'Erlkönig.'" MA 7, no. 1 (1988): 53–58.

6770. Stein, Deborah. "Schubert's *Erlkönig*: Motivic Parallelism and Motivic Transformation." NCM 13, no. 2 (1989): 145–58.

Erster Verlust, D. 226
6771. Kramer, Lawrence. "Performance and Social Meaning in the Lied: Schubert's *Erster Verlust.*" CM 56 (1994): 5–23.

Fantasies (various; *see also* specific fantasies)
6772. Godel, Arthur. "Zum Eigengesetz der Schubertschen Fantasien." M-Brusatti: 199–206.

Fantasy, D. 2e, C Minor (Formerly D. 993)
6773. Demus, Jorg. "Two Fantasies: Mozart's Fantasy in C Minor (K. 475) and Schubert's Fantasy in C Minor (D. 993)." PQ 104 (1978–1979): 9–11.

Fantasy, D. 760, C Major ("Wandererfantasie")
6774. Brody, Elaine. "Mirror of His Soul: Schubert's Fantasy in C (D. 760)." PQ 104 (1978–1979): 23–31.
6775. Fisk, Charles. "Questions About the Persona of Schubert's 'Wanderer' Fantasy." CMS 29 (1989): 19–30.
6776. Raab, Michael. "Phrygische Wendung und Mediantik: *Der Wanderer* und die Fantasie." MTH 13, no. 2 (1998): 131–43.

Fantasy, D. 934, C Major (Violin and Piano)
6777. McCreless, Patrick. "A Candidate for the Canon? A New Look at Schubert's Fantasie in C Major for Violin and Piano." NCM 20, no. 3 (1997): 205–30.

Fierrabras, D. 796
6778. Black, Leo. "Schubert and *Fierrabras*: A Mind in Ferment." OQ 14, no. 4 (1998): 17–39.
6779. Branscombe, Peter. "Schubert and the Melodrama." M-Badura-Skoda: 105–41.

Forelle, D. 550
6780. Schollum, Robert. "Schubarts und Schuberts *Forelle*-Vertonungen." ME 28 (1974–1975): 19–23.

Harfenspieler I-III, D. 478–480
6781. Salmen, Walter. "Zur Semantik von Schuberts Harfenspielergesängen." M-Grasberger: 141–49.

Heidenröslein, D. 257
6782. M-Kresky: 68–79.

Heimweh, D. 851
6783. Maier, Michael. "Franz Schuberts 'Gasteiner Lieder' Op. 79 nach Texten des Patriarchen von Venedig, Ladislaus Pyrker." AM 55, no. 4 (1998): 332–53.

Impromptus, D. 899
6784. Beach, David. "Modal Mixture and Schubert's Harmonic Practice." JMT 42, no. 1 (1998): 73–100. [No. 2]

Impromptus, D. 935
6785. Beach, David. "Modal Mixture and Schubert's Harmonic Practice." JMT 42, no. 1 (1998): 73–100. [No. 2]
6786. Levenson, Irene Montefiore. "Smooth Moves: Schubert and Theories of Modulation in the Nineteenth Century." ITO 7, nos. 5–6 (1983–1984): 35–53. [No. 4]
6787. Pierce, Alexandra. "Climax in Music: Structure and Phrase (Part III)." ITO 7, no. 1 (1983–1984): 3–30.

Introduction and Variations, D. 802 (Flute and Piano)
6788. Zbikowski, Lawrence M. "The Blossoms of 'Trockne Blumen': Music and Text in the Early Nineteenth Century." MA 18, no. 3 (1999): 307–345.

Jüngling an der Quelle, D. 300
6789. Schachter, Carl. "Motive and Text in Four Schubert Songs." M-Schachter: Chap. 8.

Jüngling und der Tod, D. 545
6790. Jackson, Timothy L. "Schubert's Revisions of *Der Jüngling und der Tod*, D. 545a-b, and *Meeresstille*, D. 216a-b [*sic*]." MQ 75, no. 3 (1991): 336–61.

Klavierstücke, D. 946
6791. Shamgar, Beth. "Drei Klavierstücke und Allegro A-Moll von Schubert: Zwei vernachlässigte Klavierwerke von 1828." MF 44, no. 1 (1991): 49–56.

Leichenfantasie, D. 7
6792. Nettheim, Nigel. "The Language of Music in Schubert's *Corpse-Fantasy.*" MR 51, no. 4 (1990): 290–95.

Liebe hat gelogen, D. 751
6793. Stein, Deborah. "Schubert's 'Das Liebe hat gelogen': The Deception of Mode and Mixture." JMR 9, nos. 2–3 (1989): 109–31.
6794. Youens, Susan. "Schubert and the Poetry of Graf August von Platen-Hallermünde." MR 46, no. 1 (1985): 19–34.

Liebende schreibt, **D. 673**

6795. Thym, Jürgen, and Ann Clark Fehn. "Sonnet Structure and the German Lied: Shackles or Spurs?" JALS 32 (1993): 3–15.

Masses

6796. Badura-Skoda, Eva. "On Schubert's Choral Works." ACR 24, nos. 2–3 (1982): 83–90. [No. 5, D. 678, A-Flat major; No. 6, D. 950, E-Flat major]

6797. Dürr, Walther. "*Dona nobis pacem*: Gedanken zu Schuberts spätem Messen." F-Dürr: 62–74.

6798. Gingerich, John. "'To how many shameful deeds must you lend your image': Schubert's Pattern of Telescoping and Excision in the Texts of His Latin Masses." CM 70 (2000): 61–99.

6799. Nafziger, Kenneth J. "The Masses of Haydn and Schubert: A Study in the Rise of Romanticism." D.M.A. diss., University of Oregon, 1970.

6800. Seidel, Wilhelm. "Schubert und die Fuge: Erwägungen über der Fugen in Franz Schuberts Missae solemnes." KJ 83 (1999): 109–36.

6801. Stringham, Ronald S. "The Masses of Franz Schubert." Ph.D. diss., Cornell University, 1964.

6802. M-Taruskin. [No. 6, D. 950, E-Flat major]

Meeresstille, **D. 215a and D. 216**

6803. Göllner, Theodor. "'Meeresstille': Goethes Gedicht in der Musik seiner Zeit." F-Kirkendale: 537–56.

6804. Jackson, Timothy L. "Schubert's Revisions of *Der Jüngling und der Tod*, D. 545a-b, and *Meeresstille*, D216a-b [*sic*]." MQ 75, no. 3 (1991): 336–61.

6805. Poos, Heinrich. "*Meeres Stille*: Versuch, den Begriff eines Schubert-Liedes zu bestimmen." M 39, no. 3 (1985): 251–58. Reprinted in *Franz Schubert "Todesmuskik,"* ed. Heinz-Klaus Metzger and Rainer Riehn, 31–42. Munich: Text + Kritik, 1997.

Mignon, **D. 321**

6806. Broeckx, Jan L., and Walter Landrieu. "Comparative Computer Study of Style, Based on Five Liedmelodies." I 1 (1972): 29–92.

Moments musicaux, **D. 780**

6807. Beach, David. "Modal Mixture and Schubert's Harmonic Practice." JMT 42, no. 1 (1998): 73–100. [Nos. 2, 6]

6808. Chesnut, John. "Affective Design in Schubert's *Moment musical* Op. 94, No. 6." F-Meyer: 295–316.

6809. Cone, Edward T. "Schubert's Promissory Note: An Exercise in Musical Hermeneutics." NCM 5 (1981–1982): 233–41.

6810. De la Motte, Diether. "Wissen, was man liebt: Zur Analyse von Schuberts *Moments musicaux*, Op. 94." MB 16, nos. 7–8 (1984): 498–502.

6811. Fisk, Charles. "Rehearing the Moment and Hearing In-the-Moment: Schubert's First Two *Moments musicaux*." CMS 30, no. 2 (1990): 1–18.

6812. Gauldin, Robert. "Schubert's *Moment musical* No. 6." ITO 6, no. 8 (1979–1981): 17–30.

6813. Holland, Mark. "Schubert's *Moment musical* in F Minor, Op. 94, No. 3: An Analysis." TP 7, no. 2 (1982): 5–32.

6814. Hughes, Matt, Lawrence Moss, and Carl Schachter. "Analysis Symposium." JMT 12, no. 1 (1968): 184–239. Reprint, M-Yeston: 141–201. [No. 1]

6815. Levenson, Irene Montefiore. "Smooth Moves: Schubert and Theories of Modulation in the Nineteenth Century." ITO 7, nos. 5–6 (1983–1984): 35–53. [No. 2]

6816. McCreless, Patrick. "Schubert's *Moment musical* No. 2: The Interaction of Rhythmic and Tonal Structures." ITO 3, no. 4 (1977–1978): 3–11.

6817. Rothgeb, John. "Another View on Schubert's *Moment musical*, Op. 94/1." JMT 13, no. 1 (1969): 129–39.

6818. Schachter, Carl. "More about Schubert's Op. 94/1." JMT 13, no. 2 (1969): 219–29.

6819. Wittlich, Gary E. "Compositional Premises in Schubert's Opus 94, Number 6." ITO 5, no. 8 (1979–1981): 31–43.

Nacht und Träume, **D. 827**

6820. M-De la Motte: 61–72.

6821. Schachter, Carl. "Motive and Text in Four Schubert Songs." M-Schachter: Chap. 8.

Octet, D. 803

6822. M-Kessler. [Movement I]

6823. Klein, Theodor. "Zu Franz Schuberts Oktett Op. 166." F-Haberl: 143–49.

Operas

6824. Citron, Marcia Smith. "Schubert's Seven Complete Operas: A Musico-Dramatic Study." Ph.D. diss., University of North Carolina, 1971.

Piano Duets (various; *see also* specific piano duets)

6825. Lechleitner, Gerda. "Zu Schuberts Ouvertüren für Klavier zu vier Händen." SZM 37 (1986): 13–26.

6826. Weekley, Dallas Alfred. "The One-Piano, Four-Hand Compositions of Franz Schubert: An Historical and Interpretive Analysis." Ed.D. diss., Indiana University, 1968.

6827. Weekley, Dallas Alfred, and Nancy Argenbright Weekley. "Schubert: Master of the Piano Duet." PQ 104 (1978–1979): 41–48.

Piano Quintet, D. 667, A Major ("Trout")

6828. Beach, David. "Phrase Expansion: Three Analytical Studies." MA 14, no. 1 (1995): 27–47. [Movement II]

6829. ———. "Schubert's Experiments with Sonata Form: Formal-Tonal Design Versus Underlying Structure." MTS 15, no. 1 (1993): 1–18.

Piano Sonatas (various; *see also* specific piano sonatas)

6830. Goldberger, David. "A Stylistic Analysis and Performance of Three Piano Sonatas by Franz Schubert." Ed.D. diss., Columbia University Teachers College, 1978.

6831. Hanna, Albert L. "A Stylistic Analysis of Some Style Elements in the Solo Piano Sonatas of Franz Schubert." Ph.D. diss., Indiana University, 1965.

Piano Sonata, D. 157, E Major

6832. Schnebel, Dieter. "Klangraume-Zeitraume: Zweiter Versuch über Schubert." F-Savoff: 111–20.

Piano Sonata, D. 537, A Minor

6833. Komma, Karl Michael. "Franz Schuberts Klaviersonte A-Moll, Op. posth. 164, D. 537: Zur Wandel des klassischen Formbegriffs." ZM 3, no. 2 (1972): 2–15. Reprint, F-Becking: 413–36.

Piano Sonata, D. 568, E-Flat Major

6834. Tusa, Michael C. "When Did Schubert Revise His Opus 122?" MR 45 (1984): 208–19.

Piano Sonata, D. 571, F-Sharp Minor

6835. Partsch, Erich Wolfgang. "Über Klang und Struktur in Franz Schuberts Sonatensatzfragment Fis-Moll (D. 571)." SZM 42 (1993): 251–56.

Piano Sonata, D. 784, A Minor

6836. Whaples, Miriam K. "Mahler's and Schubert's A Minor Sonata D. 784." ML 65 (1984): 255–63.

Piano Sonata, D. 840, C Major

6837. Cone, Edward T. "Schubert's Unfinished Business." NCM 7 (1983–1984): 222–32.

6838. Denny, Thomas A. "Schubert as Self-Critic: The Problematic Case of the Unfinished Sonata in C Major, D. 840." JMR 8, nos. 1–2 (1988): 91–117.

6839. Truscott, Harold. "Schubert's Unfinished Piano Sonata in C Major (1825)." MR 18 (1957): 114–37.

Piano Sonata, D. 845, A Minor

6840. Blumröder, Christoph von. "Zur Analyse von Schuberts Klaviersonate in A-Moll Op. 42." MF 44, no. 3 (1991): 207–20.

6841. Dommel-Diény, Amy. *Schubert-Liszt.* Dommel-Diény 9. Paris: Dommel-Diény, 1976.

6842. Thoresen, Lasse. "Un modèle d'analyse auditive: Application à la sonate Op. 42 D. 845 de F. Schubert." ANM 1 (1985): 44–59.

Piano Sonata, D. 958, C Minor

6843. Fisk, Charles. "Schubert Recollects Himself: The Piano Sonata in C Minor, D. 958." MQ 84, no. 4 (2000): 635–54.

6844. Godel, Arthur. "Schuberts drei letzte Klaviersonaten (D. 958–960)." Ph.D. diss., Zürich, n.d.

6845. Rosen, Charles. "*Ritmi di tre battute* in Schubert's Sonata in C Minor, D. 958." F-Ratner: 113–21.

Piano Sonata, D. 959, A Major

6846. Chusid, Martin. "Cyclicism in Schubert's Piano Sonata in A Major (D. 959)." PQ 104 (1978–1979): 38–40.

6847. Cone, Edward T. "Schubert's Unfinished Business." NCM 7 (1983–1984): 222–32.

6848. Godel, Arthur. "Schuberts drei letzte Klaviersonaten (D. 958–960)." Ph.D. diss., Zürich, n.d.

6849. Hatten, Robert S. "Schubert the Progressive: The Role of Resonance and Gesture in the Piano Sonata in A, D. 959." INT 7 (1993): 38–81.

6850. Jessulat, Ariane. "Zum Andantino Fis-Moll der Sonate D. 959." In *Franz Schubert "Todesmuskik,"* ed. Heinz-Klaus Metzger and Rainer Riehn, 75–87. Munich: Text + Kritik, 1997.

6851. Schwarting, Heino. "Komposition nach Vorbild: Vergleiche bei Schubert und Beethoven." M 38, no. 2 (1984): 130–38.

6852. Waldbauer, Ivan F. "Recurrent Harmonic Patterns in the First Movement of Schubert's Sonata in A Major, D. 959." NCM 12, no. 1 (1988): 64–73.

Piano Sonata, D. 960, B-Flat Major

6853. Bante-Knight, Mary Martha. "Tonal and Thematic Coherence in Schubert's Piano Sonata D. 960." Ph.D. diss., Washington University, 1983.

6854. Cohn, Richard L. "As Wonderful as Star Clusters: Instruments for Gazing at Tonality in Schubert." NCM 22, no. 3 (1999): 213–32.

6855. Godel, Arthur. "Schuberts drei letzte Klaviersonaten (D. 958–960)." Ph.D. diss., Zürich, n.d.

6856. Hill, William G. "The Genesis of Schubert's Posthumous Sonata in B-Flat Major." MR 12 (1951): 269–78.

6857. M-Kessler. [Movement I]

6858. Mainka, Jürgen. "Schuberts B-Dur-Klaviersonate: Ohnmacht und Grösse des 'Trotzdem'." MG 28 (1978): 656–62.

6859. Marston, Nicholas. "Schubert's Homecoming." JRMA 125, no. 2 (2000): 248–70. [Movement I]

6860. Pesic, Peter. "Schubert's Dream." NCM 23, no. 2 (1999): 136–44.

6861. Wolff, Konrad. "Observations on the Scherzo of Schubert's B-Flat Sonata Op. posth. (D. 960)." PQ 92 (1975–1976): 28–29.

Piano Trio, D. 898, B-Flat Major

6862. Denny, Thomas A. "Articulation, Elision, and Ambiguity in Schubert's Mature Sonata Forms: The Op. 99 Trio Finale in Its Context." JM 6, no. 3 (1988): 340–66.

6863. Levenson, Irene Montefiore. "Smooth Moves: Schubert and Theories of Modulation in the Nineteenth Century." ITO 7, nos. 5–6 (1983–1984): 35–53.

6864. Levy, Janet M. "Texture as a Sign in Classic and Early Romantic Music." JAMS 35, no. 3 (1982): 482–531.

Piano Trio, D. 929, E-Flat Major

6865. Fleischhauer, Gunther. "Franz Schubert: Trio für Klavier, Violine, und Violoncello Nr. 2 Es-Dur D. 929 (Op. 100)." NZM 144, no. 6 (1983): 31–34.

6866. M-Kessler. [Movement I]

6867. Willfort, Manfred. "Das Urbild des Andante aus Schuberts Klaviertrio Es-Dur, D.929." OMZ 33 (1978): 277–83.

Piano Works (various; *see also* specific piano works)

6868. M-Sterling.

6869. Whaples, Miriam K. "Style in Schubert's Piano Music from 1817 to 1818." MR 35 (1974): 260–80.

Rosamunde, **D. 797**

6870. Möllers, Christian. "Einfall und Darstellung: Eine Untersuchung zu Schuberts 'Rosamundethema.'" M 32 (1978): 141–46.

6871. Norman, Elizabeth. "Schubert's Incidental music to *Rosamunde*." MR 21 (1960): 8–15.

Schöne Müllerin, **D. 795**

6872. Feil, Arnold. *Franz Schubert: Die schöne Müllerin, Winterreise.* Stuttgart: Reclam, 1975.

6873. Lewin, David. "Music Theory, Phenomenology, and Modes of Perception." MP 3, no. 4 (1986): 327–92. ["Morgengruss"]

6874. Lewis, Christopher. "Text, Time, and Tonic: Aspects of Patterning in the Romantic Cycle." INT 2 (1988): 37–73.

6875. Neumann, Friedrich. *Musikalische Syntax und Form im Liederzyklus "Die schöne Müllerin" von Franz Schubert: Eine morphologische Studie.* Tutzing: Schneider, 1978.

6876. Pazur, Robert. "An Interpretation of the Pitch-Structure of *Die schöne Müllerin*." ITO 1, no. 6 (1975–1976): 9–13.

6877. Reed, John. "*Die schöne Müllerin* Reconsidered." ML 59 (1978): 411–19.

6878. Rosenberg, Herbert. "Ausdruck und Formgestaltung in Schuberts Müllerliedern." M-Lönn: 183–86.

6879. Schmidt, Karl. "Harmonie-Beispiele aus Schuberts Liederzyklus *Die schöne Müllerin*." M 32 (1978–1979): 6–12, 55–60.

6880. Steffen, Ralph. "Text and Form in Schubert's *Die schöne Müllerin*, 'Wohin?': A Schenkerian Perspective." MRF 11, no. 2 (1996): 44–59.

6881. Thigpen, Raymond Owen. "A Study of the Piano Accompaniments of Franz Schubert's *Die schöne Müllerin*." Ed.D. diss., Columbia University, 1964.

6882. Youens, Susan. *Schubert: Die schöne Müllerin.* Cambridge: Cambridge University Press, 1992.

6883. Zbikowski, Lawrence M. "The Blossoms of 'Trockne Blumen': Music and Text in the Early Nineteenth Century." MA 18, no. 3 (1999): 307–345.

Schwanengesang, **D. 957**

6884. Agmon, Eytan. "Music and Text in Schubert Songs: The Role of Enharmonic Equivalence." ISM 4 (1987): 49–58. ["Der Doppelgänger"]

6885. Atlas, Raphael. "Enharmonic *Trompe-l'oreille*: Reprise and the Disguised Seam in Nineteenth-Century Music." ITO 10, no. 6 (1988): 15–36. ["Der Atlas"]

6886. Brauner, Charles S. "Irony in the Heine Lieder of Schubert and Schumann." MQ 67 (1981): 261–81.

6887. Code, David Loberg. "Listening for Schubert's 'Doppelgaengers.'" MTO 1, no. 4 (1995).

6888. M-Code. ["Der Doppelgänger"]

6889. Dürr, Walther. "Schubert's Songs and Their Poetry: Reflections on Poetic Aspects of Song Composition." M-Badura-Skoda: 1–24. ["Die Stadt"]

6890. Goldschmidt, Harry. "Welches war die ursprüngliche Reihenfolge in Schuberts Heine-Liedern?" DJM 64 (1972): 52–62.

6891. Gruber, Gernot. "Romantisch Ironie in den Heine-Liedern?" M-Brusatti: 321–34.

6892. Kerman, Joseph. "A Romantic Detail in Schubert's *Schwanengesang*." MQ 48 (1962): 36–49. ["Ihr Bild"]

6893. Kurth, Richard. "Music and Poetry, a Wilderness of Doubles: Heine–Nietzsche–Schubert–Derrida." NCM 21, no. 1 (1997): 3–37. ["Der Doppelgänger"]

6894. Schenker, Heinrich. "Franz Schubert: 'Ihr Bild.'" Trans. William Pastille. SONUS 6, no. 2 (1986): 31–37.

6895. ———. "'Ihr Bild' (August 1828): Song by Franz Schubert to a Lyric by Heinrich Heine." Trans. Robert Pascall. MA 19, no. 1 (2000): 3–9.

6896. Schnebel, Dieter. "Klangraume-Zeitraume: Zweiter Versuch über Schubert." F-Savoff: 111–20. ["Ihr Bild"]

6897. Schwarz, David. "The Ascent and Arpeggiation in 'Die Stadt,' 'Der Doppelgaenger,' and 'Der Atlas' by Franz Schubert." ITR 7, no. 1 (1986): 38–50.

6898. Seiffert, Wolf-Dieter. "Franz Schuberts Heinelied 'Ihr Bild.'" MF 43, no. 2 (1990): 124–35.

6899. Stovall, Francis D. "Schubert's Heine Songs: A Critical and Analytical Study." D.M.A. diss., University of Texas, 1967.

6900. Thomas, J. H. "Schubert's Modified Strophic Songs with Particular Reference to *Schwanengesang*." MR 34 (1973): 83–99.

6901. Thomas, Werner. "'Der Doppelgänger' von Franz Schubert." AM 11 (1954): 252–67.

6902. Wintle, Christopher. "Franz Schubert, 'Ihr Bild' (1828): A Response to Schenker's Essay in *Der Tonwille*, Vol. 1." MA 19, no. 1 (2000): 10–28.

Songs (various; *see also* specific songs and song cycles)

6903. Baggett, Bruce A. "Analytical Guide to the Understanding and Performance of Selected Song Cycles of Franz Schubert." Ed.D. diss., Columbia University, 1964.

6904. Dommel-Diény, Amy. *Schubert-Liszt*. Dommel-Diény 9. Paris: Dommel-Diény, 1976.

6905. Dräger, Hans Heinz. "Zur Frage des Wort-Ton-Verhältnisses im Hinblick zu Schuberts Strophenlied." AM 11 (1954): 39–59.

6906. Eggebrecht, Hans Heinrich. "Prinzipien des Schubert-Liedes." AM 27 (1970): 89–109.

6907. Fischer, Kurt von. "Metrische Strukturen als Inhaltsvermittlung im Schubertschen Lied." F-Rehm: 207–13.

6908. ———. "Zur semantischen Bedeutung von Textrepetition in Schuberts Liederzyklen." M-Brusatti: 335–42.

6909. Forbes, Elliot. "'Nur wer die Sehnsucht kennt': An Example of a Goethe Lyric Set to Music." F-Merritt: 59–82.

6910. Georgiades, Thrasybulos. *Schubert: Musik und Lyrik*. Göttingen: Vandenhoeck & Ruprecht, 1967.

6911. Gray, Walter. "The Classical Nature of Schubert's Lieder." MQ 57 (1971): 62–72.

6912. Haas, Hermann. *Über die Bedeutung der Harmonik in den Liedern Franz Schuberts: Zugleich ein Beitrag zur Methodik der harmonischen Analyse*. Bonn: Bouvier, 1957.

6913. Hohlov, Jurij N. "Zur Frage vom Verhältnis der Musik und des poetischen Textes in Schuberts Liedern." M-Brusatti: 353–61.

6914. Kramarz, Joachim. "Das Rezitativ im Liedschaffen Franz Schuberts." Ph.D. diss., Freie Universität, Berlin, 1959.

6915. Kramer, Lawrence. "Decadence and Desire: The *Wilhelm Meister* Songs of Wolf and Schubert." NCM 10, no. 3 (1987): 229–42.

6916. ———. *Franz Schubert: Sexuality, Subjectivity, Song*. Cambridge: Cambridge University Press, 1998.

6917. Kramer, Richard. "Distant Cycles: Schubert, Goethe, and the *Entfernte*." JM 6, no. 1 (1988): 3–26.

6918. Krebs, Harald. "Wandern und Heimkehr: Zentrifugale und zentripetale Tendenzen in Schuberts frühen Liedern." MTH 13, no. 2 (1998): 111–22.

6919. Laitz, Steve Geoffrey. "Pitch-Class Motive in the Songs of Franz Schubert: The Submediant Complex." Ph.D. diss., University of Rochester, 1992.

6920. ———. "The Submediant Complex: Its Musical and Poetic Roles in Schubert's Songs." TP 21 (1996): 123–65.

6921. M-Lewis. [Mignon Lieder]

6922. McNamee, Ann K. "The Introduction in Schubert's Lieder." MA 4, nos. 1–2 (1985): 95–106.

6923. Moman, Carl Conway, Jr. "A Study of the Musical Setting by Franz Schubert and Hugo Wolf for Goethe's *Promethus, Ganymed*, and *Grenzen der Menschheit*." Ph.D. diss., Washington University, 1980.

6924. Porter, Ernest Graham. *Schubert's Song Technique*. London: Dobson, 1961.

6925. Schwarmath, Erdmute. *Musikalischer Bau und Sprachvertonung in Schuberts Liedern.* Tutzing: Schneider, 1969.
6926. Spirk, Arthur. "Theorie, Beschreibung, und Interpretation in der Lied-Analyse." AM 34 (1977): 225–35.
6927. Steinbeck, Wolfram. "Das Prinzip der Liedbegleitung bei Schubert." MF 42, no. 3 (1989): 206–21.
6928. Stoffels, Ludwig. "Zur Funktion des Repriseverfahrens in Schubert-Liedern: Analyse und Deutung poetisch-musikalischer Reflexionsformen." AM 43, no. 1 (1986): 46–68.
6929. Utz, Helga. *Untersuchungen zur Syntax der Lieder Franz Schuberts.* Munich: Katzbichler, 1989.
6930. Wildberger, Jacques. "Verschiedene Schichten der musikalischen Wortdeutung in den Liedern Franz Schuberts." SMZ 109 (1969): 4–9.

String Quartets (various; *see also* specific string quartets)
6931. Coolidge, Richard A. "Form in the String Quartets of Franz Schubert." MR 32 (1971): 309–25.
6932. Dahlhaus, Carl. "Formprobleme in Schuberts frühen Streichquartetten." M-Brusatti: 191–97.
6933. Sachse, Hans Martin. *Franz Schuberts Streichquartette.* Münster: Kramer, 1958.

String Quartet, D. 703, C Minor ("Quartettsatz")
6934. Beach, David. "Harmony and Linear Progression in Schubert's Music." JMT 38, no. 1 (1994): 1–20.
6935. Danckwardt, Marianne. "Funktionen von Harmonik und tonaler Anlage in Franz Schuberts Quartettsatz C-Moll, D. 703." AM 40 (1983): 50–60.

String Quartet, D. 810, D Minor ("Der Tod und das Mädchen")
6936. Hollander, Hans. "Stil und poetische Idee in Schuberts D-Moll-Streichquartett." NZM 131 (1970): 239–41.
6937. M-Kessler. [Movement I]
6938. Truscott, Harold. "Schubert's D Minor String Quartet." MR 19 (1958): 27–36.
6939. Wolff, Christoph. "Schubert's 'Der Tod und das Madchen': Analytical and Explanatory Notes on the Song D. 531 and the Quartet D. 810." M-Badura-Skoda: 143–71.

String Quartet, D. 887, G Major
6940. Beach, David. "Harmony and Linear Progression in Schubert's Music." JMT 38, no. 1 (1994): 1–20.
6941. ———. "Schubert's Experiments with Sonata Form: Formal-Tonal Design Versus Underlying Structure." MTS 15, no. 1 (1993): 1–18.
6942. Burstein, Poundie. "Lyricism, Structure, and Gender in Schubert's G Major String Quartet." MQ 81, no. 1 (1997): 51–63. [Movement I]
6943. Dahlhaus, Carl. "Die Sonatenform bei Schubert: Der erste Satz des G-Dur-Quartetts, D. 887." M 32 (1978): 125–30.
6944. Frisch, Walter. "'You Must Remember This': Memory and Structure in Schubert's String Quartet in G Major, D. 887." MQ 84, no. 4 (2000): 582–603.
6945. Gillet, Judy. "The Problem of Schubert's G Major String Quartet (D. 887)." MR 35 (1974): 281–92.
6946. Krummacher, Friedhelm. "Schubert als Konstrukteur: Finale und Zyklus im G-Dur-Quartett D 887." AM 51, no. 1 (1994): 26–50.
6947. Levy, Janet M. "Texture as a Sign in Classic and Early Romantic Music." JAMS 35, no. 3 (1982): 482–531.
6948. Truscott, Harold. "Schubert's String Quartet in G Major." MR 20 (1959): 119–45.

String Quintet, D. 956, C Major
6949. Abert, Anna Amalie. "Rhythmus und Klang in Schuberts Streichquintett." F-Fellerer: 1–11.
6950. Allen, Judith Shatin. "Schubert's C Major String Quintet, Opus 163/1: The Evolving Dominant." ITO 6, no. 5 (1981–1983): 3–16.
6951. Beach, David. "Harmony and Linear Progression in Schubert's Music." JMT 38, no. 1 (1994): 1–20.
6952. ———. "Phrase Expansion: Three Analytical Studies." MA 14, no. 1 (1995): 27–47. [Movement II]
6953. ———. "Schubert's Experiments with Sonata Form: Formal-Tonal Design Versus Underlying Structure." MTS 15, no. 1 (1993): 1–18.
6954. Cone, Edward T. "Schubert's Unfinished Business." NCM 7 (1983–1984): 222–32.
6955. Gingerich, John M. "Remembrance and Consciousness in Schubert's C-Major String Quintet, D. 956." MQ 84, no. 4 (2000): 619–34.
6956. Gülke, Peter. "Zum Bilde des späten Schubert: Vorwiegend analytische Betrachtungen zum Streichquintett, Op. 163." DJM 65 (1973–1977): 5–58.
6957. Suurpää, Lauri. "The Path from Tonic to Dominant in the Second Movement of Schubert's String Quintet and in Chopin's Fourth Ballade." JMT 44, no. 2 (2000): 451–85.

***Suleika* I and II, D. 720 and D. 717**
6958. Seelig, Harry E. "Schuberts Beitrag zu besseren Verständnis von Goethes Suleika-Gestalt: Eine literarisch-musiklische Studie der *Suleika-Lieder* Op. 14 und 31." BM 17 (1975): 299–316.

Symphonies (various; *see also* specific symphonies)

6959. Brown, A. Peter. "Performance Tradition, Steady and Proportional Tempos, and the First Movements of Schubert's Symphonies." JM 5, no. 2 (1987): 296–307.

6960. Hansen, Mathias. "Marsch und Formidee: Analytische Bemerkungen zu sinfonischen Sätzen Schuberts und Mahlers." BM 22 (1980): 3–23.

6961. Horvath, Roland. "Schuberts Symphonieschaffen." ME 26 (1972–1973): 149–53.

6962. Langevin, Paul-Gilbert. "Franz Schubert et la symphonie: Les Nouvelles donnés historiques et musicales." RM 355–357 (1982): 7–56.

6963. ———. "La Structure cellulaire dans les grandes symphonies." RM 355–357 (1982): 110–17.

6964. Levenson, Irene M. "Motivic-Harmonic Transfer in the Late Works of Schubert: Chromaticism in Large and Small Spans." Ph.D. diss., Yale University, 1981.

6965. Schulze, Werner. *Tempo Relationen im symphonischen Werk von Beethoven, Schubert, und Brahms*. Bern: Kreis und Freude um Hans Kayser, 1981.

6966. Weber, Rudolf. *Die Sinfonien Franz Schuberts im Versuch einer strukturwissenschaftlichen Darstellung und Untersuchung*. Münster: Forschungsstelle für theoretische Musikwissenschaft an der Universität, 1971; Kassel: Bärenreiter, n.d.

Symphony, D. 936a, D Major

6967. Brown, Maurice John Edwin. "Schubert's Unfinished Symphony in D." ML 31 (1950): 101–9.

6968. Halbreich, Harry. "La Symphonie no. 10 en re majeur (D. 936A): Étude musicale." RM 355–357 (1982): 83–102.

Symphony No. 2, D. 125, B-Flat Major

6969. Lek, Robbert van der. "Zur Tonartendisposition in den ersten Sätzen der 2., 3. und 4. Symphonie von Franz Schubert." AM 54, no. 4 (1997): 284–98.

Symphony No. 3, D. 200, D Major

6970. Lek, Robbert van der. "Zur Tonartendisposition in den ersten Sätzen der 2., 3. und 4. Symphonie von Franz Schubert." AM 54, no. 4 (1997): 284–98.

Symphony No. 4, D. 417, C Minor ("Tragic")

6971. Lek, Robbert van der. "Zur Tonartendisposition in den ersten Sätzen der 2., 3. und 4. Symphonie von Franz Schubert." AM 54, no. 4 (1997): 284–98.

6972. Weber, Horst. "Schuberts IV. Symphonie und ihre satztechnischen Vorbilder bei Mozart." M 32 (1978): 147–51.

Symphony No. 5, D. 485, B-Flat Major

6973. Edwards, George. "A Palimpsest of Mozart in Schubert's Symphony No. 5." CM 62 (1997): 18–39.

Symphony No. 6, D. 589, C Major

6974. Feil, Arnold. "Zur Satztechnik in Schuberts VI. Sinfonie." M-Grasberger: 69–83.

Symphony No. 7, D. 729, E Major

6975. Newbould, Brian. "La Symphonie No. 7 en mi majeur (D.729) et sa réalisation." RM 355–357 (1982): 57–70.

Symphony No. 8, D. 759, B Minor ("Unfinished")

6976. Chusid, Martin. *Schubert: Symphony in B Minor (Unfinished)*. Norton Critical Scores. New York: Norton, 1971.

6977. Cone, Edward T. "Schubert's Unfinished Business." NCM 7 (1983–1984): 222–32.

6978. Dahlhaus, Carl. "Studien zu romantischen Symphonien: Zur musikalischen Syntax in Schuberts 'Unvollendeter.'" JSIM (1972): 104–19.

6979. Kunze, Stefan. *Franz Schubert: Sinfonie G-Moll, unvollendete*. Munich: Fink, 1965.

6980. Kurth, Richard. "On the Subject of Schubert's 'Unfinished' Symphony: Was bedeutet die Bewegung?" NCM 23, no. 1 (1999): 3–32.

6981. Laaff, Ernst. "Schuberts G-Moll Symphonie: Motivische Analyse zum Nachweis von erkennbaren Grundlagen ihrer Einheitlichkeit." F-Abert/H: 93–115.

Symphony No. 9, D. 944, C Major ("Great")

6982. Bangerter, Klaus. *Franz Schubert: Grosse Sinfonie in C-Dur, D. 944*. Munich: Fink, 1993.

6983. Hinrichsen, Hans-Joachim. "Franz Schuberts Große C-Dur-Symphonie: Zu den Formbildungsprinzipien in Schuberts Spätwerk." BRS (1993): 111–18.

6984. Hollander, Hans. "Die Beethoven-Reflexe in Schuberts grosser C-Dur-Sinfonie." NZM 126 (1965): 183–85.

6985. Jernhake, Klaes-Görän. *Schubert's "stora C-dursymfoni": Kommunikationen med ett musikaliskt konstverk; En tillämpning av Paul Ricoeurs tolkningsbegrepp*. Uppsala: Uppsala University, 1999.

6986. Kopiez, Reinhard. "Die Durchführungstechnik bei Franz Schubert: Die C-dur Sinfonie (D. 944) im Vergleich mit nicht-sinfonischen Werken." M 41, no. 3 (1987): 227–30.

6987. Laaff, Ernst. "Schuberts grosse C-Dur-Symphonie: Erkennbare Grundlagen ihrer Einheitlichkeit." F-Blume: 204–13.

6988. Levenson, Irene Montefiore. "Smooth Moves: Schubert and Theories of Modulation in the Nineteenth Century." ITO 7, nos. 5–6 (1983–1984): 35–53.

6989. M-Taruskin.

6990. Truscott, Harold. "Schubert's C Major Symphony." MMR 87 (1957): 95–105.

Taucher, D. 77

6991. Dürr, Walther. "Schubert's Songs and Their Poetry: Reflections on Poetic Aspects of Song Composition." M-Badura-Skoda: 1–24.

Tod und das Mädchen, D. 531

6992. Schachter, Carl. "Motive and Text in Four Schubert Songs." M-Schachter: Chap. 8.

6993. Wolff, Christoph. "Schubert's *Der Tod und das Madchen*: Analytical and Explanatory Notes on the Song D. 531 and the Quartet D. 810." M-Badura-Skoda: 143–71.

"Trout" Quintet. *See* Piano Quintet, D. 667, A Major

Unglückliche, D. 713

6994. Dürr, Walther. "Entwurf-Ausarbeitung-Revision: Zur Arbeitsweise Schuberts am Beispiel des Liedes *Der Unglückliche* (D. 713)." MF 44, no. 3 (1991): 221–54.

Violin Sonata, D. 408

6995. Sly, Gordon. "The Architecture of Key and Motive in a Schubert Sonata." INT 9 (1995): 67–89.

Wanderer, D. 489

6996. Raab, Michael. "Phrygische Wendung und Mediantik: *Der Wanderer* und die Fantasie." MTH 13, no. 2 (1998): 131–43.

Winterreise, D. 911

6997. Agawu, V. Kofi. "On Schubert's 'Der greise Kopf.'" ITO 8, no. 1 (1984–1985): 3–21.

6998. Agmon, Eytan. "Music and Text in Schubert Songs: The Role of Enharmonic Equivalence." ISM 4 (1987): 49–58. ["Letzte Hoffnung"]

6999. Barry, Barbara R. "Time Levels and Tonal Structures in Schubert's *Die Winterreise*." MR 46, no. 3 (1985): 170–78.

7000. Carpenter, Patricia. "Music Theory and Aesthetic Form." SMUWO 13 (1991): 21–47. ["Auf dem Flusse"]

7001. Chailley, Jacques. *"Le voyage d'hiver" de Schubert.* Paris: Leduc, 1975.

7002. ———. "Le *Winterreise* et l'énigme de Schubert." SM 11 (1969): 107–12. Also in F-Szabolcsi: 107–12.

7003. Chmaj, John. "The Generative Theory as a Tool for Analysis: Multiple Metric Implications in Schubert's 'Der Leiermann.'" SONUS 6, no. 1 (1985): 39–54; 6, no. 2 (1986): 41–65.

7004. M-Code. ["Der greise Kopf"]

7005. Everett, Walter. "Grief in *Winterreise*: A Schenkerian Perspective." MA 9, no. 2 (1990): 157–75.

7006. ———. "A Schenkerian View of Text Painting in Schubert's Song Cycle *Winterreise*." Ph.D. diss., University of Michigan, 1988.

7007. Feil, Arnold. *Franz Schubert: Die schöne Müllerin, Winterreise.* Stuttgart: Reclam, 1975.

7008. Gauldin, Robert. "Intramusical Symbolism in the Last Strophe of Schubert's 'Der Wegweiser.'" ITO 3, no. 12 (1977–1978): 3–6.

7009. Georgiades, Thrasybulos. "'Das Wirtshaus' von Schubert und das Kyrie aus dem gregorianischen Requiem." F-Benz: 126–35.

7010. Greene, David B. "Schubert's *Winterreise*: A Study in the Aesthetics of Mixed Media." *Journal of Aesthetics and Art Criticism* 29, no. 2 (1970): 181–93.

7011. Grondona, Marco. "Eine Wandererfantasie." STU 24, no. 1 (1995): 87–124.

7012. Lewis, Christopher. "Text, Time, and Tonic: Aspects of Patterning in the Romantic Cycle." INT 2 (1988): 37–73.

7013. Schroeder, David P. "Schubert's 'Einsamkeit' and Haslinger's *Winterreise*." ML 71, no. 3 (1990): 352–60.

7014. Seidel, Elmar. "Ein chromatisches Harmonieiserungsmodell in Schuberts *Winterreise*." AM 26 (1969): 285–96.

7015. Youens, Susan. "Poetic Rhythm and Musical Metre in Schubert's *Winterreise*." ML 65 (1984): 28–44.

7016. ———. "'Wegweiser' in *Winterreise*." JM 5, no. 3 (1987): 357–79.

7017. Zenck, Martin. "Die romantische Erfahrung der Fremde in Schuberts *Winterreise*." AM 44, no. 2 (1987): 141–60.

Zauberharfe, D. 644

7018. Branscombe, Peter. "Schubert and the Melodrama." M-Badura-Skoda: 105–41.

7019. Newbould, Brian. "A Schubert Palindrome." NCM 15, no. 3 (1992): 207–14.

Zur guten Nacht, D. 903

7020. Gramit, David. "Lieder, Listeners, and Ideology: Schubert's *Alinde* and Opus 81." CM 58 (1995): 28–60.

Various Works

7021. Abraham, Gerald. *The Music of Schubert.* New York: Norton, 1947.

7022. ———, ed. *Schubert: A Symposium.* London: Drummond, 1946.

7023. Badura-Skoda, Paul. "Fehlende und überzählige Takte bei Schubert und Beethoven." OMZ 33 (1978): 284–94.

7024. Benary, Peter. "Zum Personalstil Franz Schuberts in seinen Instrumentalwerken." JP 2 (1979): 190–208.

7025. Bockholdt, Rudolf. "Die Kunst, heim zu finden: Über Schlüsse und Anschlüsse in Schuberts Instrumentalmusik." MTH 13, no. 2 (1998): 145–56.

7026. Boyd, Malcolm. "Schubert's Short Cuts." MR 29 (1968): 12–21.

7027. Brown, Maurice John Edwin. *Essays on Schubert.* London: Macmillan, 1966.

7028. ———. "Schubert's Settings of the Salve Regina." ML 37 (1956): 234–49.

7029. ———. *Schubert's Variations.* London: Macmillan, 1954.

7030. Bruce, Robert. "The Lyrical Element in Schubert's Instrumental Forms." MR 30 (1969): 131–37.

7031. Burdick, Michael Francis. "A Structural Analysis of Melodic Scale-Degree Tendencies in Selected Themes of Haydn, Mozart, Schubert, and Chopin." Ph.D. diss., Indiana University, 1977.

7032. Chusid, Martin. "The Chamber Music of Franz Schubert." Ph.D. diss., University of California, Berkeley, 1961.

7033. ———. "Concerning Orchestral Style in Schubert's Earliest Chamber Music for Strings." F-Jackson: 383–93.

7034. ———. "Schubert's Cyclic Composition of 1824." ACTA 36 (1964): 37–45.

7035. Clarke, F. R. C. "Schubert's Use of Tonality: Some Unique Features." CAUSM 1, no. 2 (1971): 25–38.

7036. Coren, Daniel. "Ambiguity in Schubert's Recapitulations." MQ 60 (1974): 568–82.

7037. Dale, Kathleen. "Schubert's Indebtedness to Hadyn." ML 21 (1940): 23–30.

7038. Depew, Laurienne Joyce. "Franz Schubert's Music for Violin and Piano." M.A. thesis, University of Kentucky, 1977.

7039. Downs, Philip. "On an Aspect of Schubert's Expressive Means." SMUWO 2 (1977): 41–51.

7040. Edler, Arnfried. "Hinweise auf die Wirkung Bachs im Werk Franz Schuberts." MF 33 (1980): 279–91.

7041. Federhofer, Hellmut. "Terzverwandle Akkorde und ihre Funktion in der Harmonik Franz Schuberts." M-Brusatti: 61–70.

7042. Feil, Arnold. *Studien zu Schuberts Rhythmik.* Munich: Fink, 1966.

7043. Floros, Constantin. "Parallelem zwischen Schubert und Bruckner." F-Wessely: 133–46.

7044. Gibbs, Christopher H., ed. *The Cambridge Companion to Schubert.* Cambridge: Cambridge University Press, 1997.

7045. Goldschmidt, Harry. "Die Frage der Periodisierung im Schaffen Schuberts." BM 2 (1959): 2–28.

7046. Gülke, Peter. "Musikalische Lyrik und instrumentale Grossform." M-Brusatti: 199–206.

7047. Hinrichsen, Hans-Joachim. "Die Sonatenform im Spätwerk Franz Schubert." AM 45, no. 1 (1988): 16–49.

7048. Keller, Hermann. "Schuberts Verhältnis zur Sonatenform." F-Vetter: 287–95.

7049. Krebs, Harald. "The Background Level in Some Tonally Deviating Works of Franz Schubert." ITO 8, no. 8 (1984–1985): 5–18.

7050. Kühn, Clemens. "Zur Themenbildung Franz Schuberts: Sechs Annäherungen." F-Dahlhaus: 503–15.

7051. Marggraf, Wolfgang. "Franz Schubert und die slawische Folklore." BM 23 (1981): 20–25.

7052. Misch, Ludwig. "Ein Lieblingsmotiv Schuberts." MF 15 (1962): 146–52.

7053. Newbould, Brian. "Schubert im Spiegel." Trans. Rudolf Bockholdt. MTH 13, no. 2 (1998): 101–10.

7054. Pfrogner, Hermann. "Der Dominantseptklang und seine enharmonische Stellung in Schuberts Harmonik." OMZ 2 (1947): 14–18.

7055. Porter, Ernest Graham. "Schubert's Harmonies." MR 19 (1958): 20–26.

7056. Pritchard, T. C. L. "Franz Schubert." MR 1 (1940): 103–22.

7057. Rhein, Robert. "Franz Schuberts Variationswerke." Ph.D. diss., Universität des Saarlandes, 1960.

7058. Riezler, Walter. *Schuberts Instrumentalmusik: Werkanalysen.* Zurich: Atlantis, 1967.

7059. Seidel, Elmar. "Die Enharmonik in den harmonischen Grossformen Schuberts." Ph.D. diss., Johann Wolfgang Goethe-Universität, Frankfurt am Main, 1963.

7060. Temperley, Nicholas. "Schubert and Beethoven's Eight-Six Chord." NCM 5 (1981–1982): 142–54.

7061. Webster, James. "Schubert's Sonata Form and Brahms's First Maturity." NCM 2, no. 1 (1978): 18–35; 3 (1979–1980): 52–71.

7062. Wessel, Matthias. "Die Zyklusgestaltung in Franz Schuberts Instrumentalwerk: Eine Skizze zu Anlage und Ästhetik der Finalsatze." MF 49, no. 1 (1996): 19–35.

7063. Wollenberg, Susan. "Schubert and the Dream." STU 9 (1980): 135–50.

SCHUBERT, MANFRED (b. 1937)

7064. Rienäcker, Gerd. "Die Analyse: *Cantilena e capriccio* per violino et orchestra von Manfred Schubert." MG 29 (1979): 6–7.

SCHULLER, GUNTHER (b. 1925)

7065. M-Hines: 183–202.

7066. Hopkins, Stephen. "Gunther Schuller's *In Praise of Winds.*" JBR 24, no. 1 (1988): 28–43.

7067. Larsen, Robert L. "A Study and Comparison of Samuel Barber's *Vanessa*, Robert Ward's *The Crucible*, and Gunther Schuller's *The Visitation.*" D.M.A. diss., Indiana University, 1971.

7068. M-Schweitzer.

7069. M-Wennerstrom. [*Music for Brass Quintet*]

SCHUMAN, WILLIAM (1910–1992)

7070. Broder, Nathan. "The Music of William Schuman." MQ 31 (1945): 17–28.

7071. Brown, Michael R. "*American Hymn: Variations on an Original Melody* by William Schuman." JBR 27, no. 2 (1992): 67–79.

7072. Griffin, Malcolm Joseph. "Style and Dimension in the Choral Works of William Schuman." D.M.A. diss., University of Illinois, 1972.

7073. McKinley, Lily. "Stylistic Development in Selected Symphonies of William Schuman: A Comparison of Symphonies Number Three and Nine." Ph.D. diss., New York University, 1977.

7074. M-Mize.

7075. Pye, Richard. "'Asking About the Inside': Schoenberg's 'Idea' in the Music of Roy Harris and William Schuman." MA 19, no. 1 (2000): 69–98. [Symphony No. 6]

SCHUMANN, CLARA (1819–1896)

7076. Hallmark, Rufus. "The Rückert Lieder of Robert and Clara Schumann." NCM 14, no. 1 (1990): 3–30. [Op. 12]

7077. Susskind, Pamela Gertrude. "Clara Wieck Schumann as Pianist and Composer: A Study of Her Life and Works." Ph.D. diss., University of California, Berkeley, 1977.

SCHUMANN, ROBERT (1810–1856)

Album für die Jugend, Op. 68

7078. Lester, Joel. "Substance and Illusion in Schumann's 'Erinnerung,' Op. 68: A Structural Analysis and Pictorial (geistliche) Description." ITO 4 (1978): 9–17.

Arabeske, Op. 18

7079. Fisk, Charles. "Performance, Analysis, and Musical Imagining, Part I: Schumann's Arabesque." CMS 36 (1996): 59–72.

Carnaval, Op. 9

7080. Chailley, Jacques. *"Carnaval" de Schumann, Op. 9.* Au delà des notes 2. Paris: Leduc, 1971.

7081. Kaminsky, Peter. "Principles of Formal Structure in Schumann's Early Piano Cycles." MTS 11, no. 2 (1989): 207–25.

7082. Neighbour, Oliver. "Brahms and Schumann: Two Opus Nines and Beyond." NCM 7 (1983–1984): 266–70.

7083. Simonett, Hans Peter. "Taktgruppengliederung und Form in Schumanns *Carnaval.*" Ph.D. diss., Freie Universität Berlin, 1978.

7084. Summer, Averill Vanderipe. "A Discussion and Analysis of Selected Unifying Elements in Robert Schumann's *Carnaval*, Opus 9." D.M.A. diss., Indiana University, 1979.

Cello Concerto, Op. 129

7085. Loesch, Heinz von. *Robert Schumann: Konzert für Violoncello und Orchester A-Moll Op. 129.* Munich: Fink, 1998.

Choral Works

7086. Godwin, Robert C. "Schumann's Choral Works and the Romantic Movement." D.M.A. diss., University of Illinois, 1967.

7087. Popp, Susanne. "Untersuchungen zu Robert Schumanns Chorkompositionen." Ph.D. diss., Rheinische Friedrich-Wilhelms Universität, Bonn, 1971.

Concert sans orchestre, Op. 14

7088. Alphonce, Bo H. "Dissonance and Schumann's Reckless Counterpoint." MTO 0, no. 7 (1994).

7089. Rathbun, James Ronald. "A Textual History and Analysis of Schumann's Sonatas Op. 11, Op. 14, and Op. 22." D.M.A. diss., University of Iowa, 1976.

7090. Roesner, Linda Correll. "Schumann's 'Parallel' Forms." NCM 14, no. 3 (1991): 265–78.

Concertstück, Op. 86

7091. Ahrens, Christian. "Innovative Elemente in Schumanns Konzertstück für vier Horner und Orchester F-Dur Op. 86." SMZ 123 (1983): 148–56.

Davidsbündlertänze, Op. 6

7092. Bolzani, Marco. "*Papillons* Op. 2 di Schumann: Di Jean Paul al prototipo del ciclo pianistico Davidsbundico." RIM 22 (1987): 261–309.

7093. Daverio, John. "Reading Schumann By Way of Jean Paul and His Contemporaries." CMS 30, no. 2 (1990): 28–45.

7094. Kaminsky, Peter. "Principles of Formal Structure in Schumann's Early Piano Cycles." MTS 11, no. 2 (1989): 207–25.

Dichterliebe, Op. 48

7095. Agawu, V. Kofi. "Structural 'Highpoints' in Schumann's *Dichterliebe.*" MA 3, no. 2 (1984): 159–80.

7096. M-Benary: 21–29. [No. 1]

7097. Hallmark, Rufus. "The Sketches for *Dichterliebe.*" NCM 1, no. 2 (1977): 110–36.

7098. Komar, Arthur, ed. *Schumann: Dichterliebe.* Norton Critical Scores. New York: Norton, 1971.

7099. Layton, Richard Douglas. "Large-Scale Tonal Connections in Robert Schumann's *Dichterliebe.*" Ph.D. diss., University of Maryland, College Park, 1991.

7100. Lewis, Christopher. "Text, Time, and Tonic: Aspects of Patterning in the Romantic Cycle." INT 2 (1988): 37–73.

7101. Marston, Nicholas. "Schumann's Monument to Beethoven." NCM 14, no. 3 (1991): 247–64.

7102. Maus, Fred Everett. "Agency in Instrumental Music and Song." CMS 29 (1989): 31–43. [No. 12]

7103. Meeùs, Nicolas. "Robert Schumann: Quatre Lieder du *Dichterliebe,* Op. 48." ANM 21 (1990): 23–48. [Nos. 1–2, 7, 9]

7104. Neumeyer, David. "Organic Structure and the Song Cycle: Another Look at Schumann's *Dichterliebe.*" MTS 4 (1982): 92–105.

7105. Rothgeb, John. "Comment: On the Form of 'Ich grolle nicht.'" ITO 5, no. 2 (1979–1981): 15–17.

7106. Suurpää, Lauri. "Schumann, Heine, and Romantic Irony: Music and Poems in the First Five Songs of *Dichterliebe.*" INT 10 (1996): 93–123.

7107. Turchin, Barbara. "Schumann's Song Cycles: The Cycle within the Song." NCM 8, no. 3 (1985): 231–44.

Etudes symphoniques, Op. 13

7108. Dommel-Diény, Amy. *Schumann.* Dommel-Diény 8. Neuchâtel: Delachaux et Niestlé, 1967.

7109. Kollen, John L. "Robert Alexander Schumann (1810–1856): Tema, Op. 13." F-Cuyler: 163–71.

Fantasie, Op. 17

7110. Daverio, John. "Schumann's 'Im Legendenton' and Friedrich Schlegel's *Arabeske.*" NCM 11, no. 2 (1987): 150–63.

7111. Downes, Stephen. "Kierkegaard, a Kiss, and Schumann's Fantasie." NCM 22, no. 3 (1999): 268–80.

7112. Gruber, Gernot. "Robert Schumann: Fantasia Op. 17, 1. Satz: Versuch einer Interpretation." MAU 4 (1984): 101–30.

7113. Marston, Nicholas. *Schumann: Fantasie, Op. 17.* Cambridge: Cambridge University Press, 1992.

7114. Roesner, Linda Correll. "Schumann's 'Parallel' Forms." NCM 14, no. 3 (1991): 265–78.

Frauenliebe und -leben, Op. 42

7115. Bresnick, Martin. "Convention and the Hermetic in Schumann's *Frauenlieve und Leben.*" F-Ratner: 173–93.

7116. Green, Michael D. "Mathis Lussy's *Traité de l'expression musicale* as a Window into Performance Practice." MTS 16, no. 2 (1994): 196–216. ["Seit ich ihn gesehen"]

7117. Solie, Ruth A. "Whose Life? The Gendered Self in Schumann's *Frauenliebe* Songs." HJM 15 (1998): 247–69.

7118. Turchin, Barbara. "Schumann's Song Cycles: The Cycle within the Song." NCM 8, no. 3 (1985): 231–44.

Fugen über den Namen: Bach, Op. 60

7119. Sachs, Klaus-Jürgen. "Robert Schumanns *Fugen über den Namen BACH* (Op. 60): Ihr künstliersches Vorbild und ihr kritischer Mass-stab." M-Bachfest: 151–75.

Gedichte, Op. 35

7120. Simmons, Margaret Rymer. "The Cyclic Characteristics of Robert Schumann's Lieder, Op. 35." M.M. thesis, Florida State University, 1967.

Gedichte aus F. Rückerts Liebesfrühling, Op. 37

7121. Hallmark, Rufus. "The Rückert Lieder of Robert and Clara Schumann." NCM 14, no. 1 (1990): 3–30.

Gedichte der Königin Maria Stuart, Op. 135

7122. Phillips, Edward R. "The Mary Stuart Songs of Robert Schumann: Key as an Aspect of Cycle." CAUSM 9, no. 2 (1979): 91–99.

Genoveva, Op. 81

7123. ASO 71 (1985).

7124. Oliver, Willie-Earl. *Robert Schumanns vergessene Oper "Genoveva."* Freiburg im Breisgau: Krause, 1978.

7125. Siegel, Linda. "A Second Look at Schumann's *Genoveva.*" MR 36 (1975): 17–41.

Impromptus sur une romance de Clara Wieck, Op. 5

7126. Stevens, Claudia A. "A Study of Robert Schumann's Impromptus, Op. 5: Its Sources and a Critical Analysis of Its Revisions." D.M.A. diss., Boston University, 1977.

Intermezzos, Op. 4

7127. Barela, Margaret Mary. "A Comparative Study of Metric Displacement in Schumann's Intermezzi, Op. 4, and *Waldszenen*, Op. 82." Ph.D. diss., Indiana University, 1977.

Kinderscenen, Op. 15

7128. Brendel, Alfred. "Der Interpret muss erwachsen sein: Zu Schumanns *Kinderszenen.*" M 35 (1981): 429–33.

7129. Kühn, Clemens. "*Kinderszenen*: Analytische Bausteine zu Schumanns Op. 15." M 35 (1981): 434–37.

7130. Lesznai, Lajos. "Robert Schumann: *Kinderszenen* Op. 15." SM 13 (1971): 87–94.

7131. Réti-Forbes, Jean. *"Kinderszenen" of Robert Schumann: An Interpretive and Thematic Commentary.* Tallulah Falls, Ga.: W. Stanton Forbes, 1979.

7132. Traub, Andreas. "Die *Kinderszenen* als zyklisches Werk." M 35 (1981): 424–28.

Kreisleriana, Op. 16

7133. Alphonce, Bo H. "Dissonance and Schumann's Reckless Counterpoint." MTO 0, no. 7 (1994).

7134. Crisp, Deborah. "The *Kreisleriana* of Robert Schumann and E. T. A. Hoffmann: Some Musical and Literary Parallels." MSA 16 (1993): 3–18.

7135. Fisk, Charles. "Performance, Analysis, and Musical Imagining, Part II: Schumann's *Kreisleriana* No. 2." CMS 37 (1997): 95–108.

7136. Münch, Stephan. "'Fantasiestücke in Kreislers Manier': Robert Schumanns *Kreisleriana* Op. 16 und die Musikanschauung E. T. A. Hoffmanns." MF 45, no. 3 (1992): 255–75.

7137. Rodgers, Stephen. "'The Body That Beats': Roland Barthes and Robert Schumann's *Kreisleriana.*" ITR 18, no. 2 (1997): 75–92. [No. 2]

Liederkreis, Op. 39

7138. Brinkmann, Reinhold. "Lied als individuelle Struktur: Ausgewählte Kommentare zu Schumanns 'Zwielicht.'" M-Breig: 257–75.

7139. ———. *Schumann und Eichendorff: Studien zum "Liederkreis" Opus 39.* Munich: Text + Kritik, 1997.

7140. Cacioppo, Curt. "Poem to Music: Schumann's 'Mondnacht' Setting." CMS 30, no. 2 (1990): 46–56.

7141. Ferris, David. "From Fragment to Cycle: Formal Organzation in Schumann's Eichendorff *Liederkreis.*" Ph.D. diss., Brandeis University, 1994.

7142. Henry, Margaret Elaine. "Motivic Cross References in Schumann's *Liederkreis,* Op. 39." Ph.D. diss., University of Rochester, 2000.

7143. Knaus, Herwig. *Musiksprache und Werkstruktur in Robert Schumanns "Liederkreis": Mit dem Faksimile des Autographs.* Munich: Katzbichler, 1974.

7144. Körner, Klaus. "Eichendorff/Schumann: 'Mondnacht,' ein exemplarischer Fall." MB 9 (1977): 381–84.

7145. McCreless, Patrick. "Song Order in the Song Cycle: Schumann's *Liederkreis,* Op. 39." MA 5, no. 1 (1986): 5–28.

7146. Lewis, Christopher. "Text, Time, and Tonic: Aspects of Patterning in the Romantic Cycle." INT 2 (1988): 37–73.

7147. Pierce, Alexandra. "Climax in Music: Structure and Phrase (Part III)." ITO 7, no. 1 (1983–1984): 3–30. ["Mondnacht"]

7148. Ringger, Rolf Urs. "Zu Eichendorff-Schumanns *Liederkreis.*" SMZ 106 (1966): 339–45.

7149. Schlager, Karlheinz. "Erstarrte Idylle: Schumanns Eichendorff-Verständnis im Lied Op. 39/VII ('Auf einer Burg')." AM 33 (1976): 119–32.

7150. Turchin, Barbara. "Schumann's Song Cycles: The Cycle within the Song." NCM 8, no. 3 (1985): 231–44.

Myrthen, Op. 25

7151. Geissler, William. "Vergleichende Analyse zu Robert Schumanns Vertonungen 'Die Lotosblume' nach Worten von Heinrich Heine." M-Müller: 34–41.

Nachtstücke, Op. 23

7152. Moraal, Christine. "Romantische Ironie in Robert Schumanns *Nachtstücken,* Op. 23." AM 54, no. 1 (1997): 68–83.

Overture, Scherzo and Finale, Op. 52

7153. Finson, Jon W. "Schumann, Popularity, and the *Ouverture, Scherzo, und Finale,* Opus 52." MQ 69 (1983): 1–26.

Papillons, Op. 2

7154. Bolzani, Marco. "*Papillons* Op. 2 di Schumann: Di Jean Paul al prototipo del ciclo pianistico Davidsbundico." RIM 22 (1987): 261–309.

7155. M-Chailley.

7156. Jensen, Eric Frederick. "Explicating Jean Paul: Robert Schumann's Program for *Papillons*, Op. 2." NCM 22, no. 2 (1998): 127–43.

7157. Kaminsky, Peter. "Principles of Formal Structure in Schumann's Early Piano Cycles." MTS 11, no. 2 (1989): 207–25.

7158. Stocco, Marco. "Variation der Variation der Variation . . . : Einheit als Chaos; Analytische Beobachtungen über die *Papillons* Op. 2 von Robert Schumann." MTH 11, no. 2 (1996): 139–58.

Piano Concerto, Op. 54

7159. Gerstmeier, August. *Robert Schumann: Klavierkonzert A-Moll, Op. 54*. Munich: Fink, 1986.

7160. MacDonald, Claudia. "'Mit einer eignen außerordentlichen Composition': The Genesis of Schumann's Phantasie in A Minor." JM 13, no. 2 (1995): 240–59.

Piano Quintet, Op. 44

7161. Hollander, Hans. "Das Variationsprinzip in Schumanns Klavierquintett." NZM 124 (1963): 223–25.

7162. Nelson, John C. "Progressive Tonality in the Finale of the Piano Quintet, Op. 44 of Robert Schumann." ITR 13, no. 1 (1992): 41–51.

7163. Wollenberg, Susan. "Schumann's Piano Quintet in E Flat: The Bach Legacy." MR 52, no. 4 (1991): 299–305.

Piano Sonata No. 1, Op. 11

7164. Harwood, Gregory W. "Robert Schumann's Sonata in F-Sharp Minor: A Study of Creative Process and Romantic Inspiration." CM 29 (1980): 17–30.

7165. Lester, Joel. "Robert Schumann and Sonata Forms." NCM 18, no. 3 (1995): 189–210. [Movement I]

7166. Rathbun, James Ronald. "A Textual History and Analysis of Schumann's Sonatas Op. 11, Op. 14, and Op. 22." D.M.A. diss., University of Iowa, 1976.

Piano Sonata No. 2, Op. 22

7167. Rathbun, James Ronald. "A Textual History and Analysis of Schumann's Sonatas Op. 11, Op. 14, and Op. 22." D.M.A. diss., University of Iowa, 1976.

7168. Roesner, Linda Correll. "Schumann's Revisions in the First Movement of the Piano Sonata in G Minor, Op. 22." NCM 1 (1977–1978): 97–109.

Piano Works (various; *see also* specific piano works)

7169. Beaufils, Marcel. *La musique de piano de Schumann*. Paris: Larousse, 1951.

7170. Becker, Claudia Stevens. "A New Look at Schumann's Impromptus." MQ 67 (1981): 568–86.

7171. Boetticher, Wolfgang. *Robert Schumanns Klavierwerke, Vol. 1: Opp. 1–6*. Wilhelmshaven: Heinrichshofen, 1976.

7172. ———. "Zur Zitatpraxis in Robert Schumanns frühen Klavierwerken." F-Husmann: 63–73.

7173. Brown, Thomas Alan. *The Aesthetics of Robert Schumann*. New York: Philosophical Library, 1968.

7174. Dubal, David. "Robert Schumann's Piano Music: An Overview." PQ 131 (1984–1985): 59–63.

7175. Fugo, Charles Leonard. "A Comparative Study of Melodic Motives in Selected Piano Cycles of Robert Schumann." D.M. diss., Indiana University, 1973.

7176. Hering, Hans. "Das Variation in Schumanns frühem Klavierwerk." Melos/NZM 1 (1975): 347–54.

7177. Leipold, Eugen. "Die romantische Polyphonie in der Klaviermusik Robert Schumanns." Ph.D. diss., Friedrich-Alexander-Universität, Erlangen, 1954.

7178. ———. "Vom Melodieklang in Schumanns Klaviermusik." NZM 117 (1956): 415–18.

7179. McNab, Duncan Robert. "A Study of Classical and Romantic Elements in the Piano Works of Mozart and Schumann." Ph.D. diss., University of Southern California, 1961.

7180. M-Sterling.

Presto passionato, WoO. 5

7181. Roesner, Linda Correll. "Schumann's 'Parallel' Forms." NCM 14, no. 3 (1991): 265–78.

Romanzen und Balladen, Op. 45

7182. Thym, Jürgen. "Text-Music Relationships in Schumann's 'Frühlingsfahrt.'" TP 5, no. 2 (1980): 7–25.

Scenen aus Goethes Faust

7183. Ferchault, Guy. *Faust: Une Légende et ses musiciens*. Paris: Larousse, 1948.

7184. Krummacher, Friedhelm. "'An Goethe vorbei?' Gedanken zu Schumanns *Faust*-Szenen." M-Lönn: 187–202.

7185. M-Macy.

7186. Mintz, Donald. "Schumann as an Interpreter of Goethe's *Faust*." JAMS 14 (1961): 235–36.

7187. Seyfarth, Winfried. "Die unvollendeten *Faust*-Szenen: Ein bedeutender Beitrag Robert Schumanns zu den Goethe-Gedächtnisferien im Jahre 1849." M-Müller: 42–51.

Songs (various; *see also* specific songs and song cycles)

7188. Ashley, Douglas Daniels. "The Role of the Piano in Schumann's Songs." Ph.D. diss., Northwestern University, 1973.

7189. Brauner, Charles S. "Irony in the Heine Lieder of Schubert and Schumann." MQ 67 (1981): 261–81.

7190. Broeckx, Jan L., and Walter Landrieu. "Comparative Computer Study of Style, Based on Five Liedmelodies." I 1 (1972): 29–92.

7191. Conrad, Dieter. "Schumanns Liederkomposition: Von Schubert hergesehen." MF 24 (1971): 135–53.

7192. Dommel-Diény, Amy. *Schumann.* Dommel-Diény 8. Neuchatel; Paris: Delachaux et Niestlé, 1967.

7193. Felner, Rudolf. "Schumann's Place in German Song." MQ 26 (1940): 340–54.

7194. Gerstmeier, August. *Die Lieder Schumanns: Zur Musik des frühen 19. Jahrhunderts.* Tutzing: Schneider, 1982.

7195. Hernried, Robert. "Four Unpublished Compositions by Robert Schumann." MQ 28 (1942): 50–62.

7196. Kinsey, Barbara. "Mörike Poems Set by Brahms, Schumann, and Wolf." MR 29 (1968): 257–67.

7197. M-Lewis. [Mignon Lieder]

7198. Mahlert, Ulrich. "Schumanns späte Lieder." Ph.D. diss., Freiburg Universität, Breisgau, 1982.

7199. Mayeda, Akio. "Das Reich der Nacht in den Liedern Robert Schumanns." F-Schenk: 202–27.

7200. Mertens, Paul-Heinrich. *Die Schumannschen Klangfarbengesetze und ihre Bedeutung für die Übertragung von Sprache und Musik.* Frankfurt am Main: E. Bochinsky, 1975.

7201. Sams, Eric. *The Songs of Robert Schumann.* London: Methuen, 1969.

7202. Thym, Jürgen. "The Solo Song Settings of Eichendorff's Poems by Schumann and Wolf." Ph.D. diss., Case Western Reserve University, 1974.

7203. Walsh, Stephen. *The Lieder of Schumann.* London: Cassell, 1971.

String Quartet, Op. 41

7204. Lester, Joel. "Robert Schumann and Sonata Forms." NCM 18, no. 3 (1995): 189–210. [No. 3 (Movement I)]

Symphonies (various; *see also* specific symphonies)

7205. Finson, Jon William. "Robert Schumann: The Creation of the Symphonic Works." Ph.D. diss., University of Chicago, 1980.

7206. Gebhardt, Armin. *Robert Schumann als Symphoniker.* Regensburg: Bosse, 1968.

Symphony, C Minor

7207. Finson, Jon W. "The Sketches for Robert Schumann's C Minor Symphony." JM 1 (1982): 395–418.

Symphony No. 1, Op. 38 ("Spring")

7208. Finson, Jon W. *Robert Schumann and the Study of Orchestral Composition: The Genesis of the First Symphony, Op. 38.* Oxford: Oxford University Press, 1989.

Symphony No. 2, Op. 61

7209. Finson, Jon W. "The Sketches for the Fourth Movement of Schumann's Second Symphony, Op. 61." JAMS 39, no. 1 (1986): 143–68.

7210. Newcomb, Anthony. "Once More 'Between Absolute and Program Music': Schumann's Second Symphony." NCM 7 (1983–1984): 233–48.

Symphony No. 3, Op. 97 ("Rhenish")

7211. Boetticher, Wolfgang. "Zur Kompositonstechnik und Originalfassung von Robert Schumanns III. Sinfonie." ACTA 53 (1981): 144–56.

7212. Gülke, Peter. "Zu Robert Schumanns *Rheinischer* Sinfonie." BM 16 (1974): 123–35.

7213. Musgrave, Michael. "Symphony and Symphonic Scenes: Issues of Structure and Context in Schumann's 'Rhenish' Symphony." M-Ayrey: 120–48.

Symphony No. 4, Op. 120

7214. Just, Martin. *Robert Schumann: Symphonie Nr. 4, D-Moll.* Munich: Fink, 1982.

7215. Maniates, Maria Rika. "The D Minor Symphony of Robert Schumann." F-Wiora: 441–47.

Symphony, WoO. 29

7216. Abraham, Gerald. "Schumann's Jugendsinfonie in G Minor." MQ 37 (1951): 45–60.

7217. Voss, Egon. "Robert Schumanns Sinfonie in G-Moll." NZM 133 (1972): 312–19.

Toccata, Op. 7

7218. Ensminger, Jonathan D. "'Metric Dissonance' in Robert Schumann's Toccata in C, Op. 7." TSP 2 (1985): 25–38.

7219. Lester, Joel. "Robert Schumann and Sonata Forms." NCM 18, no. 3 (1995): 189–210.

Variations on an Original Theme, WoO. 24

7220. Dommel-Diény, Amy. *Schumann*. Dommel-Diény 8. Neuchâtel: Delachaux et Niestlé, 1967.

Violin Concerto, WoO. 23

7221. Melkus, Eduard. "Schumanns letzte Werke." OMZ 15 (1960): 565–71.

7222. Struck, Michael. "Robert Schumann: Violinkonzert D-Moll (WoO 23)." NZM 147, no. 3 (1986): 32–37.

7223. ———. *Robert Schumann: Violinkonzert D-Moll (WoO 23)*. Munich: Fink, 1988.

Violin Sonatas

7224. Melkus, Eduard. "Schumanns letzte Werke." OMZ 15 (1960): 565–71. [No. 3]

7225. ———. "Eine vollständige 3. Violinsonata Schumanns." NZM 121 (1960): 190–95.

Waldscenen, Op. 82

7226. Barela, Margaret Mary. "A Comparative Study of Metric Displacement in Schumann's Intermezzi, Op. 4, and *Waldszenen*, Op. 82." Ph.D. diss., Indiana University, 1977.

Various Works

7227. Abraham, Gerald. *Schumann: A Symposium*. London: Oxford University Press, 1952.

7228. Best, Walther. *Die Romanzen Robert Schumanns*. Frankfurt am Main: Lang, 1988.

7229. Bunyan, Christine Elizabeth. "Aspects of Tradition and Originality in the Chamber Music of Robert Schumann." Ph.D. diss., Rhodes University, Grahamstown, South Africa, 1978.

7230. Helms, Siegmund. "Der Melodiebau in der Kammermusik Robert Schumanns." NZM 131 (1970): 194–96.

7231. Honsa, Melitta. "Synkope, Hemiole und Taktwechsel in den Instrumentalwerken Robert Schumanns." Ph.D. diss., Leopold Franzens Universität, Innsbruck, 1965.

7232. Johnson, Mary Imogene Evans. "Characteristic Metrical Anomalies in the Instrumental Music of Robert Schumann: A Study of Rhythmic Intention." Ph.D. diss., University of Oklahoma, 1979.

7233. Keil, Siegmar. *Untersuchungen zur Fugentechnik in Robert Schumanns Instrumentalschaffen*. Hamburg: K.D. Wagner, 1973.

7234. Kohlhase, Hans. *Die Kammermusik Robert Schumanns: Stilistische Untersuchung*. Hamburg: Wagner, 1979.

7235. Krebs, Harald. "Robert Schumann's Metrical Revisions." MTS 19, no. 1 (1997): 35–54.

7236. Longyear, Rey M. "Unusual Tonal Procedures in Schumann's Sonata-Type Cycles." ITO 3, no. 12 (1977–1978): 22–30.

7237. Marsoner, Karin. "Sonatenkonzept Robert Schumanns in Theorie und Praxis." M-Kolleritsch: 172–81.

7238. Probst, Gisela. *Robert Schumanns Oratorien*. Wiesbaden: Breitkopf & Härtel, 1975.

7239. Reiningdaus, Frieder. "Zwischen Historismus und Poesie: Über die Notwendigkeit umfassender Musikanalyse und ihre Erprobung an Klavierkammermusik von Felix Mendelssohn Bartholdy und Robert Schumann." ZM 4, no. 2 (1973): 22–29; 5, no. 1 (1974): 34–44.

7240. Sams, Eric. "Hat Schumann in seinen Werken Chriffen benutzt?" NZM 127 (1966): 218–24.

7241. ———. "The Tonal Analogue in Schumann's Music." PRMA 96 (1969–1970): 103–17.

7242. Whitesell, L. A. "E. T. A. Hoffmann and Robert Schumann: The Blending of Music and Literature in German Romanticism." JALS 13 (1983): 73–101.

7243. Wolff, Hellmuth Christian. "Robert Schumann: Der Klassizist." M 2 (1948): 47–54.

SCHURIG, WOLFRAM (b. 1967)

7244. Böttinger, Peter. "Sonic Death? (. . . Im Gegenteil): Analytische Anmerkungen zu drei Werken von Wolfram Schurig." MAS 2, no. 8 (1998): 67–82. [*CRWTH, hot powdery snow, MAUERWERK*]

SCHWAEN, KURT (b. 1909)

7245. Kleinschmidt, Klaus. "*Der neue Kolumbus*: Ein Poem von Heinz Rusch/Musik von Kurt Schwaen." MG 13 (1963): 601–3.

7246. Matties, Ludwig. "*Komm wieder zur künft'gen Nacht*: Ein Zyklus für Chor a cappella nach deutschen Volksdichtungen von Kurt Schwaen." MG 11 (1961): 92–95.

7247. ———. "Sturm und Gesang: Über Kurt Schwaens *Wartburg-Kantate*: Zu seinem 50. Geburtstag." MG 9, no. 6 (1959): 15–18.

SCHWANTNER, JOSEPH (b. 1943)

7248. Folio, Cynthia Jo. "An Analysis and Comparison of Four Compositions by Joseph Schwantner: *And the Mountains Also Rising Nowhere, Wild Angels of the Open Hills, Aftertones of Infinity*, and *Sparrows*." Ph.D. diss., University of Rochester, 1985.

7249. ———. "The Synthesis of Traditional and Contemporary Elements in Joseph Schwantner's *Sparrows*." PNM 24, no. 1 (1985): 184–96.

7250. ———. "Unity and Pluralism in Selected Works by Joseph Schwantner." EXT 5, no. 1 (1989): 77–86. [*Aftertones of Infinity, And the Mountains Rising Nowhere*]

SCHWARTZ, ELLIOTT (b. 1936)

7251. Schwartz, Elliott. "Electronic Music and Live Performance." M-Battcock: 331–38. [*Cycles and Gongs, Five Mobiles, The Harmony of Maine, Music for Napoleon and Beethoven*]

SCHWARZ-SCHILLING, REINHARD (1904–1985)

7252. Thym, Jürgen. "Reinhard Schwarz-Schilling: A Twentieth-Century Choral Composer." ACR 30, no. 2 (1988): 7–44.

SCHWEINITZ, WOLFGANG VON (b. 1953)

7253. Fehn, Ann Clark, and Jürgen Thym. "Who Is Speaking? Edward T. Cone's Concept of Persona and Wolfgang von Schweinitz's Settings of Poems by Sarah Kirsch." JMR 11, nos. 1–2 (1991): 1–31. [*Papiersterne*]

SCHWITTERS, KURT (1887–1948)

7254. Mizelle, Dary John. "Kurt Schwitters' *Ursonate* and *Quanta* and *Hymn to Matter*." Ph.D. diss., University of California, San Diego, 1977.

SCIARRINO, SALVATORE (b. 1947)

7255. Dazzi, Gualtiero. "Action invisible, drame de l'écoute." ENT 9 (1990): 117–34. [*Lohengrin*]

SCOTT, CYRIL (1879–1970)

7256. Darson, Thomas H. "The Solo Piano Works of Cyril Scott." Ph.D. diss., City University of New York, 1979.

SCRIABIN, ALEKSANDR. *See* SKRYABIN, ALEKSANDR NIKOLAYEVICH

SCULTHORPE, PETER (b. 1929)

7257. Boyd, Anne. "Peter Sculthrope's *Sun Music I*." MMA 3 (1968): 3–20.

7258. Hannan, Michael Francis. "The Music of Peter Sculthorpe: An Analytical Study with Particular Reference to Those Social and Other Cultural Forces which Have Shaped the Development of an Australian Vision." Ph.D. diss., University of Sidney, 1978.

7259. ———. *Peter Sculthorpe: His Music and Ideas, 1929–1979*. New York: University of Queensland Press, 1982.

SEARLE, HUMPHREY (1915–1982)

7260. Searle, Humphrey. "A Note on *Gold Coast Customs*." MSU 3 (1950–1951): 18–23.

SEEGER, CHARLES (1886–1979)

7261. O'Neel, Roger Lee. "Pitch Organization and Text Setting in Songs of Charles Seeger, Ruth Crawford Seeger, and Henry Cowell." Ph.D. diss., University of Texas at Austin, 1996.

SEEGER, RUTH CRAWFORD. *See* CRAWFORD, RUTH

SEIBER, MÁTYÁS (1905–1960)

7262. Carner, Mosco. "Mátyás Seiber and His *Ulysses*." M-Carner: 172–82.

7263. Seiber, Mátyás. "A Note on *Ulysses*." MSU 3 (1950–1951): 263–70.

7264. Silberman, Julian. "Some Thoughts on Mátyás Seiber." TEMPO 132 (1982): 12–14.

7265. Varro, Michael Franklin. "The Music of Mátyás Seiber (1905–1960)." D.M.A. diss., University of Washington, 1975.

7266. Weissman, John S. "Die Streichquartette von Mátyás Seiber." MELOS 22 (1955): 344–47; 23 (1956): 38–41.

SEMEGEN, DARIA (b. 1946)

7267. Lochhead, Judy. "Temporal Structure in Recent Music." JMR 6, nos. 1–2 (1986): 49–93. [*Music for Violin Solo*]

SEROCKI, KAZIMIERZ (1922–1981)

7268. Davies, Lyn. "Serocki's Spatial Sonoristics." TEMPO 145 (1983): 28–32.

7269. Zielinski, Tadeusz A. "Anmerkungen zu *Arrangements* für 1 bis 4 Blockflöten von Kazimierz Serocki." T 5, no. 6 (1980–1981): 23–28.

SEROV, ALEKSANDR NIKOLAYEVICH (1820–1871)

7270. Abraham, Gerald. "The Operas of Serov." M-Abraham: 40–55.

7271. Taruskin, Richard. "Opera and Drama in Russia: The Case of Serov's *Judith*." JAMS 32 (1979): 74–117.

7272. ———. "Serov and Musorgsky." F-Abraham: 139–61.

SESSIONS, ROGER (1896–1985)

Concertino for Chamber Orchestra

7273. Cone, Edward T. "Sessions' Concertino." TEMPO 115 (1975): 2–10.

Montezuma

7274. Laufer, Edward C. "Roger Sessions: *Montezuma*." PNM 4, no. 1 (1965): 95–108.

7275. Olmstead, Andrea. "The Plum'd Serpent: Antonio Borgese and Roger Sessions' *Montezuma*." TEMPO 152 (1985): 13–22.

Pages from a Diary (From My Diary)

7276. M-Campbell.

7277. M-Forte: 48–62. [No. 3]

Piano Sonatas

7278. Campbell, Michael Ian. "The Piano Sonatas of Roger Sessions: Sequel to a Tradition." D.M.A. diss., Peabody Conservatory, 1982.

7279. M-Campbell. [Nos. 2–3]

7280. Lochhead, Judy. "A Question of Technique: The Second and Third Piano Sonatas of Roger Sessions." JM 14, no. 4 (1996): 544–78.

7281. ———. "Temporal Processes of Form: Sessions's Third Piano Sonata." CMR 7, no. 2 (1993): 163–83.

7282. M-Mathes. [No. 2]

Quintet

7283. Imbrie, Andrew. "Roger Sessions: In Honor of His Sixty-Fifth Birthday." PNM 1, no. 1 (1962): 117–47.

7284. Wheeler, William Scott. "Harmonic Motion in the Music of Roger Sessions." Ph.D. diss., Brandeis University, 1984.

Songs

7285. Cone, Edward T. "In Defense of Song: The Contribution of Roger Sessions." CI 2, no. 1 (1975–1976): 93–112.

String Quartets

7286. Cone, Edward T. "Roger Sessions' String Quartet." MM 18 (1941): 159–63. [No. 1]

7287. M-Schweitzer.

Symphonies

7288. Cowell, Henry. "Current Chronicle." MQ 36 (1950): 94–98. [No. 1]

7289. Imbrie, Andrew. "The Symphonies of Roger Sessions." TEMPO 103 (1972): 24–32.

Violin Concerto

7290. Imbrie, Andrew. "Roger Sessions: In Honor of His Sixty-Fifth Birthday." PNM 1, no. 1 (1962): 117–47.

Violin Sonata

7291. M-Campbell.

When Lilacs Last in the Dooryard Bloom'd

7292. Black, Peter. "Inroads for Analysis: *When Lilacs Last in the Dooryard Bloom'd* by Roger Sessions." SONUS 18, no. 2 (1998): 1–17.

7293. Powers, Harold S. "Current Chronicle." MQ 58 (1972): 297–307.

Various Works

7294. Gorelick, Brian. "Movement and Shape in the Choral Music of Roger Sessions." D.M.A. diss., University of Illinois, 1985.

7295. Henderson, Ronald D. "Tonality in the Pre-Serial Instrumental Music of Roger Sessions." Ph.D. diss., University of Rochester, 1974.

7296. McClain, Charles Sharland. "The Organ Choral Preludes of Roger Sessions." D.M.A. diss., Cornell University, 1957.

7297. Olmstead, Andrea. *Roger Sessions and His Music.* Ann Arbor, Mich.: UMI Research Press, 1985.

7298. Schubert, Mark A. "Roger Sessions: Portrait of an American Composer." MQ 32 (1946): 196–214.

SÉVÉRAC, DÉODAT DE (1872–1921)

7299. Brody, Elaine. "The Piano Music of Déodat de Sévérac: A Stylistic Analysis." Ph.D. diss., New York University, 1964.

SHAPEY, RALPH (1921–2002)

7300. Greitzer, Mary. "'A World in a Grain of Sand': Ralph Shapey's Fantasy for Violin and Piano." SONUS 21, no. 1 (2000): 11–30.

SHARIF, NOAM (b. 1935)

7301. Chittum, Donald. "Current Chronicle." MQ 57 (1971): 135–38. [Chaconne for Orchestra]

SHENG, BRIGHT (b. 1955)

7302. Sheng, Bright. "*H'un (Lacerations): In Memoriam 1966–1967* for Orchestra." PNM 33 (1995): 560–603.

SHEPHERD, ARTHUR (1880–1958)

7303. Loucks, Richard. *Arthur Shepherd: American Composer.* Provo, Utah: Brigham Young University Press, 1980.

7304. Newman, William S. "Arthur Shepherd." MQ 36 (1950): 159–79.

SHIFRIN, SEYMOUR (1926–1979)

7305. Brody, Martin. "An Anatomy of Intentions: Observations on Seymour Shifrin's *Responses* for Solo Piano." PNM 19, no. 2 (1980–1981): 278–304.

7306. Fisher, George F., Jr. "Phrase Procedure in the Music of Seymour Shifrin." Ph.D. diss., Columbia University, 1995.

7307. Lochhead, Judy. "Temporal Structure in Recent Music." JMR 6, nos. 1–2 (1986): 49–93. [String Quartet No. 4]

SHINOHARA, MAKOTO (b. 1931)

7308. Landy, Leigh. "An Analysis of *Tayutai* for Koto (1972) Composed by Makoto Shinohara: A 3-Dimensional Approach." I 16, nos. 1–2 (1987): 75–96.

SHOSTAKOVICH, DMITRY (1906–1975)

Cello Concerto No. 1, Op. 107

7309. Nestjew, Iwan. "Das Cellokonzert von Schostakowitsch." MG 10 (1960): 198–203.

From Jewish Folk Poetry, Op. 79

7310. Braun, Joachim. "Shostakovich's Song Cycle *From Jewish Folk Poetry*: Aspects of Style and Meaning." F-Schwarz: 259–86.

Lady Macbeth of the Mtsensk District, Op. 29

7311. ASO 141 (1991).

7312. Shostakovitch, Dmitri. "My Opera, *Lady Macbeth of Mtzensk*." MM 12 (1935): 23–30.

Piano Quintet, Op. 57

7313. Maróthy, Jánas. "Harmonic Disharmony: Shostakovich's Quintet." SM 19 (1977): 325–48.

Piano Sonata No. 1, Op. 12

7314. Danuser, Hermann. "Dmitri Schostakowitschs musikalischpolitisches Revolutionsverständnis (1926–27): Zur Ersten Klaviersonate und zur zweiten Symphonie." Melos/NZM 4 (1978): 3–11.

Preludes, Op. 24

7315. Bowlby, Timothy J. "The Influence of Bach's *Well-Tempered Clavier* on the Opp. 34 and 87 Piano Pieces of Dmitri Shostakovich." EXT 10, no. 1 (2000): 118–40.

Preludes and Fugues, Op. 87

7316. Bowlby, Timothy J. "The Influence of Bach's *Well-Tempered Clavier* on the Opp. 34 and 87 Piano Pieces of Dmitri Shostakovich." EXT 10, no. 1 (2000): 118–40.

7317. Thomas, Robert Jay. "The Preludes and Fugues, Opus 87, of Dmitri Shostakovich." Ph.D. diss., Indiana University, 1979.

String Quartets (various; *see also* specific string quartets)

7318. Dyer, Paul Eugene. "Cyclic Techniques in the String Quartets of Dmitri Shostakovich." Ph.D. diss., Florida State University, 1977.

7319. Fay, Laurel Elizabeth. "The Last Quartets of Dmitrii Shostakovich: A Stylistic Investigation." Ph.D. diss., Cornell University, 1978.

7320. Grönke, Kadja. "Komponieren in Geschichte und Gegenwart: Studien zu den ersten acht Streichquartetten von Dmitrij Šostakovič." MF 51, no. 2 (1998): 163–90. [Nos. 1–8]

7321. Munneke, Russell Edward. "A Comprehensive Performance Project in Viola Literature and a Stylistic Study of String Quartets 1–13 of Dmitri Shostakovich." D.M.A. diss., University of Iowa, 1977.

7322. Ochs, Ekkehard. "Bemerkungen zum Streichquartettschaffen Dmitri Schostakowitschs." M-Pečman: 455–70.

7323. O'Loughlin, Niall. "Schostakovitch's String Quartets." TEMPO 87 (1968): 9–16.

7324. Siegmund-Schultze, Walther. "Meister des Streichquartetts: Eine stilkritisches Betrachtung." MG 16 (1966): 596–601.

7325. Smith, Arthur Duane. "Recurring Motives and Themes as a Means of Unity in Selected String Quartets of Dmitri Shostakovich." D.M.E. diss., University of Oklahoma, 1976.

String Quartet No. 10, Op. 118

7326. Puzan, Matthew Davis. "The Tenth String Quartet of Dmitri Shostakovich." TCM 3, no. 1 (1996): 9–10.

String Quartet No. 12, Op. 133

7327. Keller, Hans. "Shostakovich's Twelfth Quartet." TEMPO 94 (1971): 6–15.

7328. Lischke, André. "Présence et négation du dodécaphonisme dans les derniées œuvres de Chostakovitch." ANM 17 (1989): 31–37.

String Quartet No. 13, Op. 138

7329. Wildberger, Jacques. "Ausdruck lähmender Angst: Über die Bedeutung von Zwölftonreihen in Spätwerken von Schostakowitsch." NZM 151, no. 2 (1990): 4–11.

String Quartet No. 15, Op. 144

7330. Knaifel, Alexander. "'Und sichtbar wie ein Stern am Himmel stand die Wahrheit': Subjektive Bemerkungen zum zum Fünfzehnten Streichquartett von Dmitri Schostakowitsch." MTX 84 (2000): 51–54.

Symphonies (various; *see also* specific symphonies)

7331. Sabinina, Marina. "Shostakovitch as Symphonist: Dramaturgy, Aesthetics, Style." Ph.D. diss., Institute Istorii Iskusstv, 1973.

Symphony No. 2, Op. 14 ("To October")

7332. Danuser, Hermann. "Dmitri Schostakowitschs musikalischpolitisches Revolutionsverständnis (1926–27): Zur ersten Klaviersonate und zur zweiten Symphonie." Melos/NZM 4 (1978): 3–11.

7333. Lawson, Peter. "Shostakovitch's Second Symphony." TEMPO 91 (1970): 14–17.

7334. Weiss, Stefan. "Text und Form in Schostakowitschs 2. Sinfonie op. 14." AM 51, no. 2 (1994): 145–60.

Symphony No. 4, Op. 43

7335. Körner, Klaus. "Schostakowitschs vierte Sinfonie." AM 31 (1974): 116–36, 214–36.

7336. Liebert, Andreas. "Anmerkungen und Ergebnisse zum Verhältnis Mahler-Šostakovič." HJM 13 (1995): 223–52.

7337. Mattner, Lothar. "Dmitri Schostakowitsch: 4. Sinfonie Op. 43." NZM 146, nos. 7–8 (1985): 43–46.

7338. Ottaway, Hugh. "Looking Again at Shostakovich 4." TEMPO 115 (1975): 14–24.

7339. Souster, Tim. "Shostakovitch at the Crossroads." TEMPO 78 (1966): 2–9.

Symphony No. 5, Op. 47

7340. Liebert, Andreas. "Anmerkungen und Ergebnisse zum Verhältnis Mahler-Šostakovič." HJM 13 (1995): 223–52.

7341. Osthoff, Wolfgang. "'In Ketten tanzen': Symphonische Scherzi im totalitären Staat." JSIM (1994): 158–98. [Movement III]

7342. Souster, Tim. "Shostakovitch at the Crossroads." TEMPO 78 (1966): 2–9.

7343. Wildberger, Jacques. *Dmitri Schostakowitsch: 5. Symphonie D-moll Op. 47 (1937)*. Munich: Fink, 1989.

Symphony No. 6, Op. 54

7344. Liebert, Andreas. "Anmerkungen und Ergebnisse zum Verhältnis Mahler-Šostakovič." HJM 13 (1995): 223–52.

Symphony No. 9, Op. 70

7345. Osthoff, Wolfgang. "Symphonien beim Ende des Zweiten Weltkriegs: Strawinsky-Frommel-Schostakowitsch." ACTA 60, no. 1 (1988): 62–104.

Symphony No. 12, Op. 112 ("The Year 1917")

7346. Brock, Hella. "Konkretheit der emotionalen Aussage in Schostakowitschs XII. Sinfonie *Das Jahr*." MG 12 (1962): 555–59.

Symphony No. 13, Op. 113 ("Babiy Yar")

7347. Ottaway, Hugh. "Beyond Babi Yar." TEMPO 105 (1973): 26–30.

Symphony No. 14, Op. 135

7348. Lischke, André. "Présence et négation du dodécaphonisme dans les derniées œuvres de Chostakovitch." ANM 17 (1989): 31–37.

7349. Wildberger, Jacques. "Ausdruck lähmender Angst: Über die Bedeutung von Zwölftonreihen in Spätwerken von Schostakowitsch." NZM 151, no. 2 (1990): 4–11.

Symphony No. 15, Op. 141

7350. Child, Peter. "Voice-Leading Patterns and Interval Collections in Late Shostakovich: Symphony No. 15." MA 12, no. 1 (1993): 71–88.

7351. Kay, Norman. "Shostakovich's 15th Symphony." TEMPO 100 (1972): 36–40.

7352. Liebert, Andreas. "Anmerkungen und Ergebnisse zum Verhältnis Mahler-Šostakovič." HJM 13 (1995): 223–52.

7353. Lischke, André. "Présence et négation du dodécaphonisme dans les derniées œuvres de Chostakovitch." ANM 17 (1989): 31–37.

7354. Müller, Hans-Peter. "Die Fünfzehnte: Gedanken zur jungsten Sinfonie von Dmitri Schostakowitsch." MG 22 (1972): 714–20.

7355. Murphy, Edward. "A Programme for the First Movement of Shostakovich's Fifteenth Symphony: 'A Debate About Four Musical Styles.'" MR 53, no. 1 (1992): 47–62.

Violin Sonata, Op. 134

7356. Lischke, André. "Présence et négation du dodécaphonisme dans les derniées œuvres de Chostakovitch." ANM 17 (1989): 31–37.

Various Works

7357. Brockhaus, Heinz Alfred. *Dmitri Schostakowitsch.* Leipzig: Breitkopf & Härtel, 1962.

7358. Cholopov, Juri N. "Der russische Neoklassizismus bei Sergej Prokof ev und Dmitrij Sostakovi." JP 3 (1980): 170–99.

7359. Grönke, Kadja. "Kunst und Künstler in Šostakovics späten Gedichtvertonungen." AM 53, no. 4 (1996): 290–335.

7360. Masel, Leo A. "Über den Stil Dmitri Schostakowitschs." BM 9 (1967): 208–20.

7361. Ottaway, Hugh. "Shostakovich: Some Later Works." TEMPO 50 (1959): 2–14.

7362. Rosebery, Eric. "Ideology, Style, Content, and Thematic Process in the Symphonies, Cello Concertos, and String Quartets of Shostakovich." Ph.D. diss., Bristol, 1982.

7363. Slonimsky, Nicolas. "Dmitri Dmitrievitch Shostakovich." MQ 28 (1942): 425–44.

7364. Zeck, Carlferdinand. "Die Solokonzerte von Dmitri Schostakowitsch: Untersuchungen über Aufbau der Werke und ihre ästhetische Wertung." Ph.D. diss., Halle, 1972.

SIBELIUS, JEAN (1865–1957)

Aallottaret (The Oceanides)

7365. Fantapié, Henri-Claude. "*Aallottaret* de Jean Sibelius: Une question de rythme." ANM 27 (1992): 87–101.

Lemminkäinen Suite

7366. Jacobs, Robert L. "Sibelius' *Lemminkäinen and the Maidens of Saari.*" MR 24 (1963): 147–57.

Piano Quartet

7367. Revers, Peter. "Das Klavierquartett von Jean Sibelius im Kontext der Gattungsgeschichte." HJM 16 (1999): 337–53.

String Quartet, Op. 56 ("Voces intimae")

7368. Krummacher, Friedhelm. "'Voces intimae': Das Streichquartett Op. 56 von Jean Sibelius und die Gattungstradition." M 45, no. 6 (1991): 360–67.

Symphonies (various; *see also* specific symphonies)

7369. Gerschefski, Peter Edwin. "The Thematic, Temporal, and Dynamic Processes in the Symphonies of Jean Sibelius." Ph.D. diss., Florida State University, 1962.

7370. Hill, William G. "Some Aspects of Form in the Symphonies of Sibelius." MR 10 (1949): 165–82.

7371. Hollander, Hans. "Stilprobleme in den Symphonien von Sibelius." M 19 (1965): 1–4.

7372. Krohn, Ilmari. *Der Stimmungsgehalt der Symphonien von Jean Sibelius.* Helsinki: Druckerei A.G. der Finnschen Literaturgesellschaft, 1945.

7373. Matter, Jean. "Quelques aspects de l'être symphonique de Sibelius." SMZ 106 (1966): 31–36.

7374. Meyer, Alfred H. "Sibelius: Symphonist." MQ 22 (1936): 68–86.

7375. Murtomäki, Veijo. "Symphonic Unity: The Development of Formal Thinking in the Symphonies of Sibelius." Ph.D. diss., University of Helsinki, 1991.

7376. Parmet, Simon. *The Symphonies of Sibelius: A Study in Musical Appreciation.* London: Cassell, 1959.

7377. Roiha, Eino Vilho Pretari. *Die Symphonien von Jean Sibelius: Ein form-analytische Studie.* Jyväskylä, 1941.

Symphony No. 2

7378. Goddard, Scott. "Sibelius's Second Symphony." ML 12 (1931): 156–63.

Symphony No. 4

7379. Gontcharoff, Paul. "Jean Sibelius: Quatrième symphonie en la mineur, op. 63." ANM 28 (1992): 77–92.

Symphony No. 5

7380. Bisgaard, Lars. "Musikalsk hermeneutik på hierarkisk grundlag: Bidrag til en musikalsk fænomenologi." DAM 17 (1986): 69–91.

7381. Hepokoski, James A. *Sibelius: Symphony No. 5.* Cambridge: Cambridge University Press, 1993.

7382. McMullin, Michael. "Sibelius: An Essay on His Significance." MR 46, no. 3 (1985): 199–211. [Movement I]

Symphony No. 7

7383. Ballantine, Christopher. "The Symphony in the Twentieth Century: Some Aspects of Its Tradition and Innovation." MR 32 (1971): 219–32.

Tapiola

7384. Mäckelmann, Michael. "Jean Sibelius: *Tapiola*, Tondichtung Op. 112." NZM 147, no. 5 (1986): 32–36.

7385. Tammaro, Ferruccio. "Sibelius e il silenzio di *Tapiola*." RIM 12 (1977): 100–29.

Various Works

7386. Abraham, Gerald, ed. *The Music of Sibelius.* New York: Norton, 1947.

7387. Chernizvsky, David. "The Use of Germ Motives by Sibelius." ML 23 (1942): 1–9.

7388. Garden, Edward. "Sibelius and Balakirev." F-Abraham: 215–18.

7389. Mäckelmann, Michael. "Sibelius und die Programmusik: Eine Studie zu seinen Tondichtungen und Symphonien." HJM 6 (1983): 121–68.

7390. Pike, Lionel. "Sibelius's Debt to Renaissance Polyphony." ML 55 (1974): 317–26.

7391. Ringbom, Nils Eric. *Sibelius: Symphonien; Symphonische Tondichtungen; Violinkonzert; Voces intimae; Analytische Beschreibung.* Helsinki: Fazer, 1957.

7392. Tanzberg, Ernst. *Jean Sibelius: Eine Monographie.* Wiesbaden: Breitkopf & Härtel, 1962.

SIKORSKI, KAZIMIERZ (1895–1986)

7393. Marek, Tadeusz. "Composer's Workshop: The Fourth Symphony by Kazimierz Sikorski." PM 9, no. 1 (1974): 20–24.

SILVEIRA, CARLOS DA (b. 1950)

7394. Paraskevaídis, Graciela. "Música mínima: Die Komposition *Piano piano* von Carlos de Silveira." MTX 44 (1992): 17–23.

SIMPSON, ROBERT (1921–1997)

7395. Phillippo, Simon. "Symphonic Momentum and Post-Tonal Dramas: Simpson's First Symphony." TEMPO 209 (1999): 2–6.

7396. Pike, Lionel. "Robert Simpson's 'New Way.'" TEMPO 153 (1985): 20–29. [String Quartet No. 8]

7397. ———. "Robert Simpson's Ninth Symphony." TEMPO 170 (1989): 19–23.

7398. ———. "Towards a Study of Musical Motion: Robert Simpson's *Variations and Finale on a Theme of Haydn* (1948)." MR 54, no. 2 (1993): 137–48.

SITSKY, LARRY (b. 1934)

7399. Ghandar, Ann. "Melodic Structure in Two Arias from *The Fall of the House of Usher*." MMA 15 (1988): 276–83.

7400. Whiffin, Lawrence. "The Use of Recurring Imagery as a Structural Device and a Free Approach to Serialism in the Song Cycle *Music in the Mirabell Garden* for Soprano and Eight Instruments by Larry Sitsky." MSA 10 (1987): 31–40.

SKEMPTON, HOWARD (b. 1947)

7401. Müller, Hermann-Christoph. "Emanzipation der Konsonanz: Howard Skemptons Orchesterstück *Lento*." MTX 75 (1998): 77–81.

7402. Parsons, Michael. "The Music of Howard Skempton." CT 21 (1980): 12–16.

7403. Zimmermann, Walter. "Stillgehaltene Musik: Zu Howard Skemptons Kompositionen." MTX 3 (1984): 35–37.

SKILTON, CHARLES SANFORD (1868–1941)

7404. Smith, James A. "Charles Sanford Skilton (1868–1941): Kansas Composer." M.A. thesis, University of Kansas, 1979.

SKRYABIN, ALEKSANDR NIKOLAYEVICH (1872–1915)

Etudes, Op. 65

7405. Brauner, Jürgen. "Pianistisches oder kompositorisches Exerzitium? Anmerkungen zu zwei späten Klavieretüden von Claude Debussy und Aleksandr Skrjabin." MF 53, no. 3 (2000): 254–71. [No. 1]

7406. Julstrom, Rosa Drake. "Scriabin Style: Etudes, Opus 65." TCM 2, no. 7 (1995): 1–4.

7407. Schuster-Craig, John. "Contrasting Collections in Scriabin's Etudes, Op. 65." TSP 7 (1992): 99–124.

Piano Sonatas (various; *see also* specific piano sonatas)

7408. Steger, Hanns. *Materialstrukturen in den fünf späten Klaviersonaten Alexander Skrjabins.* Regensburg: Bosse, 1977.

7409. ———. *Der Weg der Klaviersonate bei Alexander Skrjabin.* Munich: Wollenweber, 1979.

7410. Woolsey, Timothy Dwight. "Organizational Principles in Piano Sonatas of Alexander Scriabin." D.M.A. diss., University of Texas, 1977.

Piano Sonata No. 2

7411. Perino, Roberto Scarcella. "Trasformazioni ritmiche nella *Sonata-fantasia* op. 19 di Aleksander Skrjabin." ANL 21 (1996): 6–14.

Piano Sonata No. 4

7412. Forte, Allen. "New Approaches to the Linear Analysis of Music." JAMS 41, no. 2 (1988): 315–48. [Movement I]

Piano Sonata No. 5

7413. M-Wise/H.

Piano Sonata No. 6

7414. Garcia, Susanna. "Scriabin's Symbolist Plot Archetype in the Late Piano Sonatas." NCM 23, no. 3 (2000): 273–300.

7415. Herndon, Claude H. "Skryabin's New Harmonic Vocabulary in His Sixth Sonata." JMR 4 (1982–1983): 353–68.

7416. Willmann, Roland. "Alexander Skrjabin: Die 6. Klaviersonate Op. 62." MF 48, no. 2 (1995): 153–66.

7417. Wai-Ling, Cheong. "Scriabin's Octatonic Sonata." JRMA 121, no. 2 (1996): 206–28.

7418. M-Wise/H.

Piano Sonata No. 7

7419. Antokoletz, Elliott. "Transformations of a Special Non-Diatonic Mode in Twentieth-Century Music: Bartók, Stravinsky, Scriabin, and Albrecht." MA 12, no. 1 (1993): 25–45.

7420. Garcia, Susanna. "Scriabin's Symbolist Plot Archetype in the Late Piano Sonatas." NCM 23, no. 3 (2000): 273–300.

7421. M-Wise/H.

Piano Sonata No. 8

7422. M-Wise/H.

Piano Sonata No. 9

7423. Garcia, Susanna. "Scriabin's Symbolist Plot Archetype in the Late Piano Sonatas." NCM 23, no. 3 (2000): 273–300.

7424. Gürsching, Andreas. "Zum Umgang mit Tonalität bei Alexander Skrjabin." MTH 14, no. 1 (1999): 65–77.

7425. M-Wise/H.

Piano Sonata No. 10

7426. Garcia, Susanna. "Scriabin's Symbolist Plot Archetype in the Late Piano Sonatas." NCM 23, no. 3 (2000): 273–300.

7427. Wait, Mark. "Liszt, Scriabin, and Boulez: Considerations of Form." JALS 1 (1977): 9–16.

7428. M-Wise/H.

Piano Works (various; *see also* specific piano works)

7429. Cook, Marcia. "Scriabin's Etudes: Form and Style." M.A. thesis, University of Southern California, 1977.

7430. Hymovitz, Edwin. "Playing the Scriabin Etudes: Problems of Keyboard Technique and Style." JALS 14 (1983): 43–58.

7431. Martins, José Eduardo. "Quelques aspects comparatifs dans les langages pianistiques de Debussy et Scriabine." CAD 7 (1983): 24–37.

7432. Meeks, John Samuel. "Aspects of Stylistic Evolution in Scriabin's Piano Preludes." D.M.A. diss., Peabody Conservatory, 1975.

7433. Pinnix, David Clemmons. "Evolution of Stylistic Elements in Selected Solo Piano Works by Scriabin." D.M.A. diss., University of Rochester, 1969.

7434. Randlett, Samuel. "Elements of Scriabin's Keyboard Style." PQ 74 (1970–1971): 20–24; 75 (1971): 18–24; 76 (1971): 22–27; 78 (1971–1972): 26–30.

7435. ———. "The Nature and Development of Scriabin's Piano Vocabulary." D.M.A. diss., Northwestern University, 1966.

7436. Ruger, Christof. "Ethische Konstanz und stilistische Kontinuität im Schaffen Alexander Nikolaevic Skrjabins unter besonderer Berücksichtigung seiner Klavierkompositionen." Ph.D. diss., Leipzig, 1971.

7437. Steger, Hanns. "Beiträge zum Klavierwerk von A. Skrjabin." Ph.D. diss., Regensburg, 1977.

Pieces, Op. 45

7438. Gürsching, Andreas. "Zum Umgang mit Tonalität bei Alexander Skrjabin." MTH 14, no. 1 (1999): 65–77. [No. 2]

Pieces, Op. 57

7439. Chapman, Alan. "A Theory of Harmonic Structures for Non-Tonal Music." Ph.D. diss., Yale University, 1978. [No. 2]

Pieces, Op. 59

7440. Benoit, Kenneth R. "Quartal Harmony as an Analytical Tool: An Analysis of Scriabin's Prelude, Op. 59, No. 2." TCM 2, no. 8 (1995): 2–4.

Preludes, Op. 11

7441. Strangeland, Robert A. "Some Structural Elements in Opus 11 of Scriabin." CAUSM 5, no. 1 (1975): 32–41.

Preludes, Op. 67

7442. Pople, Anthony. "Skryabin's Prelude, Op. 67, No. 1: Sets and Structure." MA 2 (1983): 151–74.

Prométhée

7443. Lederer, Josef-Horst. "Die Funktion der Luce-Stimme in Skrjabin's Op. 60." M-Kolleritsch/S: 128–41.

7444. Lissa, Zofia. "Zur Genesis des 'Promethesischen Akkords' bei A. N. Skrjabin." MO 2 (1963): 170–83.

7445. Peacock, Kenneth John. "Alexander Scriabin's *Prometheus*: Philosophy and Structure." Ph.D. diss., University of Michigan, 1976.

7446. Weber, Horst. "Zur Geschichte der Synästhesie, oder: Von den Schwierigkeiten, die Luce-Stimme in *Prometheus* zu interpretieren." M-Kolleritsch/S: 50–57.

Various Works

7447. Angerer, Manfred. *Musikalischer Aesthetizismus: Analytische Studien zu Skrjabins Spätwerk.* Tutzing: Schneider, 1984.

7448. Baker, James Marshall. "Alexander Scriabin: The Transition from Tonality to Atonality." Ph.D. diss., Yale University, 1977.

7449. ———. *The Music of Alexander Scriabin.* New Haven, Conn.: Yale University Press, 1986.

7450. ———. "Scriabin's Implicit Tonality." MTS 2 (1980): 1–18.

7451. Brinkmann, Reinhold. "Kette und Kreis: Hinweise zum Formdenken Skrjabins." M-Kolleritsch/S: 66–74.

7452. Cooper, Martin. "Alexander Skriabin and the Russian Renaissance." F-Abraham: 219–39.

7453. Dahlhaus, Carl. "Struktur und Expression bei Alexander Skrjabin." MO 6 (1971): 179–203.

7454. Dickenmann, P. *Die Entwicklung der Harmonik bei A. Skrjabin.* Bern: Haupt, 1935.

7455. Dickinson, Peter. "Skryabin's Later Music." MR 26 (1965): 19–22.

7456. Eberle, Gottfried. *Zwischen Tonalität und Atonalität: Studien zur Harmonik Alexander Skrjabins.* Munich: Katzbichler, 1977.

7457. Forchert, Arno. "Bemerkungen zum Schaffen Alexander Skrjabins: Ordnung und Ausdruck in der Grenzen der Tonalität." F-Pepping: 298–311.

7458. Gleich, Clemens Christoph von. *Die sinfonische Werke von Alexander Skrjabin.* Bilthoven: A.B. Creyghton, 1963.

7459. Guenther, Roy James. "Varvara Dernova's *Garmonia Skriabina*: A Translation and Critical Commentary." Ph.D. diss., Catholic University of America, 1979.

7460. Gut, Serge. "Skrjabin: Vermittler zwischen Debussy und Schöberg." M-Kolleritsch/S: 85–94.

7461. Kelkel, Manfred. *Aleksandr Skrjabin: Sa vie, l'éotéisme et le langage musical dans son oeuvre.* Paris: Champion, 1978.

7462. ———. "Esoterik und formale Gestaltung in Skrjabins Späwerken." M-Kolleritsch/S: 22–49.

7463. Macdonald, Hugh. "Skryabin's Conquest of Time." M-Kolleritsch/S: 58–65.

7464. Mast, Dietrich. *Struktur und Form bei Alexander N. Skrjabin.* Munich: Wollenweber, 1981.

7465. Nussgruber, Walther. "Über des sinfonische Werk von Alexander Skrjabin." ME 26 (1972–1973): 59–64, 106–10.

7466. Peacock, Kenneth. "Synaesthetic Perception: Alexander Scriabin's Color Hearing." MP 2 (1984–1985): 483–506.

7467. Perle, George. "Scriabin's Self-Analyses." MA 3, no. 2 (1984): 101–22.

7468. Schibli, Sigfried. "Skrjabin spricht: Sieben Stichworte zu einem Problem." NZM 143, no. 3 (1982): 22–26.

7469. Shitomirskij, Daniel Wladimirowitsch. "Die Harmonik Skrjabins." F-Boetticher: 344–58.

7470. Wai-Ling, Cheong. "Orthography in Scriabin's Late Works." MA 12, no. 1 (1993): 47–69.

SMALLEY, ROGER (b. 1943)

7471. Walsh, Stephen. "Roger Smalley's *Gloria tibi Trinitas I.*" TEMPO 91 (1970): 17–20.

SMETANA, BEDŘICH (1824–1884)

7472. Clapham, John. "Smetana's Sketches for *Dalibor* and *The Secret.*" ML 61 (1980): 136–46.

7473. Hirsbrunner, Theo. "Das Erhabene in Bedrich Smetanas *Mein Vaterland.*" AM 41 (1984): 35–41. [*Má Vlast*]

7474. Honolka, Kurt. "Smetana's *Dalibor*: Eine monothematische Oper." M 24 (1970): 554–56.

7475. Jiránek, Jaroslav. "Liszt and Smetana." SM 5 (1963): 139–92.

7476. Katz, Derek. "Smetana's Second String Quartet: Voice of Madness or Triumph of Spirit?" MQ 81, no. 4 (1997): 516–36.

7477. Large, Brian. *Smetana.* New York: Praeger, 1970.

7478. Schuffenhauser, Gerhart. "Die tschechoslowakische Volkmusik und ihr Einfluss auf die Opern Friedrich Smetanas." Ph.D. diss., Freie Universität, Berlin, 1957.

7479. Vašíček, Peter. "Bedřich Smetanas Kammermusik." M 38, no. 4 (1984): 336–40.

SMITH, HALE (b. 1925)

7480. Breda, Malcolm Joseph. "Hale Smith: A Biographical and Analytical Study of the Man and His Music." Ph.D. diss., University of Southern Mississippi, 1975.

7481. Spence, Martha Ellen Blanding. "Selected Song Cycles of Three Contemporary Black American Composers: William Grant Still, *Songs of Separation;* Hale Smith, *Beyond the Rim of Day*; John Duncan, *Blue Set.*" D.M.A. diss., University of Southern Mississipi, 1977.

SMITH, STUART SAUNDERS (b. 1948)

7482. Fiore, Linda. "Notes on Stuart Smith's *Return and Recall*: A View from Within." PNM 22 (1983–1984): 290–302.

7483. Welsh, John P. ". . . A Flight . . . *FLIGHT.*" PNM 23, no. 1 (1984–1985): 144–61.

7484. ——. "Music in the Air: *Here and There*—A Radio Landscape." I 13, no. 4 (1984): 199–223.

7485. ——. "Viewing Mobile Minds: Stuart Smith's *Gifts.*" I 16, no. 4 (1987): 219–45.

SMITH BRINDLE, REGINALD (1917–2003)

7486. Machleder, Anton. "Serialism and Poetry in Reginald Smith Brindle's *El Polifemo de Oro.*" EXT 9, no. 1 (1998): 1–11.

SOMERS, HARRY (1925–1999)

7487. Butler, Edward Gregory. "Harry Somers: The Culmination of a Pianistic Style in the Third Piano Sonata." SMUWO 9 (1984): 124–32.

7488. ——. "The Piano Sonatas of Harry Somers." D.M.A. diss., University of Rochester, 1974.

7489. Cherney, Brian. *Harry Somers.* Toronto: University of Toronto Press, 1975.

7490. Houghton, Diane. "The Solo Vocal Works of Harry Somers." D.M.A. diss., University of Missouri, 1980.

7491. Loranger, Pierre. "Harry Somers: The Picasso Suite, *Light Music* for Small Orchestra." CCM 1 (1970): 147–52.

SOMERVELL, ARTHUR (1863–1937)

7492. M-Curtis.

SOONVALD, JAAN (1890–1980)

7493. Rais, Mark. "Jaan Soonvald and His Musical System." LMJ 2, no. 1 (1992): 45–47.

SORABJI, KAIKHOSRU SHAPURJI (1892–1988)

7494. Browne, Arthur G. "The Music of Kaihosru Sorabji." ML 11 (1930): 6–16.

7495. Garvelmann, Donald. "Kaikhosru Shapurji Sorabji." JALS 4 (1978): 18–22.

7496. Gula, Robert J. "Kaikhosru Shapurji Sorabji (1892–): The Published Piano Works." JALS 12 (1982): 38–51.

7497. Habermann, Michael R. "A Style Analysis of the Nocturnes for Solo Piano by Kaikhosru Shapurji Sorabji with Special Emphasis on *Le jardin parfumé.*" D.M.A. diss., Peabody Conservatory, 1984.

7498. Rapoport, Paul. "Sorabji and the Computer." TEMPO 117 (1976): 23–26. [*Opus clavicemabalistum*]

SOUSTER, TIM (1943–1994)

7499. Jeffries, David. "Tim Souster." CT 27 (1983): 20–27.

SOWERBY, LEO (1895–1968)

7500. Guiltinan, Michael Patrick. "The Absolute Music for Piano Solo by Leo Sowerby." D.M.A. diss., University of Rochester, 1977.

7501. M-Rhoades.

7502. Rieke, Edwin Allen. "The Organ Choral Preludes of Leo Sowerby." D.M.A. diss., University of Rochester, 1975.

7503. Seeley, Robert James. "A Performer's Study of the Sacred Solo Songs of Leo Sowerby, with Organ Accompaniment." D.M.A. diss., Southwestern Baptist Theological Seminary, 1980.

7504. Tuthill, Burnet C. "Leo Sowerby." MQ 24 (1938): 249–64.

SPAHLINGER, MATHIAS (b. 1944)

7505. Weid, Jean-Noël von der. "Essai d'interprétation des conceptions du compositeur Mathias Spahlinger." DI 38 (1993): 17–23.

SPIES, CLAUDIO (b. 1925)

7506. Lansky, Paul. "The Music of Claudio Spies: An Introduction." TEMPO 103 (1972): 38–44.

SPIES, LEO (1899–1965)

7507. Brennecke, Dietrich. "Sprache des Lebens: Blick auf das Kammermusikschaffen von Leo Spies: Zum 60. Geburtstag des Komponisten." MG 9, no. 6 (1959): 8–12.

SPINNER, LEOPOLD (1906–1980)

7508. Graubart, Michael. "Leopold Spinner: The Last Phase." TEMPO 138 (1981): 2–18.

7509. ——. "Leopold Spinner's Later Music." TEMPO 110 (1974): 14–29.

7510. ——. "The Music of Leopold Spinner: A Preliminary Study." TEMPO 109 (1974): 2–14.

SPOHR, LOUIS (1784–1859)

7511. Berrett, Joshua. "Characteristic Conventions of Style in Selected Instrumental Works of Louis Spohr." Ph.D. diss., University of Michigan, 1974.

7512. Greiner, Dietrich. "Die Rolle des Rezitativs in den Opern Spohrs." F-Spohr: 35–52.

7513. Möllers, Christian. "Louis Spohr (1784–1859)." M 34 (1980): 452–56. [String Quartet Op. 29, No. 1]

7514. Schipperges, Thomas. "Satz: Streichquartett und Orchester; Spohrs *Quartett-Concert*, Op. 131 und die Tradition." F-Finscher: 492–503.

SPONTINI, GASPARO (1774–1851)

7515. Döhring, Sieghart. "Spontinis Berliner Opern." M-Dahlhaus/S: 469–89. [*Agnes von Hohenstaufen, Alcidor, Nurmahal*]

7516. Libby, Dennis A. "Gasparo Spontini and His French and German Operas." Ph.D. diss., Princeton University, 1969.

STÄBLER, GERHARD (b. 1949)

7517. Ehrler, Hanno. "Mit Morsezeichen und Zahlencodes: Zu Gerhard Stäblers Komposition *O Muro*." MTX 86–87 (2000): 13–17.

7518. Hammitt, John. "Fluktuierende Hierarchien: Zu Gerhard Stäblers *Schatten wilder Schmerzen*." MTX 38 (1991): 53–55.

7519. Heister, Hanns-Werner. "Namen und Zahlen: Gerhard Stäblers *Ruck- VERSCHioeBEN Zuck-*." MTX 38 (1991): 56–60.

7520. Stäbler, Gerhard. "*Für Später: Jetzt*: Gedanken über eine Art zu komponieren." N 3 (1982–1983): 104–19.

7521. ———. ". . . Yes, No-no." CMR 18, no. 1 (1999): 67–79. [*CassandraComplex*]

STAEMPFLI, EDWARD (b. 1908)

7522. Staempfli, Edward. "*Der Zöllner Matthäus*." SMZ 115 (1975): 131–35.

STAHNKE, MANFRED (b. 1951)

7523. Stahnke, Manfred. "Mein drittes Streichquartett *Penthesilea*: Anmerkungen zur Entstehung eines Musikstücks mit Programm." HJM 6 (1983): 347–63.

7524. ———. "Mein Weg zu Mikrotönen." F-Floros/70: 249–63.

7525. ———. "*Partch Harp*: (Er)findung einer nicht-oktavierenden Musik." F-Floros/60: 11–26.

7526. ———."Wanderung voller Abenteuer: Zu meinem Orchesterstück *Trace des sorciers*." MTX 80 (1999): 47–53.

STAMITZ, CARL (1745–1801)

7527. Jacob, Michael. *Die Klarinettenkonzerte von Carl Stamitz*. Wiesbaden: Breitkopt & Härtel, 1991.

STANFORD, CHARLES VILLIERS (1852–1924)

7528. Wilkinson, Harry. "The Vocal and Instrumental Technique of Charles Villiers Stanford." Ph.D. diss., University of Rochester, 1959.

STARER, ROBERT (1924–2001)

7529. Lewis, Dorothy. "The Major Piano Solo Works of Robert Starer: A Style Analysis." D.M.A. diss., Peabody Conservatory, 1978.

7530. Wendland, Kristin. "Choral Works by Robert Starer." ACR 36, no. 2 (1994): 2–5.

STEIGER, RAND (b. 1957)

7531. Caltabiano, Ronald. "Composers Steven Mackey and Rand Steiger: An Appreciation." CMR 10, no. 1 (1994): 133–48. [*Double Concerto, Trio in memoriam*]

STEVENS, HALSEY (1908–1989)

7532. Berry, Wallace. "The Music of Halsey Stevens." MQ 54 (1968): 287–308.

7533. Johnson, Axie Allen. "Choral Settings of the Magnificat by Selected Twentieth-Century Composers." D.M.A. diss., University of Southern California, 1968.

7534. Murphy, James Lawson. "The Choral Music of Halsey Stevens." Ph.D. diss., Texas Tech University, 1980.

STEVENS, LEITH (1909–1970)

7535. Hamilton, James Clifford. "Leith Stevens: A Critical Analysis of His Works." D.M.A. diss., University of Missouri, 1976.

STEVENSON, RONALD (b. 1928)

7536. Scott-Sutherland, Colin. "The Music of Ronald Stevenson." MR 26 (1965): 118–28.

STILL, WILLIAM GRANT (1895–1978)

7537. Shirley, Wayne D. "William Grant Still's Choral Ballad *And They Lynched Him on a Tree*." AMUS 12, no. 4 (1994): 425–61.

7538. Simpson, Ralph R. "William Grant Still: The Man and His Music." Ph.D. diss., Michigan State University, 1964.
7539. Spence, Martha Ellen Blanding. "Selected Song Cycles of Three Contemporary Black American composers: William Grant Still, *Songs of Separation;* Hale Smith, *Beyond the Rim of Day;* John Duncan, *Blue Set.*" D.M.A. diss., University of Southern Mississippi, 1977.

STOCKHAUSEN, KARLHEINZ (b. 1928)

Adieu
7540. Toop, Richard. "Mondrian, Fibonacci . . . und Stockhausen: Mass und Zahl in *Adieu.*" NZM 159, no. 4 (1998): 30–35.

Am Himmel wandre ich
7541. Gebura, Alice. "Spectral Shape as a Reflection of the Text in Stockhausen's *In the Sky* from *Indianlieder.*" SONUS 1, no. 1 (1980): 48–62.

Aus den sieben Tagen
7542. Bergstrøm-Nielsen, Carl. "Festlegen, Umreißen, Andeuten, Hervorrufen: Analytisches zu den Textkompositionen von Karlheinz Stockhausen." MTX 72 (1997): 13–16.
7543. Kohl, Jerome. "Serial Determinism and 'Intuitive Music': An Analysis of Stockhausen's *Aus den sieben Tagen.*" ITO 3, no. 12 (1977–1978): 7–19.

Elektronische Studie II
7544. Bozzetti, Elmar. "Analyse der *Studie II* von Karlheinz Stockhausen." ZM 4 (1973): 37–47.
7545. ———. "Reihenvariationen über ein Tongemisch: Analyse der *Studie II* von Karlheinz Stockhausen." MB 5 (1973): 17–24.
7546. Burow, Winfried. *Stockhausens "Studie II."* Frankfurt am Main: Diesterweg, 1973.
7547. Camilleri, Lelio. "Metodologie e concetti analitici nello studio di musiche elettroacustiche." RIM 28 (1993): 131–74.
7548. Silberhorn, Heinz. *Die Reihentechnik in Stockhausens "Studie II."* Herrenberg: Döring, 1978.
7549. M-Stockhausen: 37–42.
7550. Stroh, Wolfgang Martin. "Zur Dialektik kompositorischer Verfügungsgewalt." AM 30 (1973): 208–29.

Ensemble
7551. Gehlhaar, Rolf. "Zur Komposition *Ensemble.*" DBNM 11 (1968).

Für kommende Zeiten
7552. Bergstrøm-Nielsen, Carl. "Festlegen, Umreißen, Andeuten, Hervorrufen: Analytisches zu den Textkompositionen von Karlheinz Stockhausen." MTX 72 (1997): 13–16.

Gesang der Jünglinge
7553. Angiolini, Giuliano di. "Le son du sens: Machaut, Stockhausen." ANM 9 (1987): 43–51.
7554. Decroupet, Pascal. "Gravitationsfeld Gruppen: Zur Verschränkung der Werke *Gesang der Jünglinge, Gruppen,* und *Zeitmasze* und deren Auswirkung auf Stockhausens Musikdenken in der zweiten Hälfte der fünfziger Jahre." MTH 12, no. 1 (1997): 37–51.
7555. ———. "Timbre Diversification in Serial Tape Music and Its Consequence on Form." CMR 10, no. 2 (1994): 13–23.
7556. Decroupet, Pascal, and Elena Ungeheuer. "Through the Sensory Looking-Glass: The Aesthetic and Serial Foundations of *Gesang der Jünglinge.*" PNM 36, no. 1 (1998): 97–142.
7557. Stockhausen, Karlheinz. "Music and Speech." R 6 (1964): 40–64.
7558. M-Stockhausen: 49–68.

Gruppen
7559. Decroupet, Pascal. "Gravitationsfeld Gruppen: Zur Verschränkung der Werke *Gesang der Jünglinge, Gruppen,* und *Zeitmasze* und deren Auswirkung auf Stockhausens Musikdenken in der zweiten Hälfte der fünfziger Jahre." MTH 12, no. 1 (1997): 37–51.
7560. Misch, Imke. "On the Serial Shaping of Stockhausen's *Gruppen für drei Orchester.*" PNM 36, no. 1 (1998): 143–87.
7561. Nauck, Gisela. *Musik im Raum, Raum in der Musik,* 205–34. Stuttgart: F. Steiner, 1997.
7562. Pereira, Rosângela. "Structure acoustique et réalisation musicale: A propos d'un fragment de *Gruppen* de Karlheinz Stockhausen." MPSS 7 (1994): 12–17.

In Freundschaft
7563. Geddert, Geesche. "*In Freundschaft* von Karlheinz Stockhausen jetzt auch für Altblockflöte." T 10, no. 3 (1985): 416–19.
7564. Stockhausen, Karlheinz. "Die Kunst, zu hören." MTH 2, no. 3 (1987): 207–30.
7565. Zelinsky, Beate, and David Smeyers. "Karlheinz Stockhausens *In Freundschaft*: Ein Herausforderung für Interpretation und Publikum." T 10, no. 3 (1985): 412–16.

Inori

7566. Frisius, Rudolf. "Musik als Ritual: Karlheinz Stockhausens Komposition *Inori.*" In *Musik und Ritual*, ed. Barbara Barthelmes and Helga de la Motte-Haber, 63–77. Mainz: Schott, 1999.

7567. Leonardi, Gerson. "*Inori*: Microcosm/Macrocosm Relationships and a Logic of Perception." PNM 36, no. 2 (1998): 63–90.

Klavierstücke (various; *see also* specific Klavierstücke)

7568. Kohl, Jerome. "The Evolution of Macro- and Micro-Time Relations in Stockhausen's Recent Music." PNM 22 (1983–1984): 147–85.

7569. Pflugradt, William Charles. "Continuity and Discontinuity in the Piano Music of Karlheinz Stockhausen." M.M. thesis, Indiana University, 1972.

7570. Volans, Kevin. "The *Klavierstüke*: Stockhausen's Microcosm." B.M. thesis. Johannesburg, 1971.

Klavierstück II

7571. Marvin, Elizabeth West. "A Generalization of Contour Theory to Diverse Musical Spaces: Analytical Applications to the Music of Dallapiccola and Stockhausen." M-Marvin: 135–71. [Movement I]

7572. M-Schultz/D. [Third movement]

Klavierstück V

7573. Pereira, Rosângela. "Le *Klavierstück V* de Karlheinz Stockhausen." DI 44 (1995): 13–16.

Klavierstück VI

7574. Toop, Richard. "Last Sketches of Eternity: The First Versions of Stockhausen's *Klavierstück VI.*" MSA 14 (1991): 2–24.

Klavierstück VIII

7575. Toop, Richard. "Stockhausen's *Klavierstuck VIII* (1954)." MMA 10 (1979): 93–130. Reprint, CT 28 (1984): 4–19.

Klavierstück IX

7576. Henck, Herbert. "Karlheinz Stockhausens *Klavierstück IX*: Eine analytische Betrachtung." M-Schnitzler: 171–200.

7577. ———. "Le *Klavierstück IX* de Karlheinz Stockhausen: Considérations analytiques." Trans. Vincent Barras and Daniel Haefliger. CC (1988): 169–91.

Klavierstuck X

7578. Henck, Herbert. *Karlheinz Stockhausen's "Klavierstück X": A Contribution toward Understanding Serial Technique.* Translation of the 2d rev. ed. Cologne: Neuland, 1980.

Klavierstück XI

7579. Helffer, Claude. "La *Klavierstück XI* de Karlheinz Stockhausen." ANM 30 (1993): 52–55.

7580. Pereira de Tugny, Rosângela. "Spectre et série dans le *Klavierstück XI* de Karlheinz Stockhausen." RDM 85, no. 1 (1999): 119–37.

7581. Piencikowski, Robert. "Perspective initiale (KS IX)." DI 2 (1984): 11–13.

7582. Truelove, Stephen. "Karlheinz Stockhausen's *Klavierstuck XI*: An Analysis of Its Composition Via a Matrix System of Serial Polyphony and the Translation of Rhythm into Pitch." Ph.D. diss., University of Oklahoma, 1984.

7583. ———. "The Translation of Rhythm into Pitch in Stockhausen's *Klavierstück XI.*" PNM 36, no. 1 (1998): 189–220.

Konkrete Etüde

7584. Decroupet, Pascal, and Elena Ungeheuer. "Karel Goeyvaerts und die serielle Tonbandmusik." RBM 48 (1994): 95–118.

7585. Toop, Richard. "Stockhausen's *Konkrete Etüde.*" MR 37 (1976): 295–300.

Kontakte

7586. Blumröder, Christoph von. "Serielle Musik um 1960: Stockhausens *Kontakte.*" M-Breig: 423–35.

7587. Dack, John. "Strategies in the Analysis of Karlheinz Stockhausen's *Kontakte für elektronische Klänge, Klavier, und Schlagzeug.*" JNMR 27, nos. 1–2 (1998): 84–119.

7588. Kirchmeyer, Helmut. "Zur Entstehungs- und Problemgeschichte der *Kontakte* von Karlheinz Stockhausen." N 3 (1982–1983): 152–76.

7589. M-Kirchmeyer: 193–210.

7590. Marvin, Elizabeth West. "A Generalization of Contour Theory to Diverse Musical Spaces: Analytical Applications to the Music of Dallapiccola and Stockhausen." M-Marvin: 135–71.

7591. Schatt, Peter W. "Tendenzen des Materials in Stockhausens 'Kontaken.'" AM 45, no. 3 (1988): 206–23.

Kreuzspiel

7592. Keller, Max Eugen. "Gehörte und komponierte Struktur in Stockhausens *Kreuzspiel.*" MELOS 39 (1972): 10–18.

7593. Kinzler, Hartmuth. "Viereinhalb Marginalien zum ersten Stadium von Stockhausens *Kreuzspiel.*" MTH 12, no. 1 (1997): 71–86.

7594. Stenzl, Jürg. "Karlheinz Stockhausens *Kreuzspiel* (1951)." ZM 3, no. 1 (1972): 35–42.

Licht: Die sieben Tage der Woche

7595. Bandur, Markus. "The Composition of Meaning: Construction and Semantics in Karlheintz Stockhausen's *Luzifer-Gruss vom Samstag aus Licht.*" PNM 37, no. 1 (1999): 157–78.

7596. Decarsin, François. "Le cycle d'opéras *Licht* de Stockhausen, est-il de la musique minimale?" DI 41 (1994): 17–21.

7597. Frisius, Rudolf. "La composition comme essai de synthèse structurelle et sémantique: Karlheinz Stockhausen et son project compositionnel *Licht.*" ENT 6 (1988): 35–55.

7598. ———. "Komposition als Versuch der strukturellen und semantischen Synthese: Karlheinz Stockhausen und sein Werkprojekt *Licht.*" N 2 (1981–1982): 160–78.

7599. ———. "Zeremonie und Magie: *Evas Lied*—Karlheniz Stockhausens neues Teilstück aus *Licht.*" MTX 17 (1986): 17–20.

7600. Kohl, Jerome. "Into the Middleground: Formula Syntax in Stockhausen's *Licht.*" PNM 28, no. 2 (1990): 262–91.

7601. ———. "Stockhausen at La Scala: *Semper idem sed non eodem modo.*" PNM 22 (1983–1984): 483–501. [*Samstag*]

7602. ———. "Time and *Light.*" CMR 7, no. 2 (1993): 203–19. [*Luzifers Traum* (*Samstag*, Scene 1), *Michaels Reise um die Erde* (*Donnerstag*, Act 2)]

7603. Oehlschlägel, Reinhard. "Annäherung und Versuch: Zur Uraufführung von *Luzifers Traum* von Karlheinz Stockhausen." N 2 (1981–1982): 179–82.

7604. Stockhausen, Karlheinz. "Elektronische Musik zu *Kathinkas Gesang als Luzifers Requiem.*" N 5 (1984–1985): 31–49. English translation, PNM 23, no. 2 (1985): 40–60.

7605. ———. "Octophony: Electronic Music from *Tuesday* from *Light.*" PNM 31, no. 2 (1993): 150–70.

7606. Stoianova, Ivanka. "Der 'Coup de lune' von Stockhausen: *Montag aus Licht.*" F-Floros/60: 185–212.

Mantra

7607. Blumröder, Christoph von. "Karlheinz Stockhausens *Mantra* für 2 Pianisten: Ein Beispiel für eine symbiotische Kompositionsform." Melos/NZM 2 (1976): 94–104.

7608. Febel, Reinhard. *Musik für zwei Klaviere seit 1950 als Spiegel der Kompositionstechnik.* Herrenberg: Döring, 1978.

Mikrophonie I

7609. Günther, Ulrich. "*Mikrophonie I* von Karlheinz Stockhausen im Musikunterricht." MB 4 (1972): 84–87.

7610. Maconie, Robin. "Stockhausen's *Mikrophonie I.*" PNM 10, no. 2 (1972): 92–101.

Momente

7611. McElheran, Brock. "Preparing Stockhausen's *Momente.*" PNM 4, no. 1 (1965): 33–38.

Musik für ein Haus

7612. Raiss, Hans-Peter. "Karlheinz Stockhausen: *Musik für ein Haus* (1968)." M-Vogt: 391–99.

7613. Ritzel, Fred. "*Musik für ein Haus.*" DBNM 12 (1970).

Originale

7614. M-Stockhausen: 107–29.

Prozession

7615. Müller, Hermann-Christoph. "Plus minus gleich: Karlheinz Stockhausens *Prozession.*" MTX 67–68 (1997): 35–40.

Refrain

7616. M-Wennerstrom.

Schlagquartett

7617. M-Stockhausen: 13–18.

Stimmung

7618. Rigoni, Michel. "*Stimmung,* six chanteurs en quête d'harmonie." ANM 29 (1992): 75–83.

7619. Rose, Gregory, and Simon Emmerson. "Stockhausen–1: *Stimmung.*" CT 20 (1979): 20–25.

Studie II. See Elektronische Studie II

Telemusik

7620. Fuhrmann, Roderich. "Karlheinz Stockhausen (1928): *Telemusik* (1966)." M-Zimmerschied: 250–66.

7621. Schatt, Peter W. "Universalismus und Exotik in Karlheinz Stockhausens *Telemusik.*" M 43, no. 4 (1989): 315–20.

Tierkreis

7622. Angiolini, Giuliano di. "*Tierkreis,* œuvre pour instrument melodique et/ou harmonique: Un tournant dans le parcours musical de Stockhausen." ANM 14 (1989): 68–73.

7623. Gruhn, Wilfried. "'Neue Einfachheit?' Zu Karlheinz Stockhausens Melodien des *Tierkreis.*" In *Reflexionen über Musik heute: Texte und Analysen,* ed. Wilfried Gruhn, 185–202. Mainz: Schott, 1981.

7624. Kohl, Jerome. "The Evolution of Macro- and Micro-Time Relations in Stockhausen's Recent Music." PNM 22 (1983–1984): 147–85.

7625. Stockhausen, Christel. "Karlheinz Stockhausens *Tierkreis.*" T 3, no. 4 (1978–1979): 95–99.

Zeitmasze

7626. Decroupet, Pascal. "Gravitationsfeld Gruppen: Zur Verschränkung der Werke *Gesang der Jünglinge, Gruppen,* und *Zeitmasze* und deren Auswirkung auf Stockhausens Musikdenken in der zweiten Hälfte der fünfziger Jahre." MTH 12, no. 1 (1997): 37–51.

7627. ———. "Une genèse, une œuvre, une pensée musicale . . . en mouvement: *Zeitmaße* de Karlheinz Stockhausen." RBM 52 (1998): 347–61.

7628. Marcus, Genevieve. "Stockhausen's *Zeitmasze.*" MR 29 (1968): 142–56.

Zyklus

7629. M-Kirchmeyer: 189–93.

7630. Silberhorn, Heinz. "Analyse von Stockhausens *Zyklus* für einen Schlagzeuger." ZM 8, no. 2 (1977): 29–50.

7631. M-Stockhausen: 73–100.

Various Works

7632. Blumröder, Christoph von. *Die Grundlegung der Musik Karlheinz Stockhausens.* Stuttgart: Steiner, 1993.

7633. Brinkmann, Reinhold. "Stockhausens Ordnung: Versuch, ein Modell einer terminologischen Untersuchung zu beschreiben." In *Zur Terminologie der Musik des 20. Jahrhunderts,* ed. H. H. Eggebrecht, 205–13. Stuttgart: Walker-Stiftung, 1974.

7634. Cloete, Johan. "Pluralism and Inter-Relation: Mediation between Extremes of Materials in Stockhuasen's Works." B.M. thesis, Kapstadt, 1979.

7635. Cott, Jonathan. *Stockhausen: Conversations with the Composer.* New York: Simon & Schuster, 1973.

7636. Fass, Ekbert. "Interview with Karlheinz Stockhausen Held August 11, 1976." I 6 (1977): 187–204.

7637. Nicolas, François. "Comment passer le temps . . . selon Stockhausen." ANM 6 (1987): 44–55.

7638. Frisius, Rudolf. "Karlheinz Stockhausen: Melodie als Gestalt und Form." NZM 144, nos. 7–8 (1983): 23–29.

7639. Harvey, Jonathan. *The Music of Stockhausen: An Introduction.* Berkeley: University of California Press, 1975.

7640. ———. "Stockhausen: Theory and Music." MR 29 (1968): 130–41.

7641. Heikinheimo, Seppo. *The Electronic Music of Karlheinz Stockhausen: Studies on the Esthetical and Formal Problems of Its First Phase.* Helsinki: Suomen Musiikkitieteellienen Seura, 1972.

7642. Karkoschka, Erhard. "Stockhausen Theorien." MELOS 32 (1965): 5–13.

7643. Kelsall, John Lawrence. "Compositional Processes in the Music of Karlheinz Stockhausen." Ph.D. diss., Glasgow, 1976.

7644. Koenig, Gottfried Michael. "Karlheinz Stockhausen: Musik und Graphik." DBNM 3 (1960): 5–25.

7645. Kohl, Jerome. "Serial and Non-Serial Techniques in the Music of Karlheinz Stockhausen from 1962–1968." Ph.D. diss., University of Washington, 1981.

7646. Kramer, Jonathan. "The Fibonacci Series in Twentieth-Century Music." JMT 17 (1973): 110–48.

7647. Kruger, Walther. *Karlheinz Stockhuasen: Allmacht und Ohnmacht in der neuesten Musik.* Regensburg: Bosse, 1971.

7648. Maconie, Robin. *The Works of Karlheinz Stockhausen.* 2d ed. New York: Oxford University Press, 1990.

7649. Morgan, Robert P. "Stockhausen's Writings on Music." MQ 61 (1975): 1–16.

7650. Noller, Joachim. "Fluxus und die Musik der sechziger Jahre: Über vernachlässigte Aspekte am Beispiel Kagels und Stockhausens." NZM 146, no. 9 (1985): 14–19.

7651. Piencikowski, Robert. "Fonction relative du timbre dans la musique contemporaine: Messiane, Carter, Boulez, Stockhausen." ANM 3 (1986): 51–53.

7652. Purce, Jill. "The Spiral in the Music of Karlheinz Stockhausen." *Main Currents in Modern Thought* 30 (1973): 18–27. French translation, MJ 15 (1974): 7–23.

7653. Sabbe, Hermann. "Das Musikdenken von Karel Goeyvaerts in Bezug auf das Schaffen von Karlheinz Stockhausen: Ein Beitrag zur Geschichte der frühseriellen und elektronischen Musik 1950–1956." I 2 (1973): 101–14.

7654. Stockhausen, Karlheinz. Texte zur Musik. Vol. 4, 1970–1977. Cologne: Dumont, 1978.

7655. Toop, Richard. "Karlheinz Stockhausen: From *Kreuzspiel* to *Trans.*" In *Atti dal terzo e quarto seminario di studi e ricerche sul linguaggio musicale,* ed. Randolph Shackelford, 58–86. Padova: G. Zanibon, 1975.

7656. ———. "*O alter Duft*: Stockhausen and the Return to Melody." SMU 10 (1976): 79–97.

7657. ———. "Stockhausen–2: On Writing about Stockhausen." CT 20 (1979): 25–27.

7658. ———. "Stockhausen's Electronic Works: Sketches and Work-Sheets from 1952–1967." I 10 (1981): 149–97.

7659. Volans, Kevin. *An Introduction to the Music of Karlheinz Stockhausen.* Vortragstext Kapstadt, 1976.

7660. Westerman, Richard Martyn. "Stockhausen: The Way Ahead? A Study of Stockhausen's Orchestral Work." B.A. thesis, Liverpool, 1982.

7661. Wörner, Karl Heinrich. *Karlheinz Stockhausen: Werk und Wollen 1950–1962.* Rodenkirchen/Rhein: P. J. Tonger, 1963.

7662. ———. *Stockhausen: Life and Work.* Berkeley: University of California Press, 1973.

STOCKIGT, MICHAEL (b. 1929)

7663. Kleinschmidt, Klaus. "Die Analyse: *Orchestermusik I* von Michael Stockigt." MG 33 (1983): 397–99.

STRAESSER, JOEP (b. 1934)

7664. Berkenkamp, Heske. "Joep Straesser: Espressivity and Complexity as Constants in a Development." KN 17 (1983): 24–32. [*Intersections, Longing for the Emperor, Ramasasiri, Signal and Echoes, Splendid Isolation, Spring Quartet*]

7665. Manneke, Daan. "About Joep Straesser's *Intersections III* for Piano." SS 53 (1973): 24–36.

7666. Vermeulen, Ernst. "*Musique pour l'homme* by Joep Straesser." SS 38 (1969): 15–25.

7667. ———. "*22 Pages* by Joep Straesser." SS 31 (1967): 15–18.

7668. Vriend, Jan. "*The Autumn of Music* by Joep Straesser." SS 31 (1967): 11–14.

STRAUSS, JOHANN (1825–1899)

7669. ASO 49 (1983). [*Die Fledermaus*]

7670. Sittner, Hans. "Der Walzer bei Chopin und Johann Strauss." OMZ 4 (1949): 287–93.

STRAUSS, RICHARD (1864–1949)

Ägyptische Helena

7671. Fritz, Rebecca. *Text and Music in German Operas of the 1920s.* Frankfurt am Main: Lang, 1998.

Alpensinfonie

7672. Palmer, Christopher. "Strauss's *Alpine Symphony.*" MR 29 (1968): 106–15.

Also sprach Zarathustra

7673. Liebscher, Julia. *Richard Strauss: Also sprach Zarathustra, Tondichtung (frei nach Friedr. Nietzsche) für grosses Orchester Op. 30.* Munich: Fink, 1994.

7674. Williamson, John. *Strauss: Also sprach Zarathustra.* Cambridge: Cambridge University Press, 1993.

7675. Youmans, Charles. "The Private Intellectual Context of Richard Strauss's *Also sprach Zarathustra.*" NCM 22, no. 2 (1998): 101–26.

Arabella

7676. ASO 170 (1996).

7677. Birkin, Kenneth. *Richard Strauss: Arabella.* Cambridge: Cambridge University Press, 1989.

Ariadne auf Naxos

7678. ASO 77 (1985).

7679. Daviau, Donald G., and George Buelow. *The "Ariadne auf Naxos" of Hugo von Hofmannsthal and Richard Strauss.* Chapel Hill: University of North Carolina Press, 1975.

7680. Erwin, Charlotte E. "Richard Strauss's Presketch Planning for *Ariadne auf Naxos.*" MQ 67 (1981): 348–65.

7681. Forsyth, Karen. *Ariadne auf Naxos: Its Genesis and Meaning.* Oxford: Oxford University Press, 1982.

7682. Gräwe, Karl Dietrich. "Sprache, Musik, und Szene in *Ariadne auf Naxos* von Hugo von Hofmannsthal und Richard Strauss." Ph.D. diss., University of Munich, 1969.

7683. Schuh, Willi. "Metamorphosen einer Ariette von Richard Strauss." F-Abert: 197–208.

Capriccio

7684. ASO 152 (1993).

7685. Tenschert, Roland. "The Sonnet in Richard Strauss's Opera *Capriccio*: A Study in the Relation between Metre and the Musical Phrase." TEMPO 47 (1958): 6–11. German translation, SMZ 98 (1958): 1–6.

Don Juan

7686. Gerlach, Reinhard. *"Don Juan" und "Rosenkavalier."* Bern: Haupt, 1966.

7687. Lorenz, Alfred. "Neue Formerkenntnisse, angewandt auf Richard Strauss's *Don Juan.*" AM 1 (1936): 452–66.

Don Quixote

7688. Phipps, Graham H. "The Logic of Tonality in Strauss's *Don Quixote*: A Schoenbergian Evaluation." NCM 9, no. 3 (1986): 189–205.

7689. Rost, Cornelia. "Richard Strauss: *Don Quixote* Op. 35." NZM 148, no. 1 (1987): 26–29.

Einsame, Op. 51

7690. Roman, Zoltan. "Allegory, Symbolism, and Personification in Selected 'Night Songs' by Liszt, Mahler, and Strauss." SM 41, no. 4 (2000): 407–39.

Elektra

7691. ASO 92 (1986).

7692. Dinerstein, Norman Myron. "Polychordality in *Salome* and *Elektra*: A Study of the Application of Reinterpretation Technique." Ph.D. diss., Princeton University, 1974.

7693. Enix, Margery. "A Reassessment of *Elektra* by Strauss." ITR 2, no. 3 (1978–1979): 31–38.

7694. M-Enix.

7695. Gerlach, Reinhard. "Die Tragödie des inneren Menschen: *Elektra*-Studien." F-Stephan: 389–416.

7696. Gilliam, Bryan. *Richard Strauss's Elektra*. Oxford: Oxford University Press, 1991.

7697. Kaplan, Richard Andrew. "The Musical Language of *Elektra*: A Study in Chromatic Harmony." Ph.D. diss., University of Michigan, 1985.

7698. Kramer, Lawrence. "Fin-de-siècle Fantasies: *Elektra,* Degeneration, and Sexual Science." COJ 5, no. 2 (1993): 141–65.

7699. McDonald, Lawrence Francis. "Compositional Procedures in Richard Strauss's *Elektra*." Ph.D. diss., University of Michigan, 1976.

7700. Noe, Günther von. "Das Leitmotiv bei Richard Strauss dargestellt am Beispiel der *Elektra*." NZM 132 (1971): 418–22.

7701. Okada, Akeo. "Oper aus dem Geist der symphonischen Dichtung: Über das Formproblem in den Opern von Richard Strauss." AM 53, no. 3 (1996): 234–52.

7702. Overhoff, Kurt. *Die Elektra-Partitur von Richard Strauss: Ein Lehrbuch für die Technik der dramatischen Komposition.* Salzburg: Pustet, 1978.

7703. Puffett, Derrick. *Richard Strauss: Elektra.* Cambridge: Cambridge University Press, 1989.

7704. Wittelsbach, Rudolf. "Betrachtungen zu *Salome* und *Elektra*." F-Wiener: 93–99.

Feuersnot

7705. Morris, Christopher. "What the Conductor Saw: Sex, Fantasy, and the Orchestra in Strauss's *Feuersnot*." JMR 16, no. 2 (1996): 83–109.

Frau ohne Schatten

7706. ASO 147 (1992).

7707. Graf, Erich. "Zur Thematik der *Frau ohne Schatten*." OMZ 19 (1964): 228–33.

7708. Knaus, Jakob. *Hofmannsthals Weg zur Oper "Die Frau ohne Schatten" und Einflüsse auf die Musik.* Berlin: De Gruyter, 1971.

7709. Overhoff, Kurt. *"Die Frau ohne Schatten" von Richard Strauss.* Munich: Katzbichler, 1976.

7710. Pantle, Sherrill Hahn. *"Die Frau ohne Schatten" by Hugo von Hofmannsthal and Richard Strauss: An Analysis of Text, Music, and Their Relationship.* Bern: Lang, 1978.

Friedenstag

7711. Axt, Eva-Maria. *Musikalische Form als Dramaturgie: Prinzipien eines Spätstils in der Oper "Friedenstag" von Richard Strauss und Joseph Gregor.* Munich: Katzbichler, 1989.

7712. Potter, Pamela M. "Strauss's *Friedenstag*: A Pacifist Attempt at Political Resistance." MQ 69 (1983): 408–24.

Heldenleben

7713. M-Enix.

7714. Gerlach, Reinhard. "Die Orchesterkomposition als musikalisches Drama: Die Teil-Tonalitäten der 'Gestalten' und der bitonale Kontrapunkt in Ein Heldenleben von Richard Strauss." MTH 6, no. 1 (1991): 55–78.

Intermezzo

7715. ASO 138 (1991).

Letzte Lieder

7716. Colson, William Wilder. *"Four Last Songs* by Richard Strauss." D.M.A. diss., University of Illinois, 1975.

7717. Cooper, John Michael. "Richard Strauss's *Vier Letzte Lieder*." TSP 2 (1985): 39–51.

7718. Kaplan, Richard A. "Tonality as Mannerism: Structure and Syntax in Richard Strauss's Orchestral Song 'Früling.'" TP 19 (1994): 19–29.

7719. Kissler, John M. "The *Four Last Songs* by Richard Strauss: A Formal and Tonal Perspective." MR 50, nos. 3–4 (1989): 231–39.

7720. Strickert, Jane Elizabeth. "Richard Strauss's *Vier letzte Lieder*: An Analytical Study." Ph.D. diss., Washington University, 1975.

Liebe der Danae

7721. Birkin, Kenneth W. "The Last Meeting: *Die Liebe der Danae* Reconsidered." TEMPO 153 (1985): 13–19.

7722. Tenschert, Roland. "A 'Gay Myth': The Story of *Die Liebe der Danae*." TEMPO 24 (1952): 5–11.

Lieder (various; *see also* specific Lieder)

7723. Finscher, Ludwig. "Richard Strauss and Jugendstil: The Munich Years." MMA 18 (1984): 169–78.

7724. Jefferson, Alan. *The Lieder of Richard Strauss.* New York: Praeger, 1972.

7725. Lienenluke, Ursula. *Lieder von Richard Strauss nach zeitgenossischer Lyrik.* Regensburg: Bosse, 1977.

7726. Petersen, Barbara E. *Ton und Wort: The Lieder of Richard Strauss.* Ann Arbor, Mich.: UMI Research Press, 1980.

Lieder, Op. 10

7727. Roman, Zoltan. "Allegory, Symbolism, and Personification in Selected 'Night Songs" by Liszt, Mahler, and Strauss." SM 41, no. 4 (2000): 407–39. ["Die Nacht"]

Lieder, Op. 27

7728. Cratty, William S. "The Role of Vagrant Harmonies in Selected Lieder by Wolf, Strauss, and Schoenberg." EXT 4, no. 2 (1987–1988): 68–79. ["Ruhe, meine Seele"]

7729. Rolf, Marie, and Elizabeth West Marvin. "Analytical Issues and Interpretive Decisions in Two Songs by Richard Strauss." INT 4 (1990): 67–103. ["Morgen," "Ruhe, meine Seele"]

Malven

7730. Kissler, John M. "*Malven*: Richard Strauss's 'letzte Rose!'" TEMPO 185 (1993): 18–25.

Metamorphosen

7731. Brennecke, Wilfried. "Die *Metamorphosen*: Werke von Richard Strauss und Paul Hindemith." F-Albrecht: 268–84. Reprint, SMZ 103 (1963): 129–36, 199–208.

7732. Kusche, Ludwig, and Kurt Wilhelm. "Richard Strauss's *Metamorphosen*." TEMPO 19 (1951): 19–22.

Operas (various; *see also* specific operas)

7733. Abert, Anna Amalie. *Richard Strauss: Die Opern; Einführung und Analyse.* Hannover: Friedrich, 1972.

7734. Josephson, Nors S. "Die italienische Opernscena und ihre Weiterentwicklung in den grossen Sopranmonologen von Richard Strauss." JSIM (1999): 211–48.

7735. Lehman, Lotte. *Five Operas and Richard Strauss.* New York: Macmillan, 1964.

7736. Mann, William. *Richard Strauss: A Critical Study of the Operas.* London: Cassell, 1964.

7737. Natan, Alex. *Richard Strauss: Die Opern.* Basel: Basilius, 1963.

7738. Schulken, Samuel Benhardt. "Buffa and Seria: Musical Features in the Operas of Richard Strauss." Ph.D. diss., Florida State University, 1970.

Rosenkavalier

7739. ASO 69–70 (1984).

7740. Gerlach, Reinhard. "Die Ästhetische Ton'sprache' als Problem im *Rosenkavalier*: Die Musik der ersten Szene oder die Konst des Buchschmucks." Melos/NZM 1 (1975): 278–86.

7741. ———. *"Don Juan" und "Rosenkavalier."* Bern: Haupt, 1966.

7742. ———. "Der lebendige Inhalt und die tote Form: Marginalien zum *Rosenkavalier*." NZM 135 (1974): 411–19.

7743. Jefferson, Alan. *Richard Strauss: Der Rosenkavalier.* Cambridge: Cambridge University Press, 1986.

7744. John, Nicholas, ed. *Strauss: Der Rosenkavalier.* London: Calder, 1981.

7745. Pörnbacher, Karl. *Der Rosenkavalier.* Munich: Oldenbourg, 1964.

7746. Pryce-Jones, Alan. *Richard Strauss: Der Rosenkavalier.* London: Boosey & Hawkes, 1947.

Salome

7747. ASO 47–48 (1983).

7748. Boulay, Jean-Michel. "Monotonality and Chromatic Dualism in Richard Strauss's *Salome*." Ph.D. diss., University of British Columbia, 1992.

7749. Dinerstein, Norman Myron. "Polychordality in *Salome* and *Elektra*: A Study of the Application of Reinterpretation Technique." Ph.D. diss., Princeton University, 1974.

7750. Fuss, Hans-Ulrich. "*Salome* von Richard Strauss: Ein Rückblick aus der Perspektive neuer Musik." M 45, no. 6 (1991): 352–59.

7751. Murphy, Edward. "Tonality and Form in *Salome*." MR 50, nos. 3–4 (1989): 215–30.

7752. Okada, Akeo. "Oper aus dem Geist der symphonischen Dichtung: Über das Formproblem in den Opern von Richard Strauss." AM 53, no. 3 (1996): 234–52.

7753. Puffett, Derrick. *Richard Strauss: Salome.* Cambridge: Cambridge University Press, 1989.

7754. Schuh, Willi. "Zur harmonischen Deutung des *Salome*-Schlusses." SMZ 86 (1946): 452–58.

7755. Unseld, Melanie. "Augenblicke des Sterbens: Salome und Melisande als Entwürfe von Weiblichkeit um die Jahrhundertwende." HJM 15 (1998): 301–18.

7756. Wittelsbach, Rudolf. "Betrachtungen zu *Salome* und *Elektra*." F-Wiener: 93–99.

Schweigsame Frau

7757. ASO 199 (2000).

7758. Partsch, Erich Wolfgang. "Artifizialität und Manipulation: Studien zu Genese und Konstitution der Spieloper bei Richard Strauss unter besonderer Berücksichtigung der *Schweigsamen Frau*." Ph.D. diss., University of Vienna, 1983.

Till Eulenspiegels lustige Streiche

7759. Nieden, Hans-Jörg. *Richard Strauss: Till Eulenspiegels lustige Streiche, sinfonische Dichtung, Op. 28.* Munich: Fink, 1991.

Tod und Verklärung

7760. Armstrong, Thomas. *Strauss's Tone-Poems.* London: Oxford University Press, 1931.

7761. Longyear, Rey M. "Schiller, Moszkowski, and Strauss: *Joan of Arc's Death and Transfiguration*." MR 28 (1967): 209–17.

Various Works

7762. Adorno, Theodor W. "Richard Strauss." PNM 4, no. 1 (1965): 14–32.

7763. Albrecht, Klaus. "Untersuchungen zum Schaffensprozess von Richard Strauss." Ph.D. diss., Bochum, 1979.

7764. Del Mar, Norman. *Richard Strauss.* London: Barrie & Rockcliff, 1962.

7765. Federhofer, Hellmut. "Die musikalische Gestaltung des Krämerspiegels von Richard Strauss." F-Vötterle: 260–67.

7766. Floros, Constantin. "Richard Strauss und die Programmusik." F-Hüschen: 143–50.

7767. Forchert, Arno. "Techniken motivisch-thematischer Arbeit in Werken von Strauss und Mahler." HJM 2 (1974): 187–200.

7768. Gerlach, Reinhard. "Richard Strauss: Prinzipien seiner Kompositionstechnik (mit einem Brief von Strauss)." AM 23 (1966): 277–88.

7769. Krause, Ernst. *Richard Strauss: Gestalt und Werk.* Leipzig: Breitkopf & Härtel, 1955.

7770. Murphy, Edward W. "Harmony and Tonality in the Large Orchestral Works of Richard Strauss." Ph.D. diss., Indiana University, 1963.

7771. ———. "Tonal Organization in Five Strauss Tone Poems." MR 44 (1983): 223–33.

7772. Partsch, Erich Wolfgang. "Dimensionen des Erinnerns: Musikalische Zitattechnik bei Richard Strauss." MAU 5 (1985): 101–20.

7773. Rosenberger, Wolfram. "Prinzipien der Instrumentation, Struktur und Ästhetik in den Sinfonischen Dichtungen von Richard Strauss." MAU 19 (2000): 93–173.

7774. Schlötterer-Traimer, Roswitha. "Béla Bartók und die Tondichtungen von Richard Strauss." OMZ 36 (1981): 311–18.

7775. Schuh, Willi. "Zum Melodie und Harmoniestil der Richard Strauss'schen Spätwerke." SMZ 89 (1949): 236–43.

7776. Thurston, Richard Elliott. "Musical Representation in the Symphonic Poems of Richard Strauss." Ph.D. diss., University of Texas, 1971.

7777. Walden, Herwarth. *Richard Strauss: Symphonien und Tondichtungen erläutert von G. Brecher (et al.).* Berlin: Schlesinger, 1908.

7778. Werbeck, Walter. "Tempo und Form bei Mahler und Strauss." JSIM (1998): 210–24.

7779. Wilde, Denis S. "The Melodic Process in the Tone Poems of Richard Strauss." Ph.D. diss., Catholic University of America, 1984.

7780. Winterhager, Wolfgang. "Zur Struktur der Operndialogs: Komparative Analysen des musikdramatischen Werks von Richard Strauss." Ph.D. diss., Bochum, 1982.

STRAUSS, WOLFGANG (b. 1927)

7781. Pommer, Max. "Zur I. Sinfonie von Wolfgang Strauss." MG 20 (1970): 454–57.

STRAVINSKY, IGOR (1882–1971)

Abraham and Isaac

7782. Buell, Timothy J. "The Harmonic Language of Stravinsky's *Abraham and Isaac*." EXT 5, no. 1 (1989): 43–76.

7783. Payne, Anthony. "Stravinsky's *Abraham and Isaac* and *Elegy for J. F. K.*" TEMPO 73 (1965): 12–15.

7784. Spies, Claudio. "Notes on Stravinsky's *Abraham and Isaac*." PNM 3, no. 2 (1965): 104–26.

7785. Thomas, Jennifer. "The Use of Color in Three Chamber Works of the Twentieth Century." ITR 4, no. 3 (1980–1981): 24–40.

7786. Whittall, Arnold. "Thematicism in Stravinsky's *Abraham and Isaac*." TEMPO 89 (1969): 12–16.

7787. Young, Douglas. "*Abraham and Isaac*." TEMPO 97 (1971): 27–37.

Agon

7788. Craft, Robert. "Ein Ballett für zwölf Tänzer." MELOS 24 (1957): 284–88.

7789. Hoffman, Michael. "Stravinsky's *Agon*: An Overview Analysis." TCM 4, no. 5 (1997): 1–9.

7790. Jahnke, Sabine. "Igor Strawinskys *Agon*." MB 3 (1971): 594–99.

7791. Janzen, Howard. "A Stylistic Analysis of Stravinsky's *Agon*." M.M. thesis, University of Alberta, 1975.

7792. Michaely, Aloyse. "'Das C-Dur der seriellen Farben': Zur Reihenkomposition in Strawinskys *Agon*." HJM 16 (1999): 309–36.

7793. Pousseur, Henri. "Stravinsky selon Webern selon Stravinsky." MJ 4 (1971): 21–47; 5 (1971): 107–26. Translation published under the title "Stravinsky by Way of Webern: The Consistency of a Syntax," PNM 10, no. 2 (1972): 13–51; 11, no. 1 (1972): 112–45.

7794. Smyth, David. "Stravinsky's Second Crisis: Reading the Early Serial Sketches." PNM 37, no. 2 (1999): 117–46.

7795. Straus, Joseph. "A Principle of Voice Leading in the Music of Stravinsky." MTS 4 (1982): 106–24.

7796. M-Vogt: 293–307.

7797. Wiesel, Meir. "Motivic Unity in Stravinsky's *Agon*." OM 7 (1979–1980): 119–24.

7798. M-Wolterink.

Anthem: The Dove Descending Breaks the Air

7799. Bailey, Donald Lee. "A Study of Stylistic and Compositional Elements of *Anthem* (Stravinsky), *Fragments of Archilochos* (Foss), and *Creation Prologue* (Ussachevsky)." D.M.A. diss., University of Northern Colorado, 1976.

Apollo

7800. Gutknecht, Dieter. "Strawinskys zwei Fassungen des *Apollon musagète*." F-Fellerer/70: 199–210.

7801. Schneider, Herbert. "Die Parodieverfahren Igor Strawinskys." ACTA 54 (1982): 280–93.

Baiser de la fée

7802. Marschner, Bo. "Stravinsky's *Baiser de la fée* and Its Meaning." DAM 8 (1977): 51–83.

7803. Morton, Lawrence. "Stravinsky and Tschaikovsky." M-Lang: 47–60.

7804. Schneider, Herbert. "Die Parodieverfahren Igor Strawinskys." ACTA 54 (1982): 280–93.

Cantata

7805. Cushman, D. Stephen. "Stravinsky's 'Lyke-Wake Dirge' Revisited: A Possible Source." F-Lefkowitz: 167–74.

7806. Lindlar, Heinrich. "Cantata." MZ 12 (1955): 30–34.

7807. ———. "Igor Stravinsky: Cantata." TEMPO 27 (1953): 27–33.

7808. ———. "Igor Stravinsky's Cantata." SMZ 93 (1953): 397–401.

7809. Mason, Colin. "Serial Procedures in the *Ricercare II* of Stravinsky's Cantata." TEMPO 61–62 (1962): 6–9.

7810. M-Wolterink.

Canticum sacrum ad honorem Sancti Marci nominis

7811. Craft, Robert. "A Concert for St. Mark." SCORE 18 (1956): 35–51

7812. ———. *Le musiche religiose di Igor Stravinsky.* Venezia: Lombroso Editore, 1957.

7813. Mori, Akane. "Proportional Exchange in Stravinsky's Early Serial Music." JMT 41, no. 2 (1997): 227–59.

7814. Reck, Albert von. "Gestaltzusammenhänge im *Canticum sacrum*." SMZ 98 (1958): 49–68.

7815. ———. "Möglichkeiten tonaler Audition." MF 15 (1962): 105–22.

7816. Smyth, David. "Stravinsky's Second Crisis: Reading the Early Serial Sketches." PNM 37, no. 2 (1999): 117–46.

7817. Swarowsky, Hans. "*Canticum sacrum*." OMZ 11 (1956): 399–405.

7818. M-Wolterink.

Choral-Variationen über "Vom Himmel hoch da komm' ich her"

7819. Craft, Robert. "A Concert for St. Mark." SCORE 18 (1956): 35–51.

7820. ———. *Le musiche religiose di Igor Stravinsky.* Venezia: Lombroso Editore, 1957.

7821. ———. "Stravinsky komponiert Bach." MELOS 24 (1957): 35–39.

7822. Schilling, Hans Ludwig. "Igor Strawinskys Erweiterung und Instrumentation der canonischen Orgelvariationen, *Vom Himmel hoch, da komm ich her* von J. S. Bach." MK 27 (1957): 257–75.

7823. Straus, Joseph N. "Recompositions by Schoenberg, Stravinsky, and Webern." MQ 72, no. 3 (1986): 301–28.

Circus Polka

7824. Dunnigan, Patrick. "Stravinsky and the *Circus Polka*." JBR 30, no. 1 (1994): 35–52.

7825. Just, Martin. "'Recomposition' und Zitat in Stravinskijs *Circus Polka*." F-Göllner: 359–76.

Concertino

7826. Kielian-Gilbert, Marianne. "Stravinsky's Contrasts: Contradiction and Discontinuity in His Neoclassic Music." JM 9, no. 4 (1991): 448–80.

Concerto, E-Flat Major ("Dumbarton Oaks")

7827. Eimert, Herbert. "Stravinsky's *Dumbarton Oaks*." MELOS 14 (1947): 247–50.

7828. Straus, Joseph. "Stravinsky's Tonal Axis." JMT 26 (1982): 261–90.

Concerto for Piano and Wind Instruments. *See* Piano Concerto

Danse russe

7829. Berger, Arthur. "Problems of Pitch Organization in Stravinsky." PNM 2, no. 1 (1963): 11–42.

Double Canon

7830. Douw, André. "Sounds of Silence: Stravinsky's *Double Canon*." MA 17, no. 3 (1998): 313–35.

Dumbarton Oaks Concerto. See Concerto, E-Flat Major

Ebony Concerto

7831. Hunkemöller, Jürgen. "Igor Strawinskys Jazz-Porträt." AM 29 (1972): 45–63.

Elegy for J. F. K.

7832. Payne, Anthony. "Stravinsky's *Abraham and Isaac* and *Elegy for J. F. K.*" TEMPO 73 (1964): 12–15.

Feu d'artifice

7833. Just, Martin. "Tonordnung und Thematik in Strawinskys *Feu d'artifice*, Op. 4." AM 40 (1983): 61–72.

Firebird. See Oiseau de feu

Fireworks. See Feu d'artifice

Flood

7834. McCredie, Andrew D. "Form als Symbolik in Igor Stawinskys [*sic*] *Die Flut*." F-Floros/60: 213–32.

7835. Payne, Anthony. "Stravinsky's *The Flood*." TEMPO 70 (1964): 2–8.

7836. Rostan, Daniel. "Set Design and Formal Symmetry in Stravinsky's *The Flood*." SONUS 2, no. 2 (1982): 26–40.

Histoire du soldat

7837. Bailey, Kathryn. "Melodic Sructures in the Overture and Scene-Music of *Histoire du Soldat*." CAUSM 4 (1974): 1–7.

7838. Bradshaw, Susan. "Suite from *The Soldier's Tale*." TEMPO 97 (1971): 15–18.

7839. Heyman, Barbara B. "Stravinsky and Ragtime." MQ 68 (1982): 543–62.

7840. Marti, Christoph. "Zur Kompositionstechnik von Igor Strawinsky: Das Petit concert aus der *Histoire du soldat*." AM 38 (1981): 93–109.

7841. Reinhardt, Klaus. "Igor Strawinskys Konzertsuite nach der *Geschichte vom Soldaten*." MB 3 (1971): 548–54.

7842. Trapp, Michael. *Studien zu Strawinskys "Geschichte vom Soldaten" (1918)*. Regensburg: Bosse, 1978.

7843. Traub, Andreas. *Igor Strawinsky: L'histoire du soldat*. Munich: Fink, 1981.

7844. Van Den Toorn, Pieter C. "Stravinsky Re-Barred." MA 7, no. 2 (1988): 165–95.

7845. Zur, Menachem. "Tonal Ambiguities as a Constructive Force in the Language of Stravinsky." MQ 68 (1982): 516–26.

In Memoriam Dylan Thomas

7846. Chamberlain, Bruce B. "*In Memoriam Dylan Thomas*: Derivation of the Tone Row." CMF 1 (1989): 27–32.

7847. Clemmons, W. Ronald. "The Coordination of Motivic and Harmonic Elements in the 'Dirge-Canons' of Stravinsky's *In Memoriam Dylan Thomas*." ITO 3, no. 1 (1977): 8–21.

7848. Gauldin, Robert, and Warren Benson. "Structure and Numerology in Stravinsky's *In Memoriam Dylan Thomas*." PNM 23, no. 2 (1984–1985): 167–85.

7849. Karallus, Manfred. "Mit Quinten und chromatischen Zirkel harmonische Feldvermessung in Strawinskys Spätwerk." NZM 146, no. 1 (1985): 8–12.

7850. Keller, Hans. "*In Memoriam Dylan Thomas*: Strawinskys schönbergische Technik." MZ 12 (1955): 39–42. English translation, TEMPO 35 (1955): 13–20.

7851. Mori, Akane. "Proportional Exchange in Stravinsky's Early Serial Music." JMT 41, no. 2 (1997): 227–59.

7852. M-Straus: 142–46.

7853. M-Wolterink.

Introitus (T. S. Eliot in memoriam)

7854. Spies, Claudio. "Some Notes on Stravinsky's Requiem Settings." PNM 5, no. 2 (1967): 98–123.

7855. Straus, Joseph N. "Two 'Mistakes' in Stravinsky's *Introitus*." MPSS 4 (1991): 34–36.

7856. White, Eric Walter. "Two New Memorial Works by Stravinsky." TEMPO 74 (1965): 18–21.

King of the Stars. See Roi des étoiles

Mass

7857. Agawu, V. Kofi. "Stravinsky's Mass and Stravinsky Analysis." MTS 11, no. 2 (1989): 139–63.

7858. Bieske, Werner. "Igor Strawinsky: Messe 1948." MK 21 (1951): 12–19.

7859. Karallus, Manfred. "Mit Quinten und chromatischen Zirkel harmonische Feldvermessung in Strawinskys Spätwerk." NZM 146, no. 1 (1985): 8–12.

7860. Rehm, Gottfried. "Ein Beitrag zur tonalen-atonikalen Harmonik: Harmonische Analyse von Hindemiths 1. Orgelsonate (letztet Satz) und Strawinskys *Agnus Dei*." MK 55 (1985): 172–80.

Monumentum pro Gesualdo di Venosa

7861. Mason, Colin. "Stravinsky and Gesualdo." TEMPO 55–56 (1960): 39–48.

Movements (Piano and Orchestra)

7862. Boykan, Martin. "Neoclassicism and Late Stravinsky." PNM 1, no. 2 (1963): 155–69.

7863. Briner, Andres. "Guillaume de Machaut 1958/59 oder Stravinsky *Movements for Piano and Orchestra*." MELOS 27 (1960): 184–86.

7864. Jers, Norbert. "Strawinskys *Movements for Piano and Orchestra* (1958/59) als Schlüsselwerk seiner letzten Schaffenphase." M-Kühn: 432–34.

7865. Mason, Colin. "Stravinsky's Newest Works." TEMPO 53–54 (1960): 2–10.

7866. Rust, Douglas. "Stravinsky's Twelve-Tone Loom: Composition and Precomposition in *Movements*." MTS 16, no. 1 (1994): 62–76.

7867. Walden, William G. "Igor Stravinsky's *Movements for Piano and Orchestra*: The Relationships of Formal Structure, Serial Technique, and Orchestration." CAUSM 9, no. 1 (1979): 73–95.

7868. M-Wennerstrom.

Nightingale. See *Rossignol*

Noces

7869. Barry, Barbara. "*Les noces*, The Genesis of a Wedding." SONUS 9, no. 2 (1989): 25–35.

7870. Berger, Arthur. "Problems of Pitch Organization in Stravinsky." PNM 2, no. 1 (1963): 11–42.

7871. Horlacher, Gretchen. "Metric Irregularity in *Les noces*: The Problem of Periodicity." JMT 39, no. 2 (1995): 285–309.

7872. Jaubert, Jeanne. "Some Ideas about Meter in the Fourth Tableau of Stravinsky's *Les noces*, or Stravinsky, Nijinska, and Particle Physics." MQ 83, no. 2 (1999): 205–26.

7873. Lindlar, Heinrich. "Christ-kultische Elementen in Strawinskys Bauenhochzeit." MELOS 25 (1958): 63–66.

7874. Mazo, Margarita. "Stravinsky's *Les noces* and Russian Village Wedding Ritual." JAMS 43, no. 1 (1990): 99–142.

7875. Straus, Joseph. "A Principle of Voice Leading in the Music of Stravinsky." MTS 4 (1982): 106–24.

7876. Van Den Toorn, Pieter C. "Stravinsky Re-Barred." MA 7, no. 2 (1988): 165–95.

Norwegian Moods

7877. Kraemer, Uwe. "*Four Norwegian Moods* von Igor Strawinsky." MELOS 39 (1972): 80–84.

Octet

7878. Kielian-Gilbert, Marianne. "Relationships of Symmetrical Pitch-Class Sets and Stravinsky's Metaphor of Polarity." PNM 21 (1982–1983): 209–40.

7879. ———. "Stravinsky's Contrasts: Contradiction and Discontinuity in His Neoclassic Music." JM 9, no. 4 (1991): 448–80.

7880. Waeltner, Ernest Ludwig. "Aspekte zum Neoklassizismus Strawinskys: Schlussrhythmus, Thema und Grundriss im Finale des Bläser-Oktetts 1923." In *Bericht über den internationalen musikwissenschaftlichen Kongress, Bonn 1970*, ed. Carl Dahlhaus et al., 265–76. Kassel: Bärenreiter, 1971.

Oedipus rex

7881. Albright, Daniel. "Stravinsky's Assault on Language." JMR 8, nos. 3–4 (1989): 259–79.

7882. ASO 174 (1996).

7883. Hansen, Mathias. "Wort-Ton-Verhältnis in Igor Strawinskys *Oedipus rex*." MG 28 (1978): 329–34.

7884. Hirsbrunner, Theo. "Ritual und Spiel in Igor Strawinskys *Oedipus rex*." SMZ 114 (1974): 1–5.

7885. Liebscher, Julia. "Mythos und Verfremdung: Musikalische Ironie als Mittel der Distanzierung in *Oedipus rex* von Igor Strawinsky." F-Göllner: 345–57.

7886. Mellers, Wilfred. "Stravinsky's Oedipus as Twentieth-Century Hero." M-Lang: 34–46.

7887. Möller, Dieter. *Jean Cocteau und Igor Strawinsky: Untersuchungen zur Ästhetik und zu "Oedipus rex."* Hamburg: Wagner, 1981.

7888. Straus, Joseph. "A Principle of Voice Leading in the Music of Stravinsky." MTS 4 (1982): 106–24.

7889. ———. "Stravinsky's Tonal Axis." JMT 26 (1982): 261–90.

7890. M-Straus: 110–13. [Rehearsal nos. 167–70]

7891. Vinay, Gianfranco. "Da ΟΙΔΙΠΟΥΣ a *Oedipus rex* e ritorno: Un itinerario metrico." RIM 17 (1982): 333–45.

7892. Walsh, Stephen. *Stravinsky: Oedipus rex*. Cambridge: Cambridge University Press, 1993.

Oiseau de feu

7893. Antokoletz, Elliott. "Interval Cycles in Stravinsky's Early Ballets." JAMS 39, no. 3 (1986): 578–614.

7894. Pfaff, Herbert. "Igor Strawinsky, *Feuervogel: Danse infernale du roi Kastchei;* Eine didaktische Analyse." MB 15, no. 12 (1983): 16–19.

7895. Smyth, David. "Stravinsky's Second Crisis: Reading the Early Serial Sketches." PNM 37, no. 2 (1999): 117–46.

7896. Vial-Henninger, Mireille. "Stravinsky: *L'oiseau de feu* (version 1919), une étape dans une trajectoire." ANM 34 (1999): 16–30.

Orpheus

7897. Shatzkin, Merton. "A Pre-Cantata Serialism in Stravinsky." PNM 16, no. 1 (1977–1978): 139–43.

Petrushka

7898. Antokoletz, Elliott. "Interval Cycles in Stravinsky's Early Ballets." JAMS 39, no. 3 (1986): 578–614.

7899. ———. "Transformations of a Special Non-Diatonic Mode in Twentieth-Century Music: Bartók, Stravinsky, Scriabin, and Albrecht." MA 12, no. 1 (1993): 25–45. ["Russian Dance"]

7900. Forte, Allen. "New Approaches to the Linear Analysis of Music." JAMS 41, no. 2 (1988): 315–48. [Second tableau]

7901. Hallquist, Robert Nels, Jr. "Stravinsky and the Transcriptional: An Analytical and Historical Study of *Petrouchka*." D.M.A. diss., North Texas State University, 1979.

7902. Hamm, Charles E. *Stravinsky: Petrushka.* Norton Critical Scores. New York: Norton, 1967.

7903. Pfaff, Herbert. "Igor Strawinsky: *Petrushka*; Versuch einer Synopsis (Malerei, Grafik, Plastik, Dichtung)." MB 14, no. 11 (1982): 700–712.

7904. Schneider, Herbert. "Die Parodieverfahren Igor Strawinskys." ACTA 54 (1982): 280–93.

7905. Sternfeld, Frederick W. "Some Russian Folk Songs in Stravinsky's *Petrouchka*." NOTES 2 (1945): 95–104.

7906. Taruskin, Richard. "*Chez Pétrouchka*: Harmony and Tonality chez Stravinsky." NCM 10, no. 3 (1987): 265–86. Reprinted in *Music at the Turn of the Century*, ed. Joseph Kerman, 71–92. Berkeley: University of California Press, 1990.

Piano Concerto

7907. Benjamin, William E. "Tonality without Fifths: Remarks on the First Movement of Stravinsky's Concerto for Piano and Wind Instruments." ITO 2, nos. 11–12 (1977): 53–70.

7908. Garst, Marilyn M. "The Early Twentieth-Century Piano Concerto as Formulated by Stravinsky and Schoenberg." Ph.D. diss., Michigan State University, 1972.

7909. Nelson, David. "Analysis of the First-Movement Cadenza of Stravinsky's Concerto for Piano and Wind Instruments." JBR 32, no. 2 (1997): 76–90.

7910. Traut, Donald G. "Revisiting Stravinsky's Concerto." TP 25 (2000): 65–86.

Piano-Rag-Music

7911. Joseph, Charles M. "Structural Coherence in Stravinsky's *Piano-Rag-Music*." MTS 4 (1982): 76–91.

Piano Sonatas

7912. Boettcher, Bonna J. *A Study of Stravinsky's Sonate pour piano (1924) and Sérénade en la: A Performer's Analysis and Comparison.* San Francisco: Mellen Research University Press, 1991.

7913. Kirchmeyer, Helmut. "Optisches und analytisches zu Strawinskys Klaviersonaten." MZ 12 (1955): 57–62.

7914. Migliaccio, Carlo. "Beethoven, Stravinskij e il problema del 'bergsonismo in musica.'" RIM 29 (1994): 157–82. [Piano Sonata (1924)]

Piano Works (various; *see also* specific piano works)

7915. Chadabe, Joel. "Stravinsky and His Easy Duets for Piano." PQ 75 (1971): 27–29.

7916. Evenson, David. "The Piano in the Compositions of Igor Stravinsky." PQ 118 (1981–1982): 26–31.

7917. Joseph, Charles Mensore. *Stravinsky and the Piano.* Ann Arbor, Mich.: UMI Research Press, 1983.

7918. ———. "A Study of Igor Stravinskys's Piano Compositions." Ph.D. diss., University of Cincinnati, 1974.

7919. Shafer, Sharon Guertin. "A Survey of Igor Stravinsky's Songs." D.M.A. diss., University of Maryland, 1973.

7920. Thal, Marlene. "The Piano Music of Igor Stravinsky." D.M.A. diss., University of Washington, 1978.

Pieces (String Quartet)

7921. Döhring, Sieghart. "Strawinskys Trois pièces pour quatuor à cordes." F-Dahlhaus: 713–24.

7922. Kielian-Gilbert, Marianne. "Relationships of Symmetrical Pitch-Class Sets and Stravinsky's Metaphor of Polarity." PNM 21 (1982–1983): 209–40.

7923. Kolneder, Walter. "Strawinskys Drei Stücke für Streichquartett." OMZ 26 (1971): 631–38.

7924. Riolte, André, and Marcel Mesnage. "Analyse musicale et systèmes formels: Un modèle informatique de la 1re pièce pour quatuor à cordes de Stravinsky." ANM 10 (1988): 51–67. [No. 1]

7925. Turkalo, Alexis. "A New Approach to Similarity Relations in Set-Theory Analysis." Ph.D. diss., Michigan State University, 1980.

Pulcinella
7926. Cone, Edward T. "The Uses of Convention: Stravinsky and His Models." M-Lang 24–29.
7927. Hucke, Helmut. "Die musikalischen Vorlagen zu Igor Strawinskys *Pulcinella*." F-Osthoff/70: 241–50.
7928. Schneider, Herbert. "Die Parodieverfahren Igor Strawinskys." ACTA 54 (1982): 280–93.
7929. Straus, Joseph N. "Recompositions by Schoenberg, Stravinsky, and Webern." MQ 72, no. 3 (1986): 301–28.

Ragtime (Chamber ensemble)
7930. Heyman, Barbara B. "Stravinsky and Ragtime." MQ 68 (1982): 543–62.

Rake's Progress
7931. Abert, Anna Amalie. "Strawinskys *The Rake's Progress*: Strukturell betrachtet." M 25 (1971): 243–47.
7932. ASO 145 (1992).
7933. Carter, Lee Chandler. "The Progress in *The Rake's* Return." Ph.D. diss., City University of New York, 1995.
7934. ———. "Stravinsky's 'Special Sense': The Rhetorical Use of Tonality in *The Rake's Progress*." MTS 19, no. 1 (1997): 55–80.
7935. Chew, Geoffrey. "Pastoral and Neoclassicism: A Reinterpretation of Auden's and Stravinsky's *Rake's Progress*." COJ 5, no. 3 (1993): 239–63.
7936. Cooke, Deryck. "*The Rake* and the 18th Century." MT 103 (1962): 20–23.
7937. Craft, Robert. "Reflections on *The Rake's Progress*." SCORE 9 (1954): 24–30.
7938. Danes, Robert Harold. "Stravinsky's *The Rake's Progress*: Paradigm of Neoclassic Opera." Ph.D. diss., Washington University, 1972.
7939. Felz, Nancy. "*The Rake's Progress*: Masque élisabéthain sous un loup vénitien." RDM 77, no. 1 (1991): 59–80.
7940. Graybill, Roger. "Intervallic Transformation and Closure in the Music of Stravinsky." TP 14–15 (1989–1990): 13–34. [Duettino, Act III]
7941. Griffiths, Paul. *Igor Stravinsky: The Rake's Progress.* Cambridge: Cambridge University Pres, 1982.
7942. Hunter, Mary. "Igor and Tom: History and Destiny in *The Rake's Progress*." OQ 7, no. 4 (1990–1991): 38–52.
7943. Keever, Howard Thomas. "Stravinsky's *The Rake's Progress*: An Analysis Based on Edward T. Cone's Theory of Stratification, Interlock, and Synthesis." Ph.D. diss., Florida State University, 1988.
7944. Kerman, Joseph. "Opera à la mode." *Hudson Review* 6 (1953–1954): 560–77.
7945. Scherliess, Volker. "Mozart à la Stravinsky: Zu einer Melodie aus *The Rake's Progress*." MPSS 5 (1992): 14–18. [Act II]
7946. Schneider, Frank. "*The Rake's Progress* oder die Oper der verspielten Konventionen: Eine dramaturgische Studie." JP 3 (1980): 135–69.
7947. Schuh, Willi. "Zur Harmonik Igor Strawinskys." SMZ 92 (1952): 243–52.
7948. Straus, Joseph N. "The Progress of a Motive in Stravinsky's *The Rake's Progress*." JM 9, no. 2 (1991): 165–85.
7949. White, Eric Walter. "*The Rake's Progress*." TEMPO 20 (1951): 10–18.

Renard
7950. Van den Toorn, Pieter C. "Metrical Displacement in Stravinsky." MPSS 11 (1998): 24–28.

Requiem Canticles
7951. Cole, Vincent Lewis. "Analyses of *Symphony of Psalms* (1930, Rev. 1948) and *Requiem Canticles* (1966) by Igor Stravinsky." Ph.D. diss., University of California, Los Angeles, 1980.
7952. Payne, Anthony. "*Requiem Canticles*." TEMPO 81 (1967): 10–19.
7953. Perry, Jeffrey. "A 'Requiem for the Requiem': On Stravinsky's *Requiem Canticles*." CMS 33–34 (1993–1994): 237–56.
7954. Spies, Claudio. "Some Notes on Stravinsky's Requiem Settings." PNM 5, no. 2 (1967): 98–123.

Rite of Spring. *See Sacre du printemps*

Roi des étoiles
7955. Gottwald, Clytus. "*Swesdoliki* und die musikalische Archetype." MELOS 38 (1971): 360–64.
7956. Matthews, David. "*Zvezdoliki*." TEMPO 97 (1971): 9–14.

Rossignol
7957. ASO 174 (1996).

Sacre du printemps
7958. Antokoletz, Elliott. "Interval Cycles in Stravinsky's Early Ballets." JAMS 39, no. 3 (1986): 578–614.

7959. Boaz, Mildred Meyer. "T. S. Eliot and Music: A Study of the Development of Musical Structures in Selected Poems by T. S. Eliot and Music by Erik Satie, Igor Stravinsky, and Béla Bartók." Ph.D. diss., University of Illinois, 1977.

7960. Boulez, Pierre. "Stravinsky Remains." In *Notes of an Apprenticeship*, 72–145. New York: Knopf, 1968.

7961. Cacioppo, Curt. "Harmonic Behavior in *The Rite of Spring*." CMS 32 (1992): 129–42.

7962. De Matteis, Adriano, and Goffredo Haus. "Formalization of Generative Structures within Stravinsky's *The Rite of Spring*." JNMR 25, no. 1 (1996): 47–76.

7963. Forte, Allen. *The Harmonic Organization of "The Rite of Spring."* New Haven, Conn.: Yale University Press, 1978.

7964. ———. "New Approaches to the Linear Analysis of Music." JAMS 41, no. 2 (1988): 315–48. [Introduction]

7965. Hill, Peter. *Stravinsky: The Rite of Spring*. Cambridge: Cambridge University Press, 2000.

7966. Kielian-Gilbert, Marianne. "Relationships of Symmetrical Pitch-Class Sets and Stravinsky's Metaphor of Polarity." PNM 21 (1982–1983): 209–40.

7967. Krebs, Harald. "Neighboring Motion in Stravinsky's *Le sacre du printemps*." ITR 8, no. 1 (1987): 3–13.

7968. Morton, Lawrence. "Footnotes to Stravinsky Studies: *Le sacre du printemps*." TEMPO 128 (1979): 9–16.

7969. Petzold, Friedrich. "Formbildende Rhythmik: Zu Strawinskys *Sacre du printemps*." MELOS 20 (1953): 46–47.

7970. Pousseur, Henri. "Stravinsky selon Webern selon Stravinsky." MJ 4 (1971): 21–47; 5 (1971): 107–26. Translation published under the title "Stravinsky by Way of Webern: The Consistency of a Syntax," PNM 10, no. 2 (1972): 13–51; 11, no. 1 (1972): 112–45.

7971. Scharschuch, Horst. *Analyse zu Igor Stravinskys "Sacre du printemps."* Regensburg: Bosse, 1960.

7972. Scherliess, Volker. *Igor Strawinsky: Le sacre du printemps*. Munich: Fink, 1982.

7973. Siddons, James. "Rhythmic Structures in *Le sacre du printemps*." MAN 1 (1972): 6–11.

7974. Smalley, Roger. "The Sketchbooks of *The Rite of Spring*." TEMPO 91 (1970): 2–13.

7975. Sonntag, Brunhilde. "Die Formen in Strawinskys *Sacre du printemps*." MELOS 37 (1970): 232–35.

7976. Taruskin, Richard. "Russian Folk Melodies in *The Rite of Spring*." JAMS 33 (1980): 501–43.

7977. Travis, Roy. "Towards a New Concept of Tonality." JMT 3 (1959): 257–84.

7978. Van Den Toorn, Pieter C. "Stravinsky Re-Barred." MA 7, no. 2 (1988): 165–95. ["Evocation of the Ancestors," "Sacrificial Dance"]

7979. Vlad, Roman. "Reihenstrukturen im *Sacre du printemps*." In *Igor Stravinsky*, ed. Heinz-Klaus Metzger and Rainer Riehn, 4–64. Munich: Text + Kritik, 1984.

7980. White, Kathy Maria. "*The Rite of Spring*: A Rhythmic Prespective." Ph.D. diss., Washington University, 1987.

7981. Whittall, Arnold. "Music Analysis as Human Science? *Le sacre du printemps* in Theory and Practice." MA 1 (1982): 33–54.

Scherzo fantastique

7982. Wile, Kip. "Communication and Interaction in Stravinsky's *Scherzo fantastique* (1907–1908)." ITR 13, no. 1 (1992): 87–112.

Scherzo (Piano)

7983. Joseph, Charles M. "Stravinsky's Piano Scherzo (1902) in Perspective: A New Starting Point." MQ 67 (1981): 82–93.

Septet

7984. Hoogerwerf, Frank. "Tonal and Referential Aspects of the Set in Stravinsky's Septet." JMR 4 (1982–1983): 69–84.

7985. Schatz, Hilmar. "Igor Stravinsky: Septet." MELOS 25 (1958): 60–63.

7986. Schilling, Hans Ludwig. "Zur Instrumentation in Igor Strawinskys Spätwerk, aufgezeigt an seinem Septett 1953." AM 13 (1956): 181–96.

7987. Smyth, David. "Stravinsky's Second Crisis: Reading the Early Serial Sketches." PNM 37, no. 2 (1999): 117–46.

7988. Stein, Erwin. "Strawinsky's Septet (1953)." TEMPO 31 (1954): 7–10.

7989. M-Wolterink.

Serenade in A

7990. Boettcher, Bonna J. *A Study of Stravinsky's Sonate pour piano (1924) and Sérénade en la: A Performer's Analysis and Comparison*. San Francisco: Mellen Research University Press, 1991.

7991. Cone, Edward T. "Stravinsky: The Progress of a Method." PNM 1, no. 1 (1962): 18–26.

7992. Hays, William L. "On Voice-Leading and Syntax in the 'Cadenza Finala' from Stravinsky's *Sérénade en la*." TP 12 (1987): 55–65.

7993. Hermann, Richard. "Thoughts on Voice-Leading and Set Theory in 'Neo-Tonal' Works: The 'Hymne' from Stravinsky's *Sérénade en la*." TP 12 (1987): 27–53.

7994. Kielian-Gilbert, Marianne. "Patterns of Repetition in the 'Hymne' of Stravinsky's *Sérénade en la*: The Rhythmic Modeling of Musical Ideas." TP 12 (1987): 11–25.

7995. Straus, Joseph N. "The Problem of Coherence in Stravinsky's *Sérénade en la* (1925)." TP 12 (1987): 3–10.

Sermon, a Narrative, and a Prayer

7996. Clifton, Thomas. "Types of Symmetrical Relations in Stravinsky's *A Sermon, a Narrative, and a Prayer.*" PNM 9 (1970): 96–112.

7997. Mason, Colin. "Stravinskys's New Work." TEMPO 59 (1961): 5–14.

7998. Morton, Lawrence. "Igor Strawinskys Kantate *A Sermon, a Narrative, and a Prayer.*" MK 36 (1966): 126–29.

7999. Regamey, Constantin. "Strawinskys jüngstes Werk: *A Sermon, a Narrative, and a Prayer.*" SMZ 102 (1962): 134–41.

8000. Secondi, Pierluigi. "Simmetrie spaziali nella dodecafonia stravinskiana." ANL 18 (1995): 5–11; 19 (1996): 12–22.

Soldier's Tale. See Histoire du soldat

Sonata for Two Pianos

8001. Burkhart, Charles. "Stravinsky's Revolving Canon." MR 29 (1968): 161–64.

8002. Johns, Donald C. "An Early Serial Idea of Stravinsky." MR 23 (1962): 305–13. Translated under the title "Eine frühe Reihenarbeit Strawinskys," OMZ 19 (1964): 248–53.

8003. Kirchmeyer, Helmut. *Igor Strawinsky, Zeitgeschichte in Persönlichkeitsbild, Grundlagen und Voraussetzung zur modernen Konstruktionstechnik,* 537–46. Regensburg: Bosse, 1958.

8004. Tangeman, Robert. "Stravinsky's Two-Piano Works." MM 22 (1945): 93–98.

Songs from William Shakespeare

8005. Boge, Claire. "Idea and Analysis: Aspects of Unification in Musical Explanation." CMS 30, no. 1 (1990): 115–30. [No. 1]

8006. Eimert, Herbert. "*Die drei Shakespeare-Lieder* (1953)." MZ 12 (1955): 35–38. Reprint, M-Kirchmeyer: 186–88.

8007. Mori, Akane. "Proportional Exchange in Stravinsky's Early Serial Music." JMT 41, no. 2 (1997): 227–59.

8008. Pesson, Gérard. "*Three Songs from William Shakespeare* de Stravinsky: Une oeuvre du passage." ENT 1 (1986): 17–33.

8009. M-Wolterink.

Symphonie de psaumes

8010. Bailey, Kathryn. "Stravinsky's *Canticum Novum.*" SMUWO 10 (1985): 75–78. [Movement II]

8011. Berger, Arthur. "Problems of Pitch Organization in Stravinsky." PNM 2, no. 1 (1963): 11–42.

8012. Chittum, Donald. "Compositional Similarities in Beethoven and Stravinsky." MR 30 (1969): 285–90.

8013. Cole, Vincent Lewis. "Analyses of *Symphony of Psalms* (1930, Rev. 1948) and *Requiem Canticles* (1966) by Igor Stravinsky." Ph.D. diss., University of California, Los Angeles, 1980.

8014. Cone, Edward T. "Stravinsky: The Progress of a Method." PNM 1, no. 1 (1962): 18–26.

8015. Graybill, Roger. "Intervallic Transformation and Closure in the Music of Stravinsky." TP 14–15 (1989–1990): 13–34. [Movement II]

8016. Horlacher, Gretchen. "The Rhythms of Reiteration: Formal Development in Stravinsky's Ostinati." MTS 14, no. 2 (1992): 171–87.

8017. Kielian-Gilbert, Marianne. "Relationships of Symmetrical Pitch-Class Sets and Stravinsky's Metaphor of Polarity." PNM 21 (1982–1983): 209–40.

8018. Mellers, Wilfred. "*Symphony of Psalms.*" TEMPO 97 (1971): 19–27.

8019. Straus, Joseph. "Stravinsky's Tonal Axis." JMT 26 (1982): 261–90.

8020. M-Zimmerschied: 41–54.

Symphonies d'instruments à vent

8021. Bowles, Richard W. "Stravinsky's *Symphonies of Wind Instruments* for 23 Winds: An Analysis." JBR 15, no. 1 (1979–1980): 32–37.

8022. Cone, Edward T. "Stravinsky: The Progress of a Method." PNM 1, no. 1 (1962): 18–26.

8023. Decarsin, François. "Les *Symphonies pour instruments à vent* de Stravinsky: Déni du présent et mise en question d'une direction du temps." ANM 6 (1987): 38–43.

8024. Kramer, Jonathan. "Moment Form in Twentieth Century Music." MQ 64 (1938): 177–94.

8025. Rehding, Alexander. "Towards a 'Logic of Discontinuity' in Stravinsky's *Symphonies of Wind Instruments*: Hasty, Kramer, and Straus Reconsidered." MA 17, no. 1 (1998): 39–65.

8026. Schweizer, Klaus. "'. . . nicht zur Befriedigung sentimentaler Bedürfnisse': Anmerkung zu Igor Strawinskys 'Bläsersinfonien.'" M-Breig: 377–92.

8027. Somfai, László. "*Symphonies of Wind Instruments* (1920): Observations on Stravinsky's Organic Construction." SM 14 (1972): 355–83.

8028. Straus, Joseph. "A Principle of Voice Leading in the Music of Stravinsky." MTS 4 (1982): 106–24.

8029. Tyra, Thomas. "An Analysis of Stravinsky's *Symphonies of Wind Instruments.*" JBR 8, no. 2 (1971–1972): 6–39.

8030. Van den Toorn, Pieter C. "Metrical Displacement in Stravinsky." MPSS 11 (1998): 24–28.

8031. Walsh, Stephen. "Stravinsky's Symphonies: Accident or Design?" M-Ayrey: 35–71.

Symphony in C

8032. Babitz, Sol. "Stravinsky's *Symphony in C* (1940)." MQ 27 (1941): 20–25.

8033. Kielian-Gilbert, Marianne. "Stravinsky's Contrasts: Contradiction and Discontinuity in His Neoclassic Music." JM 9, no. 4 (1991): 448–80.

8034. Straus, Joseph. "A Principle of Voice Leading in the Music of Stravinsky." MTS 4 (1982): 106–24.

8035. ———. "Stravinsky's Tonal Axis." JMT 26 (1982): 261–90.

8036. Van den Toorn, Pieter C. "Metrical Displacement in Stravinsky." MPSS 11 (1998): 24–28.

8037. Williams, B. M. "Time and Structure of Stravinsky's *Symphony in C*." MQ 59, no. 3 (1973): 355–69.

Symphony in Three Movements

8038. Dahl, Ingolf. "Stravinsky in 1946." MM 23 (1946): 159–65.

8039. Osthoff, Wolfgang. "Symphonien beim Ende des Zweiten Weltkriegs: Strawinsky–Frommel–Schostakowitsch." ACTA 60, no. 1 (1988): 62–104.

8040. Rülke, Volker. "Strawinskys Auseinandersetzung mit der Sonatensatzform: Der Kopfsatz der *Symphony in Three Movements*." MF 47, no. 1 (1994): 42–57.

8041. Strobel, Heinrich. "Strawinskys *Symphony in Three Movements*." MELOS 15 (1948): 271–76.

Symphony, Op. 1

8042. M-Taruskin.

Threni

8043. Hogan, Clare. "*Threni*: Stravinsky's 'Debt' to Krenek." TEMPO 142 (1982): 22–25, 28–29.

8044. Pauli, Hansjörg. "On Stravinsky's *Threni*." TEMPO 49 (1958): 16–33.

8045. ———. "Zur seriellen Struktur von Igor Strawinskys *Threni*." SMZ 98 (1958): 450–56.

8046. Karallus, Manfred. "Mit Quinten und chromatischen Zirkel harmonische Feldvermessung in Strawinskys Spätwerk." NZM 146, no. 1 (1985): 8–12.

8047. Schuh, Willi. "Struckturanalyze eines Fragments aus Stravinskys *Threni*." SMZ 98 (1958): 456–60.

8048. Secondi, Pierluigi. "Simmetrie spaziali nella dodecafonia stravinskiana." Part I, ANL 18 (1995): 5–11; Part II, ANL 19 (1996): 12–22.

8049. Smyth, David H. "Stravinsky as Serialist: The Sketches for *Threni*." MTS 22, no. 2 (2000): 205–24.

8050. Vlad, Roman. "Igor Strawinskys *Threni*." MELOS 26 (1959): 36–39.

Variations (Aldous Huxley in Memoriam)

8051. Kohl, Jerome. "Exposition in Stravinsky's Orchestral *Variations*." PNM 18, nos. 1–2 (1979–1980): 391–405.

8052. Phillips, Paul Schuyler. "The Enigma of *Variations*: A Study of Stravinsky's Final Work for Orchestra." MA 3, no. 1 (1984): 69–89.

8053. Spies, Claudio. "Notes on Stravinsky's Variations." PNM 4, no. 1 (1965): 62–74.

8054. White, Eric Walter. "Two New Memorial Works by Stravinsky." TEMPO 74 (1965): 18–21.

Violin Concerto

8055. M-Hall.

8056. M-Little.

8057. Rogers, Lynne. "Stravinsky's Alternative Approach to Counterpoint." Ph.D. diss., Princeton University, 1989.

Zvezdolikiy. See *Roi des étoiles*

Various Works

8058. Andrews, Dwight Douglas. "An Analytical Model of Pitch and Rhythm in the Early Music of Igor Stravinsky." Ph.D. diss., Yale University, 1993.

8059. Babbitt, Milton. "Remarks on the Recent Stravinsky." PNM 2, no. 2 (1964): 35–55.

8060. Bass, Claude L. "Phrase Structure and Cadence Treatment in the Music of Stravinsky." Ph.D. diss., North Texas State University, 1972.

8061. Blitzstein, Marc. "The Phenomenon of Stravinsky." MQ 21 (1935): 330–37.

8062. Boys, Henry. "Stravinsky: Critical Categories Needed for a Study of His Music." SCORE 1 (1949): 3–12.

8063. Brantley, John Paul. "The Serial Choral Music of Igor Stravinsky." Ph.D. diss., University of Iowa, 1978.

8064. Browne, Arthur G. "Aspects of Stravinsky's Work." ML 11 (1930): 360–66.

8065. Cholopova, Valentina. "Russische Quellen der Rhythmik Strawinskys." MF 27 (1974): 435–46.

8066. Cholopow, Jurij N. "Die Harmonik im Frühwerk Strawinskys." BM 28, no. 4 (1986): 251–66.

8067. Cogan, Robert. "Stravinsky's Sound: A Phonological View; Stravinsky the Progressive." SONUS 2, no. 2 (1982): 4–21.

8068. Collaer, Paul. *Stravinsky*. Brussels: Larcier, 1930.

8069. Craft, Robert. "Reihencompositionen: Vom Septett zum *Agon.*" MZ 12 (1955): 43–54.

8070. Davies, Laurence. "Stravinsky as Litterateur." ML 49 (1968): 135–44.

8071. Donington, Robert. *Stravinsky Ballet Music.* London: Cassel, 1952.

8072. Edwards, William Pope, Jr. "The Variation Process in the Music of Stravinsky." Ph.D. diss., Indiana University, 1974.

8073. Fleischer, Herbert. *Strawinsky.* Berlin: Russischer Musik, 1931.

8074. M-Hart.

8075. Hirsbrunner, Theo. "Zu Strawinskys Reihentechnik." MF 35 (1982): 356–63.

8076. Hopkins, G. W. "Stravinskys's Chords." TEMPO 76 (1966): 6–12; 77 (1966): 2–9.

8077. Huff, J. A. "Linear Structures and Their Relation to Style in Selected Compositions by Igor Stravinsky." Ph.D. diss., Northwestern University, 1965.

8078. Jers, Norbert. *Igor Strawinskys späte Zwölftonwerke (1958–1966).* Regensburg: Bosse, 1977.

8079. Karallus, Manfred. "Igor Strawinsky: Der Übergang zur seriellen Kompositionstechnik." Ph.D. diss., Frankfurt am Main, 1977.

8080. Kielian-Gilbert, Marianne. "The Rhythms of Form: Correspondence and Analogy in Stravinsky's Designs." MTS 9 (1987): 42–66.

8081. Kirchmeyer, Helmut. *Igor Strawinsky, Zeitgeschichte im Persönlichkeitsbild, Grundlagen und Voraussetzung zur modernen Konstruktionstechnik.* Regensburg: Bosse, 1958.

8082. Klein, Lothar. "Stravinsky and Opera: Parable as Ethic." CCM 4 (1972): 65–71.

8083. Kraemer, Uwe. "Das Zitat bei Igor Strawinsky." NZM 131 (1970): 135–41.

8084. M-Lang.

8085. Lindlar, Heinrich. "Bläserchorale bei Strawinsky." SMZ 96 (1956): 394–98.

8086. ———. *Igor Strawinskys sakraler Gesang: Geist und Form der Christ-kultischen Kompositionen.* Regensburg: Bosse, 1957.

8087. Maconie, Robin. "Stravinsky's Final Cadence." TEMPO 103 (1972): 18–23.

8088. Mahar, William John. "Neoclassicism in the Twentieth Century: A Study of the Idea and Its Relationship to Selected Works of Stravinsky and Picasso." Ph.D. diss., Syracuse University, 1972.

8089. Mason, Colin. "Stravinsky's Contributions to Chamber Music." TEMPO 43 (1957): 6–16.

8090. Meylan, Pierre. *Une amitie celebre.* Paris: Librairie Ploix, 1962.

8091. Middleton, Richard. "Stravinsky's Development: A Jungian Approach." ML 54 (1973): 289–301.

8092. Moevs, Robert. "Mannerisms and Stylistic Consistency in Stravinsky." PNM 9, no. 2 (1971): 92–103.

8093. Monnikendam, Marius. *Igor Stravinsky.* Haarlem: Gottmer, 1966.

8094. Murrill, Herbert. "Aspects of Stravinsky." ML 32 (1951): 118–24.

8095. MZ 1 (1952). [Special issue]

8096. MZ 12 (1955). [Special issue]

8097. Reade, Eugene Walter. "A Study of Rhythm in the Serial Works of Igor Stravinsky." Ph.D. diss., Indiana University, 1979.

8098. RM 191 (1939). [Special issue]

8099. Santa, Matthew. "Chordal Tone Centers in Stravinsky's Neoclassical Music." TP 22–23 (1997–1998): 103–22.

8100. Schönberger, Elmer, and Louis Andriessen. "The Apollonian Clockwork: Extracts from a Book." Trans. Jeff Hamburg. TEMPO 142 (1982): 13–21.

8101. SCORE 20 (1957). [Special issue]

8102. Sears, Ilene Hanson. "The Influence of Rhythm on Form in Selected Chamber Works of Igor Stravinsky." Ph.D. diss., Indiana University, 1990.

8103. Stephan, Rudolf. "Aus Igor Strawinskys Spielzeugschachtel." F-Doflein: 27–30.

8104. Straus, Joseph N. "A Strategy of Large-Scale Organization in Stravinsky's Late Music." INT 11 (1997): 1–36.

8105. ———. "Stravinsky's 'Construction of Twelve Verticals': An Aspect of Harmony in the Serial Music." MTS 21, no. 1 (1999): 43–73.

8106. ———. "A Theory of Harmony and Voice Leading in the Music of Igor Stravinsky." Ph.D. diss., Yale University, 1981.

8107. Strauss, Virginia Rose Fattaruso. "The Stylistic Use of the Violin in Selected Works by Stravinsky." D.M.A. diss., University of Texas, 1980.

8108. Strube, Roger W. "Folk Music and Folk Idioms in Stravinsky's Early Works." D 5 (1973): 16–27.

8109. Struth, Sigrid. "Klassische Symphonik." MZ 12 (1955): 53–68.

8110. TEMPO 97 (1971). [Special issue]

8111. Thomason, Marshall Malone. "Neo-Tonality: A Unified Approach to Stravinsky's Neoclassical Music." Ph.D. diss., University of Texas at Austin, 1987.

8112. Van den Toorn, Pieter C. *The Music of Igor Stravinsky.* New Haven, Conn.: Yale University Press, 1983.

8113. ———. "Some Characteristics of Stravinsky's Diatonic Music." PNM 14, no. 1 (1975): 104–38.

8114. Vlad, Roman. *Stravinsky.* London: Oxford University Press, 1967.

8115. Wade, Carroll D. "A Selected Bibliography of Igor Stravinsky." MQ 48 (1962): 372–84.

8116. Ward-Steinman, David. "Serial Technique in the Recent Music of Igor Stravinsky." Ph.D. diss., University of Illinois, 1961.

8117. Webber, Allen. "Similarities of Melodic Shape in Selected Works of Igor Stravinsky." TSP 2 (1985): 11–24.

8118. White, Eric Walter. *Stravinsky: The Composer and His Works.* Berkeley: University of California Press, 1966.

8119. Wildberger, Jacques. "Eine musikalisch-rhetorische Figur bei Strawinsky." SMZ 113 (1973): 65–69.

STREICHER, THEODOR (1874–1940)

8120. Wursten, Richard Bruce. "The Life and Music of Theodor Streicher: Hugo Wolf *redivivus?*" Ph.D. diss., University of Wisconsin, 1980.

STRINGFIELD, LAMAR (1897–1959)

8121. Nelson, Douglas. "The Life and Works of Lamar Stringfield (1897–1959)." Ph.D. diss., University of North Carolina, 1971.

STSCHEDRIN, RODION (b. 1932)

8122. Gerlach, Hannelore. "*Tschastuschki-Kontraste-Poeme*: Zum Schaffen von Rodion Stschedrin." MG 22 (1972): 721–28.

SUBOTNICK, MORTON (b. 1933)

8123. VanHandel, Leigh. "Inherent Primitivism in Morton Subotnick's *All My Hummingbirds Have Alibis.*" MRF 10 (1995): 43–63.

SUCHOŇ, EUGEN (1908–1993)

8124. Zavarský, Ernest. "Modale Musik im 20. Jahrhundert, besonders im Schaffen von Eugen Suchoň." MO 10 (1986): 127–65.

SUK, JOSEF (1874–1935)

8125. Doubravová, Jarmila. "Sound and Structure in Josef Suk's *Zrání.*" IRASM 6 (1977): 73–87.

SULLIVAN, ARTHUR (1842–1900)

8126. Fink, Robert. "Rhythm and Text Setting in *The Mikado.*" NCM 14, no. 1 (1990): 31–47.

8127. Helyar, James. *Gilbert and Sullivan: Papers.* First International Conference on Gilbert and Sullivan. Lawrence: University of Kansas Libraries, 1971.

8128. Hughes, Gervase. *The Music of Arthur Sullivan.* New York: St. Martin's, 1960.

8129. Nelson, John C. "Tonal and Structural Design in the Finales of the Savoy Operas, with Some Suggestions as to Derivation." ITR 13, no. 2 (1992): 1–22. [*The Gondoliers, Iolanthe, The Pirates of Penzance*]

SWANSON, HOWARD (1907–1978)

8130. Ennett, Dorothy. "An Analysis and Comparison of Selected Piano Sonatas by three Contemporary Black Composers: George Walker, Howard Swanson, and Roque Cordero." Ph.D. diss., New York University, 1973.

SWIFT, RICHARD (1927–2003)

8131. Hanninen, Dora A. "A General Theory for Context-Sensitive Music Analysis: Applications to Four Works for Piano by Contemporary American Composers." Ph.D. diss., University of Rochester, 1996. [*Things of August*]

8132. ———. "On Association, Realization, and Form in Richard Swift's *Things of August.*" PNM 35, no. 1 (1997): 61–114.

8133. Morris, Robert D. "Not Only Rows in Richard Swift's *Roses Only.*" PNM 35, no. 1 (1997): 13–47.

8134. Swift, Richard. "On *Prime.*" PNM 26, no. 2 (1988): 26–30.

SZŐLLŐSY, ANDRÁS (b. 1921)

8135. Szesztay, Zsolt. "Further along Kodály's Path: András Szőllősy *Planctus Mariae*, an Analysis." IKSB 1988, no. 1: 31–33.

SZYMANOWSKI, KAROL (1882–1937)

8136. Bristiger, Michael, Roger Scruton, and Petra Weber-Bockholdt, eds. *Karol Szymanowski in seiner Zeit.* Munich: Fink, 1984.

8137. Cadrin, Paul. "Tonal Analysis and the First String Quartet, Opus 37, by Karol Szymanowski." Ph.D. diss., University of British Columbia, 1986.

8138. Cruz-Peréz, Horacio Antonio. "The Piano Sonatas of Karol Szymanowski." Ph.D. diss., Northwestern University, 1987.

8139. Downes, Stephen. "Szymanowski and Narcissism." JRMA 121, no. 1 (1996): 58–81. [*Metopes*, op. 29; *Narcissus*, op. 30]

8140. ———. "Themes of Duality and Transformation in Szymanowski's *King Roger*." MA 14, nos. 2–3 (1995): 257–91.

8141. Finscher, Ludwig. "Symphonie, Literatur und Philosophie: Zur 2. Symphonie Karol Szymanowskis." F-Dahlhaus: 651–58.

8142. Gray, Frances M. "Karol Szymanowski: Three Representative Works for Piano." D.M.A. diss., Indiana University, 1979. [Opp. 4, 34, 50]

8143. Helman, Zofia. "Zur Modalität im Schaffen Szymanowskis und Janke ks." M-Pečman/J: 201–11.

8144. Samson, Jim. *The Music of Szymanowski*. New York: Taplinger, 1981.

8145. ———. "Szymanowski and Tonality." STU 5 (1976): 291–312.

8146. M-Schultz: 61–62 [*Driady i Pan*, op. 30]; 63–73 [Violin Concerto No. 1, op. 35]; 74–82 [Symphony No. 3, op. 27]

– T –

TAKEMITSU, TŌRU (1930–1996)

8147. Gibson, James Robert. "Toru Takemitsu: A Survey of His Music with an Analysis of Three Works." D.M.A. diss., Cornell University, 1979. [*Landscape, Masque, Requiem*]

8148. Koozin, Timothy. "Octatonicism in Recent Solo Piano Works of Tōru Takemitsu." PNM 29, no. 1 (1991): 124–40. [*For Away, Rain Tree Sketch, Les yeux clos II*]

8149. ———. "The Solo Piano Works of Toru Takemitsu: A Linear/Set-Theoretic Analysis." Ph.D. diss., University of Cincinnati, 1989.

8150. ———. "Spiritual-Temporal Imagery in Music of Olivier Messiaen and Toru Takemitsu." CMR 7, no. 2 (1993): 185–202. [*Quatrain II*]

8151. ———. "Toru Takemitsu and the Unity of Opposites." CMS 30, no. 1 (1990): 34–44. [*For Away*]

8152. ———. "Toru Takemitsu's *Pause ininterrompue*: Linearity and Pitch-Class Set Recurrence." MRF 1 (1986): 65–81. [*Uninterrupted Rest*]

8153. O'Grady, Deborah L. "Toru Takemitsu's *Valeria*." EXT 1, no. 1 (1981): 1–17.

8154. Smaldone, Edward. "Japanese and Western Confluences in Large-Scale Pitch Organization of Tōru Takemitsu's *November Steps* and *Autumn*." PNM 27, no. 2 (1989): 216–31.

TAL, JOSEF (b. 1910)

8155. Ron, Yohanan. "Expression of the Twelve-Tone Row in the Works of Oedoen Partos and Josef Tal." OM 11 (1993–1994): 81–91. [Concerto for Cello and Chamber Orchestra]

8156. ———. "The Tone as an Idea and a Subject in the Later Works of Josef Tal." ISM 6 (1996): 71–80.

TALMA, LOUISE (1906–1996)

8157. Barkin, Elaine. "Louise Talma: *The Tolling Bell*." PNM 10, no. 2 (1972): 142–52.

TAVENER, JOHN (b. 1944)

8158. Parsons, Larry Russell. "An Analysis of Six Major Choral Works by John Tavener." D.M.A. diss., University of Illinois, 1978.

8159. Phillips, Peter. "The Ritual Music of John Tavener." CT 26 (1983): 29–30.

TAZARTÈS, GHÉDALIA (b. 1947)

8160. Stoianova, Ivanka. "Des scénarios imaginaires en impromuz: *Ghédal et son double*." MJ 29 (1977): 85–93.

8161. ———. "Multiplicité, non-directionnalité et jeu dans les pratiques contemporaines du spectacle musico-theatral (I): Théâtre instrumental et impromuz; Mauricio Kagel, *Staatstheater;* Ghedalia Tazartes, *Ghédal et son double*." MJ 27 (1977): 38–48.

TCHAIKOVSKY, PYOTR IL'YICH (1840–1893)

Ballets (various; *see also* specific ballets)

8162. Wiley, Roland John. "Dramatic Time and Music in Tchaikovsky's Ballets." F-Abraham: 187–95.

Eugene Onegin

8163. Asafev, Boris Vladimirovich. *Tschaikowsky's "Eugen Onegin": Versuch einer Analyse des Stils und der musikalischen Dramaturgie*. Potsdam: Akademische Verlagsgesellschaft Athenaion, 1949.

8164. ASO 43 (1982).

Francesa da Rimini

8165. Barricelli, Jean-Pierre. "Liszt's Journey through Dante's Hereafter." JALS 14 (1983): 3–15.
8166. Coppola, Catherine. "The Elusive Fantasy: Genre, Form, and Program in Tchaikovsky's *Francesca da Rimini*." NCM 22, no. 2 (1998): 169–89.

Hamlet

8167. Jackson, Timothy L. "Aspects of Sexuality and Structure in the Later Symphonies of Tchaikovsky." MA 14, no. 1 (1995): 3–25.

Nutcracker

8168. DeVoto, Mark. "The Russian Submediant in the Nineteenth Century." CM 59 (1995): 48–76.

Piano Concertos

8169. Niebuhr, Ulrich. "Der Einfluss Anton Rubinsteins auf die Klavierkonzerte Peter Tschikowskis." MF 27 (1974): 412–34.

Queen of Spades

8170. ASO 119–120 (1989).
8171. Leibowitz, René. "Une fantasmagorie lyrique: *La dame de pique*." Leibowitz/F: 227–58.
8172. Lobanova, Marina. "Drei, Sieben, As: Zu der Oper *Pique dame* von Pjotr Iljitsch Čajkovskij." MF 49, no. 3 (1996): 275–86.

Symphonies

8173. Hollander, Hans. "Das Finale-Problem in Tschaikowskys sechster Symphonie." NZM 118 (1957): 13–15.
8174. Jackson, Timothy L. "Aspects of Sexuality and Structure in the Later Symphonies of Tchaikovsky." MA 14, no. 1 (1995): 3–25. [Nos. 4–6]
8175. ———. *Tchaikovsky: Symphony No. 6 (Pathétique)*. Cambridge: Cambridge University Press, 1999.
8176. Kraus, Joseph C. "Tonal Conflict and Resolution in Tchaikovsky's Symphony No. 5 in E Minor." MTS 13, no. 1 (1991): 21–47.
8177. Murphy, Edward W. "The Dominant Complex/Climax in Selected Works of the Late Nineteenth Century." MR 55, no. 2 (1994): 104–18. [Symphony no. 6 (Movement I)]
8178. Pfann, Walter. "'Hat er es denn beschlossen . . .': Anmerkungen zu einem neuen Verständnis von Čajkovskijs *Symphonie Pathétique*." MF 51, no. 2 (1998): 191–209. [Symphony No. 6]
8179. Wolfurt, Kurt von. *Die sinfonischen Werke von Peter Tschaikowski: Einführungen*. Berlin: Bote und Bock, 1947.
8180. Zajaczkowski, Henry. "Tchaikovsky's Fourth Symphony." MR 45 (1984): 265–76.

Tempest

8181. Jackson, Timothy L. "Aspects of Sexuality and Structure in the Later Symphonies of Tchaikovsky." MA 14, no. 1 (1995): 3–25.

Voyevoda

8182. Jackson, Timothy L. "Aspects of Sexuality and Structure in the Later Symphonies of Tchaikovsky." MA 14, no. 1 (1995): 3–25.

Various Works

8183. Abraham, Gerald, ed. *The Music of Tchaikovsky*. New York: Norton, 1969. Reprint, 1974.
8184. ———. *Tchaikovsky: A New Study*. London: Drummond, 1945.
8185. Hanson, Lawrence, and Elizabeth Hanson. *Tchaikovsky: A New Study of the Man and His Music*. London: Cassell, 1965.
8186. Kohlhase, Thomas. "Tschaikowskij als Kirchenmusiker: Die Vsenoscnaja und ihre liturgischen Vorlagen." F-Dadelson: 189–229.
8187. Zagiba, Frantisek. *Tschaikovskij: Leben und Werk*. Zurich: Amalthea, 1953.
8188. Zajaczkowski, Henry. "The Function of Obsessive Elements in Tchaikovsky's Style." MR 43 (1982): 24–30.

TCHEREPNIN, ALEXANDER (1899–1977)

8189. Arias, Enrique Alberto. "The Symphonies of Alexander Tcherepnin." TEMPO 158 (1986): 23–31.
8190. Layton, Robert. "Alexander Tcherepnin at 75." TEMPO 108 (1974): 11–14.
8191. Thrash, Lois Leventhal. "A Stylistic Analysis and Discussion of Alexander Tcherepnin's Preludes and Etudes for Piano." D.M.A. diss., Indiana University, 1981.
8192. Wuellner, Guy. "Alexander Tcherepnin, in Youth and Maturity: Bagatelles, Opus 5, and *Expressions*, Opus 81." JALS 9 (1981): 88–94.
8193. ———. "The Complete Piano Music of Alexander Tcherepnin." D.M.A. diss., University of Iowa, 1973.
8194. ———. "The Piano Etudes of Alexander Tcherepnin." JALS 35 (1994): 1–22.

TEMPERLEY, DAVID

8195. Temperley, David. "Things I Think About, and Don't Think About, When I Compose." CM 67–68 (1999): 431–42.

TENNEY, JAMES (b. 1934)

8196. Tenney, James. "About *Changes: Sixty-four Studies for Six Harps.*" PNM 25 (1987): 64–87.

THIELE, SIEGRIED (b. 1934)

8197. Gülke, Peter. "Siegfried Thiele Sinfonie in 5 Sätzen." MG 16 (1966): 340–42.

8198. Kneipel, Eberhard. "Polarität und Metamorphose: Anmerkungen zu Siegfried Thieles Sinfonie in fünf Sätzen." MG 19 (1969): 322–28.

THILMAN, JOHANNES PAUL (1906–1973)

8199. Hauska, Hans. "Johannes Paul Thilman: *Partita piccola.*" MG 12 (1962): 679–80.

8200. Rubisch, Egon. "Eine neue Sinfonie von Thilman." MG 10 (1960): 549–99. [Symphony No. 6]

8201. Schwinger, Eckart. "Rhapsodie für Orchester von Johannes Paul Thilman." MG 16 (1966): 338–40.

THOMPSON, RANDALL (1899–1984)

8202. Brookhart, Charles E. "The Choral Works of Aaron Copland, Roy Harris, and Randall Thompson." Ph.D. diss., George Peabody College for Teachers, 1960.

8203. Forbes, Elliot. "The Music of Randall Thompson." MQ 35 (1949): 1–25.

8204. McGilvray, Byron Wendol. "The Choral Music of Randall Thompson, an American Eclectic." D.M.A. diss., University of Missouri, 1979.

8205. Urrows, David Francis. "Five Love Songs: Reflections on a Recent Work." ACR 22, no. 2 (1980): 28–38.

THOMSON, VIRGIL (1896–1989)

8206. Anagnost, Dean Z. "The Choral Music of Virgil Thomson." Ph.D. diss., Columbia University Teachers College, 1977.

8207. Chen, Shu-ling. "Music and Language in Two Twentieth-Century American Operas." Ph.D. diss., University of Maryland, College Park, 1997. [*The Mother of Us All*]

8208. Cowell, Henry. "Current Chronicle." MQ 35 (1949): 619–22. [*A Solemn Music*]

8209. Glanville-Hicks, Peggy. "Virgil Thomson." MQ 35 (1949): 209–35.

8210. Meckna, Michael. "Sacred and Secular America: Virgil Thomson's *Symphony on a Hymn Tune.*" AMUS 8, no. 4 (1990): 465–76.

8211. Sternfeld, Frederick W. "Current Chronicle." MQ 35 (1949): 115–21.

8212. Ward, Kelly Mac. "An Analysis of the Relationship between Text and Musical Shape and an Investigation of the Relationship between Text and Surface Rhythmic Detail in *Four Saints in Three Acts* by Virgil Thomson." Ph.D. diss., University of Texas, 1978.

THURM, JOACHIM (1927–1995)

8213. Gülke, Peter. "Joachim Thurms Orchestermusik 1965." MG 17 (1967): 101–2.

TIPPETT, MICHAEL (1905–1998)

Choral Works

8214. Gloag, Kenneth. *Tippett: A Child of Our Time.* Cambridge: Cambridge University Press, 1999.

8215. M-Hansler.

8216. Whittall, Arnold. "Resisting Tonality: Tippett, Beethoven, and the Sarabande." MA 9, no. 3 (1990): 267–86. [*The Mask of Time*]

Operas

8217. Clarke, David. "The Significance of the Concept 'Image' in Tippett's Musical Thought: A Perspective from Jung." JRMA 121, no. 1 (1996): 82–104. [*King Priam*]

8218. Jones, R. E. "The Operas of Michael Tippett." Ph.D. diss., Cardiff, 1976.

8219. Robinson, Suzanne. "An Opera of 'Depth': Tippett's *The Midsummer Marriage.*" MR 51, no. 2 (1990): 116–32.

8220. ———. "*The Midsummer Marriage* in *New Year*: A Comparison of Tippett's First and Latest Operas." MSA 14 (1991): 25–36.

8221. Scheppach, Margaret. "The Operas of Michael Tippett in the Light of Twentieth-Century Opera Aesthetics." Ph.D. diss., University of Rochester, 1974.

Piano Works

8222. Mason, Colin. "Tippett's Piano Concerto." SCORE 16 (1956): 63–68.

8223. Swansbourne, Clive. "The Piano Music of Sir Micheal Tippett." PQ 147 (1989): 53–58.

Songs

8224. Docherty, Barbara. "Sentence into Cadence: The Word-Setting of Tippett and Britten." TEMPO 166 (1988): 2–11. [*Heart's Assurance*]

8225. ———. "Syllogism and Symbol: Britten, Tippett, and English Text." CMR 5 (1989): 37–63. [*Boyhood's End, Heart's Assurance*]

String Quartet No. 2

8226. Puffett, Derrick. "The Fugue from Tippett's Second String Quartet." MA 5, nos. 2–3 (1986): 233–64.

Symphonies

8227. Rodda, Richard Earl. "The Symphonies of Sir Michael Tippett." Ph.D. diss., Case Western Reserve University, 1979.

Triple Concerto

8228. Clarke, David. "The Meaning of 'Lateness': Mediations of Work, Self, and Society in Tippett's *Triple Concerto*." JRMA 125, no. 1 (2000): 62–92.

Various Works

8229. Atkinson, Neville. "Michael Tippett's Debt to the Past." MR 23 (1962): 195–204.

8230. M-Hines.

8231. Kemp, Ian, ed. *Michael Tippett: A Symposium on His Sixtieth Birthday.* London: Faber & Faber, 1965.

8232. ———. "Rhythm in Tippett's Early Music." PRMA 105 (1978–1979): 142–53.

8233. Milner, Anthony. "The Music of Michael Tippett." MQ 50 (1964): 423–38.

8234. Whittall, Arnold. *The Music of Britten and Tippett: Studies in Themes and Techniques.* Cambridge: Cambridge University Press, 1982.

TISNÉ, ANTOINE (b. 1932)

8235. Matore, Daniel. "*Étude I d'après Goya* d'Antoine Tisné: Correspondances peinture-musique." ANM 4 (1986): 32–37.

TOCH, ERNST (1887–1964)

8236. Johnson, Charles Anthony. "The Unpublished Works of Ernst Toch." Ph.D. diss., University of California, Los Angeles, 1973.

8237. Konold, Wulf. "Ernst Toch—Ein vergessener Komponist?" M 41, no. 5 (1987): 427–32.

8238. Pisk, Paul. "Ernst Toch." MQ 24 (1938): 438–50.

TOEBOSCH, LOUIS (b. 1916)

8239. Geraedts, Jaap. "Louis Toebosch: *Philippica moderata*, Op. 88." SS 21 (1964): 30–35.

8240. Paap, Wouter. "Louis Toebosch." SS 21 (1964): 1–10.

8241. Visser, Piet. "Louis Toebosch: Finale from *Tryptique pour orgue*." SS 23 (1965): 35–46.

TOKUHIDE, NIIMI (b. 1947)

8242. Nuss, Stephen. "'Yes, I Wrote It, but I Didn't Mean It': Hearing the Unintended in Niimi Tokuhide's *Ohju* (1988)." PNM 37, no. 2 (1999): 51–115.

TOURNEMIRE, CHARLES (1870–1939)

8243. M-Dorroh.

TOWER, JOAN (b. 1938)

8244. Hoag, Charles. "In Quest of 'Silver Ladders' in the Americas." CMF 4 (1992): 9–16. [*Music for Cello and Orchestra, Silver Ladders*]

8245. Lochhead, Judy. "Joan Tower's *Wings* and *Breakfast Rhythms I and II*: Some Thoughts on Form and Repetition." PNM 30, no. 1 (1992): 132–56.

TREMBLAY, GILLES (b. 1932)

8246. Tremblay, Gilles. "*Les vêpres de la Vierge*." CIR 6, no. 1 (1995): 51–55.

8247. ———. "Notes pour *Cantique de durées*." CIR 6, no. 1 (1995): 43–50.

TROJAHN, MANFRED (b. 1949)

8248. Schibli, Siegfried. "Das Eigene im Fremden: Neuere Entwicklungen im Schaffen Manfred Trojahns." NZM 146, no. 5 (1985): 26–29.

TRUAX, BARRY (b. 1947)

8249. Voorvelt, Martijn. "The Environmental Element in Barry Truax's Compositions." JNMR 26, no. 1 (1997): 48–69.

TSONTAKIS, GEORGE (b. 1951)
8250. Moe, Eric. "Beyond Right and Wrong Ways to Write Music: Tsontakis, Rosenblum, and Diesendruck." CMR 10, no. 1 (1994): 149–95. [String Quartet no. 3 ("Coraggio")]

TULL, FISHER (1934–1994)
8251. Byrd, Richard William. "A Stylistic Analysis of the Solo and Chamber Music of Fisher A. Tull." Ph.D. diss., University of Kentucky, 1992.

8252. Tull, Fisher. "*Sketches on a Tudor Psalm*: Analysis by the Composer, edited by Dr. James Neilson." JBR 13, no. 1 (1977–1978): 20–26.

TURINA, JOAQUÍN (1882–1949)
8253. Powell, Linton Elzie, Jr. "The Piano Music of Joaquín Turina (1882–1949)." Ph.D. diss., University of North Carolina, 1974.

– U –

UNGER, HERMANN (1886–1958)
8254. Heldt, Gerhard. "Hermann Ungers Klavierlieder: Versuch einer Standortbestimmung des deutschen Liedes nach Max Reger." F-Schreiber: 135–58.

URBANNER, ERICH (b. 1936)
8255. Urbanner, Erich. "Mein Kontrabasskonzert 1973." ME 31 (1977–1978): 207–12.

USSACHEVSKY, VLADIMIR (1911–1990)
8256. Bailey, Donald Lee. "A Study of Stylistic and Compositional Elements of *Anthem* (Stravinsky), *Fragments of Archilochos* (Foss), and *Creation Prologue* (Ussachevsky)." D.M.A. diss., University of Northern Colorado, 1976.

– V –

VALEN, FARTEIN (1887–1952)
8257. Windebank, Florence Leah. "The Music of Fartein Valen, 1887–1952." Ph.D. diss., London, 1973.

VARÈSE, EDGARD (1883–1965)

Amériques
8258. Angermann, Klaus. *Work in Process: Varèses "Amériques."* Munich: Musikprint, 1996.
8259. Cox, David Harold. "Thematic Interrelationships between the Works of Varèse." MR 49, no. 3 (1988): 205–17.
8260. Dixon, Gail. "Some Principles of Structural Coherence in Varèse's *Amériques*." CM 48 (1990): 27–41.

Arcana
8261. Cox, David Harold. "Geometric Structures in Varèse's *Arcana*." MR 52, no. 4 (1991): 246–54.
8262. ———. "Thematic Interrelationships between the Works of Varèse." MR 49, no. 3 (1988): 205–17.
8263. Kelkel, Manfred. "*Arcana* d'Edgar Varèse: Éléments d'analyse formelle." ANM 3 (1986): 60–64.
8264. Lalitte, Philippe. "*Arcana* d'Edgar Varèse: Thématique et l'espace des hauteurs; Un univers musical en expansion." ANM 3 (1986): 65–70.

Density 21.5
8265. Baron, Carol K. "Varèse's Explication of Debussy's *Syrinx* in *Density 21.5* and an Analysis of Varèse's Composition: A Secret Model Revealed." MR 43 (1982): 121–34.
8266. Bernard, Jonathan W. *The Music of Edgard Varèse.* New Haven, Conn.: Yale University Press, 1987.
8267. ———. "On *Density 21.5*: A Response to Nattiez." MA 5, nos. 2–3 (1986): 207–31.
8268. Brower, Candace. "Pathway, Blockage, and Containment in *Density 21.5*." TP 22–23 (1997–1998): 35–54.
8269. M-Cope: 25–29.
8270. Edlund, Bengt. "Probing *Density 21.5*." MRF 11, no. 1 (1996): 48–69.
8271. Guck, Marion. "A Flow of Energy: *Density 21.5*." PNM 23, no. 1 (1984–1985): 334–47.
8272. Gümbel, Martin. "Versuch an Varèse Density *21.5*." ZM 1, no. 1 (1970): 31–38.
8273. Kloth, Timothy. "Structural Hierarchy in Two Works of Edgard Varèse: *Ecuatorial* and *Density 21.5*." CMF 3 (1991): 1–12.

8274. Koto, Takashi. "Basic Cells and Intercourse in Varèse's *Density 21.5*." SONUS 8, no. 1 (1987): 60–70.

8275. Kresky, Jeffrey. "A Path through *Density*." PNM 23, no. 1 (1984–1985): 318–33.

8276. Marvin, Elizabeth West. "The Perception of Rhythm in Non-Tonal Music: Rhythmic Contours in the Music of Edgard Varèse." MTS 13, no. 1 (1991): 61–78.

8277. Nattiez, Jean-Jacques. *"Densité 21.5" de Varèse: Essai d'analyse sémiologique.* Montreal: University of Montreal, 1975.

8278. ———. "Varèse's *Density 21.5*: A Study in Semiological Analysis." MA 1 (1982): 243–340.

8279. Siddons, James. "On the Nature of Melody in Varèse's *Density 21.5*." PNM 23, no. 1 (1984–1985): 298–316.

8280. Varèse, Edgard. *"Density 21.5."* SCORE 19 (1957): 15–18.

Ecuatorial

8281. Kloth, Timothy. "Structural Hierarchy in Two Works of Edgard Varèse: *Ecuatorial* and *Density 21.5*." CMF 3 (1991): 1–12.

Hyperprism

8282. Bernard, Jonathan W. *The Music of Edgard Varèse.* New Haven, Conn.: Yale University Press, 1987.

8283. Blyth, Andrew. "Pitch Structure and Process in Three Compositions of Edgard Varèse." MMA 16 (1989): 159–93.

8284. Meister, Christopher. "Convergence as a Mode of Musical Organization: Comparing Varèses's *Hyperprism* and Penderecki's *Polymorphia*." EXT 7, no. 1 (1994): 110–28.

8285. Morgan, Robert P. "Notes on Varèse's Rhythm." M-Van Solkema: 9–25.

Intégrales

8286. Blyth, Andrew. "Pitch Structure and Process in Three Compositions of Edgard Varèse." MMA 16 (1989): 159–93.

8287. Cox, David Harold. "Thematic Interrelationships between the Works of Varèse." MR 49, no. 3 (1988): 205–17.

8288. Koto, Takashi. "Basic Cells and Foreign Bodies in Varèse's *Integrales*." SONUS 9, no. 2 (1989): 36–45.

8289. Mâche, François-Bernard, and Gilles Tremblay. "Analyse d'*Intégrales*." RM 383–385 (1985): 111–23.

8290. Mäkelä, Tomi. "'Melodic Tonality' and Textual Form in Edgard Varèse's *Intégrales*: Aspects of Modified Tradition in Early New Music." CMR 17, no. 1 (1998): 57–71.

8291. Morgan, Robert P. "Notes on Varese's Rhythm." M-Van Solkema: 9–25.

8292. Post, Nora. "Varèse, Wolpe, and the Oboe." PNM 20 (1981–1982): 135–48.

8293. Ramsier, Paul. "An Analysis and Comparison of the Motivic Structure of *Octandre* and *Intégrales,* Two Instrumental Works by Edgard Varèse." Ph.D. diss., New York University, 1972.

8294. Strawn, John. "The *Intégrales* of Edgard Varèse: Space, Mass, Element, and Form." PNM 17, no. 1 (1978–1979): 138–60.

8295. ———. "Raum und Klangmasse in Varèses *Intégrales*." Melos/NZM 1 (1975): 446–56.

8296. Wilkinson, Marc. "Edgard Varèse: Pionier und Prophet." MELOS 28 (1961): 68–76.

Ionisation

8297. Chou Wen-Chung. "*Ionisation*: The Function of Timbre in Its Formal and Temporal Organization." M-Van Solkema: 27–74.

8298. François, Jean-Charles. "Organization of Scattered Timbral Qualities: A Look at Edgard Varèse's *Ionisation*." PNM 29, no. 1 (1991): 48–79.

8299. Gruhn, Wilfried. "Edgard Varèse (1883–1965): *Ionisation* (1931)." M-Zimmerschied: 55–72.

8300. Koto, Takashi. "Basic Cells and Combinations in Varèse's *Ionisation*." SONUS 7, no. 2 (1987): 35–45.

Octandre

8301. Blyth, Andrew. "Pitch Structure and Process in Three Compositions of Edgard Varèse." MMA 16 (1989): 159–93.

8302. Koto, Takashi. "Basic Cells and Hybridization in Varèse's *Octandre*." SONUS 8, no. 2 (1988): 59–67.

8303. Post, Nora. "Varèse, Wolpe, and the Oboe." PNM 20 (1981–1982): 135–48.

8304. Ramsier, Paul. "An Analysis and Comparison of the Motivic Structure of *Octandre* and *Intégrales,* Two Instrumental Works by Edgard Varèse." Ph.D. diss., New York University, 1972.

8305. Swan, John. "Varèse's *Octandre* as a Source Piece for the Demonstration of Three Twentieth-Century Compositional Procedures." CAUSM 2, no. 1 (1972): 53–74.

8306. Wilkinson, Marc. "Edgard Varèse: Pionier und Prophet." MELOS 28 (1961): 68–76.

Offrandes

8307. Cox, David Harold. "Thematic Interrelationships between the Works of Varèse." MR 49, no. 3 (1988): 205–17.

Poème électronique

8308. Cogan, Robert. "Varèse: An Oppositional Sonic Poetics." SONUS 11, no. 2 (1991): 26–35.

8309. M-Cope: 170–74.

8310. Lukes, Roberta Dorothy. "The *Poème électronique* of Edgard Varèse." Ph.D. diss., Harvard University, 1996.

8311. Stimson, Ann. "Analyzing *Poème électronique*: Clues from the Getty Archive and the Spectrogram." CMF 3 (1991): 13–26.

Various Works

8312. Bernard, Jonathan W. "Pitch/Register in the Music of Edgard Varèse." MTS 3 (1981): 1–25.

8313. ———. "A Theory of Pitch and Register for the Music of Edgard Varèse." Ph.D. diss., Yale University, 1977.

8314. Block, David Reed. "The Music of Edgard Varèse." Ph.D. diss., University of Washington, 1973.

8315. Carter, Elliott. "On Edgard Varèse." M-Van Solkema: 1–7.

8316. Chou Wen-Chung. "Varèse: A Sketch of the Man and His Music." MQ 52 (1966): 151–70.

8317. Cox, David Harold. "The Music of Edgard Varèse." Ph.D. diss., Birmingham, 1977.

8318. Parks, Anne Florence. "Freedom, Form, and Process in Varèse: A Study of Varèse's Musical Ideas, Their Sources, Their Development, and Their Use in His Works." Ph.D. diss., Cornell University, 1974.

8319. Stempel, Larry. "Not Even Varèse Can Be an Orphan." MQ 60 (1974): 46–60.

8320. ———. "Varèse's Awkwardness and the Symmetry in the Frame of 12 Tones: An Analytic Approach." MQ 65 (1979): 148–66. German translation, SMZ 119 (1979): 69–82.

8321. Stenzl, Jürg. "Varèsiana." HJM 4 (1980): 145–62.

8322. Tremblay, Gilles. "Acoustique et forme chez Varèse." RM 383–385 (1985): 29–46. Reprint, CIR 6, no. 1 (1995): 23–35.

8323. Wehmeyer, Grete. *Edgard Varèse.* Regensburg: Bosse, 1977.

8324. Wilheim, Andras. "The Genesis of a Specific Twelve-Tone System in the Works of Varèse." SM 19 (1977): 203–26.

8325. Wilkinson, Marc. "An Introduction to the Music of Edgard Varèse." SCORE 19 (1957): 5–14.

8326. Yannay, Yehuda. "Toward an Open-Ended Method of Analysis of Contemporary Music: A Study of Selected Works of Edgard Varèse and György Ligeti." D.M.A. diss., University of Illinois, 1974.

VAUGHAN WILLIAMS, RALPH (1872–1958)

Operas

8327. Doonan, Michael Robert. "*The Pilgrim's Progress*: An Analytical Study and Case for Performance of the Opera by Ralph Vaughan Williams." D.M. diss., Indiana University, 1980.

8328. Forbes, Anne-Marie H. "Motivic Unity in Ralph Vaughan Williams's *Riders to the Sea*." MR 44 (1983): 234–45.

8329. Reber, William Francis. "The Operas of Ralph Vaughan Williams." D.M.A. diss., University of Texas, 1977.

Symphonies

8330. Beckerman, Michael. "The Composer as Pole Seeker: Reading Vaughan Williams's *Sinfonia antartica*." CM 69 (2000): 42–67. [No. 7]

8331. Clarke, F. R. C. "The Structure of Vaughan Williams's *Sea Symphony*." MR 34 (1973): 58–61. [No. 1]

8332. Dickinson, A. E. F. "Toward the Unknown Region: An Introduction to Vaughan Williams's Sixth Symphony." MR 9 (1948): 275–90.

8333. ———. "Vaughan Williams's Fifth Symphony." MR 6 (1945): 1–12.

8334. Frogley, Alain. "Vaughan Williams and Thomas Hardy: 'Tess' and the Slow Movement of the Ninth Symphony." ML 68, no. 1 (1987): 42–59.

8335. Ottaway, Hugh. "Vaughan Williams's Eighth Symphony." ML 38 (1957): 213–25.

8336. Schwartz, Elliott Shelling. *The Symphonies of Ralph Vaughan Williams: An Analysis of Their Stylistic Elements.* Amherst: University of Massachusetts Press, 1964.

8337. Vaillancourt, Michael. "Modal and Thematic Coherence in Vaughan Williams's *Pastoral Symphony*." MR 52, no. 3 (1991): 203–17. [No. 3]

Various Works

8338. Bergsagel, John Dagfinn. "The National Aspects of the Music of Ralph Vaughan Williams." Ph.D. diss., Cornell University, 1957.

8339. M-Curtis.

8340. Dickinson, A. E. F. "The Legacy of Ralph Vaughan Williams: A Retrospect." MR 19 (1958): 290–304.

8341. Hawthorne, Robin. "A Note on the Music of Vaughan Williams." MR 9 (1948): 269–74.

8342. Hesse, Lutz-Werner. *Studien zum Schaffen des Komponisten Ralph Vaughan Williams.* Regensburg: Bosse, 1983.

8343. Kimmel, William. "Vaughan Williams's Melodic Style." MQ 27 (1941): 491–99.

8344. Payne, Elsie. "Vaughan Williams and Folk-Song." MR 15 (1954): 103–26.

8345. Rubbra, Edmund. "The Later Vaughan Williams." ML 18 (1937): 1–8.

VEGA, AURELIO DE LA (b. 1925)
8346. Eric, Ronald. "Cuban Elements in the Music of Aurelio de la Vega." LAMR 5, no. 1 (1984): 1–32.

VELKE, FRITZ (b. 1930)
8347. Velke, Fritz. "Concertino for Band." JBR 2, no. 1 (1966): 9–18.

VERBEY, THEO (b. 1959)
8348. Verbey, Theo. "Pre-Composition in *Passamezzo*." KN 31, no. 1 (1997): 17–19.

VERDI, GIUSEPPE (1813–1901)

Aida
8349. ASO 4 (1976).
8350. Bleiler, Ellen H. *Aida.* Dover Opera Guide and Libretto Series. New York: Dover, 1962.
8351. Gossett, Philip. "Verdi, Ghizlanzoni, and *Aida*: The Uses of Convention." CI 1, no. 2 (1974–1975): 291–334.
8352. John, Nicholas, ed. *Giuseppe Verdi: Aida.* London: Calder, 1980.
8353. Kahlke, Egbert. "Vers und Musik in der *Aida*." SV 11 (1996): 75–118.
8354. Lawton, David. "Tonal Systems in *Aida*, Act III." M-Abbate: 262–75.
8355. Parker, Roger. "Motives and Recurring Themes in *Aida*." M-Abbate: 222–38.
8356. Rostagno, Antonio. "Ouverture e dramma negli anni settanta: Il caso della sinfonia di *Aida*." SV 14 (1999): 11–50.
8357. Werner, Klaus G. "Verdi auf dem Weg zum Spätwerk: Zwei Ouverturen im Spannungsfeld zwischen Instrumentalmusik und Oper." MF 44, no. 2 (1991): 130–55.

Ave Maria
8358. Bister, Heribert. "Die Sept 7:4 in der Akkordfolge: Eine Untersuchung zu einigen harmonischen Zusammenhängen in Giuseppe Verdis Ave Maria–Scala enigmatica armonizzata a 4 voci miste." F-Vogel: 11–34.

Ballo in maschera
8359. ASO 32 (1981).
8360. Levarie, Siegmund. "Key Relations in Verdi's *Un Ballo in maschera*." NCM 2 (1978–1979): 143–47.
8361. ———. "A Pitch Cell in Verdi's *Un Ballo in maschera*." JMR 3 (1979–1981): 399–409.
8362. Parker, Roger, and Matthew Brown. "Motivic and Tonal Interaction in Verdi's *Un ballo in maschera*." JAMS 36 (1983): 243–65.
8363. Ross, Peter. "Amelias Auftrittsarie im *Maskenball*: Verdis Vertonung in dramaturgisch-textlichem Zusammenhang." AM 40 (1983): 126–46.

Corsaro
8364. Town, Stephen. "Observations on a Cabaletta from Verdi's *Il Corsaro*." CM 32 (1981): 59–75.

Don Carlos
8365. ASO 90–91 (1986).
8366. Chusid, Martin. "The Inquisitor's Scene in Verdi's *Don Carlos*: Thoughts on the Drama. Libretto, and Music." F-LaRue: 505–34. [Act IV, Scene II]
8367. Greenwald, Helen M. "Verdi's Patriarch and Puccini's Matriarch: 'Through the Looking-Glass and What Puccini Found There.'" NCM 17, no. 3 (1994): 220–36.
8368. Leibowitz, René. "*Don Carlo* ou les fantômes du clair-obscur." M-Leibowitz/F: 175–204.
8369. Noske, Frits R. "From Idea to Sound: Philip's Monologue in Verdi's *Don Carlos*." SV 10 (1994–1995): 76–92. [Act IV]
8370. Reti, Rudolph. "Die thematische Einheit in Verdis *Don Carlos*." OMZ 30 (1975): 342–50.

Due Foscari
8371. Biddlecombe, George. "The Revision of 'No, non morrai, ché I perfidi': Verdi's Compositional Process in *I due Foscari*." SV 2 (1983): 59–77. [Act II]

Ernani
8372. Baroni, Mario. "Un aspetto sotto alutato: Le formule d'accompagnamento." V 10 (1987): 133–41.
8373. Budden, Julian. "Il linguaggio musicale di *Ernani*." V 10 (1987): 123–32.
8374. Della Seta, Fabrizio. "L'atto di Carlo Quinto." V 10 (1995): 161–75.
8375. Gossett, Philip. "La composizione di *Ernani*." V 10 (1987): 60–91.
8376. Kerman, Joseph. "Notes on an Early Verdi opera." SN 3 (1973): 56–65.
8377. Parker, Roger. "'Infin che un brando vindice' e le cavatine del primo atto di *Ernani*." V 10 (1987): 142–60.

Falstaff

8378. ASO 87–88 (1986).

8379. Hepokoski, James A. *Giuseppe Verdi: Falstaff.* Cambridge: Cambridge University Press, 1983.

8380. John, Nicholas, ed. *Verdi: Falstaff.* London: Calder, 1982.

8381. Linthicum, David. "Verdi's *Falstaff* and Classical Sonata Form." MR 39 (1978): 39–53.

8382. Sabbeth, Daniel. "Dramatic and Musical Organization in *Falstaff.*" In *Atti del IIIo Congreso Internazionale di Studi Verdiani: Il Teatro e la musica di Giuseppe Verdi, 1972,* ed. Mario Medici, 415–42. Parma: Istituto di Studi Verdiani, 1974.

Forza del destino

8383. ASO 126 (1989).

8384. John, Nicholas, ed. *Verdi: The Force of Destiny.* London: Calder, 1984.

8385. Lawton, David. "Verdi, Cavallini, and the Clarinet Solo in *La forza del destino.*" V 2, no. 6 (1963–1965): 1723–48 (English); 2149–85 (Italian and German).

8386. Van, Gilles de. "La notion de 'tinta': Mémoire confuse et affinités thématiques dans les opéras de Verdi." RDM 76, no. 2 (1990): 187–98. [Act II]

8387. Werner, Klaus G. "Verdi auf dem Weg zum Spätwerk: Zwei Ouverturen im Spannungsfeld zwischen Instrumentalmusik und Oper." MF 44, no. 2 (1991): 130–55.

8388. Zecchi, Adone. "The Chorus in *La forza del destino.*" V 2, no. 5 (1962): 793–814.

Giorno di regno

8389. Parker, Roger. "*Un giorno di regno*: From Romani's Libretto to Verdi's Opera." SV 2 (1983): 39–58.

Luisa Miller

8390. ASO 151 (1993).

Macbeth

8391. Antokoletz, Elliott. "Verdi's Dramatic Use of Harmony and Tonality in *Macbeth.*" ITO 4, no. 6 (1978): 17–29.

8392. ASO 40 (1982).

8393. Christen, Norbert. "Auf dem Weg zum szenischen Musikdrama: Verdis *Macbeth* im Vergleich der beiden Fassungen." NZM 146, nos. 7–8 (1985): 9–15.

8394. Osthoff, Wolfgang. "Die beiden Fassungen von Verdis *Macbeth.*" AM 29 (1972): 17–44.

Messa da Requiem

8395. Roeder, John. "Formal Functions of Hypermeter in the *Dies Irae* of Verdi's *Messa da Requiem.*" TP 19 (1994): 83–104.

8396. ———. "Pitch and Rhythmic Dramaturgy in Verdi's *Lux æterna.*" NCM 14, no. 2 (1990): 169–85.

8397. Rosen, David. "The Operatic Origins of Verdi's 'Lacrymosa.'" SV 5 (1988–1989): 65–84.

8398. ———. "Reprise as Resolution in Verdi's *Messa da Requiem.*" TP 19 (1994): 105–20.

8399. ———. *Verdi: Requiem.* Cambridge: Cambridge University Press, 1995.

Nabucodonosor (Nabucco)

8400. ASO 86 (1985).

Otello

8401. Archibald, Bruce. "Tonality in *Otello.*" MR 35 (1974): 23–28.

8402. ASO 3 (1976).

8403. Di Benedetto, Renato. "Una postilla sulla tempesta." SV 12 (1997): 31–47.

8404. Hepokoski, James A. *Giuseppe Verdi: Otello.* Cambridge: Cambridge University Press, 1987.

8405. John, Nicholas, ed. *Verdi: Otello.* London: Calder, 1981.

8406. Klein, John W. "Verdi's *Otello* and Rossini's." ML 45 (1964): 130–40.

8407. Lawton, David. "On the Bacio theme in Otello." NCM 1 (1977–1978): 211–220.

8408. Natale, Marco de. "L'analisi dell'opera in musica: Un problema incombente." ANL 11 (1993): 6–25.

8409. Noske, Frits. "*Otello*: Drama through Structure." F-Fox: 14–47.

8410. Parker, Roger, and Matthew Brown. "*Ancora un bacio*: Three Scenes from Verdi's *Otello.*" NCM 9, no. 1 (1985): 50–62.

Requiem. *See Messa da Requiem*

Rigoletto

8411. ASO 112–113 (1988).

8412. Chusid, Martin. "Rigoletto and Monterone: A Study in Musical Dramaturgy." *Report of the Eleventh Congress of the International Musicological Society, Copenhagen, 1972,* vol. 1, 325–36. Copenhagen: n.p., 1974. Reprint, V 9 (1982): 1544–88.

8413. ———. "The Tonality of *Rigoletto.*" M-Abbate: 241–61.

8414. John, Nicholas, ed. *Verdi: Rigoletto.* London: Calder, 1982.

8415. Lawton, David. "Tonal Structure and Dramatic Action in *Rigoletto.*" V 9 (1982): 1559–81.

8416. Leibowitz, René. "The Orchestration of *Rigoletto.*" V 3, no. 5 (1973): 931–49 (Italian); 1248–74 (English and German).

8417. Osthoff, Wolfgang. "The Musical Characterization of Gilda." V 3, no. 8 (1973): 950–79 (German); 1275–1314 (English and Italian).

8418. Van, Gilles de. "L'introduction dans l'opéra italien comme forme musicale et prétexte dramatique: L'exemple de la 1re scène de *Rigoletto* de Verdi." ANM 27 (1992): 25–29.

8419. Zecchi, Adone. "Choruses and coryphaei in *Rigoletto.*" V 3, no. 7 (1969): 124–46 (Italian); 510–44 (English and German).

Romanze

8420. Lusk, Franklin Lynn. "An Analytical Study of the Verdi Romanze." Ph.D. diss., Indiana University, 1975.

Simon Boccanegra

8421. ASO 19 (1979).

8422. Campana, Alessandra. "Il 'menzognero incanto': Sight and insight in *Simon Boccanegra.*" SV 13 (1998): 59–87.

8423. Cone, Edward T. "On the Road to *Otello*: Tonality and Structure in *Simon Boccanegra.*" SV 1 (1982): 72–98.

8424. Kerman, Joseph. "Lyric Form and Flexibility in *Simon Boccanegra.*" SV 1 (1982): 47–62.

8425. Neuls-Bates, Carol. "Verdi's *Les vêpres siciliennes* (1855) and *Simon Boccanegra* (1857)." Ph.D. diss., Yale University, 1970.

8426. Powers, Harold. "*Simon Boccanegra* I. 10–12: A Generic-Genetic Analysis of the Council Chamber Scence." NCM 13, no. 2 (1989): 101–28.

8427. Sopart, Andreas. *Giuseppe Verdis Simon Boccanegra (1857 und 1881): Eine musikalisch-dramaturgische Analyse.* Laaber: Laaber, 1988.

Traviata

8428. ASO 51 (1983).

8429. Della Seta, Fabrizio. "Il tempo della festa: Su due scene della *Traviata* e su altri luoghi verdiani." SV 2 (1983): 108–46.

8430. John, Nicholas, ed. *Verdi: La traviata.* London: Calder, 1981.

8431. Parouty, Michel. *La traviata* de Verdi. Paris: Aubier, 1988.

Trovatore

8432. ASO 60 (1984).

8433. Balthazar, Scott L. "Plot and Tonal Design as Compositional Constraints in *Il trovatore.*" CM 60–61 (1996): 51–78.

8434. Petrobelli, Pierluigi, William Drabkin, and Roger Parker. "Verdi's *Il trovatore*: A Symposium." MA 1 (1982): 125–68.

Vêpres siciliennes

8435. ASO 75 (1985).

8436. Conati, Marcello. "Ballabili nei *Vespri*: Con alcune osservazioni su Verdi e la musica populare." SV 1 (1982): 21–46.

8437. Neuls-Bates, Carol. "Verdi's *Les vêpres siciliennes* (1855) and *Simon Boccanegra* (1857)." Ph.D. diss., Yale University, 1970.

8438. Várnai, Péter Pál. "La struttura ritmica come mezzo di caratterizzazione ne *I vespri siciliani.*" SV 10 (1994–1995): 93–103.

Various Works

8439. Balthazar, Scott L. "Analytic Contexts and Mediated Influences: The Rossinian Convenienze and Verdi's Middle and Late Duets." JMR 10 (1990): 19–45.

8440. Barbera, C. Andre. "Choruses of Revolt in Verdi's Operas of the 1840's." *Journal of Fine Arts 1, no. 1* (1977): 32–60.

8441. Baroni, Mario. "Le formule d'accompagnamento nel teatro del primo Verdi." SV 4 (1986–1987): 18–64.

8442. Budden, Julian. *The Operas of Verdi.* 3 vols. London: Cassell, 1973–1981.

8443. Gerhartz, Leo Karl. *Auseinandersetzungen des jungen Giuseppe Verdi mit dem literarischen Drama: Ein Beitrug zur szenischen Strukturbestimmung der Oper.* Berlin: Merseburger, 1968.

8444. Jablonsky, Stephen. "The Development of Tonal Coherence as Evidenced in the Revised Operas of Giuseppe Verdi." Ph.D. diss., New York University, 1973.

8445. Kerman, Joseph. "Verdi's Use of Recurring Themes." F-Strunk: 495–510.

8446. Kerman, Joseph, and Thomas S. Grey. "Verdi's Groundswells: Surveying an Operatic Convention." M-Abbate: 153–79.

8447. Kimbell, David R. B. *Verdi in the Age of Italian Romanticism.* Cambridge: Cambridge University Press, 1981.

8448. ———. "The Young Verdi and Shakespeare." PRMA 101 (1974–1975): 59–73.

8449. Lamacchia, Saverio. "Un tempo, due affetti: Una risorsa dell'aria romantica." SV 14 (1999): 51–68.

8450. Lawton, David. "Tonality and Drama in Verdi's Early Operas." Ph.D. diss., University of California, Berkeley, 1973.

8451. Noske, Frits. "Ritual Scenes in Verdi's Operas." ML 54 (1973): 415–39.

8452. ———. *The Signifier and the Signified: Studies in the Operas of Mozart and Verdi.* Gravenhage: M. Nijhoff, 1977.

8453. Osborne, Charles. *The Complete Operas of Verdi.* London: Gollancz, 1969.

8454. Osthoff, Wolfgang. "Verdi l'inattuale: Esempi e paragoni." SV 11 (1996): 13–39.

8455. Pagannone, Giorgio. "Aspetti della melodia verdiana: Periodo e barform a confronto." SV 12 (1997): 48–66.

8456. Powers, Harold. "Verdi's Monometric *Cabaletta*-Driven Duets: A Study in Rhythmic Texture and Generic Design." SAG 7, no. 2 (2000): 281–323.

8457. *Quaderni dell'Istituto di Studi Verdiana.* Venice, 1953.

8458. Siegmund-Schultze, Walther. "Some Thoughts on the Verdian Type of Melody." V 2, no. 4 (1961): 255–84 (German); 671–710 (Italian and English).

8459. Travis, Francis Irving. *Verdi's Orchestration.* Zurich: Juris, 1956.

VERESS, SÁNDOR (1907–1992)

8460. Kunkel, Michael. "Sándor Veress' *Orbis tonorum,* Nr. 4, 'Intermezzo silenzioso,' und Anton Weberns Op. 10, Nr. 3 ('Rückkehr'): ein Vergleich." MF 49, no. 4 (1996): 368–82.

8461. Sallis, Friedemann. "Formal Problems in *Threnos in memoriam Béla Bartók* (1945) by Sándor Veress." MPSS 8 (1995): 36–40.

8462. Terényi, Ede. "Laudatis musicae: Hommage à Sándor Veress à l'occasion de son 75e anniversaire." SMZ 122 (1982): 213–24.

8463. Traub, Andreas. "Melodische Artikulation: Zur Sonata per violoncello solo von Sándor Veress." SMZ 120 (1980): 15–26.

8464. ———. "Die Passacaglia concertante von Sándor Veress: Eine analytische Studie." MF 37 (1984): 122–30.

8465. ———. "Ein verlorenes Werk: Die Erste Sinfonie von Sándor Veress." MF 53, no. 3 (2000): 288–94.

8466. ———. "Zum instrumentalen Frühwerk von Sándor Veress." AM 45, no. 3 (1988): 224–47.

8467. ———. "Zur Geschichte der *Musica concertante.*" SMZ 122 (1982): 228–37.

VERMEULEN, MATTHIJS (1888–1967)

8468. Ketting, Otto. "Prelude as Postlude: On Matthijs Vermeulen's Second Symphony, *Prélude à la nouvelle journée,* and the Song *Les filles du roi d'Espagne.*" KN 3 (1976): 42–45.

8469. Vermeulen, Matthijs. "Seventh Symphony, *Dithyrambes pour les temps à venir.*" SS 29 (1966): 24–36.

8470. Wagemans, Peter-Jan. "Matthijs Vermeulen and the Dialectic of Freedom." KN 21 (1985): 3–7.

VIERK, LOIS V. (b. 1951)

8471. Carl, Robert. "Three Points on the Spectrum: The Music of Louis Karchin, Lois V. Vierk, and Paul Dresher." CMR 10, no. 1 (1994): 11–31.

VIERNE, LOUIS (1870–1937)

8472. Bölting, Ralf. "Die Orgelsinfonien Louis Viernes und ihre Vorgeschichte." MK 48 (1978): 112–18.

8473. Braas, Ton. "Matthijs Vermeulen's Second Symphony 'Prélude à la nouvelle journée': An Analysis." KN 29, no. 2 (1995): 15–19.

8474. ———. "Matthijs Vermeulen's Symphonies." KN 25 (1988–1989): 18–24.

8475. Kasouf, Edward J. "Louis Vierne and His Six Organ Symphonies." Ph.D. diss., Catholic University of America, 1970.

8476. Long, Page Carrol. "Transformations of Harmony and Consistencies of Form in the Six Organ Symphonies of Louis Vierne." D.M.A. diss., University of Arizona, 1963.

VIERU, ANATOL (1926–1998)

8477. Grigorovici, Lucian. "Elf Fragen zu Anatol Vieru." MELOS 35 (1968): 236–43.

VILLA-LOBOS, HEITOR (1887–1959)

8478. Farmer, Virginia. "An Analytical Study of the Seventeen String Quartets of Heitor Villa-Lobos." Ph.D. diss., University of Illinois, 1973.

8479. Galm, John K. "The Use of Brazilian Percussion Instruments in the Music of Villa-Lobos." In *Musicology at the University of Colorado,* ed. William Kearns, 182–99. Boulder: Regents of the University of Colorado, 1977.

8480. Oliveira, Jamary. "Black Key versus White Key: A Villa-Lobos Device." LAMR 5, no. 1 (1984): 33–47.

8481. Orrego-Salas, Juan A. "Heitor Villa-Lobos: Man, Work, Style." IAMB 52 (1966): 1–36.

8482. Peppercorn, Lisa M. *Heitor Villa-Lobos: Leben und Werk des brasilianischen Komponisten.* Zurich: Atlantis, 1972.

8483. Round, Michael. "*Bachianas Brasileiras* in Performance." TEMPO 169 (1989): 34–41. [Nos. 1–9]

VIVIER, CLAUDE (1948–1983)

8484. Tremblay, Jacques. "L'écriture à haute voix: *Lonely Child* de Claude Vivier." CIR 11, no. 1 (2000): 45–67.

VLIJMEN, JAN VAN (b. 1935)

8485. Baaren, Kees van. "Jan van Vlijmen: *Construzione* per due pianoforti." SS 9 (1961): 12–17.

8486. Bois, Rob du. "Jan van Vlijmen: *Gruppi* per 20 strumenti e percussione." SS 21 (1964): 17–21.

8487. Hartsuiker, Ton. "Jan van Vlijmen: *Omaggio a Gesualdo.*" SS 53 (1973): 1–11.

8488. ———. "Jan van Vlijmen's *Serenata I.*" SS 31 (1967): 1–9.

8489. Markus, Wim. "*Axel* or the Rejection of Life." KN 6 (1977): 19–32.

8490. ———. "*Quaterni theses.*" KN 15 (1982): 36–47.

VOEGELIN, FRITZ (b. 1943)

8491. Hirsbrunner, Theo. "Zorn über unerfülltes Dasein: Fritz Voegelins *4 Szenen für Streichquartett in memoriam F. Z.*" DI 52 (1997): 4–8.

VOGEL, WLADIMIR (1896–1984)

8492. Geiger, Friedrich. "Expressivität, konstruktiv gebändigt: Wladimir Vogels *Zwei Etüden für Orchester.*" M 50, no. 3 (1996): 189–97.

8493. M-Hines: 220–36.

8494. Oesch, Hans. "Wladimir Vogels Werke für Klavier." SMZ 97 (1957): 51–57.

8495. Schuhmacher, Gerhard. "Gesungenes und gesprochenes Wort in Werken Wladimir Vogels." AM 24 (1967): 64–80.

8496. Vogel, Wladimir. "Klaviereigene Interpretationsstudie einer variierten Zwölftonfolge (1972)." SMZ 116 (1976): 22–24.

VOLKMANN, ROBERT (1815–1883)

8497. Hopkins, William. "The Solo Piano Works of Robert Volkmann (1815–1883)." F-Kaufmann/W: 327–38.

VOORMOLEN, ALEXANDER (1895–1980)

8498. Bakker, M. Geerink. "Alexander Voormolen: *Chaconne and Fugue.*" SS 24 (1965): 12–15.

8499. Reeser, Eduard. "Alexander Voormolen." SS 22 (1965): 1–11; 23 (1965): 18–25.

8500. Wagemans, Peter-Jan. "Alexander Voormolen: From International Avant Garde to Hague Conservatism." KN 15 (1982): 14–23.

VOŘÍŠEK, JAN VÁCLAV (1791–1825)

8501. DeLong, Kenneth. "The Piano Rhapsodies of J. V. Voříšek." JALS 26 (1989): 12–28.

VRIEND, JAN (b. 1938)

8502. Vriend, Jan. "*Heterostase*: Trio for Flute, Bass Clarinet, and Piano 1980/81." I 16, nos. 1–2 (1987): 97–111.

VYSCHNEGRADSKY, IVAN (1893–1979)

8503. Beaulieu, Marc. "Cyclical Structures and Linear Voice-Leading in the Music of Ivan Wyschnegradsky." EXT 5, no. 2 (1991): 62–77.

– W –

WAGEMANS, PETER-JAN (b. 1952)

8504. Wagemans, Peter-Jan. "*Requiem*: A Composer's Analysis." KN 29, no. 4 (1995): 16–19.

WAGENAAR, BERNARD (1894–1971)

8505. Fuller, Donald. "Bernard Wagenaar." MM 21 (1944): 225–32.

WAGENAAR, DIDERIK (b. 1946)

8506. Carl, Gene. "A Sense of Escalation: Diderik Wagenaar's Discrete Evolution." KN 24 (1987): 14–22.

8507. Wagenaar, Diderik. "*Liederen*: An Analysis." KN 10 (1979): 28–32.

WAGENBRETH, PETER

8508. Oehlschlägel, Reinhard. "Zwischen Handlungsoper und absurdem Theater: Zu *Itzo-hux* von Hans-Joachim Hespos und Peter Wagenbreth." MTX 8 (1985): 46–48.

WAGNER, RICHARD (1813–1883)

Faust-Ouvertüre

8509. M-Macy.

8510. Voss, Egon. *Richard Wagner: Eine Faust-Overture.* Munich: Fink, 1982.

Feen

8511. Saar, Harold E. "*Die Feen*: Richard Wagner's First Opera." Ph.D. diss., Catholic University of America, 1964.

Fliegende Holländer

8512. ASO 30 (1980).

8513. Grey, Thomas. *Richard Wagner: Der fliegende Holländer.* Cambridge: Cambridge University Press, 2000.

8514. John, Nicholas, ed. *Wagner: The Flying Dutchman.* London: Calder, 1982.

8515. Lefrançois, André Emile. *Le vaisseu fantôme: Opera romantique de Richard Wagner: Etude thematique et analyse.* Paris: Lefrançois, 1983.

8516. Prax, Lothar. "Gestalt und Struktur von Wagners *Der fliegende Holländer.*" Ph.D. diss., University of Cologne, 1974.

Gedichte für eine Frauenstimme

8517. Gauldin, Robert. "Wagner's Parody Technique: 'Träume' and the *Tristan* Love Duet." MTS 1 (1979): 35–42.

Götterdämmerung

8518. ASO 13–14 (1978).

8519. Clark, Frank Leo. "*Götterdämmerung*: A Tonal and Formal Analysis." Ph.D. diss., University of Arizona, 1990.

8520. Darcy, Warren J. "The Metaphysics of Annihilation: Wagner, Schopenhauer, and the Ending of the *Ring.*" MTS 16, no. 1 (1994): 1–40.

8521. Daverio, John. "Brünnhilde's Immolation Scene and Wagner's 'Conquest of the Reprise.'" JMR 11, nos. 1–2 (1991): 33–66.

8522. Drake, Warren. "The Norns' Scene in *Gotterdammerung*: A Cycle within a Cycle." MMA 14 (1985): 57–77.

8523. Kinderman, William. "Dramatic Recapitulation in Wagner's *Götterdämmerung.*" NCM 4 (1980–1981): 101–12.

8524. Lefrançois, André. *"Crépuscule des Dieux" de Richard Wagner: Etude thematique et analyse.* Paris: Lefrançois, 1979.

8525. McCreless, Patrick. "Schenker and the Norns." M-Abbate: 276–97. [Act I, scene 1]

Hochzeit

8526. Tusa, Michael C. "Richard Wagner and Weber's *Euryanthe.*" NCM 9, no. 3 (1986): 206–21.

Liebesmahl der Apostel

8527. Kirsch, Winfried. "Richard Wagners biblische Szene *Das Liebesmahl der Apostel.*" HJM 8 (1985): 157–84.

Liebesverbot

8528. Engel, Hans. "Über Richard Wagners Oper Das *Liebesverbot.*" F-Blume: 80–91.

Lohengrin

8529. ASO 143–44 (1992).

8530. Breig, Werner. "Schütz und Wagner: Musik und deutsche Sprache." JP (1986–1987): 67–79.

8531. Lefrançois, André. *"Lohengrin" de Richard Wagner: Étude thematique et analyse.* Paris: Lefrançois, 1980.

8532. Leich, Robert. "'Elsa's Dream': A Musical Nightmare." MTEA 1 (1992): 7–11. [Act I, scene 2]

8533. Solyom, György. "*Lohengrin*: Höhepunkt und Zerfall der grossen romantischen Oper." SM 4 (1963): 257–87.

8534. Tusa, Michael C. "Richard Wagner and Weber's *Euryanthe.*" NCM 9, no. 3 (1986): 206–21.

8535. Whittall, Arnold. "Wagner's Great Transition? From *Lohengrin* to *Das Rheingold.*" MA 2, no. 3 (1983): 269–80.

Meistersinger von Nürnberg

8536. ASO 116–17 (1989).

8537. Finscher, Ludwig. "Über den Kontrapunkt der *Meistersinger.*" M-Dahlhaus: 303–12.

8538. Groos, Arthur. "Constructing Nuremberg: Typological and Proleptic Communities in *Die Meistersinger.*" NCM 16, no. 1 (1992): 18–34.

8539. Kinderman, William. "Has Sachs's 'Cobbler's Song,' *Tristan,* and the 'Bitter Cry of the Resigned Man.'" JMR 13, nos. 3–4 (1993): 161–84. [Act II]

8540. Komow, Ray. "The Structure of Wagner's 'Assembly of the Mastersingers' Guild.'" JMR 13, no. 14 (1993): 185–206.

8541. Kühn, Hellmut. "Der Niedergang der popularen Oper und Wagners *Meistersinger von Nürnberg.*" NZM 134 (1973): 272–79.

8542. Lefrançois, André. *"Les maître-chanteurs de Nuremberg" de Richard Wagner: Etude thematique et analyse.* Paris: Lefrançois, 1974.

8543. McDonald, William E. "Words, Music, and Dramatic Development in *Die Meistersinger.*" NCM 1 (1977–1978): 246–60.

8544. M-Stokes.

8545. Voss, Egon, ed. *Die Meistersinger von Nürnberg.* Reinbeck: Rowohlt, 1981.

8546. Warrack, John. *Richard Wagner: Die Meistersinger von Nürnberg.* Cambridge: Cambridge University Press, 1994.

Parsifal

8547. ASO 38–39 (1982).

8548. Bauer, Hans-Joachim. *Wagners "Parsifal": Kriterien der Kompostionstechnik.* Munich: Katzbichler, 1977.

8549. Beckett, Lucy. *Richard Wagner: Parsifal.* Cambridge: Cambridge University Press, 1981.

8550. Chailley, Jacques. *"Parsifal" de Richard Wagner: Opéra initiatique.* Paris: Buchet/Chastel, 1979.

8551. Clampitt, David. "Alternative Interpretations of Some Measures from *Parsifal.*" JMT 42, no. 2 (1998): 321–41. [Act III]

8552. Hollander, Hans. "Zum Symbolismus der drei *Parsifal* Vorspiele." NZM 129 (1968): 336–38.

8553. Kinderman, William. "Die Entstehung der *Parsifal*-Musik." AM 52, no. 1 (1995): 66–97; 52, no. 2 (1995): 145–65.

8554. ———. "Wagner's *Parsifal*: Musical Form and the Drama of Redemption." JM 4, no. 4 (1985–1986): 431–46.

8555. Lefrançois, André. *Parsifal: Drame sacre de Richard Wagner; Étude thématique et analyse.* Paris: Lefrançois, 1980.

8556. Lerdahl, Fred. "Tonal and Narrative Paths in Parsifal." F-Lewin: 121–46. [Act I]

8557. Lewin, David. "Amfortas's Prayer to Titurel and the Role of D in *Parsifal*: The Tonal Spaces of the Drama and the Enharmonic C-Flat/B." NCM 7 (1983–1984): 336–49.

8558. ———. "Some Notes on Analyzing Wagner: *The Ring* and *Parsifal.*" NCM 16, no. 1 (1992): 49–58.

8559. Ludwig, Ingeborg. "Die Klanggestaltung in Richard Wagners *Parsifal.*" Ph.D. diss., University of Hamburg, 1968.

8560. McCreless, Patrick. "Motive and Magic: A Referential Dyad in *Parsifal.*" MA 9, no. 3 (1990): 227–65.

8561. Murphy, Edward W. "The Dominant Complex/Climax in Selected Works of the Late Nineteenth Century." MR 55, no. 2 (1994): 104–18. [Act II]

8562. Neuwirth, Gösta. "Musik um 1900." F-Schuh: 89–134.

8563. Seelig, Wolfgang. "Ambivalenz und Erlösung: Wagners *Parsifal;* Zweifel und Glauben." OMZ 37 (1982): 307–17.

Rheingold

8564. ASO 6–7 (1976).

8565. Breig, Werner. "Der 'Rheintöchtergesang' in Wagners *Rheingold.*" AM 37 (1980): 241–63.

8566. Darcy, Warren. "*Creatio ex nihilo*: The Genesis, Structure, and Meaning of the *Rheingold* Prelude." NCM 13, no. 2 (1989): 79–100.

8567. ———. "A Wagnerian Ursatz; Or, Was Wagner a Background Composer after All?" INT 4 (1990): 1–35.

8568. ———. *Wagner's Das Rheingold.* Oxford: Oxford University Press, 1993.

8569. Dyson, J. Peter. "Ironic Dualities in *Das Rheingold.*" CM 43 (1987): 33–50.

8570. Krebs, Harald. "Dramatic Functions of Metrical Consonance and Dissonance in *Das Rheingold.*" ITO 10, no. 5 (1988): 5–19.

8571. Lefrançois, André. *"L'or du Rhin" de Richard Wagner: Étude thématique et analyse.* Paris: Lefrançois, 1976.

8572. Lewin, David. "Some Notes on Analyzing Wagner: *The Ring* and *Parsifal.*" NCM 16, no. 1 (1992): 49–58.

8573. Nitsche, Peter. "Klangfarbe und Form: Das Walhallthema in *Rheingold* und *Walküre.*" Melos/NZM 1 (1975): 83–88.

8574. Whittall, Arnold. "Wagner's Great Transition? From *Lohengrin* to *Das Rheingold.*" MA 2, no. 3 (1983): 269–80.

8575. Wiesend, Reinhard. "Die Entstehung des *Rheingold*-Vorspiels und ihr Mythos." AM 49, no. 2 (1992): 122–45.

Ring des Nibelungen (*see also Rheingold, Walküre, Siegfried*, and *Götterdämmerung*)

8576. Bailey, Robert. "The Structure of *The Ring* and Its Evolution." NCM 1 (1977–1978): 48–61.

8577. Baragwanath, Nicholas. "Alban Berg, Richard Wagner, and Leitmotivs of Symmetry." NCM 23, no. 1 (1999): 62–83.

8578. Breig, Werner. "Das Schicksalskunde-Motiv im *Ring des Nibelungen*: Versuch einer harmonischen Analyse." M-Dahlhaus: 223–33.

8579. ———. "Schütz und Wagner: Musik und deutsche Sprache." JP (1986–1987): 67–79.

8580. Buller, Jeffrey L. "The Thematic Role of *Stabreim* in Richard Wagner's *Der Ring des Nibelungen.*" OQ 11, no. 4 (1995): 59–76.

8581. Chapman, Kenneth G. "Siegfried and Brünnhilde and the Passage of Time in Wagner's *Ring.*" CM 32 (1981): 43–58.

8582. Dahlhaus, Carl. "Formprinzipien in Wagners *Ring des Nibelungen.*" In *Beiträge zur Geschichte der Oper*, ed. Heinz Becker, 95–129. Regensburg: Bosse, 1969.

8583. ———. "Tonalität und Form in Wagners *Ring des Nibelungen.*" AM 40 (1983): 165–73.

8584. Darcy, Warren Jay. "Formal and Rhythmic Problems in Wagner's *Ring* Cycle." D.M.A. diss., University of Illinois, 1973.

8585. Daverio, John. "Brünnhilde's Immolation Scene and Wagner's 'Conquest of the Reprise.'" JMR 11, nos. 1–2 (1991): 33–66.
8586. Dennison, Peter. "Musical Structuring and Its Evolution in Wagner's *Ring*." MMA 14 (1985): 29–56.
8587. Donington, Robert. *Wagner's "Ring" and Its Symbols: The Music and the Myth.* London: Faber & Faber, 1963.
8588. Floros, Constantin. "Der 'Beziehungszauber' der Musik im *Ring des Nibelungen* von Richard Wagner." NZM 144, nos. 7–8 (1983): 8–14.
8589. Gloede, Wilhelm. "Dichterisch-musikalische Periode und Form in Brünnhildes Schlussgesang." OMZ 38 (1983): 84–92.
8590. Hacohen, Ruth, and Naphtali Wagner. "The Communicative Force of Wagner's Leitmotifs: Complementary Relationships between Their Connotations and Denotations." MP 14, no. 4 (1997): 445–76.
8591. Hutcheson, Ernest. *A Musical Guide to the Richard Wagner "Ring of the Nibelung."* New York: Simon & Schuster, 1940.
8592. Jacobs, Robert L. "A Freudian View of *The Ring*." MR 26 (1965): 201–19.
8593. Jiránek, Jaroslav. "Die philosophischen Grundlagen des *Ring*-dramas." BM 5 (1963): 169–82.
8594. Kempter-Lott, Max. *Einführung in Richard Wagners dramatische Dichtung "Der Ring des Nibelungen."* Zurich: Hug, 1941.
8595. Kneif, Tibor. "Zur Deutung der Rheintöchter in Wagners *Ring*." AM 26 (1969): 297–306.
8596. Kolland, Hubert. "Zur Semantik der Leitmotive in Richard Wagners *Ring des Nibelungen*." IRASM 4 (1973): 197–212.
8597. Kroó, György. "Licht-Alberichs Lehrjahre." SM 22 (1980): 111–36.
8598. Laing, Alan Henry. "Tonality in Wagner's *Der Ring des Nibelungen*." Ph.D. diss., Edinburgh, 1973.
8599. Mackey-Stein, Christiane. "Les motifs de la femme et de l'amour dans la tetralogie: Note de recherche." MJ 31 (1978): 47–51.
8600. Orlando, Francesco. "Propositions pour une sémantique du leitmotiv dans *L'anneau des Nibelungen*." MJ 17 (1975): 73–86.
8601. Oskar, Andree. *Richard Wagners "Ring des Nibelungen."* Stuttgart: Mellinger, 1976.
8602. Osthoff, Wolfgang. "Dichterischer Rhythmus und rhythmische Melodie bei Richard Wagner." MTH 9, no. 1 (1994): 49–61.
8603. Reynaud, Bérénice. "*L'anneau de Nibelung* du mythe à l'intention musicale: Pour une analyse structurale." MJ 22 (1976): 19–63.
8604. Riedlbauer, Jörg. "Erinnerungsmotive in Wagner's *Der Ring des Niebelungen*." MQ 74, no. 1 (1990): 18–30.
8605. Rümenapp, Peter. "Hans von Wolzogen und Gottlieb Federlein–zwei Leitmotivexegeten des *Ring des Nibelungen*." ACTA 69, no. 2 (1997): 120–33.
8606. M-Stokes.
8607. Winkler, Franz Emil. *Richard Wagner: Der Ring des Nibelungen.* Schaffhausen: Novalis, 1981.

Sieger
8608. Osthoff, Wolfgang. "Richard Wagners Buddha-Projekt *Die Sieger*: Seine ideelen und strukturellen Spuren in *Ring* und *Parsifal*." AM 40 (1983): 189–211.

Siegfried
8609. ASO 12 (1977).
8610. Bailey, Robert. "Wagner's Musical Sketches for *Siegfrieds Tod*." F-Strunk: 459–94.
8611. Brinkmann, Reinhold. "'Drei der Fragen stell' ich mir frei': Zur Wanderer-Szene im 1. Akt von Wagners *Siegfried*." JSIM (1972): 120–62.
8612. Coren, Daniel. "Inspiration and Calculation in the Genesis of Wagner's *Siegfried*." F-Albrecht/S: 266–87.
8613. John, Nicholas, ed. *Wagner: Siegfried.* London: Calder, 1984.
8614. Lefrançois, André. *"Siegfried" de Richard Wagner: Étude thématique et analyse.* Paris: Lefrançois, 1979.
8615. McCreless, Patrick. *Wagner's "Siegfried": Its Drama, History, and Music.* Ann Arbor, Mich.: UMI Research Press, 1982.

Siegfried Idyll
8616. Anson-Cartwright, Mark. "Chord as Motive: The Augmented-Triad Matrix in Wagner's *Siegfried Idyll*." MA 15, no. 1 (1996): 57–71.

Sonate für das Album von Frau M. W.
8617. Dowd, John Andrew. "The Album-Sonate for Matilde Wesendonk: A Neglected Masterpiece of Richard Wagner." JALS 10 (1981): 43–47.

Tannhäuser

8618. ASO 63–64 (1984).

8619. Brinkmann, Reinhold. "Tannhäusers Lied." M-Dahlhaus: 199–211.

8620. Daverio, John. "Narration as Drama: Wagner's Early Revisions of *Tannhäuser* and Their Relation to the Rome Narrative." CMS 24. no. 2 (1984): 55–68.

8621. Lefrançois, André. *"Tannhäuser" de Richard Wagner: Étude thématique et analyse.* Paris: Lefrançois, 1982.

8622. Rosenblum, Matthew. "Sound, Structure, and Signification in Wagner's 'Evening Star' Aria." MA 16, no. 1 (1997): 77–103. [Act III, scene 2]

8623. Strohm, Reinhard. "Dramatic Time and Operatic Form in Wagner's *Tannhäuser.*" PRMA 104 (1977–1978): 1–10.

8624. Tusa, Michael C. "Richard Wagner and Weber's *Euryanthe.*" NCM 9, no. 3 (1986): 206–21.

Tristan und Isolde

8625. Abbate, Carolyn. "Wagner, 'On Modulation,' and *Tristan.*" COJ 1, no. 1 (1989): 33–58.

8626. ASO 34–35 (1981).

8627. Bailey, Robert. "The Genesis of *Tristan und Isolde* and a Study of Wagner's Sketches and Drafts for the First Act." Ph.D. diss., Princeton University, 1969.

8628. ———, ed. *Wagner: Prelude and Transfiguration from "Tristan and Isolde."* Norton Critical Scores. New York: Norton, 1985.

8629. Baragwanath, Nicholas. "Alban Berg, Richard Wagner, and Leitmotivs of Symmetry." NCM 23, no. 1 (1999): 62–83.

8630. Barford, Philip. "The Way of Unity: A Study of *Tristan und Isolde.*" MR 20 (1959): 253–63.

8631. Beeson, Roger. "The *Tristan* Chord and Others: Harmonic Analysis and Harmonic Explanation." SN 5 (1975): 55–72.

8632. Bernstein, David W. "Georg Capellen on *Tristan und Isolde*: Analytical Systems in Conflict at the Turn of the Twentieth Century." THE 4 (1989): 34–62.

8633. Brown, Matthew. "Isolde's Narrative: From Hauptmotiv to Tonal Model." M-Abbate: 180–201. [Act I, scene 3]

8634. Burstein, L. Poundie. "A New View of *Tristan*: Tonal Unity in the Prelude and Conclusion to Act I." TP 8, no. 1 (1983): 15–42.

8635. Chailley, Jacques. *"Tristan und Isolde" de Richard Wagner.* Paris: Leduc, 1972.

8636. Cone, Edward T. "Yet Once More, O Ye Laurels." PNM 14, no. 2–15, no. 1 (1975–1976): 294–306.

8637. Dahlhaus, Carl. *"Tristan: Harmonik und Tonalität."* Melos/NZM 4 (1978): 215–19.

8638. Deliège, Irène. "Wagner 'Alte Weise': Une approche perceptive." MUS special issue (1998): 63–90. [Act III, scene 1]

8639. Dommel-Diény, Amy. "Encore l'accord de *Tristan.*" SMZ 105 (1965): 31–37.

8640. Enix, Margery. "Formal Expansion through Fusion of Major and Minor: A Study of Tonal Structure in *Tristan und Isolde*, Act I." ITR 1, no. 2 (1977–1978): 28–34.

8641. M-Enix.

8642. Flechsig, Irmtraud. "Beziehungen zwischen textlicher und musikalischer Struktur in Richard Wagners *Tristan und Isolde.*" M-Dahlhaus: 239–57.

8643. Forte, Allen. "New Approaches to the Linear Analysis of Music." JAMS 41, no. 2 (1988): 315–48. [Prelude]

8644. ———. "A Schenkerian Reading of an Excerpt from *Tristan und Isolde.*" MUS special issue (1998): 15–26. [Act III, scene 1]

8645. Friedheim, Philip. "The Relationship between Tonality and Musical Structure." MR 27 (1966): 44–53.

8646. Gauldin, Robert. "Wagner's Parody Technique: 'Träume' and the *Tristan* Love Duet." MTS 1 (1979): 35–42.

8647. Giesl, Peter. "Von Stimmführungsvorgängen zur Harmonik: Eine Anwendung der Clausellehre auf Wagners *Tristan und Isolde.*" MF 52, no. 4 (1999): 403–35. [Act II]

8648. George, Graham. "Tonality and the Narrative in *Tristan.*" CAUSM 3, no. 1 (1973): 63–70.

8649. ———. "Tonality and the Narrative in *Tristan.*" CAUSM 4 (1974): 21–43. [Expansion of 8648]

8650. Gostomsky, Dieter. "Immer noch einmal: Der *Tristan*-Akkord." ZM 6, no. 1 (1975): 22–27.

8651. Grunsky, Hans. *"Tristan und Isolde*: Der symphonische Aufbau des dritten Aufzugs." NZM 113 (1952): 390–94.

8652. Hansen, Finn Egeland. "The Tristan Chord Is Nothing but a Tritone Substitution of the Characteristic Subdominant." F-Maegaard: 165–83.

8653. Hartmann, Günter. "Schon wieder: der (?) 'Tristan-Akkord.'" MF 42, no. 1 (1989): 36–52.

8654. Hyer, Brian. "Tonal Intuitions in *Tristan und Isolde.*" Ph.D. diss., Yale University, 1989.

8655. Imberty, Michel. "Du vide à l'infini: Homologies structurales repérée dans *Tristan* à partir du solo de cor anglais du III acte." MUS special issue (1998): 91–116.

8656. Jackson, Roland. "Leitmotive and Form in the *Tristan* Prelude." MR 36 (1975): 43–53.

8657. Jackson, Timothy L. "Die Wagnersche Umarmungs-Metapher bei Bruckner und Mahler." M-Riethmüller: 134–52.

8658. John, Nicholas, ed. *Wagner: Tristan and Isolde*. London: Calder, 1981.

8659. Kinderman, William. "Das 'Geheimnis der Form' in Wagner's *Tristan und Isolde*." AM 40 (1983): 174–88.

8660. Knapp, Raymond. "The Tonal Structure of *Tristan und Isolde*: A Sketch." MR 45 (1984): 11–25.

8661. Kropfinger, Klaus. "Wagners *Tristan* und Beethovens Streichquartett Op. 130: Funktion und Strukturen des Prinzips der Einleitungswiederholung." M-Dahlhaus: 259–71.

8662. Labussière, Annie. "'Die alte Weise': Une analyse sémiologique du solo de cor anglais du 3e acte de *Tristan et Isolde*." ANM 27 (1992): 30–53.

8663. Lefrançois, André Emile. *"Tristan et Isolde" de Richard Wagner: Étude thématique et analyse*. Paris: Lefrançois, 1973.

8664. Lerdahl, Fred. "Prolongational Structure and Schematic Form in *Tristan's* 'Alte Weise.'" MUS special issue (1998): 27–41. [Act III, scene 1]

8665. Luschinsky, Eva. "Studien zur Morphologie des *Tristan*: Konzept und Realisierung." Ph.D. diss., Universität Wien, 1977.

8666. Maisel, Arthur. "*Tristan*: A Different Perspective." TP 8, no. 2 (1983): 53–61.

8667. McKinney, Bruce. "The Case Against Tonal Unity in *Tristan*." TP 8, no. 2 (1983): 62–67.

8668. Metzger, Heinz-Klaus, and Rainer Riehn, eds. *Richard Wagner: Tristan und Isolde*. Munich: Text + Kritik, 1987.

8669. Mitchell, William J. "The *Tristan* Prelude: Technique and Structure." MFO 1 (1967): 162–203.

8670. Morgan, Robert P. "Circular Form in the *Tristan* Prelude." JAMS 53, no. 1 (2000): 69–103.

8671. Nattiez, Jean-Jacques. "Le solo de cor alglais de *Tristan und Isolde*: Essai d'analyse sémiologique tripartite." MUS special issue (1998): 43–62. [Act III, scene 1]

8672. Poos, Heinrich. "Zur Tristanharmonik." F-Pepping: 269–97.

8673. Raymond, Joely. "The *Leitmotiv* and Musical-Dramatic Structure in Tristan's Third Narrative of Delirium." ITR 3, no. 3 (1979–1980): 3–17.

8674. Richey, John. "History and the *Tristan* Chord." MR 55, no. 2 (1994): 97–103.

8675. Richter, Christoph. "Hermeneutische Grundlagen der didaktischen Interpretation von Musik, dargestellt am *Tristan*-Vorspiel." MB 15, no. 11 (1983): 22–26; 15, no. 12 (1983): 20–27.

8676. Rothgeb, John. "The *Tristan* Chord: Identity and Origin." MTO 1, no. 1 (1995).

8677. Scharschuch, Horst. *Gesamtanalyse der Harmonik von Richard Wagners Musikdrama "Tristan und Isolde" unter specielle Berücksichtigung der Sequenztechnik des Tristanstiles*. Regensburg: Bosse, 1963.

8678. Sievritts, Manfred. "Die emotionale Deutung des *Tristan*-Vorspiels: Eine hermeneutische Alternative." MB 16, no. 6 (1984): 436–39.

8679. M-Stokes.

8680. Straus, Joseph N. "*Tristan* and Berg's Suite." ITO 8, no. 3 (1983–1984): 33–41.

8681. Truscott, Harold. "Wagner's *Tristan* and the Twentieth Century." MR 24 (1963): 75–85.

8682. Vogel, Martin. *Der Tristan-Akkord und die Krise der modernen Harmonie-Lehre*. Düsseldorf: Gesellschaft zur Förderung des Systematischen Musikwissenschaft, 1962.

8683. Wang, Peter. "*Tristan*-akkorden opløst." DAM 19 (1988–1991): 157–70.

Walküre

8684. ASO 8 (1977).

8685. Jenkins, John Edward. "The *Leitmotiv* 'Sword' in *Die Walküre*." Ph.D. diss., University of Southern Mississippi, 1978.

8686. John, Nicholas, ed. *Wagner: The Valkyrie*. London: Calder, 1984.

8687. Kresky, Jeffrey. "A Study of the End of Act I of Wagner's *Die Walküre*." M-Kresky: 135–50.

8688. Lefrançois, André. *"La Walkyrie" de Richard Wagner: Etude thématique et analyse*. Paris: Lefrançois, 1975.

8689. Lewin, David. "Some Notes on Analyzing Wagner: *The Ring* and *Parsifal*." NCM 16, no. 1 (1992): 49–58.

8690. Nitsche, Peter. "Klangfarbe und Form: Das Walhallthema in *Rheingold* und *Walküre*." Melos/NZM 1 (1975): 83–88.

8691. Serauki, Walter. "Die Todesverkündigungsszene in Richard Wagners *Walküre* also musikalisch-geistige Achse des Werkes." MF 12 (1959): 143–151.

Wesendonck Lieder. See *Gedichte für eine Frauenstimme*

Various Works

8692. Bertram, Johannes. *Mythos, Symbol, Idee in Richard Wagners Musik-Dramen*. Hamburg: Hamburger Kulturverlag, 1957.

8693. Burbidge, Peter, and Richard Sutton, eds. *The Wagner Companion*. London: Faber & Faber, 1979.

8694. Dahlhaus, Carl. *Das Drama Richard Wagners als musikalisches Kunstwerk*. Regensburg: Bosse, 1970.

8695. ———. *Richard Wagner: Werk und Wirkung*. Regensburg: Bosse, 1971.

8696. ———. *Richard Wagners Musikdramen*. Velber: Friedrich, 1971.

8697. ——. *Richard Wagner's Music Dramas.* Trans. Mary Whittall. Cambridge: Cambridge University Press, 1979.

8698. ——. "Zur Geschichte der Leitmotivtechnik bei Wagner." M-Dahlhaus: 17–36.

8699. George, Graham. "The Structure of Dramatic Music 1607–1909." MQ 52 (1966): 465–82.

8700. Josephson, Nors S. "Tonale Strukturen im musikdramatischen Schaffen Richard Wagners." MF 32 (1979): 141–49.

8701. Knepler, Georg. "Richard Wagners musikalische Gestaltungsprinzipien." BM 5 (1963): 33–43.

8702. Laudon, Robert T. "Sources of the Wagnerian Synthesis: A Study of the Franco-German Tradition in Nineteenth-Century Opera." Ph.D. diss., University of Illinois, 1969.

8703. Lechleitner, Gerda. "Bruckner–Wagner: Ein meßbarer Unterschied: Betrachtungen zur Instrumentation in Melodie und Begleitung." BRS (1984): 123–48.

8704. Lichtenfeld, Monika. "Zur Technik der Klangflächenkomposition bei Wagner." M-Dahlhaus: 161–67.

8705. Lorenz, Alfred. *Das Geheimnis der Form bei Richard Wagners.* Tutzing: Schneider, 1966.

8706. Newcomb, Anthony. "The Birth of Music Out of the Spirit of Drama: An Essay in Wagnerian Formal Analysis." NCM 5 (1981–1982): 38–66.

8707. ——. "Ritornello Ritornato: A Variety of Wagnerian Refrain Form." M-Abbate: 202–21.

8708. Newman, Ernest. *The Wagner Operas.* New York: Knopf, 1949.

8709. Noske, Frits. "Das exogene Todesmotiv in den Musikdramen Richard Wagners." MF 31 (1978): 285–302.

8710. Overhoff, Kurt. *Die Musikdramen Richard Wagners: Eine thematisch-musikalische Interpretation.* Salzburg: Pustet, 1967.

8711. Richey, John. "A Short History of the Sequence in Wagner's Music." JALS 48 (2000): 17–34.

8712. Sommer, Antonius. *Die Komplikationen des musikalischen Rhythmus in den Bühnenwerken Richard Wagners.* Giebing über Prien am Chiemsee: E. Katzbichler, 1971.

8713. Stein, Herbert von. *Dichtung und Musik im Werk Richard Wagners.* Berlin: W. de Gruyter, 1962.

8714. Stephan, Rudolf. "Gibt es ein Geheimnis der Form bei Richard Wagner." M-Dahlhaus: 9–16.

8715. Treiber, Roland. "Die Todesszene in den Bühnenwerken Richard Wagners." Ph.D. diss., University of Heidelberg, 1976.

8716. Voss, Egon. *Studien zur Instrumentation Richard Wagners.* Regensburg: Bosse, 1970.

8717. ——. "Über die Anwendung der Instrumentation auf das Drama bei Wagner." M-Dahlhaus: 169–75.

8718. Weiner, Marc A. "Richard Wagner's Use of E. T. A. Hoffmann's *The Mines of Falun.*" NCM 5 (1981–1982): 201–9.

WALKER, GEORGE (b. 1922)

8719. De Lerma, Dominique-René. "The Choral Works of George Walker." ACR 23, no. 1 (1981): 1–29.

8720. Ennett, Dorothy Maxine. "An Analysis and Comparison of Selected Piano Sonatas by Three Contemporary Black Composers: George Walker, Howard Swanson, and Roque Cordero." Ph.D. diss., New York University, 1973.

8721. Newson, Roosevelt. "A Style Analysis of the Three Piano Sonatas (1953, 1957, 1976) of George Theophilus Walker." D.M.A. diss., Peabody Conservatory, 1977.

WALTON, WILLIAM (1902–1983)

8722. Decker, Jay C. "A Comparative Textural Analysis of Selected Orchestral Works of William Walton and Paul Hindemith." D.M.A. diss., University of Missouri, 1971.

8723. Fulton, William Kenneth, Jr. "Selected Choral Works of William Walton." Ph.D. diss., Texas Tech University, 1981.

8724. Howes, Frank Stewart. *The Music of William Walton.* London: Oxford University Press, 1965.

8725. Merrick, Frank. "Walton's Concerto for Violin and Orchestra." MR 2 (1941): 309–18.

8726. Murrill, Herbert. "Walton's Violin Sonata." ML 31 (1950): 208–15.

WANNER, DAN (b. 1971)

8727. Wanner, Dan. "Leaving the Ivory Tower." CM 67–68 (1999): 443–51.

WARD, ROBERT (b. 1917)

8728. Huband, J. Daniel. "Robert Ward's Instrumental Music." AMUS 13, no. 3 (1995): 333–56.

8729. Kellner, Hans. "Devils and Angels: A Study of the Demonic in Three Twentieth-Century Operas." JMR 2 (1976–1978): 255–72. [*The Crucible*]

8730. Larsen, Robert L. "A Study and Comparison of Samuel Barber's *Vanessa*, Robert Ward's *The Crucible*, and Gunther Schuller's *The Visitation.*" D.M.A. diss., Indiana University, 1971.

WARLOCK, PETER (1894–1930)

8731. Collins, Brian. "Rantum Tantum: Linear Techniques in Warlock's *Lillygay.*" MR 47, no. 3 (1986–1987): 184–93.

8732. Copley, Ian A. *The Music of Peter Warlock: A Critical Study.* London: Dobson, 1979.

8733. ——. "Peter Warlock's Choral Music." ML 45 (1964): 318–36.

8734. ———. "The Published Instrumental Music of Peter Warlock." MR 25 (1964): 209–23.
8735. Yenne, Vernon Lee. "Three Twentieth-Century English Song Composers: Peter Warlock, E. J. Morran, and John Ireland." D.M.A. diss., University of Illinois, 1969.

WASCHKA, RODNEY, II (b. 1958)
8736. Waschka, Rodney, II. "Computer-Assisted Composition and Performance: The Creation of *A Noite, Porém, Rangeu E Quebrou.*" LMJ 2, no. 1 (1992): 41–44.

WEBER, CARL MARIA VON (1786–1826)
Euryanthe
8737. ASO 153 (1993).
8738. Hatch, Christopher. "Weber's Themes as Agents of 'A Perfect Unity.'" MR 48, no. 1 (1988): 31–42. [Overture]
8739. Leibowitz, René. "Un opéra maudit: *Euryanthe.*" M-Leibowitz/F: 145–74.
8740. ———. "Eine verachtete Oper: *Euryanthe.*" In *Carl Maria von Weber*, ed. Heinz-Klaus Metzger and Rainer Riehn, 48–71. Munich: Text + Kritik, 1986.
8741. Tusa, Michael C. *Euryanthe and Carl Maria von Weber's Dramaturgy of German Opera.* Oxford: Oxford University Press, 1991.
8742. ———. "Richard Wagner and Weber's *Euryanthe.*" NCM 9, no. 3 (1986): 206–21.

Freischütz
8743. ASO 105–106 (1988).
8744. Bockmaier, Claus. "Nachwirkungen der Wiener Klassik in Webers *Freischütz.*" AM 56, no. 2 (1999): 110–27.
8745. Goldschmidt, Harry. "Und immer wieder *Freischütz*: Ein Befund." MG 36 (1986): 568–72. [Overture]
8746. ———. "Die Wolfsschlucht: Eine schwarze Messe?" BM 30, nos. 1–2 (1988): 8–27.
8747. Gras, Alfred H. "A Study of *Der Freischütz* by Carl Maria von Weber." Ph.D. diss., Northwestern University, 1968.
8748. Hatch, Christopher. "Weber's Themes as Agents of 'A Perfect Unity.'" MR 48, no. 1 (1988): 31–42. [Overture]
8749. Mercer-Taylor, Peter. "Unification and Tonal Absolution in *Der Freischütz.*" ML 78, no. 2 (1997): 220–32.
8750. Stephan, Rudolf. "Bemerkungen zur *Freischütz*-Musik." M-Dahlhaus/S: 491–96.

Oberon
8751. ASO 74 (1985).
8752. Hatch, Christopher. "Weber's Themes as Agents of 'A Perfect Unity.'" MR 48, no. 1 (1988): 31–42. [Overture]

Piano Works
8753. Adams, John P. "A Study of the Piano Sonatas of Carl Maria von Weber." Ph.D. diss., Indiana University, 1976.
8754. Böttinger, Peter. "Durch die Hölle unserer Gefühle." In *Carl Maria von Weber*, ed. Heinz-Klaus Metzger and Rainer Riehn, 22–47. Munich: Text + Kritik, 1986. [Piano Sonata No. 1, op. 24]
8755. Hatch, Christopher. "Weber's Themes as Agents of 'A Perfect Unity.'" MR 48, no. 1 (1988): 31–42. [*Aufforderung zum Tanze, op. 65*]
8756. Kang, Nakcheung Paik. "An Analytical Study of the Piano Sonatas of Carl Maria von Weber." Ph.D. diss., New York University, 1978.
8757. Marinaro, Stephen. "Carl Maria von Weber: His Pianistic Style and the Four Sonatas." JALS 10 (1980): 48–55.
8758. ———. "The Four Piano Sonatas of Carl Maria von Weber." D.M.A. diss., University of Texas, 1980.

Various Works
8759. Jones, Gaynor G. "Weber's Secondary Worlds: The Later Operas of Carl Maria von Weber." IRASM 7 (1976): 219–33.
8760. Sandner, Wolfgang. *Die Klarinette bei Carl Maria von Weber.* Wiesbaden: Breitkopf & Härtel, 1971.
8761. Viertel, Matthias S. *Die Instrumentalmusik Carl Maria von Webers: Ästhetische Voraussetzungen und struktureller Befund.* Frankfurt am Main: Lang, 1986.

WEBERN, ANTON (1883–1945)
Augenlicht, Op. 26
8762. Klemm, Eberhard. "*Das Augenlicht*: Analytische Betrachtung zu einer der späten Kantaten Weberns." MG 33 (1983): 696–99.
8763. McKinney, Timothy R. "A Systematic Approach to Invariance in Twelve-Tone Music." JMTP 7 (1993): 3–28.

Bagatellen, Op. 9 (String Quartet)
8764. Bauer, Jürg. "Über Anton Weberns Bagatellen für Streichquartett." M-Abraham/L: 62–68.
8765. Busch, Regina. "Oktaven in Weberns Bagatellen." DI 27 (1991): 10–12.
8766. Chrisman, Richard. "Anton Webern's Six Bagatelles for String Quartet, Op. 9: The Unfolding of Intervallic Successions." JMT 23 (1979): 81–122.

8767. Clifford, Robert. "Auditory Streaming and Contour Analysis in Webern's Sixth Bagatelle." MTEA 6 (1997): 4–18.
8768. Demske, Tom. "Registral Centers of Balance in Atonal Works by Schoenberg and Webern." ITO 9, nos. 2–3 (1986): 60–76. [No. 4]
8769. Forte, Allen. "An Octatonic Essay by Webern: No. 1 of the Six Bagatelles for String Quartet, Op. 9." MTS 16, no. 2 (1994): 171–95.
8770. Hansberger, Joachim. "Anton Webern, Die vierte Bagetelle für Streichquartett als Gegenstand einer Übung im Musikhören." M 23 (1969): 236–40.
8771. Kaufmann, Harald. "Figur in Weberns erster Bagatelle." M-Abraham/L: 69–72.
8772. Marra, James Richard. "Rhythmic Stratification in the 'Atonal' Instrumental Music of Anton Webern (1913–1914)." D.M.A. diss., Cornell University, 1977. [No. 5]
8773. Oesch, Hans. "Weberns erste Bagatelle." F-Dahlhaus: 695–712.
8774. Ogdon, Will. "How Tonality Functions in Webern's Opus 9, Nrs. 1 and 4." EXT 5, no. 1 (1989): 32–42.
8775. Schwarz, David. "Hypotaxis and Parataxis: Pitch Specificity and Color in Webern's Bagatelles for String Quartet, Op. 9." TSP 3 (1986): 1–12.

Canons nach lateinischen Texten, **Op. 16**
8776. Ligeti, György. "Die Komposition mit Reihen und ihre Konsequenzen bei Anton Webern." OMZ 16 (1961): 297–303.
8777. Dobos, Lora Gingerich. "Transformation of BACH in Webern's Op. 16, No. 4." INT 10 (1996): 1–18.

Cantata No. 1, Op. 29
8778. Hartwell, Robin. "Duration and Mental Arithmetic: The First Movement of Webern's First Cantata." PNM 23, no. 1 (1984–1985): 348–59.
8779. Klemm, Eberhardt. "Symmetrien im Chorsatz von Anton Webern." DJM 11 (1966): 107–20.
8780. Kramer, Jonathan. "The Row as Structural Background and Audible Foreground: The First Movement of Webern's First Cantata." JMT 15, nos. 1–2 (1971): 158–81.
8781. Ligeti, György. "Die Komposition mit Reihen und ihre Konsequenzen bei Anton Webern." OMZ 16 (1961): 297–303.
8782. ———. "Über die Harmonik in Weberns erster Kantate." DBNM 3 (1960): 49–64.
8783. Phipps, Graham H. "Tonality in Webern's Cantata 1." MA 3, no. 2 (1984): 125–58.
8784. Pousseur, Henri. "Webern et le silence." In *La musique et ses problemes contemporains,* 190–202. Paris: Julliard, 1963.
8785. Rochberg, George. "Webern's Search for Harmonic Identity." JMT 6 (1962): 109–22.
8786. Saturen, David. "Symmetrical Relationships in Webern's First Cantata." PNM 6, no. 1 (1967): 142–43.

Cantata No. 2, Op. 31
8787. Bailey, Kathryn. "Canon and Beyond: Webern's Op. 31 Cantata." MA 7, no. 3 (1988): 313–48.
8788. Baumann, Jon Ward. "The Cantata Number Two of Anton Webern." Ph.D. diss., University of Illinois, 1972.
8789. Brumbeloe, Joe. "Pitch Structures in Webern's Second Cantata, Opus 31." ITR 7, no. 2 (1986): 30–46.
8790. Luckman, Phyllis. "The Sound of Symmetry: A Study of the Sixth Movement of Webern's Second Cantata." MR 36 (1975): 187–96.
8791. Spinner, Leopold. "Anton Weberns Kantate Nr. 2, Op. 31: Die Formprinzipien der kanonischen Darstellung (Analyse des vierten Satzes)." SMZ 101 (1961): 303–8.
8792. William, Wolfgang. *Anton Weberns zweite Kantate Op. 31: Studien zu Konstruktion und Ausdruck.* Munich: Katzbichler, 1980.
8793. Zuber, Barbara. "Tradition und Umbruch ins Neue: Harmonische Techniken in Anton Weberns Op. 31/3." M 50, no. 5 (1996): 324–29.
8794. M-Zuber.

Concerto, Op. 24
8795. Bailey, Kathryn. "Symmetry as Nemesis: Webern and the First Movement of the Concerto, Opus 24." JMT 40, no. 2 (1996): 245–310.
8796. Boykan, Martin. "The Webern Concerto Revisited." ASUC 3 (1968): 74–85.
8797. Busch, Regina. "Taktgruppen in Weberns Konzert Op. 24." M 40, no. 6 (1986): 532–37.
8798. Cohen, David. "Anton Webern and the Magic Square." PNM 13, no. 1 (1974–1975): 213–15.
8799. Gauldin, Robert. "The Magic Squares of the Third Movement of Webern's Concerto, Op. 24." ITO 2, nos. 11–12 (1977): 32–42.
8800. ———. "Pitch Structure in the Second Movement of Webern's Concerto Op. 24." ITO 2, no. 10 (1977): 8–22.
8801. Hasty, Christopher. "Segmentation and Process in Post-Tonal Music." MTS 3 (1981): 54–73.
8802. Jones, David Evan. "Concerning Orchestration in Webern's Konzert, Opus 24." EXT 3, no. 1 (1985): 1–10.
8803. Ligeti, György. "Die Komposition mit Reihen und ihre Konsequenzen bei Anton Webern." OMZ 16 (1961): 297–303.
8804. Pasquet, Yves-Marie. "Dans les hauts pâturages weberniens." ANM 18 (1990): 61–67.

8805. Phipps, Graham. "Harmonic Thought in Webern's Sketches." MPSS 4 (1991): 31–33.

8806. Stockhausen, Karlheinz. "Weberns Konzert für 9 Instruments Op. 24: Analyze des ersten Satzes." MELOS 20 (1953): 343–48.

8807. M-Stockhausen: 24–31.

8808. Wintle, Christopher. "Analysis and Performance: Webern's Concerto Op. 24/II." MA 1 (1982): 73–100.

Gesänge aus "Viae inviae," Op. 23

8809. Alegant, Brian. "A Model for the Pitch Structure of Webern's Op. 23, No. 1, 'Das dunkle Herz'." MTS 13, no. 2 (1991): 127–46.

Kleine Stücke, Op. 11 (Cello and Piano)

8810. Batstone, Philip. "Musical Analysis as Phenomenology." PNM 7, no. 2 (1969): 94–110.

8811. Escot, Pozzi. "Towards a Theoretical Concept: Non-Linearity in Webern's Opus 11, No. 1." SONUS 3, no. 1 (1982): 18–29.

8812. Karkoschka, Erhard. "Weberns Opus 11 unter neuer analytischen Aspekten." BOGM (1972–1973): 81–92. Reprint, M-Webern: 81–92.

8813. Marra, James. "Interrelations between Pitch and Rhythmic Structure in Webern's Opus 11, No. 1." ITO 7, no. 2 (1983–1984): 3–33.

8814. ———. "Rhythmic Stratification in the 'Atonal' Instrumental Music of Anton Webern (1913–1914)." D.M.A. diss., Cornell University, 1977. [No. 3]

8815. M-Perle: 21–23.

8816. Schumann, Edgar. "Zufälligkeit oder innerer Zwang? Bemerkungen zum dritten Stück aus Op. 11 von Anton Webern." M 50, no. 5 (1996): 330–33.

8817. Williams, Edgar Warren, Jr. "On Mode 12 Complementary Interval sets." ITO 7, no. 2 (1983–1984): 34–43. [No. 3]

8818. Wintle, Christopher. "An Early Version of Derivation: Webern's Op. 11/3." PNM 13, no. 2 (1974–1975): 166–77.

Lieder (various; *see also* specific Lieder and Gesänge)

8819. Aragona, Livio. "Il lied di Abelone e il sopraciglio di Senecio: I lieder di Webern tra figura e struttura." RIM 23 (1988): 279–310.

8820. Beckmann, Dorothea. *Sprache und Musik im Vokalwerk Anton Weberns: Die Konstruktion des Ausdrucks.* Regensburg: Bosse, 1970.

8821. M-Broekema.

8822. Budde, Elmar. "Metrisch-rhythmische Probleme in Vokalwerke Weberns." M-Webern: 52–60.

8823. Marra, James. "Webern's 1904 Lieder: A Study in Late Tonal Practice." ITR 8, no. 2 (1987): 3–44.

8824. Puffett, Derrick. "Webern's Wrong Key-Signature." TEMPO 199 (1997): 21–26. [Early Lieder]

8825. Ringger, Rolf Urs. *Anton Weberns Klavierlieder.* Zurich: Juris-Atlantis, 1968.

8826. ———. "Sprachmusikalische Chiffern in Anton Weberns Klavierlieder." SMZ 106 (1966): 14–19.

8827. Schollum, Robert. "Stilistische Elemente der frühen Webern-Lieder." BOGM (1972–1973): 127–34.

8828. Stephan, Rudolf. "Zu einigen Liedern Anton Weberns." BOGM (1972–1973): 135–44. Reprint, M-Webern: 135–44.

8829. Trembath, Shirley. "Text and Texture in the Lieder of Anton Webern: The Relationship between the Contour of the Vocal and Instrumental Lines and Resultant Contrapuntal Textures in Opp. 14–25." MMA 16 (1989): 135–58.

8830. Venus, Dankmar. *Vergleichende Untersuchung zur melodischen Struktur der Singstimmen in den Liedern von Arnold Schönberg, Alban Berg, Anton Webern, und Paul Hindemith.* Göttingen: n.p., 1965.

Lieder aus "Der siebente Ring," Op. 3

8831. Brinkmann, Reinhold. "Die George-Lieder 1908, no. 9 und 1912/23: Ein Kapital Webern-Philologie." BOGM (1972–1973): 40–50.

8832. Budde, Elmar. *Anton Weberns Lieder Op. 3: Untersuchungen zur frühen Atonalität bei Webern.* Wiesbaden: Steiner, 1971.

8833. ———. "Metrisch-rhythmische Probleme im Vokalwerk Weberns." BOGM (1972–1973): 52–60.

8834. Hanson, Robert. "Webern's Chromatic Organization." MA 2 (1983): 135–50. [No. 5]

8835. Marvin, Elizabeth West, and Robert W. Wason. "On Preparing Anton Webern's Early Songs for Performance: A Collaborators' Dialogue." TP 20 (1995): 91–124.

8836. M-Park.

8837. Ringger, Rolf Urs. "Zur Wort-Ton-Beziehung beim frühen Anton Webern: Analyze von Op. 3, Nr. 1 aus 5 Lieder auf Texte von Stefan George." SMZ 103 (1963): 330–35.

8838. Wason, Robert W. "Remnants of Tonality in Webern's Op. 3/2." MPSS 4 (1991): 27–30.

Lieder (Dehmel; 1906–1908)

8839. Gerlach, Reinhard. "Die *Dehmel-Lieder* von Anton Webern: Musik und Sprache im Übergang zur Atonalität." JSIM (1970): 45–100.

8840. ———. "Die Handschriften der *Dehmel-Lieder* von Anton Webern: Textkritische Studien." AM 29 (1972): 93–113.

8841. ———. "Kompositionsniederschrift und Werkfassung am Beispiel des Liedes 'Am Ufer' (1908) von Webern." BOGM (1972–1973): 11–126. Reprint, M-Webern: 111–26.

8842. Roman, Zoltan. "From Congruence to Antithesis: Poetic and Musical *Jugendstil* in Webern's Songs." MMA 13 (1984): 191–202.

8843. Stein, Leonard. "Webern's *Dehmel Lieder* of 1906–1908: Threshold of a New Expression." In *Anton von Webern: Perspectives*, ed. Hans Moldenhauer, 53–61. Seattle: University of Washington Press, 1966.

8844. Wason, Robert W. "Signposts on Webern's Path to Atonality: The *Dehmel Lieder* (1906–08)." M-Baker: 409–32.

Lieder (George; 1908–1909)

8845. M-Park.

Lieder, Op. 4

8846. Brinkmann, Reinhold. "Die George-Lieder 1808, no. 9 und 1912/23: Ein Kapital Webern Philologie." BOGM (1972–1973): 40–50.

8847. M-Park.

Lieder, Op. 12

8848. Bach, Hans Elmar. "Anton von Webern: 'Der Tag ist vergangen,' 1915." M-Kirchmeyer: 211–18.

8849. Marvin, Elizabeth West, and Robert W. Wason. "On Preparing Anton Webern's Early Songs for Performance: A Collaborators' Dialogue." TP 20 (1995): 91–124.

Lieder, Op. 13

8850. Budde, Elmar. "Metrisch-rhythmische Probleme im Vokalwerk Weberns." BOGM (1972–1973): 52–60.

8851. Gerlach, Reinhard. "Anton Webern, 'Ein Winterabend': Op. 13, Nr. 4 zum Verhältnis von Musik und Dichtung oder Wahrheit als Struktur." AM 30 (1973): 44–68.

8852. Meyer, Felix, and Anne C. Shreffler. "Webern's Revisions: Some Analytical Implications." MA 12, no. 3 (1993): 355–79. [No. 4]

8853. Williams, Edgar Warren, Jr. "On Mode 12 Complementary Interval Sets." ITO 7, no. 2 (1983–1984): 34–43. [No. 1]

Lieder, Op. 14

8854. Cholopowa, Valentina. "Chromatische Prinzipien in Anton Weberns Vokalzyklus *Sechs Lieder nach Gedichten von Georg Trakl*, Op. 14." BM 17 (1975): 155–69.

8855. Shreffler, Anne C. *Webern and the Lyric Impulse: Songs and Fragments on Poems of Georg Trakl.* Oxford: Oxford University Press, 1994.

Lieder, Op. 25

8856. Chittum, Donald. "Some Observations on the Row Technique in Webern's Opus 25." CM 12 (1971): 96–101.

8857. Escot, Pozzi. "Webern's Opus 25, No. 1: Perception of Large-Scale Patterns." TP 4, no. 1 (1979): 28–29.

8858. Lespinard, Bernadette. "Webern et l'art poétique: À propos du lied 'Wie bin ich froh!' op. 25, no. 1 sur un poème de H. Jone." ANM 4 (1986): 50–55.

8859. M-Straus: 16–23. [No. 1]

Orchestral Pieces. *See* Pieces (Orchestra; 1913)

Orchestral Songs (1913–1914)

8860. Westergaard, Peter. "On the Problem of 'Reconstruction from a Sketch': Webern's 'Kunfttag III' and 'Leise Düfte.'" PNM 11, no. 2 (1973): 104–21.

Passacaglia, Op. 1

8861. Klein, Heribert. "Anton von Webern: Passacaglia Op. 1." NZM 147, no. 2 (1986): 30–32

8862. Nelson, Robert U. "Webern's Path to the Serial Variation." PNM 7, no. 2 (1969): 73–93.

Pieces (Orchestra; 1913)

8863. Barkin, Elaine. "Analysis Symposium: Webern, Orchestra Pieces (1913) Movement I (*Bewegt*)." JMT 19 (1975): 47–64.

8864. Hanson, Robert Frederic. "Anton Webern's Atonal Style." Ph.D. diss., Southampton University, 1976.

8865. Marvin, Elizabeth West. "The Structural Role of Complementation in Webern's Orchestra Pieces (1913)." MTS 5 (1983): 76–88.

8866. Olson, Christin. "Tonal Remnants in Early Webern: The First Movement of Orchestral Pieces (1913)." ITO 5, no. 2 (1979–1981): 34–46.

8867. Snarrenberg, Robert. "Hearings of Webern's 'Bewegt.'" PNM 24, no. 2 (1986): 386–404.

8868. Travis, Roy, and Allen Forte. "Analysis Symposium: Webern, Orchestral Pieces (1913) Movement I (*Bewegt*)." JMT 18 (1974): 2–43.

Quartet, Op. 22

8869. Fennelly, Brian. "Structure and Process in Webern's Opus 22." JMT 10, no. 2 (1966): 300–328.

8870. Hanninen, Dora A. "The Variety of Order Relations in Webern's Music: Studies of Passages from the Quartet Op. 22 and the Variations Op. 30." TP 20 (1995): 31–56.

8871. Hasty, Christopher F. "Composition and Context in Twelve-Note Music of Anton Webern." MA 7, no. 3 (1988): 281–312.

8872. M-Leibowitz: 218–23.

8873. Mead, Andrew. "Webern, Tradition, and 'Composing with Twelve Tones . . .'" MTS 15, no. 2 (1993): 173–204. [Movement I]

8874. O'Leary, Jane Strong. "Aspects of Structure in Webern's Quartet, Op. 22." Ph.D. diss., Princeton University, 1978.

8875. Pousseur, Henri. "Applications analytiques de la 'technique des réseaux.'" RBM 52 (1998): 247–98. [Movement I]

8876. Thomas, Jennifer. "The Use of Color in Three Chamber Works of the Twentieth Century." ITR 4, no. 3 (1980–1981): 24–40.

Sätze, Op. 5 (String Quartet)

8877. Archibald, Bruce. "Some Thoughts on Symmetry in Early Webern: Op. 5, No. 2." PNM 10, no. 2 (1972): 158–63.

8878. Budde, Elmar. "Anton Weberns Op. 5/IV: Versuch einer Analyse." F-Doflein: 58–66.

8879. Burkhart, Charles. "The Symmetrical Source of Webern's Opus 5, No. 4." MFO 5 (1980): 317–34.

8880. Clampitt, David. "Ramsey Theory, Unary Transformations, and Webern's Op. 5, No. 4." INT 13 (1999): 63–93.

8881. Demske, Tom. "Registral Centers of Balance in Atonal Works by Schoenberg and Webern." ITO 9, nos. 2–3 (1986): 60–76. [No. 2]

8882. Forte, Allen. "A Theory of Set-Complexes for Music." JMT 8 (1964): 136–83.

8883. Isaacson, Eric John. "Similarity of Interval-Class Content between Pitch-Class Sets: The IcVSIM Relation and Its Application." Ph.D. diss., Indiana University, 1992. [Nos. 2, 4]

8884. Lai, Eric. "Transformational Structures in Webern's Opus 5, No. 3." ITR 10 (1989): 21–50.

8885. Lewin, David. "An Example of Serial Technique in Early Webern." TP 7, no. 1 (1982): 40–43. [No. 4]

8886. ———. "Transformational Technique in Atonal and Other Music Theories." PNM 21 (1982–1983): 312–71. [No. 2]

8887. Parks, Richard S. "Pitch-Class Set Genera: My Theory, Forte's Theory." MA 17, no. 2 (1998): 206–26. [No. 4]

8888. M-Perle: 16–18.

8889. Persky, Stanley. "A Discussion of Composition Choices in Webern's *Fünf Sätze für Streichquartette*, Op. 5, First Movement." CM 13 (1972): 68–74.

8890. Santa, Matthew. "Defining Modular Transformations." MTS 21, no. 2 (1999): 200–229. [No. 3]

8891. M-Straus: 79–84. [No. 4]

String Quartet, Op. 28

8892. Bailey, Kathryn. "Rhythm and Metre in Webern's Late Works." JRMA 120, no. 2 (1995): 251–80.

8893. Döhl, Friedhelm. "Zum Formbegriff Weberns: Weberns Analyse des Streichquartette Op. 28 nebst einigen Bemerkungen zu Weberns Analyse eiegener Werke." OMZ 27 (1972): 131–48.

8894. Essl, Karlheinz. *Das Synthese-Denken bei Anton Webern: Studien zur Musikauffassung des späten Webern unter besonderer Berücksichtigung seiner eigenen Analysen zu Op. 28 und Op. 30.* Tutzing: Schneider, 1991.

8895. M-Leibowitz: 241–51.

8896. M-Pütz.

8897. Rauchhaupt, Ursula van, comp. *Die Streichquartette der Wiener Schule: Schönberg, Berg, Webern; Eines Dokumentation.* Munich: Ellermann, 1971.

8898. M-Straus: 169–73.

8899. Whittall, Arnold. "Webern and Multiple Meaning." MA 6, no. 3 (1987): 333–53.

8900. M-Zuber.

String Trio, Op. 20

8901. Haimo, Ethan. "Secondary and Disjunct Order-Position Relationships in Webern's Op. 20." PNM 24, no. 2 (1986): 406–19.

8902. M-Leibowitz: 206–9.

8903. Mead, Andrew. "Webern, Tradition, and 'Composing with Twelve Tones . . .'" MTS 15, no. 2 (1993): 173–204. [Movement II]

8904. Unverricht, Hubert. "Traditionelles in neuer Struktur: Zu Weberns Streichtrio Op. 20." F-Göllner: 377–85.

Stücke, Op. 6 (Orchestra)

8905. Baker, James M. "Coherence in Webern's Six Pieces for Orchestra, Op. 6." MTS 4 (1982): 1–27.

8906. Crotty, John E. "A Preliminary Analysis of Webern's Opus 6, No. 3." ITO 5, no. 2 (1979–1981): 23–32.

8907. Dahlhaus, Carl. "Rhythmische Strukturen in Weberns Orchesterstücken Opus 6." BOGM (1972–1973): 73–80. Reprint, M-Webern: 73–80.

8908. Davis, William. "Set Relations in No. 3 of Webern's Six Pieces for Orchestra, Op. 6 (1909)." TSP 3 (1986): 47–65.

8909. Elston, Arnold. "The Formal Structure of Opus 6, No. 1." PNM 6, no. 1 (1967): 63–66.

8910. Finney, Ross Lee. "Webern's Opus 6, No. 1." PNM 6, no. 1 (1967): 74.

8911. Hoffmann, Richard. "Webern: Six Pieces, Opus 6 (1909)." PNM 6, no. 1 (1967): 76–78.

8912. Kotani, Jeri. "Comprehensibility and Function in Webern's Six Pieces for Orchestra, Opus 6." EXT 1, no. 2 (1981): 1–29.

8913. Oliver, Harold. "Structural Functions of Musical Material in Webern's Opus 6, No. 1." PNM 6, no. 1 (1967): 67–73.

Stücke, Op. 7 (Violin and Piano)

8914. Alpern, Wayne. "Aggregation, Assassination, and an 'Act of God': The Impact of the Murder of Archduke Ferdinand upon Webern's Op. 7, No. 3." TP 21 (1996): 1–28.

8915. Berger, Christian. "Atonalität und Tradition: Anton Weberns Vier Stücke für Geige und Klavier, Op. 7." AM 53, no. 3 (1996): 183–93.

8916. Forte, Allen. "A Major Webern Revision and Its Implications for Analysis." PNM 28, no. 1 (1990): 224–55. [No. 2]

8917. Hanson, Robert. "Webern's Chromatic Organization." MA 2 (1983): 135–50. [No. 1]

8918. Harper, Steven A. "Emerging Tonality in Webern's Piece for Violin and Piano, Op. 7, No. 1." ITR 20, no. 1 (1999): 25–35.

8919. Ligeti, György. "Die Komposition mit Reihen und ihre Konsequenzen bei Anton Webern." OMZ 16 (1961): 297–303.

8920. M-Little.

8921. Morris, Robert D. "Conflict and Anomaly in Bartók and Webern." F-Lewin: 59–79. [No. 1]

Stücke, Op. 10 (Chamber Orchestra)

8922. Deliège, Célestin. "Webern: Op. 10, No. 4; Un thème d'analyse et de réflexion." RDM 61 (1975): 91–112.

8923. Gruhn, Wilfried. "Anton von Webern (1883–1945): Fünf Stücke für Orchester Op. 10 (1911/1913)." M-Zimmerschied: 13–40.

8924. Hanson, Robert Frederic. "Anton Webern's Atonal Style." Ph.D. diss., Southampton University, 1976.

8925. ———. "Webern's Chromatic Organization." MA 2 (1983): 135–50. [No. 4]

8926. Ijzerman, Job. "Die Symmetrie in Weberns Orchesterstück Op. 10 Nr. 1." MTH 5, no. 2 (1990): 165–67. [Response to 8932]

8927. Johnson, Peter. "Symmetrical Sets in Webern's Op. 10, No. 4." PNM 17, no. 1 (1978–1979): 219–29.

8928. Karkoschka, Erhard. "Nochmal: Weberns Orchesterstück Op. 10 Nr. 1." MTH 5, no. 2 (1990): 161–64. [Response to 8932]

8929. Kunkel, Michael. "Sándor Veress' *Orbis tonorum*, Nr. 4, 'Intermezzo silenzioso,' und Anton Weberns Op. 10, Nr. 3 ('Rückkehr'): ein Vergleich." MF 49, no. 4 (1996): 368–82.

8930. Marra, James Richard. "Rhythmic Stratification in the 'Atonal' Instrumental Music of Anton Webern (1913–1914)." D.M.A. diss., Cornell University, 1977. [No. 1]

8931. Meyer, Felix, and Anne C. Shreffler. "Webern's Revisions: Some Analytical Implications." MA 12, no. 3 (1993): 355–79. [No. 4]

8932. Plante, Daniel A. "Weberns Orchesterstück Op. 10, Nr. 1: Eine Untersuchung der Komposition und ihrer grundlegenden Strukturen (Source Sets)." MTH 4, no. 3 (1989): 235–46. [*See also* 8926, 8928]

8933. Russ, Michael. "Temporal and Pitch Structure in Webern's Orchestral Piece Op. 10, No. 2." MA 7, no. 3 (1988): 247–79.

8934. Smith, Charles Justice, III. "Patterns and Strategies: Four Perspectives of Musical Characterization." Ph.D. diss., University of Michigan, 1980. [No. 4]

8935. Tsang, Lee. "Musical Timbre in Context: The Second Viennese School, 1909–1925." Ph.D. diss., University of Southampton, 2000.

Symphony, Op. 21

8936. Abel, Angelika. "Adornos Kritik der Zwölftontechnik Weberns: Die Grenzen einer 'Logik des Zerfalls.'" AM 38 (1981): 143–78.

8937. Bailey, Kathryn. "Webern's Opus 21: Creativity in Tradition." JM 2 (1983): 184–95.

8938. Borris, Siegfried. "Structural Analysis of Webern's Symphony, Op. 21." F-Pisk: 231–42.

8939. ———. "Strukturanalyse von Weberns Symphonie, Op. 21." M-Reichert: 253–55.

8940. ———. "Weberns Symphonie Op. 21: Strukturanalyse." MB 5 (1973): 324–29.

8941. Bracanin, Philip K. "The Palindrome: Its Application in the Music of Anton Webern." MMA 6 (1972): 38–47.

8942. M-Cohn. [Movement II]

8943. Dagnes, Edward P. "Symmetrical Structures in Webern: An Analytical Overview of the Symphonie, Movement II, Variation 3." ITO 1, no. 9 (1975): 33–54.

8944. Fübeth, Oliver. "Die Frage nach dem 'Ausdruck' im Spätwerk Anton Weberns." MAS 3, no. 11 (1999): 43–50.

8945. Goebel, Walter F. "Anton Weberns Sinfonie." MELOS 28 (1961): 359–62.

8946. Goldthwaite, Scott. "Historical Awareness in Anton Webern's Symphony Op. 21." F-Plamenac: 65–81.

8947. Gruhn, Wilfried. "Reihenform und Werkgestalt bei Anton Webern: Die Variationen der Sinfonie Op. 21." ZM 2, no. 2 (1971): 31–37.

8948. Hiller, Lejaren, and Ramon Fuller. "Structure and Information in Webern's Symphonie, Op. 21." JMT 11, no. 1 (1967): 60–115.

8949. Hitchcock, H. Wiley. "A Footnote on Webern's Variations." PNM 8, no. 2 (1970): 123–42.

8950. Jetter, Elisabeth. "Ordnungsprinzipien im ersten Satz von Anton Weberns Symphonie Op. 21." MB 10 (1978): 151–58.

8951. Kerr, Elisabeth. "The Variations of Webern's Symphony Op. 21: Some Observations on Rhythmic Organization and the Use of Numerology." ITO 8, no. 2 (1984–1985): 5–14.

8952. M-Leibowitz: 211–18.

8953. Leleu, Jean-Louis. "Le quoi et le comment: A propos du second mouvement ('Variations') de la Symphonie op. 21 de Webern." ENT 2 (1986): 19–35.

8954. Nelson, Robert U. "Webern's Path to the Serial Variation." PNM 7, no. 2 (1969): 73–93.

8955. Rahn, John. "Webern's Symphonie Op. 21, Thema." M-Rahn: 4–18.

8956. Raiss, Hans-Peter. "Anton Webern: Symphonie Op. 21, 2. Satz (1928)." M-Vogt: 209–28.

8957. Starr, Mark. "Webern's Palindrome." PNM 8, no. 2 (1970): 127–42.

8958. Stroh, Wolfgang Martin. *Webern: Symphonie Op. 21.* Munich: Fink, 1975.

Transcriptions

8959. Gruhn, Wilfried. "Bearbeitung als kompositorische Reflexion in neuer Musik." M 28 (1974): 522–28. [J. S. Bach, *Fuga (Ricercata) a 6 voci*]

8960. Straus, Joseph N. "Recompositions by Schoenberg, Stravinsky, and Webern." MQ 72, no. 3 (1986): 301–28. [J. S. Bach, *Fuga (Ricercata) a 6 voci*]

Variations, Op. 27 (Piano)

8961. Bach, Hans Elmar. "Anton von Webern: Variationen Op. 27, 1. Satz, Takt 1–18, 1936." M-Kirchmeyer: 219–23.

8962. Bailey, Kathryn. "The Evolution of Variation Form in the Music of Webern." CM 16 (1973): 55–70.

8963. ———. "Willi Reich's Webern." TEMPO 165 (1988): 18–22.

8964. Bracanin, Philip K. "The Palindrome: Its Application in the Music of Anton Webern." MMA 6 (1972): 38–47.

8965. Brauneiss, Leopold. "Zahlen und Traditionsbestände in Anton Weberns Klaviervariationen." M-Brauneiss: 43–56.

8966. Budday, Wolfgang. "Zur Kompositionstechnik in Anton Weberns Klaviervariationen Op. 27, 3. Satz." MF 50, no. 2 (1997): 182–205.

8967. Cholopov, Juri. "Die Spiegelsymmetrie in Anton Weberns Variationen für Klavier Op. 27." AM 30 (1973): 26–43.

8968. Döhl, Friedhelm. "Weberns Opus 27." MELOS 30 (1963): 400–403.

8969. Heimann, Walter. "Autonomie und soziale Bindung." MB 10 (1978): 165–73.

8970. Huber, Nicolaus. "Die Kompositionstechnik Bachs in seinen Sonaten und Partiten für Violine solo und ihre Anwendung in Weberns Op. 27/II." ZM 1, no. 2 (1970): 22–31.

8971. Jones, James Rives. "Some Aspects of Rhythm and Meter in Webern's Opus 27." PNM 7, no. 1 (1968): 103–9.

8972. Koivisto, Tiina. "The Defining Moment: The Thema as Relational Nexus in Webern's Op. 27." ITO 13 (1997): 29–69.

8973. Kolneder, Walter. "Klang, Punkt, und Linie." In *Vergleichende Interpretationskunde.* Berlin: Merseburger, 1963.

8974. M-Leibowitz: 226–41.

8975. Leleu, Jean-Loius. "Intuition et esprit de système: Réflexions sur le schéma formel du deuxième mouvement des Variations pour piano op. 27 de Webern." RBM 52 (1998): 101–22.

8976. Lewin, David. "A Metrical Problem in Webern's Op. 27." JMT 6 (1962): 125–32.

8977. ———. "A Metrical Problem in Webern's Op. 27." MA 12, no. 3 (1993): 343–54. [Different article than 8976]

8978. Lincoln, Harry B., ed. *The Computer and Music*, 115–22. Ithaca, N.Y.: Cornell University Press, 1970.

8979. Mead, Andrew. "Webern, Tradition, and 'Composing with Twelve Tones . . .'" MTS 15, no. 2 (1993): 173–204. [Movement II]

8980. Mesnage, Marcel. "Les Variations pour piano op. 27 d'Anton Webern: Approche cellulaire barraquéenne et analyse assistée par ordinateur." ANM 14 (1989): 41–67.

8981. Nelson, Robert U. "Webern's Path to the Serial Variation." PNM 7, no. 2 (1969): 73–93.

8982. Nolan, Catherine. "Structural Levels and Twelve-Tone Music: A Revisionist Analysis of the Second Movement of Webern's Piano Variations Opus 27." JMT 39, no. 1 (1995): 47–76.

8983. Ogdon, Wilbur Lee. "A Webern Analysis." JMT 6 (1962): 133–38.

8984. Pousseur, Henri. "Applications analytiques de la 'technique des réseaux.'" RBM 52 (1998): 247–98.

8985. M-Schultz/D. [Movement II]

8986. Stadlen, Peter. "Das pointillistische Missverständnis." OMZ 27 (1972): 152–61.

8987. ———. "Das pointillistische Missverständniss [II]." BOGM (1972–1973): 173–84. Reprint, M-Webern: 173–84.

8988. Travis, Roy. "Directed Motion in Schoenberg and Webern." PNM 4, no. 2 (1966): 85–89.

8989. Wason, Robert W. "Webern's Variations for Piano, Op. 27: Musical Structure and the Performance Score." INT 1 (1987): 57–103.

8990. Westergaard, Peter. "Some Problems in Rhythmic Theory and Analysis." PNM 1, no. 1 (1962): 180–91.

8991. ———. "Webern and Total Organization: An Analysis of the Second Movement of Piano Variations, Op. 27." PNM 1, no. 2 (1963): 107–20.

Variations, Op. 30 (Orchestra)

8992. Bailey, Kathryn. "The Evolution of Variation Form in the Music of Webern." CM 16 (1973): 55–70.

8993. ———. "Formal and Rhythmic Procedures in Webern's Opus 30." CAUSM 2, no. 1 (1972): 34–52.

8994. ———. "Webern's Symmetrical Row Formations with Particular Reference to Opus 30." CCM 5 (1972): 159–66.

8995. Boynton, Neil. "Formal Combination in Webern's Variations Op. 30." MA 14, nos. 2–3 (1995): 193–220.

8996. Cholopow, Juri. "Der Wert des Webernschen Schaffens." BM 32, no. 1 (1990): 11–18.

8997. Deppert, Heinrich. "Rhythmische Reihentechnik in Weberns Orchestervariationen Opus 30." F-Marx: 84–93.

8998. Essl, Karlheinz. *Das Synthese-Denken bei Anton Webern: Studien zur Musikauffassung des späten Webern unter besonderer Berücksichtigung seiner eigenen Analysen zu Op. 28 und Op. 30.* Tutzing: Schneider, 1991.

8999. Hanninen, Dora A. "The Variety of Order Relations in Webern's Music: Studies of Passages from the Quartet Op. 22 and the Variations Op. 30." TP 20 (1995): 31–56.

9000. Hasty, Christopher F. "Composition and Context in Twelve-Note Music of Anton Webern." MA 7, no. 3 (1988): 281–312.

9001. Nelson, Robert U. "Webern's Path to the Serial Variation." PNM 7, no. 2 (1969): 73–93.

9002. Reid, John W. "Properties of the Set Explored in Webern's Variations, Op. 30." PNM 12 (1973–1974): 344–50.

9003. M-Zuber.

Volkstexte, **Op. 17**

9004. Ligeti, György. "Die Komposition mit Reihen und ihre Konsequenzen bei Anton Webern." OMZ 16 (1961): 297–303.

Various Works

9005. Abel, Angelika. *Die Zwölftontechnik Weberns und Goethes Methodik der Farbenlehre: Zur Kompositionstheorie und Ästhetik der neuen Wiener Schule.* Wiesbaden: Steiner, 1982.

9006. Anthony, Donald B. "Microrhythm in the Published Works of Anton Webern." Ph.D. diss., Stanford University, 1968.

9007. Bailey, Kathryn. "A Note on Webern's Graces." SMUWO 6 (1981): 1–6.

9008. ———. *The Twelve-Note Music of Anton Webern.* Cambridge: Cambridge University Press, 1991.

9009. Beale, James. "Weberns musikalischen Nachlass." MELOS 31 (1964): 297–303.

9010. Becker, Peter. "'Freilich ist es wieder Lyrik geworden': Auf der Suche nache dem Exemplarischen bei Webern." MB 15, no. 2 (1983): 4–10.

9011. Bradshaw, Merrill Kay. "Tonal Structure in the Early Works of Anton Webern." M.M. thesis, University of Illinois, 1962. [Opp. 1–5]

9012. Brown, Robert Barclay. "The Early Atonal Music of Anton Webern: Sound Material and Structure." Ph.D. diss., Brandeis University, 1965.

9013. M-Buccheri.

9014. Buchanan, Herbert Herman. "An Investigation of Mutual Influences among Schoenberg, Webern, and Berg (with an Emphasis on Schoenberg and Webern, ca. 1904–1908)." Ph.D. diss., Rutgers University, 1974.

9015. Busch, Regina. "Über die Musik von Anton Webern." OMZ 36 (1981): 470–82.

9016. Cone, Edward T. "Webern's Apprenticeship." MQ 53 (1967): 39–52. [Early works]

9017. Craft, Robert. "Anton Webern." SCORE 13 (1955): 9–24.

9018. Dahlhaus, Carl. "Analytische Instrumentation." F-Blankenburg: 197–206.

9019. Deppert, Heinrich. *Studien zur Kompositionstechnik im instrumentalen Spätwerk Anton Webens.* Darmstadt: Tonos, 1972.

9020. ———. "Über einige Voraussetzungen der musikalischen Analyse." ZM 4, no. 2 (1973): 10–16.

9021. ———. "Zu Weberns Klanglich-harmonischen Bewusstsein." BOGM (1972–1973): 61–72. Reprint, M-Webern: 61–72.

9022. Dimond, Chester Arthur. "Fourteen Early Songs of Anton Webern." D.M.A. diss., University of Oregon, 1971.

9023. Döhl, Friedhelm. *Webern: Weberns Beitrag zur Stilwende der neuen Musik; Studien über Voraussetzungen, Technik und Ästhetik der "Komposition mit 12 nur aufeinander bezogenen Tönen."* Munich: Katzbichler, 1976.

9024. Dreyer, Lutz. "Der tonale 'Atonale': Zur Harmonik im Spätwerk Anton Weberns." NZM 147, no. 1 (1986): 14–18.

9025. Fiehler, Judith Marie. "Rational Structures in the Late Works of Anton Webern." Ph.D. diss., Louisiana State University, 1973.

9026. Forte, Allen. "Aspects of Rhythm in Webern's Atonal Music." MTS 2 (1980): 90–109.

9027. ———. *The Atonal Music of Anton Webern.* New Haven, Conn.: Yale University Press, 1998.

9028. Gerlach, Reinhard. "Mystik und Klangmagie in Anton von Weberns hybrider Tonalität: Eine Jugendkrise im Spiegel von Musik und Dichtung der Jahrhundertswende." AM 33 (1976): 1–27. [Early works]

9029. Godwin, Paul Milton. "A Study of Concepts of Melody, with Particular Reference to Some Music of the Twentieth Century and Examples from the Compositions of Schoenberg, Webern, and Berg." Ph.D. diss., Ohio State University, 1972.

9030. Goebels, Franzpeter. "Bemerkungen und Materialen zuìn Studium neuer Klaviermusik." SMZ 113 (1973): 265–68, 329–31.

9031. Hudgens, Helen A. "Perceived Catagories in Atonal Music: Webern's Psychology of Convention." Ph.D. diss., Northwestern University, 1997. [Early instrumental works]

9032. Johnson, P. "Studies in Atonality: Non-Thematic Structural Processes in the Early Atonal Music of Schoenberg and Webern." Ph.D. diss., Oxford University, 1978.

9033. Karkoschka, Erhard. "Hat Webern seriell komponiert?" OMZ 30 (1975): 588–94.

9034. ———. *Studien zur Entwicklung der Kompositionstechnik in Frühwerk Anton Weberns.* N.p., 1959.

9035. Kolneder, Walter. Anton Webern: Einführung in Werk und Stil. Bodenkirchen/Rhein: P.J. Tonger, 1961. English translation by Humphrey Searle published under the title *Anton Webern: An Introduction to His Works.* Berkeley: University of California Press, 1968.

9036. ———. *Anton Webern: Genesis und Metamorphose eines Stils.* Vienna: Lafite/Österreichische Bundesverlag, 1974.

9037. ———. "Klangtechnik und Motivbildung bei Webern." F-Müller-Blattau/65: 27–50.

9038. Maegaard, Jan. "Webern Zwölftonreihen." M-Lönn: 249–67.

9039. Mason, Colin. "Webern's Later Chamber Music." ML 38 (1957): 232–37.

9040. McKenzie, Wallace Chesseley, Jr. "The Music of Anton Webern." Ph.D. diss., North Texas State University, 1960.

9041. ———. "Webern's Posthumous Music." BOGM (1972–1973): 185–92.

9042. Murray, Edward Michael. "New Approaches to the Analysis of Webern." Ph.D. diss., Yale University, 1979.

9043. Nielsen, Henning. "Zentraltonprinzipien bei Anton Webern." DAM 5 (1966–1967): 119–38.

9044. M-Ogdon.

9045. Olah, Tiberiu. "Weberns vorserielles Tonsystem." Melos/NZM 1 (1975): 10–13.

9046. OMZ 27 (1972). [Special issue]

9047. Overby, Patricia. "Variation Techniques in the Music of Anton Webern: An Analysis of Selected Works by Anton Webern, Demonstrating the Use of Traditional Constructive Devices in a New Stylistic Setting." M.M. thesis, University of Iowa, 1969.

9048. Perle, George. "Webern's Twelve-Tone Sketches." MQ 57 (1971): 1–25.

9049. Pisk, Paul. "Webern's Early Orchestral Works." In *Anton von Webern: Perspectives,* ed. Hans Moldenhauer, 43–52. Seattle: University of Washington Press, 1966.

9050. Poné, Gundaris. "Webern and Luigi Nono: The Genesis of a New Compositional Morphology and Syntax." PNM 10, no. 2 (1972): 111–19.

9051. R 2 (1958). [Special issue]

9052. Rubin, Marcel. "Webern und die Folgen." MG 10 (1960): 463–69.

9053. Scherzinger, Martin, with Neville Hoad. "Anton Webern and the Concept of Symmetrical Inversion: A Reconsideration on the Terrain of Gender." REP 6, no. 2 (1997): 63–147.

9054. Schollum, Robert. *Die Wiener Schule: Schönberg-Berg-Webern; Entwicklung und Ergebnis.* Vienna: Lafite, 1969.

9055. Schulz, Reinhard. *Über das Verhältnis von Konstruktion und Ausdruck in den Werken Anton Weberns.* Munich: Fink, 1982.

9056. Snow, Rosemary Allsman. "Cadence or Cadential Feeling in the Instrumental Works of Anton von Webern." Ph.D. diss., Case Western Reserve University, 1977.

9057. Somfai, László. "Rhythmic Continuity and Articulation in Webern's Instrumental Works." BOGM (1972–1973): 100–110. Reprint, M-Webern: 100–110.

9058. Spill, Angelike. "Weberns Kompositionstechnik und Goethes Methodik der Farbenlehre." Ph.D. diss., Marburg, 1980.

9059. Spring, Glenn Ernst, Jr. "Determinants of Phrase Structure in Selected Works of Schoenberg, Berg, and Webern." D.M.A. diss., University of Washington, 1972.

9060. Stadlen, Peter. "Das pointillistische Missverständnis." OMZ 27 (1972): 152–61.

9061. Stroh, Wolfgang Martin. *Anton Webern: Historische Legitimation als kompositorisches Problem.* Göppingen: Kummerle, 1973.

9062. Todd, R. Larry. "The Genesis of Webern's Opus 32." MQ 66 (1980): 581–91. [Unfinished cantata]

9063. Wilsen, William. "Equitonality as a Measure of the Evolution toward Tonality in the Pre-Opus 1 of Anton Webern." Ph.D. diss., Florida State University, 1975.

WEILL, KURT (1900–1950)

Dreigroschenoper

9064. Brock, David A. "Kurt Weill and American Jazz Banjo Style: Negotiating Stylistic Anomalies in *The Threepenny Opera.*" TCM 6, no. 4 (1999): 11–16.

Jasager

9065. Collisani, Amalia. "*Der Jasager*: Musica e 'distacco.'" RIM 17 (1982): 310–32.

Kleine Dreigroschenmusik

9066. Gresham, W. Jonathan. "Kurt Weill's *Threepenny Opera* and *Little Threepenny Music:* Comparisons and Oberservations." JBR 29, no. 2 (1994): 14–27.

9067. Hinton, Stephen. *Kurt Weill: The Threepenny Opera.* Cambridge: Cambridge University Press, 1990.

Mahagonny

9068. ASO 166 (1995).

9069. Engelhardt, Jürgen. *Gestus und Verfremdung: Studien zum Musiktheater bei Strawsinsky und Brecht/Weill.* Munich: Katzbichler, 1984.

Vom Tod im Wald, Op. 23

9070. Gresham, W. Jonathan. "Observations About Form and Style in Kurt Weill's *Vom Tod im Wald.*" JBR 33, no. 2 (1998): 14–32.

Various Works

9071. Diehl, Gunther. "'Mich so zu geben, wie ich bin, und nichts gewollt modernes zu suchen': Konturen einer Schaffensästhetik und ihre kompositorische Vermittlung im frühen Œuvre Kurt Weills." In *Kurt Weill: Die frühen Werke, 1916–1928,* ed. Heinz-Klaus Metzger and Rainer Riehn, 36–64. Munich: Text + Kritik, 1998.

9072. Harden, Susan Clydette. "The Music for the Stage Collaborations of Weill and Brecht." Ph.D. diss., University of North Carolina, 1972.

9073. Kemp, Ian. "Harmony in Weill: Some Observations." TEMPO 104 (1973): 11–15.

9074. Rienäcker, Gerd. "Thesen zur Opernästhetik Kurt Weills." JP 3 (1980): 116–34.

WEINZWEIG, JOHN (b. 1913)

9075. Keillor, Elaine. "John Weinzweig's *Wine of Peace.*" SMUWO 9 (1984): 79–92.

9076. Webb, Douglas John. "Serial Techniques in John Weinzweig's Divertimentos and Concertos (1945–1968)." Ph.D. diss., University of Rochester, 1977.

WEISGALL, HUGO (1912–1997)

9077. Balkin, Alfred. "The Operas of Hugo Weisgall." Ed.D. diss., Columbia University Teachers College, 1968.

9078. Blumenfeld, Harold. "Hugo Weisgall's Sixty-Sixth Birthday and the New *Gardens of Adonis.*" PNM 16, no. 2 (1977–1978): 156–66.

9079. Brooks, James Anthony, Jr. "Technical Aspects of the Music in the Major Operas of Hugo Weisgall." Ph.D. diss., Washington University, 1971.

9080. Saylor, Bruce. "The Music of Hugo Weisgall." MQ 59 (1973): 239–62.

WEISMANN, WILHELM (1900–1980)

9081. Köhler, Siegfried. "Ein neues Vokalwerk von Wilhelm Weismann." MG 10 (1960): 330–31. [*Lieder und Balladen (Des Knaben Wunderhorn)*]

9082. Mainka, Jürgen. "Realität und Phantastik des Volksliedes: Zu Wilhelm Weismanns Liedschaffen." JP 3 (1980): 33–53.

WEISS, ADOLPH (1891–1971)

9083. Kopp, Sister Bernadette. "The Twelve-Tone Techniques of Adolph Weiss." Ph.D. diss., Northwestern University, 1981.

WEISS, HARALD (b. 1949)

9084. Liesmann-Gümmer, Renate. "Harald Weiss: Grenzgänger unter den jungen deutschen Komponisten." NZM 144, no. 2 (1983): 14–19. [*Endstation,* other works]

WELLESZ, EGON (1885–1974)

9085. Redlich, Hans F. "Egon Wellesz." MQ 26 (1940): 65–75.

9086. ———. "Egon Wellesz: An Austrian Composer in Britain." MR 7 (1946): 69–79.

9087. Scheider, Günter. "Egon Wellesz: Studien zur Theorie und Praxis seiner Musik, dargestellt am Beispiel seiner musikdramatischen Komposition." Ph.D. diss., Innsbruck, 1981.

9088. Swedish, Stephen John. "The Piano Works of Egon Wellesz." D.M.A. diss., Indiana University, 1978. [*Drei Skizzen,* op. 6; *Idyllen,* op. 21; *Fünf Tanzstücke,* op. 42]

9089. Symons, David John. "Egon Wellesz and Early Twentieth-Century Tonality." SMU 6 (1972): 42–54.

9090. ———. "Tonal Organization in the Symphonies of Egon Wellesz." Ph.D. diss., University of Western Australia, 1981.

WENZEL, HANS JÜRGEN (b. 1939)

9091. Baethge, Wilhelm. "Die Analyse: Hans Jürgen Wenzels *Händel-Metamorphosen.*" MG 28 (1978): 273–77.

9092. Belkus, Gerd. "Die Analyse: Hans Jürgen Wenzels Konzert für Violine und Streichorchester." MG 26 (1976): 76–80.

WERZLAU, JOACHIM (b. 1913)

9093. Kleinschmidt, Klaus. "*Unser Leben im Lied:* Eine Kantate von Joachim Werzlau." MG 9, no. 1 (1959): 17–19.

WESLEY, SAMUEL SEBASTIAN (1810–1876)

9094. Hiebert, Arlis J. "The Anthems and Services of Samuel Sebastian Wesley (1810–1876)." Ph.D. diss., Northwestern University, 1965.

WESTERGAARD, PETER (b. 1931)

9095. Crumb, George. "*Variations for Six Players.*" PNM 3, no. 2 (1965): 152–59.

WEYSE, CHRISTOPH ERNST FRIEDRICH (1774–1842)

9096. Mathiassen, Finn. "Weyses klavermusik." DAM 23 (1995): 11–21.

WHITE, DONALD H. (b. 1921)

9097. White, Donald H. "*Miniature Set* for Band in Retrospect." JBR 13, no. 2 (1977–1978): 41–55.

WHITE, JOHN (b. 1936)

9098. Smith, Dave. "The Piano Sonatas of John White." CT 21 (1980): 4–11.

WHITE, MICHAEL

9099. Chittum, Donald. "Current Chronicle." MQ 55 (1969): 91–95. [*Metamorphosis*]

9100. ———. "Current Chronicle." MQ 57 (1971): 129–31. [*Opposites*]

WIDOR, CHARLES MARIE (1844–1937)

9101. Wilson, John R. "The Organ Symphonies of Charles Marie Widor." Ph.D. diss., Florida State University, 1966.

WIEGOLD, PETER (b. 1949)

9102. Barrett, Richard. "Peter Wiegold." CT 27 (1983): 28–32.

WILBRANDT, JÜRGEN (b. 1922)

9103. Mainka, Jürgen. "*Beppino*: Ein Liederzyklus von Jürgen Wilbrandt." MG 10 (1960): 10–14.

WILBY, PHILIP (b. 1949)

9104. McBride, M. Scott. "A Study of the Compositional Presuppositions of Philip Wilby and Analysis of His Three Works for Wind Orchestra." Ph.D. diss., University of Oklahoma, 1990.

WILDBERGER, JACQUES (b. 1922)

9105. Haefeli, Toni. "Kunst zwischen Herrschaft und Utopie: Zu Jacques Wildbergers neuem Werk *Du holde Kunst.*" DI 16 (1988): 4–9.

9106. Wildberger, Jacques. "*. . . die Stimme, die alte, schwacher werdende Stimme . . .*": Ein Triptychon für Solosopran, Solovioloncello, Orchester, und Tonband (1973/1974)." SMZ 117 (1977): 345–48.

WILDER, ALEC (1907–1980)

9107. Roberts, Jean Elizabeth. "The Piano Music of Alec Wilder." D.M.A. diss., University of Texas, 1984.

WILLAN, HEALEY (1880–1968)

9108. Campbell-Yukl, Joylin. "Healey Willan: The Independent Organ Works." D.M.A. diss., University of Missouri, 1976.

9109. Marwick, William. "The Sacred Choral Music of Healey Willan." Ph.D. diss., Michigan State University, 1970.

9110. Telschow, Frederick H. "The Sacred Music of Healey Willan." D.M.A. diss., University of Rochester, 1969.

WILLCOCK, IAN (b. 1959)

9111. Pace, Ian. "*Modulor* von Ian Willcock." MAS 3, no. 10 (1999): 47–58.

WILSON, DANA (b. 1946)

9112. Mathes, James. "*Piece of Mind* by Dana Wilson." JBR 25, no. 2 (1990): 1–12.

WILSON, OLLY (b. 1937)

9113. Logan, Wendell. "Olly Wilson: *Piece for Four.*" PNM 9, no. 1 (1970): 126–34.

WINTER, PETER (1754–1825)

9114. Zeller, Gary L. "The String Quartets of Peter Winter (1754–1825)." Ph.D. diss., Catholic University of America, 1977.

WISHART, TREVOR (b. 1946)

9115. Wishart, Trevor. "The Function of Text in the *VOX* Cycle." CMR 5 (1989): 189–97.

WOHLGEMUTH, GERHARD (b. 1920)

9116. Fleischhauer, Günter. "*Telemann-Variationen* von Gerhard Wohlgemuth." MG 15 (1965): 727–29.

9117. Siegmund-Schultze, Walther. "Gerhard Wohlgemuths Violinkonzert." MG 13 (1973): 599–601.

WOHLHAUSER, RENÉ (b. 1954)

9118. Wohlhauser, René. "Über kompositorische, ästhetische und philosophische Aspekte meiner Musik." DBNM 20 (1994): 98–107.

WOLF, HUGO (1860–1903)

Corregidor

9119. Cook, Peter. *Hugo Wolf's "Corregidor": A Study of the Opera and Its Origins.* London: Cook, 1976.

Gedichte von Eduard Mörike

9120. Böschenstein, Bernhard. "Zum Verhältnis von Dichtung und Musik in Hugo Wolfs *Mörikeliedern.*" *Wirkendes Wort* 19, no. 3 (May–June 1969): 175–93.

9121. Cratty, William S. "The Role of Vagrant Harmonies in Selected Lieder by Wolf, Strauss, and Schoenberg." EXT 4, no. 2 (1987–1988): 68–79. [No. 7]

9122. Gut, Serge. "Analyse musicale et musicologie: Le choix des méthodes pour l'analyse d'un lied de Hugo Wolf." ANM 2 (1986): 52–58. [No. 7]

9123. Hatch, Christopher. "Tradition and Creation: Hugo Wolf's 'Fussreise.'" CMS 28 (1988): 70–84.

9124. Kinsey, Barbara. "Mörike Poems Set by Brahms, Schumann, and Wolf." MR 29 (1968): 257–67.

9125. Schmalzriedt, Siegfried. "Hugo Wolfs Vertonung von Mörikes Gedicht *Karwoche.*" AM 41 (1984): 42–53.

9126. Sly, Gordon. "Competing Analyses as Pedagogical Strategy and Hugo Wolf's 'Das verlassene Mägdlein.'" JMTP 14 (2000): 31–46.

9127. Stein, Jack M. "Poem and Music in Hugo Wolf's Mörike Songs." MQ 53 (1967): 23–28.

9128. Tausche, Anton. *Hugo Wolfs Mörikelieder in Dichtung, Musik, und Vortrag.* Vienna: Amandus, 1947.

9129. Youens, Susan. "The Undoing of Desire: Hugo Wolf's Paired Songs in the *Mörike-Lieder.*" SAG 6, nos. 1–2 (1999): 183–212. [Nos. 2–3]

Gedichte von J. W. v. Goethe

9130. Glauert, Amanda. "'Ich singe, wie der Vogel singt': Reflections on Nature and Genre in Wolf's Setting of Goethe's *Der Sänger.*" JRMA 125, no. 2 (2000): 271–86.

9131. Hatch, Christopher. "Some Things Borrowed: Hugo Wolf's 'Anakreons Grab.'" JM 17, no. 3 (1999): 420–37.

9132. Kramer, Lawrence. "Decadence and Desire: The 'Wilhelm Meister' Songs of Wolf and Schubert." NCM 10, no. 3 (1987): 229–42.

9133. M-Lewis. [Mignon Lieder]

9134. Moman, Carl Conway, Jr. "A Study of the Musical Setting by Franz Schubert and Hugo Wolf for Goethe's *Prometheus, Ganymed,* and *Grenzen der Menschheit.*" Ph.D. diss., Washington University, 1980.

9135. Seelig, Harry E. "Goethe's *Buch Suleikas* and Hugo Wolf: A Musical Literary Study." Ph.D. diss., University of Kansas, 1969.
9136. Tenschert, Roland. "Das Verhältnis von Wort und Ton in Hugo Wolfs Goethe-Liedern." OMZ 8 (1953): 53–58.
9137. Youens, Susan. "Charlatans, Pedants, and Fools: Hugo Wolf's 'Cophtisches Lied I.'" SMUWO 8 (1983): 77–92.

Gedichte von Michelangelo
9138. Youens, Susan Lee. "'Alles endet, was entstehet': The Second of Hugo Wolf's *Michaelangelo-Lieder.*" SMU 14 (1980): 87–103.

Italienisches Liederbuch
9139. Clemens, Jon. "Combining Ursatz and Grundgestalt: A Schenkerian-Schoenbergian Analysis of Coherence in Hugo Wolf's *Italienisches Liederbuch.*" Ph.D. diss., University of Cinncinnati, 1998.
9140. Gülke, Peter. "'Sterb ich, so hüllt in Blumen meine Glieder': Zu einem Lied von Hugo Wolf." M 33 (1979): 132–40.
9141. Hantz, Edwin. "*Exempli gratia*: Le dernier cri (?); Wolf's Harmony Revisited." ITO 5, no. 4 (1979–1981): 29–32. [No. 10]
9142. Levi, Vito. "L'*Italienische Liederbuch* di Hugo Wolf." RIM 1 (1966): 203–17.
9143. Resch, Rita Marie. "The Role of the Piano in Hugo Wolf's *Italienisches Liederbuch.*" D.M.A. diss., University of Iowa, 1973.

Lieder (various; *see also* specific song cycles)
9144. Boylan, Paul C. "The Lieder of Hugo Wolf: Zenith of the German Art Song." Ph.D. diss., University of Michigan, 1968.
9145. Egger, Rita. *Die Deklamationsrhythmik Hugo Wolfs in historischer Sicht.* Tutzing: Schneider, 1963.
9146. Eppstein, Hans. "Entwicklungszüge in Hugo Wolfs frühen Liedkompositionen." STM 66 (1984): 43–58.
9147. ———. "Zum Problem von Hugo Wolfs Liedästhetik." AM 46, no. 1 (1989): 70–85.
9148. McKinney, Timothy R. "Melodic Pitch Structures in Hugo Wolf's Augmented-Triad Series." ITR 14, no. 1 (1993): 37–94.
9149. Metzger, Heinz-Klaus, and Rainer Riehn, eds. *Hugo Wolf.* Munich: Text + Kritik, 1992.
9150. Sams, Eric. *The Songs of Hugo Wolf.* London: Methuen, 1961.
9151. Stein, Deborah J. *Hugo Wolf's Lieder and Extensions of Tonality.* Ann Arbor, Mich.: UMI Research Press, 1985.
9152. Thürmer, Helmut. *Die Melodik in den Liedern von Hugo Wolf.* Giebing über Prien am Chiemsee: E. Katzbichler, 1970.

Manuel Venegas
9153. Spitzer, Leopold. "Hugo Wolfs *Manuel Venegas*: Ein Beitrag zur Genese." OMZ 32 (1977): 68–74.

Penthesilea
9154. Krones, Hartmut. "'Er hatte sich gleichsam mit seinem ganzen Körper in das Wort des Dichters verwandelt!': Hugo Wolfs *Penthesilea* als Musik gewordene Dichtung." HJM 13 (1995): 201–21.
9155. Metzger, Raphael. "Hugo Wolf's Symphonic Poem, *Penthesilea*: A History and Analysis." D.M.A. diss., Peabody Conservatory, 1980.
9156. Rosteck, Jens. "Zu Werkgenese und Formkonzeption von Hugo Wolfs Symphonischer Dichtung *Penthesilea.*" SZM 40 (1991): 205–35.
9157. Winkler, Gerhard J. "Anton Bruckner–ein Neudeutscher? Gedanken zum Verhältnis zwischen Symphonie und symphonischer Dichtung." BRS (1984): 149–62.

Various Works
9158. Eppstein, Hans. "Zum Schaffensprozess bei Hugo Wolf." MF 37 (1984): 4–20.
9159. Fellinger, Imogen. "Anton Bruckner und Hugo Wolf: Ein kompositorischer Vergleich." BRS (1984): 91–101.

WOLFF, CHRISTIAN (b. 1934)
9160. DeLio, Thomas. "Sound, Gesture, and Symbol: The Relation between Notation and Structure in American Experimental Music." I 10 (1981): 199–219. [*For 1, 2, or 3 People*]
9161. ———. "Structure as Behavior: Christian Wolff's *For 1, 2, or 3 People.*" *Percussive Notes Research Edition* 22, no. 6 (1984): 46–53. Reprint, M-DeLio: 49–67.
9162. Lovallo, Lee. "Incipient Pan-Serialism in Wolff's *Duo for Violins.*" ITO 2, nos. 1–2 (1976): 35–43.
9163. Natvig, Candace. "*Caribou Tracks*: Eine Einführung in vom Interpreten realisierbare Musik am Beispiel von Christian Wolff's *For 1, 2, or 3 People.*" N 1 (1980): 156–64.
9164. Nelson, Mark D. "Social Dynamics at the Heart of Composition: Implications of Christian Wolff's Inderterminate Music." CMF 1 (1989): 3–14. [*For 5 or 10 People*]
9165. Wilson, Peter Niklas. "Ein Kompendium nützlicher Dispositionen: Christian Wolffs *Long Peace March.*" MTX 32 (1989): 39–41.

WOLF-FERRARI, ERMANNO (1876–1948)

9166. Hamann, Peter. "Die frühe Kammermusik Ermanno Wolf-Ferraris." Ph.D. diss., Erlangen-Nürnberg, 1975.

WOLPE, STEFAN (1902–1972)

9167. Brody, Martin. "Sensibility Defined: Set Projection in Stefan Wolpe's *Form* for Piano." PNM 15, no. 2 (1977): 3–22.

9168. Hasty, Christopher. "Segmentation and Process in Post-Tonal Music." MTS 3 (1981): 54–73. [String Quartet (1969)]

9169. ———. "A Theory of Segmentation Developed from the Late Works of Stefan Wolpe." Ph.D. diss., Yale University, 1978. [*Form; Piece in Two Parts for Flute and Piano;* String Quartet (1969)]

9170. Levy, Edward. "Stefan Wolpe: For His Sixtieth Birthday." PNM 2, no. 1 (1963): 51–65. [*Piece for Two Instrumental Units*]

9171. Morehead, Patricia. "Contracting Sets, Expanding Tropes: A Discussion of Wolpe's Passacaglia for Piano." SONUS 15, no. 2 (1995): 80–112. [*Four Studies on Basic Rows*]

9172. Phleps, Thomas. "Stefan Wolpes *Stehende Musik.*" DI 41 (1994): 9–14. [Piano Sonata]

9173. Post, Nora. "Varèse, Wolpe, and the Oboe." PNM 20 (1981–1982): 135–48. [*Suite im Hexachord*]

WORK, JOHN W., II (1901–1967)

9174. Garcia, William Burres. "The Life and Choral Music of John Wesley Work (1901–1967)." Ph.D. diss., University of Iowa, 1973.

WRANITZKY, PAUL (1756–1808)

9175. Abert, Anna Amalie. "*Oberon* in Nord und Süd." F-Gudewill: 51–68.

WUORINEN, CHARLES (b. 1938)

9176. Hibbard, William. "Charles Wuorinen: The Politics of Harmony." PNM 7, no. 2 (1969): 155–66.

9177. Karchin, Louis. "Pitch Centricity as an Organizing Principle in *Speculum speculi* of Charles Wuorinen." TP 14–15 (1989–1990): 59–82.

WYNNE, DAVID (1900–1983)

9178. Jones, Richard Elfyn. *David Wynne.* Cardiff: University of Wales, 1979.

– X –

XENAKIS, IANNIS (1922–2001)

Chamber Works

9179. M-Arsenault. [*Analogique A*]

9180. DeLio, Thomas. "Structure and Strategy: Iannis Xenakis' *Linaia-Agon*." I 16, no. 3 (1987): 143–64.

9181. Frisius, Rudolf. "Xenakis und der Rhythmus." NZM 144, no. 4 (1983): 13–17. [*Persephassa*]

9182. Reish, Gregory N. "Performance Practice and Contemporary Music: A Look at *Eonta* by Iannis Xenakis." MRF 13 (1998): 36–55.

9183. Revault d'Allonnes, Olivier. "*Thalleïn* de Xenakis." INH 1 (1986): 189–95.

Choral Works

9184. Caullier, Joëlle. "Pour une interprétation de *Nuits*: Une proposition d'analyse." ENT 6 (1988): 59–69.

9185. Frisius, Rudolf. "Formalisierte Musik: Iannis Xenakis' Hörstück *Pour la Paix*." MTX 13 (1986): 39–41.

9186. ———. "Xenakis und der Rhythmus." NZM 144, no. 4 (1983): 13–17. [*Hiketides*]

9187. Prost, Christine. "*Nuits*: Première transposition de la démarche de Iannis Xenakis du domaine instrumental au domaine vocal." ANM 15 (1989): 64–70.

Orchestral Works

9188. M-Arsenault. [*Achorripsis, Pithoprakta*]

9189. Frisius, Rudolf. "Xenakis und der Rhythmus." NZM 144, no. 4 (1983): 13–17. [*Metastaseis*]

9190. M-Roberts. [*Pithoprakta*]

9191. Santana, Helena. "*Terretêktorh*: Space and Timbre, Timbre and Space." EXT 9, no. 1 (1998): 12–36.

9192. Waugh, Jane. "Xenakis and Chance." CT 10 (1974–1975): 6–13. [*Duel, Stratégie*]

9193. Wehinger, Rainer. "'Dichte': Einige Überlegungen zur Wahrnehmung am Beispiel von I. Xenakis' *Achorripsis* (1957)." MTH 12, no. 1 (1997): 87–90.

Solo Instrumental Works

9194. Castanet, Pierre-Albert. "*Mists,* œuvre pour piano de Ianis Xenakis: De l'écoute à l'analyse, les chemins convergents d'une rencontre." ANM 5 (1986): 65–75.

9195. Couroux, Marc. "Dompter la mer sauvage: Réflexions sur *Evryali* de Iannis Xenakis." CIR 5, no. 2 (1994): 55–67.

9196. DeLio, Thomas. "Iannis Xenakis' *Nomos alpha*: The Dialectics of Structure and Materials." JMT 24 (1980): 63–95.

9197. Flint, Ellen Rennie. "Metabolae, Arborescences, and the Reconstruction of Time in Xenakis' *Psappha*." CMR 7, no. 2 (1993): 221–48.

9198. Montague, Eugene. "The Limits of Logic: Structure and Aesthetics in Xenakis's *Herma*." EXT 7, no. 2 (1995): 36–65.

9199. Naud, Gilles. "Aperçus d'un analyse sémiologique de *Nomos alpha*." MJ 17 (1975): 63–72.

9200. Vriend, Jan. "*Nomos alpha* for Violoncello Solo (Xenakis 1966): Analysis and Comments." I 10 (1981): 15–82.

9201. Zeller, Hans Rudolf. "Sympolische Musik: *Herma*–auch ein Stück Mengenlehre." MTX 13 (1986): 33–34.

Tape Works

9202. Serra, Marie-Hélène. "Stochastic Composition and Stochastic Timbre: *GENDY3* by Iannis Xenakis." PNM 31, no. 1 (1993): 236–57.

Various Works

9203. Di Scipio, Agostino. "Compositional Models in Xenakis's Electroacoustic Music." PNM 36, no. 2 (1998): 201–43.

9204. Gibson, Benoît. "La théorie et l'œuvre chez Xenakis: Éléments pour une réflexion." CIR 5, no. 2 (1994): 41–54.

9205. Harley, Maria Anna. "Spatial Sound Movement in the Instrumental Music of Iannis Xenakis." JNMR 23, no. 3 (1994): 291–314.

9206. Mâche, F.-B. "The Hellenism of Xenakis." CMR 8, no. 1 (1993): 197–211.

9207. Metzger, Heinz-Klaus, and Rainer Riehn, eds. *Iannis Xenakis.* Munich: Text + Kritik, 1987.

9208. Serra, Marie-Hélène. "La synthèse dynamique stochastique de Iannis Xenakis." CAIR 2 (1993): 107–18.

9209. Solomos, Gerassimos M. "Les trois sonorites xenakiennes." CIR 5, no. 2 (1994): 21–39.

9210. Squibbs, Ronald James. "An Analytical Approach to the Music of Iannis Xenakis: Studies of Recent Works." Ph.D. diss., Yale University, 1996.

9211. Sward, Rosalie La Grow. "An Examination of the Mathematical Systems used in Selected Compositions of Milton Babbitt and Iannis Xenakis." Ph.D. diss., Northwestern University, 1981.

– Y –

YOUNG, GALE

9212. Young, Gale. "The Pitch Organizaton of *Harmonium for James Tenney*." PNM 26, no. 2 (1988): 204–11.

YOUNG, LA MONTE (b. 1935)

9213. Gann, Kyle. "La Monte Young's *The Well-Tuned Piano*." PNM 31, no. 1 (1993): 134–62.

9214. M-Mertens: 19–34.

9215. M-Potter.

9216. Schulze, Brigitte. "Im Klang sein: La Monte Young und die indische Musik." MTX 9 (1985): 40–43.

9217. Smith, Dave. "Following a Straight Line: La Monte Young." CT 18 (1977–1978): 4–9.

9218. Welch, Allison. "Meetings Along the Edge: *Svara* and *Tāla* in American Minimal Music." AMUS 17, no. 2 (1999): 179–99. [*The Well-Tuned Piano*]

YOUTZ, GREGORY (b. 1956)

9219. O'Neal, Thomas J. "Gregory Youtz's *Fire Works*." JBR 27, no. 1 (1991): 44–55.

YUN, ISANG (1917–1995)

Chamber Works

9220. Lessing, Kolja. "'Bewegtheit in der Unbewegtheit': Isang Yuns *Kontraste* für Violine solo." MTX 62–63 (1996): 84–86.

9221. Schmidt, Christian Martin. "Etüden für Flöte(n) Solo von Isang Yun." Melos/NZM 2 (1976): 16–20.

9222. Sparrer, Walter-Wolfgang. "Identität und Wandel: Zu den Streichquartetten III-VI." F-Yun: 28–57.

9223. M-Vogt: 421–35. [Sonata for Oboe, Harp, and Viola/Cello]

Orchestral Works

9224. Henseler, Ute. "'Eine Musiksprache, die Humanität hat': Zu den Solokonzerten Isang Yuns." F-Yun: 58–80. [Cello Concerto, Concerto for Flute and Chamber Orchestra, *Double Concerto* for Oboe and Harp, Violin Concerto No. 1]

9225. Lichtenfeld, Monika. "Musik, die von Widerstand und Hoffnung erzält: Isang Yuns Orchesterstück *Exemplum in memoriam Kwangju*." MTX 62–63 (1996): 74–76.

9226. Maehder, Jürgen. "Konvergenzen des musikalischen Strukturdenkens: Zur Geschichte und Klassifizierung der Klangfelder in den Partituren Isang Yuns." MTH 7, no. 2 (1992): 151–66.

9227. Schneider, Ernst Klaus. "'Man kann Musik so oder so hören. . .': Der 4. Satz der Symphonie I von Isang Yun aus der Sicht von Zuhörern." F-Yun: 81–90.

9228. Stephan, Ilja. *Isang Yun: Die fünf Symphonien.* Munich: Text + Kritik, 2000.

Vocal Works

9229. Heister, Hanns-Werner. "Zu Isnag Yuns vokalmusikalischer Idiomatik." DI 18 (1988): 14–18.

Various Works

9230. Schwake, Andreas. "Hören durch Sehen: Der latente Tanz in Kompostionen von Isang Yun." NZM 146, no. 4 (1985): 22–26.

– Z –

ZANINELLI, LUIGI (b. 1932)

9231. Fraschillo, Thomas V. "Luigi Zaninelli's Concertino for Piano and Symphonic Wind Ensemble." JBR 32, no. 1 (1996): 49–62.

ZBINDEN, JULIEN-FRANÇOIS (b. 1917)

9232. Zbinden, Julien-François. "*Concerto pour Orchestre*, Op. 57 (1977)." SMZ 117 (1977): 280–84.

ZECHLIN, RUTH (b. 1926)

9233. Röhlig, Eginhard. "*Situationen* für Orchester von Ruth Zechlin." MG 32 (1982): 75–79.

9234. Siegmund-Schultze, Walther. "Die Lidice-Kantate von Ruth Zechlin." MG 9, no. 1 (1959): 14–17.

ZEISL, ERIC (1905–1959)

9235. Cole, Malcolm S. "Eric Zeisl's 'American' Period." CM 18 (1974): 71–78.

ZELTER, CARL FRIEDRICH (1758–1832)

9236. Barr, Raymond. "Carl Friedrich Zelter: A Study of the Lied in Berlin during the Late Eighteenth and Early Nineteenth Centuries." Ph.D. diss., University of Wisconsin, 1968.

9237. Forbes, Elliot. "*Nur wer die Sehnsucht kennt*: An Example of a Goethe Lyric Set to Music." F-Merritt: 59–82.

9238. Grace, Richard M. "Carl Friedrich Zelter's Musical Settings of Johann Wolfgang Goethe's Poems." Ph.D. diss., University of Iowa, 1967.

9239. Havranek, Roger A. "Carl Friedrich Zelter: Fifteen Selected Lieder Set to Goethe Poems." D.M. diss., Indiana University, 1978.

ZEMLINSKY, ALEXANDER (1871–1942)

Lyrische Symphonie, Op. 18

9240. Fiebig, Paul. "Zu Alexander Zemlinsky's *Lyrischer Sinfonie*." NZM 134 (1973): 147–52.

9241. Michelsen, Thomas. "Form og tonal disposition i Alexander Zemlinskys *Lyrische Symphonie*." DAM 24 (1996): 39–50.

Operas

9242. ASO 186 (1998). [*Eine florentinische Tragödie*, op. 16; *Der Zwerg*, op. 17]

9243. Fuß, Hans-Ulrich. "Gesunger und verschwiegener Text: Zemlinskys *Eine florentinische Tragödie*." M 48, no. 1 (1994): 15–22.

9244. Sommer, Uwe. *Alexander Zemlinskys Oper "Der König Kandaules": Analyse und Deutung.* Munich: Text + Kritik, 1996.

9245. ———. "Alexander Zemlinskys Oper *Der König Kandaules*: Zur Entstehung eines integrativen Spätwerks." JSIM (1997): 235–64.

9246. Wildner-Partsch, Angelika. "Die Opern Alexander Zemlinskys: Betrachtungen anhand zweier repräsentativen Werke." SZM 33 (1982): 55–126. [*Eine florentinische Tragödie*, op. 16; *Der Kreidekreis*]

Seejungfrau

9247. Rooke, Keith J. "Alexander Zemlinskys *Die Seejungfrau*." SMZ 121 (1981): 85–91.

Sinfonietta, Op. 23

9248. Loll, Werner. "Ein Spiel mit Moden und Traditionen: Zur Sinfonietta Op. 23." OMZ 47, no. 4 (1992): 190–98.

Songs

9249. Hoffman, Stanley M. "Extended Tonality and Voice Leading in Twelve Songs, Op. 27, by Alexander Zemlinsky." Ph.D. diss., Brandeis University, 1993.

9250. Puffett, Derrick. "Transcription and Recomposition: The Strange Case of Zemlinsky's Maeterlinck Songs." M-Ayrey: 72–119. [Gesänge, op. 13]

9251. Weber, Horst. "Zemlinskys Maeterlinck-Gesänge." AM 29 (1972): 182–202. [Gesänge, op. 13]

String Quartets

9252. Harris, E. Scott. "Formal Archetypes, Phrase Rhythm, and Motivic Design in the String Quartets of Alexander Zemlinsky." Ph.D. diss., Indiana University, 1993. [Nos. 1–4]

9253. Jessen, Thomas von. "Metamorfose og formdualisme i Zemlinskys 2. strygekvartet op. 15." DAM 21 (1993): 49–58.

9254. Riddick, Frank Cary. "Tonality and Motivic Association in Zemlinsky's String Quartet No. 2, Op. 15." Ph.D diss., University of Colorado at Boulder, 1996.

Triumph der Zeit

9255. Weber, Horst. "'Figur und Grund': Secessionistic Instrumentation of Alexander Zemlinsky." MMA 18 (1984): 181–90.

9256. ———. "Stil, Allegorie, und Secession: Zu Zemlinskys Ballettmusik nach Hofmannsthals *Der Triumph der Zeit.*" F-Schuh: 135–50.

Various Works

9257. Neuwirth, Gösta. "Musik um 1900." F-Schuh: 89–134.

9258. Oncley, Lawrence A. "The Published Works of Alexander Zemlinsky." Ph.D. diss., Indiana University, 1975.

ZENDER, HANS (b. 1936)

9259. Gruhn, Wilfried. "Musik über Musik: Vermittlungsaspekte des Streichquartetts *Hölderlin lesen* von Hans Zender." MB 17, no. 9 (1985): 598–605. [*Hölderlin lesen I*]

9260. M-Vogt: 399–409. [*Canto IV*]

9261. Wacker, Volker. "Hans Zenders Oper *Stephen Climax*: Betrachtungen und Aspekte." HJM 10 (1988): 239–58.

ZILLIG, WINFRIED (1905–1963)

9262. Leeuwen, Andreas van. "Winfried Zillig (1905–1963): *Die Verlobung in St. Domingo*: Analyse und Interpretation einer vergessenen Funkoper." ACTA 72, no. 2 (2000): 189–218.

ZIMMERMANN, BERND ALOIS (1918–1970)

Chamber Works

9263. Ebbeke, Klaus. "Le jazz dans la musique de B. A. Zimmermann." Trans. Carlo Russi. CC 5 (1985): 102–23. [*Die Befristeten*]

9264. Hübler, Klaus-K. "Zimmermann the Conservative: Anmerkungen zu seiner Viola-Sonate." MB 18 (1981): 360–65.

9265. Imhoff, Andreas von. "Der frühe Bernd Alois Zimmermann." Melos/NZM 1 (1975): 359–65. [Sonata for Solo Violin (1951)]

9266. Schubert, Reinhold. "Bernd Alois Zimmermann." R 4 (1960): 103–13. [*Perspektiven*]

Orchestral Works

9267. Ebbeke, Klaus. "Le jazz dans la musique de B. A. Zimmermann." Trans. Carlo Russi. CC 5 (1985): 102–23. [Trumpet Concerto]

9268. Müller, Karl-Josef. "Bernd Alois Zimmermann (1918–1970): *Photoptosis,* Prelude für grosses Orchester (1968)." M-Zimmerschied: 309–29.

9269. Peters, Rainer. "Hommage à Strawinsky: Bernd Alois Zimmermanns Oboenkonzert." T 11, no. 3 (1986): 188–92.

9270. Utz, Christian. "Überwindung der Zeit als musikalische Utopie: Metamorphosen in Bernd Alois Zimmermanns Orchesterskizzen *Stille und Umkehr.*" MTH 8, no. 2 (1993): 131–47.

Piano Works

9271. Imhoff, Andreas von. *Untersuchungen zum Klavierwerk Bernd Alois Zimmermanns (1918–1970).* Regensburg: Bosse, 1976.

9272. Niehaus, Manfred. "Bernd A. Zimmermann: *Monologue* für zwei Klaviere, 1960/64 (Collage)." M-Kirchmeyer: 224–27.

Soldaten

9273. ASO 156 (1993).

9274. Ebbeke, Klaus. "Le jazz dans la musique de B. A. Zimmermann." Trans. Carlo Russi. CC 5 (1985): 102–23.

9275. Funk-Hennigs, Erika. "Zimmermanns Philosophie der Zeit: Dargestellt an Ausschnitten der Oper *Die Soldaten.*" MB 10 (1978): 644–52.

9276. Gruhn, Wilfried. "Integrale Komposition: Zu Bernd Alois Zimmermanns Pluralismus-Begriff." AM 40 (1983): 287–302.

9277. Helleu, Laurence. "*Les soldats* de B. A. Zimmermann: Aspects de la technique compositionnelle." ENT 7 (1988): 15–27.

9278. ———. "*Les soldats*, opéra de B. A. Zimmermann: Interchangeabilité de l'espace et du temps." ANM 15 (1989): 25–31.

9279. ———. "L'utilisation des formes anciennes dans *Les soldats*: L'exemple de la strophe, acte 1, scène 1." CC 5 (1985): 124–39.

9280. Herbort, Heinz Josef. "Bernd Alois Zimmermanns Oper *Die Soldaten*." MB 3 (1971): 539–48.

9281. Michaely, Aloyse. "Toccata–Ciacona–Nocturno: Zu Bernd Alois Zimmermanns Oper *Die Soldaten*." HJM 10 (1988): 127–204.

9282. Renggli, Hanspeter. "Relfex und Tropus als Verdichtung: Zum Frauenterzett in Bernd Alois Zimmermanns *Soldaten*." DI 46 (1995): 4–12.

9283. Seipt, Angelus. "Bernd Alois Zimmermann: *Die Soldaten* (1965)." M-Vogt: 371–81.

Vocal Works

9284. Danuser, Hermann. "Text- und Musikstruktur in B. A. Zimmermanns *Omnia tempus habent*." DI 16 (1988): 14–19.

9285. Ebbeke, Klaus. "'Dann trat die Figur aus dem Bild': Hinweise zur Entstehungsgeschichte von Zimmermanns *Requiem für einen jungen Dichter*." MTX 24 (1988): 39–45.

9286. Hiekel, Jörn Peter. *Bernd Alois Zimmermanns Requiem für einen jungen Dichter*. Stuttgart: F. Steiner, 1995.

Various Works

9287. Ebbeke, Klaus. "Zu Bernd Alois Zimmermanns früher Reihentechnik." MTH 2, no. 1 (1987): 33–54.

9288. Karbaum, Michael. "Zur Verfahrensweise im Werk Bernd Alois Zimmermanns." F-Schenk: 275–85.

9289. Korte, Oliver. "Zu Bernd Alois Zimmermanns später Reihentechnik." MTH 15, no. 1 (2000): 19–39.

9290. Kühn, Clemens. *Die Orchesterwerke Bernd Alois Zimmermanns*. Hamburg: Wagner, 1978.

9291. Müller, Karl-Josef. "Erleben und Messen: Zu Bernd Alois Zimmermanns Anschauung der Zeit in seinen letzten Werken." MB 9 (1977): 550–54.

ZIMMERMANN, HEINZ WERNER (b. 1930)

9292. Oehlmann, Werner. "Inmitten der pluralistischen Welt." M 29 (1975): 50–52. [*Missa profana*]

9293. Oertel, Heinz-Georg. "Kirchenmusik und Jazz: Heinz Werner Zimmermann (geboren 11.8.1930)." F-Mauersberger: 197–213.

9294. Salevič, Marion. "Heinz Werner Zimmermanns amerikanische Psalmvertonungen." MK 49 (1979): 170–77.

9295. Schütz, Adelbert. "*Missa profana* von Heinz Werner Zimmermann." MK 51 (1981): 217–23.

ZIMMERMANN, UDO (b. 1943)

9296. Böhm, Hans. "*Sonetti amorosi* von Udo Zimmermann." MG 18 (1968): 754–61.

9297. Gerlach, Hannelore. "*L'homme*: Meditationen für Orchester nach Eugène Guilleric von Udo Zimmermann." MG 23 (1973): 455–60.

ZIMMERMANN, WALTER (b. 1949)

9298. Fox, Christopher. "Walter Zimmermann's Local Experiments." CT 27 (1983): 4–9.

9299. Leukerl, Bernd. "Das nie verglühende Opfer: Zu Walter Zimmermanns *Spielwerk*." MTX 12 (1985): 21–24.

9300. McGuire, John. "In der Luft der eigenen Ätherik auflösen: Walter Zimmermanns Lokale Musik." MTX 12 (1985): 33–35.

9301. Oehlschlägel, Reinhard. "Konzeptionelle Wörtlichkeit: Walter Zimmermanns statisches Drama *Die Blinden*." MTX 15 (1989): 39–43.

9302. Schädler, Stefan. "Oper als Verfahren: Walter Zimmermanns Oper *Über die Dörfer* nach Peter Handke." NZM 149, no. 6 (1988): 27–31.

9303. Zimmermann, Walter. "Lokale Musik: Eine Projektbeschreibung." N 1 (1980): 80–86.

9304. ———. "Vom Alten zum Neuen: Zum Klavier-Stück *Beginner's Mind*." MTX 12 (1985): 38–40.

ZUMSTEEG, JOHANN RUDOLF (1760–1802)

9305. Maier, Günter. *Die Lieder Johann Rudolf Zumsteegs und ihr Verhältnis zu Schubert*. Göppingen: Kammerle, 1971.

ZWILICH, ELLEN TAAFFE (b. 1939)

9306. Schnepel, Julie. "Ellen Taaffe Zwilich's Symphony No. 1: Developing Variation in the 1980s." ITR 10 (1989): 1–19.

Appendix: Monographic Series Included

The following monographic series were thoroughly reviewed to identify analyses published in books. Although the bibliography includes citations for books that were not published in series, most of the books cited are part of one of the series listed here.

Acta Universitatis Upsaliensis. Studia musicologica Upsaliensia (Uppsala University)

Analecta musicological (Laaber)

Au delà des notes (Leduc)

Beihefte zum Archiv für Musikwissenschaft (Steiner)

Beiträge zur westfalischen Musikgeschichte (Lineppe)

Berliner musikwissenschaftliche Arbeiten (Katzbichler)

Cahiers de l'IRCAM. Compositeurs d'aujourd'hui (IRCAM)

California Studies in 19th-Century Music (University of California Press)

Cambridge Companions to Music (Cambridge University Press)

Cambridge Music Handbooks (Cambridge University Press)

Cambridge Opera Handbooks (Cambridge University Press)

Cambridge Studies in Music Theory and Analysis (Cambridge University Press)

Canadian Composers (University of Toronto Press)

Composers of the Twentieth Century (Yale University Press)

Detroit Monographs in Musicology/Studies in Music (Harmonie Park Press)

Eastman Studies in Music (University of Rochester Press)

English National Opera Guides (Calder)

Europäische Hochschulschriften. Reihe XXXVI, Musikwissenschaft (Lang)

Forschungsbeiträge zur Musikwissenschaft (Bosse)

Freiburger Schriften zur Musikwissenschaft (Katzbichler)

Garland Reference Library of the Humanities. Border Crossings (Garland)

Gesellschaft für Musikforschung (Gesellschaft für Musikforschung)

Grands opéras (Aubier)

Hamburger Beiträge zur Musikwissenschaft (Wagner)

Kontrapunkte (Tonger)

Mainzer Studien zur Musikwissenschaft (Schneider)

Meisterwerke der Musik (Fink)

Münchener Veröffentlichungen zur Musikgeschichte (Schneider)

Music in the Twentieth Century (Cambridge University Press)

Musik-Konzepte (Text + Kritik)

Musikwissenschaftliche Schriften (Katzbichler)

Neue Heidelberger Studien zur Musikwissenschaft (Laaber)

Neue musikgeschichtliche Forschungen (Breitkopf & Härtel)

Oxford Monographs in Music (Oxford University Press)

Princeton Studies in Music (Princeton University Press)
Regensburger Beiträge zur Musikwissenschaft (Bosse)
Schriften zur Musik (Katzbichler)
Schriften zur Musik des 20. Jahrhunderts (Musikprint)
Schriftenreihe zur Musik (Verlag der Musikalienhandlung)
Studien zur Musik (Fink)
Studien zur Musikgeschichte des 19. Jahrhunderts (Bosse)
Studies in Musical Genesis and Structure (Oxford University Press)
Studies in the Criticism and Theory of Music (University of Pennsylvania Press)
Veröffentlichungen des Instituts für Neue Musik und Musikerziehung Darmstadt (Schott)
Veröffentlichungen zur Musikforschung (Heinrichshofen)
Wiener musikwissenschaftliche Beiträge (Böhlau)
Wiener Veröffentlichungen zur Musikwissenschaft (Schneider)
Würzburger musikhistorische Beiträge (Schneider)
WW—Beiträge zur Musikwissenschaft (Wollenweber)

Author Index

Abbate, Carolyn, 2637, 3014, 8625
Abel, Angelika, 8936, 9005
Abendroth, Walter, 5675
Abert, Anna Amalie, 2519, 3510, 4377, 6949, 7733, 7931, 9175
Abraham, Gerald, 297, 1391–92, 2478, 3064, 3389, 3457, 5355, 6041–42, 7021–22, 7216, 7227, 7270, 7386, 8183–84
Abraham, Lars Ulrich, 861
Abravaya, Niza, 4958, 4967, 4979
Ackermann, Peter, 6475
Adams, Beverly Decker, 5240
Adams, Courtney S., 6184, 6650
Adams, Frank John, 552
Adams, John Kenneth, 2664–65
Adams, John P., 4202, 8753
Adams, Stephen, 6204
Adelson, Deborah M., 1276
Adensamer, Michael, 1985
Adlington, Robert, 1339
Adorno, Theodor W., 987, 6651, 7762
Adrio, Adam, 5612, 5619–20
Agawu, V. Kofi, 194, 742–43, 2279, 3606, 3647, 4874–75, 4888, 4909, 4980, 5005, 5395, 6760, 6766, 6997, 7095, 7857
Agmon, Eytan, 504, 639, 1684, 6884, 6998
Ahn, Suhnne, 882
Ahrens, Christian, 7091
Ahrens, Joseph, 13
Ahrens, Sieglind, 5241
Albee, David Lyman, 54
Albèra, Philippe, 1220, 6313
Albers, Bradley Gene, 5573
Albert, Thomas Russell, 4034
Albrecht, Christoph, 3780
Albrecht, Klaus, 7763
Albrecht, Michael von, 20
Albright, Daniel, 1262, 1278, 7881
Alegant, Brian, 6377, 8809
Alexander, Metche Franke, 1302
Alexander, Michael J., 2874
Alfred, Everett Maurice, 2581, 2584, 2636
Allen, Judith Shatin, 2741, 6950
Allende-Blin, Juan, 4228, 5703
Allihn, Ingeborg, 3106

Allison, Rees Stephen, 5914
Allorto, Riccardo, 2376
Almond, Frank Ward, 5720
Alpern, Wayne, 8914
Alphonce, Bo H., 7088, 7133
Alston, Charlotte LeNora, 3656
Altmann, Peter, 1236
Aluas, Luminita, 4536
Alvarez, Javier, 28
Alviani, Doric, 3250
Ameringen, Sylvia van, 116, 201, 5208
Ames, Charles, 31–32, 3786, 5415
Amiot, Emmanuel, 2724
Amman, Douglas D., 3235
Anagnost, Dean Z., 8206
Andersen, Mogens, 5486
Anderson, Gene, 3871–72
Anderson, Juliana, 3473, 5371–72
Anderson, Lyle John, 4620, 4669, 4671, 4707
Anderson, Peter James, 3445
Andersson, Magnus, 3213
Andraschke, Peter, 195, 3497, 3990, 4968, 4989, 5956, 6031
André, Naomi, 6303
Andreae, Hans, 6256
Andreani, Éveline, 2638
Andres, Hartmut, 4855
Andrewes, John, 2552
Andrews, Dwight Douglas, 8058
Andrews, Harold L., 3592, 3700
Andrews, Ralph E., 5202
Andriessen, Louis, 43, 8100
Andrieux, Françoise, 1640
Angerer, Manfred, 4644, 5397, 7447
Angermann, Klaus, 5279, 8258
Angiolini, Giuliano di, 7553, 7622
Anhalt, István, 52, 487, 1212, 1224, 4542, 4811, 6205
Ank, Matthias, 4368
Anson-Cartwright, Mark, 3642, 3644, 8616
Anthony, Carl Rheinhardt, 4260
Anthony, Donald B., 9006
Antokoletz, Elliott, 21, 169, 173, 180, 196, 327–28, 357, 383–84, 7419, 7893, 7898–99, 7958, 8391

Roeder, Michael T., 1496
Roelcke, Eckhard, 4207, 4219
Roesner, Linda Correll, 7090, 7114, 7168, 7181
Rogers, Joe, 1411
Rogers, Lynne, 8057
Rogers, Michael R., 2291
Rogge, Wolfgang, 4346, 6507
Rognoni, Luigi, 1044, 1193
Rohland, Tyll, 5014
Röhlig, Eginhard, 9233
Rohrer, Thomas P., 2182
Roig-Francolí, Miguel A., 4498, 4550, 4557
Roiha, Eino Vilho Pretari, 7377
Rolf, Marie, 2629, 7729
Roller, Dale Alvin, 1203
Roller, Jonathan Brian, 4074, 4078, 4085
Rollin, Robert, 4005, 4525–27
Roma, Catherine, 5381–82
Romain, Edwin Philip, 5730
Roman, Zoltan, 4649, 4723, 4743, 4897, 4906–8, 4912–13, 4917, 4922, 4939, 7690, 7727, 8842
Romano, Jacobo, 2675
Ron, Yohanan, 5564, 8155–56
Rooke, Keith J., 9247
Rorich, Mary Elizabeth, 5430
Rorick, William C., 3185, 3279
Rosch, Charlotte, 5529
Rose, François, 3478, 5376
Rose, Gregory, 7619
Rose, Michael Paul, 1497
Roseberry, Eric, 1775, 1799, 1802, 1850, 7362
Rosen, Charles, 942, 1433, 1436, 1444, 1597, 2162–63, 2313–14, 3723, 6698, 6845
Rosen, David, 8397–99
Rosenberg, Herbert, 6878
Rosenberg, Richard, 568–69
Rosenberg, Wolf, 4977
Rosenberger, Wolfram, 7773
Rosenbloom, Paul David, 278, 286, 345, 353
Rosenblum, Matthew, 8622
Rosenhaus, Steven L., 5627
Rosenstiel, Leonie, 1405
Rosenzweig, Morris, 4338, 4467
Rösler, Walter, 3102
Rosman, Carl, 4579
Rosner, Arnold, 3978
Ross, Mark Alan, 5211, 5252, 5261
Ross, Peter, 8363
Ross, Walter Beghtol, 3808
Rössler, Almut, 5233, 5241
Rössler, Franz-Georg, 3829
Rossum, Frans van, 4329
Rost, Cornelia, 1099, 7689
Rostagno, Antonio, 8356
Rostan, Daniel, 7836
Rostand, Claude, 445, 5299
Rosteck, Jens, 3913, 5327, 5336, 9156
Roth, Markus, 3935
Rothgeb, John, 2272, 6817, 7105, 8676
Rothkamm, Jörg, 3754, 5002

Rothstein, William, 594, 2213, 2216, 2221, 2276, 5073
Round, Michael, 8483
Rouse, Christopher Chapman, III, 2471
Routh, Francis, 6115
Routley, Nicholas, 2678, 2722–23
Rowan, Denise Cecile Rogers, 1488
Rowen, Ruth Halle, 3394
Rowlands, Jeffrey, 3402
Rowley, Vivienne Wilda, 2431
Rowold, Helge, 1851
Roy, Stéphane, 476
Rubbra, Edmund, 6125–26, 8345
Rubeli, Alfred Ulrich, 3795
Rubin, David, 5847
Rubin, Marcel, 9052
Rubisch, Egon, 8200
Rüdiger, Wolfgang, 4242
Ruf, Wolfgang, 6334
Rufer, Josef, 2501, 6472, 6699–6700
Ruger, Christof, 7436
Rülke, Volker, 363, 8040
Rümenapp, Peter, 4509, 8605
Rummenhöller, Peter, 943, 4536, 4724, 4769, 5195, 5839, 6238
Rumph, Stephen, 2579
Runestad, Cornell J., 3581
Rupprecht, Philip, 1769, 1800, 1872
Ruschenburg, Peter, 2751
Rushton, Julian, 1266, 1282, 1301, 1319, 3118
Russ, Michael, 287, 346, 5396, 5409, 8933
Russell, Armand, 6148
Russell, John, 3208
Russo, Francesco Paolo, 5533
Rust, Douglas Martin, 4824, 7866
Rust, Ezra G., 551
Rutman, Neil Clark, 3529
Ruzicka, Peter, 6237
Ryberg, James Stanley, 5751
Ryker, Harrison Clinton, 5689

Saak, Siegfried, 2203
Saar, Harold E., 8511
Saariaho, Kaija, 6156
Saathen, Friedrich, 3086
Sabatino, Trucilla Marie, 60
Sabbe, Hermann, 49, 3407, 3410, 4576, 7653
Sabbeth, Daniel, 8382
Sabin, Robert, 1166
Sabinina, Marina, 7331
Saby, Bernard, 4456
Saby, Pierre, 3452
Sachs, Klaus-Jürgen, 5896, 7119
Sachse, Hans Martin, 6933
Sadai, Yizhak, 6701
Saffle, Michael, 4686, 4770
Safránek, Milos, 5083
Saguer, Louis, 3816, 5497
Salevič, Marion, 9294
Sallis, Friedemann, 171, 4518, 8461
Salmen, Walter, 3914, 6781
Salmenhaara, Erkki, 4470, 4477, 4483, 4551

About the Author

D. J. Hoek is head of the Music Library at Northwestern University. He holds a master of library science degree with a specialization in music librarianship from Indiana University and two master of music degrees in music theory and composition from Bowling Green State University. His other publications include *Steve Reich: A Bio-Bibliography* (2002), as well as articles and reviews in *Notes, Reference and User Services Quarterly, Cataloging and Classification Quarterly,* the *Bulletin of Bibliography,* and the *All Music Guide.*

Lightning Source UK Ltd.
Milton Keynes UK
UKHW052343260120
357609UK00021B/753

9 780810 858887